Praise for
The Torah Encyclopedia of the Animal Kingdom

"*The Torah Encyclopedia of the Animal Kingdom* is beautifully produced and most informative. It will serve as a necessary aid to those who wish to comprehend the words of the Torah and appreciate its awe of the grandeur of God's world."

Rabbi Berel Wein

"Few things fascinate adults and children alike as much as the grandeur, the magnificence, and the variety of the animal kingdom. Those who appreciate the Torah and tradition will find special pleasure when these two realms come together. Rabbi Slifkin succeeds masterfully in doing this, with stunning photographs, fascinating research, and rich commentary, enabling every reader to take a sense of awe in God's creation to a new level of understanding."

Rabbi Yitzchok Adlerstein

"*The Torah Encyclopedia of the Animal Kingdom* is an extremely impressive work. It is written in such a manner as to be accessible to the non-expert, yet contains information that will be of interest to rabbis and scholars. The author has done a masterful job weaving together and integrating Torah sources and scientific knowledge while maintaining the integrity of each discipline."

Rabbi Dr. Ari Zivotofsky

"This is an important and comprehensive work on the animal kingdom from a Jewish perspective. The author demonstrates great expertise in rabbinic sources, as well as extensive knowledge of zoology. He succeeds in connecting the reader to biblical verses and sayings of the sages, clarifying both symbolic descriptions and factual accounts, in a clear writing style that is suited to diverse audiences. This volume should be in every public and private library."

Dr. Zohar Amar

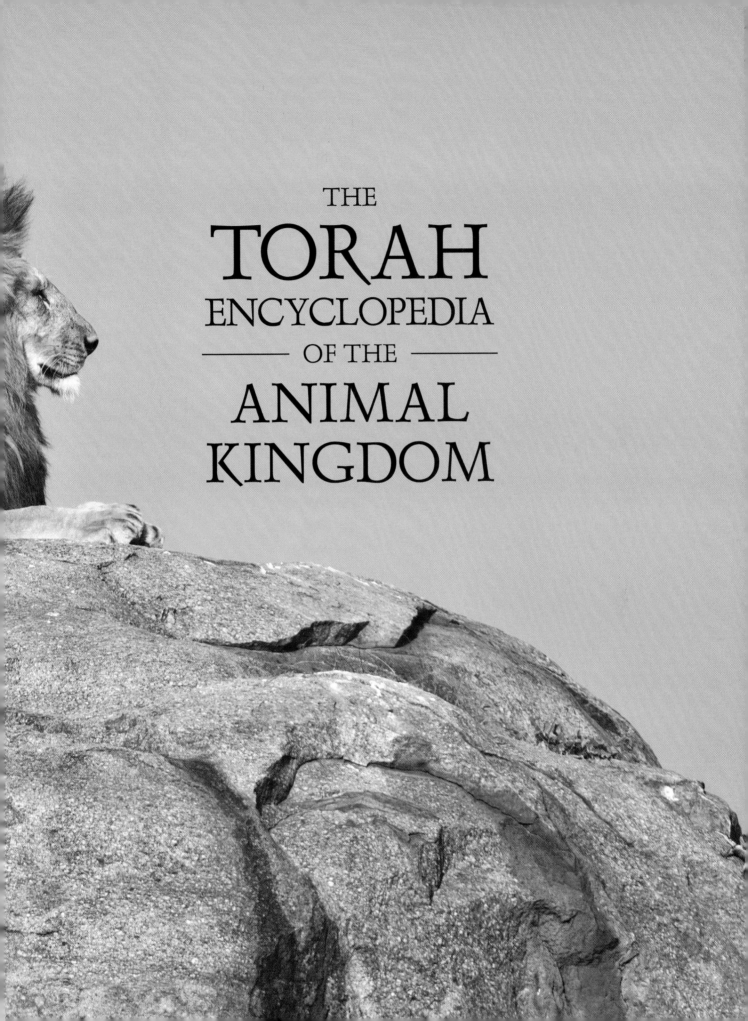

THE
TORAH
ENCYCLOPEDIA
— OF THE —
ANIMAL
KINGDOM

THE
TORAH
ENCYCLOPEDIA
— OF THE —
ANIMAL
KINGDOM

THE SAMSON EDITION

Volume One:

Wild Animals / *Chayot*

NATAN SLIFKIN

 מוזיאון הטבע התנ״כי

THE BIBLICAL MUSEUM OF NATURAL HISTORY

OUPRESS

מגיד

MAGGID

The Torah Encyclopedia of the Animal Kingdom
First English Edition, 2015

The Biblical Museum of Natural History
A project of The Torah and Nature Foundation
9200 W. Sunset Blvd., Suite #700
West Hollywood, CA 90069-3603, USA
www.BiblicalNaturalHistory.org

Maggid Books
An imprint of Koren Publishers Jerusalem, Ltd
POB 8531, New Milford, CT 06776, USA
POB 4044, Jerusalem 91040, Israel
www.korenpub.com

OU Press
An imprint of the Orthodox Union
11 Broadway
New York, NY 10004
www.oupress.org

Book design & layout by Renana Typesetting

ISBN 978-1-59264-404-9, *hardcover*

Printed in Bulgaria

מוזיאון הטבע התנ"כי

THE BIBLICAL MUSEUM OF NATURAL HISTORY

The Biblical Museum of Natural History is a unique institution that is part zoo, part natural history museum, and part Torah education center. It goes beyond the text, beyond the classroom, offering an interactive, hands-on experience of the natural world of the Torah, in order to make the biblical texts and Torah tradition come alive.

The museum showcases the mammals, birds, reptiles, amphibians and insects of Scripture, as well as related zoological topics from the Talmud. The larger species are exhibited as taxidermy specimens, while live exhibits are maintained for smaller species, and there are also a large number of biological artifacts. Through the exciting and interactive tour, visitors learn the identities and symbolism of the animals of Scripture, lessons in Torah values, law and history, and the natural history of biblical Israel.

The Biblical Museum of Natural History is located in Beit Shemesh, Israel. Tours are available by appointment.

Tel: 073-213-1662

Email: Office@TevaTanachi.org

www.TevaTanachi.org

www.BiblicalNaturalHistory.org

Dedicated in memory of Anne Samson

Michael and Susan Baum

Bill and Joan Lopatin

Moshe and Helen Sassover

Dedicated by Dr. Stephen Schloss

To our children Yakira and Gadiel Shepherd,

May your love for and curiosity of the world around you be experienced through
the warm light of our tradition in a way exemplified by this encyclopedia

Jake and Loren Shepherd

Dedicated by Drs. Chana and Gary Gelbfish in memory of

Rabbi Yitzchok Mayer and Rochel Traube, *z"l*,

Holocaust survivors who faithfully and lovingly transmitted
their Torah *mesorah* to their children and grandchildren

Dedicated in memory of Betzalel Binyamin and Grama Henny

Elisha Milstein

To our grandchildren who fill our lives daily with much joy:

Aryeh Menachem, Tamar Chana Malka, Yitzchak Yonatan, Shmuel Zanvil, Moshe,
Simcha Akiva, Yaakov Yitzchak, Temima, Rivka Bracha, Baila, Yehoshua Asher and Rachel

From your adoring grandparents who, like too many of their
generation, did not experience the love of grandparents.

Linda and Joseph Fried

Dedicated by Rhona and Eli Wilamowsky
in honor of their wonderful parents

Cantor and Mrs. Noel and Shirley Schall

Mr. and Mrs. Zvi and Zuta Wilamowsky

Dedicated to our delightful grandchildren and their
fascination, deep appreciation and love for nature

Dov & Nancy Friedberg

Dedicated in memory of my grandfather, David Polis

Jorian Polis Schutz

Dedicated by Larry and Rochelle Russak from Seattle Washington
and the Northwest Wildlife Collection

May we never cease marveling at the wonders of G-d's creations!

Dedicated by David and Miriam Rybak

In memory of Bubby and Zaidy Rybak, and Bubby and Zaidy Bock
whose commitment to Torah and mitzvos continues to inspire us

Dedicated in honor of our daughter, Sonya Kest. May you always be
blessed with a profound love and awe for all Hashem's creatures.

Lauren and Ezra Kest

TABLE OF CONTENTS

Acknowledgments

It is with deep appreciation to the Creator that I complete this work. Aside from my gratitude for the beauty and rich diversity of the natural world, and the wealth of intriguing insights in the Torah, I am truly blessed to be able to work in a field that fascinates me so deeply.

It took fourteen years to produce this work. Many people were involved in this process, but I must first mention my old next-door neighbor from England, Rabbi Hillel Gittleson. About thirty years ago, he told me that one day I could write a book about animals in the Torah. At the time, this seemed highly implausible. But I never forgot his words, and it has proved true.

Over the years I have benefited from many teachers, but my mentor with regard to the relationship between Judaism and the natural sciences was Rav Aryeh Carmell, of blessed memory. I am also grateful to my instructors at Machon Lander and Bar-Ilan University, especially my dissertation advisor Dr. David Malkiel.

Much of the material in this book was originally researched in preparation for classes that I taught many years ago at Midreshet Moriah and Yeshivat Lev HaTorah. I am grateful to these fine institutions for giving me the opportunity to teach, and to the students for their interest. My gratitude also goes to Torah in Motion for enabling me to teach this material via live internet classes and also in the considerably more exotic locations of South Africa, Botswana, Zambia and Zimbabwe, on our annual educational safari trips. My thanks as well to Shai Doron, Sigalit Dvir and Shmulik Yedvab at the Tisch Family Zoological Gardens in Jerusalem, who enabled me to run numerous educational programs there.

My teachers and colleagues in the field of biblical and talmudic zoology have been a tremendous source of knowledge and have enhanced this work greatly: Dr. Zohar Amar, Dr. Avraham Ofir-Shemesh, Dr. Moshe Raanan, Dr. David Talshir, and Rabbi Dr. Ari Zivotofsky. I am also grateful to Prof. Yoram Yom Tov, whose great expertise in the wildlife of the Land of Israel was immensely helpful.

Researching all the countless sources in this book was no easy task. I am grateful to Mrs. Bryna Epstein at the Bar-Ilan library and Rabbi Moshe Schapiro at the Mendel Gottesman Library in Yeshiva University for their assistance. I would also like to thank my friends Rabbi Nesanel Neuman and Rabbi Joshua Waxman for their learned input, and Nichie Fendrich for her insightful suggestions.

Turning a 160,000 word manuscript into a beautiful printed book was extremely challenging. I am grateful to Dr. Moshe Shoshan for his expert editing work and also for writing the glossary of rabbinic sources. Nechama Unterman proofread the text with great skill. I am deeply grateful to Peter (Avi) Kovachev for volunteering his Photoshop skills in adjusting many of the photographs; his work has greatly enhanced this book. Raphaël Freeman and Esther Malka Grodzinski at Renana Typesetting took on the herculean task of devising and executing the book's layout, and the quality of their work speaks for itself. I am grateful to Matthew Miller and Gila Fine at Koren Publishers Jerusalem, and to Rabbi Menachem Genack and Rabbi Simon Posner at OU Press, for taking on the co-publishing, distribution and marketing of this work.

The funding of this project took place through the Torah and Nature Foundation. I am very grateful to Mr. Steven Plotnick for his work in setting up the foundation, and to the directors: Rabbi Yitzchak Adlerstein, Dr. Charles Hall, Mr. Ronny Hersh, Mr. Lee Samson, and Rabbi Dr. Tzvi Hersh Weinreb. I am also indebted to the directors of the foundation's counterpart in Israel, Keren Torah V'Teva: Rabbi David Bar-Cohn and Rabbi Scott Kahn. On behalf of the readers, I would also like to express gratitude to all the people whose support of this work made its publication possible.

The final stages of the publication of this book coincided with the establishment of The Biblical Museum of Natural History, which brings the contents of this work to life. I am deeply grateful to Mr. and Mrs. Shlomo Yehuda and Tamar Rechnitz, Mr. Lee Samson, and Dr. Stephen Schloss, for their generous support of this unique project. My thanks also to the staff at the museum, Shlomo Horowitz, Noah Persky, Chaya Leah Maierovits, and especially administrative director Maayan Steele, whose hard work enabled me to take some time away from the museum in order to complete this book.

My father, Professor Michael Slifkin of blessed memory, always encouraged my fascination with animals and my career as a writer. When I was growing up, we took countless trips together to exotic animal dealers, as well as nature walks and safari trips. A distinguished scientist, he also guided me in understanding the natural sciences. I am deeply saddened that he was unable to see the completed version of this book, but I hope that it honors his memory. My mother, Mrs. Marietta Slifkin, may she live long, also indulged my obsession with animals as a child, despite being traumatized by many of the creatures that I brought into the house. In her home, she has a framed cartoon on the shelf of books that I have written, depicting a "Meet the Author" event at which there is also an option to "Meet the Author's Mother." She truly deserves all the pleasure that she will receive from this book and its reception.

My father-in-law, Mr. Lee Samson, is an invaluable source of guidance and support, for which I am eternally grateful. This takes place in so many ways, whether it is helping me word difficult pieces of writing, guidance with developing projects and negotiating challenges, or chairing the foundation that operates my publications and the museum. My mother-in-law, Mrs. Anne Samson of blessed memory, was always so enthusiastic about my work, and her sudden loss was extremely painful. Several of the sponsors of this work dedicated their support in her memory, and I hope that it brings honor to her name.

I began writing this book shortly after marrying my beloved wife Tali, for whose support no words can do justice. There were times when the sheer scale of this project tempted me to give up, but her encouragement helped me persevere. May we enjoy continued blessings from our children Tikvah, Simcha, Michaella, Chaviva, and Menachem Asher, a.k.a. Ashi.

Natan Slifkin
Ramat Beit Shemesh

About This Book

Writing this work has been a difficult process of finding a balance that will be suitable for a broad range of people. The primary audience of this encyclopedia is Orthodox Jewry, but it will undoubtedly also be of interest to the wider Jewish community and also to non-Jews. Yet even within the primary readership of Orthodox Jews, there are a range of different approaches to subject matter such as that of this encyclopedia. Is this to be a work of religious inspiration or an academic study? A popular work or a scholarly work? It is intended to balance the nature of all of these.

The different tastes and requirements of the diverse audience of this book are reflected in numerous aspects. These include Hebrew transliterations – Bereshit or Genesis? Moshe or Moses? The question was also raised whether to include Hebrew texts for the verses cited; the solution chosen was to present the Hebrew verses as a separate graphic feature on the same page where the English translation is quoted. (Only verses which actually mention the names of animals are presented in Hebrew.)

An additional complexity in writing this work is that the subject matter is inherently highly uneven. When discussing the animal described in the Torah as the *yachmur*, for example, the primary discussion revolves around a very technical investigation into its identification. With the lion, on the other hand, its identification is clear, and most of the discussion revolves around its symbolism in Scripture and Midrash. In introducing the section on kosher wild animals, the discussion is very different again, being largely focused on intricacies in Jewish law.

In order to assist the reader with navigating each chapter, the material has been divided into sections that are labeled according to various categories. While the chapters are designed to be a coherent whole, some readers may wish to skip certain types of sections. The six section categories are as follows:

1. "Natural History" reviews basic zoological information about the animal, including its historic and current status in the wild in the Land of Israel. This usually appears at the beginning of the chapter, unless the very identity of the animal mentioned in the Torah is unclear, in which case the "Identification" section appears first.
2. "Identification" explores the process of correctly identifying the animal named in the Torah, and the methodology for this is explained in part II of the introduction. Note that in several cases, it is not possible to identify the animal with certainty; in such cases, a question mark is placed next to the Hebrew name of the animal at the beginning of the chapter.
3. "Symbolism" surveys the symbolism of the animal in Scripture, Midrash, and later works of Jewish thought; these sections sometimes venture into homiletic discourses.
4. "Law and Ritual" discusses references to the animal in the Talmud or later works of halakha that deal with legal issues pertaining to the animal or its use in ritual practices.

5. "Theology, Philosophy, and Science" explores complex issues of Jewish thought, often relating to the science of modern zoology.

6. "Jewish History" is used rather loosely to include any way in which the animal correlates with the history of the Jewish people, even post-scriptural and talmudic eras; thus, it also includes accounts of remarkable efforts by the Israel Parks and Nature Authority to restore wild animals to the Land of Israel.

Another challenge raised in preparing this work for a wide range of readers is with regard to dealing with conflicts between rabbinic literature and modern science. This is a potentially sensitive area in which the approach to dealing with such questions varies considerably depending on one's religious worldview. Some reject the assessments of modern science; some interpret the statements of the Sages as being a metaphor, or as reflecting spiritual truths; and others follow the view that the Sages of the Talmud were adopting the scientific beliefs of their era. Consequently, it was decided to avoid delving into such topics in this work. When a statement made by the Sages of the Talmud conflicts with the assessments of modern zoologists, this is merely noted; the reader can follow his or her own preferred approach with regard to such issues. Topics such as the age of the universe and the evolution of life are not relevant to this work and are not discussed.

As noted in the introduction, the term "Torah" in the title of this work does not only refer to the Five Books of Moses. Rather, it is used in a broad sense, to refer to all twenty-four books of Scripture, as well as Mishna, Talmud, Midrash, and the entirety of literature relating to these texts. In discussing each animal's role in the Torah, the goal is to be as comprehensive as possible. Every scriptural reference to specific animals is quoted in both English and Hebrew (where a verse is quoted on more than one occasion, the Hebrew only appears alongside the first instance where it is referenced). Virtually every reference to the animal in Mishna, Talmud, and Midrash is also quoted; where the same passage appears in multiple texts with only minor variations, these are referenced at the end of the citation or in the endnotes. The only instances where references to animals in rabbinic literature are not mentioned are some cases where the reference to the animal clearly has nothing to do with the particular nature of that animal (for example, when a lion is mentioned merely as an example of a dangerous animal). Scriptural citations appear with a parchment-textured sidebar; citations from rabbinic literature appear with a pale green sidebar.

In general, full bibliographic references are given in the endnotes. The exception is for general works on biblical zoology and the wildlife of the Land of Israel, which are cited in virtually every chapter of this book. Full bibliographic information for these works is listed in a special bibliography at the end of the book, and there is also a review of works on biblical zoology in part IV of the introduction, "A History of Biblical and Rabbinic Zoology." A more comprehensive bibliography of literature relating to biblical and talmudic zoology can be found online at www.BiblicalNaturalHistory.org/resources. Bibliographic information is not given for traditional rabbinic works; instead, there is a glossary of rabbinic sources at the end of the book, briefly describing the nature and era of each such work cited.

The animals featured in this book are not presented in alphabetical order, which would have no significance beyond convenience. Instead, the animals are presented in a thematic sequence relating to their role in the Torah. The animals are divided into three categories: predators, kosher wild animals, and other wild animals. Within the category of predators, the animals are ordered with regard to their power as predators, which roughly correlates to their size (but not always – lions are not as large as bears, yet are superior predators). With kosher animals, the animals are listed in the order in which they appear in the list of kosher animals presented in the Book of Deuteronomy, and the significance of this order is discussed in the introduction to that section. The remaining animals are presented in an order relating to their thematic role in Scripture and Talmud.

General Introduction

The Role of Animals in Torah

Defining Torah

The Torah Encyclopedia of the Animal Kingdom discusses the animals of the Torah; but before doing so, we must first clarify the meaning of "Torah."

"Torah" is in fact a term with diverse meanings. Often, it is used specifically to refer to the Five Books of Moses and in contrast to the books of Prophets (*Nevi'im*) and Writings (*Ketuvim*). However, in classical Judaism, there is both the Written Torah and the Oral Torah. The Written Torah includes all twenty-four books of Scripture. The Oral Torah is found in the Mishna, Talmud, Midrash, and certain other texts from that period.

But the term "Torah" is often not only limited to such classical works of the Jewish canon. It is commonly used in reference to any discussion relating to any of these texts, or anything contributing toward the goals of Judaism. Thus, the word "Torah" often refers to the entire gamut of Jewish religious works.

This broad usage of the word "Torah" is the meaning that is intended with the title of this work.[1] It is an encyclopedia of animals in all twenty-four books of Scripture, Mishna, Talmud, Midrash, and throughout Jewish texts, tradition, and history. Animals appear in these for a variety of different reasons, which we shall explore in this section.

The wild ram that Abraham found trapped in the thicket would probably have been a mouflon

Animals as Participants

Sometimes, animals appear in the Torah as participants in events described in a narrative. Examples from Scripture include the animals that were on Noah's Ark, the ram slaughtered by Abraham in place of Isaac, the animals in the plagues of Egypt, the bears that attacked the children who mocked Elisha, the lion that was killed by Samson, and the monkeys that were presented to King Solomon. Examples from the Talmud include the fox encountered by R. Akiva, and the lions encountered by R. Shimon b. Chalafta.[2]

Beyond the general concept that everything in this world is directed by God, there is a prevalent theme in Jewish tradition of animals, especially predators, being specific emissaries of God. Most famously, we have the creatures that were involved in the plagues that were inflicted upon Egypt. There are also numerous mentions in Scripture of predatory animals being sent by God to punish people for acts of wickedness, as we shall explore in the introduction to the section on predators.

Animals are generally not presented in the Torah as characters with personalities, aside from the serpent in the Garden of Eden and Balaam's ass. Still, it is the inherent characteristics of the various species that are significant for their role in events. Therefore, there is much discussion in rabbinic tradition regarding the symbolism and significance of animals that are described as participating in events.

The hoopoe, recently voted national bird of Israel, is mentioned in Scripture in the list of non-kosher birds, under the name dukhifat.

Animals in Laws and Rituals

A second context in which animals are mentioned in Scripture, Midrash, and Talmud is in various laws and rituals. In Scripture, this most obviously occurs with regard to the laws of kosher and non-kosher animals, and with sacrificial offerings. However, there are also laws concerning animals relating to spiritual purity. These differ depending on the type of animal, and thus involve identifying the type of animal under consideration. Other laws relate to man's interactions with animals. This latter category includes not only man's treatment of animals, but also how to deal with animals that attack people or property; the Talmud elaborates on which types of animals are rated as dangerous from the outset.

Some of these laws are relevant to the animal kingdom as a whole, rather than to a specific type of creature. These are not discussed in this work.[3] However, laws that relate to particular types or groups of animals are discussed in the relevant sections. For example, laws relating to kosher wild animals are discussed in the introduction to that section, laws relating to damages caused by predatory animals are discussed in the introduction to that section, and laws relating to the acquisition of elephants are discussed in the chapter on that animal.

Inspiration from Animals

A third category of references to animals are those that provide inspiration and awe. Examples include various references to animals in the Books of Psalms, Proverbs, and Job. Psalm 104 describes the beauty and harmony of the natural world and its inhabitants, from hyraxes to storks to whales. It also includes a famous verse that speaks of the wonders of all nature:

> How great are Your works, O God! In wisdom You have made them all; the earth is full of Your creatures. (Ps. 104:24)

The wonder of animals stems not just from extraordinary aspects of individual creatures, but also from the rich diversity and sheer numbers of the animal kingdom:

GABOR NEDECKY / SHUTTERSTOCK

"How great are your works, O God!" Come and see how many types of domestic and wild animals and birds there are in the world, and how many types of fishes in the sea. Is the voice of one like that of another? Is the appearance of one like that of another? Is the personality of one like that of another? Is the taste of one like that of another? (*Tanna DeVei Eliyahu Rabba*, ch. 2)

Sometimes, the inspiration being described in Scripture is not from wondrous aspects of the animals themselves. Instead, it stems from the providential manner in which the animal survives. The line between these two, however, is not always distinct.

The most extensive accounts of the animal kingdom occur in the Book of Job. In response to Job's protests about the terrible suffering that he underwent, God gives detailed descriptions of a variety of animals. These may be intended to humble Job in the face of such marvels of nature. Alternatively, or in addition, they may be intended to demonstrate God's providence over the animal kingdom, in order to impress upon Job that there is plan and purpose to existence, even if it is not always apparent to man.

RICHMONDPEST / FLICKR

Proverbs 30:19 describes the movement of a snake as being beyond human understanding.

The result of all this is that the animal kingdom is seen as praising God:

Praise God from the land, the sea-monsters, and all the depths…the beasts and every animal, insect, and winged bird. (Ps. 148:7, 10)

This does not mean that animals are actually uttering praise. Instead, it means that through the wonder of their very existence, the animal kingdom is living testimony to the glory of its Creator. This is echoed in the prayer *Nishmat kol chai*, "The soul of every living thing shall bless Your Name."

Animals as Symbols and Metaphors

The fourth type of references to animals in Scripture is that in which animals are mentioned to create imagery or for their symbolic value. (This is also often explored for animals that appear as participants in narratives, based on the understanding that these particular animals were involved for a reason.)

The prophets often make use of imagery involving animals. For example, Jeremiah and Ezekiel describe animals that inhabit desolate areas, in order to conjure up imagery of destruction. Various people and nations are metaphorically represented by different animals. God Himself is compared to a variety of different creatures, including a vulture, a lion, and a bear. The Talmud describes how Boaz pounced like a leopard, and the Midrash engages extensively in describing how animals symbolize various people, nations, and concepts. In the medieval period, Berechiah ben Natronai HaNakdan published an extensive series of animal fables, adapted from those of Aesop, featuring a wide range of creatures displaying different personalities.[4]

ANGELFISH / FLICKR

Genesis 48:16 records Jacob's blessing that his descendants should reproduce like fish.

"Praise God from the land, the sea-
monsters, and all the depths…"
(Psalms 148:7)

In Jacob's blessings for the Twelve Tribes, many of the blessings use animal symbolism. The Talmud stresses that even those tribes that did not receive blessings comparing them to animals, are elsewhere compared to animals:

> "And the midwives said to Pharaoh: For the Hebrew women are not like the Egyptian women; they are *chayot*" (Ex. 1:19). What are *chayot*? If you say actual midwives (the usual understanding of the word here) – does a midwife not need another midwife in order to give birth?! Rather, they said to him, this nation is compared to animals (*chayot*): "Judah is a young lion," "Dan shall be a serpent," "Naphtali is a hind set loose," "Issachar is a strong ass," "Joseph is the firstling of an ox," "Benjamin is a predatory wolf." Those [tribes] that have [such imagery] written with regard to them, have it written; for those who do not have it written, it is written: "What was your mother? A lioness, crouching amongst the lions" (Ezek. 19:2) (i.e. that they are all compared to lions). (Sota 11b[5])

This also explains how animal names became popular as human names. In Scripture, there are numerous Jews who are named after animals: Rachel (ewe), Shual (fox),[6] Shafan (hyrax),[7] Chuldah (marten),[8] Yael (ibex),[9] Deborah (bee),[10] and Jonah (dove).[11] The practice of naming people after animals appears to have subsequently disappeared, and was restarted by Ashkenazi Jews in the fourteenth century.[12] Originally, it was only German/Yiddish names for animals that were used, added to a person's Hebrew name. In the nineteenth century, people began to use Hebrew animal names. Animals used as names include the lion (Leib – Aryeh), bear (Baer – Dov), wolf (Vulf – Ze'ev), bird (Feigel – Tzipporah), and deer (Hirsch – incorrectly considered in Europe to be synonymous with Tzvi).

Animals as Educators

A consequence of animals representing various characteristics is that they can be mentioned not to describe people, but also in order to educate people. There is a verse in the Book of Job that is commonly translated as follows:

> He teaches us more than the animals of the land,
> and makes us wiser than the birds of the heavens.
> (Job 35:11)

However, there is a different way of translating it:

> He teaches us *from* the animals of the land, and *from* the birds of the heavens He makes us wise.

The Talmud elaborates upon this verse according to this alternative translation:

> R. Chiyya said: What does it mean, "He teaches us from the animals of the land, and from the birds of the heavens He makes us wise"? It means, He makes us wise. "He teaches us from the animals of the land" – this refers to the female mule, which squats to urinate; "And from the birds of the heavens He makes us wise" – this refers to the rooster, which appeases and then mates. R. Yochanan said: Had the Torah not been given, we would

*"Had the Torah not been given, we would have learned … [the prohibition of] theft from the ant …"
(Eiruvin 100b)*

ANDREY PAVLOV / SHUTTERSTOCK

have learned modesty from the cat, [the prohibition of] theft from the ant, [the prohibition of] forbidden relationships from the dove, and the proper method of conjugal relations from fowl. (Eiruvin 100b)

The Mishna highlights four creatures for the character traits that they symbolize, which we are enjoined to emulate:

R. Yehuda b. Teima said: Be as brazen as a leopard, as light as a vulture, as swift as a gazelle, and as mighty as a lion to fulfill the will of your Father in Heaven. (Mishna Avot 5:24)

This was taken further in *Perek Shira*, a text of unclear origins that is first referenced in the tenth century.[13] *Perek Shira* lists many different elements of the universe – the luminaries, geographical features, plants, birds, animals, insects – each of which "recites" a verse from Scripture. There have been many different interpretations of *Perek Shira*, but one approach is that each element of the natural world teaches us a lesson, which is alluded to in the verse – the "message" of each creature.

In conclusion, we see that animals are mentioned in Scripture, Talmud, Midrash, and Jewish tradition for a variety of different purposes. If we are to understand the narratives that are being described, the laws that are being legislated, the inspiration that is being presented, the symbolism that is being conveyed, and the lessons that are being taught by these sources we have to familiarize ourselves with the identities and nature of these animals.

Identifying the Animals of the Torah

The Importance of Identification

Identifying the animals of the Torah is not an easy task. Biblical Hebrew has not been a spoken language for thousands of years. The meanings of the names of animals in Modern Hebrew are not always the same as their meanings in Biblical Hebrew. They are simply the assessments of those who created Modern Hebrew, who might not even have been trying to replicate the biblical meaning of the terms. Even if they were trying to do so, sometimes errors occurred due to animal names taking on different meanings while Jews were in Europe and were surrounded by different animals than those that live in the Land of Israel.

One may wonder if it is indeed important to expend effort in precisely identifying the animals of the Torah. What difference does it make if a person thinks that the *tzvi* is the gazelle, the deer, the ibex, or the antelope?

In fact, there are several reasons why it is important to be able to accurately identify the animals of the Torah. One simple reason is that this, too, is part of the fulfillment of the mitzva of Torah study. We are duty bound to understand the precise meaning of every word in the Torah, including the names of the animals.

Another reason is that every animal is mentioned in the Torah for a specific purpose, and this purpose can be negated if we make a mistake regarding the identity of the animal. For example, many creatures are mentioned in the context of the laws of kosher and non-kosher animals. Obviously, in order to be able to correctly observe the laws of *kashrut*, one has to know exactly which animals are in each category. In fact, in this context, Maimonides states that there is a mitzva that is fulfilled by knowing how to identify the animals:

> It is a positive commandment to know the signs by which those domestic and wild animals, birds, fish, and locusts that are permitted to be eaten are distinguished from those that are not permitted to be eaten, as it is written, "And you shall distinguish between the clean and unclean animals, and between the unclean and clean birds" (Lev. 20:25); and it is also written, "To distinguish between the unclean and the clean, and between the animal that may be eaten and the animal which may not be eaten" (Lev. 11:47). (Maimonides, *Mishneh Torah, Hilkhot Maakhalot Assurot* 1:1)

In many cases, animals are mentioned in order to convey symbolic or moralistic concepts. But if one does not know the identity of the animal mentioned, these messages are lost. For example, the prophets often portray the destruction of Israel by evoking the sound of the *tanim*. This phrase is carried through into several of the lamentations recited on the Ninth of Av. Some, however, leave this name untranslated, due to uncertainty about its correct translation. Yet in doing so, the intent of the author is entirely lost. But if one knows that the *tanim* are jackals, and one is familiar with their mournful-sounding howls, one understands the message that the prophet was trying to convey.

This is a reason not only to be able to identify the animals of the Torah, but also to be familiar with their nature and way of life. The prophets conveyed messages to us in terms of the world in which they lived. This was not a world of cars and computers. It was a world in which the stork migration heralded spring, the crocodile symbolized Egypt, and the great hippopotamus was an unstoppable force of nature. If we are to understand their messages, we have to understand the world in which they lived.

In the biblical Land of Israel, the arrival of the stork heralded the spring. This is a sight that can still be seen today.

MURATART / SHUTTERSTOCK

Methodology

In order to identify the animals mentioned in the Torah, we need to establish a systematic methodology. This takes six factors into account:

1. All references to the creature in Torah literature;
2. Comprehensive and accurate zoological knowledge;
3. The names of the creature in other ancient languages;
4. Knowing when it is and when it is not viable to posit that the animal is unknown or extinct;
5. Zoogeography – the realization that the animals of the Torah are those indigenous to the region of the Land of Israel;
6. A thorough review of previous research in this area, with a proper evaluation of each source.

We shall now proceed to discuss these factors in detail, and apply them by way of example to some of the animals in the Torah.

1. All References in Torah Literature

The first factor to take into account is that one must study all references to the creature concerned in the entire gamut of Torah literature. Additional clues to the creature's identity may be found elsewhere in Scripture or in the Talmud. One must also ascertain that the presumed conclusion is not contradicted by conflicting information elsewhere in the Torah.

For example, in listing non-kosher animals, the Torah mentions the *shafan* as an animal that brings up the cud but lacks true hooves. One might be tempted to identify it as a member of the camel family, such as a llama. However, in Proverbs, the *shafan* is described as a small animal, and in Psalms it is described as hiding under rocks. These descriptions would not match any member of the camel family.

2. Comprehensive Zoological Knowledge

The second factor is that one's knowledge of zoology must be comprehensive, and the information as accurate as possible. In past times, when knowledge of the animal world was very poor, some people made mistakes about the identities of the animals of the Torah. Even today, the most accurate information is not to be found in the average encyclopedia of animals found in homes and libraries. Such books usually contain second- or third-hand information which is sometimes inaccurate. Most of us are not able to make detailed studies of animals in the field. But our information should ideally come from those who have specialized in individual groups of creatures, either via authoritative publications, scientific journals, or personal communication.

At the same time, it is important to realize that such information was not necessarily available in antiquity. Thus, descriptions of animals from antiquity would reflect beliefs about animals in antiquity rather than modern zoology.[14] As such, knowledge of the history of natural history can be just as relevant as knowledge of natural history itself.

3. Names in Other Languages

Another valuable technique in identifying the names of creatures found in the Torah is to look at which creatures possess the same or similar names in other languages. Of the thousands of languages in the world, clearly not all of them concern us. The languages of importance to us are those closest to the region and preferably the era of the giving of the Torah. This includes not only various dialects of Arabic, but also other Semitic languages and also languages in the broader Afro-Asiatic family.

Rabbi Avraham ibn Ezra utilizes this method in identifying the *nesher*, pointing out that there is a bird by this name in the language of Ishmael (Arabic).[15] Ibn Ezra adds that the Arabic name is "somewhat of a proof, in that the two languages are very similar." It transpires that the bird known as *nasr* in Arabic is the griffon vulture, which may be surprising to many as the identity of the *nesher*, but for which there are ample further lines of proof.

The limitations of this technique must be recognized. As Ibn Ezra states, it is "somewhat" of a proof, but it is not foolproof. Among the many different dialects of Arabic, for example, one can find the same name used for several very different species. Still, this technique is an important one of which to be aware, although its implementation can be difficult, due to the difficulty in deciphering ancient languages.

The nesher is identified by Ibn Ezra as the griffon vulture.

4. Difficulties with Unknowns and Extinctions

In many cases, perhaps even the majority, identifying the animals of Scripture is extremely difficult. Often there is no known creature that accurately matches the clues at hand. In face of these difficulties, it is sometimes suggested that the creature is unknown or extinct. For example, since it is difficult to interpret the Torah's description of the *shafan* as a ruminating animal that lacks split hooves, some posit that the true *shafan* is extinct.

While this concept is freely used, it is actually highly difficult to substantiate. That a creature from Scripture should be living and unknown to us is extraordinarily unlikely. Although there are still new discoveries in the animal kingdom, these are exclusively from remote regions of the world. Israel and the surrounding area, on the other hand, has been a center of human society for thousands of years. There are countless artifacts from ancient civilizations of the area which give us enormous information about the world in which these people lived, including its animal life.

Another important source of information for establishing a picture of the animals formerly in existence is the fossil record. In some cases, the fossil record gives us important information about animals that we would not otherwise think to be mentioned in the Torah. There are remains of animals that were formerly living in the region of Israel, but now only live elsewhere, such as the hippopotamus. We also find evidence of some animals that are now entirely extinct, such as the aurochs. But we should be skeptical of claims that a creature formerly existed if there is no evidence for it in the fossil record.

One might argue that there is insufficient evidence to determine that a given creature did *not* exist, as it is only under very specific conditions that an animal will fossilize. However, since the fossil record provides extensive evidence for the overwhelming majority of known animals, this indicates that we do possess very comprehensive coverage. And while the fossil record is poor for some parts of the world and some parts of history, for the Land of Israel in the biblical period it is superb. Overall, then, in most cases it is unreasonable to argue that the true creature discussed in the Torah is altogether unknown to us from current animal life, ancient accounts, and the fossil record.

Furthermore, extinction due to natural causes (i.e. before the destruction by man in the last few centuries) is a very rare event. The likelihood of a given species becoming extinct in the last few thousand years is very low.

The aurochs, mentioned several times in the Torah, is now extinct.

5. Zoogeography

"Zoogeography" refers to the geographical distribution – past and present – of animals. The Creator of the World obviously knows every creature that He created. And the Torah is binding at all times and in all places. However, the Torah would only mention animals that were familiar to the generation that received it. These are the animals that are indigenous to the region of the Land of Israel. If we look at the reasons as to why animals are mentioned in the Torah in the first place, this becomes clear.

Animals are mentioned in Scripture for three reasons. Sometimes, an animal is recorded as having been involved in a historical event. If so, it must have been an animal found in that region. A qualification to this is that some animals, while not indigenous to that region, were nevertheless familiar to people due to their being imported to the area. The animals in this category are the monkeys and peacocks that are explicitly described as being shipped to King Solomon.

A second category of animals mentioned in the Torah are those listed in the laws of kosher and non-kosher animals. Since many of these laws are transmitted by means of stating the names of the animals, this means that the animals themselves had to be familiar to the people. Otherwise, their names would be meaningless and useless as a means of transmitting the laws.

The overwhelming majority of animals in the Torah are mentioned to convey concepts, which would be meaningless if people didn't know what the animal was. There is a principle in rabbinic literature that "the Torah speaks in the language of man." This does not mean mankind in general, but rather the people who initially received the Torah. For example, the Torah contains figures of speech and references that were used by the Jewish people at that time. This principle is all the more true with the rest of Scripture – the books of Prophets and Writings. Prophecies were received and transmitted by the prophets in terms of concepts that were familiar to them and their intended audience. The animals mentioned in Scripture, usually to symbolize and convey concepts, were animals familiar to the audience – which are the animals of the region of the Land of Israel.

Thus, in all cases, the Torah would only mention animals that were familiar to the Jewish people at that time. It is often not appreciated that these are very different from the animals of Europe or America, as discussed in the section on the wildlife of the Torah.

Furthermore, the animals of the Torah are not the animals that live in Israel today, but rather they are animals that lived in the biblical Land of Israel. This includes many species that are no longer found in the region, such as lions, aurochsen, hartebeest, and crocodiles. There are also some species living in Israel today that were introduced to the area, deliberately or accidentally, relatively recently and were not native to the region in biblical times. Some of these newcomers have also led people astray in identifying the animals of Scripture.

SERGEY URYADNIKOV / SHUTTERSTOCK

Crocodiles were found in the Land of Israel until the early twentieth century.

Returning to our example of the *shafan*, we now have a further reason why it could not refer to a llama, aside from the llama not being a small animal. The *shafan* is mentioned by both King David in Psalms and King Solomon in Proverbs, and was thus an animal that they knew of. Furthermore, it is described in the context of its natural habitat, as something familiar to the audience. But llamas have only ever been found in South America. Even if one were to posit the highly unlikely possibility that a llama was shipped to King Solomon, he would not have been able to describe its existence in its natural habitat to the Jewish people for them to relate to. Furthermore, since his goal was to describe a small animal that hides in rocks, and there is a local animal that fulfills that description – the hyrax – there would be no reason for him to look elsewhere.

6. Prior Research

Serious research to determine the identities of the animals in the Torah should include a review of all previous scholarship in this area. But it is also important to correctly prioritize and evaluate past scholarship.

One very important factor to take into account when studying prior Jewish scholarship with regard to identifying animals is zoogeographical awareness. Since the destruction of the Temple, and until very recently, most Jewish scholars did not live in the Land of Israel. Furthermore, it was generally not appreciated that the animals of the Land of Israel are very different from the animals of other lands. As a result, many rabbinic scholars identified the animals of the Torah as animals which they knew from Europe. Later rabbinic scholars often recognized the drawbacks of following earlier scholars who lived outside of the Land of Israel and were not familiar with it, in fields such as geography and botany.[16] However, it is often not appreciated that this is also very relevant to identifying animals in the Torah. Authorities such as Rashi are often given priority over authorities such as Rav Saadia Gaon in explicating words in the Torah. But in the case of identifying animals, it is Rav Saadia Gaon who should receive priority, since he lived in Egypt, Israel, and Babylonia, whereas Rashi lived in France.

In reviewing previous efforts at identifying the animals of the Torah, there is a tremendous quantity of research by non-Jewish scholars. With regard to analyzing Scripture and Talmud, there were some classical Jewish commentators such as Abarbanel who themselves made use of non-Jewish interpretations,[17] following Rambam's maxim was that one should adopt the truth from wherever it comes. Nevertheless, the general trend was, of course, to stick with Jewish approaches. In this volume, the emphasis with regard to the significance and symbolism of animals in Scripture has been very much upon traditional Jewish interpreters. However, in the case of identifying animals, a broader approach was utilized, although traditional views are discussed extensively.

It should be noted that some historical non-Jewish scholarship with regard to the identification of animals was itself ultimately based on Jewish sources. For example, Jerome, who wrote the Latin translation of Scripture known as the Vulgate, consulted with rabbinic scholars in ancient Israel regarding the meaning of various terms. Meanwhile, some Jewish scholarship incorporated insights from non-Jewish scholars.

In general, although there is a vast chasm between traditional approaches to Torah and academic Jewish studies, the field of biblical and talmudic zoology is one area in which the two worlds meet.[18] This is because we are not dealing here with principles of Jewish ideology or belief, but rather with the technical matter of identifying animals mentioned in the Torah. As we have discussed, in most cases this relates to expertise in zoology, geography, and languages rather than religious belief and values.

The Classification of Animals

Torah vs. Zoology

The classification of animals embodies two related concepts: how various different types of animals are grouped together, and how one type of animal is differentiated from another. The Torah's system of animal classification is very different from modern zoology in both of these aspects. It is what is known in academic discourse as a "folk taxonomy" rather than a "scientific taxonomy."[19]

There is nothing disparaging in speaking of a "folk taxonomy." It is crucial to note that there is no "right" or "wrong" method of classification. A system of classification has no independent reality. It is simply a means by which we measure and describe the animal kingdom, depending upon our purpose. For the purposes of science, the animal kingdom is evaluated on its own terms. For the Torah's system of classification, the animal kingdom is presented in terms of the relationship between animals and human beings, and their perception by the common person. Neither system is more correct than the other; they are just serving different purposes.[20]

To illustrate this principle further, consider the court case regarding whales that took place in New York in the nineteenth century. The question under judgment was whether taxes on fish oil should also apply to whale oil. Whalers, naturalists, philosophers, and lawyers all weighed in on the question. It is important to recognize that there is no objective right or wrong answer. Everyone, on both sides, agreed that whales are warm-blooded animals that give birth to live young and nurse them on milk. But who defines the term "fish"? Naturalists defined it as referring to cold-blooded creatures, with whales being mammals instead. But whalers, who knew whales just as well, used the word "fish" to refer to any fishlike creature, including whales – and the jury agreed that this was a legitimate meaning of the word.[21]

Zoology itself employs different terms of classification depending on the purpose. For example, "nekton" is a term that refers to all aquatic life possessing independent motion,

A beluga whale nursing its young. It is a mammal, but it can potentially still be called a "fish," depending upon how one defines the term.

as opposed to plankton, which drifts in whichever direction the water moves. Thus, certain microscopic organisms, fish, and whales are all nekton, even though they are from very different classes of creatures.

Grouping Animals in the Zoological System

Generally, zoological science groups animals using the phylogenetic system, which is based upon shared anatomical features. Thus, for example, since the internal anatomy of a whale is far more similar to that of a dog than to that of a shark, it is classified along with the dog as being a mammal, despite its superficial resemblance to a shark. However, there are numerous controversies as to how much weight to give to various features, and this leads to disputes regarding how to group various families. For instance, there was a dispute for many decades as to whether pandas should be grouped with raccoons or with bears.

The animal kingdom is divided into the primary categories of mammals, birds, reptiles, amphibians, fishes, and invertebrates (and other members of the animal kingdom such as sponges and jellyfish). Following this are various subdivisions into orders, families, genera, and so on. The hierarchical system used in the zoological system is as follows; the example shows the classification of the domestic cow:

Class	*Mammalia* (Mammals)
Order	*Artiodactyla* (Even-toed hoofed mammals)
(& sometimes: Suborder)	*Ruminantia* (Ruminants)
Family	*Bovidae* (Cloven-hoofed ruminants)
(& sometimes: Subfamily)	*Bovinae* (Cattle, buffalo, and antelope)
(& sometimes: Tribe)	*Bovini* (Cattle and buffalo)
Genus	*Bos* (Cattle)
Species	*primigenius* (Aurochs)
(& sometimes: Subspecies)	*taurus* (Domesticated version of aurochs)

When referring to an animal, only the genus and species is used (and sometimes the subspecies, if it exists). The genus is always capitalized, and the species and subspecies written in lower case. Thus, the domestic cow is *Bos primigenius taurus.*

Following the internal anatomy of a whale, zoology classifies it along with dogs and cats as being a mammal.

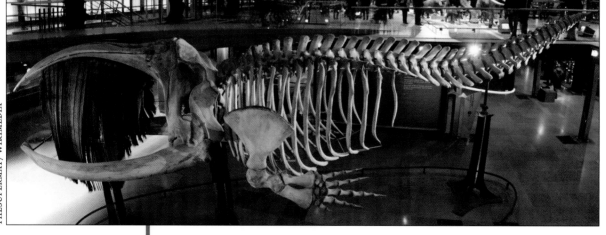

Grouping Animals in the Torah System

The Torah's system of dividing animals into groups is considerably different from that used in zoology. It is based on their overall external appearance, the habitat in which they live, and their relationship to man.

Terrestrial animals of significant size are divided into *behemot* (domestic animals) and *chayot* (wild animals). *Sheratzim* ("creeping" or "swarming" creatures) refers to small terrestrial creatures, including certain reptiles such as lizards; but it also refers to certain mammals, such as most rodents and certain small carnivores. *Remes* refers to terrestrial insects and other invertebrates (which are also sometimes termed *sheretz haaretz*). *Of* is a category including birds and also bats, which are superficially similar to birds. *Sheretz haof* are winged insects. In aquatic environments, there are *dagim* (fishes), *chayat hayam* (aquatic animals), and *sheretz hayam* (aquatic invertebrates).

It is important to note that aspects of classification which we take for granted may be based on premises of modern zoology that are not shared by different systems. It is not just a matter of zoology grouping animals into mammals, birds, reptiles, and so on, and Torah using different categories. The entire system of categorization may be different.

For example, we are used to the idea that if something fits in one category (say, it is a reptile), then it cannot be in another category (say, a fish). Modern zoological taxonomy is a nested hierarchy in which there is absolutely no overlap. But it is possible that the Torah system may allow an animal to simultaneously be in two categories,[22] or even to move from one category to another as it develops.[23]

Bats are not birds, but this has no bearing on their being classified as of *in the biblical system of taxonomy.*

Defining Species in Zoology

It may come as a surprise to learn that there is no unequivocal definition of a "species" in zoology. It is popularly assumed that species can be defined simply as animals that do not reproduce with others, and that it is thus an objectively real definition. But matters are not so simple. There are animals that can interbreed and even produce fertile offspring, such as lions and tigers, and yet nobody would consider them to be the same species, due to the vast physical and behavioral differences. Conversely, there are populations that are somewhat physically different and do not interbreed with each other, but which should still be considered the same species.

As an example of the complexities involved, consider domestic dogs, which are descended from wolves (*Canis lupus*). Dogs and wolves can still interbreed, and their offspring are fertile. Nevertheless, all zoologists agree that due to the extensive physical and behavioral differences, dogs should be classified differently from wolves. But how exactly should they be classified? There is no unequivocal answer. Some consider that they

Two ligers, hybrids of lions and tigers

17

have developed into an entirely different species, *Canis familiaris*. But many others consider that they are simply a subspecies of wolves, and name them *Canis lupus familiaris*.

More than twenty different definitions of "species" have been offered.[24] Many argue that there is no single definition of "species," and that it is therefore not a real category in nature, as is commonly thought.

Defining Types in Torah

With regard to the level at which individual animals are differentiated from each other, Torah does not use the zoological concept of species. Instead, it uses its own unique concept of *min*, "type." The definition of *min* is even less clear than the concept of species.[25] There are, however, some general observations that can be made.

ALASTAIR RAE

The gerbil would presumably be rated in the Torah as being of the same min *as the mouse.*

As discussed earlier, the Torah's system of classification is a folk taxonomy, presented in terms of the animal kingdom's relationship to human beings. The differences between many zoological species are simply irrelevant from the human standpoint. This is especially true in the case of smaller species, where the differences may not even be noticeable. All the different species of bats in the Land of Israel – over two dozen – would presumably be classified as the same *min*. So would all the different species of mice, which would also include voles, gerbils, hamsters, and other rodents.

At the other end of the scale, large animals of great significance to humans can be classified as different *minim* even if they are not different species from a zoological standpoint. As noted earlier, there is dispute amongst zoologists as to whether domesticated versions of wild animals are classified as an entirely separate species, or merely a subspecies. In the Torah system, however, it seems that such animals, which differ greatly in their relationship vis-à-vis humans, are classified as entirely different *minim*.

Additionally, it seems that there are different levels of *min*-classification, i.e. regular *minim* and subspecies of *minim*. This is similar to the concept of species and subspecies in zoology, although here there are not distinct terms for the two levels of taxa.[26] For example, the Torah gives a list of twenty-four types of birds that are not kosher. With several of these, after mentioning the bird's name, it says *lemino*, "according to its kind." The Talmud states that this serves to include many dozens, even hundreds, of different types:

HENRIQUE OLIVEIRA PIRES / FLICKR

The common buzzard, described in the Talmud as having a hundred different varieties.

> There are a hundred birds in the East, all of which are the *min* of the buzzard. (Chullin 63b)

We see here that *min* can have a very broad definition, referring to many different zoological species.[27] Several authorities state that while the Torah states "according to its kind" for birds whose sub-types differ greatly, even those birds for which the Torah does not state "according to its kind" have sub-types that differ to some degree.[28]

Furthermore, it seems that *min* can sometimes refer to a related variety. For example, the Torah's reference to "the crow, after its kind" is explained by the Talmud to include the *zarzir* (jackdaw or starling).[29] This does not mean that the *zarzir* is a subcategory of the crow family. Rather, it means that it is a related and associated variety. There are extensive disputes in the Talmud and amongst the great medieval rabbinic scholars regarding how to categorize various creatures, and the very concept of *min* itself, just as there are disputes amongst zoologists regarding the definition of species.[30]

A pair of wolfdogs – hybrids between wolves and dogs.

Matters become even more complicated when we investigate the prohibitions of *kilayim* – mating different animals together[31] or harnessing them to the same plow.[32] Nahmanides, with regard to the laws of *kilayim*, relates the differences between *minim* to their inability to produce fertile hybrids.[33] But there is a ruling in the Mishna which explicitly states that even animals of very similar species that produce fertile hybrids can sometimes nevertheless be considered as two *minim*:

> A wolf with a dog, and a "village dog" with a fox, and goats with gazelles, and ibex with ewes, and a horse with a mule, and a mule with a donkey, and a donkey with an onager – even though they are similar to each other, they are *kilayim* with each other. (Mishna Kilayim 1:6)

Wolves and dogs can produce offspring, and yet they are defined here as different types. This gives an even narrower definition to the term *min*. The Tosefta adds further animals to the list of forbidden mixtures:

The wild boar is fully interfertile with the domestic pig, but it is nevertheless rated as being a forbidden mixture with the pig.

> An ox and a wild ox, an ass and a wild ass, a pig and a wild boar – even though they are similar to each other, they are *kilayim* with each other. (Tosefta, Kilayim 1:5)

The domestic pig and the wild boar can interbreed and produce fertile offspring. Nevertheless, for the laws of *kilayim*, they are considered to be different *minim*.

But the problem with declaring the pig and wild boar to be different *minim* is that when discussing the laws of non-kosher animals, the Torah only mentions the pig. Does this mean that the Torah omitted mentioning the wild boar, in accordance with the view of some that the list of non-kosher animals is not necessarily comprehensive?[34] Or does it mean that the definition of *min* in the laws of *kashrut* is broader than that used for *kilayim*, and that the "pig" includes both the domestic pig as well as the wild boar?

The answer is unclear. Some rabbinic authorities appear to be of the view that the definition of *min* for the laws of *kilayim* is different from the definition used in the classification of kosher types.[35] But others are of the view that it is the same.[36] As such, we cannot draw any unequivocal conclusions regarding the relationship between the two applications of *min* classification.

In conclusion, we see that the system of classification used in the Torah is very difficult to untangle, and that it often differs considerably from that employed by modern zoology. The result of all this is that the reader should not be surprised to learn that the *namer* refers to both leopard and cheetah, that the *shual* refers to both jackal and fox, or that different types of deer are all the *ayal*.

A History of Biblical and Talmudic Zoology

Rabbinic Scholarship That Aids Biblical Zoology

In the world of Jewish scholarship, the most important texts after the Written Torah are the Mishna and Talmud. The Sages of the Talmud discuss many of the animals in Scripture and give various clues about their identities. However, no less a figure than Rashi suggests that the Sages themselves were not fully proficient in the identities of all the creatures in Scripture.[37] This would especially be the case with those Sages who lived in Babylonia rather than the Land of Israel. Furthermore, identifying the animals that the Talmud discusses, whether the Talmud is referring to the animals of Scripture or introducing other animals, is itself often challenging.

Furthermore, the Talmud does not present a systematic translation of every animal in Scripture. Such a resource can however be found in the Aramaic translation of the Torah, *Targum Onkelos*, and that of the Prophets, *Targum Yonatan*. Of course, difficulties remain with regard to identifying the animals referred to in the Aramaic translations, but these works are still an important aid.

A somewhat earlier effort to translate every animal mentioned in Scripture is the ancient Greek translation of Scripture known as the Septuagint, from the Latin word for "seventy." This name derives from the story related in Talmud as well as several earlier sources, that the Torah was first translated into Greek by seventy Jewish scholars for King Ptolemy of Egypt.[38] The translations of the different books of Scripture were undertaken by different translators in Egypt over the course of many years. As such, it is not surprising to find that the Septuagint will often translate the same Hebrew animal name into a different Greek translation in different places.

Another ancient translation of the Torah is the Vulgate. This is an early fifth-century translation of the Bible into Latin by the Christian scholar Jerome (Eusebius Sophronius Hieronymus, circa 340–420 CE). Unlike most other Christian translators of his day, who based themselves on the Septuagint, in his translation Jerome returned to the original Hebrew source. He consulted with several Jewish scholars regarding difficult Hebrew words.[39] As such the Vulgate can be a useful resource for identifying biblical animal terms. However, Jerome sometimes translates biblical animal names using their European counterparts rather than the proper Middle Eastern terms (e.g. identifying the *tinshemet* as the mole rather than the mole-rat).

Since the Septuagint and Vulgate were written so long ago, they provide an important record of how people in ancient times understood the Torah's references to animals. But it is also important to research ancient zoological writings even when not connected to the Bible. By comparing beliefs about the animal kingdom in the Jewish and non-Jewish communities, evidence can be accumulated regarding the identities of the animal being discussed. For example, there is discussion in Torah literature about the *korei*, a bird that is described as stealing the eggs of other birds and raising their young itself. While there is strong evidence for identifying the *korei* as the partridge, some have rejected this identification on the grounds that the partridge is not known to demonstrate this behavior. However, since a survey of ancient literature such as the *Physiologus* and medieval bestiaries reveals the same description of the partridge, this indicates that the talmudic references are to the same bird.

After the Vulgate, the next translation of every animal listed in the Torah is found in the writings of Rav Saadia Gaon (882–942 CE). Rav Saadia does not engage in discussions concerning each animal, but he does give an Arabic translation. Rav Saadia Gaon's identifications of the Torah's creatures carry more weight than those of later Torah scholars of Europe. This is because he lived in the Middle East and was therefore more familiar with the wildlife of the area. Furthermore, as noted earlier, the Arabic names for animals provide additional evidence for their identities in cases where they are similar.

An illustration from a medieval bestiary of a partridge stealing eggs

Amongst the *Rishonim* (literally "the early ones") – the important Torah scholars of the tenth to fifteenth centuries – we find various brief comments about the identities of the animals in Scripture. Rashi (Rabbi Shlomo Yitzchaki, 1040–1105 CE), Radak (Rabbi David Kimche, 1160–1235), and Chizkuni (Rabbi Chizkiya ben Mano'ach, thirteenth century) all give local translations, and sometimes brief descriptions, of the animals. There were also dictionaries, such as that of Yona ibn Janach (c. 990–c. 1050). However, despite the great stature of these authorities, their comments in this field cannot be taken as the last word. These scholars lived in Europe and therefore were only familiar with European animals, which are very different from the animals described in Scripture. This geographical disparity caused some of their translations to be inaccurate.[40] A particularly striking example of this is found in Rashi's commentary to the Talmud, where he admits that the common translation of *tzvi* as "deer" cannot be accurate, since it does not match the description of the *tzvi* given in the Talmud.[41] Rashi instead suggests that it is the ibex; but *Tosafot* points out that this causes other difficulties. The true *tzvi*, which is the gazelle, does not live anywhere in Europe, and therefore Rashi did not know of its existence. Few scholars were actually familiar with the Land of Israel; notable exceptions are Ishtori HaParchi (1280–1355), who wrote *Kaftor VaFerach* (Venice, 1549), a description of the geography of *Eretz Yisrael*, and Tanchum Yerushalmi (thirteenth century), whose writings came to light only recently. Both of these scholars have scattered references to the animals of the Torah.

A number of Jewish zoological works appeared in the medieval period. However, these were simply translations, adaptations, or commentaries of the writings of Aristotle and other such works. They did not attempt to elucidate any references to animals in the Torah.[42]

Biblical Zoology Begins

Biblical zoology, as a specialized study of the animals in Scripture, began in the seventeenth century.[43] The first, and perhaps still the most remarkable, work on this topic was written by Samuel Bochart (1599–1667), a Protestant minister in France, and was titled *Hierozoïcon sive bipertitum opus de animalibus Sacrae Scripturae*, "Sacred Life: A Two Volume Work on Animals of the Sacred Scriptures." This work, the result of thirty years' labor, was first published in two enormous volumes in 1663. Bochart was a tremendous scholar, fluent in eighteen languages. The *Hierozoïcon* is written primarily in Latin, but also includes lengthy citations in Hebrew, Arabic, and Greek. His knowledge of ancient languages such as Coptic, Egyptian, Ethiopic, Phoenician, Chaldaean, Syriac, and Persian was invaluable in assisting him with identifying the animals of Scripture. Bochart was also familiar with a tremendous range of talmudic literature, which he also analyzed in his work, and he himself was cited by subsequent rabbinic scholars. He was able to rediscover correct animal identifications that had been lost for thousands of years, such as his naming of the behemoth in the Book of Job as the hippopotamus.

Despite Bochart's outstanding scholarship, his work was limited in value. Scientific knowledge was far more limited in his day than it is now. Bochart did not live in the Land of Israel and was not intimately familiar with the unique wildlife of that region. He was also criticized for quoting extensively from other literature without performing adequate analysis on the animal's identity.[44] But notwithstanding such flaws, the *Hierozoïcon* remains a seminal work in identifying the animals of Scripture.

In the eighteenth century, the new developments in the field of "biblical natural history" came from Europeans who traveled to biblical lands and were able to learn about their flora and fauna. Thomas Shaw (1694–1751) published *Travels, or, Observations Relating to Several Parts of Barbary and the Levant*, which included a section on zoology.[45] While he only rarely related his findings to Scripture, his zoological information provided data that was utilized by later scholars of biblical natural history. It appears that Shaw was the first Western writer to correctly identify the *shafan* as the hyrax.

Another such work was that of Frederick Hasselquist (1722–1752), a Swedish traveler and naturalist. His teacher, the great naturalist Carolus Linnaeus, had often expressed regret at the lack of knowledge concerning the natural history of Palestine. Hasselquist subsequently traveled there, making a large collection of specimens and writing copious notes. After Hasselquist's untimely death during his expedition, Linnaeus published Hasselquist's notes, later translated into English under the title *Voyages and Travels in the Levant, in the Years 1749, 50, 51, 52*.

James Bruce (1730–1794) was a Scottish traveler who journeyed throughout the Levant. In his resultant work, *Travels to Discover the Source of the Nile*, the sixth volume was entitled *Select Specimens of Natural History*. Bruce wrote that he "... made it a constant rule to give the preference to such of each kind as are mentioned in Scripture, and concerning which doubts have arisen. Many

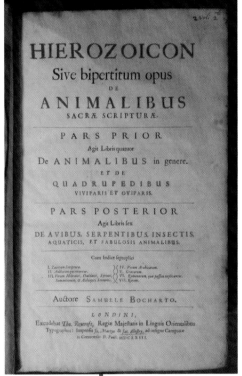

The title page of Bochart's Hierozoicon. From the author's collection.

23

learned men have employed themselves with success upon these topics, yet much remains still to do; for it has generally happened that those perfectly acquainted with the language in which the Scriptures were written have never travelled, nor seen the animals of Judea, Palestine, or Arabia; and again, such as have travelled in these countries and seen the animals in question, have been either not at all, or but superficially, acquainted with the original languages of Scripture. It has been my earnest desire to employ the advantage I possess in both these requisites to throw as much light as possible upon the doubts that have arisen."

In 1753, the biblical scholar Johann David Michaelis recommended "…a mission of learned men into the east, that by travelling through Syria, Palestine, and Egypt, and observing the animals, plants, & c. of those regions, and investigating their nature and qualities, they might ascertain those which are named in Holy Writ." King Frederick V of Denmark supported the expedition, which began in 1761, but unfortunately its naturalist, Peter Forsskål, died of malaria during the trip. The only surviving member of the expedition, Carsten Niebuhr, subsequently published Forsskål's notes.[46]

The nineteenth century saw an explosion of works on the topic of biblical natural history. One of the earliest of these was the *Handbuch der Biblischen Alterthumskunde* ("Handbook of Biblical Antiquities") by Ernst Friedrich Karl Rosenmüller (1768–1835). The fourth volume, entitled *Biblische Naturgeschichte*, dealt with natural history; the first part with mineralogy and botany, and the second part with zoology. Rosenmüller was a professor of Arabic and Oriental languages who, as noted above, re-edited Bochart's *Hierozoïcon*. His intimate familiarity with Bochart's work, coupled with nearly two centuries of advances in zoological knowledge, made his work an important advance in the field.[47]

THE LEOPARD.

"*As a Leopard by the way will I observe them.*"—Hos. xiii. 7.

An illustration of a biblical scene with a leopard from John Wood's Bible Animals

Many English studies of biblical natural history were published during the nineteenth century. Of these, some were merely popular adaptations of prior works, while others were detailed studies. One of the first such works was *Scripture Natural History* by William Carpenter (1797–1874). John George Wood (1827–1889), a prolific popularizer of natural history, published the extremely detailed *Bible Animals*. Jonathan Fisher published *Scripture Animals*, notable for its charming poems. William Houghton (1828–1895), a naturalist and clergyman, wrote studies of the "Natural History of Palestine" and the "Natural History of the Bible" and various articles in other journals on the identities of different scriptural animals. William Groser and Henry Chichester-Hart, who traveled throughout southern Palestine, authored two volumes of *Scripture Natural History*, the former on plants and the latter on animals.

One of the most famous and important works of the nineteenth century about the natural history of the Bible was that of Canon Henry Baker Tristram (1822–1906). He engaged in extensive travels throughout the Land of Israel during 1863–64, accompanied by botanical and zoological collectors sent by the Zoological Society of London. The result is *The Natural History* of the Bible; Being a Review of the Physical Geography, Geology, Meteorology of the Holy Land, With a Description of Every Animal and Plant Mentioned in the Bible. Tristram also published *The Fauna and Flora of Palestine*. Both of these are detailed works that provide a precious record of animal life in the Land of Israel before the modern intensive human settlement.

Jewish Zoological Studies in the Modern Period

In the Jewish world, the first writers on zoology in the modern period generally did not relate it to the Bible or Talmud. There are, however, two notable exceptions from Italy.[48] Johanan Alemanno (1435–early sixteenth century) wrote a work entitled *Chai HaOlamim*.[49] This work, a form of encyclopedia, includes extensive discussion of natural history, based mainly upon Hebrew adaptations of Aristotle. But it also occasionally quotes the Talmud and medieval Jewish authors. More significantly, he adopted names from the Bible and Talmud for the animals that he described.

Avraham ben David Portaleone of Mantua (1542–1612) wrote *Shiltei HaGiborim*. This work was purportedly about the Temple, but he used this as a springboard to provide an encyclopedia of the natural sciences. The laws of sacrifices launch an extensive discussion of natural history, including relating it to the Talmud's laws regarding the characteristics of kosher and non-kosher animals, and an extended effort to identify the ten kosher types of mammals enumerated in Scripture. Still, this work was far from a comprehensive study of zoology and Scripture.[50]

In the early period of the Enlightenment, Baruch Linda (1759–1849) wrote a book on the natural sciences entitled *Reishit Limudim*. The third volume included several pages of discussion about animals, although it rarely related to Scripture or Talmud. Seven editions of this book were published, which points to its popularity.

A few years later, Rabbi Pinchas Eliyahu Hurwitz of Vilna (1765–1821) published *Sefer HaBrit*, originally anonymously.[51] The book came with several approbations from important rabbis. It was immensely popular, being reprinted many times, and translated into Yiddish and Ladino. The fourteenth treatise of the first part (*Ktav Yosher*) was devoted to the animal kingdom, and was largely based on Baruch Linda's *Reishit Limudim*. In eight chapters, it covered a variety of mammals, birds, reptiles, and insects. It made no attempt to be comprehensive (for example, it does not mention the fox or wolf), and only occasionally refers to sources from Scripture, Talmud, and rabbinic authorities.

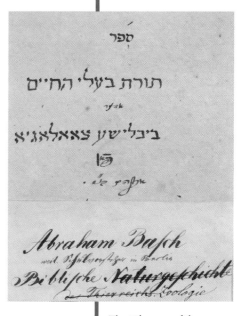

The title page of the first rabbinic work dedicated to biblical zoology, Torat Baalei HaChayim *by Abraham Basch*

Jewish Biblical Zoology in the Nineteenth Century

The nineteenth century saw, for the first time, a number of Jewish publications that dealt with the topic of scriptural natural history in a comprehensive manner. The earliest such work was by Abraham Basch (1800–1841), a school principal in Berlin.[52] He wrote a treatise on biblical zoology entitled *Sefer Torat Baalei HaChayim*. Unfortunately, Basch died at a young age, and the manuscript was never published. Fortunately, however, it did survive.[53]

Rabbi Yosef Schonhak (1812–1870) published *Toledot HaAretz*, a three-volume work which is a general study of zoology, botany, and mineralogy. However, it also includes many footnotes which contain countless invaluable insights into the identities of animals in Scripture, or the explanation of statements in the Talmud and Midrash. Schonhak, who possessed great expertise in linguistic studies, quotes extensively from Bochart and also from the lexicographer Wilhelm Gesenius, to whom he refers not by name but instead with the appellation "a certain Nazarene (Christian) scholar."

Shalom Yaakov Abramowitz (1835–1917), later to become known as Mendele Mokher Sefarim, published a set of works on natural history entitled *Toledot HaTeva* ("Natural History").[54] The first of these volumes, on mammals, was a Hebrew translation of Harald Othmar Lenz's *Gemeinnützige Naturgeschichte* ("Natural History for General Use"). The second volume, which incorporated material from other sources as well as Lenz, was on birds, and the third on reptiles. He also began a volume on fish, but only managed to publish a small portion of it. Abramowitz also included a number of references to scriptural citations and talmudic discussions in footnotes and especially in endnotes; only a few in the first volume, but many more in the subsequent volumes. Although nowhere near as systematic as Schonhak's work, he did make some contributions in the field of identifying animals of Scripture and Talmud, as well as in creating new Hebrew names for species that were not previously named.

A very different but equally valuable work is that of Rabbi Yosef Schwartz (1804–1865). Born at Flosz, Bavaria, his father, Rabbi Menachem Schwartz, was the community rabbi, and after completing his school studies at Kaltenbrunen, Yosef Schwartz went on to study in the yeshiva of Frankfurt that had been established by Rabbi Nathan Adler. He then spent five years at the University of Würzburg, where he devoted himself to the geography and history of the Holy Land. In 1833 he emigrated to Palestine, where he spent about fifteen years traveling around the country and researching its geology, geography, history, fauna, and flora. This enabled him to write *Tevuot HaAretz*, first published in Jerusalem in 1845. The zoological section includes a list of most of the creatures mentioned in Scripture together with their Arabic names and brief descriptive notes. An English translation by Isaac Leeser, entitled *A Descriptive Geography and Brief Historical Sketch of Palestine*, was published in Philadelphia in 1850, and another edition incorporating material from Rabbi Schwartz's other works was published in 1900.[55]

Another important publication from within the Jewish community was that of Rabbi Dr. Yehuda Leib Ludwig Lewysohn, *Die Zoologie des Talmuds*, "The Zoology of the Talmud," which inevitably also dealt with the zoology of Scripture. Ludwig Lewysohn (1819–1901) delivered sermons in Frankfurt on the Oder and Worms, and later became a rabbi in Stockholm. He was an exceptional scholar in many fields, and published hundreds of historical, philosophical, and archeological pieces in English, French, German, and Hebrew publications. *Die Zoologie des Talmuds* is an extremely thorough

Rabbi Yosef Schonhak, author of Toledot HaAretz

Rabbi Yosef Schwartz, the first rabbinic scholar to write about biblical zoology based on actual experience with the wildlife of the Land of Israel

study of all talmudic references to animals (including, of course, many that are not mentioned in Scripture). As well as being learned in traditional talmudic commentaries, Lewysohn also made use of Bochart and other non-Jewish scholars. *Die Zoologie des Talmuds* became an invaluable reference that is frequently cited in later works such as the *Encyclopedia Talmudit*. However, Lewysohn was handicapped by his lack of familiarity with the wildlife of the Land of Israel.

Jewish Biblical Zoology in the Twentieth Century

The twentieth century saw a new type of investigator in the field of identifying the animals of the Torah: the modern Israeli scientist. First and foremost of these was Dr. Yisrael Aharoni (1880 Lithuania–1946 Israel). Aharoni expended great effort in studying the animal life of Israel and in identifying the animals of the Torah, and he was responsible for many of the assignments of animal names in Modern Hebrew. As well as authoring *Memoirs of an Israeli Zoologist*, he also published a number of invaluable articles in the journal *Tarbitz* on identifying specific species.

Prof. Frederick (Fritz) Shimon Bodenheimer (1897–1959) specialized in entomology, but also studied the entire spectrum of animal life in the Land of Israel both in present times, and in the fossil record and writings of antiquity.[56] His important works include *HaChai BeEretz Yisrael*[57] and *HaChai BeArtzot HaMikra*,[58] translated into English as *Animal and Man in Bible Lands*,[59] both of which are of great assistance in identifying the Torah's animals. Rabbi Immanuel Löw (1854–1944) is mainly renowned for his seminal work on the plant life of Scripture and Talmud, but also wrote several articles about animal life, which were posthumously collected by Alexander Scheiber and published as *Fauna und Mineralien der Juden*.[60] An invaluable but difficult to obtain work is that of zoologist Dr. Menachem Dor (1901-1998), *HaChai BiYemei HaMikra, HaMishna VeHaTalmud*, "Animals in the Era of Scripture, Mishna and Talmud."[61]

Probably the most famous Israeli scientist in the field of biblical natural history is Dr. Yehuda Feliks (1922–2005). Born in Poland, he immigrated to Israel at sixteen and studied Talmud and biology at the Hebrew University. He authored many works on this topic, including *The Animal World of the Bible*,[62] *HaChai BaMishna*,[63] and *Nature and Man in the Bible*.[64]

Within the world of the yeshiva, some insights on the animals of the Torah appear in commentaries on the talmudic tractate Chullin, which deals in part with animal identification. Rabbi Yisrael Meir Levinger, a veterinarian as well as a Talmud scholar, has published *Maor LeMasekhet Chullin*[65] and *Mazon Kasher Min HaChai*.[66] Rabbi Amitai Ben David's *Sichat Chullin*[67] is a valuable collection of sources in several areas. Rabbi David Tzvi Feldman's *Yalkut Kol Chai*[68] is a very comprehensive compilation of talmudic statements about animals and their rabbinic interpretations, but unfortunately only one volume has so far been published.

Important research in biblical and talmudic zoology continues today.[69] This is largely undertaken by Jewish academic scholars who live in Israel and

are thus intimately familiar with the wildlife of the region. Several valuable articles and works have been published by Dr. Mordechai Kislev, Dr. David Talshir, Dr. Avraham Ofir-Shemesh, Rabbi Dr. Ari Zivotofsky, and especially Dr. Zohar Amar of the Land of Israel Studies Department at Bar-Ilan University. Dr. Amar performs invaluable practical research, such as testing the Talmud's principle that only the milk of kosher animals can curdle, and teaches academic courses on the natural history of Scripture. And thus the study of

The Wildlife of the Torah

the animals of the Torah, which began as a dedicated study by Bochart, has finally become a formal discipline.

Zoogeography

As noted in the earlier section on identifying animals in the Torah, the animals of the Torah are the animals from the Land of Israel and the surrounding regions (with the exception of those that are mentioned as being imported, such as the monkeys and peacocks that were brought to King Solomon). It is often not adequately appreciated that the makeup of animals that inhabit the countryside varies greatly from one place to another. Most readers of this book live in North America, and the wildlife of that continent is very different from that of the Land of Israel. North America has plenty of rabbits; Israel has none. Israel has plenty of hyraxes; North America has no hyraxes, and most Americans have never even heard of a hyrax, much less seen one.

However, there are many animals that are the North American equivalent of species found in the Land of Israel. For example, the coyote is the equivalent of the jackal, the condor is the equivalent of the griffon vulture, and the alligator is the equivalent of the crocodile. These species are not exactly the same, but they are very similar and fill an equivalent role in the ecosystem. As such, residents of North America may be able to understand references to various animals in the Torah in terms of local equivalents with which they are more familiar.

It should be noted that the borders of the biblical Land of Israel do not precisely correlate with the borders of the modern State of Israel. The biblical borders of the Land of Israel did not reach as far south as the modern State of Israel, which reaches the Red Sea at Eilat. However, it extended much further northwards, into the forested, hilly country that is today Lebanon and part of Syria.

The dugong is sometimes found off the shores of Eilat, but this is not part of the biblical Land of Israel

The ostrich, native
to biblical Israel but
subsequently hunted
to extinction, has
since been returned
to the wild

NATAN SLIFKIN

VILLIERS STEYN / SHUTTERSTOCK

30

Cheetahs used to
live wild in the
Land of Israel

This work is, however, not limited to discussing the species native to the Land of Israel. There were some animals that were not native to the area, but which were imported, such as monkeys, elephants, and giraffes. In addition, this is an encyclopedia of animals in the Oral Torah as well as the Written Torah. The Sages of the Babylonian Talmud lived in what today forms Iran and Iraq. The wildlife found in those countries is mostly, but not entirely, the same as that found in the Land of Israel.

The Biodiversity of Israel

The Land of Israel is home to a spectrum of animal life that is uniquely rich and diverse relative to the small size of the country. For example, Israel has over one hundred species of mammals. This is about half the number of species found in Europe, despite the fact that Europe is three hundred times larger. There are several reasons for this biodiversity.

One is that although small in area, the Land of Israel has a wide range of ecological habitats. It is home to snowy mountains and Mediterranean forest. It has freshwater lakes and arid desert. This wide range of habitats provides homes for a greater number of species than would be found in a single habitat of equivalent size.

Another reason for the great biodiversity in the Land of Israel is that, as described in the Midrash, it is the "center of the world."[70] It is geographically located at the junction of three continents: Europe, Asia, and Africa. Species native to the temperate forests of Europe and the Mediterranean region reach the south-eastern limit of their distribution in the Land of Israel. African species reach the northern limits of their distribution in the Land of Israel. And Asian species reach their western limit in the Land of Israel. (It is for this reason that it is difficult to determine whether the lion of the Torah was the Asiatic lion, the African lion, or even both.) The Land of Israel is also a main migration route for birds, with over 150 million birds passing through on their way between Europe and Africa.

As a result, the Land of Israel was historically home to a curious mix of species. There were creatures from the temperate forests of Europe and Asia, such as bears, wolves, fallow deer, and squirrels. There were animals from the deserts of Africa and Asia, such as cheetah, oryx, ostriches, and monitor lizards. And there were also tropical animals such as crocodiles and hippopotami. The biblical Land of Israel was an astonishingly rich zoological landscape.

Extinction, Conservation, and Reintroduction

Unfortunately, many of the animals that are most prominent in the Torah are now extinct from the region, and in some cases from the entire world. The hippopotamus disappeared from Israel around three thousand years ago; the lion became extinct from the region sometime after the thirteenth century; cheetahs, bears, and crocodiles endured until the early twentieth century. The mighty aurochs became entirely extinct in the seventeenth century, having disappeared from the Land of Israel long before that.

Meanwhile, non-native species have been introduced to the region. Examples include the water buffalo, brown rat, nutria, and Indian myna bird. This can cause problems not only for ecology, but also for those attempting to identify the animals of the Torah.

The extinction of animals from the region occurred for several reasons. One was habitat destruction. The biblical Land of Israel boasted thick forests – the cedars of Lebanon, oaks, and terebinths, amongst many others. But over the tumultuous history of the land, many of these trees were cut down or burned down. The final straw was the construction of the railroad for the Ottoman Empire in the nineteenth century, for which many trees were cut down for charcoal or for use as rail ties. Animals died out as they lost the habitats in which they lived and sought refuge.

Another cause of extinction was hunting. Lions, bears, and leopards posed a real threat to people and were killed wherever possible. Other animals, such as fallow deer and hartebeest, presented an opportunity for food, and were hunted without regard to preserving a viable population. The introduction of firearms sealed the fate of many animals.

After the establishment of the State of Israel, matters became worse in some aspects. The spread of civilization meant further habitat loss. Agriculture caused various problems. In one case, a farmer, furious after some cattle had been killed by wolves, laced some meat with pesticides. It didn't kill any wolves, but it did kill seven jackals, three wild boar, one wild cat, three Egyptian vultures, and twenty-seven griffon vultures.[71]

The nutria and myna bird are commonly seen in Israel today, but were only introduced in the last few decades.

But on the other hand, for the first time, efforts were made at conservation.[72] General Avraham Yoffe, a founding member of the Hagana, and commander of the army division that captured Sharm el-Sheikh in 1956, was the head of the newly-created Israeli Nature and Parks Authority. Hunting and trapping animals were banned. The Hai-Bar nature reserve was set up in the Arava, with a smaller branch in the Carmel, to form breeding groups of endangered species and prepare animals for reintroduction to the wild. Some animals that had become extinct from Israel were obtained from elsewhere – often via extraordinary efforts – and were ultimately successfully reintroduced to Israel. These include the Mesopotamian fallow deer, oryx, and onager, as described in the relevant chapters in this volume. While it will never be possible to reintroduce dangerous creatures such as lions and bears and crocodiles, due to the density of human population, at least some animals from the biblical landscape are returning home. ∎

TYLINEK / SHUTTERSTOCK

STUBBLEFIELD PHOTOGRAPHY

A herd of rare Arabian oryx at the Hai-Bar nature reserve

Notes

1 For the sake of precision, however, in the body of this work, we shall generally use the word "Torah" only with regard to the Five Books of Moses.

2 Sanhedrin 59b.

3 For an extensive discussion of laws relating to animals, see *Man and Beast* by this author.

4 See Moses Hadas, *Fables of a Jewish Aesop* (Boston: Godine/Nonpareil, 2001). For discussions of other animal characters in Jewish folk literature, see Dan Ben-Amos, "Jewish Folk Literature," *Oral Tradition* 14:1 (1999), pp. 140–274, and Dov Noy, "Animal Tales," *Encyclopedia Judaica* (2nd edition, Gale, 2008).

5 Similarly in *Shir HaShirim Rabba* 4:15.

6 I Chronicles 7:36.

7 II Kings 22:3.

8 II Kings 22:14.

9 Judges 4:17.

10 Genesis 35:8, Judges 4:4.

11 II Kings 14:25, Jonah 1:1.

12 See Alexander Beider, *A Dictionary of Ashkenazic Given Names* (Bergenfield, NJ: Avotaynu, 2001).

13 For a thorough academic study of *Perek Shira*, see Malachi Bet Arie, "Perek Shirah," critical ed., 2 vols. (Ph.D. thesis, Hebrew University of Jerusalem, 1966). For an extensive commentary on *Perek Shira*, see *Perek Shirah: Nature's Song* (Jerusalem: Zoo Torah/Gefen Books, 2010), by this author.

14 This may well also be true for descriptions of animals that are found in sacred literature, and even in Scripture itself. This is as per the principle, "The Torah speaks in the language of man," which according to several important rabbinic authorities, means that the messages and laws of the Torah are packaged within the scientific worldview of antiquity. See Rambam, *Guide for the Perplexed* 2:8 and 3:3, with the commentaries of Efodi, Shem Tov, Narvoni, and Abarbanel in *Taanot*, 4, and Rabbi Shlomo Fisher, *Derashot Beit Yishai, Maamar Hamo'ach VeHaLev*, fn. 4; Ralbag, commentary to Genesis 15:4, and commentary to Job, end of ch. 39; Rabbi Dr. Isadore Twersky, "Joseph ibn Kaspi: Portrait of a Medieval Jewish Intellectual," *Studies in Medieval Jewish History and Literature*, vol. 1 (Harvard University Press, 1979), pp. 239–242; Rabbi Samson Raphael Hirsch, *Collected Writings* vol. 7, p. 57 and commentary to Genesis 1:6; and Rabbi Avraham Yitzchak Kook, *Eder HaYekar*, pp. 37–38. For a study of the history of this phrase, see Zion Ukshi, "The Torah Speaks Like the Language of Men – The Development of the Expression and its Nature" (Hebrew), *Derekh Efrata* 9–10 (5761), pp. 39–59.

15 Commentary to Leviticus 11:13.

16 Rabbi Yosef Karo discounts a ruling of Rabbi Yaakov son of Rosh (better known as the *Tur*) regarding sugarcane, on the grounds that sugarcane did not grow in his region and he was unfamiliar with how it is eaten (*Kesef Mishneh* on Rambam's *Hilkhot Berakhot* 8:5). Radvaz negates the view of Rabbi Eliyahu Mizrahi (and many others) who identified the "River of Egypt," stated to be the border of the Land of Israel, as the river Nile, pointing out that they were unfamiliar with the geographical reality due to their living in Europe (Responsa Radvaz 6:2:2206). Rabbi Yom Tov Lipman Heller, discussing the location of Akko and Keziv, rejects the views of those who did not live in Israel and were unfamiliar with it (*Tosafot Yom Tov, Shevi'it* 6:1). Rabbi Akiva Yosef Schlesinger writes that European medieval authorities who rated the halakhic quantity of an olive in terms of a large fraction of an egg did so only because they did not have access to actual olives (*Tel Talpiot*, Shevat 5661 p. 103).

17 See, for example, his commentaries to I Samuel 28:10 and I Kings 8:11.

18 Note that in the wide range of strictly Orthodox literature published by ArtScroll/Mesorah, one of the few academic works cited is Professor Yehuda Feliks' *Plants and Animals of the Mishnah*.

19 For a fuller discussion, see *The Camel, The Hare And The Hyrax* by this author. See too Mordechai Kislev, "Principles of Classification of Animals in the Torah, and an Example with the Eight *Sheratzim*" (Hebrew), *Hallamish* 7 (Winter 1988), pp. 27–40. For academic studies, see Scott Atran, "Folk Biology and the Anthropology of Science: Cognitive Universals and Cultural Particulars," *Behavioral and Brain Sciences* 21 (1998), pp. 547–609; Richard Whitekettle, "Where the Wild Things Are: Primary Level Taxa in Israelite Zoological Thought," *Journal for the Study of the Old Testament* 93 (2001), pp. 17–37; idem, "Rats are Like Snakes, and Hares are Like Goats: A Study in Israelite Land Animal Taxonomy," *Biblica* 82 (2001), pp. 345–62.

20 In the words of one specialist: "From a scientific standpoint, folk-biological concepts such as the generic species are woefully inadequate for capturing the evolutionary relationships of species over vast dimensions of time and space.... This does not mean that folk taxonomy is more or less preferable to the inferential understanding that links and perhaps ultimately dissolves taxa into biological theories. This 'commonsense' biology may just have different conditions of relevance than scientific biology: the one, providing enough built-in structural constraint and flexibility to allow individuals and cultures to maximize inductive potential relative to the widest possible range of everyday human interests in the biological world; and the other, providing new and various ways of transcending those interests in order to infer the structure of nature in itself, or at least a nature where humans are only incidental" (Scott Atran, "Folk Biology and the Anthropology of Science: Cognitive Universals and Cultural Particulars," *Behavioral and Brain Sciences* 21 (1998), pp. 547–609).

21 See John Dupré, "Are Whales Fish," in Medin, D.L. and Atran, S. (eds.), *Folkbiology* (MIT Press, 1999), pp. 461–476. For a comprehensive and fascinating study of the New York trial, see Graham Burnett, *Trying Leviathan: The Nineteenth-Century New York Court Case That Put the Whale on Trial and Challenged the Order of Nature* (Princeton University Press, 2007).

22 Rambam, *Mishneh Torah, Hilkhot Maakhalot Assurot* 2:23 rules that creatures can fall into several categories simultaneously – an insect that walks on the ground, can fly, and breeds in water is simultaneously a *sheretz haaretz, sheretz haof*, and *sheretz hamayim*. He adds that such a creature could even simultaneously be an *of*.

23 Rambam, *Mishneh Torah, Hilkhot Maakhalot Assurot* 3:8 rules that a mostly-formed embryo of a non-kosher bird is classified as *sheretz haof* (the category of flying insects) rather than *of*. This could mean that locusts, which metamorphose through different phases, could be considered different *minim* at each stage.

24 See Marc Ereshefsky, ed., *The Units of Evolution: Essays on the Nature of Species* (Cambridge: MIT, 1991), for a collection of essays revealing some of the complexity and debates involved.

25 Rabbi Malkiel Zevi Tannenbaum, *She'elot UTeshuvot Divrei Malkiel* (Kronenburg: 1905) 4:56 discusses various physical characteristics that differentiate *minim* for *kashrut* purposes, but there is insufficient information for a definition of *min*.

26 See *Tosafot*, Chullin 63b s.v. *V'dilma*.

27 In this vein, several traditional sources state that not all the species found today were always in existence. Netziv explains that the phrase "according to their *min*" is repeatedly used in Genesis to indicate that God only created one type of each *min*, from which the later sub-*minim*

evolved. Ran, Commentary to Genesis 6:14–15, uses this to explain how Noah managed to fit all the animals into the Ark, stating that there were simply far fewer types of animals in existence back then. Rabbi David Luria, in his commentary on *Pirkei DeRabbi Eliezer*, makes the same point, and also emends a passage to read that there are 365 *minim* each of birds, vermin, domesticated and wild animals.

28 Rabbi Chayim ibn Attar, *Or HaChayim* to Deuteronomy 14:13; Netziv, *Haamek Davar* to Leviticus 11:14.

29 Chullin 63a.

30 See Chullin 62a–63b. As a further example, Rashi to Chullin 61a states that any bird which possesses four certain non-kosher characteristics is by definition the *min* of the griffon vulture (*nesher*); but *Tosafot* there disagrees.

31 Leviticus 19:19.

32 Deuteronomy 22:10.

33 Ramban, Commentary to Leviticus 19:19.

34 Rabbi Avraham Portaleone, *Shiltei HaGiborim* (Mantova: 1612), was under the impression that the hippopotamus, like the pig, has split hooves and does not chew its cud, and asks why it was not mentioned in the Torah's list of non-kosher animals. He answers that the Torah does not mention the hippo either because it isn't fit for eating anyway, or because its non-kosher status can be inferred from the pig. The latter would provide a reason for the Torah not mentioning the wild boar.

35 Rashi on Nidda 50b, s.v. *tarnegolta*, and the first opinion in *Tosafot* (ibid.), consider that with reference to birds, even within one species the male can be non-kosher and the female kosher (yet there is presumably no prohibition of *kilayim* in such a case). But *Peri Chadash* (*Yoreh De'ah* 86:6) and *Peri Megadim* (*Yoreh De'ah* 82 *Siftei Daat* 8) consider it unthinkable that one *min* could contain both kosher and non-kosher types.

36 Rabbi Moshe Sofer (*Chatam Sofer, Yoreh De'ah* 74) transfers *minim* principles between the laws of *kashrut* and the laws of *kilayim*, but he acknowledges that Rashi, cited above, causes difficulties with this.

37 See Rashi to Chullin 61b s.v. *Mahu DeTeymah* as explained by Rabbi Yonatan Eybeshitz in *Kreiti UPleiti, Kuntrus Pnei Nesher*.

38 See Megilla 9a. For a brief survey of the development of this tradition in classical and early rabbinic sources see Moshe Simon-Shoshan, "The Tasks of the Translators: The Rabbis, the Septuagint, and the Cultural Politics of Translation," *Prooftexts* 27:1 (2007), pp. 1–39.

39 See Jerome, preface to Job. For an extensive discussion of Jerome's relationship to Judaism and Jews, see Hillel Newman, *Jerome and the Jews* (Hebrew), Ph.D. Thesis (Jerusalem: Hebrew University, 1997).

40 It likewise affected the accuracy of their comments regarding the geography of the Land of Israel. See Rabbi Yom Tov Lippman Heller, *Tosafot Yom Tov* to Shevi'it 6:1.

41 Rashi to Chullin 59b, s.v. *Veharei tzvi*.

42 See Resianne Fontaine, "Meteorology and Zoology in Medieval Hebrew Texts," in Gad Freudenthal, *Science in Medieval Jewish Cultures* (Boston/Cambridge: Cambridge University Press, 2011), 217–229; Mauro Zonta, "Mineralogy, Botany and Zoology in Medieval Hebrew Encyclopaedias: 'Descriptive' and 'theoretical' approaches to Arabic sources," *Arabic Sciences and Philosophy* (1996), 6:263–315, Cambridge University Press; and idem, "The Zoological Writings in the Hebrew Tradition: The Hebrew approach to Aristotle's zoological writings and to their ancient and medieval commentators in the Middle Ages," in C. Steel, G. Guldentops, P. Beullens (ed.), *Aristotle's Animals in the Middle Ages and Renaissance*, 'Mediaevalia Lovaniensia' s. I / Studia, n. 27 (Leiden University Press, Leiden, 1999), 44–68.

43 A bibliography can be found online at www.BiblicalNaturalHistory. org/resources.

44 Menachem Dor, *HaChai BiYemei HaMikra, HaMishna VeHaTalmud* (Tel Aviv: Grafor-Daftal Books, 1997), p. 18.

45 Pp. 238–261 in the first edition, and much more material in the second edition.

46 *Descriptiones Animalium – Avium, amphiborum, insectorum, vermium quæ in itinere orientali observavit Petrus Forskål* (1775).

47 A short supplement to his work, entitled *Beiträge zur Biblischen Zoologie* (Leipsig: 1836), was written by a Dr. Friedrich Carl Zeddel.

48 See Abraham Melamed, "The Hebrew Encyclopedias of the Renaissance," in Steven Harvey (ed.), *The Medieval Hebrew Encyclopedias of Science and Philosophy* (Netherlands: Kluwer Academic Publishers, 2000), pp. 441–464.

49 Ms. Mantua 21. Fols. 141v–164r deal with the natural sciences, including zoology.

50 N. Shapiro, "R. Abraham Portaleone – Physician and Encyclopaedist – and his book *Shiltei HaGiborim*" (Hebrew), in *HaRofeh HaIvri* 33 (1960), 137–144.

51 See Resianne Fontaine, "Natural Science in *Sefer HaBrit*: Pinchas Hurwitz on Animals and Meteorological Phenomena," in: *Sepharad in Ashkenaz: Medieval Knowledge and Eighteenth-Century Enlightened Jewish Discourse,* eds. Irene Zwiep, Andrea Schatz, and Resianne Fontaine (Amsterdam: Royal Netherlands Academy of Arts and Sciences, 2007), pp. 157–181.

52 His obituary appears in *Der Orient* (1841) vol. 46, pp. 286–7, and vol. 47, p. 295.

53 The manuscript, written in Judeo-German, is held in the Berlin Staatsbibliothek, Or. Qu. 698.

54 A survey of these works can be found in Joseph Klausner, *Historiya Shel HaSifrut HaIvrit HaChadasha*, 2nd edition (Jerusalem: Achiasaf, 1950), vol. 6, pp. 408–418.

55 This edition, published by Avraham Moshe Luntz, was republished in Jerusalem by Ariel in 1979.

56 For a fascinating biography of Bodenheimer, see Isaac Harpaz, "Frederick Simon Bodenheimer (1897–1959): Idealist, Scholar, Scientist," *Annual Review of Entomology* (January 1984) 29:1, pp. 1–23.

57 Tel Aviv: Dvir 1953.

58 Jerusalem: Mossad Bialik 1957.

59 Leiden, Netherlands: E. J. Brill 1960.

60 Hildesheim: Georg Olms 1969. He had also written two books on this topic, but they were destroyed in the Holocaust before being published.

61 Tel Aviv: Grafor-Daftal Books 1997.

62 Tel Aviv: Sinai 1962.

63 Jerusalem: Institute for Mishna Research 1972.

64 Jerusalem: The Soncino Press 1981.

65 Jerusalem: Maskil LeDavid 1995.

66 Jerusalem: Institute for Agricultural Research According to the Torah 1980.

67 Jerusalem: Medrash Bikkurei Yosef 1995.

68 Jerusalem: Makhon Shaarei Tziyon 1997.

69 A bibliography can be found online at www.BiblicalNaturalHistory. org/resources.

70 *Midrash Tanchuma, Kedoshim* 10.

71 Walter W. Ferguson, *The Mammals of Israel*, pp. 18–19.

72 See Alon Tal, *Pollution in a Promised Land: An Environmental History of Israel* (Los Angeles, CA: University of California Press, 2002), Chapter Six: "A General Launches a War for Wildlife," and Bill Clark, *High Hills and Wild Goats: Life Among the Animals of the Hai-Bar Wildlife Refuge.*

Wild Animals

Chayot / חיות

Wild Animals: Introduction

The Prestige of Wild Animals

This volume of the *Torah Encyclopedia of the Animal Kingdom* is devoted to wild animals. While a distinction between wild animals and domestic animals is of relatively minor significance in modern zoological taxonomy, it is of overriding significance in the biblical system of classifying animals, which primarily views them in their role vis-à-vis human beings. Domestic animals are of such great importance to man that they stand in a class by themselves. All other land-dwelling large mammals default to the category of wild animals.

However, while wild animals are less important than domestic animals from a human perspective, they are, as far as most people are concerned, the most interesting members of the animal kingdom. They are often large, often very strong, mostly fast, and always proud of spirit. Domestic animals are more part of our lives, but precisely for that reason we are desensitized to them. Insects are more diverse and ingenious, but they are too small and alien to be of major interest. Zoos house all sorts of creatures, but when we go to a zoo, it is primarily wild animals – lions and bears and elephants and monkeys and giraffes – that we go to see.

The Midrash notes that the Jewish people is compared to various wild animals, and explains why it is important:

The tribe of Naphtali, depicted in a stained glass window in a synagogue

ARTWORK BY DAVID ASCALON, © "ASCALON STUDIOS"

> R. Yochanan said: The Holy One said, I refer to Israel as a dove, as it is written, "Ephraim is like a dove…" (Hos. 7:11). With Me, they are like a dove; but vis-à-vis the nations of the world, they are like wild animals, as it is written, "Judah is a young lion," "Naphtali is a hind set loose," "Dan shall be a serpent," "Benjamin is a predatory wolf." And all twelve tribes are compared to animals (such as in verses that compare Israel to a family of lions[1]). This is because the nations fight against Israel, and say to Israel, Why are you interested in Shabbat and circumcision? And so the Holy One empowers Israel, and makes them like wild animals in front of the nations, to subdue them before the Holy One and before Israel. (*Shir HaShirim Rabba* 2:30)

Note that this midrash does not refer to those tribes that are compared to domestic animals – Issachar, who is compared to an ass, and Joseph, who is compared to an ox. However, Naphtali is mentioned, even though the wild animal to which he is compared – the deer – is a herbivore rather than a carnivore. All wild animals, even deer, embody a certain vitality, a strength of spirit as well as of body. For a nation that has been persecuted for most of its history, the symbolism of wild animals provides an important source of strength and inspiration.

Terminology: *Chaya* vs. *Behema*

In Hebrew, wild animals are called *chaya* in the singular and *chayot* in the plural. The term "*chaya*" literally means "possessing life," which describes the vitality of wild animals. The category stands in opposition to domesticated animals, which are called *behema* in the singular, and *behemot* in the plural. The term *behema* is explained by some to have the connotation of raw material that is bent to man's will,[2] and thus describes domestic animals, that are subordinate to human control.[3]

It should be noted that the Hebrew terms for these groups are not always used in a precise manner in Scripture. As the Talmud and Midrash note: "*Chaya* is (sometimes) included in *behema*, and *behema* is (sometimes) included in *chaya*."[4] In the introduction to the laws of kosher mammals, both terms are used interchangeably:

> This is the *chaya* that you shall eat, from every *behema* that is on the land. (Lev. 11:2)

Sometimes, we find the term *behema* being used to describe both domestic and wild animals.[5] According to the view that the term *behema* has the connotation of something that is bent to man's will, this is because wild animals are also under man's subjugation, albeit less so than domestic animals.[6] Thus, the list of ten kosher mammals, which includes both domestic and wild animals, is described as being a list of *behemot*:

> This is the *behema* that you shall eat; the ox, the sheep, and the goat; the deer, the gazelle, the hartebeest, the ibex, the oryx, the aurochs, and the wild sheep. (Deut. 14:4)

Similarly, the term *chaya* is also sometimes used to refer to all animals. This is because it literally means "possessing life," and domestic animals also possess life – albeit without as much vitality as wild animals. Thus, when Scripture describes the creation of animal life, domestic animals are also called *chaya*, since they also possess the spirit of life:

> And the Lord God formed out of the earth every *chaya* of the field and all the birds of the sky, and brought them to the man to see what he would call them; and whatever the man called each living creature (*nefesh chaya*), that would be its name. (Gen. 2:19)

However, in the very next verse, the terms *behema* and *chaya* are used more precisely, to refer to distinct groups: And the man gave names to all the *behema* and to the birds of the sky and to every beast of the field (*chayat hasadeh*). (Gen. 2:20)

And later, describing the animals that were in Noah's Ark, a distinction is likewise drawn between domestic and wild animals:

> God remembered Noah and every *chaya* and every *behema* that was with him in the ark, and God caused a wind to blow across the earth, and the waters subsided. (Gen. 8:1)

On other occasions, as well, the term *chaya* is used to specifically refer to wild animals. For example, it is only with wild animals that there is a commandment that, after slaughtering it for food, its blood must be covered with earth:

> Any man of the Children of Israel, or of the strangers who sojourn among you, who hunts and traps any beast or bird that may be eaten; he shall pour out its blood, and cover it with earth. (Lev. 17:13)

In the Talmud, the terms *behema* and *chaya* are generally used specifically to refer to domestic and wild animals, respectively.

Terminology: Beasts of Land, Field, and Forest

IDENTIFICATION

In Scripture, the term *chaya* is often given a qualifying description: *chayat haaretz* (the "beasts of the land"), *chayat hasadeh* (the "beasts of the field"), or *chayot hayaar* (the "beasts of the forest"). While some usages of these expressions may refer to a particular subgroup of wild animals, such as carnivores or herbivores, the terms themselves include all wild animals.

The first expression, *chayat haaretz*, the "beasts of the land," is used at creation to describe everything other than domestic animals:

> And the Lord made the beasts of the land after their kind, and the *behema* after its kind, and every creeping creature of the earth after its kind, and the Lord saw that it was good. (Gen. 1:25)

However, on other occasions, it is intended to refer specifically to carnivores, such as in God's promise that His people shall be safe from predation:

> They shall no longer be a spoil for the nations, and the beasts of the land (*chayat haaretz)* shall not devour them; they shall dwell secure and untroubled. (Ezek. 34:28)

The second expression, *chayat hasadeh*, the "beasts of the field" (with "field" referring not to farmland, but to wilderness) is also a generic term for all wild animals. For example, in the account of man naming all the animals, the term is used to cover all animals aside from domestic animals:

> And the man gave names to every domestic animal (*behema*) and to the birds of the sky and to every beast of the field (*chayat hasadeh*); but for the man, no fitting helper was found. (Gen. 2:20)

© THE ISRAEL MUSEUM, JERUSALEM

In the fifteenth-century compilation of Jewish texts from Italy known as the Rothschild Miscellany, the Nishmat *prayer depicts a variety of wild animals being called upon to praise God*

39

However, sometimes the expression "beasts of the field" is used with a particular sub-group of wild animals in mind. For example, in some cases, it refers to herbivores, such as in the reference to the land being desolate in the Sabbatical year, and the produce being food for the *chayat hasadeh*:

> In the seventh year, you shall let it rest and lie fallow. Let the needy among your people eat of it, and what they leave, let the beasts of the field (*chayat hasadeh*) eat. You shall do the same with your vineyards and your olive groves. (Ex. 23:11[7])

On other occasions, the term "beasts of the field" refers to wild carnivores. For example, God tells the Jewish people that He will drive out the pagan nations from the Land of Israel very gradually, such that there should not be an increase in the number of "beasts of the field":

> I will not drive them out before you in a single year, lest the land become desolate, and the beasts of the field (*chayat hasadeh*) increase against you. (Ex. 23:29)

Here, the reference is to wild beasts that would pose a threat to human beings, not to herbivores that are a source of food. Another verse, in which God compares His people to a flock of sheep that has not been guarded, describes such a flock as falling prey to the *chayat hasadeh*:

> As I live, declares the Lord God, My flock has been a spoil, My flock has been food for all the beasts of the field, for lack of anyone to tend them, because My shepherds have not sought the welfare of My flock, for the shepherds tended themselves instead of tending the flock. (Ezek. 34:8)

Yet another verse describes the *chayat hasadeh* devouring a victim, and thus appears specifically to refer to carnivores:

> All you beasts of the field, come and devour, all you beasts of the forest! (Is. 56:9)

This verse also mentions the third expression, *chayot hayaar*, which in this verse also seems to refer specifically to wild carnivores. This last expression is only mentioned on two other occasions in Scripture. One reference to the "beasts of the forest" describes them as being active at night, and juxtaposes them with lions; this seems to indicate that the reference is specifically, or primarily, to predators:

> You bring on darkness and it becomes night, in which all the beasts of the forest roam. The young lions roar for their prey, and to seek their food from God. (Ps. 104:20–21)

But another occurrence of this phrase is in a declaration of God's ownership over the entire animal kingdom, where it is used in contrast to domestic animals, and thus the phrase appears to refer to all wild animals:

"The young lions roar for their prey, and to seek their food from God." (Ps. 104:21)

> For all the beasts of the forest are Mine; the *behemot* on a thousand hills. I know every bird of the mountains, and the crawlers of the field are subject to Me. (Ps. 50:10–11)

Thus, the terms "beasts of the land," "beasts of the field," and "beasts of the forest" can all refer to all wild animals.

Classification: Defining Wild Animals

THEOLOGY, PHILOSOPHY, AND SCIENCE

All domestic animals are descended from wild animals.[8] Domestication is a process by which wild animals with suitable characteristics are selectively bred for desirable traits, such as a passive nature and a high yield of meat or wool. But while domestic animals are descended from wild animals, their current nature places them in a different category.

Differentiating between wild and domestic animals is important in Jewish law. With regard to kosher animals, there are different requirements in the slaughter and consumption of wild and domestic animals, which are discussed in the introduction to the section on kosher wild animals. With regard to non-kosher animals, there is a prohibition of forbidden mixtures between domestic and wild animals. This not only applies to crossbreeding them,[9] but even to working them together:

> …a domestic animal with a wild animal, a wild animal with a domestic animal…are forbidden for plowing, pulling and leading. (Mishna Kilayim 8:2)

The distinction between wild and domesticated animals is not absolutely clear. Zoologists differentiate between truly domestic animals and animals that are merely exploited captives (sometimes referred to as "domesticated" rather than "domestic"). A truly domesticated animal is an entire population that is reproductively isolated from wild populations, and exhibits unique morphological, physiological, and/or behavioral characteristics.[10] Exploited captives, on the other hand, are individual animals that have been made more tractable, such as elephants. This definition appears to basically correlate with that employed by the Sages. Thus, the Mishna points out that the monkey and elephant are not rated as domestic animals, even though they can be trained.

Elephants can be trained, but they are nevertheless rated as wild animals

However, there may also be cases where secular zoology differs from Judaism. For example, some (but not all) zoologists consider that the camel is not a domestic species, due to its not fulfilling the above-mentioned criteria.[11] But in Jewish thought, the camel is certainly rated as a domestic animal.[12]

The definitions of wild vs. domestic are not always easy to apply, either in secular zoology or in Jewish law. Is a cat a domestic animal? What about water buffalo? The answer is unclear for both systems. The Mishna itself records a dispute regarding whether certain animals – the dog and the "wild ox" (probably referring to the aurochs) – are classified as wild or domesticated.[13] Domes-

APIRUT / SHUTTERSTOCK

tic cattle are the descendants of wild aurochs, which were gigantic, wild oxen that were hunted to extinction a few hundred years ago. But is the aurochs to be classified as a wild animal, or is it a primordial domestic animal? Dogs are the descendants of wolves. But is the dog a truly domesticated animal, or is it merely a tractable wild animal? The answers to these questions are unclear, and hence form a dispute in the Mishna.

The Sages also note that some animals are extremely similar, such as the domestic pig and wild boar, and the domestic donkey and wild ass.[14] Nevertheless, they are considered different types, with one being classified as a domestic animal and the other as a wild animal. This is even though they can interbreed and produce fertile offspring.

(The Talmud does suggest a method of distinguishing between kosher wild and domestic animals vis-à-vis certain laws that are relevant to their slaughter for food and consumption, based on the characteristics of their horns. However, it appears that this method was not intended to conclusively resolve the question for all species. We shall explore it in detail in the introduction to the section on kosher wild animals.)

In addition, in order for an animal to be classified as a *chaya*, it is not enough that it is not a domestic animal. A shark is not a domestic animal, but it is not a *chaya*. The category of *chaya* only includes terrestrial animals. Thus, although a whale is a mammal, it is not a *chaya*; rather, it is classified as an aquatic creature. There is a dispute in the Mishna regarding the status of a semi-aquatic animal known as the "water-dog," which is probably the otter, as discussed in that chapter. And although a bat is classified by zoologists as a mammal, due to its possessing hair and lactating, it is rated by the Torah in the category of birds rather than being a *chaya*.

DAVID HOWLETT

It is unclear as to whether the marbled polecat would be rated as a sheretz *or a* chaya

Furthermore, the category of *chaya* only includes terrestrial animals of significant size. Small mammals such as mice, rats, and even martens and polecats are rated as *sheratzim*, "swarming" or "creeping" creatures rather than *chayot*.[15] But here, too, there is no clear dividing line between the categories. There is a continuum of sizes and body shapes amongst terrestrial mammals, from the smallest shrew to the elephant. Thus, even in the Mishna we find Beit Shammai in doubt as to whether a creature called the *chuldat sena'im*, which we shall discuss in the chapter on the mongoose, is rated as a *chaya* or a *sheretz*. Another question occurs with the snake: is it to be rated as a *chaya*, or a *sheretz*? The answer is unclear and disputed.[16]

The allocation of animals to various volumes of this encyclopedia follows the Torah classification of *chayot* rather than the zoological category of mammals. Thus, this volume does not include bats or whales. But it will also take into account editorial considerations, including ease of use, as well as balancing the various volumes in the set. Thus, the dog will be discussed in the volume on domesticated animals, even though there is a view in the Mishna that it is rated as a wild animal. The snake, and small carnivores such as martens, will be discussed in the volume on *sheratzim*. ∎

Notes

1   See *Midrash Shir HaShirim Rabba* 4:15 and Sotah 11b, quoted in the general introduction.

2   See Rabbi Samson Raphael Hirsch, *Commentary to the Torah*, Genesis 1:24.

3   Ramban, in his commentary to Genesis 1:24, inexplicably defines *behemot* as herbivores and *chayot* as carnivores. Netziv, in *Haamek Davar* ad loc., challenges this explanation, and point out that there are herbivorous *chayot* (such as deer and gazelles). There are also carnivorous *behemot*, such as dogs, according to one opinion in the Mishna.

4   Chullin 70b–71a, 84a; *Midrash Sifrei* 94.

5   Genesis 1:26 is also an example of this, according to Ramban and Radak, but not according to Netziv in *Haamek Davar*. For an academic perspective regarding this verse, see Richard Whitekettle, "Where The Wild Things Are: Primary Level Taxa in Israelite Zoological Thought," *Journal for the Study of the Old Testament* 93 (2001), pp. 17–37.

6   Rabbi Samson Raphael Hirsch, *Commentary to the Torah*, Leviticus 11:2.

7   In Psalms 104:11, where *chayat hasadeh* is juxtaposed with wild asses, it likewise seems to be used to refer specifically to herbivores, in contrast to the "beasts of the forest" that are juxtaposed with lions in 104:20–21.

8   See Malbim to Genesis 1:28, 2:20, 7:3, and Leviticus 11:2.

9   However, the prohibition only applies to manually coupling them; if they are housed in the same pen and interbreed, there is no transgression. See Bava Metzia 91a and Rambam, *Mishneh Torah, Hilkhot Kilayim* 9:2.

10   See Juliet Clutton-Brock, *A Natural History of Domesticated Mammals* (University of Texas Press, 1989), p. 104.

11   Ibid., pp. 104–5.

12   See Mishna Shabbat 5:1; Rambam, *Mishneh Torah, Hilkhot Maakhalot Assurot* 1:2, and *Mirkevet HaMishneh* and *Or Same'ach* ad loc.

13   Mishna Kilayim 8:5.

14   Tosefta, Kilayim 1:5; see too Mishna Kilayim 1:6.

15   See David Talshir, *Shemot Chayim* (Jerusalem: Bialik, 2012), pp. 95–106.

16   For an extensive review of sources, see Rabbi David Weiss, "Is the Snake a Type of *Chaya* or a *Sheretz*?" (Hebrew), *Otzrot Yerushalayim* (1970) 43, pp. 684–5.

PART ONE

Predators

Predators: Introduction

A Distinct Category

We often divide terrestrial animals into the categories of carnivores and herbivores. The Torah does not explicitly make such a distinction.[1] However, there are various contexts in Scripture, Mishna, and Talmud where various different predators are grouped together. Some of these are specifically referring to predators that are dangerous to human beings – the lion, bear, leopard, and sometimes the less dangerous wolf, hyena, and cheetah. But in the Mishna and Talmud, this grouping sometimes also explicitly includes even smaller predators – in particular, with regard to laws pertaining to how all these animals can inflict fatal wounds on their prey. As such, it makes sense to categorize all the predators into a distinct group from other wild animals, and to introduce this group with a discussion of the contexts in which they are placed together.

As discussed in the introduction to *Chayot*, Wild Animals, the term *chaya* in Scripture is often given a qualifying description: *chayot haaretz* (the "beasts of the land"), *chayot hasadeh* (the "beasts of the field"), or *chayot hayaar* (the "beasts of the forest"). While some usages of these expressions may refer to a particular subgroup of wild animals, such as carnivores or herbivores, the terms themselves include all wild animals. However, we find one qualifying description of *chayot* which specifically refers to predators – in fact, specifically to predators that pose a particular threat. The term *chaya raah*, literally "evil beasts," is used to describe wild animals that are dangerous to human beings, such as in the following verse:

While not as large as a bear, the lion is indisputably the top predator

> I will grant peace in the land, and you shall lie down untroubled by anyone; I will give the land respite from evil beasts, and no sword shall cross your land. (Lev. 26:6)

E2DAN / SHUTTERSTOCK

The expression "evil beasts," found in a number of places,[2] should not be understood to mean that these animals are consciously engaging in acts of wickedness. In Jewish thought, animals do not possess free will such as to make moral choices.[3] Rather, these animals are "evil" in the sense of being vicious. Alternately, Scripture is describing these animals in terms of their harmful effects on people. It is similar to the warning that was printed on entry permits to Palestine in the early twentieth century, when there was a great danger of malaria: "The mosquito is your enemy!"

Emissaries of God

SYMBOLISM

Predators present a threat not only to animals, but also to man. In the comfort of Western civilization today, it is hard for us to imagine being actually afraid of an attack from a predator. But in the ancient world, this was the reality. These animals posed a clear and present danger, no different from bandits or enemy soldiers:

There are four agents (of damage): Those which see and are seen, those which are seen but do not see, those which see but are not seen, and those which do not see and are not seen. Those which see and are seen – such as the wolf, lion, leopard, bear, cheetah,[4] snake, bandits, and troops – these can see and can be seen. (*Avot DeRabbi Natan* 40:10)

However, since God controls everything, this means that an attack on a person by a predator is not mere happenstance. The Midrash states it can only occur if the predator is on a divinely-arranged mission:

The powerful bear is second only to the lion in the scriptural hierarchy of dangerous animals

"If the snake bites, it is because it has not been charmed" (Eccl. 10:11) – R. Abba bar Kahana said, The snake never bites unless it has been thus charmed from Above, and the lion does not maul unless it has been thus charmed from Above, and an empire does not oppress people unless it has been thus charmed from Above. (*Kohelet Rabba* 10:14)

In fact, predators are seen as being ideal agents via which God can exercise divine retribution if people sin:

(If you reject My laws and spurn My rules, so that you do not observe all My commandments and you break My covenant . . .) I will send the beasts of the field against you, and they shall bereave you of your children and wipe out your cattle. They shall decimate you, and your roads shall be deserted. (Lev. 26:22)

This is seen as being an integral part of the purpose of these creatures' existence, since creation:

"The heaven and earth were completed, and all their hosts (or: armies)" (Gen. 2:1). . . . The Holy One appointed many armies to demand retribution for man's wrongs; many bears, many lions, many snakes, many venomous snakes, many scorpions. (*Midrash Bereshit Rabba* 10:5)

While this midrash describes them as "armies," elsewhere the Sages describe predators that act as God's executioners as "judges":

> Whoever negates themselves from words of Torah, is given over to those who will negate him, such as a lion, wolf or leopard . . . as it says, "There are judges in the land for God" (Ps. 58:12). (*Avot DeRabbi Natan* 29:2)

A moving account in the Talmud relates how the righteous Lulianus and Pappus gave themselves to be killed in order to save their brethren. They told the Roman Emperor Trajan that in killing them, he is no better than a predatory animal that is following God's will, and is in fact in a worse position:

> When Trajan was about to execute Lulianus and his brother Pappus in Lydia, he said to them, "If you are of the people of Hananiah, Mishael and Azariah, let your God come and deliver you from my hands, in the same way as he delivered Hananiah, Mishael and Azariah from the hands of Nebuchadnezzar." They replied: "Hananiah, Mishael and Azariah were perfectly righteous men and they merited that a miracle should be wrought for them, and Nebuchadnezzar also was a king worthy for a miracle to be wrought through him, but as for you, you are a common and wicked man and are not worthy that a miracle be wrought through you; and as for us, we have deserved of the Omnipresent that we should die, and if you will not kill us, the Omnipresent has many other agents of death. The Omnipresent has in His world many bears and lions who can attack us and kill us; the only reason why the Holy One, blessed be He, has handed us over into your hand is that at some future time He may exact punishment of you for our blood." (Taanit 18b[5])

The prophet Hosea, describing God's response to the sins of Israel, speaks of Him first as metaphorically acting toward them like predators – lion, leopard, and bear – and finally states that actual predators, the *chayot hasadeh*, will attack them:

> Therefore I will be to them as a lion; as a leopard by the way will I observe them; I will meet them like a bear that is bereaved of her cubs, and I shall tear their closed-up heart, and there I will devour them like a lion; the beast of the wilderness shall tear them apart. (Hos. 13:7–8)

Another account goes into greater detail of how predators will function as agents of divine retribution:

> O mortal, if a land were to sin against Me and commit a trespass . . . and if I were to send evil beasts (*chaya raah*) to roam the land and make it bereft, and it became a desolation with none passing through it because of the beasts. (Ezek. 14:13, 15)

Predators do not always need to actually kill people in order to fulfill their divine mission. Sometimes, their mission is just to present a deterrent, as when the Children of Israel, leaving Egypt and arriving at the Red Sea, wished to turn back:

*The leopard is the third
of the great predators
in the Land of Israel*

When Israel saw the stormy sea, they turned back to the wilderness. The Holy One summoned evil beasts, which did not allow them to pass, as it says, "He shut the wilderness against them" (Ex. 14:3), and "shutting" means nothing other than by way of evil beasts, as it says, "Who shut the mouths of the lions" (Dan. 6:23). (*Mekhilta, Beshalach* 1[6])

Sometimes, the predators follow divine instruction in going against their nature and *not* killing someone:

The Caesar said to R. Tanchum, "Come, let us all be one people." "Certainly!" he replied, "But we, who are circumcised, cannot possibly become like you; so you should circumcise yourselves and become like us." The Caesar replied: "You have spoken well; nevertheless, anyone who gets the better of the king must be thrown into the arena." They threw him in, but he was not eaten. A Sadducee said, "The reason that they did not eat him is that they are not hungry." They threw the Sadducee in, and he was eaten. (Sanhedrin 39a)

It is not only the Jewish nation that suffers retribution at the hand of carnivores. Ezekiel describes the divine judgment upon Gog and Magog, destined to take place at the End of Days, in terms of their corpses being eaten by scavengers:

And you, O mortal, say to every winged bird and to all the beasts of the wilderness: Thus said the Lord God: Assemble, come and gather from all around for the sacrificial feast that I am preparing for you – a great sacrificial feast – upon the mountains of Israel, and eat flesh and drink blood. You shall eat the flesh of warriors and drink the blood of the princes of the land; rams, lambs, he-goats, and bulls – all fatlings of Bashan. (Ezek. 39:17–18)

The Hordes That Plagued Egypt

IDENTIFICATION

Perhaps the most famous appearance of predators in the Torah as agents of divine retribution is in the fourth plague that was inflicted upon Egypt. It may come as a surprise, then, to learn that it is far from unequivocal that the plague actually consisted of wild animals. The word used in the Torah, *arov*, simply means "mixture" or "swarm." The Sages disputed whether this was a swarm of wild beasts, or of birds and flying insects, or of both:

The cheetah appears in the Mishna as another animal that is potentially dangerous to man

BILDAGENTUR ZOONAR / SHUTTERSTOCK

"I will let loose hordes against you" (Ex. 8:17). From where did they come? Some say, from above (i.e. birds and insects), some say from below (i.e. wild animals), and R. Akiva says from above and below. (*Midrash Shemot Rabba* 11:2)

Another view is that it was a mixture of specific types of insects alone:

R. Nechemiah says, They were types of wasps and mosquitoes. (*Midrash Shemot Rabba* 11:2)

The Midrash proceeds to argue against this view, on the grounds that the only reason why the hordes are described as eventually disappearing,[7] as opposed to dying like the frogs, must have been to avoid a benefit to the Egyptians – namely, that dead wild animals are of benefit for their meat and hides.

Nevertheless, there is support for R. Nechemiah's view. The Septuagint, for example, renders *arov* as referring to a type of dogfly. Others point out that the ten plagues fall into a pattern of five pairs: blood and frogs related to the Nile, pestilence and boils were diseases, hail and locusts come from the sky and destroy crops, and darkness and the death of the firstborn are both forms of darkness (literal darkness, and the darkness of death, at midnight); accordingly, *arov*, which is paired with lice, should be insects.[8]

Still, it became popularly accepted that the plague involved wild animals. While one view is that it was only wolves,[9] others are of the view that it was a mixture of different animals:

> R. Shimon b. Lakish said: The Holy One said, You massed yourselves against My children, I shall also mass the birds of the skies and the beasts of the land against you, as it says, "I will let loose hordes (lit. "a mixture") against you" – beasts and birds mixed together. (*Shemot Rabba* 11:2)

Which types of animals would it have been? Many people envision lions and tigers and bears. In fact, no sources mention tigers, since these are native only to Asia. Lions and bears, on the other hand, are indeed mentioned, as being involved due to poetic justice:

MENNO SCHAEFER / SHUTTERSTOCK

Although foxes are predators, they are not dangerous to man unless rabid

> Why was there the plague of hordes? Because the Egyptians would say to Israel, "Go and bring us bears and lions," so that they could hunt[10] them. Therefore, the Holy One brought a mixture (*arov*) of wild animals, as it says, "And heavy hordes came" (Ex. 8:20) – these are the words of R. Yehuda. (*Shemot Rabba* 11:2[11])

Other sources mention additional creatures, such as leopards, wolves, and even eagles:

> They schemed to have the Israelites encumbered as tutors, so He sent the hordes against them, of lions, wolves, leopards, bears, and eagles.[12] If an Egyptian had five sons, and he gave them to an Israelite to take them to the market, a lion would come and seize one, a wolf another, a bear another, a leopard another, and an eagle another. (*Midrash Tanchuma*, Bo 4[13])

And another source adds snakes, also due to poetic justice:

> The Holy One said, Let lions and bears[14] and snakes come and exact retribution from Egypt, which sought to destroy a nation that is compared to wild animals: "Judah is a lion cub," "Dan is a lion cub," "Dan is a snake along the way," "Benjamin is a predatory wolf," etc. (Midrash, *Yalkut Shimoni, Shemot* 182)

Other, later midrashim even add the giant octopus.[15]

The Predators of Scripture and Enemy Nations

In Scripture, there are various contexts in which the five most dangerous predators – the lion, bear, leopard, wolf, and sometimes the snake – are grouped together. One is with regard to the Messianic Era:

> The wolf shall live with the lamb, and the leopard shall lie down with the kid; and the calf and the young lion and the fatling together; and a small child shall lead them. And the cow and the bear shall graze; their young ones shall lie down together; and the lion shall eat straw like the ox. (Is. 11:6–7)

> The wolf and the lamb shall graze as one, and the lion shall eat straw like cattle, and the snake shall eat dirt. They shall not cause harm or destruction in all My holy mountain, says God. (Is. 65:25)

A late midrash of indeterminate origin relates this prophecy to statues of animals that were incorporated into King Solomon's throne:

The wolf is the fourth and least of the animals described in Scripture as predators

> There was a lion facing an ox.... R. Yochanan said: King Solomon set them on his throne, one on the right and one on the left: A sheep on the right and a wolf on the left, a gazelle on the right and a bear on the left ... and the Holy One engraved them on Solomon's throne to show an example for Israel for the future era, in which these will dwell as one, as it says, "And the wolf shall dwell with the lamb" (Is. 11:6). (*Midrash Kisei VeIpudrumin shel Shlomo HaMelekh*[16])

There is a dispute in rabbinic tradition regarding the interpretation of these prophecies. Some explain them literally, to mean that predatory animals will actually change their nature and become herbivorous.[17] Maimonides and others, however, interpret them metaphorically.[18] Instead of referring to actual animals, these verses refer to wicked people and nations that are symbolized by these animals. Such people will no longer pose a threat, and will live in peace with us.

The predators also symbolize wicked nations in a prophetic vision experienced by Daniel:

> In the first year of Belshazzar, King of Babylon, Daniel saw a dream and vision in his mind in bed; he then wrote down the dream, and related an account of it. Daniel told the following: "In my vision at night, I saw the four winds of heaven stirring up the great sea. Four mighty beasts, each different from the other, emerged from the sea.... The first was like a lion ... and behold, another beast, a second one, similar to a bear.... Afterwards I beheld, and there was another, similar to a leopard.... After that, as I looked on in the night vision, there was a fourth beast – fearsome, dreadful, and very powerful, with great iron teeth – that devoured and crushed, and stamped the remains with its feet." (Dan. 7:1–7)

In classical Jewish thought, the four beasts in Daniel's vision – the lion, bear, leopard, and a fictitious monster with similarities to the wild boar – represent four kingdoms to which the Jewish people have been subjected: Babylon, Persia-Media, Greece, and Rome.[19] (These parallels shall be explored in detail in the relevant chapters.) These metaphors are also seen in a rebuke by Amos to those who sought God's destruction of the Babylonian empire, little appreciating that, before the Messianic Era, any redemption would only be temporary:

> Ah, you who desire the day of the Lord! Why would you want the day of the Lord? It is darkness, not light! It is like a man who fled from a lion, and a bear encountered him; or if he came into a house, and leaned his hand on the wall, and a snake bit him. (Amos 5:18–19)

Escaping from a lion is little reason to celebrate if one is then attacked by a bear. By the same token, escaping the tyranny of Babylon is little reason to celebrate if one is then under the subjugation of Persia-Media.[20] The Sages present a similar metaphor in describing how the tribulations of Gog and Magog will eclipse all previous events:

> "Do not remember the first things" (Is. 43:18) – this refers to subjection to other nations; "and do not contemplate the previous events" (ibid.) – this is the Exodus from Egypt. "I am about to do something new, it is now sprouting" (ibid. v. 19) – Rav Yosef taught: This is the war of Gog and Magog. It is comparable to a person who was walking along the road and encountered a wolf and was saved from it, and would tell everyone about the incident with the wolf. Then he encountered a lion and was saved from it, and would tell everyone about the incident with the lion. Then he encountered a snake and was saved from it, and forgot about both earlier incidents, and would tell everyone about the incident with the snake. So, too, with Israel; the later sorrows cause the earlier ones to be forgotten. (Berakhot 13a[21])

Normally, it is always the lion that is mentioned first. But here, the first animal in the story is the wolf. This is because the scriptural reference is understood as referring to the subjugation to a nation preceding that of the four empires, namely Egypt. The lion, which always represents Babylon, thus appears second.[22]

These animals, representing the nations that have oppressed Israel, are mentioned in one of the *selichot*, the prayers that are recited between Rosh HaShana and Yom Kippur. To the list of predators is added the wild boar, which is a dangerous and destructive animal that represents Rome:

> There are four primary damagers: The [Median] wolf, the [Babylonian] lion, the [Persian] bear, and their young, the [Greek] leopard poised over their cities, and the [Roman] wild boar with them. Give them according to their deeds, and the evil of their endeavors! (*Selicha* 80)

It should be noted, however, that the symbolism of predators is not wholly evil. Indeed, some of the Jewish tribes themselves are likened to lions and wolves.

There are those who classify the snake as a wild animal, but others classify it as a sheretz, *creeping creature*

Legal Aspects of Predators

Predators appear in a number of contexts in Jewish law. If a person takes on the role of guardian for someone else's livestock, there is discussion of his liability in a case where there are attacks by predators. The ruling is that the liability depends upon which type of predator is involved in the attack:

> There are maulings for which [a guardian] is obligated to pay, and there are mauled animals for which he does not pay. Which is the mauling for which he must pay? For example, mauling by a cat, fox, or mongoose.... And which is the mauling for which he is exempt from payment? For example, mauling by a wolf, a lion, a bear, a leopard, a cheetah, or a snake ... for in any case where it is impossible for him to rescue it, he is exempt from paying. (*Mekhilta DeRabbi Yishmael, Mishpatim* 16)

The caracal is one of several species of wild cat in the Land of Israel

Cats, foxes, and mongooses are not considered to be dangerous to man, and it is easy to fend them off. It is only the predators which are potentially dangerous to man – the lion, bear, leopard, wolf, cheetah, and snake – which can present situations of unavoidable harm:

> [An attack by] one wolf is not unavoidable, but [an attack by] two wolves is avoidable. The lion, bear, leopard, cheetah, and snake, are cases of unavoidable damage. This is only where they came of their own accord, but if he took [the flock] to a place that is infested with wild beasts and bandits, it is not a case of unavoidable damage. (Mishna Bava Metzia 7:9)

Elsewhere, the Mishna discusses a situation where these predators are privately owned. The Mishna classifies these animals as dangerous, such that the owner is already considered warned about them[23] and is thus fully liable for any damage that they do:

> The wolf, the lion, the bear, the leopard, the cheetah, and the snake, are all rated as animals about which one is warned. R. Elazar says: When they are tamed, they are not in the category of warned. (Mishna Bava Kama 1:4)

R. Elazar is of the view that it is possible to tame these animals, to the extent that they are no longer considered necessarily dangerous. As such, if they launch an attack, one is not fully liable.

Elsewhere, the Mishna discusses the circumstances under which such animals can be put to death:

> The wolf, the lion, the bear, the leopard, the cheetah, and the snake – their death is via a court of twenty-three.[24] R. Eliezer says: Whoever goes ahead and kills them (i.e. even without a court ruling), merits.[25] (Mishna Sanhedrin 1:4)

Why are these animals being put to death? The Talmud records a discussion as to whether the Mishna is discussing a situation where the predator killed someone, or even a case where the animal did not yet kill anyone:

Resh Lakish said: "It is only if they actually killed [that there is a dispute as to whether these animals must be tried in court or anyone can kill them], but if they did not kill, it is not [permitted for them to be put to death]." We see that he is of the view that these can be tamed and they can [legally] have owners.

R. Yochanan said: "[R. Eliezer is of the view that these animals may be killed, and by anyone,] even if they did not actually kill." We see that he is of the view that they cannot be tamed, and [therefore] they cannot [legally] have owners. (Sanhedrin 15b)

We see that there are diverse views regarding whether an allegedly tame predatory animal can ever be truly considered harmless.[26] Indeed, while there are certain facilities today that house allegedly tame predators such as lions, bears, and leopards, accidents have been known to happen. Of course, accidents happen with dogs and cows too; the question is whether the incidence of attacks with predators is high enough to mean that they are never truly considered tame. This is precisely the point of dispute in the Talmud.

There are other legal issues involved in owning dangerous predators. There is a limitation placed upon the sale of such animals:

The mongoose is a small predator which attacks small animals, but poses no harm to man

KLAUS RUDLOFF

One may not sell (to heathens) bears, lions, or anything that can cause damage to the public. (Mishna Avoda Zara 1:7)

The concern here is not about selling animals to a zoo. Rather, it refers to an era in which lions and bears were commonly placed in the arena to attack people. If one owns a dangerous animal, one may not sell it to someone who may put it to such a use.

When Predators Maul

THEOLOGY, PHILOSOPHY, AND SCIENCE

Further legal aspects of predators relate to domestic animals that survive being attacked by various predators. An animal is only kosher for consumption if it is in good physical health at the time of slaughter. The Mishna lists various *tereifot*, fatal defects, which render an animal prohibited for use as food. One of these fatal defects is a mauling by a predator:

These are the *tereifot* in domesticated animals... if it fell from a roof, if most of its ribs were broken, a mauling by a wolf; R. Yehuda says, a mauling by a wolf [is considered a fatal defect] with a small domestic animal, and a mauling by a lion [is considered a fatal defect] with a large animal. (Mishna Chullin 3:1)

Unfortunately, these laws give rise to several difficult contradictions with our knowledge of zoology. One difficulty is that the Talmud states that the result of such maulings is that venom is injected into the prey animal.[27] Needless to say, this is not consistent with modern zoological knowledge.

One solution presented for such difficulties is that the Talmud is not referring to a chemical venom generated by the animal, but rather to infections caused by bacteria that accumulates under the claws.[28] (A variation on this would be to say that bacterial infections led to the belief that venom is injected.) Such infections can prove fatal.[29]

With regard to such maulings, there is also extensive discussion in the Talmud[30] and later rabbinic authorities[31] regarding which predators are rated as able to inflict them. This also hinges upon which type of animal is being attacked; thus, while a wound inflicted upon a cow by a lion is considered fatal, a marten can only inflict a fatal injury on a bird.

The claws of a lion cub

Whatever the nature of attacks by predators, the results are that the animal being mauled is extremely unlikely to survive. For this reason, the Talmud notes that in such cases, the owners are assumed to have forfeited their ownership:

> R. Shimon b. Elazar says, Someone who saves [an animal] from a lion or from a bear or from a leopard or from a cheetah…it is his, as the owners have given up hope on them. (Bava Metzia 24a; Avoda Zara 43a; Y. Shekalim 29b)

Other legal aspects of predators, which relate to specific species, are discussed in the relevant chapters. ∎

Notes

1 Ramban, Commentary to Genesis 1:24, states that *chaya* refers to carnivores and *behema* refers to herbivores; Netziv, *Haamek Davar* ad loc., points out that this is not the case.

2 Genesis 37:20, 33; Leviticus 26:6; Ezekiel 5:17; 14:15, 21; 34:25.

3 For further discussion, see *Man and Beast* by this author.

4 Or: hyena. The term used is *bardelas*, which refers to the cheetah when used in the Mishna, but which the Babylonian Talmud defines as a hyena.

5 Also *Kohelet Rabba* 3:22.

6 Similarly in *Midrash Shemot Rabba* 15:15.

7 Exodus 8:27.

8 Rabbi Moshe David (Umberto) Cassuto, in *A Commentary on the Book of Exodus* (Jerusalem: Magnes Press, 1997), p. 93. See Gary A. Rendsburg, "Beasts or Bugs? Solving the Problem of the Fourth Plague," *Bible Review* 19:02 (Apr. 2003), pp. 19–23.

9 Rashbam, commentary to Exodus 8:17. Rabbi Yosef Schonhak in *Toledot HaAretz* (p. 59) claims that these wolves that plagued Egypt, along with the "wolves of dusk" referred to in Scripture, are hyenas. See too *Midrash Tehillim* 78 and *Shemot Rabba* 11:2 with the commentary of Maharzu ad loc. See too the discussion in the chapter on wolves.

10 Following the emendation of *Etz Yosef* and *HaTirosh*.

11 Also *Midrash Tanchuma, Va'era* 14. A longer version is in *Tanna DeVei Eliyahu Rabba* 7, where it states that the goal of the Egyptians was for the Israelite men to be out hunting for animals in the wilderness, and unavailable for their wives, thus making it impossible for them to have children.

12 The term *nesher* probably refers to a vulture, but we are translating it as eagle for the comfort of the reader.

13 In *Midrash Yalkut Midrashei Teiman, Va'era*, it appears with certain differences, such as that the bear and eagle are replaced by two different types of lions.

14 The source verses regarding the tribes mention wolves, not bears. However, the two are sometimes interchanged, as we shall discuss in the chapter on wolves, due to the Aramaic name for the wolf being similar to the Hebrew name for the bear.

15 *Midrash Vayosha, Sefer HaYashar*, and *Yalkut Me'am Loez*. See the extensive discussion in *Sacred Monsters*, by this author, Chapter Two: Mermaids, Krakens and Wild Men.

16 In J.D. Eisenstein, *Otzar HaMidrashim* (New York, 1915), vol. II, p. 527.

17 *Metzudot* and Malbim to Isaiah 11:7; Abarbanel to Hosea 2:18.

18 Rambam, *Mishneh Torah, Hilkhot Melakhim* 12:1; Ibn Ezra to Isaiah 11:6. Radak to Isaiah 11:6–7 suggests that, as well as the allegorical meaning, it is also referring to actual animals, but it is only stating that the

animals in the Land of Israel will not kill, and will satisfy themselves with animals that have died naturally; outside of Israel, however, they will kill as usual.

19 For an academic study of the symbolism of the animals in rabbinic thought, see Rivka Raviv, "Shaping the Four Kingdoms in Daniel in the Rabbinical Literature," *Jewish Studies Internet Journal* 5 (2006), pp. 1–20 (Hebrew).

20 See Abarbanel ad loc.

21 Also Tosefta, Berakhot 1:13, and Y. Berakhot 11b.

22 Maharsha ad loc.

23 See Exodus 21:29: "If, however, that ox has been in the habit of goring, and its owner, though warned, has failed to guard it, and it kills a man or a woman – the ox shall be stoned and its owner, too, shall be put to death."

24 See the chapter "Animals on Trial" in *Man and Beast*, by this author, for a discussion on why animals appear in court and require so many judges in order to be put to death.

25 The Talmud (Sanhedrin 15b) explains that according to R. Yochanan, when R. Eliezer says that anyone can kill these animals and "merits," it means that they merit to acquire the hides. According to Resh Lakish, on the other hand, R. Eliezer cannot mean that they acquire the hides; since Resh Lakish understands that Rav Yochanan is only licensing people to kill the animal once the animal has already killed, at which point it becomes forbidden to derive benefit from the animal. Accordingly, R. Eliezer means that one merits heavenly reward.

26 See too *Tosafot* to Bava Kama 16b s.v. *Rabbi Elazar* and *Tosafot* to Sanhedrin 15b s.v. *veRabbi Yochanan*, and Rashba to Avoda Zara 16b.

27 Chullin 53a.

28 See Rabbi Aryeh Carmell, in *Mikhtav MiEliyahu*, vol. IV, p. 355, footnote 4, who records Rabbi Dessler as stating that the Talmud was giving an explanation for a law for which the real reasons have been lost in antiquity. See too Rabbi Amitai Ben-David, *Sichat Chullin* to Chullin 52b, and the debate between Rabbi Carmell and Prof. Shlomo Sternberg in *BDD* (Winter 1998) vol. 6. Cf. the section "How Lions Kill" in the chapter on lions, and the section "How Wolves Attack" in the chapter on wolves.

29 "Many people mauled by lions have died from wounds that should have been survivable: the meat caked under the attackers' claws and teeth injected the victims with disease, and they died in a gangrenous fever" – Gordon Grice, *The Red Hourglass: Lives of the Predators* (London: Penguin Books, 1998), p. 104.

30 Chullin 52b–53b.

31 See Rosh, Chullin 3:40, *Tur, Yoreh De'ah* 57; *She'iltot, Vayikra* 68; Rashba, Chullin 52b; *Peri To'ar, Yoreh De'ah* 57:7; *Tzemach Tzedek, Yoreh De'ah* 269:1.

LION

Lion

אֲרִי, אַרְיֵה, לַיִשׁ, לָבִיא, כְּפִיר, שַׁחַל, שַׁחַץ

Ari, Aryeh, Layish, Lavi, Kefir, Shachal, Shachatz

The Lions of the Land of Israel

NATURAL HISTORY

אִתִּי מִלְּבָנוֹן כַּלָּה אִתִּי מִלְּבָנוֹן תָּבוֹאִי תָּשׁוּרִי מֵרֹאשׁ אֲמָנָה מֵרֹאשׁ
שְׂנִיר וְחֶרְמוֹן מִמְּעֹנוֹת אֲרָיוֹת מֵהַרְרֵי נְמֵרִים:
שיר השירים ד:ח

וְיִגְאֶה כַּשַּׁחַל תְּצוּדֵנִי וְתָשֹׁב תִּתְפַּלָּא בִי:
איוב י:טז

The lion is by far the most prominent of all wild animals mentioned in Scripture, Midrash, and Talmud. It is mentioned on over 150 occasions in Scripture, under a variety of different names,[1] and in nearly two hundred different contexts in the Talmud and Midrash.[2] Most of these invoke the lion as a metaphor – which itself indicates its prominence – while others describe actual lions as part of a narrative.

Lions used to be widespread in the Land of Israel. They are described in Scripture as living in the Jordan valley,[3] in the central territory of Samaria,[4] and in the Negev desert in the south.[5] The reference to the tribe of Dan as being a lion, "leaping from Bashan,"[6] indicates that lions also lived in the portion of Dan, the Golan; ancient synagogues in the Golan often contain depictions of lions. There is also an indication that lions were prevalent in the hills of the northern region:

> Come with me from Lebanon, my bride, come with me from Lebanon; look from the peak of Amana, from the peak of Senir and Hermon, from the lions' dens, from the mountains of the leopards. (Song. 4:8)

Why did lions disappear? One reason is that they were captured for use in the Roman amphitheater. Some indication of how many lions suffered this fate can be seen in the following account:

> R. Yehoshua b. Beteira said: There was an incident where they were spearing wild asses for lions in the royal arena, and those who came up for the festivals were wading up to their knees in blood. (Menachot 103b; Y. Shekalim 31b)

Lions were also hunted for sport by kings. There may be an allusion to this in Job's cries of despair, depending upon the interpretation of the verse:

> If my head is lifted up proudly, You hunt me like a lion; and again work wonders against me. (Job 10:16)

Job may be describing God's oppression of him as being like a lion hunting him.[7] But another interpretation is that Job is saying that God hunts him in the way that a lion is hunted.[8] A lion may "lift up its head proudly," but precisely for that reason, it was a favored target for kings to hunt.

Through a combination of trapping, hunting, and habitat destruction, the biblical lions were doomed. The last evidence for lions being found in the Land of Israel dates to the twelfth century, though it appears that they survived in neighboring countries for much longer. It is unclear when they finally became extinct from the region.[9]

The lion of biblical Israel was not, however, the African lion that is familiar to us and which lives today in central and southern Africa. Instead, it was a different subspecies: either the Asiatic lion (*Panthera leo persica*), or the Barbary lion, also known as the Atlas lion (*Panthera leo leo*). It is not known which of the subspecies was in the Land of Israel; this may have been the south-westernmost part of the range of the Asiatic lion, or the north-easternmost part of the range of the Barbary lion.[10] It is also possible that the ranges of both types of lion overlapped in the Land of Israel.

The Asiatic lion is slightly smaller than the African lion, with a sparser mane, and a distinct fold of skin along its belly. Unlike African lions, it lives in wooded areas, and Scripture speaks about lions living in forests[11] and thickets.[12] (It should be remembered that in biblical times, the Land of Israel was much more heavily forested than it is today.) The Asiatic lion survived in Syria and Iran until the nineteenth century, but today lives only in a single forest in India. A number of Asiatic lions are also maintained in captivity, including at the Jerusalem Biblical Zoo. The lion that was familiar to the Sages of the Babylonian Talmud would have been the Asiatic lion.

The Barbary lion is often described as being larger than African lions, although this is disputed by some. It was distinctive for its huge mane, very dark in coloration, which

Asiatic lion

Barbary lion

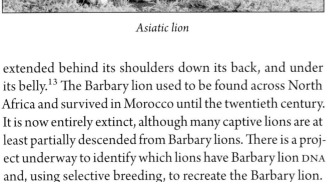

שַׁאֲגַת אַרְיֵה וְקוֹל שָׁחַל וְשִׁנֵּי כְפִירִים נִתָּעוּ: לַיִשׁ אֹבֵד מִבְּלִי טָרֶף וּבְנֵי לָבִיא יִתְפָּרָדוּ:

איוב ד:י-יא

extended behind its shoulders down its back, and under its belly.[13] The Barbary lion used to be found across North Africa and survived in Morocco until the twentieth century. It is now entirely extinct, although many captive lions are at least partially descended from Barbary lions. There is a project underway to identify which lions have Barbary lion DNA and, using selective breeding, to recreate the Barbary lion.

The Names of the Lion

—————————————————— IDENTIFICATION

There are several different names for the lion in Scripture, which attests to the prominence of the lion. While some of these names refer to different stages of the lion's life, with others it is unclear as to whether they refer to particular types of lion (e.g. lions of particular ages or appearances), or are simply synonyms used for literary purposes.[14] In just two consecutive verses in the Book of Job, there are no less than five different appellations for lions:

> [As I have seen, those who plow iniquity, and sow wickedness, reap the same. By the blast of God they perish, and by the blast of his anger are they consumed.] The roaring of the *aryeh*, and the voice of the *shachal*, and the teeth of the *kefirim* – they are broken. The *layish* perishes for lack of prey, and the young of the *lavi* are scattered. (Job 4:10–11)

The Talmud adds another name to the end of this list, *shachatz*:

> R. Yochanan said: The lion has six names – *ari, kefir, lavi, layish, shachal, shachatz.* (Sanhedrin 95a[15])

Elsewhere, the Rabbis distinguish between the names *ari* and *aryeh*, and also propose explanations for each of these seven different names:

The lion has seven names, and they are as follows: *Aryeh, ari, kefir, lavi, layish, shachal, shachatz. Aryeh* – when it is young. *Ari* – when it is old.[16] *Kefir* – that it rejects (*kofer*) its father and mother. *Lavi* – that it seizes the hearts (*lev*) of people when it roars. *Layish* – that everything is like dough (which is kneaded, *lash*) in its mouth. *Shachal* – that all tremble (*shechalim*) before it. *Shachatz* – that it tears (*meshachetz*) with its mouth. (*Avot DeRabbi Natan,* Version B, Shechter ed., ch. 43)

A later midrashic compilation subsumes the *aryeh* into the *ari,* but adds a seventh name, *gur,* which means "cub":

> R. Levi said: The lion has seven names, and they are as follows: *Ari, shachal, kefir, lavi, layish, shachatz,* and *gur aryeh. Ari* – in accordance with its plain meaning, that all are in awe of it (*yir'a*). *Kefir* – that all who see it are in denial (*kofer*) of their life. *Lavi* – that it seizes the hearts (*lev*) of people. *Layish* – that the flesh of man is kneaded (*lash*) in its teeth. *Shachal* – that all tremble (*shechalim*) before it. *Shachatz* – that it is proud;[17] alternatively, that it tears (*meshachetz*) with its teeth. (*Midrash Yalkut Shimoni, Mishlei* 20:959)

We shall survey each of these names in turn.

1. Ari/Aryeh

Ari and *aryeh* appear to be two versions of the same word; the reason for the variant spelling is unclear. These appear in Scripture more often than any other name for the lion. *Ari/ aryeh* is a generic term for a lion, though it seems to often specifically refer to an adult male lion (just as the English

61

term "lion" is used both in reference to the species as a whole, yet often is intended to refer to an adult male lion). Some suggest that the name *aryeh* comes from the root *orah*, fire, due to the lion's fiery nature and/or appearance.[18]

2. Kefir

Kefir, a term that appears on thirty-one occasions in Scripture, refers to a young lion. It does not refer to a cub – the *kefir* can hunt on its own, and is at adult size and strength, or close to that.[19] However, it is only just transitioning to adulthood. All this is clear from the following verses:

> What a lioness was your mother! She lay down among lions, she nourished her cubs among young lions. And she brought up one of her cubs; he became a young lion (*kefir*), and he learned to catch the prey; he devoured men. (Ezek. 19:2–3)

In line with this, the Midrash says that the young lion is called *kefir* because it rejects (*kofer*) its parents.[20] The boldness and independence of the young adult lion also appears to lie behind its name being invoked as a metaphor:

> Sheba, and Dedan, and the merchants of Tarshish, with all its *kefirim*, shall say to you, Have you come to take booty? Have you gathered your company to plunder? To carry away silver and gold, to take away cattle and goods, to take a great booty? (Ezek. 38:13)

A kefir – a young lion

וְאָמַרְתָּ מָה אִמְּךָ לְבִיָּא בֵּין אֲרָיוֹת רָבָצָה בְּתוֹךְ כְּפִרִים רִבְּתָה גוּרֶיהָ: וַתַּעַל אֶחָד מִגֻּרֶיהָ כְּפִיר הָיָה וַיִּלְמַד לִטְרָף טֶרֶף אָדָם אָכָל:

יחזקאל יט:ב-ג

שְׁבָא וּדְדָן וְסֹחֲרֵי תַרְשִׁישׁ וְכָל כְּפִרֶיהָ יֹאמְרוּ לְךָ הֲלִשְׁלֹל שָׁלָל אַתָּה בָא הֲלָבֹז בַּז הִקְהַלְתָּ קְהָלֶךָ לָשֵׂאת כֶּסֶף וְזָהָב לָקַחַת מִקְנֶה וְקִנְיָן לִשְׁלֹל שָׁלָל גָּדוֹל:

יחזקאל לח:יג

הֵן עַם כְּלָבִיא יָקוּם וְכַאֲרִי יִתְנַשָּׂא לֹא יִשְׁכַּב עַד יֹאכַל טֶרֶף וְדַם חֲלָלִים יִשְׁתֶּה:

במדבר כג:כד

כִּי גוֹי עָלָה עַל אַרְצִי עָצוּם וְאֵין מִסְפָּר שִׁנָּיו שִׁנֵּי אַרְיֵה וּמְתַלְּעוֹת לָבִיא לוֹ:

יואל א:ו

The commentaries explain that sharp and aggressive traders are metaphorically referred to as young lions, which boldly go out to fulfill their desires.[21]

3. Lavi

Lavi is a name for lions that occurs on fourteen occasions in Scripture. This is translated by some as "lioness," but this is an error.[22] It is true that lionesses are specifically referred to with this name on two occasions,[23] but this is with the feminine gender of the term, *leviya*. *Lavi*, in the masculine form, refers to a male lion. Some are of the view that it refers to a lion of greater size than an *ari*,[24] while others posit that it refers to a smaller lion.[25] In Scripture, sometimes the *lavi* appears before the *ari*, and sometimes after, making it difficult to definitively state that it refers to either a greater or lesser lion:

> Behold, the people shall rise up as a *lavi*, and lift himself up as an *ari*; he shall not lie down until he eats of the prey, and drinks the blood of the slain. (Num. 23:24)

> For a nation has come up upon my land, strong, and without number, whose teeth are the teeth of an *ari*, and he has the fangs of a *lavi*. (Joel 1:6[26])

It would appear impossible to determine the true understanding of the nuance of the term *lavi*. One speculative suggestion is that it relates to the word *lavah*, meaning "to blow ablaze," and thus refers to a flame-colored lion,[27] or perhaps the fiery appearance of a lion due to its mane. In the absence of anything more concrete, we will translate *lavi* as "fiery lion."

4. Layish

The term *layish* occurs on three occasions in Scripture. One of these perhaps indicates that it refers to a particularly powerful lion:[28]

"What a lioness was your mother!"

(Ezek. 19:1)

לַיִשׁ גִּבּוֹר בַּבְּהֵמָה וְלֹא יָשׁוּב מִפְּנֵי כֹל:

לֹא הִדְרִיכֻהוּ בְנֵי שָׁחַץ לֹא עָדָה עָלָיו שָׁחַל:

אֶת כָּל גָּבֹהַּ יִרְאֶה הוּא מֶלֶךְ עַל כָּל בְּנֵי שָׁחַץ:

שִׁוִּיתִי עַד בֹּקֶר כָּאֲרִי כֵּן יְשַׁבֵּר כָּל עַצְמוֹתָי מִיּוֹם עַד לַיְלָה תַּשְׁלִימֵנִי:

בְּנָיָה בֶן יְהוֹיָדָע בֶּן אִישׁ חַיִל רַב פְּעָלִים מִן קַבְצְאֵל הוּא הִכָּה אֵת שְׁנֵי אֲרִיאֵל מוֹאָב וְהוּא יָרַד וְהִכָּה אֶת הָאֲרִי בְּתוֹךְ הַבּוֹר בְּיוֹם הַשָּׁלֶג:

משלי ל:ל

איוב כח:ח

איוב מא:כו

ישעיה לח:יג

דברי הימים א יא:כב

The *layish* is the mightiest of animals, and turns away before no one. (Prov. 30:30)

In the absence of any stronger evidence for the meaning of the term, we will translate *layish* as "mighty lion."

5. Shachal

Shachal is a term that occurs on seven occasions in Scripture. Its precise nuance is difficult to determine with any certainty, and as with the *lavi*, diametrically opposed views exist. Some have suggested that it refers to a large[29] or old[30] lion, while others argue that it refers to a medium-sized[31] or young[32] lion. At least, then, there is something of a consensus that it refers to a lion at a particular stage of life! With no grounds to choose any particular translation, we shall use "mature lion."

6. Shachatz

There are two instances in the Book of Job of the term *shachatz*, which the Sages interpret as referring to a lion:

The sons of *shachatz* have not trodden it, nor has the *shachal*-lion passed by it. (Job 28:8)

[Leviathan] sees all that is haughty; he is king over all the sons of *shachatz*. (Job 41:26)

As noted earlier, the Talmud and Midrash understand *shachatz* to refer to the lion.[33] This fits with the first verse in Job, which parallels the *shachatz* with the *shachal*-lion, and can also fit with the second verse, in which Leviathan is mightier even than the proud king of beasts. While the aforementioned midrash relates the etymology of *shachatz* to the lion's tearing of its prey, another midrash interprets it as referring to pride, which also fits well with the second verse above:

"With me [you will be exiled] from Lebanon…from the dens of lions" (Song. 4:8) – This refers to Sichon and Og. Just as the lion is proud (*shachutz*),[34] so too Sichon and Og were proud and mighty; for there was only the

distance of a day's travel between them, and yet they did not come to each other's assistance. (*Shir HaShirim Rabba* 4:19)

In light of the verse and midrash, perhaps it is best to render *shachatz* as "proud lion."

7. Gur

The term *gur* simply refers to a cub. It is also used in Scripture in reference to the cubs of the jackal.[35] As such, it is not a distinct name for lions, notwithstanding its famous mention by Jacob in his reference to Judah as a lion cub.[36]

The Power of the Lion

— SYMBOLISM

The most distinctive aspect of lions is their sheer power as predators. Wild oxen and bears possess more brute strength, and leopards possess greater speed and cunning. But when one factors in everything together, including size (lions weigh up to five hundred pounds), strength, claws, teeth, and hunting ability, the lion emerges as the leader, standing right at the top of the food chain, as stated in a verse cited earlier:

The lion[37] is the mightiest of animals, and turns away before no one. (Prov. 30:30)

The strength of a lion defies belief. A single blow from its powerful paw is often enough to kill livestock or people.[38] It can kill and carry away animals much larger than itself. King Hezekiah, reminiscing upon the terrible pains of his illness, likens them to being mauled by a lion:

Then it was as though a lion were breaking all my bones; I cried out until morning; from daybreak to nightfall You shall finish me. (Is. 38:13)

There are even halakhic ramifications of the power of a lion:

One who traps a lion on Shabbat is not liable until he brings it into its cage. (Shabbat 106b)

Due to the lion's great strength, merely having caught it in a trap does not mean that one has successfully captured it. It can only be truly considered secured when it is locked up in a cage.

One verse simultaneously demonstrates that powerful warriors were compared to lions, and that the greatest act of human power was to kill a lion:

Benaiah the son of Jehoiada of Kabzeel, was a brave man who performed great deeds; he slew two lion-like men of Moab; and once, on a snowy day, he went down and slew a lion in a pit. (1 Chr. 11:22)

Benaiah's bravery and great deeds are demonstrated by slaying two powerful warriors who are likened to lions, and by slaying an actual lion.[39] But the most famous example of a person whose strength is demonstrated by killing a lion is Samson:

> Then Samson and his father and his mother went down to Timnath. When he came to the vineyards of Timnath, behold, a young lion came roaring to meet him. And the spirit of the Lord came mightily upon him, and he tore it apart with his bare hands as he would have torn a kid. (Judges 14:5–6)

When Samson later discovered that bees had made a nest and honey in the lion's carcass, this inspired him to present the people of Timnath with a riddle: "Out of the eater came something to eat, out of the strong came something sweet."[40] After Delilah had gotten the answer out of him and told it to the people of Timnath, they went to Samson and presented it as follows:

> And the men of the town said to him, "What is sweeter than honey, and what is stronger than a lion?" (Judges 14:18)

The lion is not merely strong; it epitomizes strength, even though a bear or ox might be technically more muscular. Some point out that the *gematria* (numerical value of the Hebrew letters) of *aryeh*, "lion," equals that of *gevura*,

וַיֵּרֶד שִׁמְשׁוֹן וְאָבִיו וְאִמּוֹ תִּמְנָתָה וַיָּבֹאוּ עַד כַּרְמֵי תִמְנָתָה וְהִנֵּה כְּפִיר אֲרָיוֹת שֹׁאֵג לִקְרָאתוֹ:

שופטים יד:ה

וַיֹּאמְרוּ לוֹ אַנְשֵׁי הָעִיר בַּיּוֹם הַשְּׁבִיעִי בְּטֶרֶם יָבֹא הַחַרְסָה מַה מָּתוֹק מִדְּבַשׁ וּמֶה עַז מֵאֲרִי וַיֹּאמֶר לָהֶם לוּלֵא חֲרַשְׁתֶּם בְּעֶגְלָתִי לֹא מְצָאתֶם חִידָתִי:

שופטים יד:יח

שָׁאוּל וִיהוֹנָתָן הַנֶּאֱהָבִים וְהַנְּעִימִם בְּחַיֵּיהֶם וּבְמוֹתָם לֹא נִפְרָדוּ מִנְּשָׁרִים קַלּוּ מֵאֲרָיוֹת גָּבֵרוּ:

שמואל ב א:כג

"power." The Midrash relates a story teaching that it is a sin to describe the lion as being anything other than mighty:

> There was an incident with R. Chanina b. Dosa that he saw a lion and said to it, "Weak king! Did I not make you swear that you shall not be seen in the Land of Israel?" Immediately it ran away. R. Chanina ran after it and said to it: "I have sinned to you, that I called you weak, and the One who created you called you powerful, as it says, 'The lion is the mightiest of animals'" (Prov. 30:30). (*Midrash Tanchuma, Vayigash* 3)

The lion is therefore a symbol of power, used whenever Scripture seeks to describe a person in such a way:

> Saul and Jonathan were loved and dear in their lives, and in their death they were not divided; they were swifter than eagles, they were stronger than lions. (II Sam. 1:23)

The lion's great power is further visually accentuated by its mane

65

N. SLIFKIN

אַיֵּה מְעוֹן אֲרָיוֹת וּמִרְעֶה הוּא לַכְּפִרִים אֲשֶׁר הָלַךְ אַרְיֵה לָבִיא שָׁם
גּוּר אַרְיֵה וְאֵין מַחֲרִיד: אַרְיֵה טֹרֵף בְּדֵי גֹרוֹתָיו וּמְחַנֵּק לְלִבְאֹתָיו
וַיְמַלֵּא טֶרֶף חֹרָיו וּמְעֹנֹתָיו טְרֵפָה: הִנְנִי אֵלַיִךְ נְאֻם יְהוָה צְבָאוֹת
וְהִבְעַרְתִּי בֶעָשָׁן רִכְבָּהּ וּכְפִירַיִךְ תֹּאכַל חָרֶב וְהִכְרַתִּי מֵאֶרֶץ טַרְפֵּךְ
וְלֹא יִשָּׁמַע עוֹד קוֹל מַלְאָכֵכֵה:

נחום ב:יב-יד

The Talmud also presents this metaphor when describing the reaction of David and Avishai to the prospect of killing a fearsome Philistine called Yishbi:

> They said, Shall two lion cubs kill a lion?! (Sanhedrin 95a)

And the mighty lion is also used to represent powerful wicked nations, as in the following prophecy regarding the destruction of the enemy city of Nineveh:

> What has become of that lions' den, that pasture of young lions, where lion and fiery lion walked, and the lion cub with no fear? What of the lion that tore prey for his cubs, and strangled for his lionesses, and filled his lairs with prey, and his dens with mangled flesh? I am going to be against you, declares the Lord of Hosts; I will burn down her chariots in smoke, and the sword shall devour your young lions; I will stamp out your killings from the earth, and the sound of your messengers shall be heard no more. (Nahum 2:12–14)

In the Midrash, this leonine power is described as being present in someone who drinks too much wine:

> The Rabbis said: When Noah came to plant a vineyard, Satan came and...brought a lamb and slaughtered it under the vine, and after this he brought a lion and killed it.... He alluded to him that before a man drinks wine, he is innocent as a lamb, that knows nothing, and like a ewe silent before being sheared; if he drinks in appropriate quantities, he becomes as powerful as a lion and says there is no one like him in the world. (*Midrash Tanchuma, Noach* 13[41])

The Talmud also describes the evil inclination of idolatry as being represented by a lion, when the Sages prayed for it to depart:

> They fasted for three days and three nights, and it was given over to them. Out of the Sanctuary came a lion of fire. The prophet said to Israel: "This is the evil inclination for idolatry." (Yoma 69b)

A lion, with its golden flowing mane, visually looks similar to fire; and its powerful predatory nature is like a burning lust for evil. Thus, when the Jewish people cried out to God that He should cause the evil inclination to surrender its power, it appeared as a fiery lion.[42]

"Be as mighty as a lion" – from the historic Rymanow synagogue

Positive Power

SYMBOLISM

The power of the lion presents a terrible danger to people. But this does not mean that it is necessarily seen as a negative phenomenon. The Mishna instructs man to emulate this power of the lion for noble purposes:

> Yehuda b. Teima said: Be ... as mighty as a lion to fulfill the will of your Father in Heaven. (Mishna Avot 5:20; Pesachim 112a)

Simply speaking, this is referring to the lion's physical strength, which man is encouraged to emulate in a non-literal sense. But perhaps we can homiletically explain it to refer to a unique aspect of lions.

Big cats are aggressive carnivores by nature, which makes it hard for them to get along with each other. All the other big cats – tigers, leopards, jaguars, cheetahs, cougars – therefore lead solitary lives. But lions, unique among cats, live in large groups. These are called prides and typically consist of one to four males, five or six females, and their cubs. These large family groups successfully cooperate in hunting their prey – the family that preys together, stays together. Such sociability is remarkable; in the words of one zoologist: "Hitherto we have known little more than the savage side of big cats, for we have relied on the stories of big-game hunters. But in recent years zoologists have been investigating a multitude of astonishing details in the tender family life of lions.... The lion is undoubtedly a creature with a highly aggressive disposition. But within his clan he controls his bloodthirstiness so effectively that he can be called a friendly, even a tender-hearted beast. What is it that inhibits his aggressiveness when in the presence of fellows he knows well?"[43]

Perhaps the real might of the lion is not in its great power as a predator, but in its ability to *overcome* this in the pres-

The lion is unique among big cats in that it lives in large family groups

ence of other lions. This would be in accordance with the definition of power given elsewhere in the Mishna:

> Who is mighty? He who conquers his [evil] inclination. (Mishna Avot 4:1)

This power, to subdue and override the animalistic drives that try to destroy us, is the leonine trait that man is encouraged to emulate.[44] The Talmud relates that King David – who, as we shall later see, is deeply connected to the lion – exercised this leonine strength in overcoming the fatigue of night:

> David said: Midnight never passed me by in my sleep. R. Zeira said: Until midnight, David slept like a horse, and from then on, he strengthened himself like a lion. (Berakhot 3b)

And Rabbi Yosef Karo uses this analogy at the very start of his monumental halakhic code, the *Shulchan Arukh*:

> A person should strengthen himself like a lion to arise in the morning for the service of his Creator. (*Shulchan Arukh, Orach Chayim* 1:1[45])

Due to the lion's great power, it is unafraid of any creature. A person who lacks fear is therefore described as having the heart of a lion:

וְהוּא גַם בֶּן חַיִל אֲשֶׁר לִבּוֹ כְּלֵב הָאַרְיֵה הִמֵּס יִמָּס כִּי יֹדֵעַ כָּל יִשְׂרָאֵל כִּי גִבּוֹר אָבִיךָ וּבְנֵי חַיִל אֲשֶׁר אִתּוֹ: שמואל ב יז:י

נָסוּ וְאֵין רֹדֵף רָשָׁע וְצַדִּיקִים כִּכְפִיר יִבְטָח: משלי כח:א

> Even if he is a brave man, with the heart of a lion. (II Sam. 17:10)

Such a lack of fear can lead to the negative trait of haughtiness:

> "With me [you will be exiled] from Lebanon... from the dens of lions" (Song. 4:8) – This refers to Sichon and Og. Just as the lion is proud,[46] so too Sichon and Og were proud and mighty; for there was only the distance of a day's travel between them, and yet they did not come to each other's assistance. (*Shir HaShirim Rabba* 4:19)

However, Scripture presents such lion-like fearlessness as characteristic of a righteous person who trusts in God's help:

> The wicked flee, though no man is chasing them; but the righteous are as confident as a young lion. (Prov. 28:1)

If one exercises the power of the lion correctly, then one can be as confident as a lion to gain God's help.

וּדְמוּת פְּנֵיהֶם פְּנֵי אָדָם וּפְנֵי אַרְיֵה אֶל הַיָּמִין לְאַרְבַּעְתָּם וּפְנֵי שׁוֹר
מֵהַשְּׂמֹאול לְאַרְבַּעְתָּן וּפְנֵי נֶשֶׁר לְאַרְבַּעְתָּן:
יחזקאל א:י

וְאַרְבָּעָה פָנִים לְאֶחָד פְּנֵי הָאֶחָד פְּנֵי הַכְּרוּב וּפְנֵי הַשֵּׁנִי פְּנֵי אָדָם
וְהַשְּׁלִישִׁי פְּנֵי אַרְיֵה וְהָרְבִיעִי פְּנֵי נָשֶׁר:
יחזקאל י:יד

The Lion King

—————————————————————— SYMBOLISM

The lion is universally regarded as the king of beasts. For the most part, this is due to it being the most powerful of predators, and its resultant position at the very top of the food chain. The lion may also earn this title due to its regal appearance. From head to tail, the lion exudes majesty. Its head is adorned by a luxurious mane, like a royal crown upon a king. Lions are also unique in having tufts of hair on their elbows and a tuft of hair at the tip of the tail; these tassels contribute to their ornate, regal appearance. The Talmud explicitly describes the lion as the king of beasts:

> Resh Lakish said: What does it mean by, "I shall sing to God because He is most exalted" (Ex. 15:1)? A song for the One who is exalted over the exalted, as it was said, the king of beasts is the lion, the king of domestic animals is the ox, the king of birds is the eagle,[47] and man is exalted over all of them, and the Holy One is exalted over them all and over the entire world. (Chagiga 13b)

The Midrash relates a story presenting even animals as being aware of the lion's status as king:

> "Save me from the mouth of the lion as you have answered me from the horns of *reimim*" (Ps. 22:22). When David was grazing the sheep, he went and found an aurochs sleeping in the wilderness. Thinking it was a mountain, he climbed upon it to watch the sheep. The aurochs shook itself and awoke, and David was riding upon it, and reached the heavens.... What did the Holy One do? He summoned a lion; when the aurochs saw the lion, it was afraid, and crouched down before it, because it is the king; and David descended to the ground. Then when David saw the lion, he was in fear of it, and thus it states, "Save me from the mouth of the lion as you have answered me from the horns of aurochsen." (*Midrash Tehillim* 102)

Scripture does not explicitly describe the lion as the king of beasts. However, it is implicit in the lion's symbolism for the tribe of Judah, as we shall see. It is also implicit in the prophet Ezekiel's visions of the divine:

> I looked, and behold, a stormy wind came sweeping out of the north.... In the center of it were also the figures of four creatures.... As for the likeness of their faces, the four had the face of a man, and the face of a lion on the right side; each of the four had the face of an ox on the left side; the four also had the face of an eagle. (Ezek. 1:4–5, 10)

> And each one had four faces; the first face was the face of a cherub, and the second face was the face of a man, and the third the face of a lion, and the fourth the face of an eagle. (Ezek. 10:14)

The Midrash explains that the lion appeared in this vision due to its pre-eminent role vis-à-vis all the other wild animals:

> The greatest of wild animals is the lion, and it became a figurehead (literally, "a face") for the wild animals, as it says, "and the face of a lion" (Ezek. 1:10). (*Midrash Tanchuma, Emor* 16)

But why is it necessary for the king of animals to appear on the divine chariot? The Midrash explains that it is not only to teach man about who is the King of kings, but even to teach the king of beasts himself:

> R. Avin said: There were four types of proud ones created in the world. The proudest of creatures is man, the proudest of birds is the eagle, the proudest of domestic animals is the ox, the proudest of wild beasts is the lion, and they all took reign, and greatness was given to them, and they are affixed under the Holy One's chariot, as it says, "And the image of the faces was the face of a man, the face of a lion, the face of an ox, and the face of an eagle," (Ezek. 1:10). Why was all this necessary? So that they should not lord it over the world, and they should know that there is the Heavenly reign over them. (*Shemot Rabba* 23:13[48])

The lion is the king of beasts, but there is also a King of kings.

The 15th-century compilation of Jewish texts from Italy known as the Rothschild Miscellany includes a fable about the king of beasts, drawn complete with a royal crown

Judah the Lion King

———————————————— SYMBOLISM

When Jacob blessed his sons, he described Judah as being similar to a lion, and as destined to be king:

> Judah is a lion cub; you have risen from the prey,[49] my son. He kneels down, he crouches like a lion, and as a fiery lion; who shall rouse him up? The scepter shall not depart from Judah, nor the rule's staff from between his feet. (Gen. 49:9–10)

The first point to ponder in this blessing is that Judah is described not just as a lion, but as a cub (*gur*). The Midrash sees this as praising Judah as having the qualities of both adult and young lions:

> "Judah is a lion cub" (Gen. 49:9) – This teaches that he was given the power of the lion and the *chutzpa* of its cubs. (*Bereshit Rabba* 98:7)

Others see it as describing Judah's current state and foretelling his destiny as king. Judah had not yet attained royalty; he was still only a cub. But he was a *lion* cub, already demonstrating leadership vis-à-vis his brothers. Later, he would become an adult lion; he would give rise to kings – David, Solomon, and others. Crouching at rest, as a mature lion, nobody would dare "rouse him up," i.e. challenge his reign.[50]

Judah had demonstrated his lion-like nature with his actions in Egypt. When the viceroy of Egypt, who unbeknownst to Judah was actually his brother Joseph, threatened to keep Benjamin as a slave, Judah was not afraid to challenge this immensely powerful man:

> "And Judah drew near to him…" (Gen. 44:18) – This is what Scripture refers to with, "The lion is the strongest of animals, and does not retreat from anyone" (Prov. 30:30). (*Midrash Tanchuma, Vayigash* 3)

Another midrash elaborates upon the lion-like nature of Judah's approach:

> Another explanation: "And Judah drew near to him…"…When Joseph seized Benjamin and told his brothers that "The man in whose possession is found the goblet shall become my slave"…Judah grew angry and roared in a great voice…. Job said, "The roar of the lion…" (Job 4:10) – the roar of the lion refers to Judah…. "The lion perishes for lack of prey" (Job 4:11) – this refers to Judah, who was ready to sacrifice himself for Benjamin (i.e. for failing to accomplish his mission, like a lion that has not managed to obtain its prey). He

The tribe of Judah, depicted in a stained glass window in a synagogue

> said, May the Holy One forgive me for the sin of deceiving my father, telling him that I will bring Benjamin back for him. At that moment he was filled with rage against Joseph. (*Bereshit Rabba* 93:7)

Judah was the tribe of lions, and the lion was therefore the emblem depicted on the flag of the tribe of Judah in the wilderness.[51] The city of Jerusalem, originally established by King David of the house of Judah in the portion of Judah, today has the lion emblazoned on both its flag and its coat-of-arms.

David and Davidic Kingship

———————————————— SYMBOLISM

The Midrash points to a contrast between the leonine description given by Jacob, and that in the blessings reluctantly given by Balaam. The former describes the lion as kneeling and crouching, while the latter describes him as crouching and lying down:

> He kneels down, he crouches like a lion, and as a fiery lion; who shall rouse him up? (Gen. 49:9–10)

"Judah is a lion cub..."

(Gen. 49:9)

He crouches, he lies down like a lion, and as a fiery lion; who shall rouse him up? (Num. 24:9)

The Midrash sees the difference between kneeling/crouching and crouching/lying down as reflecting two different periods of the line from Judah through Davidic kingship. Whereas kneeling and crouching are only a partial state of relaxation, lying down with the head upon the ground signifies absolute ease. The former symbolizes the state of matters until David, whereby Judah's descendants had a certain level of superiority over their brothers, but it was not unequivocal. Only with the appointment of David as king was the kingship at rest, clear and unchallenged.

"Judah is a lion cub…he kneels down, he crouches" (Gen. 49:9) – from Peretz until David. "He crouches, he lies down" (Num. 24:9) – From David until Zedekiah (Tzidkiyahu). (*Bereshit Rabba* 98:7[52])

However, the Midrash also presents an entirely different view. This sees crouching as a superior state, symbolizing the regal poise of a king securely in charge. Lying down, on the other hand, is a state of sleep which represents the lack of active kingship. Accordingly, Jacob's blessing alluded to the period of active leadership, whereas Balaam's statement referred to the period of dormancy in the kingship:

And some say: "He kneels down, he crouches" – from Peretz until Zedekiah. "He crouches, he lies down" (Num. 24:9) – from Zedekiah until the King Messiah. (*Bereshit Rabba* 98:7)

Jacob's blessing is explained by some as alluding to a microcosm of the story of Judah's descendant David. At first he was just a lion cub; he demonstrated leadership, but had not yet been appointed king. Later, however, he became an adult lion, appointed as king over Israel.[53]

David also had another connection with the lion, which he described when offering to fight Goliath:

Saul said to David, You are not able to go against this Philistine to fight with him; for you are just a youth, whereas he is a man of war since he was young. And David said to Saul, Your servant shepherded his father's sheep, and there came a lion, and a bear, taking a lamb from the flock; And I went out after him, and struck him, and rescued it from his mouth; and when he arose against me, I caught him by his mane, and struck him, and slew him. Your servant slew both the lion and the bear; and this uncircumcised Philistine shall be like one of them, seeing he has defied the armies of the living God. God, Who saved me from the paw of the lion, and from the paw of the bear, He will save me from the hand of this

כָּרַע שָׁכַב כַּאֲרִי וּכְלָבִיא מִי יְקִימֶנּוּ מְבָרֲכֶיךָ בָרוּךְ וְאֹרֲרֶיךָ אָרוּר:

במדבר כד:ט

וַיֹּאמֶר דָּוִד אֶל שָׁאוּל רֹעֶה הָיָה עַבְדְּךָ לְאָבִיו בַּצֹּאן וּבָא הָאֲרִי וְאֶת הַדּוֹב וְנָשָׂא שֶׂה מֵהָעֵדֶר: וְיָצָאתִי אַחֲרָיו וְהִכִּתִיו וְהִצַּלְתִּי מִפִּיו וַיָּקָם עָלַי וְהֶחֱזַקְתִּי בִּזְקָנוֹ וְהִכִּתִיו וַהֲמִיתִּיו: גַּם אֶת הָאֲרִי גַּם הַדּוֹב הִכָּה עַבְדֶּךָ וְהָיָה הַפְּלִשְׁתִּי הֶעָרֵל הַזֶּה כְּאַחַד מֵהֶם כִּי חֵרֵף מַעַרְכֹת אֱלֹהִים חַיִּים: וַיֹּאמֶר דָּוִד יְהוָה אֲשֶׁר הִצִּלַנִי מִיַּד הָאֲרִי וּמִיַּד הַדּוֹב הוּא יַצִּילֵנִי מִיַּד הַפְּלִשְׁתִּי הַזֶּה וַיֹּאמֶר שָׁאוּל אֶל דָּוִד לֵךְ וַיהוָה יִהְיֶה עִמָּךְ:

שמואל א יז:לד-לז

וְאָמַרְתָּ מָה אִמְּךָ לְבִיָּא בֵּין אֲרָיוֹת רָבָצָה בְּתוֹךְ כְּפִרִים רִבְּתָה גוּרֶיהָ: וַתַּעַל אֶחָד מִגֻּרֶיהָ כְּפִיר הָיָה וַיִּלְמַד לִטְרָף טֶרֶף אָדָם אָכָל: וַיִּשְׁמְעוּ אֵלָיו גּוֹיִם בְּשַׁחְתָּם נִתְפָּשׂ וַיְבִאֻהוּ בַחַחִים אֶל אֶרֶץ מִצְרָיִם: וַתֵּרֶא כִּי נוֹחֲלָה אָבְדָה תִּקְוָתָהּ וַתִּקַּח אֶחָד מִגֻּרֶיהָ כְּפִיר שָׂמָתְהוּ: וַיִּתְהַלֵּךְ בְּתוֹךְ אֲרָיוֹת כְּפִיר הָיָה וַיִּלְמַד לִטְרָף טֶרֶף אָדָם אָכָל: וַיֵּדַע אַלְמְנוֹתָיו וְעָרֵיהֶם הֶחֱרִיב וַתֵּשַׁם אֶרֶץ וּמְלֹאָהּ מִקּוֹל שַׁאֲגָתוֹ: וַיִּתְּנוּ עָלָיו גּוֹיִם סָבִיב מִמְּדִינוֹת וַיִּפְרְשׂוּ עָלָיו רִשְׁתָּם בְּשַׁחְתָּם נִתְפָּשׂ: וַיִּתְּנֻהוּ בַסּוּגַר בַּחַחִים וַיְבִאֻהוּ אֶל מֶלֶךְ בָּבֶל יְבִאֻהוּ בַּמְצֹדוֹת לְמַעַן לֹא יִשָּׁמַע קוֹלוֹ עוֹד אֶל הָרֵי יִשְׂרָאֵל:

יחזקאל יט:ב-ט

Philistine. And Saul said to David, Go, and God be with you. (1 Sam. 17:33–37)

The Midrash states that on four such occasions David killed a lion.[54] Being able to slay a lion indicates that one is as powerful as a lion. The Talmud notes that David also demonstrated leonine strength in another way:

David said: Midnight never passed me by in my sleep. R. Zeira said: Until midnight, David slept like a horse, and from then on, he strengthened himself like a lion. (Berakhot 3b)

While David epitomized the traits of the lion,[55] the entire lineage of Davidic kingship earns this appellation:

The kingship of David is called "lion," as it says, "What a lioness was your mother! She lay down among lions" (Ezek. 19:2). (*Shemot Rabba* 29:9)

The Midrash is referring to the following lamentation of Ezekiel:

And you, raise a lamentation for the princes of Israel, And say, What a lioness was your mother! She lay down among lions, she raised her cubs among young lions. And she brought up one of her cubs; he became a young lion, and he learned to catch the prey; he devoured men. The nations heard of him; he was trapped in their pit, and they brought him with hooks to the land of Egypt. And when she saw that, although she had waited, her hope was lost, she then took another of her cubs, and made him a young lion. And he roamed among the lions; he became a young lion, and learned to catch prey, and devoured men. He smashed their castles and laid waste their cities; the land and all in it became desolate at the sound of his roaring. Nations from the countries on every side set themselves against him. They spread their net over him, and he was caught in their snare. They put him in a cage with hooks, and they carried him off to the king of Babylon, and confined him in a fortress, so that his roar should never again be heard on the hills of Israel. (Ezek. 19:1–9)

The first lion cub in this lamentation clearly alludes to King Jehoahaz (Yehoachaz). He ascended to the throne at the young age of twenty-three, and reigned for only three months before being captured and taken down to spend the rest of his life in Egypt.[56] The second lion cub seems to refer his successor, Jehoiakim (Yehoyakim),[57] but it may refer instead, or in addition, to Jehoiachin (Yehoyakhin) or Zedekiah, who are known to have been captured by Babylon.[58] All these kings are considered the young of the mother lioness, who represents the royal lineage.[59]

The Lion and the Ox

SYMBOLISM

Scripture describes how, in the Messianic Era, predatory animals will dwell in peace alongside their prey (with a long-standing dispute in rabbinic tradition regarding whether this is to be understood literally or allegorically[60]). It is popularly believed that Scripture speaks of how the lion shall lie down with the lamb. But in fact, it is the wolf that lies down with the lamb. The lion is paired with a different animal: the ox.

> The wolf shall live with the lamb, and the leopard shall lie down with the kid; and the calf and the young lion and the fatling together; and a small child shall lead them. And the cow and the bear shall feed; their young ones shall lie down together; and the lion shall eat straw like the ox. (Is. 11:6–7)

> The wolf and the lamb shall feed together, and the lion shall eat straw like the ox; and dust shall be the serpent's food. They shall not hurt nor destroy in all My holy mountain, says the Lord. (Is. 65:25)

In the African savannah, lions eat zebra and wildebeest; in the wilds of ancient Israel, lions would have eaten deer and aurochsen. When there is a shortage of such natural food, lions will readily switch to preying upon domestic cattle. As seen with Ezekiel's vision, the ox is the king of domestic animals; but it can be killed by the king of

וְגֵר זְאֵב עִם כֶּבֶשׂ וְנָמֵר עִם גְּדִי יִרְבָּץ וְעֵגֶל וּכְפִיר וּמְרִיא יַחְדָּו וְנַעַר קָטֹן נֹהֵג בָּם: וּפָרָה וָדֹב תִּרְעֶינָה יַחְדָּו יִרְבְּצוּ יַלְדֵיהֶן וְאַרְיֵה כַּבָּקָר יֹאכַל תֶּבֶן:
ישעיה יא:ו-ז

זְאֵב וְטָלֶה יִרְעוּ כְאֶחָד וְאַרְיֵה כַּבָּקָר יֹאכַל תֶּבֶן וְנָחָשׁ עָפָר לַחְמוֹ לֹא יָרֵעוּ וְלֹא יַשְׁחִיתוּ בְּכָל הַר קָדְשִׁי אָמַר יְהוָֹה:
ישעיה סה:כה

wild beasts. Whereas wolves are able to prey upon sheep, and leopards are able to prey upon goats, lions are strong enough to prey upon cattle:

> "And God shall seek the pursued" (Eccl. 3:15).... R. Eliezer son of R. Yose b. Zimra said: It is even the case with offerings; the Holy One said, "The ox is pursued by the lion, the goat is pursued by the leopard, and the sheep by the wolf: do not bring offerings before Me from the pursuers, but only from the pursued." (*Vayikra Rabba* 27:5)

There are ramifications of this in Jewish law. An animal may not be slaughtered for food if it is already fatally wounded. The Mishna discusses which types of predator are rated as capable of inflicting life-threatening wounds on various animals:

> The following are considered fatal wounds...the mauling of a wolf. R. Yehuda says: The mauling of a wolf [is only considered a fatal wound] with small livestock (i.e. sheep and goats), the mauling of a lion [is considered a fatal wound] with large livestock (i.e. cattle).[61] (Mishna Chullin 3:1[62])

The Talmud relates that R. Abahu was encouraged by his son not to slaughter his three-year-old calf – whereupon it was promptly eaten by a lion.[63] Elsewhere, the Talmud notes that the presence of a lion nearby will prevent an ox from eating.[64]

Conversely, an ox is powerful enough to inflict severe damage upon a lion, with its horns or hooves. The Talmud notes that under certain circumstances, even if a lion is present amongst oxen, there is no concern that one of them might have been mauled by it:

> If the lion is roaring and the oxen are bellowing, then they are both frightened of each other (and the lion has not injured the oxen). (Chullin 53a)

The lion is the mortal enemy of the ox, which is why the notion of a lion living alongside an ox is inconceivable in this world – it is a motif of the Messianic Era, and of the Heavens:

> In this world, the ox cannot tolerate the lion, but Above, the ox and the lion are both on the Divine Chariot. (*Midrash Shir HaShirim Zuta* 1:1)

72

Lions are strong enough to take down large prey such as buffalo

Judah the Lion vs. Joseph the Ox

SYMBOLISM

The motif of the lion as the nemesis of the ox also finds expression in a metaphorical sense. The tribe of Judah is symbolized by the lion, and the Midrash draws upon the imagery of an ox's fear of a lion to illustrate Judah's relationship with another tribe:

Moses blessed eleven tribes, but did not bless the tribe of Simeon, because he was disheartened at them regarding their actions at Shittim (where they were seduced by Moab). R. Yehoshua of Sichnin said in the name of R. Levi: Even so, they were taken care of with Judah, as it says, "the inheritance of the sons of Simeon was in the portion of the sons of Judah" (Josh. 19:9). To what is Simeon comparable? To an ox that misbehaved. What did they do? They tied a lion to its trough, and when the ox saw it, its vigor was weakened. So, too, Judah is compared to a lion, as it states, "Judah is a lion cub," and therefore they took care of Simeon. (*Midrash Tehillim* 90⁶⁵)

However, in most cases where the motif appears of Judah as the lion being the enemy of the ox, it is with regard to Joseph. This is because in Moses' blessings to the tribes, Joseph is represented by an ox.

Joseph is an ox, as it says, "The firstling of his ox, grandeur is his" (Deut. 33:17) and Judah is a lion, as it says, "Judah is a lion cub" (Gen. 49:9). Who stands opposite the ox? The lion! As it states, "And Judah drew near to him" (referring to Judah approaching Joseph in Egypt in order to challenge him). (*Midrash Tanchuma Vayigash* 3⁶⁶)

The enmity between lion and ox reflects that between Judah and Joseph. The Midrash notes that Jacob was aware of Judah's enmity with Joseph, to the extent that he even suspected him of killing him:

Our forefather Jacob thought that Judah had killed Joseph, when they brought him the coat (of Joseph, dipped in blood), as it says, "And he recognized it, and he said, This is the coat of my son – an evil beast has consumed him!" (Gen. 37:33) – and the "evil beast" is none other than the lion. (*Bereshit Rabba* 95:2)

Another midrash explains that, despite Joseph's successes, Judah would always come out on top:

In whatever Joseph triumphs, Judah comes and conquers him … it is comparable to an ox that goes out and causes all the animals to flee from before it, kicking and goring them all. But the lion came, and the ox could not stand up to it. (*Midrash Tanchuma-Buber, Vayigash*)

The Midrash explains that when Jacob sent Judah at the head of the procession to meet Joseph, this symbolized the reconciliation of the lion with the ox:

It is written, "The lion shall eat straw like the ox" (Is. 65:25).... The lion is Judah, as it says, "Judah is a lion cub" (Gen. 49:9), and the ox is Joseph, as it says, "The firstling of his ox, grandeur is his" (Deut. 33:17). They are found to be eating together, as it says, "They were seated by his direction … portions were served" (Gen. 43:33–34), fulfilling, "The lion shall eat straw like the ox"; therefore, "he sent Judah before him" (Gen. 46:28). (*Bereshit Rabba* 95:1⁶⁷)

73

However, it appears that this reconciliation was only temporary. The Midrash states that this enmity between the tribes endures throughout history, and is only solved when the Messiah arrives:

> When Judah and Joseph are quarreling with each other, the ministering angels say to each other, Come, let us descend and watch the ox and lion goring each other! The normal way of the world is that the ox is afraid of the lion, but this ox and lion stand attacking each other, and the jealousy between them endures until the coming of the Messiah. (*Midrash Tanchuma, Vayigash* 4)

The Other Lion Tribes: Dan and Gad

———————————————————— SYMBOLISM

Judah is not the only tribe to be symbolized by a lion. In the blessings that Moses gave to the Children of Israel before his death, he likened two other tribes to the lion. One was the tribe of Dan:

> And of Dan he said, Dan is a lion cub; he shall leap from Bashan. (Deut. 33:22)

The Midrash explains this as alluding to their ferocity in battle:

> He shall leap with Har HaBashan – just as the lion leaps upon an animal, so too the sons of Dan jump upon people in war. (*Midrash Lekach Tov, Vezot HaBerakha*)

Another reference to Dan as a lion is found in the Midrash describing Judah approaching Joseph in Egypt, not knowing that he was his brother. The Midrash states that "he was joined by Chushim son of Dan, and they roared like lions."[68]

The second tribe that Moses likens to a lion is the tribe of Gad:

> And of Gad he said, Blessed be he who enlarges Gad; he dwells as a fiery lion, and tears the arm with the crown of the head. (Deut. 33:20)

Much later, Scripture describes this tribe as being lion-like warriors:

> And from the Gadites men of valor went over to David at the fortress in the wilderness; men of war, fit for battle, who could wield shield and spear, whose faces were like the faces of lions, and who were as fast as the gazelles on the hills. (1 Chr. 12:9)

The Midrash notes that the tribes of Dan and Gad lived adjacent to the border of the Land of Israel, and were compared to lions since they provided border defense.[69]

Israel as a Lion

———————————————————— SYMBOLISM

The Midrash sees Jacob's blessing to Judah, in which he compares him to a lion, as providing this symbolism not just for Judah himself, or even just for his tribe, but for all Israel:

> Israel is called "lion," as it says, "Judah is a young lion" (Gen. 49:9). (*Shemot Rabba* 29:9)

Earlier, we cited part of Balaam's blessing to the Jewish people, which the Midrash expounded as alluding to an aspect of Davidic kingship. But Balaam draws out the parallel to the lion at length, and it goes beyond Davidic kingship to referring to the entire Jewish nation:

> Behold, the people shall rise up as a fiery lion, and lift up himself as a lion; he shall not lie down until he eats of the prey, and drinks the blood of the slain.... He crouches, he lies down like a lion, and as a fiery lion. Who shall stir him up? Blessed is he who blesses you, and cursed is he who curses you. (Num. 23:24, 24:9)

"Rising up like a lion" is explained by some to prophetically allude to Israel's future conquest of the Canaanite nations.[70] Others explain it more simply to be an inversion of Balaam's goals; he had wanted to curse the Jewish people, but was forced instead to praise them in the highest terms.[71] The Midrash interprets it as alluding to the lion-like strength that Israel exerts in its service of God:

> "Behold, the people shall rise up as a lion" (Num. 23:24) – there is no nation in the world like them. When they are sleeping, uninvolved in Torah and mitzvot, they then arise from their sleep like lions and hasten to recite *Shema*, and appoint the Holy One as king, and they become like lions, and then they depart for their worldly business affairs. (*Bemidbar Rabba* 20:20)

Elsewhere we also find the Jewish people being compared to a lion:

The remnant of Jacob shall be among the nations, in the midst of many peoples, like a lion among the beasts of the forest, like a young lion among the flocks of sheep; which tramples wherever it goes, and tears apart with no one to save. (Micah 5:7)

The Midrash refers to this blessing as having materialized during the episode of the Book of Esther:

"The Jews congregated in their cities . . . and no man stood before them, for the fear of them had fallen upon all the nations" (Est. 9:2). Israel was strengthened like a lion that falls upon a flock of sheep, continually striking, with no one saving them from it. That is what is meant by, "the remnant of Jacob shall be among the nations, in the midst of many peoples, like a lion among the beasts of the forest, like a young lion among the flocks of sheep" (Micah 5:7). (*Esther Rabba* 10:11)

The question is posed as to why fear would render the enemies of the Jewish people incapable of fighting back. It is answered that it is similar to a lion attacking sheep, with which the fear of the lion is so great that the sheep simply freeze in shock.[72] The shock mechanism prevents the sheep from feeling excessive pain.[73]

A lion embroidered on the cover of a Torah scroll

וְהָיָה שְׁאֵרִית יַעֲקֹב בַּגּוֹיִם בְּקֶרֶב עַמִּים רַבִּים כְּאַרְיֵה בְּבַהֲמוֹת יַעַר כִּכְפִיר בְּעֶדְרֵי צֹאן אֲשֶׁר אִם עָבַר וְרָמַס וְטָרַף וְאֵין מַצִּיל:

מיכה ה:ז

שֵׁשׁ מַעֲלוֹת לַכִּסֵּה וְרֹאשׁ עָגֹל לַכִּסֵּה מֵאַחֲרָיו וְיָדֹת מִזֶּה וּמִזֶּה אֶל מְקוֹם הַשָּׁבֶת וּשְׁנַיִם אֲרָיוֹת עֹמְדִים אֵצֶל הַיָּדוֹת: וּשְׁנֵים עָשָׂר אֲרָיִים עֹמְדִים שָׁם עַל שֵׁשׁ הַמַּעֲלוֹת מִזֶּה וּמִזֶּה לֹא נַעֲשָׂה כֵן לְכָל מַמְלָכוֹת:

מלכים א י:יט-כ

וְשֵׁשׁ מַעֲלוֹת לַכִּסֵּא וְכֶבֶשׁ בַּזָּהָב לַכִּסֵּא מָאֳחָזִים וְיָדֹת מִזֶּה וּמִזֶּה עַל מְקוֹם הַשָּׁבֶת וּשְׁנַיִם אֲרָיוֹת עֹמְדִים אֵצֶל הַיָּדוֹת: וּשְׁנֵים עָשָׂר אֲרָיוֹת עֹמְדִים שָׁם עַל שֵׁשׁ הַמַּעֲלוֹת מִזֶּה וּמִזֶּה לֹא נַעֲשָׂה כֵן לְכָל מַמְלָכָה:

דברי הימים ב ט:יח-יט

וְעַל הַמִּסְגְּרוֹת אֲשֶׁר בֵּין הַשְׁלַבִּים אֲרָיוֹת בָּקָר וּכְרוּבִים וְעַל הַשְׁלַבִּים כֵּן מִמַּעַל וּמִתַּחַת לַאֲרָיוֹת וְלַבָּקָר לֹיוֹת מַעֲשֵׂה מוֹרָד:

מלכים א ז:כט

וַיְפַתַּח עַל הַלֻּחֹת יְדֹתֶיהָ וְעַל מִסְגְּרֹתֶיהָ כְּרוּבִים אֲרָיוֹת וְתִמֹרֹת כְּמַעַר אִישׁ וְלֹיוֹת סָבִיב:

מלכים א ז:לו

In Throne, Temple, Synagogue, and Scroll

—— SYMBOLISM

Due to the lion's position as king of beasts, it is a creature that symbolizes royal honor. For this reason, the lion was depicted in places that were associated with such honor. Solomon's throne was flanked by statues of lions:

The throne had six steps, and the top of the throne was round behind; and there were arm rests on either side on the place of the seat, and two lions stood beside the armrests. And twelve lions stood there on one side and on the other upon the six steps; the like of it was never made in any kingdom. (1 Kings 10:19–20; similarly in II Chr. 9:18–19[74])

And the Holy Temple was decorated with images of lions:

And on the borders that were between the ledges were lions, oxen, and cherubim; and upon the ledges there was a base above; and beneath the lions and oxen were wreaths of hanging work. . . . For on the plates, on its stays, and on its borders, he engraved cherubim, lions, and palm trees, according to the space between each one, and wreaths were around. (1 Kings 7:29, 36)

Similar lion-inspired décor is to appear in the Third Temple:

And all over the wall, both in the inner one and in the outer, ran a pattern. It consisted of cherubs and palm trees, with a palm tree between every two cherubs. Each

75

cherub had two faces: a human face turned toward the palm tree on one side and a lion's face turned toward the palm tree on the other side. (Ezek. 41:17–19)

In Scripture, there is a curious word, Ariel, which can be translated as "lion of God":

"Oh, Ariel, Ariel, city where David camped." (Is. 29:1).

The Midrash sees this word as referring to the Temple:

The Temple is called "lion," as it says, "Oh, Ariel" (Is. 29:1). (*Shemot Rabba* 29:9)

The Talmud describes the very shape of the Temple itself as being similar to the shape of a lion:

The Sanctuary was narrow at the rear, and wide at the front, similar to a lion, as it says, "Oh, Ariel, Ariel, the city where David camped." Just as the lion is narrow at the rear and wide at the front, so too the Sanctuary was narrow at the rear and wide at the front. (Mishna Middot 4:7)

Some, on the other hand, sees the word Ariel in this verse as referring to the altar.[75] This follows the Talmud's description of the altar:

Five things were reported about the fire of the pile of wood: It was lying like a lion. (Yoma 21b)

Simply speaking, this refers to the flames, which burned with majesty; but Rashi explains that it refers to a coal that fell from Heaven in the days of Solomon and was shaped like a crouching lion.

Today, we have neither throne nor Temple; but the royal imagery of the lion appears in similar places. Synagogues have long been decorated with illustrations and carvings of lions, especially on the Holy Ark. (However, this has not been without controversy; a number of medieval halakhic authorities strongly opposed this practice.[76]) If a creature is ever depicted on the covers of Torah scrolls themselves, the holiest items in our possession, it is only the lion. This powerfully demonstrates the significance of lions for royal symbolism.[77]

Due to the lion's deep chest and especially its mane, it is described as being "narrow at the rear and wide at the front."

NATAN SLIFKIN

God as a Lion

Due to it being the king of beasts, the lion is not only the symbol of human kings, but also of the King of kings – God Himself. Sometimes this symbolism is positive, but on other occasions, as we shall see later, the lion represents God as a destructive force of overwhelming power. On yet other occasions, the symbolism combines both aspects: fear of the lion not as a negative motif, but as representing awe in the face of supremacy.

> The lion has roared, who shall not be afraid? The Lord God has spoken, who shall not prophesy? (Amos 3:8)

The Midrash notes the irony of comparing God to one of His creations, but concludes that there is no better way for the human mind to begin to appreciate His nature:

> "The lion has roared, who shall not be afraid?" (Amos 3:8) – And who gave the strength and power to the lion – was it not He Himself? However, we characterize Him by way of His creations so as to ease a person's ear by way of that which he can understand. (*Midrash Tanchuma, Yitro* 13)

Still, the Sages elsewhere stress that He cannot really be compared to a lion; at least, not to any single lion:

> "The lion roars, who shall not be afraid? The Lord God has spoken, who shall not prophesy?" – Not like one lion alone, but like every lion in the world. (*Avot DeRabbi Natan* 2:6)

Nevertheless, it is the might of the lion that is invoked when God's revelation to the Jewish people is portrayed:

> "I am God your Lord" – that is as it is written, The lion has roared; who shall not be afraid?! (Amos 3:8). (*Shemot Rabba* 29:9)

And when God is described as fighting for Zion against the other nations, the imagery used is that of a lion fearlessly standing its ground against a multitude of people:

> For thus has the Lord said to me: Like the lion and the young lion growling over its prey, when a multitude of shepherds is called forth against it, it will not be afraid of their voice, nor be subdued by their mob; so shall the Lord of Hosts descend to fight for Mount Zion, and on its hill. (Is. 31:4)

> He has gone forth from His lair like a young lion, for their land is desolate because of the oppressive wrath, and because of His fierce anger. (Jer. 25:38)

אַרְיֵה שָׁאָג מִי לֹא יִירָא אֲדֹנָי יֱהֹוִה דִּבֶּר מִי לֹא יִנָּבֵא:
עמוס ג:ח

כִּי כֹה אָמַר יְהֹוָה אֵלַי כַּאֲשֶׁר יֶהְגֶּה הָאַרְיֵה וְהַכְּפִיר עַל טַרְפּוֹ אֲשֶׁר יִקָּרֵא עָלָיו מְלֹא רֹעִים מִקּוֹלָם לֹא יֵחָת וּמֵהֲמוֹנָם לֹא יַעֲנֶה כֵּן יֵרֵד יְהֹוָה צְבָאוֹת לִצְבֹּא עַל הַר צִיּוֹן וְעַל גִּבְעָתָהּ:
ישעיה לא:ד

עָזַב כַּכְּפִיר סֻכּוֹ כִּי הָיְתָה אַרְצָם לְשַׁמָּה מִפְּנֵי חֲרוֹן הַיּוֹנָה וּמִפְּנֵי חֲרוֹן אַפּוֹ:
ירמיה כה:לח

הִנֵּה כְּאַרְיֵה יַעֲלֶה מִגְּאוֹן הַיַּרְדֵּן אֶל נְוֵה אֵיתָן כִּי אַרְגִּיעָה אֲרִיצֶנּוּ מֵעָלֶיהָ וּמִי בָחוּר אֵלֶיהָ אֶפְקֹד כִּי מִי כָמוֹנִי וּמִי יוֹעִדֶנִּי וּמִי זֶה רֹעֶה אֲשֶׁר יַעֲמֹד לְפָנָי:
ירמיה מט:יט

הִנֵּה כְּאַרְיֵה יַעֲלֶה מִגְּאוֹן הַיַּרְדֵּן אֶל נְוֵה אֵיתָן כִּי אַרְגִּעָה אֲרִיצֵם מֵעָלֶיהָ וּמִי בָחוּר אֵלֶיהָ אֶפְקֹד כִּי מִי כָמוֹנִי וּמִי יוֹעִדֶנִּי וּמִי זֶה רֹעֶה אֲשֶׁר יַעֲמֹד לְפָנָי:
ירמיה נ:מד

אַחֲרֵי יְהֹוָה יֵלְכוּ כְּאַרְיֵה יִשְׁאָג כִּי הוּא יִשְׁאַג וְיֶחֶרְדוּ בָנִים מִיָּם:
הושע יא:י

As with David, who killed a lion and was subsequently symbolized by a lion, God's power is also described in terms of His being able to vanquish lions:

> Behold, it shall be like when a lion comes up from the jungle by the Jordan against a strong sheepfold; I can suddenly make him run away from there, and I can appoint over it whoever I choose. (Jer. 49:19, 50:44)

And in *Perek Shira*, a Midrash which lists the "songs" of the natural world, the lion's verse does not mention lions specifically, but describes God in lion-like terms:

> The lion is saying: "God shall go out as a mighty man, He shall arouse zeal, He shall cry, even roar, He shall prevail over His enemies" (Is. 42:13). (*Perek Shira*)

The Talmud also likens God to a lion:

> There are three watches at night, and over each and every watch the Holy One sits and roars like a lion, as it says, "God shall roar from upon high, and from the abode of His dwelling place, He shall give voice, He shall roar, roar on His abode." (Berakhot 3a)

The roaring of the lion is a significant theme in the Torah, especially vis-à-vis God's representation as a lion, as we see in the following verse:

> They shall walk after the Lord; He shall roar like a lion. When He shall roar, then the children shall come trembling from the west. (Hos. 11:10)

We shall now explore the roar of the lion in more detail.

77

This picture shows a lion roaring; when lions are photographed with their mouths wide open, they are actually yawning rather than roaring.

The Roar of the Lion

SYMBOLISM

Lions are very vocal animals with a wide repertoire of sounds, including grunting, growling, humming, snarling, and moaning.[78] But the most prominent of their vocalizations is the roar. Not only does the lion have several different names in Scripture, but there are also several different terms for the lion's roar.[79] The roar itself is not of a single variety; rather, there is a range of different volumes and intensities at which the lion may emit the roar. Lionesses also roar, but not as loudly or deeply as do males.

Lions roar for many different reasons.[80] One is in order to proclaim ownership of a territory, signaling lions of rival prides to stay away, often emitted immediately before a hunt. They will also roar to maintain contact with other lions from their own pride, to intimidate hyenas and other opponents, and communal roaring may strengthen the bonds with the group. A lion's roar can be heard from several miles away.

Sometimes, scriptural descriptions of lions roaring reflect what is known about the circumstances under which lions roar. In one verse, describing typical lion behavior (as opposed to presenting a metaphor), it is describing the pre-hunt roar:

הַכְּפִירִים שֹׁאֲגִים לַטָּרֶף וּלְבַקֵּשׁ מֵאֵל אָכְלָם: תהלים קד:כא

עָלָיו יִשְׁאֲגוּ כְפִרִים נָתְנוּ קוֹלָם וַיָּשִׁיתוּ אַרְצוֹ לְשַׁמָּה עָרָיו נִצְּתוּ מִבְּלִי יֹשֵׁב: ירמיה ב:טו

The young lions roar for their prey, and to seek their food from God. (Ps. 104:21)

The typical roar, emitted as a proclamation over territory, is mentioned by Jeremiah, in reference to the destruction of the Land of Israel:

The young lions roared against him, they gave their cries, and they have made his land a waste; his cities are burned, without inhabitant. (Jer. 2:15)

This verse might be understood as referring to actual lions that have overrun a land made desolate, but the commentaries explain it to be a metaphor, alluding to the foreign rulers and soldiers who conquered Israel. Either way, the roaring is a declaration of territory conquered.[81]

The account of a lion roaring as it approached Samson (discussed in the section "The Power of the Lion") appears

78

to be a case of the roar that lions emit when confronting potential threats:

> When he came to the vineyards of Timnath, behold, a young lion came roaring to meet him. (Judges 14:5)

Similarly, when describing the rage of a king as being similar to the roaring of a lion, it would appear to refer to the roars that lions utter during fights with other predators, including other lions:

> The king's rage is like the roaring of a young lion; but his favor is like dew on the grass. (Prov. 19:12)

On other occasions, when Scripture refers to the lion's roar as part of a poetic metaphor, it does not necessarily correlate with circumstances under which lions actually roar. Thus, in a prophecy referring to the king of Assyria conquering Israel, it seems to describe the lion roaring as part of a hunt, which does not occur with real-life hunts:

> He has a roar like a lion; he will roar like the young lions, and he will growl and seize his prey, and he will carry it away and none will rescue it. (Is. 5:29[82])

Another verse, referring to wicked false prophets, likewise uses the imagery of a lion roaring during a predatory attack:

> There is a conspiracy of her prophets in her midst, like a roaring lion tearing its prey; they have devoured souls; they have taken treasure and precious things; they have made many widows in her midst. (Ezek. 22:25)

Yet another verse, in an allusion to the mighty ones of Israel whose strongholds were shattered, anthropomorphically describes the lion roaring in anger at its habitat[83] being destroyed:

> There is a sound of the howling of the shepherds; for their glory is gone; a sound of the roaring of young lions, for the jungle along the Jordan is destroyed. (Zech. 11:3)

The prophet Amos, presenting a metaphor for there always being a reason for God's actions, speaks of how a lion will only roar when he has reason to do so – namely, having successfully hunted his quarry:

> Does a lion roar in the forest, when he has no prey? Does a young lion cry out from his lair, if he has caught nothing? (Amos 3:4)

This notion is reflected in a statement in the Talmud describing the excesses of behavior that result from being overly satiated:

> Moses said before the Holy One: Master of the Universe, it was due to the silver and gold that You bestowed upon

נַהַם כַּכְּפִיר זַעַף מֶלֶךְ וּכְטַל עַל עֵשֶׂב רְצוֹנוֹ: משלי יט:יב

שְׁאָגָה לוֹ כַּלָּבִיא יִשְׁאַג\ כַּכְּפִרִים וְיִנְהֹם וְיֹאחֵז טֶרֶף וְיַפְלִיט וְאֵין מַצִּיל: ישעיה ה:כט

קֶשֶׁר נְבִיאֶיהָ בְּתוֹכָהּ כַּאֲרִי שׁוֹאֵג טֹרֵף טָרֶף נֶפֶשׁ אָכָלוּ חֹסֶן וִיקָר יִקָּחוּ אַלְמְנוֹתֶיהָ הִרְבּוּ בְתוֹכָהּ: יחזקאל כב:כה

קוֹל יִלְלַת הָרֹעִים כִּי שֻׁדְּדָה אַדַּרְתָּם קוֹל שַׁאֲגַת כְּפִירִים כִּי שֻׁדַּד גְּאוֹן הַיַּרְדֵּן: זכריה יא:ג

הֲיִשְׁאַג אַרְיֵה בַּיַּעַר וְטֶרֶף אֵין לוֹ הֲיִתֵּן כְּפִיר קוֹלוֹ מִמְּעֹנָתוֹ בִּלְתִּי אִם לָכָד: עמוס ג:ד

נַהַם כַּכְּפִיר אֵימַת מֶלֶךְ מִתְעַבְּרוֹ חוֹטֵא נַפְשׁוֹ: משלי כ:ב

Israel until they said "Enough!" that caused them to make the Golden Calf. The School of R. Yannai noted: A lion does not maul and roar (*nohem*) from having a trough of hay, but from having a dish of meat. (Berakhot 32a; Sanhedrin 102a)

As noted earlier, a primary reason why lions roar is in order to declare ownership of a territory. Such proclamations are often made immediately before hunting prey. Therefore, for human beings, the lion's roar is a sign of imminent danger and justifiably causes terror:

> The terror of a king is like the roaring of a young lion; whoever provokes him to anger forfeits his life. (Prov. 20:2)

A graphic description of the terror that this roar can inspire is given by Colonel John Patterson, who was in charge of a railroad construction camp that suffered from the notorious man-eating lions of Tsavo at the turn of the twentieth century. Although himself an exceptionally brave man, he writes: "In the whole of my life I have never experienced anything more nerve-shaking than to hear the deep roars of these dreadful monsters growing gradually nearer and nearer, and to know that some one or other of us was doomed to be their victim before morning dawned. Once they reached the vicinity of the camps, the roars completely ceased, and we knew that they were stalking for their prey. Shouts would then pass from camp to camp, "*Khabar dar, bhaieon, shaitan ata*" ("Beware, brothers, the devil is coming"), but the warning cries would prove of no avail, and sooner or later agonizing shrieks would break the silence, and another man would be missing from roll-call next morning."[84] With such an account in mind, we can better understand the statement by Amos, which as we noted in the section "God as a Lion," is presented as a suitable metaphor for the awe experienced with of God's revelation:

> The lion has roared; who shall not be afraid?! (Amos 3:8)

When Lions Attack

——————————————————— JEWISH HISTORY

It is very difficult for us today to grasp the impact that lions have on people who live in proximity to them. At the turn of the twentieth century, a Scottish hunter who traveled extensively in Africa wrote that "People living in the perfect safety of their homes in a Western country have no conception of the insecurity that is felt by blacks in their kraals in the interior of Africa. The cause of this feeling of insecurity is chiefly the man-eating lion and no other animal of the forest inspires such terror into the black man's heart. In villages far in the heart of the pori, where the white man is never seen, not hundreds but thousands of Africans are annually eaten by these monsters."[85]

Apparently, however, the situation in biblical lands, while dangerous, was not quite as bad as that in Africa. In Scripture, we find that claims of lions being present were invoked by those looking for an excuse to avoid leaving their homes:

> The lazy man says, There is a lion outside, I shall be slain in the streets.... The lazy man says, There is a mature lion in the way; a lion is in the streets. (Prov. 22:13, 26:13)[86]

It seems that the person described in these verses is lazy rather than prudent because the risk is not as great as he claims. In the Talmud, we also see that fatal attacks by lions, while conceivable, were rare. In discussing the case

NEJRON PHOTO / SHUTTERSTOCK

An angry lion presents a terrifying sight

80

of a sick man who gave his wife a conditional bill of divorce, which would only take effect in the event that he would not recover, the Sages of Israel ruled that if he dies instead from a different sickness, the divorce is still valid; but "if a lion ate him, this is not considered a valid divorce."[87] Their reason was that this eventuality was unusual and was not covered by the person's declaration. However, it was not all that unusual, since the Talmud discussed it!

The Talmud contains several references to the threat posed to people by lions. In discussing the responsibilities of prayer, the Talmud recounts that "there was an incident with a man who was eaten by a lion at a distance of three parasangs from R. Yehoshua b. Levi, and Eliyahu did not speak with him for three days as a result [of his not praying sufficiently for the people around him]."[88] Elsewhere, the Talmud notes that although a woman's immersion in a *mikve* (ritual bath) is supposed to take place at night, "R. Idi ordained at Narash that immersion should be performed on the eighth day before nightfall, on account of lions [that roamed at night in that area]."[89] The Midrash tells the story of a person who learned of a certain herb that had the ability to revive the dead. He came across a dead lion, and used the herbs to restore it to life, whereupon it ate him. The Midrash deduces that "one should not help evil people, lest evil befall you."[90]

Lions also have a place in the language of talmudic legal discussions. There is a repeated talmudic metaphor of a crouching lion rendering a place non-usable.[91] The Talmud also discusses a hypothetical case in which a person makes a lion crouch somewhere in order to drive away people or animals.[92] Such behavior is sometimes used as a figure of speech to denote an un-neighborly action.[93] There is also a talmudic expression *mavriach ari*, "driving a lion away from a neighbor's property," which is a frequent metaphor for a normative act of goodwill with which no payment can be charged.[94]

When Lions Don't Attack

LAW AND RITUAL

The Sages of the Talmud observed that lions do not automatically kill people merely because they have the opportunity and ability to do so. The Talmud rules that "if a person fell into a lion's den, we do not attest that he is dead [such that his wife can remarry]."[95] The reason is that it is by no means certain that the lions killed him; they might not be hungry, and he could have escaped.[96] In another context, discussing how a person is only prosecuted for murder if his actions were certain to lead to the victim's death, the sage Rava rules that a person is not prosecuted for murder if he tied up the victim and left him in the presence of a lion.[97] While a variety of explanations are offered for this ruling, one explanation is that lions do not automatically kill people.[98]

In another discussion, the Talmud introduces an interesting factor into the question of whether a lion will attack people:

> Rav Pappa said: "We have a tradition: A lion does not attack two people." But surely we see that this does happen? That can be explained in accordance with Rami bar Abba, who said that a wild animal does not have power over a person until he appears to it like an animal, as it says, "Man does not abide in glory; appearing like an animal, he is ruled" (Ps. 49:13; literally, "he is compared, he is likened to an animal"). (Shabbat 151b[99])

Ordinarily, a lion is wary of attacking a human, and especially if there are two people.[100] But if they are not fulfilling their unique destiny as human beings, says the Talmud, then the lion perceives them as merely other animals on the menu.

What about the possibility of a person successfully defending against a lion attack? As noted earlier, Scripture describes several people who were able to not only defend against a lion attack, but even kill the lion. Yet these people were singled out for being outstanding heroes; an ordinary person is not usually expected to be able to defeat a lion. As such, a person looking after someone's animals is not responsible in the case of an attack by a lion, unless he took the animals to a place where such an attack was bound to happen:

> The lion, bear and leopard…are cases of unavoidable damage. This is only where they came of their own accord, but if he took [the flock] to a place that is infested with wild beasts and bandits, it is not a case of unavoidable damage. (Mishna Bava Metzia 7:9)

The Talmud does, however, note that it can sometimes be possible to successfully fend off an attack by a marauding lion:

> If a shepherd was tending a flock and he abandoned them to enter town, and a wolf came and tore or a lion came and mauled, we do not say that had the shepherd been there he could have saved them (and he is therefore liable). Rather, we assess whether he could indeed have saved them (had he been present), in which case he is liable, and if not, he is exempt…. This is referring to where he heard the roar of the lion and went up (to the town in panic to save himself, rather than negligently leaving his job early). But what is there to assess – what could he possibly have done? – We assess whether he could have challenged the lion with shepherds and sticks. (Bava Metzia 93b[101])

Indeed, Masai tribesmen in Africa will graze their cattle with a stick and a spear to fend off attacks by lions. Another way of defending against lion attacks is to satisfy the lion with something more expendable:

> Rav Safra was traveling in a caravan, and a certain lion accompanied them. Every night, they would give over the donkey of one of them for it to eat. (Bava Kama 116a[102])

Some explain that the lion was divinely guided in order to protect Rav Safra's group, and the donkey was to reward it for its assistance.[103] But it may simply be that the lion was stalking the group, and they expediently decided to satisfy it with a donkey rather than risk it eating a person.

The Sages also occasionally refer to the possibility of a lion being trained. This is mentioned as a legal scenario in the Talmud,[104] and the Talmud elsewhere, in discussing the recommended vocalizations to emit when training various animals, includes the call *zeh, zeh* for a lion.[105] A trained lion also appears as part of a parable in the Midrash:

> "And [the angel of Esau] saw that he could not overcome him" – A parable: To what is this comparable? To a king who had a feral dog and a tame lion. The king would take his son and endear him to the lion, so that if the dog were to come to confront him, the king would say, "The lion could not overcome him, and you think that you can confront him?!" Likewise, if the nations of the world come to assail Israel, the Holy One will say to them: Your angel could not overcome him, and you seek to confront his children?! (*Bereshit Rabba* 77:3)

It is indeed possible to train lions such that even children can approach them without harm. However, there is always an element of risk involved. At certain animal facilities today, where visitors are allowed and even encouraged to pet "tame" lions, accidents have been known to happen. In fact, there is a dispute in the Talmud with regard to whether a trained lion can ever be considered harmless; according to one view, it is always a menace to society, and as a result an unrestrained lion can never be considered the rightful property of a person and can be freely killed.[106]

In prophecies describing the tranquility and safety of the Messianic Era, a key feature is that lions will no longer pose a danger. One prophecy, already discussed, describes lions as becoming docile (and is interpreted by some as alluding to dangerous human enemies). Another prophecy states that there will be a complete absence of lions in the Land of Israel:

NATAN SLIFKIN

Even allegedly trained lions, such as this lion which is used in the film industry, can suddenly turn aggressive, as shown here in a filming session with the author

82

No lion shall be there, and the deviant beast shall not ascend there; they shall not be found there, and the redeemed shall walk it. (Is. 35:9)

This is one aspect of the Messianic Era that has already come to fruition. And while people may understandably lament the loss of biblical wildlife from the Land of Israel, the fact is that the complete lack of danger of fatal attacks by lions is a good thing.

Metaphors for Enemies and Destruction
SYMBOLISM

While we usually think of the lion as positive symbol, by far the most common symbolic usage of the lion in Scripture is as a motif of death and destruction. We must bear in mind that today, lions are usually experienced in the safety of a zoo environment, or anthropomorphized in cartoons. But in biblical and talmudic times, as we shall later discuss, lions posed a genuine threat to people's lives. As such, they are a symbol for powerful and dangerous people:

As a roaring lion, and a charging bear, so is a wicked ruler over the poor people. (Prov. 28:15)

King David, in Psalms, spoke of God saving him from lions in the literal sense:

You shall tread on the lion and on the viper; the young lion and the serpent shall You trample underfoot. (Ps. 91:13)

But on most occasions, he mentioned lions as representing his human enemies:

Lest like a lion they tear my soul, rending it in pieces, while there is none to save. (Ps. 7:3)

They open wide their mouths at me, like a tearing and roaring lion … a pack of evil ones has surrounded me, they seize my hands and my feet like a lion…. Save me from the lion's mouth. (Ps. 22:14, 17, 22)

Lord, how long will you look on? Rescue my soul from their attacks, my precious life from the young lions. (Ps. 35:17)

My soul is among lions; and I lie down among those who are set on fire, the sons of men, whose teeth are spears and arrows, and their tongue a sharp sword. (Ps. 57:5)

Break their teeth, O God, in their mouth; shatter the fangs of the young lions, O Lord. (Ps. 58:7)

The Midrash elaborates upon how David was using the lion to symbolize his many foes:

לֹא יִהְיֶה שָׁם אַרְיֵה וּפְרִיץ חַיּוֹת בַּל יַעֲלֶנָּה לֹא תִמָּצֵא שָׁם וְהָלְכוּ גְּאוּלִים:
ישעיה לה:ט

אֲרִי נֹהֵם וְדֹב שׁוֹקֵק מֹשֵׁל רָשָׁע עַל עַם דָּל:
משלי כח:טו

עַל שַׁחַל וָפֶתֶן תִּדְרֹךְ תִּרְמֹס כְּפִיר וְתַנִּין:
תהלים צא:יג

פֶּן יִטְרֹף כְּאַרְיֵה נַפְשִׁי פֹּרֵק וְאֵין מַצִּיל:
תהלים ז:ג

פָּצוּ עָלַי פִּיהֶם אַרְיֵה טֹרֵף וְשֹׁאֵג:…כִּי סְבָבוּנִי כְּלָבִים עֲדַת מְרֵעִים הִקִּיפוּנִי כָּאֲרִי יָדַי וְרַגְלָי:…הוֹשִׁיעֵנִי מִפִּי אַרְיֵה וּמִקַּרְנֵי רֵמִים עֲנִיתָנִי:
תהלים כב:יד, יז, כב

אֲדֹנָי כַּמָּה תִרְאֶה הָשִׁיבָה נַפְשִׁי מִשֹּׁאֵיהֶם מִכְּפִירִים יְחִידָתִי:
תהלים לה:יז

אֱלֹהִים הֲרָס שִׁנֵּימוֹ בְּפִימוֹ מַלְתְּעוֹת כְּפִירִים נְתֹץ יְהוָה:
תהלים נח:ז

הָיְתָה לִּי נַחֲלָתִי כְּאַרְיֵה בַיָּעַר נָתְנָה עָלַי בְּקוֹלָהּ עַל כֵּן שְׂנֵאתִיהָ:
ירמיה יב:ח

שָׂרֶיהָ בְקִרְבָּהּ אֲרָיוֹת שֹׁאֲגִים שֹׁפְטֶיהָ זְאֵבֵי עֶרֶב לֹא גָרְמוּ לַבֹּקֶר:
צפניה ג:ג

"Lest he tear me apart like a lion" (Ps. 7:3) – Just as a lion sits over his prey and tears it apart, so Doeg and Ahitophel sit over me to tear me apart. (*Midrash Tehillim* 7)

For the prophets, on the other hand, lions did not represent personal enemies, but instead the wicked of all Israel:

My heritage is to me like a lion in the forest; it cries out against me; therefore have I hated it. (Jer. 12:8)

Her princes in her midst were as roaring lions; her judges were the wolves of dusk; they [leave] no bones for the morning. (Zeph. 3:3)

And in the story of Job, Eliphaz compares the wicked, in the punishment that they receive, to lions that are destroyed (as previously quoted in the section "The Names of the Lion"):

As I have seen, those who plow iniquity, and sow wickedness, reap the same. By the blast of God they perish, and by the blast of His anger are they consumed. The lion roars, and the mature lion gives voice, and the teeth of the young lions are broken. The mighty lion perishes for lack of prey, and the young of the fiery lion are scattered. (Job 4:8–11)

The Midrash relates that when the Jewish people was once distressed at the decrees of the non-Jewish ruler, R.

לַשָּׁוְא הִכֵּיתִי אֶת בְּנֵיכֶם מוּסָר לֹא לָקָחוּ אָכְלָה חַרְבְּכֶם נְבִיאֵיכֶם
כְּאַרְיֵה מַשְׁחִית:

ירמיה ב:ל

כִּי אָנֹכִי כַשַּׁחַל לְאֶפְרַיִם וְכַכְּפִיר לְבֵית יְהוּדָה אֲנִי אֲנִי אֶטְרֹף
וְאֵלֵךְ אֶשָּׂא וְאֵין מַצִּיל:

הושע ה:יד

וָאֱהִי לָהֶם כְּמוֹ שָׁחַל כְּנָמֵר עַל דֶּרֶךְ אָשׁוּר: אֶפְגְּשֵׁם כְּדֹב שַׁכּוּל
וְאֶקְרַע סְגוֹר לִבָּם וְאֹכְלֵם שָׁם כְּלָבִיא חַיַּת הַשָּׂדֶה תְּבַקְּעֵם:

הושע יג:ז-ח

קַדְמָיְתָא כְאַרְיֵה וְגַפִּין דִּי נְשַׁר לַהּ חָזֵה הֲוֵית עַד דִּי מְּרִיטוּ גַפַּהּ
וּנְטִילַת מִן אַרְעָא וְעַל רַגְלַיִן כֶּאֱנָשׁ הֳקִימַת וּלְבַב אֱנָשׁ יְהִיב לַהּ:

דניאל ז:ד

שֶׂה פְזוּרָה יִשְׂרָאֵל אֲרָיוֹת הִדִּיחוּ הָרִאשׁוֹן אֲכָלוֹ מֶלֶךְ אַשּׁוּר וְזֶה
הָאַחֲרוֹן עִצְּמוֹ נְבוּכַדְרֶאצַּר מֶלֶךְ בָּבֶל:

ירמיה נ:יז

Yehoshua consoled them with a fable about a lion,[107] which represented the ruler:

> He expounded: There was once a lion that was mauling and eating its prey, and a bone became lodged in its throat. The lion announced, I will reward whoever will come and remove it! That Egyptian bird with the long beak came, inserted its beak and removed the bone. It said to the lion, Give me my reward! The lion replied, Go – and boast that you entered the mouth of a lion and departed in peace. So, too, with us, it is sufficient that we entered this nation in peace and depart in peace. (*Bereshit Rabba* 64:10)[108]

Earlier, we saw that God is often symbolized by a lion. This symbolism is also used to describe how, when Israel sins, God Himself is like an attacking lion in His response to them:

> In vain did I strike your children; they received no correction; your own sword has devoured your prophets, like a destroying lion. (Jer. 2:30)

> For I will be to Ephraim as a lion, and as a young lion to the house of Judah; I will tear and go away; I will take away, and none shall save him. (Hos. 5:14)

> Therefore I will be to them as a lion; as a leopard by the way I will watch them; I will meet them like a bear that is bereaved of her cubs, and I shall tear their closed-up heart, and there I will devour them like a lion; the beast of the wilderness shall tear them apart. (Hos. 13:7–8)

As a result of all this, the Talmud considers that seeing a lion in a dream is a potentially serious matter, and steps should be taken to ensure that it is actualized in a positive manner:

One who sees a lion in a dream should arise and say, "The lion roars, who shall not be afraid?" (Amos 3:8) (causing the vision to be fulfilled through God's salvation) before another verse pre-empts him – "The lion arose from the thicket (referring to Babylon's persecution)" (Jer. 4:7). (Berakhot 56b)

The lion is a constant metaphor for Israel's enemies. Hence, the Sabbath song *Yah Ribon* includes the prayer *perok yat anakh mipum aryvata*, "redeem Your flock from the mouth of the lion."[109]

The Lion and Babylon

— SYMBOLISM

While the lion can be a symbol for any sort of threat, it most often appears in Torah literature as representing a particular enemy. The prophet Daniel had a vision in which he saw several strange beasts:

> I saw in my vision by night.... Four great beasts came up from the sea.... The first was like a lion, and had eagle's wings; I looked till its wings were plucked off, and it was lifted up from the earth, and made to stand upon its feet as a man, and a man's heart was given to it. (Dan. 7:2–4)

In classical Jewish thought, the four beasts in Daniel's vision represent the four kingdoms to which the Jewish people have been subjected.[110] First of these was Babylon, under the reign of the wicked Nebuchadnezzar, who destroyed the Temple and sent the nation into exile. It appeared in Daniel's vision as a lion, symbolizing the great power of this nation; indeed, Nebuchadnezzar's palace, excavated in the twentieth century, was decorated with lions. The lion in Daniel's vision also had the wings of an eagle, symbolizing the spread of this empire. Nebuchadnezzar was explicitly likened to a lion by Jeremiah:

> Israel is a scattered sheep, the lions have driven him away; first the king of Assyria has consumed him, and in the end King Nebuchadnezzar of Babylon has broken his bones. (Jer. 50:17)

However, when the Sages connect Daniel's vision of a lion to Babylon, they mention a different verse:

> "The first was like a lion" (Dan. 7:4) – this is Babylon. Jeremiah saw Babylon as a lion, as it is written, "The lion has come up from his thicket" (Jer. 4:7). (*Vayikra Rabba* 13:5)

This refers to another prophecy by Jeremiah:

> The lion has come up from his thicket, and the destroyer of the nations is on his way; he has gone out from his

place to make your land desolate; and your cities shall be laid waste, without inhabitant. (Jer. 4:7)

There are also other occasions on which Jeremiah refers to persecutors as being lions:

Therefore the lion of the forest shall slay them, and the wolf of the plains shall destroy them, a leopard shall watch over their cities; everyone who goes out there shall be torn in pieces; because their transgressions are many, and their apostasies are great. (Jer. 5:6)

Here, there is also mention of wolves, but the Midrash understands that it is specifically the lion which is referring to Babylon:

"Therefore the lion of the forest has attacked them" (Jer. 5:6) – This refers to Babylon. (*Bereshit Rabba* 99:2)

Indeed, the Talmud consistently interprets scriptural references to lions as alluding to Babylon:

"The lion roars, the bear growls, the wicked man rules over a poor nation" (Prov. 28:15). "The lion roars…"

עָלָה אַרְיֵה מִסֻּבְּכוֹ וּמַשְׁחִית גּוֹיִם נָסַע יָצָא מִמְּקֹמוֹ לָשׁוּם אַרְצֵךְ לְשַׁמָּה עָרַיִךְ תִּצֶּינָה מֵאֵין יוֹשֵׁב:
ירמיה ד:ז

עַל כֵּן הִכָּם אַרְיֵה מִיַּעַר זְאֵב עֲרָבוֹת יְשָׁדְדֵם נָמֵר שֹׁקֵד עַל עָרֵיהֶם כָּל הַיּוֹצֵא מֵהֵנָּה יִטָּרֵף כִּי רַבּוּ פִּשְׁעֵיהֶם עָצְמוּ מְשׁוּבוֹתֵיהֶם:
ירמיה ה:ו

refers to the wicked Nebuchadnezzar, as it is written, "The lion arose from the thicket" (Jer. 4:7). (Megilla 11a)

The Talmud notes that Nebuchadnezzar was even more terrible than the Assyrian leader Sennacherib:

"Lift up thy voice, O daughter of Gallim, cause it to be heard unto Layish" (Is. 10:30). Do not fear this man (Sennacherib), but be in dread of the wicked Nebuchadnezzar, who is likened to a mighty lion (*layish*), as it is written, "The lion has come up from his thicket." (Sanhedrin 94b)

The relationship between Nebuchadnezzar and Sennacherib is explained to be alluded to in the following verse:

"I saw in my vision by night.… Four great beasts… The first was like a lion, and had eagle's wings" (Dan. 7:2-3)

One of the many lions depicted on the Ishtar gate of Nebuchadnezzar's royal palace in Babylon

> For the waters of Dimon shall be full of blood; for I will bring more upon Dimon, a lion for those who escape Moab, and upon the remnant of the land. (Is. 15:9)

The verse is explained to mean that those who survived the invasion of Sennacherib were taken by Nebuchadnezzar.[111]

There is only one verse in which the Midrash expounds Nebuchadnezzar as being symbolized by a different animal:

> "He is a bear lying in wait for me" (Lam. 3:10) – this refers to Nebuchadnezzar; "a lion in hiding" – this refers to Nebuzaradan. (*Eikha Rabba* 3:4[112])

But the only reason why Nebuchadnezzar is explained to be the bear rather than the lion is that the lion is a more terrible predator than the bear, and it thus must signify an even more terrible Babylonian figure: Nebuzaradan. He was the commander of Nebuchadnezzar's guard, who was in charge of the destruction of the Temple and the deportation of the Jews. The Midrash later states that Nebuzaradan is even referred to in Scripture as a lion, and explains why:

> Nebuzaradan is Arioch (the "commander of the king's guard" mentioned in Daniel 2:14). And why is he called Arioch? Because he would roar over the captives like a lion (*ari*), until they reached the Euphrates. (*Eikha Rabba* 5:5)

> כִּי מֵי דִימוֹן מָלְאוּ דָם כִּי אָשִׁית עַל דִּימוֹן נוֹסָפוֹת לִפְלֵיטַת מוֹאָב אַרְיֵה וְלִשְׁאֵרִית אֲדָמָה:
>
> ישעיה טו:ט

Some explain that Ariel, the name used for the Temple,[113] is comprised of two words: Ari-El, "lion-(of)-God." When the Jewish people sinned, leading to the destruction of the Temple, God left them. The El departed from Ariel, leaving the Ari, the predatory lion Nebuchadnezzar.

The Redemption from Babylon
— SYMBOLISM

The lion represents the Babylonian destruction. But this was not a permanent destruction: there was a longing for God to reunite with His people:

> "From Lebanon come with me; from Lebanon, my bride, with me! Travel down from Amana's peak, from the peak of Senir and Hermon, from the dens of lions…" (Song 4:8).… "From the dens of lions" – from the Babylonian exile. (*Shemot Rabba* 23:6)

The Midrash states that God, in anger at the destruction of His lions by the Babylonian lion, Himself becomes the ultimate lion:

> Nebuchadnezzar is called "Aryeh," as it says, "The lion arose from his thicket" (Jer. 4:7), and he destroyed the

Holy Temple, took the kingship of the House of David, and exiled Israel. And the Holy One said, "What has become of the den of lions?" (Nahum 2:12) – Where are My children? At that time, "He roars over His abode" (Jer. 25:30). (*Shemot Rabba* 29)

Another midrash elaborates upon this theme, seeing the Babylonian destruction and eventual redemption as being symbolized by lions at every step of the way:

R. Avin said: A lion arose in the constellation of the lion (Leo), and destroyed the Lion of God. A lion arose – this is the wicked Nebuchadnezzar, as it says, "The lion arose from his thicket" (Jer. 4:7). In the constellation of the lion: "when Jerusalem went into exile in the fifth month" (Jer. 1:3). And destroyed the Lion of God (Ariel, i.e. the Temple): "O, Lion of God, Lion of God, city where David camped!" (Is. 29:1). This is so that a lion shall come during the constellation of the lion and rebuild the Lion of God. A lion shall come – this is the Holy One, about whom it is written, "The lion has roared, who shall not be afraid?" (Amos 3:8). During the constellation of the lion – "And I shall change their mourning to rejoicing…" (Jer. 31:13). And rebuild the Lion of God – "God is the builder of Jerusalem, He shall gather in the exiled of Israel" (Ps. 147:2). (*Midrash Pesikta DeRav Kahana* 13:15)

And another midrash presents yet more leonine symbolism relating to this theme:

Let a lion come, and build the Holy Temple, for a lion, in the portion of the lion. "Let a lion come" – this is Bezalel, who was from the tribe of Judah, as it says, "Judah is a young lion." And "a lion" – is Oholiav, who was from the tribe of Dan, as it says, "Dan is a young lion." "And build the Holy Temple" – as it is written, "Lion of God, city where David camped." For the lion – this is the Holy One, as it is written, "The lion has roared, who shall not be afraid?" In the portion of the lion – this is Israel, for God's portion is with us. (*Yalkut Midrashei Teiman*)

And the ultimate fate of Babylon was to become symbolized by lions in a negative way:

Babylon shall become rubble, a den for jackals, an object of horror and hissing, without inhabitant. They roar together like young lions, they roar together, they growl like lion cubs. (Jer. 51:37–38)

"The lion has roared, who shall not be afraid?"

Indeed, the Midrash notes that while lions embody the cause of the destruction of the Temple as well as the agents of the destruction, they will ultimately represent the cessation of such threats:

> God says: With that which I punish, I heal ... they sinned with lions, as it is written, "Her princes in her midst were as roaring lions (in their terrorization of the people)" (Zeph. 3:3); they were punished with lions: "The lion (Nebuchadnezzar) arose from his thicket ..." (Jer. 4:7); and they shall be comforted with lions: "The lion shall eat straw like an ox" (Is. 11:7). (*Pesikta Rabbati* 33)

Daniel in the Lions' Den

The fall of Babylon is linked to the fate of Daniel. As a young man, Daniel was brought to the Babylonian court of Nebuchadnezzar. But instead of assimilating into Babylonian culture, Daniel remained loyal to the God of Israel. He successfully interpreted Nebuchadnezzar's dreams, including one that foretold that Nebuchadnezzar would lose his mind. After the rise of Nebuchadnezzar's successor, Belshazzar, Daniel correctly interpreted a mysterious sign, the handwriting on the wall, to mean that the Babylonian kingdom would fall to the Medes and Persians. Daniel is thus described as having a share in the downfall of Babylon, in a midrash that links Daniel to the lion symbolism mentioned earlier:

> Judah corresponds to the Kingdom of Babylon – both are symbolized by a lion. This one is compared to a lion: "Judah is a young lion" (Gen. 49:9), and this one is compared to a lion: "The first was like a lion" (Dan. 7:4). The kingdom of Babylon falls by the hand of Daniel, who comes from the tribe of Judah. (*Bereshit Rabba* 99:2)

But Daniel's connection to lions does not, of course, end there. One of the most famous stories involving lions in Scripture is the story of Daniel in the lions' den. The lions were owned by King Darius, though he did not necessarily keep them for the purpose of executing criminals. He might have owned them for display, as a sign of his royal status. Alternately, he may have even kept them for hunting purposes; the Assyrian king Ashurnasipal II is known to have kept a group of lions at Nimrud in order to breed them for this purpose. An ancient cylinder seal depicts King Darius hunting a lion from a horse-drawn chariot; this may well have been a lion that he bred for the purpose of a "canned" lion hunt.

Daniel, an official in the court of King Darius, was a God-fearing Jew. The other officials, jealous of him, sought to find

בֵּאדַיִן מַלְכָּא בִּשְׁפַרְפָּרָא יְקוּם בְּנָגְהָא וּבְהִתְבְּהָלָה לְגֻבָּא דִי
אַרְיָוָתָא אֲזַל: וּכְמִקְרְבֵהּ לְגֻבָּא לְדָנִיֵּאל בְּקָל עֲצִיב זְעִק עָנֵה
מַלְכָּא וְאָמַר לְדָנִיֵּאל דָּנִיֵּאל עֲבֵד אֱלָהָא חַיָּא אֱלָהָךְ דִּי אַנְתָּה
פָּלַח לֵהּ בִּתְדִירָא הַיְכִל לְשֵׁיזָבוּתָךְ מִן אַרְיָוָתָא: אֱדַיִן דָּנִיֵּאל
עִם מַלְכָּא מַלִּל מַלְכָּא לְעָלְמִין חֱיִי: אֱלָהִי שְׁלַח מַלְאֲכֵהּ וּסֲגַר
פֻּם אַרְיָוָתָא וְלָא חַבְּלוּנִי כָּל קֳבֵל דִּי קָדָמוֹהִי זָכוּ הִשְׁתְּכַחַת לִי
וְאַף קָדָמָיִךְ מַלְכָּא חֲבוּלָה לָא עַבְדֵת: בֵּאדַיִן מַלְכָּא שַׂגִּיא טְאֵב
עֲלוֹהִי וּלְדָנִיֵּאל אֲמַר לְהַנְסָקָה מִן גֻּבָּא וְהֻסַּק דָּנִיֵּאל מִן גֻּבָּא וְכָל
חֲבָל לָא הִשְׁתְּכַח בֵּהּ דִּי הֵימִן בֵּאלָהֵהּ:

דניאל ו כ-כד

a way to destroy him. They established a law that anyone who asks a petition from any god or man, aside from the King, shall be cast into the lions' den. Daniel disregarded this law, and continued to pray to God, despite the fact that he was visible through the windows of his home. The officials gleefully reported his actions and, to the dismay of the king, Daniel was thrown to the lions. A stone was placed on the mouth of the den, and sealed with the king's signet; the Midrash says that God sent an angel, in the form of a lion, to sit on the stone, such that Daniel's enemies would not harass him.[114] Miraculously, Daniel survived unharmed:

> The king arose very early in the morning, and rushed to the lions' den. When he came to the den, he cried in an anguished voice to Daniel, and said, "O Daniel, servant of the living God, is your God, whom you serve continually, able to save you from the lions?" Then Daniel said to the king, "O king, live forever. My God has sent His angel, who shut the lions' mouths, so that they have not hurt me; because I was found innocent before Him; and also before you, O king, I have done no wrong." Then the king was extremely glad for him, and commanded that Daniel should be taken out of the den. So Daniel was taken out of the den, and he was found to be entirely unhurt, because he believed in his God. (Dan. 6:20–24)

The Midrash explains that the lions could not harm Daniel, because he was the true lion:

> Why was Daniel saved from the lions? Because he prayed before the Holy One, who is called a lion, as it is written, "They shall go after God, He shall roar as a lion" (Hos. 11:10); and Daniel was from the tribe of Judah, which is called a lion, as it says, "Judah is a lion cub" (Gen. 49:9); and it is written, "Daniel was from the sons of Judah" (Dan. 1:6). Let a lion (God) come and save a lion (Daniel) from the mouth of a lion.[115] Another explanation: Because (in the eyes of the lions[116]) he was similar to lions, being a lion, therefore they did not harm him. (*Bemidbar Rabba* 13:6)

"The lion is the mightiest
of animals, and turns
away before no one."
(Prov. 30:30)

Yossipon, a tenth-century work of Jewish chronology, describes how "the beasts in the den received Daniel as faithful dogs might receive their returning master, wagging their tails and licking him."[117] Another midrash elaborates upon the interactions between Daniel and the lions:

When Daniel descended into the pit, an angel said to the lions, "Receive your relative – Judah is a young lion!" Immediately, the lions leaped onto each others' backs until they reached the mouth of the pit and received him.... Because their breath reeks,[118] Daniel placed their mouths on the ground, so that he should not smell the odor.... And when it was time for him to ascend, the lions leaped onto each others' backs and lifted him up.... "He delivered Daniel from the hand of the lions" (Dan. 6:28) – It does not say "from the mouth of the lions" but rather "from the hand of the lions" – this teaches that they did not harm him, not with their hand, nor their foot, nor their mouth nor their stench. (*Bereshit Rabbati* [Albeck ed.], *Vaychi* 49:9)

The king, relieved that his favorite courtier had survived, decided to exact punishment upon the ministers who had conspired against him:

And the king commanded, and those men who had accused Daniel, were brought and thrown in the den of lions; they, their children, and their wives; and the lions overpowered them and broke all their bones into pieces before they reached the bottom of the den. (Dan. 6:25)

According to the midrash, Daniel's enemies claimed to the king that the reason why he was unharmed is that the lions were not hungry. The king responded that if so, all the ministers, along with their wives and children, should spend a night with the lions. As a result, says the midrash, the enemies of Daniel were torn apart, with every person being pulled apart by four lions, one seizing each of his limbs.[119] Another midrash relates that the ministers claimed that Daniel had fed and tamed the lions, and so the king had the ministers likewise feed the lions, but they were killed anyway.[120] The midrash sees one of David's psalms as describing how the efforts of Daniel's enemies rebounded on them, and explains the connection between Daniel and David:

ENCIKTAT / SHUTTERSTOCK

A lion and lioness on a hunt

And regarding [Daniel's enemies] David says, "God shall shoot them with arrows, they shall be struck down suddenly, their tongue shall be their downfall" (Ps. 64:8–9). "The righteous shall rejoice in the Lord" (ibid. v. 11) – This is Daniel.... Why did David recite a Psalm for Daniel? For both were descended from the tribe of Judah, and both were from the lineage of kings, and both were saved from lions, and both founded the Temple.[121] (Bereshit Rabbati [Albeck ed.], Vaychi 49:9)

The miraculous survival of Daniel in the lions' den has earned an important place in Jewish history, such that, if a person were to ever come across the remains of that den, a blessing is to be pronounced:

> If a person sees the lions' den, he should say, Blessed is the One who performed miracles for our fathers in this place. (Berakhot 57b; Y. Berakhot 62b)

Agents of Divine Retribution

——————————————— SYMBOLISM

In the story of Daniel, the lions followed God's will in refraining from killing him; but ordinarily, lions follow God's will in the opposite role. As the dominant predator, the lion is perfectly suited to being a naturalistic agent of divine retribution. There are several instances in Scripture of the lion fulfilling this role.[122] One such instance is a story related about a prophet who disobeyed God's command, with grave consequences. After departing on his donkey, he encountered a lion:

> When he set out, a lion met him by the way, and killed him. His corpse was cast onto the road, and the donkey stood by it, with the lion also standing by the corpse. Some men passed by, and saw the corpse lying in the road, and the lion standing by the corpse; and they went and told it in the city where the old prophet lived. And when the prophet who brought him back from the road heard of it, he said, "That is the man of God, who was disobedient to the word of the Lord; therefore the Lord has delivered him to the lion, who has torn him, and killed him, according to the word of the Lord, which He spoke to him." And he said to his sons, "Saddle me the donkey," and they did so. He went and found the corpse lying in the road, and the donkey and the lion standing by the corpse; the lion had not eaten the corpse, nor mauled the donkey. (I Kings 13:24–28)

Normally, a lion would be much more likely to attack a donkey than a human being, since a donkey more closely resembles its natural prey in the wild.[123] Furthermore, it would be unusual for a lion to make a kill and then make no

וַיֵּלֶךְ וַיִּמְצָאֵהוּ אַרְיֵה בַּדֶּרֶךְ וַיְמִיתֵהוּ וַתְּהִי נִבְלָתוֹ מֻשְׁלֶכֶת בַּדֶּרֶךְ וְהַחֲמוֹר עֹמֵד אֶצְלָהּ וְהָאַרְיֵה עֹמֵד אֵצֶל הַנְּבֵלָה: וְהִנֵּה אֲנָשִׁים עֹבְרִים וַיִּרְאוּ אֶת הַנְּבֵלָה מֻשְׁלֶכֶת בַּדֶּרֶךְ וְאֶת הָאַרְיֵה עֹמֵד אֵצֶל הַנְּבֵלָה וַיָּבֹאוּ וַיְדַבְּרוּ בָעִיר אֲשֶׁר הַנָּבִיא הַזָּקֵן יֹשֵׁב בָּהּ: וַיִּשְׁמַע הַנָּבִיא אֲשֶׁר הֱשִׁיבוֹ מִן הַדֶּרֶךְ וַיֹּאמֶר אִישׁ הָאֱלֹהִים הוּא אֲשֶׁר מָרָה אֶת פִּי יְהֹוָה וַיִּתְּנֵהוּ יְהֹוָה לָאַרְיֵה וַיִּשְׁבְּרֵהוּ וַיְמִיתֵהוּ כִּדְבַר יְהֹוָה אֲשֶׁר דִּבֶּר לוֹ: וַיְדַבֵּר אֶל בָּנָיו לֵאמֹר חִבְשׁוּ לִי אֶת הַחֲמוֹר וַיַּחֲבֹשׁוּ: וַיֵּלֶךְ וַיִּמְצָא אֶת נִבְלָתוֹ מֻשְׁלֶכֶת בַּדֶּרֶךְ וַחֲמוֹר וְהָאַרְיֵה עֹמְדִים אֵצֶל הַנְּבֵלָה לֹא אָכַל הָאַרְיֵה אֶת הַנְּבֵלָה וְלֹא שָׁבַר אֶת הַחֲמוֹר:
מלכים א יג כד-כח

וַיֹּאמֶר לוֹ יַעַן אֲשֶׁר לֹא שָׁמַעְתָּ בְּקוֹל יְהֹוָה הִנְּךָ הוֹלֵךְ מֵאִתִּי וְהִכְּךָ הָאַרְיֵה וַיֵּלֶךְ מֵאֶצְלוֹ וַיִּמְצָאֵהוּ הָאַרְיֵה וַיַּכֵּהוּ:
מלכים א כ לו

וַיְהִי בִּתְחִלַּת שִׁבְתָּם שָׁם לֹא יָרְאוּ אֶת יְהֹוָה וַיְשַׁלַּח יְהֹוָה בָּהֶם אֶת הָאֲרָיוֹת וַיִּהְיוּ הֹרְגִים בָּהֶם: וַיֹּאמְרוּ לְמֶלֶךְ אַשּׁוּר לֵאמֹר הַגּוֹיִם אֲשֶׁר הִגְלִיתָ וַתּוֹשֶׁב בְּעָרֵי שֹׁמְרוֹן לֹא יָדְעוּ אֶת מִשְׁפַּט אֱלֹהֵי הָאָרֶץ וַיְשַׁלַּח בָּם אֶת הָאֲרָיוֹת וְהִנָּם מְמִיתִים אוֹתָם כַּאֲשֶׁר אֵינָם יֹדְעִים אֶת מִשְׁפַּט אֱלֹהֵי הָאָרֶץ:
מלכים ב יז כה-כו

attempt to eat it. This aberrant behavior demonstrated that its attack of the person was not part of ordinary predatory behavior, but instead was the result of its being on a divine mission.[124]

Later, another lion attack on a disobedient person takes place. Here, evidence of the killing being a divine mission comes not from the lion changing its behavior, but instead from the fact that the event was foretold by a prophet:

> Then he said to him, "Because you have not obeyed the voice of the Lord, behold, as soon as you leave me, a lion shall kill you." And as soon as he departed from him, a lion found him, and killed him. (I Kings 20:36)

In both of these incidents, it was individuals who were killed by lions. But in a later incident, there were mass attacks by lions on people who defied God's laws:

> The king of Assyria brought [people] from Babylon, Cuthah, Avva, Hamath, and Sepharvaim, and he settled them in the towns of Samaria in place of the Israelites; they took possession of Samaria and dwelt in its towns. When they began living there, they did not fear the Lord; so the Lord sent lions among them, which killed some of them. It was told to the king of Assyria: "The people that you exiled and resettled in the towns of Samaria do not know the judgments of the God of that land. He has sent lions among them, which are killing them, because the people do not know His judgments." (II Kings 17:24–26)

מַשָּׂא בַּהֲמוֹת נֶגֶב בְּאֶרֶץ צָרָה וְצוּקָה לָבִיא וָלַיִשׁ מֵהֶם אֶפְעֶה
וְשָׂרָף מְעוֹפֵף יִשְׂאוּ עַל כֶּתֶף עֲיָרִים חֵילֵהֶם וְעַל דַּבֶּשֶׁת גְּמַלִּים
אוֹצְרֹתָם עַל עַם לֹא יוֹעִילוּ:

ישעיה ל:ו

Scripture proceeds to describe how, in order to avoid the problem of lion attacks, the people learned how to practice the laws of Judaism. The people described in these verses, collectively known as Kuthim, are described in the Talmud as *gerei arayot*, "converts due to lions."[125]

Some see another reference in Scripture to lions being sent by God to attack sinners. There is a prophecy regarding those who traveled through the desert to seek aid from Egypt, without first seeking counsel from God:

> The pronouncement of the beasts of the south; to the land of trouble and anguish, from where the fiery lion and the mighty lion come. (Is. 30:6)

This is explained by some to mean that the people would be attacked by wild animals, as a punishment for their actions.[126]

The lion is regarded as being so likely to be an agent of divine retribution that any encounter with a lion is seen as being a close encounter with God's judgment of death:

> If a person encounters a lion, and it did not eat him, he should give blessings and praise to the Name of the Holy One; perhaps he was destined for this lion [to eat him], and the Holy One had mercy on him and it did not eat him. (*Tanna DeVei Eliyahu Rabba* 18)

The Midrash relates an extraordinary account of how someone was voluntarily exposed to lions in order to check if any divine retribution was required. R. Meir was tricked by a woman into becoming drunk, and when he fell asleep, she entered his bed. When he discovered what had happened, he was stricken with guilt. R. Meir went to ask the Rosh Yeshiva what he should do in order to atone, even if it meant being fed to wild animals. After deliberating, the Rosh Yeshiva said that R. Meir should be offered to the lions. He ordered two men to tie him up in a place where lions were found, with the instruction that if R. Meir is eaten, his bones should be returned for a eulogy in which he would be praised for accepting divine judgment. They tied him up, and a lion approached in the night, but did not touch him. The Rosh Yeshiva ordered them to tie him up again on the following night, and the same happened again. The Rosh Yeshiva ordered that R. Meir be tied up for a third and final night. This time, the lion bit him, dislocated a rib, and ate a tiny amount of flesh. The Rosh Yeshiva, concluding that R. Meir was now exempt from further retribution, ordered that R. Meir be taken to a doctor for healing. When R. Meir

returned home, says the Midrash, a voice from the Heavens announced that he had earned his place in the World to Come.[127]

The lion can sometimes serve as an agent of divine protection rather than retribution, due to its ability to present a lethal threat:

> There was an incident with a person who forgot to bring in his wheat into his home before ascending on the festival pilgrimage, and when he returned, he found lions encircling his wheat. (*Shir HaShirim Rabba* 7:3[128])

The Hunger of the Lion

THEOLOGY, PHILOSOPHY, AND SCIENCE

The Talmud relates how the Sages once appeared before King David in order to inform him of the people's economic distress:

> The sages of Israel entered to King David and said, Our master the king, your people Israel needs sustenance. He said to them, Let them go and derive sustenance from each other (i.e. by mutual trade). They said to him, A handful does not satisfy the lion, and nor can a cistern fill up from its ring. (Berakhot 3b, Sanhedrin 16a).

TAMBAKO / FLICKR

Lions eat vast quantities of meat at a single sitting

A cistern cannot fill up only from the rain that falls directly into the stone ring placed on its mouth; runoff from a larger area must be channeled into the cistern for it to be effective. And a lion will not be satiated with a handful of food – it usually eats from forty to as much as ninety pounds of meat at a sitting![129] King David, understanding that the nation lacked sufficient resources to sustain itself, advised them to launch raids in order to obtain resources that would provide sustenance for all the people.[130]

The prodigious appetite of the lion is also demonstrated in a verse which shows how little of a sheep is left when a shepherd manages to retrieve it from a marauding lion:

Thus says the Lord: As the shepherd rescues out of the mouth of the lion two legs, or the tip of an ear; so shall the people of Israel who dwell in Samaria be rescued with the corner of a bed, and the corner of a couch. (Amos 3:12)

There is an inherent contradiction in the nature of the lion vis-à-vis its food. On the one hand, the lion is the king of beasts and the most powerful animal, which should mean that it has the easiest time of procuring food. But on the other hand, as a meat-eater, and the largest one at that, the lion has the ultimate challenge in finding sufficient food. This tension is seen as being reflected in the following verse, well known from appearing in the final paragraph of *Birkat HaMazon*:

The young lions suffer want and hunger; but those who seek God shall not lack any good thing. (Ps. 34:11)

Some see the reference to young lions in this verse as metaphorically referring to powerful people.[131] But others explain it as referring to actual lions. Rabbi Bachya ibn Pekuda, the renowned medieval philosopher, notes that helpless creatures, such as fetuses in the womb and the humble ant, have their needs readily provided for them. Lions, on the other hand, despite being the mightiest of animals, have to struggle to survive. This is a lesson for man that it is ultimately God who determines one's sustenance, rather than physical power.[132] Note that the lion mentioned in this verse is the *kefir*, the young lion that has just learned to hunt for itself.[133] Perhaps this emphasizes that having the power and the skills to obtain one's needs does not guarantee success.

Elsewhere in Scripture, this concept is presented from the opposite perspective. It is pointed out that when young lions roar for their food (as referenced in the section "The Roar of the Lion"), this is due to the way that God has set up the world:

You bring on darkness and it becomes night, when all the beasts of the forest roam. The young lions roar for

their prey, and to seek their food from God. When the sun rises, they are gathered in, to crouch in their lairs. (Ps. 104:20–22)

The commentaries explain that this does not mean that the lions are consciously addressing God with their roaring. Rather, it means that the lions roar to seek their food, which is arranged by God through various natural causes.[134] The circle of life is arranged such that each animal carves out its own unique niche in the ecosystem, finding its sustenance in its own way.[135] God has set up the world in such a way that even lions, with their prodigious appetites, are able to find food.

This point is made in the story of Job. Job is protesting his suffering, wondering why it befell him. God's response is to make Job realize his limitations as a human being, such that he will not expect to understand the ways of his Creator. In addition, God stresses that His providence does indeed extend over all the world. Both these points are conveyed by an account of how God is able to provide for the needs of lions:

Will you trap prey for the lion? Or satisfy the appetite of the young lions, when they crouch in their lairs, and lie in ambush in the undergrowth? (Job 38:39–40)

The hunger of the lions can only be provided for via God's providential arrangement of the world.[136]

The Lurking Lion
THEOLOGY, PHILOSOPHY, AND SCIENCE

Zoologists have observed that while the lion's method of obtaining prey takes many forms, there is one method that is most common. This involves co-operative hunting in which several lions will stalk their prey, fan out, and some will then rush the prey animal and chase it toward the others. Zoological studies also describe lionesses as doing most of the killing of prey, with males enjoying the results of the lionesses' kills. One oft-cited study of lion behavior, performed in the Serengeti, describes how out of a total of 1,210 lions observed stalking and chasing after their prey, only three percent were males.[137]

93

כֹּה אָמַר יְהֹוָה כַּאֲשֶׁר יַצִּיל הָרֹעֶה מִפִּי הָאֲרִי שְׁתֵּי כְרָעַיִם אוֹ בְדַל אֹזֶן כֵּן יִנָּצְלוּ בְּנֵי יִשְׂרָאֵל הַיֹּשְׁבִים בְּשֹׁמְרוֹן בִּפְאַת מִטָּה וּבִדְמֶשֶׁק עָרֶשׂ:
עמוס ג:יב

כְּפִירִים רָשׁוּ וְרָעֵבוּ וְדֹרְשֵׁי יְהֹוָה לֹא יַחְסְרוּ כָל טוֹב:
תהלים לד:יא

הֲתָצוּד לְלָבִיא טָרֶף וְחַיַּת כְּפִירִים תְּמַלֵּא: כִּי יָשֹׁחוּ בַמְּעוֹנוֹת יֵשְׁבוּ בַסֻּכָּה לְמוֹ אָרֶב:
איוב לח:לט-מ

Male lions attack by bursting out of the thicket in a surprise ambush

Such co-operative stalking and chasing by lionesses is, however, never described in Scripture. Instead, all accounts of lion attacks – most of which are metaphorical, but which should still be using an image drawn from reality – are of male lions that are lying in ambush:

> He lies in wait secretly, like a lion in his den; he lies in wait to catch the poor; he catches the poor, when he draws him into his net. (Ps. 10:9)

> He is like a lion that is greedy for its prey, and like a young lion lurking in secret places. (Ps. 17:12)

> [God] is to me like a bear lying in ambush, and like a lion in secret places. (Lam. 3:10)

The Talmud even describes the motif of a lion in ambush as a figure of speech that has entered popular discourse, in order to refer to someone who is suspected of being able to cause harm:

> If the assailant says to the injured person: "I can personally act as your healer," the other party can retort "You are in my eyes like a lurking lion." (Bava Kama 85a[138])

Why does Scripture describe male lions hunting via ambush, if the zoological accounts of hunting involve lionesses hunting via stalking and chasing? The reason is that the zoological accounts of hunting were, until very recently, necessarily selective. Most zoological studies of lions hunting have taken place in open savannah such as the Serengeti, where it is easy to observe such behavior. But new studies using GPS devices fitted to lions and laser-based terrain-mapping technology have shown a different side to how lions obtain their prey. While in the open savannah, the

יֶאֱרֹב בַּמִּסְתָּר כְּאַרְיֵה בְסֻכֹּה יֶאֱרֹב לַחֲטוֹף עָנִי יַחְטֹף עָנִי בְּמָשְׁכוֹ בְרִשְׁתּוֹ:

תהלים י:ט

דִּמְיֹנוֹ כְּאַרְיֵה יִכְסוֹף לִטְרוֹף וְכִכְפִיר יֹשֵׁב בְּמִסְתָּרִים:

תהלים יז:יב

דֹּב אֹרֵב הוּא לִי אֲרִי בְּמִסְתָּרִים:

איכה ג:י

hunting is mostly done via lionesses stalking and chasing, in forested regions it is different: male lions hunt alone, via ambushing their prey.[139]

The reason for this has to do with the physical differences between male and female lions. Males are much more powerfully built, with a heavy mane. This makes them well suited for fighting other males for control of the pride, but it makes them slower and less agile than females, and the mane harms their ability to camouflage themselves in grass. Whereas lionesses can engage in group hunting involving stalking and speed, male lions must use a technique of ambushing. Such a technique is most effective in dense forest. This terrain is not very common in the African savannah, but there would have been much of it in biblical Israel, which was much more densely forested than the Israel of today.

> The lion has come up from his thicket…a lion from the forest shall slay them. (Jer. 4:7, 5:6)

The typical lion attack in biblical Israel would not have been the stalking and chasing done by groups of lionesses in the Serengeti, but instead an ambush from a solitary male lion in a thicket, just as described in Scripture.

How Lions Kill

How do lions kill their prey? This has been extensively researched by contemporary zoologists studying African lions, and there is little reason to believe that it would have been any different for the Barbary or Asiatic lions that were familiar in biblical and talmudic times.

When a lion hunts its preferred prey – large herbivores such as cattle – it usually first kills it in a safe manner, so that it cannot be injured from its horns and hooves.[140] The first stage in this process is to bring the animal down. Sometimes, the lion can do this by using its paws to drag the animal down. If the prey animal is too big for this, the lion will leap onto the victim's flanks, using its claws to grip the victim, often using one paw to grasp its muzzle, while using its teeth to grasp the animal by its neck. This causes the animal to topple down onto the ground, and will sometimes cause it to break its neck. If the animal is still alive, the lion will kill it by biting its neck from the front, in order to clamp the trachea shut, or its muzzle, in order to seal the mouth, thereby causing asphyxiation.[141] The lion will then sometimes eat its prey on the spot, but if it fears disturbance (as may well be the case when having killed cattle), it will drag its victim a considerable distance to suitable shelter.[142] It will also carry away its prey if it is going to feed its cubs. If several lions are present, the kill is torn to pieces and each lion retreats with its portion.[143]

The Talmud discusses two different types of lion attacks, one of which is considered normal and the other abnormal. The normal form of attack is rated in the legal category of *shen* – literally, "tooth" – which applies to damage sustained by animals eating their food in a normal way. This form of damage is normally very common, in terms of domestic cattle eating whatever produce they come across. As a result, the owners of the damaging animals are not liable if the food consumed was in a public domain – the person who left it there should have been more careful.[144] This is a blanket exemption applied across the board to owners of all animals that cause such normal damage in the course of eating – even in the case of a pet lion eating its usual food, which could be someone else's cow.[145] On the other hand, if an animal causes damage in an abnormal way, this is rated in the legal category of *keren* – literally, "horn" – and the owner of the animal is liable.

However, the terms that the Talmud uses to describe the different forms of lion attack are difficult to translate and understand. One type of attack is called *dores*, which literally usually means "trample," while the other is called *toref*, which literally means "tear":

> Shmuel said: If a lion tramples and eats an animal in a public area, the owner is exempt (from full damages); if it tears and eats the animal, he is liable. If it tramples and eats he is not liable – because it is usual for it to eat by way of trampling, and it is therefore equivalent to eating fruit and vegetables, which would be categorized as *shen* in a public area and exempt. But if it tore, this is not the normal behavior (and it is rated as *keren*, for which the owner is liable). (Bava Kama 16b)

The Talmud proceeds to query whether "tearing" is truly an abnormal way for a lion to eat, based on scriptural verses which seem to present this as the norm, and explains that the verses are referring to particular scenarios:

> Is it really the case that "tearing" is not normal behavior? Surely it is written, "The lion tears for its cubs" (Nahum 2:13)? – That is for the sake of its cubs (and not for its own food, which would be abnormal). "And strangles for its lionesses" – for the sake of its lionesses. "And

GERRIT DE VRIES / SHUTTERSTOCK

A lion seizing a wildebeest

fills its lair with its prey" – for the sake of stocking its lair. "And its den with prey" – for the sake of its den. (Ibid.[146])

There are different opinions amongst the traditional commentaries regarding how to explain the differences in the terms "trampling" and "tearing." Some explain "trampling" to refer to eating the prey animal while it is still alive, whereas "tearing" refers to killing it first;[147] but in light of what is known today about lion attacks, this is difficult. On occasion, lions will indeed eat their prey, even buffalo, without killing it first, but this is the exception rather than the rule, whereas the Talmud is specifically describing "trampling" as being the typical hunting method of the lion and "tearing" as being unusual.[148]

Alternately, perhaps "trampling" means killing it first, in the normal ways that lions do (with claws and teeth), and "tearing" means tearing chunks off it while it is still alive. A variation on this would be to explain "trampling" as killing and eating it immediately, while "tearing" means dismembering it and eating it later.

Understanding the Talmud's conception of the lion's normal method of killing also sheds light on different references in the Talmud to the lion killing. One is a presentation of a lion kill as a metaphor for the attitude of an *am haaretz* (ignorant or boorish person) to his wife:

One who marries off his daughter to *am haaretz* is as though he has bound her and placed her before a lion. Just as a lion tramples and eats and has no shame, so too a boor beats his wife and cohabits without shame. (Pesachim 49b)

The idea of the lion "trampling and eating without shame," as opposed to dismembering its prey for later consumption, is that the lion is consumed with savagery and does not bide his time to eat, nor delay out of caution. This recalls the infamous man-eating lions of Tsavo, about which Patterson writes that "Nothing flurried or frightened them in the least, and except as food they showed a complete contempt for human beings. Having once marked down a victim, they would allow nothing to deter them from securing him, whether he were protected by a thick fence, or inside a closed tent, or sitting round a brightly burning fire. Shots, shouting and firebrands they alike held in derision.... [I recall on one occasion] the brutes carried off their unfortunate victim and began their horrible feast close beside the camp. The Inspector, Mr. Dalgairns, fired over fifty shots in the direction in which he heard the lions, but they were not to be frightened and calmly lay there until their meal was finished." This is a metaphor for the boor, who, rather than being courteous with his wife, beats her into immediate submission.

A white lion (a paler variety) tearing away at its meat

Another reference to the lion's method of killing is a metaphor for how an *am haaretz* who is a *kohen* (priest) reacts to tithes of produce that are given to him:

> Rav Acha bar Ada said in the name of Rav Yehuda: Whoever gives tithes to a *kohen* who is an *am haaretz*, is as though he gives it to a lion. Just as with a lion it is uncertain if it will trample and eat or not, so too with the *kohen* who is an *am haaretz*, it is unclear if he will eat it in a state of ritual purity or ritual impurity. (Sanhedrin 90b)

The precise nature of this metaphor is unclear, and a variety of different explanations are suggested.[149] Perhaps it means that the lion will usually eat its prey immediately, but occasionally will dismember it for later; similarly, the *am haaretz* will usually eat the food immediately, rather than waiting until he is ritually pure.

In Noah's Ark

Lions are mentioned in several different contexts regarding Noah's Ark, in various different statements by the Midrash. One midrash describes how God established a covenant with Noah to prevent unauthorized passengers on the ark:

> A lion would come to enter the Ark, and it would be turned back (lit. "its teeth would be blunted"), just as it is written, "The roaring of the lion, and the voice of the mature lion, and the teeth of the young lions – they are broken" (Job 4:10). (*Bereshit Rabba* 31:12)

Another midrash describes how God used lions as His emissaries to keep away hostile people:

> When the people saw that they were doomed, they sought to overturn the Ark. What did the Holy One do? He surrounded the Ark with lions, as it says "And God closed it for him" – "closing" means nothing other than with lions, just as it says, "My God sent His angel and closed the lions' mouths" (Dan. 6:23). (*Midrash Tanchuma Noach* 7[150])

The Talmud, in discussing how various animals were sustained on Noah's Ark, states that the lion fell sick and was thereby able to survive without having to prey upon other animals:

> The lion was nourished by a fever, as Rav said, fever can sustain for not less than six and not more than twelve. (Sanhedrin 108b)

The commentaries differ as to whether Rav meant that a fever can sustain life for six to twelve *days*[151] or six to twelve *months*.[152] Those who take the latter view argue that if a fever only sustains for a matter of days, this would not have been of much help to Noah, since the animals were on the Ark for a year. Those who take the former view presumably feel that it is impossible for a fever to sustain life for months, and the Talmud's intent was only that Noah's job was temporarily eased.

Feeding the lion posed other problems, aside from obtaining enough food, as we see in the following midrash:

> For twelve months, Noah and his sons did not taste sleep, for they had to feed all the animals and birds.... Once Noah was late in feeding the lion, it struck him and he emerged wounded, as it says, "And only Noah remained" – "only" (a word that always serves to exclude something) i.e. that he was not complete, and was not fit to bring an offering, which had to be brought by his sons in his place. (*Midrash Tanchuma* 9)

Another midrash notes that Noah was not the only person to be mauled by a lion:

> R. Shimon opened up the verse: "For the same fate is in store for all: for the righteous, and for the wicked" (Eccl. 9:2). "For the righteous" – this is Noah, about whom it is said, "A righteous man" (Gen 6:9). R. Yochanan said in the name of R. Eliezer, son of R. Yose HaGelilee – When Noah emerged from the Ark, a lion struck him and broke him, and he was not fit to bring an offering, which had to be brought by his sons in his place. "For the wicked" – this is Pharaoh Necho, who sought to sit on the throne of Solomon but did not know the procedure, and a lion struck him and injured him.[153] This one died wounded and this one died wounded – that is what is written, "one happening for the righteous and the wicked." (*Vayikra Rabba* 20:1)

The commentaries ask how the Midrash deduces that is was specifically a lion that mauled Noah, rather than another animal. One ingenious answer given is that the letters of וישאר אך, "and only he remained," can be rearranged to read אכשו ארי, "a lion struck him."[154] Others explain that the lion would be the animal to take particularly aggressive exception to a delay in its meal.[155] Another explanation can be based upon the mystical concept that if a person is deficient in a particular trait, he is punished by the animal that embodies that trait.[156] In being late to feed the animals, Noah exhibited a lack of *gevura*, the trait of energy that is required to overcome lethargy. The manifestation of this trait is the powerful lion; we are told "a man should strengthen himself like a lion to arise in the mornings."[157] The lion is *gevura* incarnate, and thus when Noah's trait of *gevura* was not implemented properly, its physical incarnation in the lion also malfunctioned.

The Tiger-Lion of Ila'i

The Talmud mentions a creature that it describes as a form of lion:

> R. Yehuda said: The *keros*[159] is the deer of the region of Ila'i; the *tigris* is the lion of the region of Ila'i (*aryeh d'bei ila'i*). (Chullin 59b)

The name Ila'i is of uncertain meaning; Ila'i means "of high" and it thus may refer to a mountainous region. But there can be little doubt that the *tigris* is the tiger (and this is also the more correct term for the tiger in Modern Hebrew, instead of *namer*[160]). The *tigris* is described as being extremely large:

> Rav Kahana said: There are nine cubits between the lobes of the lion of the region of Ila'i. (Ibid.)

Nine cubits is a little over thirteen feet, but what are the "lobes" of the lion of Ila'i? Some explain the term to refer to its ears; but even as an exaggeration, it would be strange to describe the tiger as measuring thirteen feet between the ears. However, the term may perhaps mean "between its extremities," i.e. "from end to end." As such, it would refer to the length of the tiger from the tip of its nose to the tip of its tail, which is often described in English as its length "between the pegs."[161] This can indeed approach thirteen feet.

However, the Talmud proceeds to relate a story that does not match the tiger as we know it, or indeed any big cat:

> Caesar said to R. Yehoshua b. Chananiah: "Your God is compared to a lion, as it is written, 'The lion has roared; who shall not be afraid?! (Amos 3:8).' But what is His greatness? A warrior can kill a lion!" R. Yehoshua replied: "He is not compared to such a lion, but rather He is compared to the lion of the region of Ila'i." Caesar said: "I want you to show it to me." R. Yehoshua replied: "You are not capable of looking at it." Caesar said: "Indeed, I will look at it!" R. Yehoshua prayed, and the lion set out from its place. When it was four hundred parasangs away, it emitted a single roar, and all the pregnant women miscarried, and the walls of Rome collapsed. When it was three hundred parasangs away, it emitted another roar, and all the men's teeth fell out, and Caesar fell from his throne to the ground. Caesar said: "I beg of you, pray for it to return to its place!" He prayed, and it returned to its place. (Ibid.)

There are several different approaches taken by classical rabbinic authorities to fantastic stories such as these.[162]

A Bengal tiger

Some interpret them literally, notwithstanding any empirical difficulties.[163] Others see them as including exaggerations.[164] Still others interpret them metaphorically[165] or metaphysically.[166]

With this story, too, we find diverse approaches. Some interpret it literally, with the incidents surrounding this lion being of a miraculous nature.[167] Others interpret it metaphorically; indeed, the phrase *aryeh d'bei ila'i*, "Lion of the Higher Realm," so obviously lends itself to a metaphoric explanation that in later centuries it became a common figure of speech used to praise great Torah scholars.[168] Some thus explain that the "lion" here is a metaphor for God's power.[169] Still others propose an elaborate allegorical explanation for the entire discussion of the *tigris*. According to this view, *tigris* refers to the Tigris river, the "lion of high" refers to the Babylonians and Persians, and R. Yehoshua was reminding Caesar of how the Persians drove the Romans back across the Tigris.[170]

בֶּן אָדָם שָׂא קִינָה עַל פַּרְעֹה מֶלֶךְ מִצְרַיִם וְאָמַרְתָּ אֵלָיו כְּפִיר
גּוֹיִם נִדְמֵיתָ וְאַתָּה כַּתַּנִּים בַּיַּמִּים וַתָּגַח בְּנַהֲרוֹתֶיךָ וַתִּדְלַח מַיִם
בְּרַגְלֶיךָ וַתִּרְפֹּס נַהֲרוֹתָם: יחזקאל לב:ב

כִּי מִי אֲשֶׁר יְחֻבַּר אֶל כָּל הַחַיִּים יֵשׁ בִּטָּחוֹן כִּי לְכֶלֶב חַי הוּא טוֹב
מִן הָאַרְיֵה הַמֵּת: קהלת ט:ד

Pharaoh's Lions

The pharaohs of Egypt associated themselves with the lion, seeing themselves as sharing its nature as noble king and ruler, albeit with this claim being disputed by God:

> Son of man, raise a lamentation for Pharaoh king of Egypt, and say to him, You consider yourself a young lion of the nations, but you are like a crocodile in the seas; and you burst forth in your rivers, and trouble the waters with your feet, and foul their rivers. (Ezek. 32:2)

The sphinx is in the form of the head of a Pharaoh on the body of a lion, and Ramses II had a pet lion named "Slayer of his Foes" which accompanied him in battle.[158] In ancient Egypt, deities which guarded the fiery sun as it rose and set were portrayed as lions. We can thus understand why Pharaoh is described as having lions guarding his palace:

> There were four hundred entrances to the palace of Pharaoh, and on each entrance were lions, bears, and fearsome beasts, and nobody could enter until they were fed with meat so that they would not attack. But when Moses and Aaron came, the beasts all gathered around them and were licking their feet, and escorted them until they arrived before Pharaoh. (*Midrash Yalkut Shimoni* 1:181)

Another midrash highlights lions in particular as being used for this task:

> Pharaoh had lions in his palace, and these lions would open their mouths and growl and roar at everyone who entered, whereupon they would be fainting in terror. But when Moses entered, the lions were like dogs before him, to the astonishment of Pharaoh and his magicians. (*Midrash Lekach Tov, Shemot*)

And another midrash elaborates upon this episode:

> Afterwards, Moses and Aaron came, and it was when they reached the gates of the king's house that there were two young lions tied up with iron chains. No one could leave or enter between them aside from he that the king commanded alone, whereupon the handlers would remove the lions with their commands. Moses quickly waved his staff over the lions and released them, and he came to the king's house with the lions accompanying them in great joy, just as a dog rejoices when its master comes in from the fields. (*Yalkut Shimoni* 1:176)

Similarly to later heroes of Israel such as Samson, Benaiah, David, and Daniel, the greatness of Moses is described in terms of his being able to overcome lions.

Weaknesses of the Lion

Notwithstanding the lion's status as the king of beasts, there are circumstances in which the lion holds little status. One example is when it is dead:

> For to him who is joined to all the living there is hope; for a living dog is better than a dead lion. (Eccl. 9:4)

Commenting on this verse, the Midrash bemoans the fact that, in this imperfect world, the distinction between those who are like lions and those who are like dogs is not always as clear as it should be:

> In this world, someone who is a dog can become a lion, and someone who is a lion can become a dog. But in the future era, someone who is a lion cannot become a dog, and someone who is a dog cannot become a lion. (*Ruth Rabba* 3:2)

The gulf between lions and canids is so great that the Sages utilize them in teaching a lesson regarding with which kinds of people one should associate:

> Be a tail to lions, rather than being a head to jackals. (Mishna Avot 4:15)

The Talmud notes that even a live lion also has its limitations. It is afraid of a small creature called a *mafgia*:

> The Rabbis taught: There are five fears with which the fear of the weak is upon the mighty: The fear of the *mafgia* upon the lion, the fear of the mosquito upon the elephant, the fear of the gecko upon the scorpion, the fear of the swallow upon the vulture, and the fear of the *kilbit*-fish upon the whale.[171] R. Yehuda said: What is the scriptural source? "He grants the robbed one power over the mighty" (Amos 5:9). (Shabbat 77b)

Similarly, the Midrash notes that the lion is afraid of a creature called the *ankakta*, which may well be another name for the *mafgia*:

> "How great are Your works, O God!" (Ps. 104:24) – Such as the lion, *ankakta*, and dog, which were once all in the same place. The lion sought to attack the dog, but it saw the *ankakta*, and was afraid of it, for it is an enemy of the lion. The dog is the enemy of the *ankakta*. And thus they

did not harm each other. R. Akiva saw it, and said, "How great are Your works, O God!" (*Midrash Tehillim* 118)

The lion wanted to kill the dog, but did not do so because only the dog could overpower the *ankakta*. The dog, in turn, would have killed the *ankakta*, but did not do so because only the *ankakta* could save it from the lion. The *ankakta*, in turn, did not kill the lion, because only the lion could defeat the dog. As a result, there was a stalemate, and no animal killed any other.

But what is the mysterious *mafgia/ankakta*, of which the lion is afraid? There is an ancient Greek and Roman view that the lion is afraid of the rooster. However, the rooster has an established name in the Talmud, and it is thus not being referred to with the unusual name *mafgia*.

There are several different views as to the Talmud's intent in describing the *mafgia*. Unfortunately, it is impossible to determine which is correct. Amongst the Torah scholars of the medieval period, some say that the *mafgia* is a tiny creature which has a loud cry and deceives the lion into thinking that it is enormous.[172] Others claim that it is a bird that punctures the lion's skull with its sharp claws.[173] More recent scholars describe a legend, dating back to the Alexandrians in Syria, of the leontophone (also called leontophonos), a tiny creature which is a deadly poison to lions.[174] Yet another suggestion, which is perhaps related to both of the previous views, is that the *mafgia* is a type of gnat.[175] The lion is aware of the painful stings that it can inflict upon its face, and thus is terrified even of the buzzing sound that it makes. Other creative suggestions abound.[176]

Whatever the nature of the *mafgia*, the point of the Talmud's statement is that size does not always count. Even the lion, mighty king of beasts, is afraid of a small creature. Lions are indeed deservedly afraid of porcupines; a face-full of quills can cause immense pain to the lion and even lead to its death. Recently, a single porcupine was filmed scaring off a pride of seventeen lions.[177] Lions are also known to fear a small animal called the zorilla, a type of polecat that, skunk-like, emits a foul-smelling spray.

Some see the Talmud's account of the *mafgia* as presenting a theological problem. How can the existence of the *mafgia* be reconciled with all the descriptions in Torah literature of the lion fearing no other creature?[178]

The answer is less complicated than one might suppose. The *mafgia* is simply an exception. There are countless precedents for seemingly absolute statements about reality having exceptions. For example, Ecclesiastes 7:20 states that "There is no righteous man in the world who does good and does not sin." One of the Tosafists challenges this, based on a statement in the Talmud which lists four people who died

Lions learn to fear porcupines

without sin.[179] He answers that the verse is not an absolute statement, just a generality, which can have exceptions. Numerous other rabbinic authorities discuss exceptions to rules that should be seen as generalities, not absolute.[180] Notwithstanding the rare case of the mysterious *mafgia*, it is acceptable to state that the lion is indeed the mightiest of beasts, fearing nothing.

Lion by Nature, Lion by Name
— SYMBOLISM

With the lion being the mightiest of beasts, and powerful people being metaphorically described as lion-hearted, it comes as no surprise to find that mighty people are actually referred to as "Lion." The Talmud relates a person's story regarding one such hero:

> "He and I were walking with a man along the road, and a band of robbers chased us, and he grabbed an olive branch and tore it off, and chased the band away with it. I said to him, 'Well done, Aryeh!' He said to me, 'How did you know my name? For that is what they call me in my city, Yochanan b. R. Yehonatan Aryeh from the village of Sichay.'" (Yevamot 122b; Y. Yevamot 84a)

Of course, the point is that the man did not know the hero's name beforehand; he was calling him Aryeh/Lion in acknowledgment of the bravery and power that he had exhibited.[181] Acknowledgment of such mighty deeds is valued even for a person who would not normally be praised:

> A heathen (slave[182]) or a (Jewish) servant – one does not busy himself with them at all (regarding their funeral), but one may eulogize them with, "O, the lion, the lion, O, the mighty one." (Talmud, *Evel Rabbati* (*Semachot*) 1:5)

We find that people were referred to as "lions" not merely for their physical strength or courage in battle, but also for their strength of intellect and/or character as displayed in matters regarding Torah:

After R. Eleazar died, four sages entered to give rejoinders to his positions. R. Yehoshua said: We do not respond to a lion after his death. (Gittin 23b)

There are numerous occasions in the Talmud in which sages are described as lions, or as sons of lions.[183] To give but one example:

When Rav Kahana came to Palestine, Resh Lakish told R. Yochanan that "A lion has ascended from Babylon!" (Bava Kama 117a).

In Europe, people named Yehuda (Judah) were often called also Leib, the Yiddish word for the lion, symbol of Judah. Subsequently, the Hebrew name Ari was often given as a first name, with Leib following as a direct translation. The family name Lowy, and its many variants, is taken from the German Löwe, for lion.

The Lion Hunter of Zion

—————————————————— JEWISH HISTORY

As we have seen, several heroes of Jewish history, from Samson to Benaiah to David to Daniel, demonstrated their strength and courage by overcoming lions. In modern times, too, one of the greatest heroes for the Jewish nation gained fame as a slayer of lions. These were not just any lions, but were amongst the most feared and dangerous lions in recorded history. Their slayer, although an outstanding hero who fought on behalf of the Jewish people, was not even Jewish.

On several occasions in this chapter, we have made reference to the notorious man-eating lions of Tsavo in Kenya. These two maneless but huge lions, working together, were estimated to have killed and eaten well over a hundred people working on the railroad at the turn of the twentieth century. Colonel John Patterson, an Irish soldier and engineer in charge of the railroad, was faced with the task of killing the lions.[184]

Night after night, Patterson sat in a tree, hoping to shoot the lions when they came to the bait that he set for them. But the lions demonstrated almost supernatural abilities, constantly breaking through thorn fences to take victims from elsewhere in the camp, and seemingly immune to the bullets that were fired at them. Finally, after many months, Patterson eventually shot both lions. He himself was nearly killed in the process on several occasions, such as when approaching the body of one lion, that he had shot several times, which suddenly leaped up to attack him. Patterson published a blood-curdling account of the episode in *The Man-Eaters of Tsavo*,[185] which became a best-seller, and earned him a close relationship with US President Roosevelt.

Upon returning to England, Patterson was a hailed as a hero. When World War I broke out, however, Patterson traveled to Egypt and took on a most unusual task: forming and leading a unit of Jewish soldiers, comprised of Jews who had been exiled from Palestine by the Turks.[186] As a child, Patterson had been mesmerized by stories from the Bible. He viewed this task as being of tremendous, historic significance. The unit, called the Zion Mule Corps, was tasked with providing supplies to soldiers in the trenches in Gallipoli. Patterson persuaded the reluctant War Office to provide kosher food, as well as matza for Passover, and he himself learned Hebrew and Yiddish in order to be able to communicate with his troops.

In 1916 Patterson joined forces with Vladimir Jabotinsky to create a full-fledged Jewish Legion in the British Army, who would fight to liberate Palestine from the cruel reign of the Ottoman Empire and enable the Jewish people to create a home there.[187] The War Minister, Lord Derby, succumbed to anti-Zionist agitators and attempted to prevent the Jewish Legion from receiving kosher food, from serving in Palestine, and from having "Jewish" in their name. Patterson promptly threatened to resign and risked a court-martial by protesting Derby's decision as a disgrace. Derby backed down and

Colonel John Patterson alongside the first of the man-eating lions that he killed

Part of Colonel Patterson's Jewish Legion

The notorious man-eaters of Tsavo, now on display at the Field Museum in Chicago

Patterson's Jewish Legion was successfully formed. During training, Patterson again threatened the War Office with his resignation if his men (many of whom were Orthodox) were not allowed to observe Shabbat, and again the army conceded. Meanwhile, Patterson brought Rabbi Avraham Yitzchak Kook to address and inspire his troops.

Patterson clashed repeatedly with antisemitic officers in the British Army. Once, when a visiting brigadier called one of his soldiers "a dirty Jew," Patterson demanded an apology, ordering his men to surround the brigadier with bayonets until he did so. The apology was produced, but Patterson was reprimanded by General Allenby. On another occasion, Patterson discovered that one of his Jewish soldiers had been sentenced to execution for sleeping at his post. Patterson circumvented the chain of authority and contacted Allenby directly in order to earn a reprieve. The reprieve came, but a notoriously antisemitic brigadier by the name of Louis Bols complained about Patterson's interference to General Shea. Shea summoned Patterson and, rather than discipline him, revealed that his children were great fans of *The Man-Eaters of Tsavo*. The Jewish Legion fought well, and Palestine was liberated from the Turks. But Patterson himself was the only British officer in World War I to receive no promotion at all – a result of his outspoken efforts on behalf of the Jewish people.

After the war, Patterson dedicated himself to assisting with the creation of a Jewish homeland. The achievements of the Jewish Legion gained sympathy for the cause, but there was much opposition from both Jews (who feared being forced to move to Israel) and non-Jews. One Jewish delegation, seeking to explore an alternate option of creat-ing a Jewish homeland in Africa, was dissuaded after reading *The Man-Eaters of Tsavo*. Meanwhile, against Patterson's strenuous efforts, Bols was appointed Military Governor of Palestine, and filled the administration with antisemites who attempted to undermine the Balfour Declaration and empowered hostile elements in the Arab world.

When World War II broke out, Patterson, now an old man, fought to create another Jewish Legion. After great effort, the Jewish Infantry Brigade was approved. Aside from fighting the Germans, members of the Brigade succeeded in smuggling many concentration camp survivors into Palestine. Many other survivors had been cruelly turned away, and Patterson protested this to President Truman, capitalizing on his earlier relationship with Roosevelt that had been formed via his lion-hunting activities. This contributed to Truman's support for a Jewish homeland.

Patterson spent most of his later years actively campaigning for a Jewish homeland and against the British Mandate's actions toward the Jews in Palestine. Tragically, he passed away a month before the State of Israel was created. The newly formed country would not have won the War of Independence without trained soldiers – and the soldiers were trained by veterans of Patterson's Jewish Legion and Jewish Infantry Brigade. Colonel John Patterson had ensured the survival of the Jewish homeland.

Alas, Patterson has been all but forgotten. The two lions were mounted and are still on display at the Field Museum in Chicago. But his legacy lived on in another way, too. Close friends of his named their child after him, and the boy grew up to be yet another lion-hearted hero of Israel. His name was Yonatan Netanyahu. ∎

Notes

1 For an extremely extensive academic analysis of the lion in Scripture, see Michael Matthew Kaplan, *The Lion in the Hebrew Bible: A Study of a Biblical Metaphor* (Ph.D. Thesis, Brandeis University, 1981), and Brent Strawn, *What is Stronger Than a Lion? Leonine Image and Metaphor in the Hebrew Bible and the Ancient Near East* (Switzerland: Academic Press Fribourg, 2005) (henceforth, Strawn, *What is Stronger Than a Lion?*).

2 In this chapter, we will review all the sources in which the reference to the lion is significant in terms of its specific nature as a lion. There are also sources which mention a lion simply as an example of a predator; we shall not be reviewing all of those sources. Some of them are discussed in the introduction to the section on predators. A full list of sources can be found in Rabbi David Feldman, *Yalkut Kol Chai* (Jerusalem, 1997), vol. I.

3 Jeremiah 49:19; 50:44; Zechariah 11:3.

4 II Kings 17:25.

5 Isaiah 30:6.

6 Deuteronomy 33:22.

7 *Metzudat David.*

8 Rashi. There thus may be an allusion here to the Neo-Assyrian royal lion hunt; cf. Michael B. Dick, "The Neo-Assyrian Royal Lion Hunt and Yahweh's Answer to Iyov."

9 Various opinions on the matter are reviewed by Strawn, *What is Stronger Than a Lion?* pp. 28–30. See too Yehuda Feliks, *Nature and Man in the Bible*, pp. 96–97.

10 Professor Yoram Yom-Tov, personal communication, 13 May, 2008.

11 Jeremiah 5:6; 12:8; Amos 3:4; Micah 5:7.

12 Jeremiah 4:7.

13 Bruce D. Patterson, *The Lions of Tsavo* (New York: McGraw-Hill, 2004), pp. 110–111.

14 For a detailed review of traditional rabbinic views regarding the different names of the lion, see David Feldman, *Yalkut Kol Chai*, pp. 142–150. For an exhaustive study from an academic perspective, see Michael Kaplan, *The Lion in the Hebrew Bible: A Study of a Biblical Metaphor*, Part I, and Brent Strawn, *What is Stronger Than a Lion?*, Appendix I.

15 Also *Avot DeRabbi Natan* 39:2.

16 With regard to the lion aging, some (*Or HaChayim* to Numbers 23:24, and Maharzu to *Midrash Bereshit Rabba* 98:7) reference a statement of the Sages in which the lion is listed as one of the creatures that increase in strength as they age. However, in the versions of this statement found in our editions of the Talmud (Shabbat 77b, Avoda Zara 30b) only the snake, fish, and pig are listed in this category.

17 Following the textual emendation suggested by Jastrow, consistent with *Shir HaShirim Rabba* 4:19.

18 *Alufei Yisrael.* Later, we shall explore various references to the lion which mention fire.

19 Note how Samson's strength is demonstrated by his killing a *kefir* that came roaring to meet him (Judges 14:5), and Pharaoh is described as seeing himself as a *kefir* amongst the nations (Ezek. 32:2).

20 *Avot DeRabbi Natan*, Version B, Shechter ed., ch. 43.

21 Rashi and Radak ad loc. Cf. Psalms 34:11.

22 For an explanation of how this translation error arose, see Strawn, *What is Stronger Than a Lion*, pp. 311–318.

23 Ezekiel 19:2, Nahum 2:13.

24 Radak to Joel 1:6

25 Ramban to Numbers 23:24; Baal HaTurim, Numbers 24:9.

26 The verse is actually describing a plague of locusts, metaphorically comparing their destructive mouths to those of lions.

27 Jastrow, *Dictionary of the Talmud*, p. 689.

28 Radak, commentary to Judges 14:5.

29 Malbim to Proverbs 26:13.

30 Vilna Gaon to Proverbs 26:13.

31 Rashi to Job 4:10.

32 Mahari Kara to Hosea 5:14.

33 Others see the term as having the connotation of some sort of serpent or dragon, which may have even been combined with the lion in various ancient cultures. See Scott C. Jones, "Lions, Serpents, and Lion-Serpents in Job 28:8 and Beyond," *Journal of Biblical Literature* 130:4 (2011), pp. 663–686.

34 The Hebrew word is *shachutz*; cf. *shachatz* as one of the names of the lion.

35 Lamentations 4:3.

36 Genesis 49:9.

37 The term used here is *layish*, rather than the more common name of *ari*.

38 Bruce Patterson, *The Lions of Tsavo*, p. 50.

39 The Talmud expounds these verses as alluding to Benaiah's strength in Torah: "'Once, on a snowy day, he went down and slew a lion in a pit' – some say that this indicates that he broke blocks of ice and went down and bathed (in order to study Torah in purity), others say that he went through the Sifra of the School of Rav on a winter's day" (Berakhot 18b).

40 The Midrash notes that Samson was struck by the irony of an animal at the top of the food chain being itself the source of food: "'This is the offering of Aaron and his sons' (Lev. 6:13) refers to that which Scripture states, 'And he said to them, Out of the eater came food' (Judges 14:14).... When he returned from Timnath he said, I shall go and show them the downfall of the lion, as it states, 'He returned after some time to marry her...he scraped [the honey from inside the lion] onto his hands' (Judges 14:8–9), and Samson was wondering to himself: The lion eats all the animals, and now food emerges from it! So too, Aaron consumes all the offerings, and now an offering emerged from him – and which is that? 'the offering of Aaron and his sons'" (*Vayikra Rabba* 8:2).

41 Cf. *Midrash Yalkut Shimoni* I:61.

42 Cf. the Talmud's description of the fire on the altar being like "a crouching lion" (Yoma 21b), discussed later.

43 Vitus B. Dröscher, *The Friendly Beast* (London: W. H. Allen & Company, 1970), pp. 127–131.

44 Perhaps it is necessary to become a lion in order to defeat a lion: "A man is compared to the twelve constellations. At first, when he is born, he is compared to a tender lamb. Then he strengthens himself like an ox as he grows, and he becomes as twins – that is to say, complete – and an evil inclination grows within him. At first it is as weak as a crab; but afterwards, as he grows, it becomes as powerful as a lion" (*Midrash Tanchuma, Haazinu* 1)

45 Cf. *Bemidbar Rabba* 20:20: "'Behold, the people shall rise up as a lion...' (Num. 23:24) – ...When the Jewish people are sleeping, uninvolved in Torah and mitzvot, they then arise from their sleep like lions and hasten to recite *Shema*, and appoint the Holy One as king, and they become like lions, and then they depart for their worldly business affairs."

46 The Hebrew word is *shachutz*; cf. *shachatz* as one of the names of the lion.

47 Technically, the term *nesher* refers to a griffon vulture. However, since the purpose here is to refer to the king of birds, and in Europe and North

America the eagle is perceived as the king of birds, we are adopting the term eagle as a cultural translation.

48 Variations in *Midrash Tehillim* 103, *Midrash Shir HaShirim Rabba* 3:23, *Tanna DeVei Eliyahu Rabba* 31.

49 Perhaps this alludes to the quality of restraint that is necessary in a king and is the ultimate demonstration of power (as per the earlier discussion of the positive power of the lion). See Amichai Nachshon, "The King of Beasts and the King of Trees in Scripture – The Words of Sages and their Riddles" (Hebrew), *Oreshet* 1 (5770), pp. 103–111.

50 Thus *Targum Onkelos*: "Dominion shall be in the beginning, and in the end the kingdom shall be increased from the house of Judah, because from the judgment of death, my son, you have withdrawn. He shall rest, and abide in strength as a lion, and as a lioness; there shall be no king that may cut him off."

51 *Midrash Bemidbar Rabba* 2:7.

52 The Midrash later in the same section, following the premise that lying down is a superior state to crouching, states that it refers to the Messianic Era or to times of successful military conquest.

53 Rashi, commentary ad loc., referencing II Samuel 5:2.

54 *Midrash Aggadat Shmuel* 20.

55 We also find the following midrash: "David said…Judah is 'a lion cub,' and I am 'as the heart of a lion' (II Sam. 17:10) (*Yalkut Shimoni, Devarim* 6:845).

56 II Kings 23:31–34.

57 Rashi, Radak, *Metzudot* ad loc., and Ibn Ezra to Daniel 1:1.

58 Abarbanel, Rabbi Eliezer of Beaugency.

59 *Metzudot* explains it as referring to the royal house of Josiah (Yoshiyahu), the immediate ancestor of these kings, while the Midrash sees it as referring to the larger line of Davidic kingship. Radak explains that the "lioness" alludes to the Jewish people as a whole.

60 See the introduction to Predators.

61 For discussion regarding the nature of the mauling described by the Mishna, see the section "Legal Aspects of Predators" in the introduction to Predators.

62 The Talmud, Chullin 53a, discusses further scenarios of mauling by lions.

63 Shabbat 119b.

64 Bava Metzia 90b.

65 *Pesikta DeRav Kahana* 32 has a similar account, except that the lion is a picture drawn on the ox's trough rather than an actual lion tied to it.

66 Also *Midrash Bereshit Rabba, Vayigash* 44:18.

67 Also *Midrash Tanchuma, Vayigash* 8.

68 *Midrash Bereshit Rabba* 93:7.

69 Sifrei, *Vezot HaBerakha* 14; *Lekach Tov, Vezot HaBerakha*.

70 Ibn Ezra and Rabbeinu Bachya ad loc.

71 *Bekhor Shor* and *Daat Zekeinim* ad loc.

72 *Etz Yosef* ad loc.

73 "Stress itself is a mechanism that protects animals from extreme pain. For example, when certain antelopes are attacked by big cats, their nervous systems automatically shift into a state of stress, manifesting physiological changes such as increased adrenal activity and other metabolic changes, increased heartbeat, and several other phenomena that usually help normal, healthy animals deal better with a dangerous situation…. But if the animal is eventually cornered by the big cat, and it becomes obvious that there is no escape, it will slip into a state of shock. This is the nervous system's response to a hopeless situation, and it virtually reverses all of the 'keyed-up' aspects of stress. Shock is a state of collapse. Blood flow is severely reduced. The physiological responses become anesthetized, and the animal reacts as if it had been drugged…. This shock mechanism protects prey animals from the extreme pain of being pulled down and killed by a predator…. The predation of many wild animals isn't really as tortuous or cruel as it appears." Bill Clark, *High Hills and Wild Goats* (Boston: Little, Brown and Company, 1990), pp. 60–61.

74 *Midrash Yalkut Shimoni* 2:1046 has a dramatic account of the throne statues being mechanized.

75 *Targum Yonatan*, as per Ezekiel 43:16.

76 For example, Responsa Radvaz 4:107. For further sources, see Yitzchak Zev Kahana, "*Umanut Beit HaKnesset BeSifrut HaHalakha*," in *Mechkarim BeSifrut HaTeshuvot* (Jerusalem: Mossad HaRav Kook, 1972), pp. 354–360.

77 For a historical survey, see Ilia Rodov, "Papal Lions on the Torah Ark: A Heraldic Symbol Converted," *Materia Giudaica* 17–18 (2012–2013), pp. 215–227.

78 George B. Schaller, *The Serengeti Lion: A Study of Predator-Prey Relations* (Chicago: University of Chicago Press, 1972), pp. 103–106. (Henceforth, Schaller, *The Serengeti Lion*.)

79 These include נוער, נתן קול, המם, יהגה, שאג. It is, however, possible that some of these terms may refer to the other vocalizations. See Strawn, *What is Stronger Than a Lion?*, pp. 34–35. The Talmud also uses the term נוהם.

80 Schaller, *The Serengeti Lion*, pp. 105–110; Bruce Patterson, *The Lions of Tsavo*, pp. 134–6.

81 The same explanation might be advanced for a verse in which a sentry is described as calling like a lion, though the precise significance of the lion in this context is unclear: "And he called, like a lion: I stand continually upon my Lord's lookout in the daytime, and I stand on guard at my watch every night" (Is. 21:8). See the commentaries of Radak and *Metzudot* ad loc.

82 Following the interpretation of Radak ad loc.

83 See Jeremiah 19:19, 50:44.

84 John Patterson, *The Man-Eaters of Tsavo* (London: Macmillan, 1908), p. 67.

85 James Sutherland, *The Adventures of an Elephant Hunter* (London: Macmillan, 1912), p. 69.

86 *Midrash Devarim Rabba* 8:6 elaborates as to how these are excuses presented by a lazy person who does not want to go to learn Torah from his rabbi. Ralbag, Ibn Ezra, and *Metzudot*, on the other hand, explain the verses as referring to a person who is seeking excuses to avoid working for a living.

87 Gittin 73a.

88 Makkot 11a.

89 Nidda 67b.

90 *Midrash Bemidbar Rabba* 18:22.

91 Eiruvin 78b, Shavuot 22b.

92 Bava Metzia 12a, 90b.

93 Bava Kama 114a.

94 Nedarim 33a, Bava Kama 58a, Bava Batra 53a.

95 Berakhot 33a, Yevamot 121a.

96 Me'iri, commentary ad loc.

97 Sanhedrin 77a.

98 Rabbi Meir Abulafia, *Yad Rama* ad loc., consistent with the previously discussed ruling. Other views are those of Rashi, who explains that the victim is doomed if in the presence of a lion even if he is not tied up, and Me'iri, who explains that the Talmud is referring to the case of a tame lion that was not expected to kill.

99 The Midrash (*Bereshit Rabba* 34:12) states that a lion flees from even a one-day-old baby. *Etz Yosef* objects that lions and snakes will even attack

adults! He suggests that it is a textual error, and that it is only supposed to refer to martens and mice, as in the version that appears in the Talmud (Shabbat 151b). *Matnot Kehuna* says that the Midrash is referring to a person who does the will of God, and that a lion will flee from such a person; however, this is difficult, since the Midrash is referring to a baby.

100 Regarding the Talmud drawing a difference between one person and two people, see *Ben Yehoyada*, Riaf in *Ein Yaakov*, and *Sefat Emet* ad loc.

101 See Bava Metzia 41a and 106a for further discussion.

102 The Talmud continues: "When Rav Safra's turn came, he handed over a donkey but it did not eat it. Rav Safra quickly performed an act of (re)acquisition with it. Rav Acha of Difti said to Ravina: Why was it necessary for him to acquire it? Surely when he abandoned it, it was only with regard to the lion; he did not abandon it vis-à-vis everyone else! Ravina replied: Rav Safra only did this as an added precaution."

103 See Rashi and *Tosafot* ad loc.

104 Bava Kama 16b. See too Chullin 53a, which discusses a lion that enters a herd of oxen without attacking them, and Rashi's explanation that it is referring to a trained lion. See also Avoda Zara 16b.

105 Pesachim 112b. Rashbam (commentary ad loc.) suggests that this call is either to chase it away or to induce it to follow instructions. In light of it appearing in between the ox and camel, the latter seems to be the more likely meaning.

106 Sanhedrin 15b. See *Tosafot* ad loc. s.v. *veRabbi Yochanan*.

107 Several further fables that feature lions are mentioned in the chapter on the fox and jackal.

108 Possibly an ibis. This story is also one of Aesop's fables, where the bird is a stork.

109 Cf. Daniel 6:23.

110 For an academic study of the symbolism of the animals in rabbinic thought, see Rivka Raviv, "Shaping the Four Kingdoms in Daniel in the Rabbinical Literature," *Jewish Studies Internet Journal* 5 (2006), pp. 1–20 (Hebrew).

111 Rashi ad loc.

112 The Midrash continues: "Another view: 'He is a bear lying in wait for me' – this refers to Vespasian; 'A lion in hiding' – this refers to Tarquinius."

113 See above, section "In Throne, Temple, Synagogue, and Scroll."

114 *Midrash Tehillim* 64.

115 Similarly in *Midrash Tehillim* 64, but regarding an angel sent in the form of a lion to save Daniel.

116 *Etz Yosef* ad loc.

117 *Yossipon* iii 8b.

118 Lions are notorious for their bad breath, a fact also commented upon by the Roman naturalist Pliny the Elder.

119 *Midrash Tehillim* 64.

120 *Bereshit Rabbati* (Albeck ed.), *Vaychi* 49:9.

121 The Midrash proceeds to correlate aspects of Yaakov's lion-blessing for Judah with the events of Daniel in the lion's den.

122 A mild account is found in the following midrash: "These twenty years that I have been with you ... I never brought you anything mangled, I myself would bear the loss (*anokhi achatena*), from me you would exact it" (Gen. 31:38–39). I would sin (*chotei*) against the lion; for the Holy One decreed upon the lion to prey and eat from Laban's flocks every day (yet I saved them in my merit), and should you suggest that another shepherd might have saved them, it teaches, "...Like the lion and the young lion roaring on his prey, when a multitude of shepherds is called forth against him, he will not be afraid of their voice, nor abase himself for the noise of them" (Is. 31:4)' (*Genesis Rabba* 74:11).

123 See Berakhot 60b, where R. Akiva's donkey is eaten by a lion.

124 Ralbag to 13:24, Malbim to 13:25, Radak to 13:28. The Sages explain that it demonstrated divine compassion: "If at a time of anger the righteous God has compassion on them [in that the lion didn't eat the ass], how much more so at a time of compassion" (Tosefta, Berakhot 4:15).

125 Kiddushin 75b.

126 Ibn Ezra and Radak.

127 *Midrash Aseret HaDibrot, Dibbur Shevi'i*. Printed in *Midrashim VeAggadot* (Warsaw, 1924), pp. 36–38.

128 Also Y. Pe'ah 17b.

129 Schaller, *The Serengeti Lion*, p. 270.

130 With regard to the implications of this passage regarding the propriety of solving the economic problems through wars of conquest, see Moshe Simon-Shoshan, "*Ein Yaakov* – The World of Talmudic Aggada," Lecture 9: Daf 3b–4a, at http://vbm-torah.org/archive/taggada/09taggada.htm.

131 Ibn Ezra and *Metzudot* ad loc. Cf. Ezekiel 38:13 and Rashi ad loc.

132 Rabbeinu Bachya ibn Pekuda, *Chovot HaLevavot, Shaar HaBitachon*, introduction, also cited by Rabbeinu Bachya ben Asher, *Kad HaKemach, Shaar HaBitachon*.

133 See Ezekiel 19:3.

134 Me'iri, Radak, and Malbim ad loc.

135 Cf. Rabbi Yehuda HaLevi, *The Kuzari* 3:11: "I see that the wise and just Manager of the world equipped the lion with the means for hunting, with ferocity, strength, teeth and claws.... Can I say anything but that this is the fruit of a wisdom which I am unable to grasp, and that I must submit to Him who is called 'The Rock whose doing is perfect' (Deut. 2:4)?"

136 In the Talmud, a story is related where lions are directly given their food by God: "R. Shimon b. Chalafta was walking along the road. He encountered some lions, that began roaring at him. He said, 'The young lions roar for their prey, and to seek their food from God' (Ps. 104:21). Two pieces of meat descended from Heaven, and they ate one of them" (Sanhedrin 59b).

137 Schaller, *The Serengeti Lion*, p. 242.

138 The same phrase is used in Bava Metzia 101b and Bava Batra 168a to describe a person who is not trusted.

139 Scott R. Loarie, Craig J. Tambling and Gregory P. Asner, "Lion hunting behaviour and vegetation structure in an African savanna," *Animal Behaviour* 85:5 (May 2013), pp. 899–906.

140 Contrast the view of Rashi and *Tosafot*, who write that lions normally consume their prey while it is still alive. It should be noted that lions were largely extinct from Europe in the medieval period.

141 Bruce Patterson, *The Lions of Tsavo*, pp. 49–50; Schaller, *The Serengeti Lion*, pp. 263–7.

142 Patterson, ibid., p. 51; Schaller, ibid. p. 267.

143 Schaller, ibid., p. 269.

144 See the commentaries of Rif and Rosh to Bava Kama 16v.

145 Several commentators ask that surely the reason for the exemption of *shen* in a public domain does not apply to a pet lion mauling someone's cow. It may well be the normal way of a lion to do that – but it is precisely for this reason that one should not be letting it roam in the public domain in the first place! *Pnei Yehoshua* concludes that the exemption for *shen* is a scriptural decree with no known reason. *Yam Shel Shlomo*, however, says that the reason for *shen* is as stated, but since it is highly unusual for people to keep pet lions anyway, the Torah was not concerned to remove the rule in these exceptional cases. It should be noted, however, that even though there is no liability for the lion's damage, one would still have to pay for the benefit received (i.e. for having one's lion fed), and one would transgress the prohibition against keeping a dangerous pet (see Bava Kama 15b discussing the prohibition against keeping a dangerous dog, and *Yam Shel Shlomo* ad loc.)

146 The Talmud proceeds to raise further questions: "But surely it was taught in a *baraita* that if a wild beast entered a courtyard and tore an animal and ate it, it pays full damages? – That is talking about where it tore it and set it aside [which is thus normal]. But surely it states that it ate it? – It is talking about when it changed its mind and ate it. But how could we know that it originally intended otherwise? And furthermore, perhaps this could also be the case with the situation ruled upon by Shmuel? – Rav Nachman bar Yitzchak said: The *baraita* was speaking about alternate scenarios – that if it tore an animal and set it aside, *or* it trampled it and ate it, the owner pays full damages. Ravina said: Shmuel's ruling was referring to the case of a trained lion, and following the view of R. Eleazar, that it is not considered normal for the lion to do this. But if so, then even if it trampled, he should be liable! – Rather, Ravina was referring to the *baraita*, that it was speaking in the case of a trained lion, and following the view of R. Eleazar, that it is not considered normal for the lion to do this."

147 Rashi and *Tosafot*.

148 Rabbeinu Chananel explains that "trampling" refers to an act of killing that involves only the claws, and which is done when the lion wants to eat, whereas "tearing" refers to an unusual form of attack in which the lion uses only its teeth. But this, too, is difficult to reconcile with observed behavior of lions.

149 See Rashi, *Yad Rama* (two suggestions), Maharsha, and *Arukh LaNer* ad loc.

150 This also appears with slight variations in *Midrash Bereshit Rabba* 32:8.

151 Rashi, Maharsha.

152 *Yad Rama*.

153 This refers to the mechanized lion statues on Solomon's throne. A more elaborate account of this incident appears in *Midrash Yalkut Shimoni* 1:1046.

154 *Etz Yosef*.

155 Rabbi David Feldman in *Yalkut Kol Chai*; *Likkutei Yehuda* cites similarly from *Imrei Emet*. *Torat Chayim* to Sanhedrin 108b suggests that because (as mentioned earlier) the lion caught a fever and temporarily did not require food, Noah was late in his assessment of the date that it required feeding again.

156 Cf. Chanoch Zundel Luria, *Knaf Renanim al Perek Shira, Dov*, discussed in the chapter on the bear, in the section Elisha and the Bears.

157 *Shulchan Arukh, Orach Chayim* 1:1.

158 Henry G. Fischer, "More Ancient Egyptian Names of Dogs and Other Animals," *Metropolitan Museum Journal*, Vol. 12 (1977), pp. 173–178.

159 This appears to refer to the rhinoceros. See *Sacred Monsters*, Chapter One: Unicorns of Different Colors.

160 Avraham Even-Shoshan, *The Even-Shoshan Dictionary*.

161 See R. G. Burton, *The Tiger Hunters* (London: Hutchinson, 1936), p. 189.

162 For an extensive survey of approaches, see the introduction to *Sacred Monsters* by this author.

163 For example, Maharsha and Vilna Gaon, in their commentaries to the stories of Rabba bar bar Chana.

164 Rabbi Yeshayah of Trani II (Riaz), Introduction to *Perek Chelek* of *Sanhedrin*.

165 Rambam, commentary to the Mishna, Introduction to *Perek Chelek* of *Masekhet Sanhedrin*.

166 Maharal, *Be'er HaGola*.

167 Rabbi Yosef Chayim, *Ben Yehoyada* ad loc.

168 See, for example, the title page of *Mechir Yayin* by Rabbi Moshe Isserles.

169 Maharal, *Chiddushei Aggadot* ad loc.

170 Rabbi Chaim Hirschenson, *Motza'ei Mayim* (Budapest, 1924), pp. 96–100.

171 Or: the fear of the mongoose is upon the crocodile. See Rabbi Benzion (Benedetto) Raphael Kohen Frizzi, *Petach Einayim* (Livorno, 1815), vol. II, pp. 28a–b.

172 Rashi and Rabbeinu Chananel ad loc. Such a creature is also described by the sixteenth-century Italian naturalist Ulisse Aldrovandi, as cited by Rabbi Benzion (Benedetto) Raphael Kohen Frizzi, *Petach Einayim*, vol. II, p. 27b.

173 Ritva, as cited by Rabbi Yehuda Kook, *Nofet Tzufim* to Shabbat 77b.

174 Yosef Schonhak, *Toledot HaAretz*, p. 309 footnote 205, citing Bochart; F. S. Bodenheimer, *Animals and Man in Bible Lands*, p. 42.

175 Bochart, *Hierozoicon*, 1663 ed., vol. II, col. 566–7 and 792 (vol. III, pp. 769–770 in 1796 Rosenmueller ed.). Also cited by Lewysohn, *Die Zoologie des Talmuds*, p. 316.

176 Rabbi Benzion (Benedetto) Raphael Kohen Frizzi, *Petach Einayim*, vol. II, p. 27b, suggests that the *mafgia* is any person who encounters (*poge'a*) a lion; lions are afraid of people, who often succeed in scaring them away with only light weapons. This creative suggestion does, however, seem unlikely; there would be simpler ways for the Talmud to refer to a human being. Rabbi Yosef Chayim of Baghdad, better known as the Ben Ish Chai, in *Ben Yehoyada* to Shabbat 77b, states that it is a creature with dozens of small sharp claws that leaps onto the lion and punctures its brain. While there is no known creature matching this description, he gives it the Arabic name for a porcupine.

177 http://blog.londolozi.com/2014/10/a-prickly-encounter-lions-vs-porcupine.

178 Rabbi Yehuda Kook, *Nofet Tzufim* to Shabbat 77b. He leaves the question unresolved.

179 *Tosafot* to Shabbat 55b.

180 See too Rabbi Yonatan Eybeschitz, *Kreiti, Yoreh De'ah* 83:3; Rabbi Yaakov Tzvi Mecklenburg, *HaKetav VeHaKabbala* to Leviticus 11:9. See also Ritva to Nidda 24a; *Tosafot* to Nidda 10b s.v. *dehavya*; *Tosafot* to Nidda 26b s.v. *yalda*; Rashba to Menachot 6b; *Yam Shel Shlomo, Chullin, Eilu Tereifot* 80; Ramban, *Hasagot* to *Sefer HaMitzvot, Shoresh* 1; Rabbi Shlomo Schick, *Torah Sheleima* (1909) vol. I *Vayishlach* 32:16.

181 "You are a mighty man of valor, with the heart of a lion" – Rashi ad loc.

182 *Nachalat Yaakov* ad loc.

183 Yoma 78a, Chagiga 14a, Avoda Zara 31b, Bava Metzia 84b; Kiddushin 48b (*ari shebechabura*, "the lion of our company"); Y. Shevi'it 26a, Shabbat 12a. Some of these are discussed in the chapter on jackals.

184 Denis Brian, *The Seven Lives of Colonel Patterson: How an Irish Lion Hunter Led the Jewish Legion to Victory* (Syracuse University Press, 2008).

185 John Patterson, *The Man-Eaters of Tsavo* (London: Macmillan and Co., 1907).

186 John Patterson, *With the Zionists in Gallipoli* (London: Hutchinson, 1916).

187 John Patterson, *With the Judaeans in the Palestine Campaign* (London: Hutchinson, 1922).

BEAR

Bear

דב

Dov

The Biblical Bear

NATURAL HISTORY

There are several different species of bears in the world, including polar bears, brown bears, black bears, spectacled bears, and sloth bears. The bear of Scripture, mentioned on thirteen occasions, is a subspecies of the brown bear. It is known as the Syrian brown bear, *Ursus arctos syriacus*. This is the smallest of the many subspecies of brown bear, and is distinguished by the pale, sandy coloration of its fur.

Today, the Syrian brown bear is found in several areas of the former Soviet Union, Iran, Iraq, and Turkey. But before modern firearms facilitated the hunting of bears, they were more widespread. In former times, the Syrian brown bear also lived in Egypt (in the Sinai Peninsula), Syria and Lebanon (until at least the 1990s), and the Land of Israel.

In 1863, Henry Tristram, the chronicler of the natural history of Palestine, recorded that he saw a bear in the Arbel wadi, near the Sea of Galilee.[1] He also relates reports that bears were very common at that time in the vicinity of Mount Hermon. In 1916, a bear was sighted in Kefar Giladi, which is near Kiryat Shemona.[2] The last bear in what would be the modern State of Israel was shot in the Druze village of Majdal Shams in the Golan Heights in 1917.[3] Due to the dense human population of Israel, bears cannot be reintroduced to the wild.

The Syrian brown bear

YORY FRENKLAKH / SHUTTERSTOCK

108

Beware the Bereft Bear

SYMBOLISM

Today, we generally perceive bears in the safety of zoos, or in various popular cultural incarnations as objects of entertainment. But bears are extremely powerful and dangerous animals, which can and do kill people. During the Holocaust, Jewish prisoners in the Buchenwald concentration camp were thrown to bears at the local zoo.[4] Further back in history, when bears were more widespread, they presented a very real danger to anyone in the countryside.

Virtually all references to bears in Scripture present them in the role of dangerous predators. This is also implicit in the messianic description of predators and prey living in harmony, in which the bear is described as coexisting with cattle:

> The wolf shall live with the lamb, and the leopard shall lie down with the kid; and the calf and the young lion and the fatling together; and a small child shall lead them. And the cow and the bear shall graze; their young ones shall lie down together, and the lion shall eat straw like the ox. (Is. 11:6–7)

There is a dispute in rabbinic tradition as to whether these prophecies are to be interpreted literally or allegorically;[5] but, either way, these verses describe each predator as living in peace with an animal that is normally its prey. The bear is matched with the cow, largest of domestic animals.[6] This demonstrates the great power and danger presented by the bear; in the wild, bears sometimes kill even moose and bison.[7]

In fact, bears are mentioned three times in Scripture as examples of the most dangerous of all opponents. But the description in all these three cases is of bears in a very specific circumstance:

> It is better to meet a mother bear bereft of her cubs than a fool in his madness. (Prov. 17:12)[8]

> And now they sin more and more...I am the Lord your God...I will meet them like a bear bereft of her cubs, and I will tear open their closed hearts. (Hos. 13:2–8)

> And Ahithophel said to Absalom, Let me now choose out twelve thousand men, and I will arise and pursue after David this night; and I will come upon him while he is tired and weak.... And Hushai said to Absalom, Ahithophel's counsel is not good at this time, for you know your father and his men, that they are mighty men, and they are embittered in their minds, as a bear bereft of her cubs in the field; and your father is a man of war, and will not spend the night with the people. (II Sam. 17:1–8)

וּפָרָה וָדֹב תִּרְעֶינָה יַחְדָּו יִרְבְּצוּ יַלְדֵיהֶן וְאַרְיֵה כַּבָּקָר יֹאכַל תֶּבֶן:

ישעיה יא:ז

פָּגוֹשׁ דֹּב שַׁכּוּל בְּאִישׁ וְאַל כְּסִיל בְּאִוַּלְתּוֹ:

משלי יז:יב

אֶפְגְּשֵׁם כְּדֹב שַׁכּוּל וְאֶקְרַע סְגוֹר לִבָּם וְאֹכְלֵם שָׁם כְּלָבִיא חַיַּת הַשָּׂדֶה תְּבַקְּעֵם:

הושע יג:ח

וַיֹּאמֶר חוּשַׁי אַתָּה יָדַעְתָּ אֶת אָבִיךָ וְאֶת אֲנָשָׁיו כִּי גִבֹּרִים הֵמָּה וּמָרֵי נֶפֶשׁ הֵמָּה כְּדֹב שַׁכּוּל בַּשָּׂדֶה וְאָבִיךָ אִישׁ מִלְחָמָה וְלֹא יָלִין אֶת הָעָם:

שמואל ב יז:ח

A mother bear with her playful cubs

GIEDRIIUS / SHUTTERSTOCK

The phrase used in all these cases is *dov shakul*, and the word *shakul* is based on a root meaning destroy or consume. Some are of the view that the conjugation here refers to the bear destroying others – "an attacking bear."[9] But most interpret it as referring to the bear having been destroyed itself, in that its cubs have been killed – "a bereft bear."[10] But why is it specifically bears, rather than any other animal, that the mother is singled out as so dangerous when her young are taken from her? Why does Scripture not speak of lions or leopards? The answer relates to a peculiar aspect of bears.

As noted above, bears are huge animals. Yet their young are tiny. Bear cubs are smaller in proportion to the size of the mother than is the case with any other placental mammal. Even the largest brown bears, which may weigh 1500 pounds, weigh only about half a pound at birth, less than one per cent of their mother's weight. This means that the mother bear has to invest enormous effort into raising and weaning her cubs.[11] Producing and raising cubs can result in a forty percent total body weight loss for mother during hibernation. Bears in the tropics do not hibernate, but their cubs are highly dependent on their mothers, and the mothers stay in the den with their nursing cubs, fasting for several weeks or months. The cubs will then normally stay with the mother for the first two and a half years.

Because the mother bear has to give so much to her young, they are very important to her and she forges an especially powerful bond with them. That is why she becomes so aggressive when her young are taken away from her. Cubs would have been captured by people in order to train them for entertainment purposes, and the mother bear would react with overwhelming rage.

The word for "love" in Hebrew is *ahava*, which some homiletically relate to the Aramaic word *hav*, "give." While many think that we give to someone because we love them, the opposite can also be true; that the more we give to someone, the more we come to love them. The tremendous anger of the mother bear relates to her unparalleled investment in her young.[12]

The devotion of the mother bear for her cubs may shed light on a statement in the Midrash. When Abraham attempted to dissuade God from destroying Sodom, he argued that righteous people would also end up being killed if destruction was unleashed upon the city. The Midrash compares such unwanted results to a bear whose anger does not find the correct target:

> R. Levi said: [It is comparable] to a bear that was raging against an animal, and could not find the animal to rage against, and raged against her cubs. (*Bereshit Rabba* 49:8)

Such a thing would never happen, since a bear's protective urges toward her children are so powerful.[13] But perhaps this is the very point – that just as it is absurd to suppose that a bear, raging against a threat, would take out its anger upon its young, so too Abraham was arguing that it makes no sense for God, raging at the sin in Sodom, to take out His anger upon those who are innocent of sin.

The raging anger of the bear may also account for a talmudic reference. The Talmud states that the united prayers of R. Chiyya and his sons were so powerful that Elijah sought to prevent them from taking place, lest they cause the Messiah to arrive before the appropriate time. Elijah is described as having accomplished this as follows:

> He appeared to them as a fiery bear, went amongst them and distracted them. (Bava Metzia 85b)

Why did he appear as a bear? Perhaps because the bear is the epitome of a creature that rages around, causing people to panic and scatter.[14]

A brown bear roaring in rage

וַיִּפֶן אַחֲרָיו וַיִּרְאֵם וַיְקַלְלֵם בְּשֵׁם יְהֹוָה וַתֵּצֶאנָה שְׁתַּיִם דֻּבִּים מִן
הַיַּעַר וַתְּבַקַּעְנָה מֵהֶם אַרְבָּעִים וּשְׁנֵי יְלָדִים:

מלכים ב ב:כד

דֹּב אֹרֵב הוּא לִי אֲרִי בְּמִסְתָּרִים:

איכה ג:י

Elisha and the Bears

———————————————— SYMBOLISM

The prophet Elisha, a disciple of Elijah, lived in the Kingdom of Israel at the time of the First Temple. He once found himself in the city of Jericho, where the waters were bitter, and he miraculously caused them to become sweet. But after this wonderful event, an unfortunate incident took place:

> He went up from there to Bet-El; and as he was going up on the way, small boys came out of the city and jeered at him, and said to him, "Get up, baldy, get up, baldy!" He turned around and looked at them, and he cursed them in the name of God. And two she-bears came out of the forest and tore up forty-two of the children. (II Kings 2:23–24)

Why was it specifically bears that appeared as result of Elisha's curse? The question is especially significant in light of the fact that in the other three instances in the Book of Kings where predators are used as agents of retribution, it is lions that appear.[15] Why here was it bears?

Perhaps the answer relates to the character traits of the bear. Scripture highlights these bears as being female.[16] Presumably, this relates to other scriptural references to mother bears, bereft of their young, as being the most dangerous animals – killing not in order to eat, but out of rage and bitterness of spirit.

This in turn could connect to the story in two possible ways. One is that it might correspond to the trait exhibited by the youths. The Talmud states that they were from families that had formerly earned money by bringing sweet water from elsewhere to the city of Jericho.[17] Now that Elisha, in sweetening the well, had rendered their work redundant, they lashed out at him in fury. When they misused the trait of anger, they were punished by way of its animal manifestation.[18]

Alternately, the bitter anger of the bears may reflect Elisha's own bitter anger. He was bereft of his teacher, Elijah, who had died not long earlier. And he was being mocked by the youths as being a poor successor for Elijah (who is described as having much hair;[19] taunting Elisha for being bald was thus a way of saying that he is no equal to his teacher). This caused Elisha to have a bear-like bitter anger: "They are embittered in their minds, as a bereft bear bereft of her cubs" (II Sam. 17:8). Elisha was embittered in his mind, and his unfortunate[20] curse was therefore manifest in the bitter rage of bears bereft of their cubs.[21]

The Bears and the Woods

———————————————— THEOLOGY, PHILOSOPHY, AND SCIENCE

The bears that appeared as result of Elisha's curse are the subject of a fascinating discussion in the Talmud:

> "And two she-bears came out of the forest and tore up forty-two of the children" (II Kings 2:24). There was a dispute between Rav and Shmuel; one said that this was a miracle, and the other said that it was a miracle within a miracle. The one who said that it was a miracle is of the opinion that there was [already] a forest, but there were not any bears. The one who said that it was a miracle within a miracle is of the opinion that there was [previously] neither forest nor bears.[22] But let there be bears without a forest? Because they would be afraid. (Sota 46b–47a)

Some explain the last part to mean that the bears would be afraid to attack without a forest to which they can retreat; accordingly it was necessary to create a forest along with the bears.[23] Others, however, question whether fear would impede bears that were supernaturally summoned, and therefore conclude that the Talmud is referring to the children; had there not been a forest, the children would have seen the bears from afar and would have been afraid to approach.[24]

The obvious question is that, whether the reference is to the bears or the children being afraid, let there simply be a miracle of their not being afraid. The answer given by some is that there is generally a trend of minimizing the miraculous.[25] But it is interesting that creating an entire forest is seen as less of a miracle than creating bears or children that are not afraid under circumstances where they ordinarily would be afraid. According to these views, it is less of a miracle to create something than to change a character trait.

Daniel's Bear

———————————————— SYMBOLISM

One scriptural reference to a bear refers to its mode of attack:

> "[God] is to me like a bear lying in ambush." (Lam. 3:10)

As we shall see later, bear attacks do not generally happen due to the bear deliberately waiting to attack people; instead, when a person stumbles across a bear at rest, the bear feels threatened and seeks to neutralize the threat. This may convey the perception that the bear has been deliberately lying in wait for the person to walk by. But bears sometimes actually do attack via ambush; grizzly bears have been seen lying in ambush on the edges of forests near meadows, waiting for herds of elk or caribou to enter.[26] There are thus two ways in which bears can be described as lying in

> *"And behold another beast, a second, like a bear, and it raised itself up on one side, and it had three ribs in its mouth between its teeth"*
>
> (Dan. 7:5)

וַאֲרוּ חֵיוָה אָחֳרִי תִנְיָנָה דָּמְיָה לְדֹב וְלִשְׂטַר חַד הֳקִמַת וּתְלָת עִלְעִין בְּפֻמַּהּ בֵּין שִׁנַּיהּ וְכֵן אָמְרִין לַהּ קוּמִי אֲכֻלִי בְּשַׂר שַׂגִּיא:

דניאל ז:ה

wait for their victims, which the verse invokes to represent God's harsh treatment of the Jewish people at the time of the destruction of the First Temple. But the Midrash on this verse sees it as alluding to a later era in history:

> "[God] is to me like a bear lying in ambush..." – This refers to the kingdom of Persia. (*Midrash Lekach Tov*)

Why does the Midrash see a reference to the bear as alluding to Persia? For the answer, we have to look elsewhere in Scripture. The prophet Daniel had a dream in which he saw several beasts, one of which was a bear:

> Daniel spoke, and said, "I saw in my vision by night... four great beasts.... The first was like a lion.... And behold another beast, a second, like a bear, and it raised itself up on one side, and it had three ribs in its mouth between its teeth; and it was told, Arise, devour much flesh." (Dan. 7:2–5)

In Daniel's vision, the four beasts represented four empires under which the Jews were subjects.[27] The lion represented the Babylonian empire of Nebuchadnezzar. After the Babylonians had destroyed the Temple and dispersed the Jews, they were themselves conquered by the combined armies of King Darius of Media and King Cyrus of Persia. In Daniel's prophecy, the Medo-Persian kingdom is represented by the bear,[28] for a variety of reasons. Let us analyze each aspect of Daniel's description:

"…It raised itself up on one side…"

According to Rashi, the description of the bear raising itself up on one side, indicating an imbalance, alludes to an inequality in the succession of power. The second empire was a coalition; the Medes and the Persians were united into one empire. Historically, the Medes initially formed the kingdom. Cyrus, a Persian, was a dependent vassal king under the Median King Astyages. But Cyrus overcame Astyages, defeated resistance within the Median empire, and within a few years was able to reign over all of it. The verse is describing this shift in the balance of power, with Persia's portion eventually becoming more dominant and powerful than the Median portion.[29]

Perhaps we can read an allusion in the bear's method of locomotion to this shifting in the balance of powers. The most common method of locomotion with four-legged creatures is that which is sometimes called the diagonal walk, used by most hoofed animals as well as cats and dogs. In this walk, the animal uses diagonally opposing legs, i.e. the front left and right hind legs move forwards, then the front right and left hind legs, and so on. But a few animals, such as giraffes, camels, and brown bears, first move both legs on one side, and then both legs on the other side. In some cases the hind leg starts first, so there is a slight lag. This is also called "pacing." The line of support is farther from the center of mass than with the diagonal walk, and pacing animals consequently sway from side to side as they move. The bear, with its movement that sways it from side to side, alludes to the shifting balances of power within the Persia-Median empire.[30]

"…it had three ribs in its mouth between its teeth…"

One opinion is that these three ribs refer to three areas that wavered in and out of Persia's control; hence the ribs were between its teeth, i.e. only partly in its mouth.

> "And three ribs in its mouth between its teeth" – R. Yochanan said, This refers to Holvan, Adiabena, and Netzivin, which it sometimes absorbed and sometimes excluded. (Kiddushin 72a)

Alternatively, it may refer to the three major conquests of Persia: Lydia, Babylon, and Egypt. Another explanation is that the three ribs refer to three kings that arose in the Persian Empire: Cyrus, Ahasuerus, and Darius.[31]

"…and it was told, Arise, devour much flesh…"

According to Rav Saadia Gaon, this phrase alludes to the great material wealth of the Persian empire, as demonstrated by Ahasuerus' spectacular feast.[32]

The Persian Bear in the Talmud

SYMBOLISM

In the Talmud, various Sages offer "keys" to the Purim Megilla, single verses from elsewhere in the Torah which express the essence of the entire episode according to each Sage's perception. One in particular is based on a verse that mentions the bear:

> The lion roars, the bear growls, the wicked man rules over a poor nation. (Prov. 28:15)

The Talmud explains this to refer to the Babylonian and Persian empires:

Resh Lakish opened up that episode [of the Purim story] based on this: "The lion roars, the bear growls, the wicked man rules over a poor nation" (Prov. 28:15). "The lion roars" refers to Nebuchadnezzar.... "The bear growls" refers to Ahasuerus.... "The wicked man rules" refers to Haman. "Over a poor people" refers to Israel, who were impoverished from mitzvot. (Megilla 11a)

As king of Persia, Ahasuerus is described as the animal which symbolizes his nation. The Talmud goes to explain the use of the bear as a metaphor for Persia, as follows:

> "And afterwards was an animal like a bear" (Dan. 7:5) – R. Yosef taught that this refers to the Persians, who eat and drink like a bear, and are clothed in flesh like a bear, and are hairy like a bear, and have no rest like a bear.[33]

We shall now analyze each of these comparisons in turn.

"…they eat and drink like a bear…"

Bears eat an enormous range of food. Brown bears feed on nuts, roots, bulbs, berries, fruit, grasses, clams, moths, grubs, ants, and other insects, fish, rodents, carrion, and animals of all sizes that they hunt.

Bears not only eat a huge range of food, but also huge quantities. This is especially true of bears that live in colder climates, which must eat enough to store huge amounts of fat needed to sustain them through up to six months of winter in their den. The bear's ability to eat large quantities of rich food and store fat without suffering from heart disease or cholesterol problems is of great interest to medical scientists. Bears living off their accumulated body fat have cholesterol levels more than twice as high as the normal cholesterol levels of most humans, yet they suffer no ill effects.

TORY KALLMAN / SHUTTERSTOCK

113

Bears have enormous appetites

The enormous appetite of the bear parallels the greed of the Persians. The feast of Ahasuerus is described as lasting for one hundred and eighty days.[34] Aside from displaying all the riches that his kingdom had consumed, there was food and wine in abundance.

"…they are clothed in flesh like a bear…"

Bears are the largest terrestrial carnivores in the world. The very largest brown bears are found on the west coast of British Columbia and Alaska, and on offshore islands along coastal Alaska, such as Kodiak and Admiralty. There, males commonly reach over 700 pounds, but on occasion can reach as much as 1800 pounds. Of all carnivores, it is the bear that represents physicality to the extreme. This, too, symbolizes the physical excesses of the Persian Empire.

"…they are hairy like a bear…"

Brown bears are covered with a heavy shaggy fur that ranges in color from black to brown to reddish brown to blond. They have dense fur close to the skin and long, coarse guard hairs. In summer they shed much of the lower layer of fur, giving them a shaggy look. R. Yosef draws an analogy to Persians, referring to their body and facial hair.

"…they have no rest, like a bear."

The home ranges of brown bears are among the largest of all land mammals. These can extend up to eight hundred square miles, encompassing diverse forests interspersed with meadows and grasslands, usually in or near mountains. Bears spend most of their time wandering around looking for food. And bears in captivity will often pace to and fro in their enclosure.[35] Some relate the Hebrew name for the bear, *dov*, to the word *davav*, which refers to motion.[36]

This constant motion is analogous to Persia. The Persians ruled over a vast empire, stretching over three continents. Governing over this enormous territory required a constant stream of messengers, and Persia was forced to create the world's first postal system. Messengers were carrying mail by day and night; relay stations were built close enough to each other so that a horse could gallop from one to another without resting or feeding, at which point the messenger would be transferred to a new horse. Thousands of miles of roads were constructed in order to facilitate the delivery of mail throughout the Persian Empire, and there was huge investment in canals, such as that joining the Tigris and Euphrates, in order to facilitate trade. Like the bear, the Persians were constantly in motion:

> When R. Ami saw a Persian riding, he would say, "There is a wandering bear!" (Kiddushin 72a)

Lions and Bears

SYMBOLISM

Of further potential relevance to the bear's Persian symbolism is its standing vis-à-vis the lion. Lions and bears were the two great carnivores in the Land of Israel. Both are

Angels and Demons

As we have seen, the bear repeatedly appears as representing Persia, beginning with the Book of Daniel and continuing throughout numerous statements in the Talmud and Midrash. It thus comes as no surprise when the Talmud states that the angel of Persia is called Dubi-el, which means "bear of God."[37]

Ingeniously, this analogy between Persians and bears has an additional layer of meaning. There was a burning issue in Iran regarding whose religion was demonic – demons were said to be the armies of the evil spirit. The Persians, who were Zoroastrians, claimed to be members of an anti-demonic religion, and recited this daily as part of their confession of faith. They claimed that Judaism, on the other hand, is demonic. In response, R. Yosef demonstrated himself to have been well versed in Zoroastrian beliefs and

Middle Persian literature. R. Yosef's statement is based on a play on words: *dov* is Hebrew for "bear," and *dêv* is Middle Persian for "demon." Demons were reputed to engage in excessive eating and drinking, to have disheveled hair, and to have no rest, since they flit from place to place.[38] Thus, R. Yosef was countering that the Persians themselves are like demons.

mentioned by David as having attacked his flocks, but the lion naturally takes first place:

> Saul said to David, You are not able to go against this Philistine to fight with him; for you are just a youth, whereas he is a man of war since he was young. And David said to Saul, Your servant shepherded his father's sheep, and there came a lion, and a bear, taking a lamb from the flock; and I went out after him, and struck him, and rescued it from his mouth; and when he arose against me, I caught him by his mane, and struck him, and slew him. Your servant slew both the lion and the bear; and this uncircumcised Philistine shall be like one of them, seeing he has defied the armies of the living God. David said, God who saved me from the paw of the lion, and from the paw of the bear, He will save me from the hand of this Philistine. And Saul said to David, Go, and God be with you. (I Sam. 17:33–37)

Perhaps this provides further insight into why the bear is explained as referring to Persia. Just as the Medo-Persian Empire followed the Babylonian Empire, so too the bear is secondary to the lion in its danger as a predator. The prophet Amos presents a similar sequence of lion and bear:

> Ah, you who desire the day of the Lord! Why would you want the day of the Lord? It is darkness, not light! It is like a man who fled from a lion, and a bear encountered him; or if he came into a house, and leaned his hand on the wall, and a snake bit him. (Amos 5:18–19)

The Midrash explicitly relates this verse to the sequence of empires:

> "Who fled from a lion" – this is Babylon, as per "The first was like a lion" (Dan. 7:3). "And a bear met him" – this is Media, as per "And behold another beast, a second, like a bear" (Dan. 7:4). "He came into the house" – when they started to rebuild the walls of the Temple ("he leaned with his hand on the wall"), the wicked Haman and his son Shimshi tried to stop them ("a snake bit him"). (Yalkut Shimoni, Amos 545)

Relating to this sequence of predators and empires is an account in the Talmud about the future judgment of the nations, which is described as taking place in order of their importance. First is Rome; second is Persia:

> The kingdom of Rome leaves, and then the kingdom of Persia enters. Why? Because it follows Rome in prestige. How do we know this? As it is written, "And behold another beast, a second, like a bear" (Dan. 7), and Rav Yosef taught that this refers to the Persians. (Avoda Zara 2b)

וַיֹּאמֶר דָּוִד אֶל שָׁאוּל רֹעֶה הָיָה עַבְדְּךָ לְאָבִיו בַּצֹּאן וּבָא הָאֲרִי וְאֶת הַדּוֹב וְנָשָׂא שֶׂה מֵהָעֵדֶר: וְיָצָאתִי אַחֲרָיו וְהִכִּתִיו וְהִצַּלְתִּי מִפִּיו וַיָּקָם עָלַי וְהֶחֱזַקְתִּי בִּזְקָנוֹ וְהִכִּתִיו וַהֲמִיתִּיו: גַּם אֶת הָאֲרִי גַּם הַדּוֹב הִכָּה עַבְדֶּךָ וְהָיָה הַפְּלִשְׁתִּי הֶעָרֵל הַזֶּה כְּאַחַד מֵהֶם כִּי חֵרֵף מַעַרְכֹת אֱלֹהִים חַיִּים: וַיֹּאמֶר דָּוִד יְהֹוָה אֲשֶׁר הִצִּלַנִי מִיַּד הָאֲרִי וּמִיַּד הַדֹּב הוּא יַצִּילֵנִי מִיַּד הַפְּלִשְׁתִּי הַזֶּה וַיֹּאמֶר שָׁאוּל אֶל דָּוִד לֵךְ וַיהֹוָה יִהְיֶה עִמָּךְ:

שמואל א יז:לד-לז

כַּאֲשֶׁר יָנוּס אִישׁ מִפְּנֵי הָאֲרִי וּפְגָעוֹ הַדֹּב וּבָא הַבַּיִת וְסָמַךְ יָדוֹ עַל הַקִּיר וּנְשָׁכוֹ הַנָּחָשׁ:

עמוס ה:יט

The commentary of *Tosafot* raises the question that if we are judging the prominence of nations via their symbolism with animals, then surely the lion, as king of beasts, is more important than the bear. Since the lion represents Babylon, then surely Babylon should be judged before Persia!

Tosafot first answers that even though the lion is king of beasts, the bear is more powerful and more devious. But this answer is difficult. While bears certainly are stronger than lions, there is no context in which they ever receive precedence.

However, *Tosafot* provides another answer: that Babylon was only compared to a lion when it was in its prime. In a variation on this, we can explain that the Talmud was only interested in discussing kingdoms that were significant at the time. Babylon had not been a player on the world stage since the fall of the Neo-Babylonian Empire in 539 BCE. The verse from Daniel shows that Persia is second to Babylon, and since Babylon was no longer relevant, Persia comes right after Rome.[39] Accordingly, the bear still takes second place to the lion; but the lion is simply not relevant in this context.

Joseph and the Bear

SYMBOLISM

We have seen many references to the bear in the Midrash and Talmud which allude to Persia. But there is another set of references to the bear in the Midrash and Talmud which occur in a very different context. When Joseph's brothers presented their father with Joseph's bloodstained coat, Jacob bemoaned the fate that had befallen his son:

> "And he said, My son's coat! A wild beast has consumed him…" (Gen. 37:33). R. Huna said, the Divine Spirit was enkindled within him; "A wild beast has consumed him" – this is the wife of Potiphar. (Bereshit Rabba 84:19)

The reference to the wife of Potiphar, who tried to seduce Joseph, as a "wild beast," is very significant. As we shall see, she is likened to a very specific wild animal.

115

"The lion roars, the bear growls, the wicked man rules over a poor nation."

(Prov. 28:15)

The Midrash cites an opinion that whenever a passage in the Torah begins with "And it was…," then it introduces a time of travails. Another opinion states that it can introduce either something very negative or something very positive. Then there is a third opinion:

> R. Shmuel b. Nun came and made a compromise: Whenever it says, "And it was," it denotes a time of travails, whereas "And it shall be" denotes a joyous period.… It was pointed out to him, surely it is written, "And God was with Joseph"? He responded, This was not something entirely happy, as that bear became attached to him. (*Bereshit Rabba* 42:3)

By virtue of feeling that God was with him, Joseph glowed with happiness. His resultant beauty caused a certain "bear" to be attracted to him. Another midrash relates that this bear was a challenge for him:

> "And Joseph was beautiful of form and appearance" – like a mighty man standing in the street, fussing over his eyes, fixing his hair, pivoting on his feet, and saying, For me, it is befitting, I am a handsome man of might! They said to him, If you are a man of might, if you are handsome, here is a bear for you – arise and overcome it! (*Bereshit Rabba* 87:3)

The motif of the bear is used again and again. Another midrash states:

> Joseph was pondering, and said, When I was in my father's house, my father would look for the best por-

tion, and he would give it to me, and my brothers would give me the evil eye; now that I am here, I am grateful to You, that I am in tranquility. The Holy One said to him, Layabout! By your life, I shall set the bear upon you! (*Bereshit Rabba* 87:4)

And yet another midrash uses the bear to describe the threat to Joseph:

> "And Joseph brought evil talk of them…" (Gen. 37:2). What was it?…R. Shimon said: They are moving their eyes to the young girls of the land…. The Holy One said…you say that they are moving their eyes to the young girls of the land?! By your life! I will set the bear upon you! (*Bereshit Rabba* 84:7)

Why is the bear repeatedly used as the metaphor in the story of Joseph and Potiphar's wife? It may relate to the Roman arena, in which bears were set against gladiators and criminals, providing the audience with a competition to see who would triumph. Joseph declared himself to be a "mighty man," and was considered by God to have acted inappropriately, and so he was put in the arena with a bear.[40]

But another possibility is that the answer relates to the use of the bear as the symbol of Persia. The ferocity represented by the bear is used against the Jewish people in a specific situation. In order to understand this properly, we need to understand how bears differ from man-eaters such as lions and leopards in their threat to man.

Syrian brown bears fighting

EVGENIY AYUPOV / SHUTTERSTOCK

When Bears Attack

In biologist Stephen Herrero's definitive study, *Bear Attacks: Their Cause and Avoidance*,[41] one of the first chapters is titled by what is considered the primary type of bear attack: "Sudden Encounters With Grizzlies." The chapter begins: "Hikers, hunters, or other persons traveling on foot in bear country may suddenly confront a grizzly. If this happens, a grizzly may attack because it perceives a threat."

Attacks by bears are not like attacks by lions and leopards. The latter attack as part of a planned hunt. In the case of bear attacks, on the other hand, the attack occurs when a person is nonchalantly taking a relaxing stroll in the countryside, enjoying the peace and tranquility of his surroundings, and happens across a bear. The bear, which did not hear the person coming, is taken by surprise, assumes that it is being threatened, and seeks to neutralize that threat – often with lethal results. And if it is a female bear with cubs to protect, then the bear is especially paranoid and even more dangerous.

> "As if a man fled from a lion, and a bear met him..." (Amos 5:19) – The lion alludes to Laban, who pursued Jacob like a lion, to seize his life. The bear alludes to Esau, who encountered him on the trail like a bear to kill mother with child; a lion has shame, but a bear has no shame. (*Midrash Pirkei DeRabbi Eliezer* 36[42])

Lions attack as part of a planned hunt due to hunger, and thus pick a single target.[43] But bears attack out of unbridled rage, reacting to threats either real or perceived, and thus attack indiscriminately.

In *Bear Attacks: Their Causes and Avoidance*, the author is very clear about how best to avoid them: "Your best weapon to minimize the risk of a bear attack is your brain. Use it as soon as you contemplate a trip to bear country, and continue to use it throughout your stay.... Careful travel in grizzly country requires alertness, attention, intelligence, and knowledge. Alertness and attention to your immediate environment are important." Bear attacks happen when, instead of being alert to the potential presence of danger and taking appropriate precautions, people relax and enjoy the tranquility of their surroundings. This is why bear attacks are the perfect analogy for retribution that occurs as a result of people inappropriately relaxing and enjoying their surroundings when they are not supposed to do so.

Exile is a period of banishment during which the Jewish people are not able to live in Israel and fulfill all the commandments of the Torah. This is supposed to be an unsatisfactory state of affairs for the Jewish people, one that spurs them to improve their observance of the Torah and merit redemption.

A mother bear with cubs is particularly likely to attack if she is surprised

DAVID RASMUS / SHUTTERSTOCK

However, people sometimes do not miss having a Temple, and they feel no stimulus to improve their ways. They relax in exile and feel comfortable. But if you go down to exile this way, you are in for a big surprise. For it is against this sort of complacency that the bear is sent.

One example of this is with Joseph. As a slave in Egypt, with his father mourning his presumed death, he was not supposed to be content with his state of affairs. But as he rose in position to be the controller of his master Potiphar's affairs, he became complacent about his lifestyle:

> "Joseph was beautiful of form and appearance" (Gen. 39:6) – since he saw himself as a ruler, he began eating and drinking and curling his hair. God said: "Your father is in mourning and you are curling your hair? I will set the bear upon you!" Immediately, "his master's wife lifted her eyes toward Joseph, and she said, Lie with me." (Rashi to Gen. 39:6)

The bear is always wandering and has no rest, says the Talmud. Such is supposed to be the lot of the Jew in exile. If the Jew considers himself at rest, then the bear is sent to remind him otherwise. Perhaps this is why Potiphar's wife is metaphorically described as a bear.[44]

So, too, was the situation in the Persian exile at the time of Ahasuerus. The Jews indulged themselves in his feast, ignoring their position in exile. Their complacency called for an attack by the bear. Sure enough, Ahasuerus turned against them and sealed a decree to annihilate them. It was only when they returned to God through fasting and prayer that the decree was rescinded. They finally learned the lesson that the Jew in exile is to view his situation as strictly temporary and yearn for redemption.[45]

Joseph's bear was the wife of Potiphar, the "wild animal" who attempted to seduce him. Yet Joseph managed to overcome this test:

"And God was with Joseph, and he was a successful (*matzliach*) man" (Gen. 39:2). R. Berechiah said, A jumping man, as it says, "And they passed over (*vetzalchu*) the Jordan before the king" (II Sam. 19:18). (*Bereshit Rabba 86:4*)

The phrase used to describe the fording of the Jordan refers to them leaping over it in a light and joyous way. Since the Hebrew word used, *vetzalchu*, is similar to the word used to describe Joseph's success, *matzliach*, this indicates that Joseph was dancing opposite his evil inclination. The Midrash continues:

> It is comparable to a bear that was standing in the street, decorated with precious stones and pearls. They said, Anyone who jumps on it can take what is on it. There was one wise man there who said to them, You are looking at what is on it, and I am looking at its teeth! R. Berechiah said, That she-bear is doing nothing other than jump at you, and yet you are greater than that! (Ibid.)

True victory over the enemy means using their trait for the good. Joseph was the great jumper, because the more she jumped at him, the more he jumped away.[46] He ultimately triumphed over the bear because he shed his mood of tranquility. He was a "jumping man," not relaxing in the bear's company, but jumping out of the way.

Identifying with Bears

In all the scriptural references to bears that we have seen, bears always represent dangerous enemies. In this, the bear presents an interesting contrast with lions and wolves, which appear in Scripture with positive symbolism. In light of that, it is interesting that a few centuries ago Jews began to use the name Dov, "Bear."[47] How did this happen, in light of the negative imagery of the bear in Scripture? The name Dov is often joined with the name Yissachar, which is strange, because in Scripture, Yissachar is associated with the donkey rather than the bear. Perhaps the bear, as a more impressive animal, was substituted for the donkey; both animals share traits of strength and endurance.[48] Aside from lions, deer, and mythical creatures, the only animal to be frequently depicted on Jewish tombstones in Europe was the bear.[49] In some cases, this was due to the deceased being named Dov, while in other cases it may relate to the bear being the emblem of the household.[50] Illustrations of bears also appeared on the title pages and end-pages of numerous Jewish works in the seventeenth and eighteenth centuries.[51]

Although there is no positive symbolism associated with the bear in Scripture, Talmud, or Midrash, perhaps we can trace a history of identifying with bears. There is one verse in Scripture in which the bear is identified with the speaker rather than representing an enemy:

GIEDRIIUS / SHUTTERSTOCK

This bear cub is sitting upright, in a very humanlike position

Bears have large, flat paws, similar to human palms.

נֶהֱמֶה כַדֻּבִּים כֻּלָּנוּ וְכַיּוֹנִים הָגֹה נֶהְגֶּה נְקַוֶּה לַמִּשְׁפָּט וָאַיִן לִישׁוּעָה רָחֲקָה מִמֶּנּוּ:

ישעיה נט:יא

We all groan (*nehemeh*) like bears, and moan like doves; we hope for judgment, but there is none; for salvation, but it is far from us. (Is. 59:11)

This verse presents an interesting contrast between the huge, tough bear, and the small, frail dove, both of which emit similarly mournful sounds. When bears feel threatened by more dominant bears, or when they are otherwise afraid (such as when in a trap), they emit mournful-sounding groaning and moaning. Isaiah, speaking on behalf of the people in exile, describes them as being like bears in their groaning.

It is not only due to their vocalizations that people would identify with bears. Bears are also seen as humanlike in hav-ing front paws that are similar to hands. In the biblical laws of impurity transmitted by animal carcasses, there is refer-ence to animals that "walk on their hands,"[52] i.e. referring to their possessing paws rather than hooves. The medieval European commentaries give the example of bears, dogs, and cats. Dogs and cats are very familiar animals, and it is thus no surprise to see them mentioned, but why are bears listed? Presumably this is because bears have very distinc-tive large and flat paws, which are even more hand-like (and different from hooves) than the paws of dogs and cats. Dogs and cats are digitigrade, which means that they walk on the digits of their hands and feet – the equivalent of human fingers and toes, with the heels elevated. Bears, on the other hand, are plantigrade – their paws incorporate the podial and metatarsal bones of their hands and feet. This results in large, flat, paws, which are very much like the hands and feet of humans. Rabbi Yehuda HaChasid, the twelfth-century author of the important work *Sefer Chasidim*, notes that bears, monkeys, and humans are all similar in their hands,

120

which enable them to fulfill functions that other animals cannot do with their paws.[53] And in order to use their hands, bears will sit upright on their haunches, or even stand fully erect on their feet, just like humans.

Bears are not only humanlike in their vocalizations and appearance, but also in their behavior. Their intelligence, playfulness, and the relative ease with which they are trained means that they have long been captured for entertainment purposes[54] (which may be an unfortunate reason why people were familiar with the sound of their moans). We have already seen a midrash describing a bear decorated with gemstones, perhaps referring to the common practice of training bears to dance. Another midrash refers to the practice of kings to keep bears for entertainment:

> Another explanation: "If the anointed priest shall sin..." ...It is a parable to a bear handler who was eating the bear's food rations. The king said, Since he is eating the bear's food rations, let the bear eat him. So, too, the Holy One said, since he benefited from sanctified items, let the fire consume him. (*Vayikra Rabba* 5:6)

In modern times, we identify with bears when we play with teddy bears as children. The history of the teddy bear is itself an extraordinary Jewish story, which begins with a person who, like the prophet Isaiah, identified with the distress of a bear.

The American President Theodore "Teddy" Roosevelt was once on a hunting trip, searching for bears. But after several days in the wilderness, he still had not found one. One of the guides finally managed to find a bear, which he wore down with the aid of hounds, and tied it to a tree. When Roosevelt was brought to shoot the bear, he took pity on the injured and weary animal, and refused to shoot it. The scene was illustrated in a newspaper, which was read in Brooklyn by a poor Jewish immigrant couple from Russia, Morris and Rose Michtom. Rose made a toy bear out of scraps of fabric, with buttons for eyes, and Morris placed it in their store window with the name "Teddy's bear." It was an instant hit, and the Michtoms' resultant toy empire brought them great wealth and enabled them to become major philanthropists who, remembering their own difficulties as immigrants, supported Jewish immigrants in America and Palestine and developed land for the settlement in Israel.[55] While the real (and dangerous) bears were disappearing from the Land of Israel, toy bears were supporting its resettlement by the Jewish people.   ∎

Notes

1 H.B. Tristram, *The Natural History of the Bible*, p. 49.

2 Uzi Paz, "*Hayo hayu dubim...*" (Hebrew), *Teva VeAretz*, Tamuz/Av 5752/July 1992, vol. 250.

3 Aharoni, *Zikhronot Zoolog Ivri*.

4 Ari L. Goldman, "Time 'Too Painful' to Remember," *The New York Times*, November 10, 1988.

5 See the introduction to Predators.

6 In rabbinic law, there is discussion as to whether a cow that survives being attacked by a bear is considered to be fatally wounded. See Rosh, Chullin 3:40, *Tur, Yoreh De'ah* 57; *She'iltot, Vayikra* 68; Rashba, Chullin 52b; *Peri To'ar, Yoreh De'ah* 57:7; *Tzemach Tzedek, Yoreh De'ah* 269:1.

7 National Park Service, Yellowstone, at http://www.nps.gov/yell/naturescience/bisonqa.htm.

8 Maimonides cites this verse in his commentary to Mishna Avot 5:14, in explaining why a person lacking all intellectual and spiritual qualities is compared to a dangerous animal.

9 Ralbag to II Samuel 17:8.

10 Radak and *Metzudot* to II Samuel 17:8.

11 Maimonides, in *Pirkei Moshe* (*Medical Aphorisms*) 24:28, cites the ancient belief that a bear cub is born as an unshaped mass, which the mother must lick into its correct form (the origin of the expression "to lick into shape"). He presents this as an example of the wonders of nature.

12 Radak to Hosea 13:8.

13 The version found in the Midrash *Yalkut Shimoni, Bereshit* 18:83, reads that the bear's rage was redirected *babehema*, to a domestic animal, rather than reading that it was directed *bevaneha*, to her cubs.

14 For another explanation, see Chakham Yosef Chayim, *Ben Yehoyada* ad loc., who relates it to the scriptural description of a bereft bear "tearing open hearts."

15 I Kings 13:24–26; I Kings 20:35–36; II Kings 17:24–26.

16 In Biblical Hebrew, there is no gender specificity apparent from the name "bears" (*dubim*); however, when the verse describes them as emerging from the forest, the feminine form of the verb is used, thus revealing that the bears were female.

17 Sota 46b. Note that Jericho would not have had any forests, which (as we shall see) one view in the Talmud states to have been a miraculous creation. The verses can also be read to mean that the youths came from Bet-El, where there were (in antiquity) forests.

18 Chanoch Zundel Luria, *Knaf Renanim al Perek Shira, Dov*.

19 II Kings 1:8.

20 The Talmud sees Elisha's curse and its results as a tragedy which resulted in Elisha being punished. See Sota 47a and the commentary of Rashi ad loc.

21 Rabbi Elchanan Samet, *Pirkei Elisha* (Yediyot Sefarim, 2010).

22 This is the source of the Modern Hebrew expression *lo dubim velo yaar*, "no bears and no forest," which means that something never occurred at all.

23 Rashi ad loc.

24 Maharsha ad loc. Chakham Yosef Chayim in *Ben Yehoyada* argues that it refers instead to Elisha's escorts.

25 See Rabbi Moshe Betzalel Luria, *Torat HaKenaot* (Warsaw, 1899) to Sota ad loc., who, following Maharsha's understanding that the Talmud is referring to the children being afraid, explains that interfering with free will is more difficult than creating a forest. An alternate answer is presented by Rabbi Chaim Kanievsky, in *Sefer Taama D'Kra*, citing his father, the Steipler Gaon. He suggests that it was a message to the youths who had thought that Elisha had deprived them of their livelihood. God clothed the supernatural miracle of the bears in the natural environment of the forest, so that the youths would realize that everyone's livelihood is also a "miracle within a miracle" – a miracle within nature, which is itself a miracle. In a different approach, Rabbi Avraham ben Musa, in *Minchat Sota*, suggests that it was important for there to be a forest as a memorial to the miracle.

26 Spencer Heffernan, "Ursus arctos horribilis – the Grizzly Bear," at the Tree Of Life web project.

27 For an academic study of the symbolism of the animals in rabbinic thought, see Rivka Raviv, "Shaping the Four Kingdoms in Daniel in the Rabbinical Literature," *Jewish Studies Internet Journal* 5 (2006), pp. 1–20 (Hebrew).

28 The word for bear, *dov*, is written here (as in many, but not all, instances) without the letter *vav*. It can therefore be read as *dev*, which is the Aramaic word for a wolf. Accordingly, the verse "the wolf of the plains has plundered them" (Jer. 5:6) is explained to refer to Persia/Media; see *Midrash Bereshit Rabba* 99:2 and *Midrash Vayikra Rabba* 13:5. For further discussion, see Rabbi Shaul Chona Kook, *Iyunim VeMechkarim* (Jerusalem: Mossad HaRav Kook 1959), *Mikra VeLashon*, pp. 15–16.

29 Rashi ad loc.

30 See Malbim ad loc.

31 Rashi, Rav Saadia Gaon, *Metzudat David* to Daniel 7.

32 Rav Saadia Gaon.

33 This passage also appears in Avoda Zara 2b and Kiddushin 72a.

34 Est. 1:1–7.

35 See Rashi to Kiddushin 72a.

36 Yosef Schonhak, *Toledot HaAretz*, p. 48, citing Gesenius. Cf. Song of Songs 7:10.

37 Yoma 76.

38 See Yaakov Elman, "*Rav Yosef BeIdan Ratcha*," *Bar-Ilan* 30–31 (5766), pp. 9–20; my thanks to Rabbi Dr. Elman for further discussing this topic with me.

39 My thanks to Rabbi Dr. Yaakov Elman for his insights on this.

40 Joshua Levinson, "Cultural Androgyny in Rabbinic Literature," in *From Athens to Jerusalem: Medicine in Hellenized Jewish Lore and in Early Christian Literature*, ed. Samuel Kottek (Rotterdam: Erasmus Publishing, 2000), pp. 119–141. Levinson also suggests that Joseph is being described as effeminate, "fussing over his eyes, fixing his hair, pivoting on his feet," and is thus challenged by Potiphar's wife who is described as a bear, i.e. hirsute and aggressively mannish. However, the Midrash here compares Joseph to a "mighty man" (*gibbor*), which seems to rule out any intent to describe him in feminine terms.

41 Stephen Herrero, *Bear Attacks: Their Cause and Avoidance* (New York: Lyons Press, 2002).

42 In *Pirkei DeRabbi Eliezer* 43, Amalek is compared to a bereft bear that kills mother and child.

43 "A lion does not fall upon two people" – Shabbat 151b.

44 For a different approach, see Joshua Levinson, "Cultural Androgyny in Rabbinic Literature," in Samuel Kottek, ed., *From Athens to Jerusalem* pp. 119–140.

45 *Perush Maharzu* to *Midrash Bereshit Rabba* 84:7 explains the usage of the bear as a symbol for Potiphar's wife in terms of the bear's lack of shame, based on *Pirkei DeRabbi Eliezer* 36.

46 *Etz Yosef* and *Matnot Kehuna* to *Midrash Bereshit Rabba* ad loc. *Imrei Yosher* explains instead that Joseph is described as the great jumper because he *refrained* from jumping at her, and the truly expert jumper is the one who knows when not to jump.

47 Rabbi Shlomo Kluger, in Responsa *HaElef Lekha Shlomo*, *Even HaEzer* 188 notes that it is used infrequently.

48 Alexander Beider, *Dictionary of Ashkenazic Given Names*. Beider also points out that the Yiddish name Ber became popular before Yissachar, and this may have caused it to be assigned to an existing less popular Hebrew name; the Hebrew translation of Dov came much later.

49 Several examples can be found in David N. Goberman, *Jewish Tombstones in Ukraine and Moldova* (Moscow, 1993).

50 *The Jewish Encyclopedia* (1902 ed.), "Tombstones."

51 Marvin J. Heller, *Further Studies in the Making of the Early Hebrew Book* (Brill, 2013), Chapter Three, "The Bear Motif On Seventeenth-Eighteenth Century Hebrew Books," pp. 57–76.

52 Leviticus 11:27.

53 *Sefer Chasidim* 589.

54 Cf. *Responsa Terumat HaDeshen* 168, which discusses the case of a captive bear, used for entertainment purposes, that was suspected of mauling a cow.

55 Michael Feldberg, "The Jewish Teddy Bear," in *Blessings of Freedom: Chapters in American Jewish History* (Hoboken, NJ: The American Jewish Historical Society/ Ktav Publishing, 2002), pp. 66–67. Also available online at http://www.ajhs.org/scholarship/chapters/chapter.cfm?documentID=239.

LEOPARD

Leopard

נמר

Namer

The Leopards of Israel

NATURAL HISTORY

The strikingly beautiful leopard is the most widespread of all the big cats. It lives in a variety of habitats in much of Africa, the Middle East, and Asia. In former times, leopards were abundant throughout Israel, especially in the hilly and mountainous regions:

> With me from Lebanon, O bride, come with me from Lebanon, look from the peak of Amana, from the peak of Senir and Hermon, from the dens of lions, from the mountains of leopards. (Song. 4:8).

The leopard of the mountains was the Anatolian leopard, *Panthera pardus tulliana*, which was found in much of the hilly regions of Israel. After the 1834 Arab pogrom in Safed, leopards moved into the destroyed town.[1] The Anatolian leopard was still recorded in the Carmel region in 1866,[2] and was found in the Galilee until as recently as the 1960s. These were one of the largest subspecies of leopards, weighing up to 170 pounds, and preying on wild boar, porcupines, hyrax, and livestock. They were also undoubtedly dangerous to humans; leopards of this size are known to be man-eaters in other parts of the world, and are hunted as a result. In the

אִתִּי מִלְּבָנוֹן כַּלָּה אִתִּי מִלְּבָנוֹן תָּבוֹאִי תָּשׁוּרִי מֵרֹאשׁ אֲמָנָה מֵרֹאשׁ
שְׂנִיר וְחֶרְמוֹן מִמְּעֹנוֹת אֲרָיוֹת מֵהַרְרֵי נְמֵרִים:
שיר השירים ד:ה

first decade of the twentieth century, at least five leopards were killed in between Jerusalem and Beit Shemesh; one of them badly mauled a person after being shot.[3] The last specimen was killed by a shepherd near Hanita in 1965.[4] Another leopard subspecies that lived in the area was the Sinai leopard, *Panthera pardus jarvus*. It was hunted by the Bedouin upon whose goats it preyed, and is now extinct.

Today, the Arabian leopard, *Panthera pardus nimr*, is the only subspecies of leopard to be found in Israel. It is one of the smallest subspecies of leopards, weighing only up to about seventy pounds. The Arabian leopard usually preys on ibex and hyrax, and rarely attacks livestock. But it, too, faces extinction. Some leopards of this subspecies formerly inhabited the popular Ein Gedi area, and learned that an easy source of food was to be found in the dogs and cats of the local kibbutz. As a result, two females were trapped and taken into captivity, causing the collapse of the leopard population in that area. A DNA study of leopard droppings,

EYAL BARTOV

וְקַלּוּ מִנְּמֵרִים סוּסָיו וְחַדּוּ מִזְּאֵבֵי עֶרֶב וּפָשׁוּ פָּרָשָׁיו וּפָרָשָׁיו מֵרָחוֹק
יָבֹאוּ יָעֻפוּ כְּנֶשֶׁר חָשׁ לֶאֱכוֹל:

חבקוק א:ח

performed in 2006, showed an estimated population size of just five males and three females of the Arabian leopard in the Negev and Judean desert regions. The chances of encountering a leopard in Ein Gedi today are so slim that, on the sign warning visitors about leopards, somebody once scribbled, "Watch out for polar bears too!"

There are also some names of places in Scripture that are derived from the leopard. There was a fortified city of the Tribe of Gad named Nimrah (leopardess),[5] and there was a region in Moab referred to as Nimrim (leopards).[6] The Talmud refers to cities named Namer and Nameri.[7] With regard to names of people, Nimrod's name may relate to the leopard; but although the lion, bear, and wolf have long been popular as Jewish names (Aryeh, Dov and Zev), the leopard has never received such an honor.[8] This may be because naming people after animals was a European custom, and leopards were absent from Europe.

Leopards, Tigers, and Cheetahs

——————————————————————— IDENTIFICATION

There is both a strong tradition and clear evidence that the *namer* of Scripture (pronounced *nah-mehr*) is the leopard. This animal is often cited in Scripture as one of the great predators in the Land of Israel, along with lions, bears, and wolves, which is indeed the status of the leopard. The coat of the *namer* is described as spotted; as we shall see later, perhaps "blotched" is a more accurate translation, and this perfectly describes the leopard. There is also evidence for the leopard from cognate languages; in Akkadian and Arabic, the leopard is known as *nimr* (plural, *nimrin*). The Aramaic name for the leopard is *nimra*.

However, today there is some confusion regarding the term *namer*. Beginning in at least the nineteenth century, and possibly earlier, the word *namer* was commonly understood to refer to the tiger.[9] Illustrations of the Mishna's maxim that one should be "as bold as a *namer*" sometimes depict a tiger instead of a leopard. Even in Modern Hebrew today, the word *namer* is often used for the tiger, despite the fact that *tigris* is the more correct term.[10] However, tigers are natives of central and eastern Asia and are not found anywhere near the Land of Israel. They would not therefore be the subject of discussion in Scripture.

There is one reference to the *namer* in Scripture that might not refer to the leopard. It occurs in the context of a prophecy describing the terror of the Chaldeans:

Their horses are lighter than *nemerim*. (Hab. 1:8)

The description of the horses tells us that the *namer* is a creature that is renowned for being "light." The definition of this is a little difficult to pinpoint with accuracy. It could

mean "agile." Leopards are certainly very agile creatures, able to lightly bound up trees and pounce on their prey. However, it more likely means "swift." Leopards are very fast over short distances; they catch their prey either by ambush or by stalking it to within a close range and then making a very short and fast rush. But this description would certainly far better apply to the cheetah. The cheetah, which is described more thoroughly in the following chapter, is able to run much faster than the leopard, reaching speeds of up to seventy miles an hour over short distances.

The name *namer* could not refer exclusively to cheetahs; there are references to the *namer* that do not match the cheetah at all. As we shall see later, the Mishna describes the *namer* as being brazen, which can only refer to the leopard; cheetahs, being relatively weak animals, are wary and shy. It seems most likely that the term *namer* is a generic term for both leopards and cheetahs. The very name of the leopard in Hebrew appears to refer to the variegated coloring of its coat, which would also be applicable to the cheetah. The Mishna uses the term *hamenamer* to describe someone who sows his field in uneven patches, which is explained to be based on the word *namer*:

> "*Hamenamer*" – that he sows in various places in the field, like the appearance of the skin of a leopard, which is spotted. (Rambam, commentary to Mishna Pe'ah 3:2[11])

Cheetahs and leopards are basically similar in terms of their coloration; although cheetahs have spots and leopards have blotchy markings, both would certainly be described as variegated in their coloration. However, it is interesting to note the wording of the famous verse that refers to the leopard's markings:

In the historic Rymanow synagogue, the namer *is illustrated as a tiger instead of a leopard*

125

◀ *This Arabian leopard is poised on a hill in the Judaean Desert*

הֲיַהֲפֹךְ כּוּשִׁי עוֹרוֹ וְנָמֵר חֲבַרְבֻּרֹתָיו גַּם אַתֶּם תּוּכְלוּ לְהֵיטִיב
לִמֻּדֵי הָרֵעַ:

ירמיה יג:כג

בָּאתַר דְּנָה חָזֵה הֲוֵית וַאֲרוּ אָחֳרִי כִּנְמַר וְלַהּ גַּפִּין אַרְבַּע דִּי עוֹף
עַל גַּבַּיהּ וְאַרְבְּעָה רֵאשִׁין לְחֵיוְתָא וְשָׁלְטָן יְהִיב לַהּ:

דניאל ז:ו

> Can the Cushite change his skin, or the leopard his
> blotches (*chavarburotav*)? So too, can you, in whom
> evil is ingrained, do good? (Jer. 13:23)

The word used to describe the leopard's markings, *chavarburotav*, is conventionally translated as "spots," but this is not a precise translation. Amongst the traditional commentators, some translate *chavarburotav* as *ketem*, which is used elsewhere to refer to a stain.[12] Others relate it to the term *chabura*, "wound," and explain that it refers to the mark left by a wound.[13] Thus, this particular verse seems to specifi-cally refer to the bruise-like blotching of the leopard rather than the more perfect circular spots that a cheetah possesses.

The Greek Leopard

SYMBOLISM

One of the most intriguing appearances of the leopard in Scripture is in a prophetic vision of Daniel:

> Daniel told the following: "In my vision at night, I saw the four winds of heaven stirring up the great sea. Four mighty beasts, each different from the other, emerged from the sea.... The first was like a lion...and behold, another beast, a second one, similar to a bear.... Afterwards I beheld, and there was another, similar to a leopard, which had upon its back four wings of a bird; the beast also had four heads; and dominion was given to it." (Dan. 7:2–6)

"Afterwards I beheld, and there was another, similar to a leopard, which had upon its back four wings of a bird; the beast also had four heads, and dominion was given to it."

(Daniel 7:6)

STEVE CREITZ

In classical Jewish thought, the four beasts in Daniel's vision represent the four exiles to which the Jewish people have been subjected.[14] The leopard was the parallel of *Yavan* – Ancient Greece.[15] The four wings on its back symbolize the rapid expansion of the Greek empire to all four corners of the world;[16] alternatively, they represent the division of the empire after Alexander's death into four regions.[17] The four heads of the leopard refer to the four generals between whom the empire was divided after Alexander's death: Lysimachus, Cassander, Seleucus, and Ptolemy.

But what is the inherent similarity of leopards to Ancient Greece? Is it just that the leopard was the third greatest predator in biblical Israel, and Greece was the third oppressive empire? There may also be symbolic similarities between leopards and Ancient Greece. One possible explanation for this is that leopards are strikingly beautiful animals. Greece, too, was renowned for its aesthetic values; and the Torah itself speaks of beauty being promised to Japeth, one of whose descendants was Yavan.[18] Another explanation is that, as we have seen earlier, Scripture highlights the *namer* (whether leopard or cheetah) for its swiftness. This may represent the amazingly rapid expansion of Alexander's empire. But, as we shall now see, there may be a more fundamental reason why the leopard represents Ancient Greece.

The Brazen Leopard

SYMBOLISM

The Mishna describes the fundamental character traits of various animals, including the leopard:

> Yehuda b. Teima said: Be as brazen as a leopard, as light as a vulture, as swift as a gazelle, and as powerful as a lion to fulfill the will of your Father in Heaven. (Mishna Avot 5:20)

The term used here for *"brazen"* is the word *az,* which generally means "strength." However, leopards are not the strongest of animals, and thus it must relate to inner rather than outer strength. Some translate the Mishna's use of the term as "energetic,"[19] but it is usually understood as referring to "boldness," "brazenness," or "*chutzpa.*" Leopards are often described as "boldly marked," but their boldness is not limited to their coloration; it is their fundamental nature. In the words of the former curator of the Hai-Bar nature reserve in Israel, Bill Clark: "They don't have the speed of a cheetah, nor can they claim the brute force of a lion. Instead, they rely on their wits. They're smart, and, pound for pound, they're the scrappiest of the big cats.... No other predator confronts its victims with such rampaging fury."[20] Famous lion hunter Colonel John Patterson,

who later became a heroic commander of Jews in Palestine,[21] records that a leopard once broke into his shed and killed his entire flock of thirty sheep and goats.[22] It had no desire or capability of eating so many animals; the attack was an act of brazen aggression.

This brazenness, in Hebrew *azut,* of the leopard is mentioned on several occasions in rabbinic literature. We shall explore some of these references later, but for now we shall cite just one such instance. The Midrash expounds the verse that we mentioned earlier, "With me from Lebanon, O bride ... from the dens of lions, from the mountains of leopards" (Song. 4:8), as referring to a variety of people and nations in our history:

> "From the mountains of leopards" – These are the Canaanites. Just as the leopard is brazen, so too the Canaanites were brazen. This is as it is written, "Not a man was left in Ai or in Beth-El who did not go out after Israel" (Josh. 8:17). (*Shir HaShirim Rabba* 4:8)

The brazen aggression of the leopard also explains why this animal was chosen as a symbol of Ancient Greece. Alexander of Macedon began his reign by killing all potential rivals to the throne. Under his military direction, the Greek Empire expanded its conquests with unparalleled ferocity.

The word *az* also carries the connotation of defiance. The brazen defiance of the leopard is presented by Maharal of Prague as symbolizing the clash between Ancient Greece and the nation of Israel.[23] Although the early Hellenistic kingdom of Ptolemaic Egypt, and the Syrian Seleucid dynasty of King Antiochus III, were relatively tolerant vis-à-vis Judaism, this was not to last. The tolerance toward the

DEREK HAINES

This leopard is brazenly attacking a kudu antelope many times its size

Jews ended with Antiochus IV Epiphanes, who promulgated various decrees against the practice of Judaism along with cruel measures. The Greeks defiled the Temple, and they forced the Jewish people to discard their Torah lifestyle:

> "I saw in my vision...another, like a leopard" (Dan. 7:1, 6) – this refers to Greece, which set up decrees and told Israel: "Write on the horn of an ox that you have no share in the World to Come!" (*Vayikra Rabba* 13:5[24])

Good and Brazen

———————————————————————————— SYMBOLISM

The evil nature of *azut* was not limited to the Greeks; it is something that is a danger for all of us. Brazenness stands at odds with a person's sense of shame, which is supposed to keep him from sin. Yet no character trait is *entirely* good or bad. All traits can be used either way, and *azut* is no exception.

> Yehuda b. Teima said: Be as brazen as a leopard, as light as a vulture, as swift as a gazelle, and as powerful as a lion to fulfill the will of your Father in Heaven. (Mishna Avot 5:20)

An example of this positive application of brazenness is discussed in the Talmud, discussing a person who is too poor to afford delicacies for Shabbat:

> The School of R. Eliyahu taught: Even though R. Akiva says that it is better to make one's Shabbat like a weekday rather than to receive charity, one should do something small in one's home to honor Shabbat. What is "something small"? Rav Pappa said: It is fish fried in its own

BENO ROTHENBERG / WIKIMEDIA COMMONS

This 1500-year-old mosaic of a leopard is from the ancient Maon synagogue at Nirim in Israel.

128

oil with flour. This is as R. Yehuda b. Teima taught: Be as brazen as a leopard...to fulfill the will of your Father in Heaven. (Pesachim 112a)

Rashi explains that the Talmud is urging a person to strengthen himself in the commandment to honor Shabbat beyond his natural ability. He should brazenly purchase something beyond his means, albeit something small, in honor of Shabbat. This is analogous to the leopard, which boldly exceeds its limitations in its willingness to tackle animals much larger than itself.

The brazenness of the leopard is explained by the fourteenth-century halakhic authority Rabbi Yaakov ben Asher to refer to the need for a person not to be intimidated by those who would dissuade him from doing the right thing:

> It specifies four areas in the service of the Creator, blessed is He, and it begins with "Be as brazen as the leopard," for it is a great principle in the service of the Creator. For there are times when a person desires to do a mitzva, but he refrains from doing it, because there are people who are mocking him. Therefore, it instructs that a person should be brazenfaced against all those who mock him, and he should not refrain from doing the mitzva. (*Tur, Orach Chayim* 1)

Just as the leopard is not intimidated, so too a person should not be intimidated. This, too, is explained to relate to the battle between the Greeks and the Hasmoneans. In mystical Jewish thought, victory does not just mean military or even ideological conquest; it means that one takes the enemy's evil trait and uses it for the good. Then one has truly conquered the enemy, which is really the enemy within.

The Greeks used brazenness in a negative way. But the Hasmoneans took the trait of brazenness and used it for the good. The leopard stands unafraid of creatures that outweigh it or outnumber it. Likewise, even though the Hasmoneans were far outnumbered by the gigantic Greek army, they brazenly stood firm and fought back.[25]

Leopard Infidelity

———————————————————————————— SYMBOLISM

The word "leopard" is a combination of the words "leo," which refers to the lion, and "*pard*," which refers to the panther (based on the Greek *párdos* and Latin *pardus*). It was believed that the leopard was a hybrid of the lion with the panther, and this is how the leopard received its name.

But what exactly is a panther? The Midrash refers to a "panther" that was sent amongst the Egyptians, but it is difficult to know which animal is being referenced:

"Be as brazen as a leopard... to fulfill
the will of your Father in Heaven."

(Mishna Avot 5:20)

"He sent the swarms amongst them to devour them" (Ps. 78:45) – ...R. Chama and R. Yehoshua both say that it was a type of wild beast, called *panther*, that the Holy One brought. (*Midrash Tehillim* 78)

The Midrash is borrowing the Greek term *pánthēr*. Today, the name "panther" is often a source of confusion; it usually refers to the American cougar, while the term "black panther" is often used to describe a black leopard or black jaguar, which are two entirely different species. In antiquity, the term "panther" is likewise of unclear meaning (though it could not refer to the cougar or jaguar, which are both American species). It appears that in antiquity, the distinctions between lions, leopards, and cheetah were not necessarily the same as those of modern zoology. This relates at least in part to a belief that hybridization was an ordinary occurrence with these creatures.[26]

It is not only with the Greeks and Romans that the leopard was thought to be a product of crossbreeding. Two prominent fifteenth-century rabbinic authorities write that the leopard is a product of such infidelity:

The leopard is born from a wild boar and a lioness. For when lions come into heat, the lioness pokes her head into the forest thickets and roars to summon a mate, and the boar hears her voice and cohabits with her; the offspring of this pair is the leopard. (Rabbi Ovadiah MiBartenura, commentary to *Pirkei Avot* 5:20; also Rabbi Shimon ben Tzemach Duran, *Magen Avot* 3:4)

Yet as Rabbi Samuel Strashun (Rashash) already noted in the nineteenth century, this is problematic from a scientific standpoint.[27] It is possible to crossbreed some animals, such as wolves and dogs, because they are genetically closely related. Likewise, one can crossbreed horses, donkeys, and zebras because all of these are closely related (although the offspring are mostly sterile). But it is impossible to crossbreed pigs and lions, because they are genetically very different from each other. Ramban likewise notes that it is inconceivable for animals that are very different to produce offspring.[28]

However, others see a metaphor in these rabbinic references to the leopard being a hybrid of the lion and boar. Rabbi Tzaddok HaKohen of Lublin interprets this explanation allegorically, writing that the lion, which often symbolizes Babylon, here represents the talmudic knowledge of the Jewish academies in Babylon. The boar represents the wisdom of the Edomite Empire, Rome. The leopard therefore represents Greece, which caused the adulteration of the wisdom of Torah with the wisdom of Rome.[29]

Although, in a biological sense, leopards do not originate from interspecies hybridization, they do seem to have a pro-pensity for interbreeding with other big cats. Koshien Zoo in Japan bred a leopard to a lioness, which subsequently gave birth to a litter of "leopons." The Hagenbeck Tierpark in Hamburg mated a puma with a leopardess, producing "pumapards," and a tiger with a leopardess, producing a "tigard." A facility in the US first mated a jaguar with a leopardess, giving birth to a single female "jagulep," which was in turn mated by a male lion, producing a litter of "lijaguleps"!

Nor are such hybrids necessarily limited to artificial circumstances. A rare spotted lion, known as the *marozi*, is thought by many to be an example of natural crossbreeding between the lion and the leopard, although other explanations have been offered. And in the early 1900s, Indian natives regularly spoke of an animal they knew as the *dogla*, which was claimed to be a natural hybrid between the leopard and the tiger. Although it was never established that hybridization was the cause, there were reports of some large leopards in the area with striping on their abdomens.

Whether in ancient ideas about its ancestry, its crossbreeding ability with other big cats, or mystical imagery, the leopard is a symbol of hybridization and infidelity. This is a theme found in Jewish sources. The Talmud refers to leopard-like behavior when describing a dark period in the history of the Jewish people:

The Lord said, "I said that Israel should be considered before Me as the cherubs, and they set themselves as a leopard.[30] Another version: R. Avahu said, The Lord said, "Even though they put themselves as a leopard, they are considered before Me as the cherubs." (Kiddushin 70a)

God wanted the Jewish people to be as cherubs, which represent innocence and fidelity. But instead, the Jewish people "set themselves as a leopard." What does this mean? Some explain that just as the leopard is full of dark spots,

A rare photograph of a leopon (a hybrid of a leopard with a lioness)

An artist's rendition of the legendary marozi, *believed by some to be a naturally-occuring hybrid of a leopard with a lion*

so too were the Jewish people spotted with sinners.[31] But Rashi explains that the Jews were disloyal to God in the same way that a leopard is disloyal to its partner.[32]

This may be another reason why the leopard represents the Greek empire in Daniel's prophecy and in Jewish mystical thought. The Jews' preference for keeping apart from other nations led to resentment and persecution.[33] The Greeks did not want to kill the Jewish nation, but there was a creeping Hellenizing influence upon the Jewish religion. Judaism was under the threat of hybridization, symbolized by the leopard.

The infidelity of the leopard is also inherently linked by some to the leopard's brazenness. The progeny of forbidden

relationships, such as a mother and son, brother and sister, etc., is known as a *mamzer*. According to the Mishna, this person will also possess certain character traits: "A *mamzer* is brazen" (*Masekhet Kalla* 2).[34] Later, we shall return to this mishna's linkage of the *mamzer* with brazenness.

The Jews were threatened by Ancient Greece with hybridization, with merging into Hellenistic culture. They won by remaining separate, by retaining their identity as Jews. This is part of the symbolism of the olive oil that is lit in the menora:

> Other liquids mix together, but olive oil remains separate. So, too, Israel is separate from other nations. (*Shemot Rabba* 36:1)

Olive oil represents the singularity of Jewish identity. Rather than succumb to Greek culture, a significant number of Jews remained true to the Torah. The Written Torah was translated into Greek and stolen from Israel; but with the Oral Torah, they retained their uniqueness. The thirty-six lights that are lit in total over Chanukka also represent the thirty-six tractates of the Babylonian Talmud with which the Jews resisted Hellenism. Chanukka thereby also symbolizes victory over the leopard, symbol of Greece and hybridization.

Can the Leopard's Spots Disappear?

A lion has spots at birth, which quickly fade. So does the Florida panther. But a leopard never, ever, changes its spots:

> Can the Cushite change his skin, or the leopard his spots? So too, can you, in whom evil is ingrained, do good? (Jer. 13:23)

Yet although a leopard cannot change its spots, it does have a way of making them effectively disappear. With melanistic (black) leopards, which are a color variety of normal leopards, the spots are still present, but they are mostly obscured by the dark color of the rest of the animal's coat. Irregularities no longer stand out when the entire area resembles them. Homiletically, if we recall the idea that the leopard symbolizes hybridization with other cultures, and that a leopard's spots represent a person being "spotted" with sin, there is an analogy here. Adulterations of Torah

that begin with hybridizations with other cultures, and small distortions of religion, can end up losing any and all resemblance to Judaism.

הֲיַהֲפֹךְ כּוּשִׁי עוֹרוֹ וְנָמֵר חֲבַרְבֻּרֹתָיו גַּם אַתֶּם תּוּכְלוּ לְהֵיטִיב לִמֻּדֵי הָרֵעַ:

ירמיה יג:כג

A Persian leopard, the largest subspecies

Brazenness in Torah

——————————————————— SYMBOLISM

As we mentioned earlier, brazenness does have its positive applications. One of these relates to Torah study:

> It was taught in the name of R. Meir: Why was the Torah given to Israel? Because they are brazen. (Beitza 25b)

Some explain this to mean that Torah was given to the brazen Jews in order to temper them and keep them in line.[35] But others explain precisely the opposite: that the Jewish people's brazenness enables them to stick it out in plumbing the depths and truths of the Torah.[36] Brazenness is an essential tool for success in Torah:

> A bashful person cannot learn. (Mishna Avot 2:5)

Although a sense of shame is usually a virtue, and one of the hallmarks of the Jewish people, it is not always desirable in the study of Torah. Someone who is afraid to ask questions, fearful of being mocked for his ignorance, will always remain with doubts and ignorance. A person needs to be courageous enough to ask about that which he does not understand, or he will never learn.[37]

Furthermore, when learning Torah, one must seek the truth. When two people are arguing over the correct understanding of a section of Talmud, each must be concerned only with reaching the true explanation. A person must never cower into submission to accept an explanation he has reason to feel is incorrect.[38]

As we noted earlier, Rabbi Yaakov ben Asher discusses the maxim that one should be brazen as a leopard. He presents King David as the quintessential example of the type of brazenness that is required:

> He begins with "Be as brazen as the leopard," for it is a great principle in the service of the Creator.... Similarly, he is speaking regarding embarrassment; that sometimes, a person is more embarrassed in front of people than he is before the Creator. Therefore, he warns that a person should be brazen in front of those who mock him, and not be ashamed. In this vein, David said, "And I shall speak of Your statutes in front of kings, and I shall not be ashamed" (Ps. 119:46). Even though he was pursued and was fleeing from the heathens, he strengthened his Torah and studies, even though they were mocking him. (Rabbi Yaakov ben Asher, *Tur, Orach Chayim* 1)

King David spoke that which he felt to be the truth, and was not ashamed to do so. This is one of the reasons why he is described as embodying the essence of the Oral Torah.[39] This trait of brazenness, which also enabled David to stand in combat against the giant Goliath, was his heritage from his ancestors Boaz and Ruth.

Boaz wished to marry Ruth, but faced opposition. For Ruth was from the nation of Moab. As such, it was thought that Boaz was prohibited from marrying her, since the Torah states that "an Ammonite or Moabite shall not enter into the congregation of God" (Deut. 23:4). Yet Boaz proposed that one must take into account the precision of the wording; the law was specifically speaking about a Moabite, and not a Moabitess. The Talmud refers to Boaz's actions with particularly intriguing terminology:

> He pounced like a leopard and explained the law ... a Moabite, and not a Moabitess. (Y. Yevamot 48b)

It is not by chance that the Talmud picks the leopard here as its metaphor; rather, it is due to the Sages' exquisite sensitivity to the nature of the animals around them. Boaz had the brazenness, *azut,* of the leopard within him – hence the name *Bo-az,* "in him is brazenness." And Ruth herself was the product of an illegitimate relationship – Lot's incest with his daughter gave rise to Moab, the ancestor of Ruth. As noted earlier, the Mishna states that the products of such relationships are prone to brazenness. Thus, their descendant David had a tendency to brazenness based upon both lines of his ancestry. He implemented this trait for the good, which enabled him to triumph in Torah against all opposition.

Leopards and Goats

In a utopian prophecy of the Messianic Era, there is a description of some unexpected comradery between predators and their prey:

> The wolf also shall live with the lamb, and the leopard shall lie down with the kid, and the calf and the young lion and the fatling together; and a little child shall lead them. (Is. 11:6)

There is a dispute as to whether these verses are intended as a literal description of biological changes, or if they are a metaphor for the future harmony of the nations represented by these animals.[40] In any case, it is interesting to note that later sources consistently present the same pairings of animals: the lion with cattle, the wolf with the lamb, and the leopard with the goat:

"God seeks the pursued" (Eccl. 3:15).... It is even so with offerings. The Holy One said: The ox is pursued by the lion, the goat is pursued by the leopard, the lamb is pursued by the wolf; do not bring offerings before Me from the hunters, only from the hunted. (*Vayikra Rabba* 27:5; *Pesikta DeRav Kahana* 9:4)

In the statues of animals on the throne of King Solomon, the same pairings were made:

> On every step there were kosher animals facing non-kosher ones. On the first step, an ox, and opposite, a lion; on the second, a lamb facing a wolf; on the third, a goat facing a leopard. (*Midrash Aba Gurion* 1)

These pairings can be simply explained as referring to each predator's preferred prey. Lions are the only predators big enough to take on cattle, while wolves must settle for sheep. Leopards habitually prey upon goats – not only domestic goats, but also wild goats (ibex), since, unlike lions and wolves, they are agile enough to chase ibex in their steep terrain.

133

When goats are not available, leopards readily eat other small hoofed animals

The Vigilance of the Leopard

—————— SYMBOLISM

Another attribute of the leopard highlighted in Scripture is its vigilance:

But the prey animals in these pairs are not only the preferred prey of each predator. In all these cases, the two are related in another way. Both animals in each pair represent the same attribute. The lion and ox both express the trait of pride. The wolf and sheep both live in groups. And the leopard and goat are both brazen:

> The goat is the brazen one of the domesticated animals. (Beitza 25b)[41]

> And I am the Lord your God since the land of Egypt, and you know no god but Me; for there is no savior beside Me. I knew you in the wilderness, in the land of great drought. When they grazed, they became full; when they were full, they became haughty; and so they have forgotten Me. Therefore I will be to them as a lion; as a leopard on the way I shall be watching (*ashur*). (Hos. 13:4–7)

A ferocious leopard, ready to spring

A leopard vigilantly watching over its surroundings

Some understand the word *ashur* to refer to the name of a place: Assyria, which is the native home of the Anatolian leopard. Thus, the verse is read, "as a leopard on the way of Assyria."[42] But others explain the word *ashur* here as deriving from the root *shur*, "to see," as in "I shall observe him (*ashurenu*), but not from near" (Num. 24:17).[43] It thus refers to the leopard's nature of stealthily stalking its prey. This technique enables them to catch a wide variety of prey, and is perhaps one the reasons that they are the most widespread member of the cat family.[44] This vigilance is referred to elsewhere in the Torah with a specific word:

> Therefore the lion from the forest shall slay them, and the wolf of the deserts shall destroy them, the leopard is poised alert (*namer shokeid*) over their cities; everyone who goes out there shall be torn in pieces, because their transgressions are many, and their rebellion is great. (Jer. 5:6)

עַל כֵּן הִכָּם אַרְיֵה מִיַּעַר זְאֵב עֲרָבוֹת יְשָׁדְדֵם נָמֵר שֹׁקֵד עַל עָרֵיהֶם כָּל הַיּוֹצֵא מֵהֵנָּה יִטָּרֵף כִּי רַבּוּ פִּשְׁעֵיהֶם עָצְמוּ מְשֻׁבוֹתֵיהֶם:

ירמיה ה:ו

This verse refers to the leopard's alertness and vigilance with the term *shekeida*. This is inherently linked to the leopard's brazenness. It is all very well to possess the trait of brazenness, but one might not make use of this trait without the zeal of *shekeida*. It is not enough to just be *able* to stand up against the threat of an enemy – one has to actually *do* so. The Hasmoneans utilized the characteristic of brazenness only with the benefit of their *shekeida*. The combination of these two properties enabled them to defeat Ancient Greece.[45] The vigilance of the leopard was the key to the victory of Chanukka. ∎

135

Notes

1 Menachem Mendel meKamenitz, *Korot HaItim LiYeshurun BeEretz Yisrael* (Vilna, 1839), p. 2b; Rabbi Yosef Schwartz, *Tevuot HaAretz*, p. 371.

2 Henry Tristram, *The Natural History of the Bible* (London, 1883), p. 113.

3 Pater Schmitz, writing in 1911, cited by Yossi Leshem, "Zoological Treasure in Jerusalem," in *Israel – Land and Nature* 4:2 (Winter 1978–79), pp. 56–61; translated from *Teva VaAretz* 20:3 (March–April 1978).

4 Heinrich Mendelssohn and Yoram Yom-Tov, *Fauna Palaestina: Mammalia of Israel*, p. 225.

5 Numbers 32:3. In Numbers 32:36 it is referred to as Bet-Nimrah.

6 Isaiah 15:6 and Jeremiah 48:34, describing the "waters of Nimrim."

7 Bekhorot 55a.

8 The leopard is also conspicuously absent from *Perek Shira*, the Midrash which records the "songs" of various creatures and elements of the natural world.

9 Yosef Schonhak, in *Toledot HaAretz*, p. 64, identifies the *namer* as the tiger, although he explains it to be a generic term that would also extend to the leopard (which he calls "panther") and the South American jaguar. Rabbi Pinchas Eliyahu Hurwitz of Vilna (d. 1821) in *Sefer HaBrit* 1:14:6 translates *namer* as "tiger," but he describes its coat as blotched and thus appears to be describing the leopard.

10 See Eliezer Ben Yehuda's dictionary.

11 This is as per the more accurate Kapach edition, which has *baherot*, whereas the regular edition has *nekudot*.

12 Radak and *Metzudat David* ad loc.

13 *Metzudat Tziyon* and Malbim. Cf. Shabbat 107b, which relates the term as used in this verse to a wound.

14 For an academic study of the symbolism of the animals in rabbinic thought, see Rivka Raviv, "Shaping the Four Kingdoms in Daniel in the Rabbinical Literature," *Jewish Studies Internet Journal* 5 (2006), pp. 1–20 (Hebrew).

15 *Midrash Vayikra Rabba* 13:5.

16 Malbim to Daniel 7:6.

17 Rav Saadia Gaon.

18 Genesis 9:26, 10:2.

19 See Jastrow, *A Dictionary of the Talmud*, p. 1060, apparently contrasting the unqualified term *az* with the term *az panim*.

20 Bill Clark, *High Hills and Wild Goats* (Boston: Little, Brown and Company, 1990), p. 110.

21 The extraordinary life of John Patterson is related by Denis Brian, *The Seven Lives of Colonel Patterson* (Syracuse University Press, 2008).

22 John Patterson, *The Man-Eaters of Tsavo* (London: Macmillan and Co., 1919), p. 114.

23 Maharal, *Ner Mitzva* p. 16. The word "brazen" also refers to something made out of brass, a strong alloy of copper. Maharal also points out that in another prophetic vision, Greece was represented by copper.

24 Cf. *Midrash Yalkut Shimoni Vayikra* 11:546.

25 *Shem MiShmuel*, Chanukka 5673, sixth night; Rabbi Gedaliah Schorr, *Or Gedalyahu*, Mo'adim, Chanukka 5, 6.

26 George Jennison, in *Animals for Show and Pleasure in Ancient Rome* (Manchester, UK: Manchester University Press, 1937), includes an appendix (pp. 183–7) dedicated to untangling the various Greek terms for big cats. He notes: "Ancient writers were faced with two great difficulties in putting correct names to these spotted cats great and small; they believed in the breeding of hybrid forms in nature, and the Romans had the additional difficulty of naming a foreign animal." See too Benjamin Moser, "The Roman Ethnozoological Tradition: Identifying Exotic Animals in Pliny's Natural History" (University of Western Ontario, 2013), Electronic Thesis and Dissertation Repository, Paper 1206, pp. 69–96.

27 Rashash, commentary ad loc. He describes it as "novel and bizarre," and aside from his objection that the offspring would be sterile, he further notes that he has not read any such thing in books of natural history. See too the comments of Rashash to Chullin 79b. Rabbi Chanoch Henoch ben Rabbi Yosef David Teitelbaum (1884–1943), in Responsa *Yad Chanokh*, questions Rabbi Ovadiah's statement based on the talmudic dictum (Bekhorot 8a) that they could not interbreed since their gestations periods are not equal. He claims that there is a printing error and that Rabbi Ovadiah was actually talking about a lion interbreeding with a tiger or leopard.

28 Ramban, commentary to Leviticus 19:19.

29 Rabbi Tzaddok HaKohen, *Divrei Soferim, Likutei Maamarim, Siyum HaShas*, s.v. *ulekach parashiyot*.

30 The Talmud is expounding a verse, "These are the ones who went up from Tel-melach, Tel-charsha, Keruv, Adon, and Immer" (Neh. 7:61). The reference to the Lord is a play on the word *Adon*, and the reference to cherubs is a play on the word *Keruv*. The reference to a leopard may be a play on *AdoN Immer = Namer*. Another possibility is that the leopard is not directly alluded to in the verse, but is instead simply used a symbol of infidelity.

31 Rabbi Pinchas Horowitz, *Sefer HaMiknah* to Kiddushin ad loc.

32 Rashi, commentary ad loc.

33 Frank William Walbank, *The Hellenistic World* (Harvard University Press, 1982), pp. 222–223, referring to the writings of the Greek historian Diodorus.

34 For a mystical explanation of why a *mamzer* is described as feeling no shame, see Rabbi Yaakov Moshe Charlap, *Mei Marom*, vol. 13 p. 40.

35 Rashi, commentary ad loc.

36 *Pnei Yehoshua*, commentary ad loc.

37 Rabbi Ovadiah MiBartenura, commentary ad loc. and to *Pirkei Avot* 5:20.

38 In the words of Rabbi Chaim of Volozhin: "It is forbidden for a student to accept the words of his teacher when he has difficulties with them. And sometimes, the truth will lie with the student. This is just as a small branch can ignite a larger one" (*Ruach Chayim* to Avot 1:4).

39 Rabbi Tzaddok HaKohen, *Tzidkat HaTzaddik* 167; *Dover Tzedek, Mitzvot asei* 1; *Kometz HaMincha* 2:6.

40 Rambam, *Mishneh Torah*, Hilkhot Melakhim 12:1, takes the position that the verses are allegorical.

41 It therefore comes as no surprise that the goat is also used as a metaphor for Ancient Greece: "And the rough goat is the king of Greece" (Daniel 8:21).

42 Cf. Malbim, who explains that this alludes to Ancient Greece entering the Land of Israel.

43 Rashi, Radak, *Metzudot*, Malbim.

44 Brian Bertram, in *The Unwin Encyclopedia of Mammals*, p. 45.

45 Note that almonds are called *shekeidim*. This is because the almond tree is the very first tree to blossom each year, as soon as the rains ease off. The almond thus represents assiduousness and zeal. It is explained that for this reason we find that the menora, symbol of the Chanukka victory, is constructed with a design involving *shekeidim* (Exodus 25:31, 33; see Rabbi Samson Raphael Hirsch, commentary ad loc.). And Maharal (*Netivot Olam* 1, p. 62), commenting on the Mishna which states that one should "Be vigilant (*shokeid*) in learning Torah, and know what to answer a heretic" (Avot 2:14) explains that an attitude of *shekeida* toward Torah is a prerequisite for dealing with Ancient Greece. Cf. Rabbi Shmuel Bornsztain, *Shem MiShmuel*, Mikeitz 5680.

CHEETAH

Cheetah

The Cheetah of Israel

NATURAL HISTORY

Many people confuse cheetahs with leopards, but they are very different animals. The most immediately visible difference between the two is in their coloration; leopards have blotchy markings, whereas cheetahs have neat circular spots, and distinctive black stripes running down their face. However, the differences go much further than mere coloration. Leopards are powerfully built, highly aggressive big cats, which hunt their prey via ambush or stalking. Cheetahs, on the other hand, have a very slender build. They hunt their prey – typically gazelles, but also guinea-fowl, hares, and young wildebeest – via a high-speed chase. When the cheetah catches up with the gazelle, it brings it down not by pouncing on it, like other big cats, but by sticking out its paw and tripping it. It then kills the gazelle via clamping down on its neck and suffocating it. The exertion of the high-speed chase leaves the cheetah so weakened that it may take half an hour before it has the strength to actually eat its prey.

Cheetahs are associated today with the African savannah. However, there is a subspecies of cheetah that lives outside of Africa, the Asiatic cheetah, *Acionyx jubatus venaticus*. It was once widespread throughout Arabia, Iran, central Asia, and India. But cheetahs were widely hunted and captured, and their habitat was converted to farmland. Today, the Asi-

Note the very large dewclaws on the lower part of the cheetah's front legs, used for hooking its fleeing prey off-balance

וְקַלּוּ מִנְּמֵרִים סוּסָיו וְחַדּוּ מִזְּאֵבֵי עֶרֶב וּפָשׁוּ פָּרָשָׁיו וּפָרָשָׁיו מֵרָחוֹק
יָבֹאוּ יָעֻפוּ כְּנֶשֶׁר חָשׁ לֶאֱכוֹל:

חבקוק א:ח

A Bedouin with a cheetah and her kitten, shot in Iraq in 1925

scarce, the cheetah was still found in his day in different parts of the country, including Tabor, the hills of the Galilee, and Gilead.[1] In the early twentieth century, Bedouins in Beersheba hunted them and sold their skins.[2] The last cheetah in Israel was seen in 1959, in the Arava valley, where it ran for a few minutes in front of a truck that was traveling at fifty miles per hour.[3]

Leopards and "Hunting Leopards"

IDENTIFICATION

There is both a strong tradition and clear evidence that the *namer* of Scripture is the leopard. However, there is one reference to the *namer* in Scripture that would perhaps match the cheetah better than the leopard. It occurs in the context of a prophecy describing the terror of the Chaldeans:

Their horses are lighter than *namerim*. (Hab. 1:8)

The term "lighter" probably means "swifter." The *namer* is used in this verse as an example of a very swift animal, with the horses being poetically described as even faster than them. Thus, this verse is likely to refer to the cheetah rather than the leopard. Leopards catch their prey either by ambush or by stalking it to within a close range and then making a very short and fast rush, whereas cheetahs are renowned for their high-speed chases. Cheetahs can reach speeds of up to seventy miles an hour over short distances, and take just three seconds to accelerate to such speeds.

atic cheetah is critically endangered, with just a few dozen individual surviving in Iran and Pakistan.

The Asiatic cheetah was found in the Land of Israel in biblical times. Tristram, chronicler of animal life in the Land of Israel in the nineteenth century, writes that while

In these illustrations from the fifteenth-century Rothschild Miscellany, the leopard and cheetah are clearly distinguished.
The leopard has a stocky build and is patterned with blotches, whereas the cheetah has a slender build and is spotted, and bears a collar.

A cheetah chasing a young gazelle in the Masai Mara, Kenya

The cheetah's rangy build and flexible spine enables it to take strides of enormous length, and it seems to fly above the ground as it runs, making it appropriate to describe it as being "light."

The Hebrew name of the *namer* appears to refer to the variegated coloring of its coat, which would also be applicable to the cheetah. The Mishna uses the term *hamenamer* to describe someone who sows his field in uneven patches, which is explained to be based on the word *namer*:

> "*Hamenamer*" – that he sows in various places in the field, like the appearance of the skin of a leopard, which is spotted[4]. (Rambam, commentary to Mishna Pe'ah 3:2)

Cheetahs and leopards are basically similar in terms of their coloration. Although cheetahs have spots and leopards have blotchy markings, both would certainly be described as variegated in their coloration.

It seems that the term *namer* is a generic term for both leopards and cheetahs. In fact, cheetahs were formerly known as "hunting leopards," due to their being leopard-like cats that can be trained to hunt. Thus, in Tristram's nineteenth-century account of the cheetah in Israel, he describes it as an "animal of the leopard kind, the well-known chetah (sic.), or hunting leopard of India."[5]

The Danger of the *Bardelas*

Although the cheetah may well be included with the leopard in the scriptural term *namer*, elsewhere it is differentiated from the leopard. The Mishna discusses the laws of damages incurred by a person's animals. If your cow or sheep goes on a rampage, Jewish law does not hold you fully accountable, since it could not have been expected. Only if such an animal causes damage on three occasions is it then rated as a dangerous animal, for which one is fully responsible.

But there are some animals that are rated as dangerous predators from the outset. The owner is considered to be forewarned about the risk that they present. If a person owns one of these animals, and it causes harm, he is therefore fully liable:

> The wolf, the lion, the bear, the leopard (*namer*), the *bardelas*, and the snake, are all rated as animals about which one is forewarned. (Mishna Bava Kama 1:4[6])

140

What is the *bardelas*? The Babylonian Talmud understands the *bardelas* of this mishna to be the hyena, whereas the Yerushalmi understands the hyena to be a different animal, as we shall see in that chapter. But the word *bardelas* can be traced to the almost identical Greek word *pardalis*,[7] which generally referred to the leopard. Yet it cannot refer to the leopard in the Mishna's list, since the *namer*, which is certainly the leopard, is listed separately. It therefore appears that the term *pardalis* became a generic term for spotted cats,[8] and was then used in this mishna, in the Hebraized version *bardelas*, to refer specifically to the cheetah.[9] Based on this interpretation of the Mishna's usage of the term, the cheetah is called *bardelas* in Modern Hebrew.

When Cheetahs Attack

LAW AND RITUAL

The aforementioned mishna refers to the laws regarding damages caused by captive cheetahs. In antiquity, cheetahs were often kept in captivity. Sometimes, they were used for hunting other animals, but they were also kept as pets by royalty. They can be easily trained, and are relatively weak and unaggressive compared to other predators, being built for speed rather than fighting. Cheetahs never attack people in the wild, and are often reported as never having killed a human. It may therefore appear odd that this mishna classifies the cheetah as a potentially dangerous animal.

But it would be a mistake to think that cheetahs are harmless. Accounts of cheetahs attacking people are rare, but they do exist. One person chasing cheetahs on horseback was faced with a cheetah that leaped onto the horse and bit him in the face. In another case, a cheetah escaped from its enclosure in a zoo and attacked a child. Another zoo visitor once entered a cheetah enclosure and was killed.[10] As the Mishna rules, a captive cheetah is to be considered a potentially dangerous animal. ∎

While a cheetah is far less dangerous than a lion or leopard, it is still not to be underestimated

Notes

1 Tristram, *The Natural History of the Bible*, pp. 113–4.

2 Bodenheimer, *Animal Life in Palestine*, p. 105.

3 Heinrich Mendelssohn and Yoram Yom-Tov, *Fauna Palaestina: Mammalia of Israel*, p. 25.

4 This is as per the Kapach edition, which has *baherot*, whereas the regular edition has *nekudot*.

5 Tristram, *The Natural History of the Bible*, pp. 113–4.

6 This list of dangerous predators also appears in Mishna Sanhedrin 1:4, Bava Metzia 7:9, and *Mekhilta DeRabbi Yishmael, Mishpatim* 16.

7 See Binyamin Mussafia, *Mussaf HaArukh*, in *Arukh HaShalem, erekh bardelas*. Note that in one manuscript edition of *Mekhilta DeRabbi Yishmael, Mishpatim* 16 (Cam. Or. 1080c), the word is written as *pardalis* (פרד־לס).

8 It should be noted that defining *pardalis* is doubly difficult since these ancient writers themselves may not have had a clear idea of which species they were referring to. George Jennison, in *Animals for Show and Pleasure in Ancient Rome* (Manchester, UK: Manchester University Press, 1937), includes an appendix (pp. 183–7) dedicated to untangling the various Greek terms for big cats. He notes: "Ancient writers were faced with two great difficulties in putting correct names to these spotted cats great and small; they believed in the breeding of hybrid forms in nature, and the Romans had the additional difficulty of naming a foreign animal." See too Benjamin Moser, "The Roman Ethnozoological Tradition: Identifying Exotic Animals in Pliny's Natural History," (University of Western Ontario, 2013), Electronic Thesis and Dissertation Repository, Paper 1206, pp. 69–96.

9 Jennison, *Animals for Show and Pleasure*, notes that the Greek term *pardalis* (πάρδαλις) usually refers to the leopard, but in Oppian of Syria's *The Chase*, part III, the term seems to also refer to the cheetah: it describes a race of *pardalis* that is smaller and slimmer but with a longer tail. See too Menachem Dor, *HaChai BiYemei HaMikra, HaMishna VeHaTalmud*, p. 64; Avraham Ofir-Shemesh, "The *Bardelas* in Ancient Rabbinic Literature: A Test Case of Geographic Identification" (in Hebrew), *Mo'ed* 14 (5764), pp. 70–80. Note that, as discussed by Ofir-Shemesh, there are other references to the *bardelas* in the Talmud which appear to be corrupted versions of a different term, *mandaris*, that probably refers to a mongoose, as discussed in that chapter.

10 All these incidents are recorded by Gordon Grice, *Deadly Kingdom: The Book of Dangerous Animals*, pp. 43–44.

The author encountering an allegedly tame cheetah in South Africa. After this picture was taken, the author discovered that a few weeks earlier, this cheetah had mauled someone.

WOLF

Wolf

זאב

Ze'ev

The Quintessential Opportunist

NATURAL HISTORY

The gray wolf, *Canis lupus*, is distributed throughout the world. However, there are numerous subspecies which vary tremendously in size and coloration. The Arabian wolf may weigh as little as thirty-five pounds, while the huge wolves of Alaska can weigh over 170 pounds. In different parts of the world, wolves can be white, gray, yellowish, reddish, brown and black.

If there is a single trait that best characterizes the wolf, it is opportunism. When hunting their prey, although wolves can and occasionally do take animals in their prime, they usually look for the injured, the very old, the very young – easier opportunities for a meal. Wolves will often make "test runs" against animals to assess whether they would make an easier kill.

Wolves are opportunistic not only in their selection of individual prey animals, but also in the entire range of their diet. "Wolves are flexible and opportunistic predators…adapted to feeding on a diverse array of foods."[1] The wolves in Israel hunt prey ranging in size from rodents to gazelles and cattle calves, and they also scavenge carcasses, eat sweet fruit, and raid garbage.[2]

The opportunism of the wolf is especially relevant to farmers raising livestock, who must be vigilant against wolves snatching their animals. Likewise, the Hai-Bar nature reserve in the Negev desert suffers from wolves finding ways of getting through the fence, especially in the spring, when

בִּנְיָמִין זְאֵב יִטְרָף בַּבֹּקֶר יֹאכַל עַד וְלָעֶרֶב יְחַלֵּק שָׁלָל:

בראשית מט:כז

the wolves know that there is an opportunity to prey upon newborn animals. In the words of the curator of the Hai-Bar, "the best fences in the world won't keep a persistent wolf out unless they are frequently patrolled."[3] As we shall see, this opportunism plays a significant part in the wolf's symbolism in Jewish thought.

Wolves were formerly widespread in the Land of Israel. However, many were eradicated by means of heavy poisoning in the 1950s, and today only a few hundred remain. Most of these are of the subspecies *Canis lupus arabs*, the Arabian wolf, living in the Negev desert in the south. There is also a population of the larger Southern-East Asian Wolf (*Canis lupus pallipes*), which averages seventy pounds in weight and is darker in color. These are based in the north of the country, in the Golan, but have begun to move out to the Galilee and Jezreel Valley. Wolves are a protected species in Israel, but they suffer from conflicts with livestock farmers, and crossbreeding with dogs.

The Benjaminite Wolf

SYMBOLISM

The wolf is called *ze'ev* in Hebrew (a female wolf is called a *ze'eva*[4]). The name Zev has been popular over the centuries as a name for boys, which may seem somewhat odd in light of the nature of this creature as a dangerous menace. However, in the Torah, the wolf is the symbol of the tribe of Benjamin. The primary source in the Torah about wolves, the verse which serves as a basis for countless midrashic expositions, appears in Jacob's blessing of his son Benjamin:

> Benjamin is a predatory wolf; in the morning he devours his prey, and in the evening he divides his spoils. (Gen. 49:27)

As the symbol of the tribe, the wolf also appeared on the tribe's banner in the wilderness, as the Midrash describes:

> Benjamin's [stone on the priestly breastplate] was jasper, and the color of his flag was similar to all the colors, to

ALEX KANTAROVICH

144

An Arabian wolf in Israel

all twelve colors [of the tribes], and there was an illustration of a wolf on it, as "Benjamin is a predatory wolf." (*Bemidbar Rabba* 2:7)

What is the characteristic of the wolf which is reflected in Benjamin? According to the Midrash, it is the opportunism of the wolf that we described above. The Midrash relates the opportunism of the wolf to the tribe of Benjamin in several ways, beginning with an episode that occurred with the Benjaminite clan of Givah. The men of Givah raped and killed a concubine. Facing an outcry by the rest of Israel, the tribe of Benjamin rallied around the men of Givah in defense. As a result, the rest of the nation declared war upon the entire tribe, and forbade anyone from giving them wives. Later, the nation relented, and circumvented the oath by telling the Benjaminites to snatch women at the Shiloh festival: "So they directed the sons of Benjamin, saying, Go and lie in wait in the vineyards, and see, and, behold, if the daughters of Shiloh come out to perform the dances, then come out of the vineyards, and every man can snatch a wife from the daughters of Shiloh, and go to the land of Benjamin" (Judges 21:15–21). The Benjaminites lay in wait and snatched these women, just as a wolf opportunistically snatches its prey:

> "Benjamin is a predatory wolf…" – a large and powerful tribe. Just as the wolf snatches, so too the descendants of Benjamin snatched women in defiance of the oath, for the Jewish people were sworn by oath, "Cursed is he that gives a woman to Benjamin" (Judges 21:18), and it is written, "And you shall snatch for yourselves" (ibid. v. 21). (*Midrash Lekach Tov, Parashat Vaychi*[5])

Snatching by Judges, Kings, and Land
SYMBOLISM

The Midrash continues to give other examples of how the opportunistic snatching of prey by wolves is reflected in the tribe of Benjamin:

> "Benjamin is a predatory wolf…" – this refers to his judges. Just as the wolf snatches, so too Ehud snatched the heart of Eglon. (*Bereshit Rabba* 99:3)

Ehud, of the tribe of Benjamin, engineered a cunning attack upon Israel's enemy Eglon, King of Moab. He requested a private meeting with the king, in which he took advantage of the opportunity to pull out a sword that he had hidden in his clothing and stab him to death. Another midrash mentions this opportunism of Benjamin's descendant, and also relates the last part of the verse in Jacob's blessing to the wolf-like snatching of Ehud:

> "Benjamin is a predatory wolf…"…likewise with his judges…. What is written with Ehud? "He took the

The tribe of Benjamin, depicted in a stained glass window in a synagogue

sword from upon his thigh, and thrust it into Eglon's belly." "In the morning he devours his prey" – referring to his thrusting his sword into Eglon's belly – "And at dusk he divides his spoils" (referring to his ultimately conquering Eglon's lands[6]). (*Midrash Tanchuma, Parashat Vaychi*)

The Midrash proceeds to give a further example of how Benjamin snatched like a wolf:

> "Benjamin is a predatory wolf…" Alternatively: It refers to his kingdom. Just as the wolf snatches, so too Saul

145

Benjamin is a predatory wolf; in the morning he devours his prey, and in the evening he divides his spoils.

(Gen. 49:27)

TAMBAKO / EVJICKR

snatched the kingdom, as it says "And Saul consolidated (lit., "captured") the kingship on Israel" (1 Sam. 14:47). (*Bereshit Rabba* 99:3)

Benjamin's descendant Saul became the first king, thereby effectively snatching it away from the line of Judah. Another midrash likewise sees Saul as being compared to a wolf:

"And you shall not fear from the beasts of the land" (Job 5:22) – from Saul, who was of the tribe of Benjamin, which is compared to a wolf, as it says "Benjamin is a predatory wolf." (*Midrash Iyov* 29)

The Midrash also relates the last part of the verse in Jacob's blessing to the wolf-like snatching of King Saul:

"In the morning he devours his prey" – "And he fought all around with all his enemies" (I Sam. loc cit.). "And in the evening he divides his spoils" – "And Saul died due to the desecration that he had committed (i.e. his kingship was given away to others)" (1 Chr. 10:13). (*Bereshit Rabba* 99:3)

The Midrash further relates Jacob's blessing to the Land of Israel:

"Benjamin is a predatory wolf..." It refers to his land: Just as the wolf snatches, so too the land of Benjamin snatches its crops (i.e. makes them ripen quickly).[7] "In the morning he devours his prey" – this is Jericho, where the crops ripen early. "And at dusk he divides his spoils" – this is Beth-El, where the crops ripen late. (*Bereshit Rabba* 99:3)

In every way, the tribe of Benjamin displayed opportunistic snatching, just like a wolf opportunistically snatches its prey.

The Wolf-Altar of Benjamin

SYMBOLISM

Another view relates Jacob's blessing to the Temple, which was built in the portion of Israel that was allocated to the tribe of Benjamin. It sees an allusion to the Temple in a Psalm describing the Temple being situated in the forest, which brings to mind a certain wild denizen of the forest:

"Benjamin is a predatory wolf" – This teaches that the Temple was built in the portion of Benjamin.... "(David swore to God...I will not allow sleep to my eyes, slumber to my eyelids, before I find a place for God...), Behold, we heard of it in Efrat, we found it in the fields of the forest" (Ps. 132:6) – in the fields of the one who is compared to the beast of the forest. Who is this? It is Benjamin, as it says, "Benjamin is a predatory wolf." (*Sifrei, Vezot HaBerakha* 352[8])

A symbolic connection between the Temple and Benjamin is mentioned in another midrash. It refers specifically to one component of the Temple: the Altar. The Altar was partially built on a strip of land belonging to Judah which was enclosed by the territory of Benjamin, thereby being snatched by it, just like a wolf snatches its prey.[9]

"Benjamin is a predatory wolf" – the Temple was built in the portion of Benjamin. *Ze'ev* (wolf) is [an acronym for] "*Zeh Av*" ("this is the father"). This refers to the Holy Temple. It has been established that Jerusalem was not divided amongst the Tribes, and a strip extended from the portion of Judah into the portion of Benjamin, and the Altar was built there...and that corner stood in the portion of Benjamin, who is called a "snatcher." (*Midrash Aggada, Parashat Vaychi*[10])

A further symbolic connection between the Altar and the wolf is that the fire that descended from the Heavens snatched and consumed the offerings, just like a wolf snatching and devouring its prey:

"Benjamin is a predatory wolf..." R. Pinchas interpreted the verse in reference to the Altar; just as the wolf snatches, so too the Altar would snatch the offerings. "In the morning he devours his prey" – "Offer one lamb in the morning" (Num. 28:4). "And in the evening he divides his spoils" – "And offer the second lamb in the afternoon." (*Bereshit Rabba* 99:3)

The midrashic comparison between the Altar's dramatic consumption of offerings and the wolf's consumption of its prey perhaps reflects a particularly unusual characteristic of wolves. Wolves always eat their food very quickly; unlike with humans, no digestion takes place with the saliva in the mouth, and so there is no reason to chew it. Another reason for their rapid swallowing of food is to prevent it from being stolen by other animals. The phrase "wolfing down food" thus entered the English language to refer to anyone devouring food very rapidly. In addition, because wolves are often unable to obtain food, they have to be able to take full opportunity when it is available. They thus consume very large quantities of food after a kill; a wolf's stomach enables it to eat as much as twenty-two pounds of meat in one meal.[11]

This great capacity of the Altar to devour offerings is also referred to in a non-too-complimentary way, in a story recounted by the Talmud:

There was an incident with Miriam of Bilgah, who switched her religion, and went and married an officer of one of the Greek kings. When the Greeks entered the Sanctuary, she kicked with her sandal on top of the Altar

147

These wolves are fighting over the carcass of a wild sheep

and said, "*Lukas, Lukas!* How long will you consume the money of Israel, and yet you do not stand by them in time of need?!" (Sukka 56b)

Lukas is the Greek name for a wolf.[12] The woman referred to the Altar by this name in reference to its devouring the sheep belonging to Israel.[13]

Wolves, Bears, and Medes

— SYMBOLISM

The wolf appears in Scripture, along with the lion and leopard, as a dangerous predator:

Therefore the lion of the forest has struck them, the wolf of the plains has plundered them, the leopard prowls over their cities; all who emerge from there shall be preyed upon, for their sins are numerous and their waywardness is intense. (Jer. 5:6)

The Midrash, however, notes that such references allude to various nations that have menaced the Jewish people:

R. Yochanan said: "Therefore the lion of the forest has struck them" refers to Babylon, "the wolf of the plains has plundered them" refers to Media, "the leopard prowls over their cities" refers to Greece. (*Vayikra Rabba* 13:5)

The Persian-Median Empire followed that of Babylon in oppressing the Jewish people. Yet while this verse's citation of the lion in reference to Babylon is consistent with its symbolism elsewhere, and likewise with its mention of the

עַל כֵּן הִכָּם אַרְיֵה מִיַּעַר זְאֵב עֲרָבוֹת יְשָׁדְדֵם נָמֵר שֹׁקֵד עַל עָרֵיהֶם כָּל הַיּוֹצֵא מֵהֵנָּה יִטָּרֵף כִּי רַבּוּ פִּשְׁעֵיהֶם עָצְמוּ מְשׁוּבוֹתֵיהֶם:

ירמיה ה:ו

וַאֲרוּ חֵיוָה אָחֳרִי תִנְיָנָה דָּמְיָה לְדֹב וְלִשְׂטַר חַד הֳקִמַת וּתְלָת עִלְעִין בְּפֻמַּהּ בֵּין שִׁנַּהּ וְכֵן אָמְרִין לַהּ קוּמִי אֲכֻלִי בְּשַׂר שַׂגִּיא:

ספר דניאל ז:ה

leopard to refer to Greece, the wolf is not the animal usually used to allude to the Persian/Median Empire. Instead, we find that the bear is normally mentioned, most notably in Daniel's prophetic dream in which he sees the enemies of Israel represented by predatory animals:

Daniel spoke, and said, "I saw in my vision by night...four great beasts.... The first was like a lion.... And behold another beast, a second, like a bear.... Afterwards I beheld, and there was another, similar to a leopard." (Dan. 7:2–6)

The Midrash, however, notes that the spelling used for the Hebrew name of the bear can also be read as the Aramaic name for the wolf:

"And after, I saw another one, similar to a bear" – It is written, "to a *dev* (דב)";[14] this refers to Media. This is the view of R. Yochanan, as R. Yochanan said: "Therefore the lion of the forest has struck them" refers to Babylon, "the wolf of the plains has plundered them" refers to Media. (*Vayikra Rabba* 13:5)

TAMBAKO / FLICKR

The Aramaic name for the wolf is *diva*.[15] The Talmud sometimes uses this word to refer to the wolf:

> Adda bar Chavu had a *ben pakua* (an animal that was removed alive from the womb of its slaughtered mother, which may be eaten without kosher *shechita*) that was attacked by a *duva*. He came before Rav Ashi, who told him, Go slaughter it (and eat it, and the fact that it had a fatal defect as a result of being mauled by a wolf is of no concern[16]). (Chullin 75b)

The commentaries of Rashi and *Tosafot* both explain *duva* to refer to a wolf. Likewise, although the animal in the Book of Daniel is usually understood to be a bear, it can also be read as referring to a wolf. Some explain that the dual possibilities are intended to refer to the dual nature of this empire; a union of Persia with Media, with the former being represented by the bear, and the latter being represented by the wolf.[17]

Benjamin vs. Media: Wolf vs. Wolf
SYMBOLISM

Earlier, we discussed how the tribe of Benjamin was prophetically compared with a wolf. With the Median Empire being represented by the wolf too, the Midrash points out how Benjamin is therefore the natural nemesis of Media:

> "For the Lord God will do nothing, without revealing His secret to His servants the prophets" (Amos 3:7).... Benjamin correlates to the kingdom of Media – each is compared to a wolf. Benjamin is compared to a wolf in

"Benjamin is a predatory wolf" and Media is compared to a wolf in "And after, I saw another one, similar to a bear"; R. Chanina said, It is written *ledaiv*, its name was *daiv* (wolf). This is the view of R. Yochanan, as R. Yochanan said: "Therefore the lion of the forest has struck them" (Jer. 5:6) refers to Babylon, "the wolf of the plains has plundered them" (ibid.) refers to Media. In whose hand does Media fall? In the hand of Mordekhai, who comes from the tribe of Benjamin. (*Bereshit Rabba* 99:2[18])

Mordekhai, who was from the tribe of Benjamin, is the one naturally empowered to defeat the Medes. We further find that the principal enemy of the Jews at that time, Haman, is indirectly linked to a wolf in the following midrash:

> "When you go out to battle" (Deut. 20:1). What is written above? "And your eyes shall not have mercy," and after it says "And you shall see a horse and rider." He said to them: If you have compassion upon them, they will go out to war against you. A parable: A shepherd was shepherding his flock in the forest, and found a wolf cub. He had compassion upon it and raised it, suckling from the goats. A worker came and saw it and said, "Kill it, and do not have pity, so that no harm should come to your flock!" but he did not listen to him. When it grew up, it would see a sheep and kill it, and eat goats. The worker said, "Did I not tell you not to have compassion on it?" So too Moses said: If you have compassion upon them, "those of them who you leave shall be pins in your eyes" (Num. 33:55). And thus we find with Saul, that he had

It may be tempting to adopt a wolf cub as a pet, but the results can be disastrous

וְקַלּוּ מִנְּמֵרִים סוּסָיו וְחַדּוּ מִזְּאֵבֵי עֶרֶב וּפָשׁוּ פָּרָשָׁיו וּפָרָשָׁיו מֵרָחוֹק
יָבֹאוּ יָעֻפוּ כְּנֶשֶׁר חָשׁ לֶאֱכוֹל:

חבקוק פרק א:ח

שָׂרֶיהָ בְקִרְבָּהּ אֲרָיוֹת שֹׁאֲגִים שֹׁפְטֶיהָ זְאֵבֵי עֶרֶב לֹא גָרְמוּ לַבֹּקֶר:

צפניה ג:ג

pity upon Agag, and Achav had pity upon Ben-Hadad.
(*Midrash Yalkut Shimoni* 1:923)

This midrash describes how King Saul's compassion
upon King Agag is comparable to a shepherd's compassion
upon a wolf cub, with similarly disastrous results. Agag's
eventual descendant was Haman.[19] Thus, this wolf cub
turned into a truly menacing wolf – the prime minister of
the Median Empire.

Another view relates the verse in Jacob's blessing to
how Esther, who was also from the tribe of Benjamin, took
Vashti's place as queen to King Ahasuerus. This relates to the
verse not only in terms of Esther being a Benjaminite, but
also in connection to the wolf's devouring of its prey and
division of its spoils:

"Benjamin is a predatory wolf…" It refers to his kingdom: Just as the wolf snatches, so too Esther snatched
the kingship. This is what is written, "And Esther was
taken…" (Est. 2:8). "In the morning he devours his
prey" – "On that day, the king Ahasuerus gave Queen
Esther the house of Haman" (Est. 8:1). "And at dusk he
divides his spoils" – "And Esther placed Mordekhai in
charge of the house of Haman." (*Bereshit Rabba* 99:3)

Finally, another midrash notes that the morning and
evening mentioned in this verse conceptually relate to these
events in the history of the tribe of Benjamin; the dawn of
the tribe was with King Saul, and the evening relates to the
dark exile of the Median Empire:

Our forefather Jacob alluded to [the Purim story] in his
blessings to the tribes. This is what is written, "Benjamin
is a predatory wolf; in the morning he devours his prey."
This refers to Saul, who was the morning of Israel in
that he was the first of their kings, and he was from the
tribe of Benjamin, and he smote Amalek and destroyed
all that they had. "And in the evening, he shall divide
the spoil" – this refers to Mordekhai and Esther, who
stood up for Israel in their exile, which is compared
to the evening, and divided the spoil of Haman. For
[Mordekhai] is compared to a wolf, and the Holy One
set up him in opposition to the wolf of the kings of Persia
and Media, who are likened to the wolf…the Holy One
set up Mordekhai and Esther against them, for they are
from the tribe of Benjamin about which it is written,
"Benjamin is a predatory wolf." (*Esther Rabba* 10:13)

Dawn and Dusk

—————————————— SYMBOLISM

Let us return once more to the primary source in Scripture
for understanding the role of the wolf in Jewish thought, the
verse comparing Benjamin to a wolf: "Benjamin is a predatory wolf; in the morning he eats his prey, and in the evening
he divides his spoils" (Gen. 49:27). This verse highlights
the activities of the wolf as occurring at two times: dawn
and dusk. This is well known to be typical of all wolves, as
noted by the curator of the Hai-Bar nature reserve: "Like
wolves around the world, Israel's desert wolves are generally
crepuscular – that is, they are active in the early morning
and evening hours and tend to sleep through the middle of
the day and middle of the night."[20] Another verse likewise
associates the wolf with dusk:

For behold, I am establishing the Chaldeans, that bitter
and impetuous nation.… It is awesome and terrifying.…
Its horses are swifter than leopards, and they are sharper
than the wolves of dusk, and its horsemen are many.
(Hab. 1:6–8)

Scripture describes the Chaldeans as being even quicker
to attack than wolves at dusk, which are hungry after not
having eaten all day.[21] But if the wolves are so hungry by
dusk, why don't they hunt earlier? The answer is to be found
in another verse which compares the sinning city of Jerusalem to these evening wolves:

She did not listen to the voice; she did not take rebuke;
she did not trust in God, she did not draw near to her
Lord. Her princes in her midst were as roaring lions, her
officers were the wolves of dusk, not [leaving] a bone for
the morning. (Zeph. 3:2–3)

The verse is comparing the crafty, bribe-taking officers
to the cunning wolf who attacks under cover of darkness and consumes its prey so entirely that not even a
bone remains to show what happened.[22] The wolf, ever
conscious of picking the right opportunity, waits for the
concealment of dusk in order to give its attacks a greater
chance of success.

In a prominent work on wolf biology and lore by Barry
Lopez, it is noted that this feature of wolf behavior is so
striking as to form a basis for the wolf's symbolism: "From
classical times he had been a symbol of things in transit.
He was a twilight hunter, seen at dawn and dusk."[23] The
time of wolf activity also relates to a halakhic ruling in the
Talmud:

From when may one recite the *Shema* prayer in the
morning? …R. Meir said: From when one can distinguish between a wolf and a dog. (Berakhot 9b)

"Her officers were the wolves of dusk..."

(Zeph. 3:3)

One could explain this in several ways. Simply speaking, it is referring to a level of light, enough to enable one to distinguish between the gaunt gray wolf and the stockier, brown dog. But one could also note that wolves are commonly seen at such an hour, and therefore it is appropriate to use them as a frame of reference for determining the level of light. This would also account for why this frame of reference became a way of obliquely referring to dawn:

> "In that night Belshazzar the Chaldean king was slain" (Dan. 5:30). At what hour was he killed? R. Eleazar and R. Shmuel bar Nachman gave different answers. R. Eleazar said: At the time when sleep is sweetest (i.e. at the beginning of night). R. Shmuel said: At the time when a man can distinguish between a wolf and a dog[24] (i.e. at dawn). (*Shir HaShirim Rabba* 3:3)

Some offer additional depth to the Talmud's ruling regarding the recital of the *Shema* prayer. It is written in the *Shema* prayer that it should be recited "when one goes out on the trail" (*uvelekhtekha baderekh*), and it is further stated in the Talmud that one should only begin one's trav-els at daybreak, so that there is enough light to avoid danger. Thus, only when one can ascertain the difference between a dog and a wolf – a predator active at dawn – is it safe enough to travel. Only at that level of light should one "go out on the trail," and therefore only at that time is one obligated to recite the *Shema*.[25]

But there may be still another level of meaning to the Talmud's statement that the dawn prayer of *Shema* should be recited when one can distinguish a wolf: that the wolf is a creature that is symbolically related to such times of half-light. Lopez notes that this is a pervasive theme in wolf lore: "The link between the wolf and a period of halflight – either dawn or dusk, though dawn is more widely known as the hour of the wolf… the wolf as a creature of dawn, representing an emergence from darkness into enlightenment… the association is old enough to have been the basis for the Latin idiom for dawn, *inter lupum et canem*, between the wolf and the dog. Darkness and savagery are symbolized in the wolf, while enlightenment and civilization are symbolized in the tame wolf, the dog."[26]

Wolves howl most frequently at dawn and dusk

The wolf is a symbol of transition. Behaviorally, it is active at times of transition. Taxonomically, it is a creature that, within a single species (for wolves and dogs are both *Canis lupis*), can be either a savage killer or man's best friend. And thus, in Jewish law, it becomes the barometer for times of transition.

Of the two periods of half-light, Lopez writes that it is dawn that was more widely rated as the hour of the wolf. Scripture, on the other hand, places greater emphasis on dusk:

> His horses are swifter than cheetahs, and quicker than the wolves of dusk. (Hab. 1:8)

> Her princes in her midst were as roaring lions, her officers were the wolves of dusk, not [leaving] a bone for the morning. (Zeph. 3:2–3)

> Therefore the lion from the forest has struck them, the wolf of the dusk has plundered them. (Jer. 5:6[27])

There is another possible reference in Scripture to wolves as being creatures of dusk. The name of the fourth of the plagues that befell Egypt, *arov*, is a word of unclear meaning. But some suggest that it is based on the word *erev*, dusk, and it refers to the creature that is known for being active at that time: the wolf.[28] It was a plague of "duskies"!

The description of the wolf as a creature of dusk may convey another concept about wolves; but in order to appreciate it, we must first explore one more aspect of wolves.

Wolves and Ravens

SYMBOLISM

Very few mammals have symbiotic relationships with other creatures. One of the rare exceptions is the wolf. When wolves howl before starting a hunt, this attracts ravens. They follow the wolves on the chase, and feed on the remains of the kill.[29] The wolves also benefit, since the ravens will sometimes alert the wolves to the presence of prey, or to potential danger at a kill site.[30]

Some zoologists speculate that the relationship between wolves and ravens may be assisted by their psychological make-up.[31] Both species are highly social, which means that they possess the psychological mechanisms necessary for forming social attachments. It appears that wolves and ravens have been able to extend this beyond their own species to include each other. Whatever the cause, this relationship is so common that the raven is sometimes called the "wolf-bird."

This unusual partnership also finds expression in Scripture. The only person in Scripture named after the wolf, the Midianite chieftain Ze'ev, had a partner named Orev – Raven!

A raven near a wolf at a kill site

And they captured the two chieftains of Midian, Orev and Ze'ev; and they executed Orev in the Rock of Orev, and they executed Ze'ev at the Winepress of Ze'ev, and they pursued Midian; and they brought the heads of Orev and Ze'ev to Gideon, across the Jordan. (Judges 7:25)[32]

It may be that since wolves and ravens have a well-known association, the Midianites called their two chieftains by these names. Alternately, it may be that these were not their real names, but Scripture calls them by these names in order to tell us something about them, as we shall see.[33]

Aside from the social and symbiotic relationship between wolves and ravens, there is another connection between them. The Hebrew name for raven, *orev*, is comprised of the same letters as the word *erev*, dusk. Dusk, the time which is so epitomized by wolves that they are repeatedly referred to as "the wolves of dusk" and according to some are even referred to solely by the name "dusky" in the Egyptian plague, is the same word used as the name of the raven. The Midrash also records a view that that the Egyptian plague of *arov* was comprised of a variety of ravens and other such birds, while another view maintains that it was both wolves and ravens.[34]

The etymology of the name *orev* for raven is simple to explain in terms of the raven's black plumage, reminiscent of the onset of night. But one can also see other ways in which the raven is related to this word. *Erev*, dusk, is the time when day mixes with night; in fact, the word for mixture in Hebrew is *ervuv*.[35] Ravens are a mixture in that they are the only bird to possess two of the signs of kosher birds as well as two of the signs of non-kosher birds – a true mixture. The Midrash notes that the raven also has a tendency to mix even when mixing is forbidden:

153

There were three that engaged in conjugal relations while in the Ark: Ham, the raven, and the dog. (Sanhedrin 108b)

Males and females of all species were to remain separate for the duration of their stay on the Ark, but the ravens negated this, mingling together and mating. Perhaps it is for this reason that the chieftains of Midian are called Ze'ev and Orev by the Torah. The crime of Midian was to send their girls to mix and intermingle with the Jewish people.[36] Ravens and wolves are thus both creatures that represent dusk, the mixture of light and dark, and also mixing in general – and furthermore they mix with each other, mammal with bird. The dusky ravens and the wolves of dusk are both symbols of the mixing of two distinct realms.

Hunting Habits

NATURAL HISTORY

A number of aspects of wolf behavior and biology are brought out by various accounts in the Talmud. Several of these relate to the wolf's hunting and feeding habits.

A fast was once decreed because wolves ate two children in Transjordan. R. Yose said: It was not that they ate the children, but that they were seen. (Mishna Taanit 3:6)

Three women brought their nests of birds [as a Temple offering]…one said that it was for her *ziva*…they thought that she meant that it was for her untimely menstrual flow (*zava*), but she said that a wolf (*zev*) had come to take her son. (Y. Shekalim 21b)

It is popularly stated today that there is no documented case of a wolf ever killing a person in North America. This is inaccurate; there are in fact several such cases.[37] Still, it is true that wolves in North America are, on the whole, much less dangerous than people imagine. But wolves in many other parts of the world are every bit as deadly as their reputation. In 1878, a particularly bad year in India, wolves killed 624 people (mostly children). In 2008, a wolf broke into a house in the Golan Heights in Israel and attacked a child.[38]

A story in the Talmud of wolves killing and eating people further reflects the wolf's gruesome eating habits:

Ulla said in the name of R. Shimon b. Yehotzadak: It once happened that wolves devoured two children, and they passed them out through their anal canal. The question came up before the Sages, and they declared that the flesh [of the children] was clean but that their bones were unclean. (Taanit 22b[39])

Wolves will crush the bones of their prey to get at the marrow, but they will also eat the bone itself as an important

A wolf chewing on its prey

source of calcium and phosphorus. Fragments of bone will be excreted, coated in hair to protect the internal lining of the gut.[40] A human corpse transmits ritual impurity – but what if it has passed through the digestive system of an animal? In this case mentioned in the Talmud, the ruling was that the flesh had been sufficiently digested such that by the time it was excreted, it no longer transmitted ritual impurity. The bones, on the other hand, were not fully digested, and when they were excreted, they did transmit ritual impurity.

Another discussion in the Talmud may shed further light on which parts of its prey a wolf will eat:

R. Abba asked of Rav Huna: If a wolf took the innards of a slaughtered animal, what is the law?[41] (Chullin 9a[42])

The term used for "innards," *benei me'ayim*, is usually translated as intestines. While several popular works on natural history state that wolves do not eat intestines, certain studies by experts show that they do eat them.[43] They shake the intestines vigorously to remove most of their contents and then consume them. The mucous membranes that form the walls of the intestines provide them with a source of fatty acids, and the microflora remaining inside the intestines may be a source of vitamins that maintain their skin and hair. However the Talmud elsewhere establishes that the term *benei me'ayim* can refer to other internal organs, such as the heart and liver.[44] These are favored food items for wolves, and thus the Talmud may be speaking here of innards in general.[45]

How Wolves Attack

THEOLOGY, PHILOSOPHY, AND SCIENCE

An animal is only kosher for consumption if it is in good physical health at the time of slaughter. The Mishna lists various *tereifot*, fatal defects, which render an animal prohibited for use as food. One of these fatal defects is a mauling by a wolf:

These are the *tereifot* in domesticated animals... if it fell from a roof, if most of its ribs were broken, a mauling by a wolf; R. Yehuda says, a mauling by a wolf [is considered a fatal defect] with a small domestic animal, and a mauling by a lion [is considered a fatal defect] with a large animal. (Mishna Chullin 3:1)

Although wolves usually hunt in packs, single wolves are capable of bringing down even very large prey such as moose[46] or bison.[47] They usually prefer not to take on such prey, however, since one kick from a moose can disembowel the wolf. Furthermore, the wolves of North America, which bring down such large prey, are much bigger animals than the wolves of Israel and the surrounding region. While North American wolves average 100 pounds, with one record specimen weighing 175 pounds, the wolves of the Middle East average only about 50 pounds and take much smaller prey. Thus, from a halakhic standpoint, if a wolf mounts an unsuccessful attack against a large animal such as a cow, the animal is not considered to be mortally wounded and it may still be slaughtered for human consumption. Only with small livestock, such as sheep and goats, is a mauling by a wolf considered a fatal defect. The

Talmud further clarifies that a wolf is the smallest creature with which a mauling on a small domestic animal renders it as possessing a fatal defect.[48]

In the introduction to the section on predators, we have discussed one difficulty with these laws, regarding the Talmud's statement that the result of such maulings is that "venom" is injected into the prey animal. It has been suggested that this refers to bacterial infection.[49] But another potential difficulty is that the Talmud cites Abaye's tradition that maulings which are rated as causing fatal defects are only maulings inflicted with the claws, not with the teeth.[50] This conflicts with contemporary observations of wolves, which reveal that wolves attack prey with their teeth rather than with their claws. The reason for this reflects the very different hunting strategy of wolves compared to members of the cat family such as lions and leopards. A big cat is an ambush predator; it is not built for running at speed, but rather for firmly seizing its prey. It uses its strong arms and claws to grasp its prey, enabling it to inflict a killing bite in a precise spot. Wolves, on the other hand, are pursuit predators. The legs of a wolf are slender, and the paws are not jointed for grasping; its body is built for long-distance pursuit, not for bringing down prey. The wolf's claws are

A wolf attacks its prey with its jaws rather than its claws

155

strong, but very blunt, because the tips are worn off by constant contact with the ground. These are used for digging and gripping the earth while running, not for seizing or killing prey, which is usually done with a large number of slashing bites.

However, there is a possible resolution to this difficulty. The fifth digit of the wolf's front paws is a sharp claw higher up the leg, known as a dewclaw. This is sometimes used for holding on to very large prey. The dewclaw may be the subject of the Talmud's reference.

Yet in any case, it seems that the Talmud itself elsewhere notes that wolves kill with their teeth rather than with their claws:

> If a shepherd was tending a flock, but left them and went to the town, and a wolf came and was *taraf*, or a lion came and was *dores*. (Bava Metzia 93b)

Here we seem to have a contrast presented between the typical modes of attack of a wolf and a lion. A lion is *dores*. A wolf, on the other hand, is *toref*. But what is the difference between these two modes of attack? Some explain that *dores* refers to attacking to immediately kill and consume, whereas *toref* refers to wounding the sheep and then dragging it back to a lair for later consumption.[51] But others

explain that *dores* refers to killing with claws, whereas *toref* refers to killing with its teeth.[52] Accordingly, this passage, expressing the typical difference between attacks by lions and attacks by wolves, is consistent with our knowledge of how wolves kill.

What, then, are we to make of the other talmudic passage, regarding maulings that create a fatal defect being only those caused by claws? It may represent a dissenting view. Alternately, perhaps that statement was based upon attacks by other types of predators.

Front and Rear
THEOLOGY, PHILOSOPHY, AND SCIENCE

The Torah tells us to "Remember the Sabbath" (Ex. 20:8) and "Guard the Sabbath" (Deut. 5:12). A curious midrash about this dual terminology makes an unexpected mention of the wolf:

> "Remember" and "Guard" – Remember it in front, and guard it at the back. From here they said that one should add from the secular onto the sanctified (i.e. one should extend the Sabbath at both ends). A parable is to be drawn with a wolf, which is *tored* from the front and the rear. (*Mekhilta, Parashat Yitro*, 7:4)

In this picture of a wolf's feet one can see that most of the claws are blunt, but the higher dewclaws are sharp.

The wolf is described here as being *tored*. The word *tored* can mean "quarrel," "make unsteady," "cause trouble," "cause anxiety," and so on. In English, the word "worry" originally referred to such physical attack, and gradually began to be used to refer to verbal harassment, until eventually the word "worry" began to refer to feeling harassed and troubled. Dogs and wolves, however, are still described sometimes as "worrying at their prey." This may reflect the way in which the word *tored* is being used in this midrash; referring to the wolf attacking its prey by harassing it and biting at it. This is also consistent with the meaning of an alternate text in the Midrash, which speaks of how the wolf is *toref* (attacks) from the front and rear.

Numerous studies of wolves confirm that they worry at their prey beginning at the rear, followed by attacking the front.[53] It appears to be in this vein that some suggest that the Midrash is referring to Shabbat snatching sparks of sanctity that are absorbed within the surrounding weekdays.[54] Just as the wolf is renowned for snatching at its prey from the front and rear, so too Shabbat snatches some of the preceding and following days for itself. In this interpretation, Shabbat is represented by the wolf. But another interpretation is that Shabbat is the animal (or flock) being attacked by the wolf. Just as the prey animal (or flock) is most vulnerable at its front and back, so too Shabbat is most vulnerable to being transgressed at the beginning and end, which is where precautions must be taken.[55]

However, others explain the midrash very differently. *Tored* can also mean to "banish" or "drive away," and it would therefore refer to the wolf scaring people into keeping their distance from it, whether they are in front of it or behind it.[56] This would be consistent with a different version of the midrash quoted in some works, in which the midrash refers to a lion rather than a wolf, and speaks of how all are in fear of it and keep a safe distance from it.[57] By the same token, people are in awe of Shabbat, and fear transgressing it, and they therefore take the precaution of adding time to the beginning and end of Shabbat during which they refrain from engaging in work.[58]

Surplus Killing

NATURAL HISTORY

Another aspect of wolf predation is mentioned in Scripture:

> Her officers within her are like wolves mauling their prey, shedding blood, to destroy lives, and for the sake of unjust gain. (Ezek. 22:27)

The nineteenth-century commentator Rabbi Meir Leibush Wisser (better known as Malbim) explains this verse to refer to the fact that unlike lions, which kill only to eat, wolves will sometimes kill even not for the purposes of food. This wanton destruction is reflected in the verse describing the officers as being like wolves in that they shed blood simply in order to destroy lives as well as for unjust gain.

The phenomenon of wolves killing many more animals than they can eat is well documented. Researchers in Canada's Northwest Territories once found thirty-four dead calves, scattered over a large area, of which the wolves had eaten only a few parts from half the calves and not touched the rest at all. In 1969, during a harsh winter in Minnesota which left deer in deep snow, wolves killed almost every deer they came across, leaving many of them entirely uneaten.[59] With attacks on domestic animals, the same phenomenon sometimes occurs, with many dozens more sheep being killed than the wolves actually eat:[60]

> There was a case involving the children of Yehuda b. Shamui, in which wolves tore apart three hundred of their sheep. (Y. Beitza 2b)

Why does this happen? It is thought that the wolves' predatory impulse is sometimes sparked by the stimulus of so many helpless prey animals, in such a way that the desire to kill is not shut off. Another explanation is that if an ordinary sequence of killing is interrupted or altered in some way, the normal instinct to end the kill is not activated. Either way, when wolves attack, the number of animals slaughtered can be immense; the shepherd cannot assume that only one or two animals were taken, and he must count the number that remain to assess the devastation:

> It is written, "And those that died in the plague numbered twenty-four thousand" (Ex. 25:9), to teach you that whenever there were casualties, they were counted. It is comparable to a wolf who fell upon some sheep; the owner of the sheep said to the shepherd, "Count how many are missing." (*Bemidbar Rabba* 20:25)

Sometimes, the devastation is so massive that the shepherd gives up in despair:

> "God said to Moses, Your day to die has drawn near" (Deut. 31:14).... To what may this be compared? To a shepherd with whom a wolf has entered to his flock and torn them asunder. What did he do? He raised his cloak over his shoulder, placed it upon his head, and left in despair, just as it says, "as the shepherd folds his garment" (Jer. 43). So too, with me (said Moses), if I do not enter the land of Israel, I am toiling in despair, without reward.

157

A wolf and raven in the Arava valley, Israel

The Holy One said to him: By your life! I am giving you all your complete reward in the future era, more than all Israel." (*Midrash Tanna'im, Parashat Vayelekh* 31:14)

There are indications in the Mishna that wolves are extremely prone to launch attacks. The Mishna lists wild animals which are rated as dangerous, such that if they are privately owned, their owner is considered to be warned from the outset that they may cause damage and he is fully liable if this happens. As expected, all the dangerous predators of the Torah are in this list, but they are listed in an intriguing order:

The wolf, the lion, the bear, the leopard, the cheetah, and the snake, are all rated as animals about which one is warned. (Mishna Bava Kama 1:4)

The same order appears in the Mishna that describes the procedure by which such animals are put to death if they kill someone:

The wolf, the lion, the bear, the leopard, the cheetah, and the snake – their death is via a court of twenty-three. (Mishna Sanhedrin 1:4)

One would expect the lion to head this list, followed in turn by bear and leopard. Yet the wolf appears at the beginning of the list, even though it is a much lesser predator than the lion, bear, or leopard. There are other instances, too, where the wolf is mentioned before the lion.[61] Perhaps this is because wolf attacks are a much more common scenario.

Wolves and Sheep

—————————————————————— SYMBOLISM

Although wolves will kill whatever kind of livestock is available to them, they are best known as predators of sheep. This is probably because sheep are the most vulnerable to attack. While most attacks on horses or cattle result in only one animal being killed or wounded, attacks on sheep usually result in several being killed.

"[And Laban put a distance of three days] between him and Jacob" (Gen. 30:36) – three days between the sheep that he gave to his sons, and those sheep that he gave to Jacob, so that the sheep of Jacob should not return and mix with the remaining sheep of Laban. As soon as Jacob left them, immediately wolves came and took many of them. (*Midrash Aggada, Parashat Vayetzeh*)

The wolf is known as the predator of sheep; the sheep is known as the prey of the wolf. This connection is noted in a midrash which describes several different such predator-prey relationships:

"God seeks [to protect] the pursued" (Eccl. 3:15). R. Eliezer b. Rav Yosef b. Zimra said: This is even the case with offerings. The Holy One said: The ox is pursued by the lion, the goat is pursued by the leopard, the sheep from the wolf; do not bring Me offerings from the pursuers, but only from the pursued. (*Vayikra Rabba* 27:5)

The common phenomenon of wolves eating sheep becomes a convenient way of accounting for any loss to the flock, as Jacob observed:

"And I did not eat the rams of your sheep" (Gen. 31:38) – as is the way of other shepherds, who eat the rams and claim that they were eaten by wolves. (*Midrash Lekach Tov, Parashat Vayetzeh*)

While lions, leopards, and wolves are all known as predators of various types of livestock, the phenomenon of wolves killing sheep is so tragically familiar that it became the archetypical predator-prey relationship, cited as an analogy for evil nations attacking the Jewish people. For example, the Midrash states that when Moses pleaded with God for assistance in shepherding the Children of Israel, arguing that it was not befitting God's honor that he should end up failing in his task, he compared such a failure to one who mourns the loss of his flock to wolves:

"Why should I be like one veiled (in mourning) [among the flocks of your friends]" (Song. 1:7) – That I should not be like a shepherd with whom wolves have entered into his flock and torn them apart, while he covered himself with a cloak and escaped. (*Shir HaShirim Rabba* 1:44)

The Children of Israel likewise saw themselves as sheep threatened by a wolf:

"[The people said to Moses and Aaron], May God look upon you and judge, for you have made our very scent abhorrent in the eyes of Pharaoh and his servants, to place a sword in their hands to murder us!" (Ex. 5:21). R. Yehuda b. R. Shalom said: They said to Moses, We are comparable to a lamb which the wolf comes to take,

and the shepherd runs after it to save it from the wolf; between the shepherd and the wolf, the lamb is torn apart. Thus Israel said: Moses, between you and Pharaoh, we are dead! (*Shemot Rabba* 5:21)

The parable given is explained to mean that while the shepherd is running to get his weapon, the lamb is killed; so too, said the people to Moses, while you were hiding to trick Pharaoh, he is killing us.[62] An instantaneous rescue would be welcomed, but a delayed rescue causes more suffering, just as the shepherd's delay enables the wolf to make a final, ferocious attack.[63] However, in another midrash, the Jewish people are presented as sheep that are successfully protected from wolves, by virtue of their shepherd being God rather than Moses:

"You led Your people like sheep, in the hand of Moses and Aaron" (Ps. 77:21).... Just as the shepherd is careful day and night to protect his sheep from wolves, so too the Holy One is careful with Israel, as it says, "And the pillar of cloud did not depart" (Ex. 13:22). (*Midrash Yalkut Shimoni* II:818)

The same structure, with God rather than Moses as the shepherd, is seen in another midrash, which details how wolves symbolize their enemies:

R. Yehuda b. R. Shimon said: A parable: It is like a person who had a staff and a basket (i.e. meager resources). He collected and saved, until he was able to buy sheep, but wolves came and tore them apart. The shepherd

Wolves consuming a sheep

said: I will return to the staff and basket. The shepherd is the Holy One, as it says, "Listen, O shepherd of Israel, You who leads Joseph like a flock; appear, O You who is enthroned upon the Cherubim" (Ps. 80:2). The sheep are Israel, as it says, "Now, you are My sheep, the sheep of My pasture" (Ezek. 34:31). The wolves entering to the flock and tearing them apart – these are the haters, who entered the Temple. At that moment, the Holy One said: "If only My head would be water (i.e. if only I could return to the primeval world where My presence hovered over the waters unchallenged)" (Jer. 8:23). (*Eikha Rabba* 1:52)

While there is a general metaphor in which the Jewish people are sheep and their foes are wolves, a more specific version of this metaphor has the Jewish people being a single lamb, the weakest of sheep, facing seventy wolves, corresponding to the multitude of other nations:

David said: A lamb amongst seventy wolves – what can it do? Israel is amongst seventy powerful nations – what could it do, were it not that You stand on their behalf at every moment? (*Midrash Pesikta Rabbati* 9)

The wolf is renowned as the relentless predator of sheep, even when it is a single wolf against an entire flock of sheep. The motif of a single sheep standing against seventy wolves is thus especially powerful, and is mentioned on several occasions in midrashic literature.

"The Jews gathered in their cities…and nobody could stand before them, for their fear had fallen upon all the peoples…" (Est. 9:2). Caesar Andrianus said to R. Yehoshua, Great is the lamb that can stand before seventy wolves! He replied, Great is the shepherd who saves them and breaks [their enemies] before them! (*Esther Rabba* 10:11[64])

Defense Against Wolves

LAW AND RITUAL

The Mishna, in discussing the law that certain types of guardians are not accountable for unavoidable damage to the items or livestock they are guarding, explains which types of wolf attacks are considered unavoidable:

[An attack by] a single wolf is not considered unavoidable, but [an attack by] two wolves is considered

There are usually less than ten wolves in a pack

BILDAGENTUR ZOONAR GMBH / SHUTTERSTOCK

unavoidable. R. Yehuda says: When there is an outbreak of wolves, even an attack by a single wolf is considered unavoidable. (Mishna Bava Metzia 7:9)

Such an attack on the flock is so difficult to prevent that the guardian is not held accountable. However, in terms of protecting oneself against an outbreak of wolves, the Talmud does note, in passing, a popular method:

A daughter of an Israelite (who may not eat priestly tithes) who comes to light a candle from a *kohenet* (the single daughter or wife of a priest) may dip the wick in oil of tithes, that is due to be burned, and light it. [But how is a non-*kohen* allowed to benefit from tithes?] R. Chuna said in the name of the academy of R. Yannai: The permission was given at a time of an outbreak of wolves. (Y. Shevi'it 4:2)

Using such oil would ordinarily be forbidden, but when there is an outbreak of wolves, it is permitted as a security measure. This may refer to the person being able to light her path to see her surroundings and avoid danger.[65] Alternately, it may be that fire protects a person against wolves, which are afraid of fire.[66]

Various different measures were taken to protect flocks of sheep from wolves. The Mishna, when discussing which items may be transported by an animal through the public domain on Shabbat, makes a cryptic reference to rams being allowed to go out while "*levuvin*." The meaning of *levuvin* is obscure, and amongst the interpretations presented in the Talmud is one that relates to wolves:

"Rams may go out *levuvin*." What does *levuvin* mean?… Ulla said: A piece of leather is bound around their heart, so that wolves do not attack them. – But do wolves only attack males, and not females (i.e. why specify rams)? – It is because rams are at the head of the flock. – But do wolves only attack at the head of the flock, not at the rear? – Rather, rams are attacked because they are fat. – But are there no fat females? And can the wolves know (when they want to attack females at the rear, that there are males at the front)? – Rather, the males are vulnerable because they walk with their noses up and as though looking out. (Shabbat 53b)

Why would walking with their nose up make the rams particularly vulnerable? One explanation of the Talmud is that the rams are thereby provoking the wolves.[67] Another view is that the rams adopt a more aggressive stance vis-à-vis other rams, which simultaneously makes their underbellies more vulnerable to attacks by wolves.[68]

Defense Against Metaphorical Wolves
———————————————————————— SYMBOLISM

One strategy of protecting sheep from a wolf is to divert the wolf's attention by sending a particularly challenging prey animal in his path:

R. Chama bar Rav Chanina said, when Israel left Egypt the angel Samael stood up to accuse them, and R. Chama explained in the name of his father, it is comparable to a shepherd who was crossing his flock over a river when a wolf came to attack the sheep. The experienced shepherd took a large goat and gave it to the wolf, saying, "Let him struggle with this while we cross the river, and then I will bring it." So, too, when Israel left Egypt, the angel Samael stood up to accuse them and said before the Holy One: "Master of the Universe! Until now they were worshipping idols, and You are going to split the sea for them?!" What did the Holy One do? He handed over Job, who was one of Pharaoh's advisors, about whom it is written, "A wholesome and straightforward man" (Job 1:1), and said, "Here is this one in your hand." The Holy One said, "While he is busy with Job, Israel is crossing the sea, and afterwards I will save Job." (*Shemot Rabba* 21:7[69])

The Talmud notes that it was difficult for Samael (Satan) to deal with Job, since although he was allowed to cause him immense suffering, he had to be careful not to kill him.[70] God could therefore (so to speak) leave Job with Satan, so that Satan would have his hands full, while He took the Children of Israel through the sea, returning to rescue Job later. The metaphor given is that of a shepherd, who buys time to cross his flock over the river by sending a large goat to the approaching wolf. The wolf will not be able to kill the goat immediately, giving the shepherd time to cross his sheep over the river and return to fight off the wolf. Both male and female goats have been known to successively fend off attacking wolves, due to their aggressive disposition and sharp horns. With sheep, too, large males can pose a challenge to wolves:

"And Esau went to meet him, and they hugged" (Gen. 33:4). – Esau sought to bite him, but his neck turned to marble…"and they wept" (ibid.). Why did they weep? A parable: To what can this be compared? To a wolf which came to snatch a ram. The ram began to butt him, and the wolf's teeth were caught up in the ram's horns. Each began to weep; the wolf cried because it could not do anything to it, and the ram cried that it might return and kill it. So too with Esau and Jacob: Esau cried because Jacob's neck became like marble. And Jacob wept in case Esau would return and bite him. (*Midrash Tanchuma, Vayishlach* 4)

161

SONJA PAUEN / FLICKR

The Czechoslovakian wolfdog was originally produced by crossing German shepherd dogs with Carpathian wolves

But the best solution (from the shepherd's perspective) is to attempt to actually capture and kill the wolf.

> "He shall bathe his feet in the blood of the wicked" (Ps. 58:11) – This refers to Balaam. Moses said to Pinchas and to the men of the army: I know that the wicked Balaam is there (in Midian) to take his payment; while the wolf is coming to the sheep, spread a trap for him! (*Bemidbar Rabba* 22:5)

Another parable of a wolf being trapped seems particularly odd in that the wolf is used as a metaphor for the Jewish people rather than for their enemies:

> "And all the servants of the king who were within the king's gate would bow down and prostrate themselves before Haman, for so the king had commanded about him..." (Est. 3:2). R. Yose bar Chanina expounded: "The arrogant have hidden a snare for me" (Ps. 140:6). The congregation of Israel said before the Holy One: "Master of the Universe! The heathens have spread a trap for me to cause my downfall! They tell me to worship idols; if I listen to them I will be punished, and if I do not listen to them they will kill me!" It is comparable to a wolf who thirsted for water, and they spread a trap over the well for him. The wolf said, "If I go down to drink, I will be trapped, and if I don't go down, I will be trapped of thirst!" (*Esther Rabba* 7:6)

Perhaps this can be understood in light of the fact that this midrash is in reference to the Book of Esther. As discussed earlier, while the oppression of the Persian/Median empire is symbolized by a wolf, so too is Mordekhai, hero of the resistance. The wolf seems to have no way out of being trapped, but eventually its opportunism enables it to find a way to survive and triumph. So, too, Mordekhai did manage to avoid bowing down to Haman and to avoid being killed.

Wolves and Dogs

— SYMBOLISM

There is a general consensus amongst zoologists that the wolf is the ancestor of the domestic dog. However, there is great controversy as to whether the dog and wolf should now be considered as the same species (*Canis lupus*), two separate species (with the dog being *Canis familiaris*), or whether the dog should be rated as a subspecies of the wolf (*Canis lupus familiaris*). Such disputes relate to differences of opinion regarding how much weight should be given to various morphological and behavioral differences. In the Mishna, these differences are considered significant enough to rate dogs and wolves as separate types with regard to the prohibition against crossbreeding animals:

> The wolf and the dog, the *kufri* dog and the fox, the goats and the gazelles, the ibex and the ewes, the horse and the mule, the mule and the donkey, and the donkey and the onager – even though they are all similar to each other, they are considered forbidden mixtures. (Mishna Kilayim 1:6)

Such crossbreeding is a sign of corruption:

> R. Azariah said in the name of R. Yehuda bar Shimon: All corrupted their ways in the generation of the Flood; the dog mixed with the wolf, the rooster with the pea-

162

cock. This is what is written, "For all flesh had become corrupted" – it does not say "Every person had become corrupted" but rather "For all flesh had become corrupted." (*Bereshit Rabba* 28:8)

The behavior described by the Midrash is a sign of corruption because it is an aberration. Although it does happen on occasion, wolves and dogs generally do not voluntarily interbreed.[71] In cases where they do interbreed, the resultant hybrids are not only corrupt from the standpoint of the halakhic prohibition of crossbreeding; they are also corrupt from a behavioral standpoint. "Wolfdogs," as they are commonly known, are less predictable in their behavior than either wolves or dogs, and are considered especially dangerous to humans.[72]

One reason why wolves and dogs do not generally interbreed is that there is great enmity between them. The Midrash, in discussing a verse describing someone who mixes in to another conflict, applies this to Balak of Moab and Balaam of Midian deciding to take sides after witnessing the conflict between Israel and Amalek. It gives the example of a dog picking a fight with a wolf:

"The evil one sees and becomes angry" (Ps. 112:10) – this is Balak. "The ambition of the wicked shall perish" (ibid.) – this is Balak and Balaam, whose ambition perished. Regarding them, Scripture states: "The one who mixes in to a quarrel that is not his is like someone who grabs a dog's ears" (Prov. 26:17). A parable – to what can this be compared? To a wolf who comes and snatches a goat from a flock. A potter's dog was there, and came out to bark at it and fight with it. The wolf said to it, You are a potter's dog, why are you fighting with me – have I taken anything of yours? I only took from the shepherd's flock, what business is it of yours? This is grabbing a dog's ears. (*Midrash Yalkut Shimoni* I:765, II:961)

Such a fight, however, would likely end badly for the dog. Wolves will kill and eat dogs almost wherever they have opportunity to do so. In some places, dogs even outrank sheep as the most common domestic prey of wolves.[73] This predation is noted by the Talmud, which again likens Moab and Midian to dogs that run into trouble with a wolf. In this case, the Talmud notes that just as such an encounter spells disaster for the dog, Moab and Midian realized that they had to put their differences aside in order to unite against their common enemy:

"And Moab said to the Elders of Midian" (Num. 22:4). It was taught: Midian and Moab had never been at peace. It is comparable to two dogs that were with a flock and

were fighting with each other, and a wolf came to attack one of them. The second said to himself, If I don't help him, today the wolf will kill him and tomorrow he will come to attack me! And so they both went to kill the wolf. (Sanhedrin 105a[74])

In all these texts, we see that notwithstanding the great similarities between wolves and dogs, they are mortal enemies who should never come together.

The Wolf in *Perek Shira*

— SYMBOLISM

Perek Shira is an ancient text that lists the "songs" of various elements of the natural world, including astronomical and geological phenomena, plants, and animals. Each recites a verse from Scripture, which, according to some schools of thought, is intended to illustrate a lesson to be learned from that creature.[75] The wolf's song is a verse referring to a thief:

The wolf is saying, "For every matter of iniquity, for the ox, the donkey, the lamb, the garment, for every lost item about which he says, 'This is it,' the matter of both of them shall come before the judge; he who the judge finds guilty shall pay double to the other" (Ex. 22:8). (*Perek Shira*, chapter five)

The consequences of the wolf's predation on sheep have been catastrophic for wolves. They have been perpetually hated and hunted, with the gray wolf severely endangered in many areas and the red wolf on the brink of extinction. That which began as a way of getting easy meals has sentenced the wolf to a grim struggle for survival.

Symbolically, this represents is a profound illustration of justice. The criminal has become the victim, the hunter has become the hunted. Contemplation of the wolf's fate, as per *Perek Shira*, hopefully leads people to the realization that crime just doesn't pay.

A further look at the wolf's situation reveals this lesson with greater detail. The punishment meted out to the wolf is somewhat unequal. Shepherds have killed wolves wherever possible, without knowing if a given wolf was actually responsible for the losses to their flock. A wolf new to the raiding game may well pay the price for his more experienced friends.

The same is true for a human thief. If he is caught and dealt with by the victim himself, the victim will make him pay the price for all the losses that he has ever suffered, whether from this person or not. If the *Beit Din*, the Torah court, catches him, he will be fined double the cost of the stolen goods. One rationale for this may be that since, as often as not, thieves are not caught, the punishment has to be doubly severe in order to serve as a deterrent.

A similar explanation can be made for the four- and five-fold fines incurred for slaughtering and selling a stolen animal. Such actions indicate a degree of professionalism to the criminal – he is clearly an old hand at this game. Thus, he is made to pay even more for all the earlier crimes for which he has evaded capture.[76] All in all, the price that the thief will pay on capture should make him think twice before pursuing a career in crime.

This message is expressed in the song of the wolf. "For every matter of iniquity" – for all kinds of crimes, whether committed by this thief or by others. "For every lost item about which he says 'this is it'" – the owner is likely to vent out his frustration over previous losses on this thief. "He who the judge finds guilty shall pay double to the other." It is a severe sentence, but one that will fulfill its intended goal of dissuading people from crime.[77]

Of course, the multiple payments of the thief are God's rules. That many crimes go unpunished does not grant us permission to punish a captured criminal for other crimes that he or others may have committed. The ultimate justice of the punishments is ensured by God alone.

Similarly, the wolf's crimes do not permit man to indiscriminately hunt the wolf to extinction. And even though a shepherd must take precautions to protect his flock, and will even kill wolves where necessary, he should not view his role as an enforcer of divine justice. Rather, when his flock suffers losses, he should examine his own deeds to see which sins he has committed to incur such a loss. The song of the wolf can also be taken to be teaching us this lesson.

"For every matter of iniquity" – examine all of your ways, and search for your sins that have brought these troubles upon you. The matter shall then "come before the judge (*elohim*)" – the true judge, God. If you have performed sincere repentance, you shall be repaid double.[78]

Wolf Legends and Fables

— SYMBOLISM

The well-known legend of Romulus and Remus, raised by a wolf, is referenced in the Midrash:

> It is written, "You do see! For you observe trouble and strife; it is in Your hand to deal accordingly, the helpless rely upon You; for the orphan, You were the helper" (Ps. 10:14). The assembly of Israel said before the Holy One: Master of the Universe! You see that the wicked Esau is coming, and is destined to destroy the Temple! …For the orphan, You were the helper" – there were two orphans that were left out, Romulus and Remus, and You gave permission for a she-wolf to nurse them, and ultimately they arose and built two great powers in Rome. (*Esther Rabba* 3:5[79])

The wolf also makes several appearances in fables. The famous fox fables of Rabbi Berechiah ben Natronai HaNakdan, of late twelfth/early thirteenth century France, include a number of ancient fables that mention the wolf. One particularly entertaining fable is as follows: A man taught the letters of the alphabet to a wolf. He said to him, Say "A," and the wolf said "A." Then he said, Say "B," and the

וְגָר זְאֵב עִם כֶּבֶשׂ וְנָמֵר עִם גְּדִי יִרְבָּץ וְעֵגֶל וּכְפִיר וּמְרִיא יַחְדָּו וְנַעַר קָטֹן נֹהֵג בָּם:

ישעיה יא:ו

זְאֵב וְטָלֶה יִרְעוּ כְאֶחָד וְאַרְיֵה כַּבָּקָר יֹאכַל תֶּבֶן וְנָחָשׁ עָפָר לַחְמוֹ לֹא יָרֵעוּ וְלֹא יַשְׁחִיתוּ בְּכָל הַר קָדְשִׁי אָמַר יהוה:

ישעיה סה:כה

Illustration by Fritz Kredel from Fables of a Jewish Aesop, *edited by Moses Hadas*
Reprinted with permission of David R. Godine, Publisher, Inc.

wolf repeated "B" after him, and so on for all the letters of the alphabet. The man said, "Now listen to everything that I set before you, so that you will learn all the letters and be able to string them together and say whatever you want to say. When you are able to combine the letters together, we shall be one people. Put the letters together, just like me!" The wolf responded with its first word: "Sheep!" Rabbi Berechiah HaNakdan explains the allegory:

The parable is to one whose eye and heart are bent upon gain. His mouth will reveal his wickedness and his lips will testify against him to reveal the duplicity in his heart. Wickedness issues from his belly when evil is found in his mouth, and his thoughts can be recognized from his deeds. He despises Jacob and chooses Esau. His righteousness goes before the righteous but the perverseness of transgressors shall destroy them. Solomon's proverb retains its force: "They that devise evil go astray" (Prov. 14:22). (Fable 113, Haberman edition, Jerusalem, 1945)

This and all other fables mentioning the wolf present it as a bloodthirsty, evil predator. Still, it is important to remember that the wolf is also presented in a very positive light in Jewish thought.

Wolf Reversal

SYMBOLISM

On some occasions, we find mention of bizarre reversals of normal situations with wolves. For example, the Talmud cites a view that one indication of Job's original success in life was that his flocks were able to overcome wolves:

What does it mean, "And his flocks breached out in the land" (Job 1:10)? R. Yose bar Chanina said: The flocks of Job breached all norms. The way of the world is that wolves kill goats; with the flocks of Job, the goats killed the wolves. (Bava Batra 15b)

Similarly, the Talmud relates a story of how the goats of the righteous R. Chanina b. Dosa turned the tables on the wolves:

R. Chanina b. Dosa had goats. On being told that they were doing damage, he exclaimed, "If they indeed do damage, then may wolves devour them; but if not, may each of them at evening time bring home a wolf on their horns." In the evening each of them brought home a wolf on their horns. (Taanit 25a[80])

And the Midrash similarly refers to sheep killing wolves:

"And Moses was shepherding…and he led the sheep…" (Ex. 3:1). Once, wolves came upon the sheep, but the wolves' mouths were sealed shut, and the sheep trampled them. When Moses awoke in the morning, he saw the sheep lying on top of the wolves in their paddock. This is the explanation of "The sheep of Moses – these are Israel." (*Yalkut Midrashei Teiman, Parashat Shemot*)

In Scripture, we find messianic predictions involving wolves and sheep making peace with each other:

And the wolf shall dwell with the sheep, and the leopard shall crouch with the goat, and the young lion shall be together with the cattle, with a young boy leading them. (Is. 11:6)

The wolf and the lamb shall graze as one, and the lion shall eat straw like cattle, and the snake shall eat dirt. They shall not cause harm or destruction in all My holy mountain, says God. (Is. 65:25)

As with other such predictions, there is a dispute between rabbinic authorities as to whether these verses are referring to actual changes in the behavior and physiology of these predators, or if the animals are a metaphor for nations and evil character traits.[82] One midrash appears to support an allegorical interpretation, relating the messianic prophesy to other events involving "wolves" that are clearly metaphorical:

"I, I am your comforter" (Is. 51:12). The Holy One said: Thus is my practice: The tool that I use to smite, I use to heal…they sinned with wolves, as it is written, "Her judges are the wolves of dusk" (Zeph. 3:3), they were smitten with the wolf – "The wolf of the plains shall plunder them" (Jer. 5:6) – and they shall be consoled with the wolf – "The wolf and the lamb shall graze as one" (Is. 65:25). (*Midrash Pesikta Rabbati* 33)

While debate about the literalness of such forecasts has gone on for many hundreds of years, we do find that the Midrash presents an explicit rebuttal of a certain messianic prediction concerning the wolf:

R. Meir sat and expounded: The wolf is destined (in the Messianic Era) to have a fleece of fine wool, and the dog will have the coat of ermine (to make clothing for the righteous). They said to him, "Enough, R. Meir! There is nothing new under the sun." (*Kohelet Rabba* 1:28)

Interestingly, of all the various supernatural predictions for the Messianic Era, this one is the least out of the ordinary; wolves living in very northern countries do grow a thick undercoat of soft fur during the winter. Still, the disputants of R. Meir stated that for the wolves of the Middle East to grow a fleece of fine wool would be a contravention of the dictum that there is nothing new under the sun.

The future peaceful coexistence of wolves and sheep is not only taken as a metaphor for peace between the Jewish people and their enemies, but also as a metaphor for internal peace between particular elements of the Jewish people:

"And he sent Judah before him" (Gen. 46:28). It is written, "The wolf and the lamb shall graze as one, and the lion shall eat straw like cattle" (Is. 65:25)…. The wolf is Benjamin, and the lamb is the tribes, as it says, "Israel is as a scattered lamb" (Jer. 3:17). "Shall graze as one" – When was this? When [Joseph decreed that] Benjamin would descend [to Egypt] with his brothers, and Jacob said to them, "My son shall not go down with you"; but when the time came, he went down with them, and they surrounded him and protected him. (*Bereshit Rabba* 95:1[83])

The commentaries raise the question that the verse from Isaiah is prophesying about the future, so why does the Midrash state that it refers to an event from the past? The answer given is that *maase avot siman lebanim* – "the deeds of the ancestors forecast the future of their descendants."[84] Joseph's brothers were able to overcome their prior jealousy of their father's favored youngest sons and their disregard for his feelings, and resolved to protect Benjamin. This is represented by the wolf and the lamb living in harmony, and it foretells the future state of the Jewish people. ∎

When the Wolf Lay with the Lamb

In 1940, Professor Aharon Shulov established the Biblical Zoo in Jerusalem. His vision was for the zoo to feature not only animals from the Bible, but also animal-related scenes from the Bible. In particular, he wanted to exhibit the wolf lying down with the lamb. But the problem with creating a wolf-lamb exhibit was that it would be prohibitively expensive, due to the need to replace the lamb on a regular basis! However, Professor Shulov was determined to find a way around this problem, and he did.

Israeli author Meir Shalev relates that when he was a child, in the 1950s, he would often visit the Biblical Zoo, and his family was friendly with Professor Shulov.[81] One day, said Shalev, they saw a wolf lying spreadeagled on the ground, with a look of abject misery and exhaustion. "What happened?" he asked Professor Shulov. Shulov replied that it had just returned from the new wolf-lamb exhibit.

It turns out that Professor Shulov had decided upon a rather novel solution to displaying a wolf with a lamb. The wolf was barely more than a cub, just eight months old. The lamb, on the other hand, was a strapping two-year-old, well on its way to becoming a ram. It had spent its time together with the wolf using its head and horns to butt it all around the cage!

Notes

1 Rolf O. Peterson and Paolo Ciucci, "The Wolf as a Carnivore," in David Mech (ed.), *Wolves: Behavior, Ecology and Conservation* (Chicago: University of Chicago Press, 2003), p. 104.

2 Heinrich Mendelssohn and Yoram Yom-Tov, *Fauna Palaestina: Mammalia of Israel*, p. 186.

3 Bill Clark, *High Hills and Wild Goats*, pp. 122–124.

4 *Midrash Esther Rabba* 3:5, *Midrash Shocher Tov* 10, *Midrash Yalkut Shimoni* 2:652.

5 Similarly in *Midrash Tanchuma, Vaychi* 14.

6 *Etz Yosef*.

7 However, see *Yefeh To'ar*.

8 Similarly in *Midrash Bereshit Rabba* 99:1.

9 See *Etz Yosef* to *Midrash Bereshit Rabba* 99:3.

10 Similarly in the earlier *Midrash Tanchuma, Vaychi* 14, but with less elaboration.

11 David Mech (ed.), *Wolves: Behavior, Ecology and Conservation*, p. xv. "Their feeding habits and digestive systems are adapted to a feast-or-famine existence and to procuring and processing massive amounts of food in a relatively short time" – Barry Lopez, *Of Wolves and Men* (New York: Charles Scribner's Sons, 1978), p. 53.

12 The Talmud (Gittin 11b) notes that Lukas was used as a person's name, but rarely by Jews.

13 See Maharsha ad loc. For a mystical discussion on the relationship between wolves, the Altar, and Benjamin, see Rabbi Tzaddok HaKohen, *Peri Tzaddik, Parashat Vayigash* 16, and *Kuntrus Eit HaOkhel* 9.

14 The word for bear, *dov*, is written here (as in many, but not all, instances) without the letter *vav*. It can therefore be read as *dev*, which is the Aramaic word for a wolf. For further discussion, see Rabbi Shaul Chona Kook, *Iyunim VeMechkarim* (Jerusalem: Mossad HaRav Kook, 1959), *Mikra VeLashon*, pp. 15–16.

15 See Rashi and *Minchat Shai* to Daniel 7:5. This name is used for the wolf in *Midrash Yalkut Shimoni* 1:923.

16 Rav Ashi required *shechita*, even though it was a *ben pakua*, since it had placed its hooves on the ground, and permitting it without *shechita* might mislead people into thinking that animals do not require *shechita* (since it is not externally recognizable as a *ben pakua*). However, since there was no biblical requirement for *shechita*, the fact that it was a *tereifa* from the wolf-mauling did not prohibit its consumption.

17 Rabbi Yeshayah Horowitz (Shlah), *Masekhet Taanit, derush leParashat Matot*. He also discusses mystical aspects of this symbolism.

18 Similarly in *Tanchuma, Vaychi* 14, and in *Midrash Shocher Tov, Parashat Vaychi*: "'Each man according to his blessing, he blessed them' (Gen. 49:28). According to what was appropriate to them; according to what the Holy One placed in his mouth, for He revealed their secrets to him. What was destined to be with them, thus he blessed them... He blessed Benjamin with the power of the wolf, such that his descendant Mordekhai would stand in opposition to the kingdom of Media, about which it is written, 'The wolf of the plains has plundered them.' And it is written, 'And after, I saw another one, similar to a bear' – It is written, 'to a *daiv*,' which is the wolf."

19 Esther 3:1.

20 Bill Clark, *High Hills and Wild Goats*, p. 164.

21 *Metzudat David*, Mahari Kara, Seforno.

22 Malbim, commentary ad loc.

23 Barry Lopez, *Of Wolves And Men*, p. 209.

24 The commentary of Maharzu, noting that the Midrash explains Belshazzar to have been killed by Koresh, future king of Persia, and Darius, future king of Media, notes that these nations are symbolically represented by the wolf, which lends further significance to the Midrash's statement.

25 Rabbi Yaakov Yehoshua Hirsch (1752–1780), in his talmudic commentary *Pnei Yehoshua* ad loc.

26 Barry Lopez, *Of Wolves And Men*, p. 209.

27 According to *Targum Yonatan*, Mahari Kara, Radak, and Malbim.

28 Rashbam, commentary to Exodus 8:17. Rabbi Yosef Schonhak in *Toledot HaAretz* (p. 59) claims that these wolves that plagued Egypt, along with the "wolves of dusk" referred to in Scripture, are hyenas. See too *Midrash Tehillim* 78 and *Midrash Shemot Rabba* 11:2 with the commentary of Maharzav ad loc.

29 Barry Lopez, *Of Wolves And Men*, p. 67.

30 Bernd Heinrich, *Mind of the Raven: Investigations and Adventures with Wolf-Birds*, pp. 237–238. See too D.R. Stahler, B. Heinrich, and D.W. Smith, "The Ravens' Behavioral Association with Wolves," *Animal Behaviour* (2002), 64:283–290. For a contrasting view which sees wolves forming packs in response to ravens stealing their kills, see J.A. Vucetich, R.O. Peterson, and T.A. Waite, "Raven scavenging favours group foraging in wolves," *Animal Behavior* (2004), 67(6):1117–1126.

31 David Mech, *The Wolf: The Ecology and Behaviour of an Endangered Species* (Garden City, NY: The Natural History Press, 1970), p. 288.

32 Ze'ev is always mentioned together with his partner Orev. See Judges 8:3 and Psalms 83:12.

33 Precedent for this can be found in the writings of Maharal, who says that Abel (Hevel) was not called this by his parents; rather the Torah gives that name in order to tell us certain things about him (Maharal, *Drasha LeShabbat HaGadol*).

34 See too *Midrash Tehillim* 78 and *Midrash Shemot Rabba* 11:2 with the commentary of Maharzu ad loc.

35 This etymology for *erev* is given by Ibn Ezra in *Sefer Moznayim* and Radak in *Sefer HaShorashim*.

36 See Numbers 25:6.

37 For a thorough discussion, see Steven Fritts, Robert Stephenson, et al., "Wolves and Humans," in David Mech (ed.), *Wolves: Behavior, Ecology and Conservation*, p. 289–316.

38 *Yediyot Acharonot*, 21.6.08.

39 Also cited in Menachot 69b.

40 See *Likutei HaGra* to Habakkuk 1:8 – "The wolf breaks the body, and bones, and all the body parts."

41 The Talmud proceeds to explain that the question is being raised in a scenario where the wolf took the innards of a slaughtered animal, and when they were retrieved, they were found to be punctured. The question is whether we need be concerned that it punctured them in a place where there was already a hole, in which case the animal was a terminally injured creature even before it was slaughtered, and it may not be eaten.

42 See too Chullin 49a and Y. Beitza 14a.

43 David Mech, personal communication, 16.10.07; Rolf O. Peterson and Paolo Ciucci, "The Wolf as a Carnivore," in David Mech (ed.), *Wolves: Behavior, Ecology and Conservation*, pp. 123–124.

44 Chullin 56b.

45 Rolf O. Peterson and Paolo Ciucci, "The Wolf as a Carnivore," loc. cit.

46 J.M. Thurber and R.O. Peterson, "Effects of population density and pack size on the foraging ecology of gray wolves," *Journal of Mammology* (1993), 74:879–889.

47 L.N. Carbyn, S.M. Oosenbrug, and D.W. Anions, *Wolves, bison and the dynamics related to the Peace-Athabasca Delta in Canada's Wood Buf-*

falo National Park (Edmonton, Alberta: Canadian Circumpolar Institute, 1993).

48 Chullin 52b.

49 Such suggestions still run into the problem that the wolf is rated as an animal that can cause such damage whereas a dog is not, even though a wolf is physiologically essentially the same as a dog rather than a cat.

50 Chullin 53a.

51 Rashi ad loc.

52 Rabbeinu Chananel to Bava Kama 16b.

53 "It is evident…that the first point of attack on a moose is the animal's rump or ham area…. A second important point of attack is the nose of the moose." L. David Mech, *The Wolf: The Ecology and Behavior of an Endangered Species*, p. 217. "From May 1974 to September 1977 the senior author examined 11 moose that had been injured or killed by wolves. All had cuts on the posterior surface of one or both rear legs…. Injuries on the rear legs were apparently made by canine teeth of wolves as they gripped the legs of moose from the rear…. Another sign of wolf attack on moose which we observed on two occasions was tooth punctures of the fleshy nose…. Simultaneous attacks on a calf and a cow moose by three wolves were observed by several park visitors…the calf moved away from the others and was attacked by two wolves. One wolf held the calf by the nose while the second wolf attacked from the rear. A cow, presumably the mother of the calf, approached and was attacked from the rear by the third wolf" – Buskirk, S. W. and P. S. Gipson, "Characteristics of wolf attacks on moose in Mount McKinley National Park, Alaska," *Arctic* (1978), 31 pp. 499–502.

54 *Magen Avraham, Zayit Raanan*, 261. See too Rabbi Yaakov Baruch Trab, *Yaateh Moreh, Mo'adim*, p. 253.

55 Rabbi Yechiel Epstein, *Arukh HaShulchan*, 2:261:1; *Mei Zahav, Parashat Emor*, p. 389; Rabbi Yisrael Fischleder, *Mivtzar Yisrael*, p. 169.

56 This may also be more consistent with the wording of the Midrash, which speaks of the wolf being *tored* from in front and behind *of it*, i.e. it itself.

57 *Menorat HaMaor* III.

58 Rabbi Yehuda Leib Graubard, Responsa *Chavalim BeNe'imim* 3:11; Rabbi Yosef Chayim, *Ben Ish Chai, Bereshit* II, *Even Chai* 34.

59 Barry Lopez, *Of Wolves and Men*, p. 56.

60 Steven H. Fritts, Robert O. Stephenson, et al., "Wolves and Humans," in David Mech (ed.), *Wolves: Behavior, Ecology, and Conservation*, p. 306.

61 The Mishna (Bava Metzia 7:9) discusses attacks by wolves before attacks by lion, bear, leopard, cheetah, and snake. The wolf is also mentioned before the lion elsewhere: "If a shepherd was tending a flock and he abandoned them to enter town, and a wolf came and tore or a lion came and mauled" (Bava Metzia 93b).

62 *Etz Yosef* ad loc.

63 Maharzu ad loc.

64 See too *Midrash Yalkut Shimoni* I:923: "'When you go out to battle against your enemies, and you see horses and chariots, a people more powerful than you, do not be afraid of them' (Deut. 20:1). Someone said to R. Akiva: Is this sheep not audacious, to graze amongst seventy wolves? Rabbi Akiva replied: It grazes by the power of the shepherd; were it not for the power of the shepherd, it would not be able to graze amongst seventy wolves, for he saves it from them."

65 *Pnei Moshe* ad loc.

66 *Gilyon Efraim* ad loc.

67 Rashi, commentary ad loc.

68 Me'iri, commentary ad loc.

69 A shorter version is in *Midrash Bereshit Rabba* 57:4

70 Bava Batra 16a.

71 Ronald M. Nowak, "Wolf Evolution and Taxonomy," in David Mech (ed.), *Wolves: Behavior, Ecology, and Conservation*, p. 257.

72 Robert A. Willems, "The Wolf-Dog Hybrid: An Overview of a Controversial Animal," *Animal Welfare Information Center Newsletter*, Winter 1994/1995, vol. 5 no. 4.

73 Steven H. Fritts, Robert O. Stephenson, et al., "Wolves and Humans," in David Mech (ed.), *Wolves: Behavior, Ecology, and Conservation*, p. 306.

74 Also *Midrash Bemidbar Rabba* 20:4 and *Yalkut Midrash Teiman, Parashat Balak*.

75 For a full commentary on *Perek Shira*, see *Perek Shirah: Nature's Song* by this author.

76 Chanoch Zundel Luria, *Kenaf Renanim* on *Perek Shira*.

77 Ibid.

78 *Zimrat HaAretz VeHaShamayim* on *Perek Shira*.

79 A briefer version is in *Midrash Shocher Tov* 10. Romulus and Remus are also mentioned in *Midrash Bereshit Rabba* 49:9.

80 Although some English translations of the Talmud render the subjects of this story as bears rather than wolves, it appears that the reference is to *deivei*, the Aramaic for "wolves," rather than *duvei*, which is Aramaic for bears. Bears are not known for eating goats (either in the Talmud or otherwise), whereas wolves are the classical predators of goats, such as in the statement from Bava Batra 15b cited above: "The way of the world is that wolves kill goats." The talmudic manuscript MS Munich 95, although it has דובא on the first occasion in this passage, in fact does have דיבי on the second (and Sokolof, in his *Dictionary of Babylonian Aramaic*, p. 326, col. 1, reads דיבי for both). Furthermore, the letters *yod* and *vav* interchange easily. Thus, the original reference was presumably to wolves. Cf. Rashi, who says "*Dubei* – and wolves." Presumably, this means that although Rashi's text referred to bears, he wanted it to also refer to wolves, because it is wolves rather than bears that are typically known for preying upon goats.

81 Heard from Meir Shalev at the symposium on the occasion of the 20th anniversary of the Tisch Family Zoological Gardens in Jerusalem, July 1st 2013.

82 See the introduction to Predators.

83 Similarly in *Midrash Aggadat Bereshit* 79:6.

84 *Etz Yosef, Maharzav, Imrei Yosher* ad loc.

HYENA

NARA SINHAN

Hyena

The Hyena of Israel

———————————————————— NATURAL HISTORY

The hyena is a strange animal. It has a large head, a mane running down its back (in some species), and its front legs are longer than its back legs, which gives it a peculiar loping gait. There is much confusion surrounding the nature of hyenas and their place in the animal kingdom. The eighteenth-century explorer James Bruce, one of the first to give eyewitness accounts to Europeans of the animals of the Levant, noted that "There are few animals, whose history has passed under consideration of naturalists, that have given occasion to so much confusion and equivocation as the Hyena has done. It began very early among the ancients, and the moderns have fully contributed their share."[1] Hyenas look somewhat like dogs, but are actually rated by zoologists as being more closely related to cats, and even more closely related to the mongoose family.

There are four members of the hyena family, two of which are relevant to our discussion. The hyena which is native to the Land of Israel is a subspecies of the striped hyena, *Hyaena hyaena*. The striped hyena lives in northern Africa and its range extends to the Middle East and Asia. It measures a little less than four feet in length and up to three feet tall at the shoulder; its weight ranges from 55 to 120 lbs. They are a grayish-brown color, with black stripes on their body and legs. They have a medium-sized mane that forms

a crest on their neck and extends down their back, which is erected when they are excited or frightened. Striped hyenas do not have the famous hyena "laugh," which is a feature only of the spotted hyena (and is not a sign of amusement at all), but it seems that the reputation for laughing spread to all hyenas; in Yiddish, the hyena is known as *lachan chaya*, "the laughing animal." Striped hyenas mainly scavenge from that which other animals have killed. They rarely kill livestock, but they do hunt smaller prey, such as porcupines, foxes, rodents, birds, turtles, lizards, and insects. They also readily eat fruit, vegetables, and refuse.

The British explorer Henry Tristram, who studied the fauna and flora of the Land of Israel in the nineteenth century, writes about how hyenas "prowl about the graveyards to attack the buried corpses, on which they feast, and unless the grave be well protected by a covering of heavy stones, they will rapidly exhume the body. Indeed, after these precautions, they are often known to burrow alongside, and so to reach the body."[2] Another nineteenth-century chronicler of life in the Land of Israel, Ermete Pierotti, describes how he personally saw hyenas digging out bodies from graves that had not been covered by stones.[3] It is probably due to hyenas that the Talmud describes a practice of sealing tombs with a heavy stone.[4]

The subspecies of striped hyena found in Israel, *Hyaena hyaena Syriaca*, is found across Israel even today, though

At left, a spotted hyena; at right, a striped hyena

NATAN SLIFKIN

NATAN SLIFKIN

the entire national population is estimated to number only around 150–200 individuals. They can be found even close to areas of human habitation; this author once came across a dead striped hyena just outside his home town of Ramat Bet Shemesh.

A very different animal, the spotted hyena, *Crocuta crocuta*, lives only in Africa, but reports of its unusual habits and physiology spread beyond that continent, and are the subject of a discussion in the Talmud that we shall later explore. In addition, there are two other species of hyena which are not relevant here. The brown hyena, *Hyaena brunnea*, is similar to the striped hyena, but lives only in the far south of Africa. The aardwolf, *Proteles cristatus*, is the smallest member of the hyena family, and feeds mostly on termites; it lives in eastern and southern Africa.

Valley of the Hyenas

————— IDENTIFICATION

The Hebrew term for hyena is *tzavua*, meaning "colored" or "patterned,"[5] which is a good description of both the striped and spotted varieties of the hyena. Alternately, the name might not refer to the coloration of their fur, but rather to the coloration that they acquire due to their eating habits; that is to say, it may mean "bloodstained."

While this term appears a number of times in later literature, there are only a few uses of the word in Scripture, none of which unequivocally refers to hyenas.[6] The first reference is in the Book of Samuel, which describes how a raiding camp of Philistines passed through a place known as "the valley of the *tzevo'im*":

> Saul and his son Jonathan, and the troops who remained with them, stayed in Geba of Benjamin, while the Philistines were encamped at Michmas. The raiders came out of the Philistine camp in three columns: One column headed for the Ophrah road that leads to the district of Shual, another column headed for the Beth-horon road, and the third column headed for the border road that overlooks the valley of *tzevo'im* toward the desert. (1 Sam. 13:16–18)

It is generally assumed that "the valley of the *tzevo'im*" means "the valley of the hyenas." As Rashi explains:

> The valley of the *tzevo'im* – that many *tzavuim* are found there. (Rashi, Commentary ad loc.)

This may be the valley in Israel known today in Arabic as Shaqq-ud-Diba (meaning "cleft of the hyenas") and Wadi-Abu-Diba (meaning "valley of the hyenas"). There is also mention in Scripture of a city of the tribe of Benja-

וְהָרֹאשׁ אֶחָד יִפְנֶה דֶרֶךְ בֵּית חֹרוֹן וְהָרֹאשׁ אֶחָד יִפְנֶה דֶרֶךְ הַגְּבוּל הַנִּשְׁקָף עַל גֵּי הַצְּבֹעִים הַמִּדְבָּרָה: שמואל א יג:יח

הַעַיִט צָבוּעַ נַחֲלָתִי לִי הַעַיִט סָבִיב עָלֶיהָ לְכוּ אִסְפוּ כָּל חַיַּת הַשָּׂדֶה הֵתָיוּ לְאָכְלָה: ירמיה יב:ט

min by the name of Tzevo'im, which might similarly mean "hyenas."[7] The Mishna further mentions a place called "Har Tzevo'im," "Mountain of the Hyenas."[8]

Another possible reference to the hyena in Scripture is found in the book of Jeremiah:

> My heritage is to Me like an *ayit tzavua*, with the bird of prey around her. Go, gather all the wild beasts, bring them to devour! (Jer. 12:9)

Ayit is a generic term for scavenging birds of prey, and most of the commentaries understand *tzavua* to be an adjective of *ayit*, describing it being colored. Thus, the verse is understood to be speaking of "the colored bird of prey"[9] or "the bloodstained bird of prey."[10] However, the Septuagint renders the term *tzavua* here as *huaine*, which means hyena. It also translates *ayit* not as a bird of prey, but as a cave. Thus, in the Septuagint's reading the term *ayit zavua* means "a hyena's cave."[11] Others suggest that while *tzavua* refers to the hyena, *ayit* still refers to a bird of prey, and that the verse is describing two scavengers: "the bird of prey, the hyena."[12] The two are grouped together in this verse as being carrion-eaters, perfectly symbolizing a heritage gone to waste.

A brown hyena

My heritage is to Me like a hyena's
cave, with the bird of prey around her.
Go, gather all the wild beasts, bring
them to devour!

(Jer. 12:9)

The Riddle of the *Bardelas*

IDENTIFICATION

In rabbinic literature there is another term which, according to some, may also refer to the hyena. The Mishna discusses the laws regarding which animals are classified as dangerous, such that their owners have a higher degree of liability for damage that they cause:

> The wolf, the lion, the bear, the leopard, the *bardelas,* and the snake are *muadin* (rated as expected to cause damage). (Mishna Bava Kama 1:4)

What is the *bardelas*? As discussed in the chapter on the cheetah, this is not a Hebrew or Aramaic term but rather a Greek term. In Greek, it refers primarily to the leopard but also to the "lesser leopard", i.e. the cheetah. The leopard is already mentioned prior to the *bardelas* in the Mishna's list, under its usual name of *namer*, and thus the term *bardelas* must refer to the cheetah.[13] As we shall see, this is apparently the view of the Yerushalmi. The Babylonian Talmud, on the other hand, queries the meaning of the term *bardelas*, presumably due to the Sages of Babylonia being relatively isolated from Greek culture and language. It answers that the *bardelas* is the hyena:

> What is the *bardelas*? Rav Yehuda said: The *nafraza*. What is the *nafraza*? Rav Yosef said: the *afeh* (אפא). (Bava Kama 16a)

Afeh is the Aramaic equivalent of the Hebrew *tzavua*.[14] Thus, according to the Babylonian Talmud the *bardelas* is to be identified with the *tzavua*, which is the hyena. But this leads the Talmud to raise a difficulty with this interpretation:

> Let us raise a question: R. Meir said, also the *tzavua*, and R. Eleazar said, also the snake, and Rav Yosef said, the *tzavua* is the *afeh*! (Bava Kama 16a)

The question being posed by the Talmud is that since the *tzavua* is listed by R. Meir as a separate creature from the *bardelas* in the Mishna, then they must be different types of animals. The Talmud answers that this need not be the case:

> This is no difficulty; one refers to a male *tzavua*, while the other refers to a female *tzavua*. (Ibid.)

The Talmud considers that both male and female hyenas are dangerous. It takes the term *bardelas* as referring to one gender of hyena, and the term *tzavua* as referring to the other gender of hyena. But while this is the view of the Babylonian Talmud, the Yerushalmi is of a different view, for two reasons. First, it apparently understood the term *bardelas* as referring to the cheetah, and second, the

Yerushalmi is of the view that only a male hyena is considered potentially dangerous:

> It was taught: R. Meir said, also the *tzavua*. R. Yose, son of R. Avin, said, R. Meir was only talking about a male *tzavua*, which has its hour when it is as dangerous as a lion. (Y. Bava Kama 6b)

Later, we shall further explore the danger posed by the hyena, as well as other aspects of the views of the Talmud regarding male and female hyenas. For now, let us note that the Babylonian Talmud identifies the *bardelas* with the *tzavua*, which in turn refers to the hyena. This identification was accepted by Maimonides, who gave the Arabic name of the hyena:

> *Bardelas* – an animal that is called *al-tzaba* in Arabic. (Maimonides, commentary to the Mishna, Bava Kama 1:4)

In 1338, Shlomo ben Shmuel of Gurgang published a Hebrew-Persian dictionary, in which he identified the *bardelas* as "an animal that lives in cemeteries, digs up the dead and eats them."[15] This undoubtedly refers to the hyena. A little over three hundred years later, Rabbi Yaakov Yisrael Chagiz (1620–1674), a resident of the Land of Israel, refers

173

A tame striped hyena at the Tel Aviv Zoo in the 1930s

to Maimonides' description of the *bardelas*, and writes about it at length. He describes it as somewhat similar to a donkey; presumably this is a reference to the hyena's mane, longish neck and large ears.[16]

Rabbi Moshe Reischer was a nineteenth-century resident of Palestine who was forced to emigrate and moved to Galicia. He wrote a popular work about the Land of Israel which includes a brief section on its fauna, in which he discusses the *bardelas* at length – presumably because his European readership was unfamiliar with this animal.[17] He cites Maimonides' Arabic translation of *al-tzaba*, and notes that the Arabs of his day refer to it as *al-daba*, which is synonymous due to the common transposition of "*tz*" with "*d*." Rabbi Reischer says that he saw the hide of a hyena, but apparently did not see a living specimen. He gives a fairly accurate description of the hyena, describing its mane as extending down its back, though exaggerating its size somewhat in describing it as being as big as a donkey.[18]

While in this passage the Talmud identifies the *bardelas* as the hyena, it seems that other references to the *bardelas* in the Talmud do not refer to this animal.[19] Instead, they are apparently a corruption of the word *mandris*. This appears to refer to the mongoose or similar such creature, as we shall discuss in the chapter on the mongoose.[20]

The Strange Nature of Hyenas
THEOLOGY, PHILOSOPHY, AND SCIENCE

As we saw previously, in explaining the Mishna's list of dangerous animals, the Babylonian Talmud states that the terms *bardelas* and *tzavua* both refer to hyenas, with one term referring to the male and the other to the female. It presupposes that we might have a reason to present male and female hyenas not merely as two genders of the same animal, but as different creatures.[23] In order to understand why this would be, let us first look at the Yerushalmi, which makes a remarkable statement about male and female hyenas:

> The male hyena turns into a female. (Y. Shabbat 1:3, 8a)

The notion that hyenas change gender was widely accepted in antiquity. The Roman writer Aelian described this phenomenon in his work on natural history,[24] and it was also mentioned by other writers.[25] Many African and Asian legends report that a male hyena turns into a female after seven years. A related belief, repeated in the twentieth century by the famous author Ernest Hemingway, is that hyenas are hermaphrodites.[26] Such beliefs are not supported by contemporary biological theory or empirical observation; although some fishes and frogs can change gender, this is not known to occur amongst mammals. But there is an extraordinary feature of the spotted hyena that would account for such beliefs.

Mad Dogs and Hyenas

The Talmud, when discussing remedies for rabies, suggests one solution that involves writing an incantation on the hide of a male hyena, here called by its Aramaic name of *afeh*:

> Someone who is bitten by a mad dog will die. What is the remedy? Abaye said: Bring the hide of a male hyena (*afeh*) and write upon it, "I, so-and-so, son of so-and-so, write upon the skin of a male hyena, *kanti, kanti, kloros*, God, God, Lord of Hosts, Amen, Amen, Selah." (Yoma 84a)

The use of hyena hides against rabies is found in other ancient sources.[21] In modern science, there is an interesting connection between hyenas and rabies. It has recently been discovered that spotted hyenas are able to carry the rabies virus without suffering any ill effects. They are the only wild animals known to possess this ability.[22]

The striped hyena can erect its remarkable crest the instant it is alarmed

Female spotted hyenas are by far the most masculinized females in the animal kingdom.[27] In clans of spotted hyenas, which may number up to eighty individuals, all of the adult females are dominant to the males, which leave the group when they reach puberty. Females are far more aggressive than the males at every stage in their lives; even as newborns, they will attempt to kill their siblings, and a quarter of newborn hyenas die in this way. The females possess large amounts of the male testosterone hormone, and grow considerably larger than males. Most extraordinarily of all, their reproductive organs look identical to those of a male.

(This bizarre phenomenon is of great interest to medical science. Some cases of human infertility result from a disorder known as polycystic ovarian syndrome, in which women produce abnormally high levels of androgen. This may be cause by a hormonal event similar to that which occurs in pregnant hyenas, and learning how female hyenas accommodate to high doses of hormones without suffering ill effects may shed light upon the actions of hormones in humans.)

As a result, spotted hyenas that to all appearances are male, may in fact be female. Thus, the belief arose that male spotted hyenas actually transform into females. It may be that this belief spread to include the striped hyena of the Land of Israel. Alternatively, the belief that striped hyenas change gender may relate to the fact that male striped hyenas have very small scrota and are not easily identified as males.[28]

The notion that male hyenas undergo an extraordinary metamorphosis is reported in the Babylonian Talmud in an even more remarkable form. The Bavli explains that the male *tzavua* has a different name from the female and is listed separately because it is a very different creature from the female, undergoing a series of metamorphoses:

> … as it was taught in a *baraita*: the male *tzavua* turns into an *atalef*-bat after seven years; the *atalef*-bat turns into an *arpad*-bat after seven years; the *arpad*-bat turns into a nettle after seven years; the nettle turns into a thorn after seven years; the thorn turns into a demon after seven years. (Bava Kama 16a)

The idea that hyenas transform into different creatures and demons is not unique to the Talmud and is found in many cultures throughout Asia and Africa.[29] The belief in the demonic nature of the hyena is probably related to its macabre habit of stealing corpses from graves. Some, however, explain this passage in allegorical terms. It has been suggested that the lesson behind this teaching is that evil sinks deeper and deeper until it reaches the lowest degree of depravity.[30]

A hyena's teeth and massively powerful jaws are capable of inflicting serious, even fatal, wounds

When Striped Hyenas Attack

LAW AND RITUAL

As we have seen, R. Meir adds the hyena to the Mishna's list of animals that are rated as dangerous, such that its owner is considered forewarned if it causes damage. The Babylonian Talmud suggests that R. Meir was referring to both genders of hyena, while the Yerushalmi states that he was referring only to the male hyena. As mentioned previously, the female spotted hyena from Africa is larger and more aggressive than the male. With the striped hyenas of the Land of Israel, on the other hand, the male is around ten percent larger than the female. But is it actually dangerous to man?

It is often claimed that striped hyenas, unlike their larger and much more dangerous spotted cousins, are entirely harmless to humans. It is true that striped hyenas are usually shy and avoid confrontation. But this is not always the case. In 1974, nineteen children were killed by striped hyenas in the Bihar district of India.[31]

Nor are adults immune from harm. Joanna Greenfield, an American working at the Hai-Bar wildlife reserve in the Arava, was badly mauled by a striped hyena.[32] The animal was a young male that had been rejected by its parents and raised by people. As it grew older, it began nipping at people, and was kept caged. One day, while Greenfield was placing fresh water in the hyena's enclosure, it attacked her, taking chunks out of her arm and leg before she managed to summon help. There are also reports that hyenas will attack people who block the exits to their lair, and that females will attack people who appear to threaten their cubs.[33]

Striped hyenas are sometimes today sold as pets by exotic animal dealers. But, as R. Meir observes, they can occasionally be dangerous. The owner of a hyena cannot claim that he had no reason to expect it to cause problems.

Hour of the Hyena

SYMBOLISM

As we saw earlier, the Yerushalmi describes the hyena as "having its hour" when it is dangerous:

> Mishna: The wolf, the lion, the bear, the leopard, the cheetah, and the snake are *muadin*.... Gemara: It was taught: R. Meir said, also the hyena. R. Yose, son of R. Avin, said, R. Meir was only talking about a male hyena, which has its hour when it is as dangerous as a lion. (Y. Bava Kama 6b)

The phrase "having its hour" is a curious figure of speech. It appears in only one other place in all of Mishna, Talmud, and Midrash:

> He (the son of Azzai) used to say, do not be scornful of any person and do not be dismissive of anything, for there is no person who does not have his hour, and there is nothing that does not have its place. (Mishna Avot 4:3)

Some explain this to mean that a person should not underestimate the ability of another person to harm him.[34] This is similar to the concept as presented with the hyena, that it has its hour when it is extremely dangerous.

Others, however, explain this mishna to mean that one should not underestimate the value of anyone or anything in the world, even if it seems harmful, such as repulsive or dangerous creatures, as everything has a valuable function.[35] This, too, would relate well to the hyena.

Hyenas have always been much loathed by man, due to their mangy appearance, bizarre sexual characteristics, unearthly howls, aggressive natures, and most of all their scavenging habits. It is natural for people to think that the world would be a better place without them. Indeed, as we saw earlier, even the prophet Jeremiah likens the horror of the Destruction to that associated with the hyena:

> My heritage is to me as a hyena's cave, with the bird of prey around her. Come, assemble all the beasts of the field, come to devour. (Jer. 12:9)

But, as the Talmud states, albeit in a different context, even the hyena has its hour. The hyena fulfills a vital role in the natural world – especially from a spiritual perspective.

Contrary to popular belief, spotted hyenas are not just scavengers, but often actively hunt down prey themselves. Lions feed off the remains of a kill made by hyenas just as often as hyenas feed from the remains of a kill made by lions. By killing herbivores, hyenas fulfill a vital function in keeping these animals' numbers under control. If wil-

This hyena is transporting carrion for its cub, which is standing next to its hind leg ▶

debeest and gazelle were to breed unchecked, the pastures would be overgrazed and mass famine would ensue. Second, the prey animals that the hyenas kill are usually the sick and weak individuals. This is because hyenas chase their prey, rather than stalking it, and it is the sick and weak individuals that are caught more easily. Killing these individuals has the effect of ensuring that the population of prey animals remains healthy.

Spotted hyenas also, of course, scavenge from dead animals, and striped hyenas do so almost exclusively. Hyenas possess immensely strong jaws with enables them to crush and chew up bones, which they digest with their very powerful acid stomach secretions. The result is that a pack of hyenas can entirely consume a dead animal within a short space of time. By so doing, they are fulfilling an important role in disposing of these carcasses, and preventing them from being a source of disease.

Repulsive as the scavenging hyena may be, we should not underestimate its value in this world. Even the hyena has its hour.   ■

VIJAY CAVALE

Notes

1 James Bruce, *Travels to Discover the Source of the Nile*, volume 6, p. 131. See also Holger Funk, *Hyaena: On the Naming and Localisation of an Enigmatic Animal* (Grin Verlag, 2010).

2 Henry B. Tristram, *The Natural History of the Bible*, pp. 108–9.

3 Ermete Pierotti, *Customs and Traditions of Palestine: Illustrating the Manners of the Ancient Hebrews* (Cambridge: Deighton, Bell and Co., 1864), p. 39.

4 E.g. Y. Mo'ed Katan 3:5; Sanhedrin 47b.

5 See Radak to 1 Samuel 13:18: "The *afeh* is called *tzavua* because it has different shades and colors." *Bereshit Rabba* 7:4 (Theodor-Albeck edition) also mentions the *tzavua* as possessing 365 colors, but the commentaries of Rabbi David Luria and Maharif suggest that it is a textual error and should actually be referring to the *tavas*, a type of bird. See, however, the note in the Albeck edition of the Midrash.

6 Two important and extensive studies of hyenas in rabbinic literature and in the Land of Israel have been produced by Avraham Ofir-Shemesh: "The Striped Hyena in Eretz Yisrael Sources: Between Legend and Reality" (Hebrew), *Al Atar* 12 (5763), pp. 7–28; "The *Bardelas* in Ancient Rabbinic Literature: A Test Case of Geographic Identification" (Hebrew), *Mo'ed* 14 (5764), pp. 70–80. The Apocryphal book of *Ben Sira* also mentions the *tzavua* and apparently refers to the hyena: "Is there peace between the *tzavua* and the dog? Is there peace between the wealthy man and the pauper?" (*Ben Sira* 13:17).

7 Nehemiah 11:34.

8 Mishna Challa 4:10 and Bikkurim 1:3.

9 *Metzudat David* and *Metzudat Tziyon* ad loc.

10 Rashi and Radak ad loc.

11 The difficulties with the Septuagint's translation are discussed by Benjamin Foreman, *Animal Metaphors and the People of Israel in the Book of Jeremiah* (Göttingen, Germany: Vandenhoeck & Ruprecht, 2011), p. 224.

12 Menachem Dor, *HaChai BiYemei HaMikra, HaMishna VeHaTalmud*.

13 See Binyamin Mussafia, *Mussaf HaArukh*; Menachem Dor, *HaChai BiYemei HaMikra, HaMishna VeHaTalmud*, p. 64; Avraham Ofir-Shemesh, "The *Bardelas*."

14 See *Targum* and Radak to 1 Samuel 13:18 and Avraham Ofir-Shemesh, "The *Bardelas*."

15 Cited in Wilhelm Bacher, *Ein hebräisch-persisches Wörterbuch aus dem vierzehnten Jahrhundert* (Strassburg, 1900).

16 Yaakov Yisrael Chagiz, *Korban Mincha* (Izmir, 1675), Chapter 7; also cited by Rabbi Eliyahu HaKohen in *Midrash Talpiyot* (Izmir, 1736), *anaf bardelas*. Rabbi Chagiz also relates a belief that the hyena hypnotizes people by dancing and singing, after which it lures them to its lair and kills them.

17 Rabbi Moshe Reischer, *Shaarei Yerushalayim* (Warsaw, 1868), pp. 18–19.

18 Rabbi Reischer also relates a belief that the hyena hypnotizes a person. According to Rabbi Reischer, it does this by dancing in front of him on two legs while drumming on its belly, causing the onlooker to fall into hysterical laughter and lose his mind. The person then follows the hyena to its lair, whereupon it kills him, eating only his brain.

19 Rabbi Yaakov Yisrael Chagiz and Rabbi Moshe Reischer, loc. cit. See *Tosafot* to Sanhedrin 15b s.v. *Vehabardelas*.

20 Avraham Ofir-Shemesh, "The *Bardelas* in Ancient Rabbinic Literature."

21 The Roman physician Scribonius Largus, in *Compositiones Medicamentorum* 172, attests to the use of hyena hide as a prophylactic against rabies.

22 M.L. East, H. Hofer, et al., "Regular exposure to rabies virus and lack of symptomatic disease in Serengeti spotted hyenas," *Proceedings of the National Academy of Sciences of the United States of America* 98:26 (2001): 15026–15031.

23 This is not as odd as it might appear. Pliny, in *Historia Naturalis* VIII, seems to treat the leopard and cheetah as males and females of the same species, yet giving them each different names.

24 Aelian, *On the Characteristics of Animals* 1:25. Aristotle, on the other hand, disputed this notion; see *Historia Animalium* 6:32, *On the Generation of Animals* 3:6.

25 Ovid, *Metamorphoses* 15:408–9; Oppian, *Cynegetica* 3:289–92.

26 Hemingway, *Green Hills of Africa* (1935), p. 38.

27 See Natalie Angier, *The Beauty of the Beastly* (New York: Houghton Mifflin, 1995), pp. 131–144.

28 Giora Ilani, "Hyenas in Israel," in *Israel – Land and Nature* 1:1 (1975), pp. 10–18. See too Reginald I. Pocock, *Fauna of British India: Mammals* vol. II (London: Taylor and Francis, 1941), p. 63.

29 Mikita Brottman, *Hyena* (London: Reaktion Books, 2012), pp. 77–78.

30 Lewysohn, *Die Zoologie Des Talmuds*, p. 76.

31 Gordon Grice, *Deadly Kingdom* (New York: The Dial Press, 2010), p. 53.

32 Joanna Greenfield, "Hyena," *The New Yorker*, November 11, 1996, pp. 74–81.

33 Ilani, "Hyenas in Israel," loc. cit.

34 Rabbi Ovadiah MiBartenura, ad loc.

35 *Tiferet Yisrael*, commentary ad loc.

FOX AND JACKAL

Fox and Jackal

שועל, תן (?)

Shual, Tan

Foxes and Jackals

IDENTIFICATION

The *shual*, known in Aramaic as *taal* (תעל) or *taala* (תעלא), is the subject of several famous verses in Scripture and stories in the Talmud. The word *shual* also appears in Scripture as the name of certain people[1] and of certain places.[2] Most people assume, based on traditional European translations, that this animal is the fox. The Vulgate translates it with the term *Vulpes*, which is the Latin name for the fox.

But in fact, it seems that many or even all references to the *shual* in Scripture do not refer to the fox.[3] Instead, they appear to refer to another member of the dog family which does not live in Europe and was thus largely unknown to Europeans: the jackal. The jackal is somewhat similar to a fox, with the most obvious differences being its considerably larger size, smaller ears, and shorter tail. The name *shual* may be a generic term for both species; indeed, jackals and foxes go by the same name in several languages. Etymologists rate the word jackal as being related to the word *shual*,[4] which, with the more authentic Hebrew pronunciation of a guttural *ayin*, would be transliterated as *shu'gal* or *shu'kal*.[5] But in contrast to the scriptural *shual*, we shall see that many talmudic references to the *shual* seem to refer to the fox rather than the jackal.

A golden jackal

GAURIKA WIJERATNE

180

The red fox

Jackals and Foxes of Israel

NATURAL HISTORY

The species of jackal found in Israel is the golden jackal, *Canis aureus*. The Israeli subspecies of the golden jackal, smaller than its African counterpart, is the Syrian jackal, *Canis aureus syriacus*. It is patched gold to greyish-brown in color, with a dark tip to its tail, and weighs around 9kg (20 pounds). The Syrian jackal is found in most of Israel, except for the southern desert region. It usually lives in pairs or small family groups, but when food is plentiful jackals form packs. The jackal is an omnivore, eating fruit and killing animals up to the size of calves.[6]

There are four species of fox in Israel. Best known and most common is the red fox, *Vulpes vulpes*. The subspecies of red fox found in North America and Europe is easily recognizable by its red coat and long bushy tail with a white tip. The various subspecies of red fox found in Israel, on the other hand, are gray or yellow in color and have a slimmer tail. *Vulpes vulpes palaestina* is the subspecies usually found in central and northern Israel, while *Vulpes vulpes arabica* is found in desert regions. The red fox in Israel is smaller than those of Europe and North America, weighing up to 4kg (10 pounds). It is found throughout the country, but usually lives alone, except during the breeding season. The red fox is an omnivore.

There are also three other species of fox in the desert regions of Israel that are smaller and much rarer: the sand fox, *Vulpes rueppellii*; Blanford's fox, *Vulpes cana*; and the tiny fennec fox, *Vulpes zerda*. They would doubtless be collectively included with the red fox in scriptural taxonomy.[7]

The Fox and the Grapes

IDENTIFICATION

One famous reference to the *shual* is as a creature that enjoys grapes and causes damage to vineyards:

> Seize for us the *shualim*, the little *shualim*, that spoil the vineyard, for the vineyard is in blossom. (Song. 2:15)

This may shed light upon a curious expression in the Talmud regarding the fox:

> R. Asi said: When R. Yochanan and Resh Lakish were analyzing the laws of the Red Heifer (for a consistent methodology), they were not able to come up with anything more than that which a fox brings up from a plowed field. (Yoma 43b)

> Ulla said: When R. Yochanan and Resh Lakish were discussing the chapter on the "Young Girl," they were not able to come up with anything more than that which a fox brings up from a plowed field. (Nidda 65b)

In other words, R. Yochanan and Resh Lakish were not able to come up with anything, just as a fox only brings up flecks of dirt on its feet when it walks through a plowed field.[8] But why mention a fox? Perhaps because it presents a sharp contrast with the ordinary scenario of a fox taking a lot of a farmer's produce.

The motif of a vineyard being threatened by *shualim* is also mentioned in the Midrash. The Midrash derives this theme from the similar-sounding word *mish'ol*, which refers to a lane in a vineyard. This occurs in the context of a verse describing an angel standing in such a lane and blocking the way of Balaam, who sought to harm the Jewish people:

> "And the angel of God stood in the lane (*mish'ol*) of the vineyards" (Num. 22:24). He said to him: Shall

181

The fennec fox is the smallest species of fox found in Israel

כְּשֻׁעָלִים בָּחֳרָבוֹת נְבִיאֶיךָ יִשְׂרָאֵל הָיוּ:
יחזקאל יג:ד

עַל הַר צִיּוֹן שֶׁשָּׁמֵם שׁוּעָלִים הִלְּכוּ בוֹ:
איכה ה:יח

וְטוֹבִיָּה הָעַמֹּנִי אֶצְלוֹ וַיֹּאמֶר גַּם אֲשֶׁר הֵם בּוֹנִים אִם יַעֲלֶה שׁוּעָל
וּפָרַץ חוֹמַת אַבְנֵיהֶם:
נחמיה ג:לה

the vineyards (i.e. the Jewish people[9]) be given over to the *shualim*? (i.e. to their enemies, Balak and Balaam). (*Midrash Tanchuma, Balak* 8[10])

While this is the only appearance of the word *mish'ol* and it is of uncertain derivation, some suggest that the word itself originally derives from *shual*, due to the propensity of the *shual* to walk along the lanes in a vineyard.[11] Others suggest precisely the opposite; that the fox derived its name due to its propensity for being in hollowed-out areas such as vineyard lanes.[12]

But does the association of the *shual* with the vineyard assist with its identification? Some presume that, even if other mentions of the *shual* refer to the jackal, this grape-eating *shual* is the fox.[13] Yet there does not seem to be any basis for this. Both foxes and jackals eat grapes and cause great damage to vineyards.

Why are the *shualim* of this verse described as "little"? It may serve to specify that it is the fox being described, not the larger jackal. However, this is inconclusive; it may be nothing more than a figure of speech.

There is, however, an entirely different interpretation of the "little *shualim*" in this verse, according to which, unlike the other scriptural references to the *shual*, it is describing a very little type of fox: the "flying fox." This is an alternate name for the Egyptian fruit bat, which has a fox-like head and was already called "flying fox" by Aristotle. There is also some evidence that this bat was referred to as a "fox" in the Jerusalem Talmud.[14] It has been proposed that this bat, which farmers rate as an agricultural pest, is the "little fox" of this verse.[15] Others add that this unprepossessing "bird" would fit well as a contrast to the beautiful doves described a few verses earlier.[16]

However, all this seems a little far-fetched. The "little foxes" could adequately refer to either foxes or jackals. Furthermore, while fruit bats have been recorded as eating grapes in some countries,[17] this does not appear to happen in Israel.[18]

The Fox of Destruction – Or the Jackal

SYMBOLISM

Most references to the *shual* in Scripture describe it as a creature that inhabits ruined areas and thus symbolizes desolation.

> Thus said the Lord God: Woe to the degenerate prophets, who follow their own fancy, without having had a vision! Your prophets, O Israel, have been like the *shualim* in the ruins. You did not enter the breaches and repair the walls for the House of Israel, that they might stand up in battle in the day of the Lord. They prophesied falsehood and lying divination; they said, "Declares the Lord," when the Lord did not send them, and then they waited for their word to be fulfilled. (Ezek. 13:3–6)

Some interpret the verse as referring to "breaches" rather than ruins, and understand it to refer to *shualim* entering breaches in the fence around vineyards in order to devastate the fruit.[19] Others, however, interpret it as referring to ruined buildings. This is the context in which the *shual* appears in other verses:

> Because of this our hearts are sick, because of these our eyes are dimmed; for Mount Zion which is desolate, *shualim* walk in it. (Lam. 5:17–18)

> When Sanballat heard that we were rebuilding the wall, it angered him, and he was extremely vexed. He mocked the Jews, saying in the presence of his brothers and the Samarian force, "What are the miserable Jews doing? Will they restore, offer sacrifice, and finish one day? Can they revive those stones out of the dust heaps, burned as they are?" Tobiah the Ammonite, alongside him, said,

EYAL BARTOV

The sand fox, another species of fox found in Israel

182

"That stone wall they are building – if a *shual* climbed it, he would breach it!" (Neh. 3:33–35)

יַגִּירֻהוּ עַל יְדֵי חָרֶב מְנָת שֻׁעָלִים יִהְיוּ:
תהלים סג:יא

וַיֵּלֶךְ שִׁמְשׁוֹן וַיִּלְכֹּד שְׁלֹשׁ מֵאוֹת שׁוּעָלִים וַיִּקַּח לַפִּדִים וַיֶּפֶן זָנָב אֶל זָנָב וַיָּשֶׂם לַפִּיד אֶחָד בֵּין שְׁנֵי הַזְּנָבוֹת בַּתָּוֶךְ:
שופטים טו:ד

All these references could equally refer to either foxes or jackals. Henry Tristram, who explored Palestine and the region in the nineteenth century, wrote that "the fox is to be found everywhere, especially about ruins."[20] Constantin-François Volney (1757–1820), who also traveled to Palestine, reported that jackals are found "among the ruins and tombs."[21]

But there is another mention of the *shual* which may be more determinative. This occurs in a psalm of David describing his hopes for his enemies:

May those who seek to destroy my life enter the depths of the earth. They shall be given over to the power of the sword; they shall be a portion for *shualim*. (Ps. 63:10–11)

Some interpret this verse as referring to a place becoming a habitation for *shualim*.[22] As such, it could equally refer to either foxes or jackals. But most adopt a more straightforward understanding of the verse, as referring to the victims of the sword becoming literally a portion for *shualim* – that is to say, it is referring to the *shual* eating corpses.[23] As such, it would refer to jackals rather than foxes; it is jackals that are known for eating carrion.[24]

The Fire-Foxes of Samson

IDENTIFICATION

A key mention of the *shual* in Scripture is the story involving Samson:

And it was in the days of the wheat-harvest.... Samson went and trapped three hundred *shualim*. He took torches and, turning them tail to tail, he placed each torch in between the tails. Then he set fire to the torches,

Unlike foxes, jackals frequently consume carrion

Blanford's fox, one of the four species of fox found in Israel, lives in desert habitats and has a distinctively large tail

and sent them amongst the standing grain of the Philistines, setting fire to stacked grain, standing grain, vineyards, and olive trees. (Judges 15:1, 4–5)

Some rabbinic authorities saw this story as a source for the principle that causing pain to animals is permitted for a human need.[25] But others negated it as a proof, however, because there were exceptional circumstances of battle.[26] History reveals many instances of nations using animals to wage warfare. In ancient times, rats and other animals were sometimes set on fire and launched into enemy encampments; in World War II, the United States military experimented with using bats to deliver miniature bombs.

As we shall see, this story is used by some to prove that the *shual* is the fox, while others use it to prove that it is the jackal. The interpretation of this story by various scholars of Scripture is also affected by their religious outlook, i.e. whether it is understood as a historical event (and if so, to what degree it might involve a supernatural element), or whether it is non-historical.

The Talmud understood this account as referring to foxes rather than jackals:

"And he captured three hundred *shualim*" – why specifically *shualim*? R. Ibo bar Nagdai said: R. Chiyya bar Aba said in the name of R. Shimon – Let the one that doubles back on itself come and exact retribution from the Philistines, who reneged on their oath (that Avimelech swore to Abraham). (Sota 10a)

Foxes will often double back on their tracks to throw off enemies that are pursuing their scent. Jackals are not known to do this; hence, the Talmud understood Scripture as refer-

ring specifically to foxes, and saw this as being of symbolic significance.

The medieval Jewish commentator Rabbi David Kimche explains that foxes are ideally suited to this task. Other animals would run away in opposite directions from each other, causing the firebrand to detach. Foxes, on other hand, will twist and turn in order to escape, preventing the firebrand from being detached.[27]

Other arguments for the *shualim* of Samson being foxes were based on the writings of the first-century poet Ovid, who recorded an unusual circus custom in the Roman town of Carceoli. Lit torches were tied to the tails of foxes, which were then let loose to run in the ring of the Circus Maximus until they burned to death. This custom was performed as a punishment to foxes, in response to an event in which a fox, which had been set alight by a mischievous child, ran through a cornfield and burned it. The Roman custom was presented by early Christian biblical scholars as attesting to this being a known practice in antiquity. However, there would not appear to be any connection; the Roman practice was a local custom, initiated in response to a particular event. This does not appear related to Samson's story of a thousand years previously.[28]

But from the early seventeenth century, people began to wonder if it was actually possible to catch so many foxes. Voltaire and other Bible critics ridiculed the account, and it became a topic of intense discussion for Bible scholars.[29] Some Christian Bible scholars sought to explain that *shualim* refers to sheaves rather than to any kind of animal,[30] but this ran into numerous textual difficulties. There were those who considered that Samson had supernatural skills and aid, thereby rendering any questions obsolete, but others were reluctant to resort to such an approach in the absence of clear scriptural direction.

However, others suggested that the *shualim* of this story were not foxes, but rather jackals (which were hitherto unknown in Europe).[31] Whereas foxes are solitary animals, jackals band together in large groups.[32] In the eighteenth century, Constantin-François Volney reported that "the wolf and the real fox are very rare; but there is a prodigious quantity of the middle species, named *Shacal* (jackal) which in Syria is called *wauwee* in imitation of its howl…these jackalls go in droves";[33] elsewhere, he wrote that "jackals are concealed by hundreds."[34] Capturing three hundred animals, presumably within a reasonably short period of time, is far more likely to happen with jackals than with foxes.

Tristram further argued that jackals are more suitable than foxes for the grisly task of spreading fire, using precisely the opposite argument to that used by Rabbi David Kimche. Foxes, as solitary animals, would, when tied together, strain to run apart from each other in opposite directions, which would not lead them to cover much ground. Jackals, however, will run together, and with the firebrands tied at some distance to their tails, they would run and spread the devastation over the maximum area.[36]

Modern academic scholars, on the other hand, note that fire is often associated with foxes, and especially fox-tails. This occurs in many cultures, from the Celts to the Japanese;[37] in Arabic, the words for "fox" and "fire" are similar. This connection presumably stems from the fiery coloration of the red fox, and especially its bushy, blazing tail. Indeed, the fox was called *lampouris*, meaning "torch-tail," in ancient colloquial Greek. Exactly how this may relate to the story with Samson is disputed and unclear.[38] Nevertheless, the result is that while some insist that the account is referring to jackals, others are convinced that foxes are the subject of the story.

In conclusion, then: While the early European tradition was to identify the *shual* as the fox, this was only because people in Europe were unfamiliar with the jackal. Since the early modern period, *all* scholars have all agreed that the scriptural term *shual* is a generic term for both foxes and jackals. There are certain references to the *shual* in Scripture – namely, those referring to it eating grapes and living in ruined areas – which could equally well refer to either the fox or the jackal. But the description of victims of the sword being "a portion for *shualim*," if it is (as seems likely) referring to their actually being eaten, would be referring to jackals rather than foxes. Whether the account of Samson should be interpreted as referring to foxes or to jackals is the subject of disagreement.

No Dead Foxes in a Foxhole

IDENTIFICATION

Although scriptural references to the *shual* may appear more likely to refer to the jackal, Talmud references to the *shual* appear to better match the fox. The Talmud discusses

EYAL BARTOV

A young fox at the entrance to its hole

the laws relating to which kinds of vow made by a married woman can be annulled by her husband. He is permitted to annul vows to act in ways which interfere with physical intimacy. The Talmud relates a dispute as to whether a woman's vows to neglect her personal hygiene fall into this category:

> Regarding matters (of intimacy) between him and her: Rav Huna says that the husband may annul them; Rav Ada bar Ahava says that the husband may not annul them, for we do not find a fox that dies in the dirt of its burrow. (Ketubot 71b; Nedarim 81a[39])

A fox is intimately familiar with the dirt in its burrow; it will not become trapped in it and die. So, too, a husband will not be prevented from conjugal relations, no matter what the state of his spouse.[40]

In this passage, the animal being described is a fox rather than a jackal. Jackals do not dig burrows, except occasionally for breeding purposes. Foxes, on the other hand, predominantly live in burrows that they tunnel into the earth. (The Talmud also reports an account of a fox that tunneled out a nest inside an enormous gourd.[41])

Fox's Tails and Teeth in the Talmud

— IDENTIFICATION

There are further cases in the Talmud where *shual* apparently refers to the fox rather than the jackal. A certain grain

mentioned in the Talmud, *shibbolet shual*, is named after the *shual*.[42] Theoretically, this could be for a variety of reasons, such as that the *shual* is known for eating them.[43] However, the consensus of traditional and scholarly opinion is that the ears of this grain resemble the *tail* of the *shual*. There is a wide-ranging dispute as to the precise identity of this grain.[44] The medieval rabbinic authorities of Ashkenaz identified it as oats, but it is difficult to see any resemblance between oats and the tail of either a fox or jackal. Other medieval rabbinic authorities identified it as rye, or as wild barley, which are slightly similar to a fox's tail, but not bearing a strong resemblance. Some modern authors propose that it is the foxtail millet (*Setaria italica*), which, as its English name suggests, does indeed look strikingly similar to a fox's tail; however, there are technical difficulties with identifying it as the *shibbolet shual* of the Talmud. The identity of this grain remains unclear. But in any case, since the fox has a far more distinctive tail than the jackal, this would indicate that the Talmud is referring to a fox.

Another talmudic mention of the tail of a *shual* may also indicate that it is referring to a fox rather than a jackal:

> A horse may not go out [on the Sabbath] with a fox tail, nor with a ribbon between its eyes [due to the prohibition against transporting items]. (Shabbat 53a)

Pheasants' tails, bright ribbons, wolf-skins, and other such gaudy, bushy items were often placed on the bridles of horses in antiquity in order to absorb the harmful effects of the evil eye and prevent the horse itself from being harmed.[45] The large and bushy tail of a fox would be a natural choice for this task. This is a further indication of the term *shual* referring to the fox rather than the jackal, which has a much shorter, thinner tail.

There are further references to supernatural associations with the *shual*, which can perhaps be assumed to likewise refer to the fox. The Mishna describes people wearing a fox's tooth for its assumed ability to promote or prevent sleep, depending on whether it was taken from a live or a dead animal.[46] The Talmud criticizes a superstitious belief that passing a fox on one's left side is an evil omen.[47]

The Lowliest of the Wild Beasts

—————————————————————— SYMBOLISM

The Book of Daniel presents a prophetic vision of various predators from the animal kingdom – the lion, bear, leopard, and a fourth, mythical beast. These are interpreted as representing the four kingdoms that have opposed the Jewish people: Babylon, Persia-Media, Greece, and Rome. The Midrash states that the *shual*, described as "little" in Scripture, is smaller than any of these, and thus represents Egypt, which was the least of these kingdoms. While the jackal is also smaller than these other predators, the focus here may be on the fox, which is much smaller than the jackal:

> "And God said to Moses: Stretch out your hand over the sea, and the waters shall return..." (Ex. 14:26) – This is what is referred to by "Seize for us the foxes, the little foxes" (Song. 2:15). When parables were sought for the kingdoms, they were symbolized by wild animals, as it says, "And four great beasts emerged from sea" (Dan. 7:3). And when Egypt is spoken of allegorically, it is symbolized by foxes. Just as the fox is smaller than the four beasts (of Daniel's vision), so too Egypt is the smallest of kingdoms (that oppressed the Jewish people), as it says, "It shall be the lowest of kingdoms" (Ezek. 29:15). (*Shemot Rabba* 22:1)

The motif of the *shual* being the lowliest of all the wild beasts appears on several occasions in the teachings of the Sages. Most famous of these is the following recommendation:

> Be a tail to lions, rather than being a head to *shualim*. (Mishna Avot 4:15)

It is suggested that the reference here is to a fox, due to its reputation for craftiness and trickery.[48] It thereby alludes to Torah scholars of small stature, who attempt to vanquish their colleagues in debate via tricks such as sarcasm, rather than by using superior argumentation. Maimonides describes such unsuitable rabbinic judges as destroying "the vineyard of the Lord," and sees an allusion to them in the verse speaking of the "little foxes who ruin the vineyard."[49] One should not attempt to be part of such a gathering, even as its head; rather, one should strive to attach oneself to a group of greater people.

However, the Mishna's parable may well be referring to jackals rather than foxes. First of all, as noted earlier, foxes are solitary animals, whereas jackals roam in packs. Since the Mishna speaks of being the head to a group of *shualim*, this would better refer to jackals. Second, jackals often follow after lions, seeking to scavenge whatever is left from the lions' kills after the lions have eaten their fill. Accordingly,

Jackals often attempt to scavenge from lions' kills

Even if a lion is not at a kill, jackals may follow it in the hope that a kill will take place

the juxtaposition of the *shualim* with the lions may indicate that it is jackals, which follow after lions, to which the Mishna is referring.

Whether fox or jackal (and we shall proceed to assume the latter), the message of the Mishna is that a person should strive to place himself in the company of those greater than himself (the "lions"), such that he can learn from them, rather than surrounding himself with lesser people (the "jackals"). The Talmud applies this principle even to a situation where there is nothing wrong per se with the lesser group, teaching that it is still better to be at the tail end of the greater group:

> "Three rows of the disciples of the sages would sit before them, each recognizing his place. If they needed to ordain someone, they would ordain someone from the first row, and then one from the second row would move up to the first" (Mishna Sanhedrin 4:4). Abaye said: "We see from here that when they move, everyone would move." But let someone say, "Until today I was sitting at the head of the row, and now you are making me sit at the end!" Abaye said: "They can tell him as follows: Be a tail to lions rather than a head to jackals." (Sanhedrin 37a)

The symbolism of lions and jackals to refer not just to greater versus lesser groups but also to the relative placement of Torah scholars also appears elsewhere in the Tal-

mud. The Talmud relates that when Rav Kahana came to the Land of Israel, Resh Lakish was very impressed, and told R. Yochanan that "A lion has ascended from Babylon!" They placed Rav Kahana in the first row of the study hall, but after several classes in which he did not speak up, he was moved to the back. He was then compared to a different animal:

> R. Yochanan said to Resh Lakish: The lion of which you spoke has turned into a jackal! (Bava Kama 117a)

The motif of describing greater scholars vis-à-vis lesser scholars in terms of lions and jackals appears on several occasions in the Talmud:

> R. Yitzchak bar Radifa had a case. He came to ask R. Yirmiyah, who said to him: "Lions are before you, and you ask the jackal?!" (i.e. "There are great scholars here, why are you asking me?"). (Y. Shevi'it 26a)

> He said to him, My son, do not be dejected; he is a lion that is the son of a lion, whereas you are a lion that is the son of a jackal. (Bava Metzia 84b)

Notwithstanding the jackal's lowly status, however – or precisely because of it – the Sages saw fit to note that sometimes even a jackal is worthy of respect. This is a metaphor used in elaborating upon the reunification of Joseph with his family in Egypt:

> "And his brothers also went, and they fell before him" (Gen. 50:18). R. Binyamin bar Yefet said that R. Eleazar said: "That is just as people say, When the jackal has his moment, bow down to him." But how was Joseph inferior to his brothers [such as to be described as a jackal with regard to them]? Rather, if this was said, it is to be applied as follows: "And Israel (i.e. Jacob) bowed down at the foot of his (son Joseph's) bed" (Gen. 47:31) – When the jackal has his moment, bow down to him. (Megilla 16b)

Even the jackal has his day; as Rudyard Kipling wrote in *The Jungle Book*, "Even the tiger runs and hides when little Tabaqui (the jackal) goes mad." The Talmud employs this aphorism with reference to Joseph; although vis-à-vis his father, Joseph was a "jackal," nevertheless there was a time for this jackal to be shown respect.

Mauling and Biting

LAW AND RITUAL

Jackals and foxes are the smallest of the predatory wild animals, and this causes them to be the subject of halakhic discussion. An animal is only kosher for consumption if it is in good physical health at the time of slaughter. The Mishna lists various *tereifot*, fatal defects, which render an animal prohibited for use as food. One of these fatal defects is described as *derusa*, "clawing,"[50] inflicted by a predator such as a lion, leopard, or wolf. The Talmud discusses whether a fox (or jackal) can inflict such a fatal defect on its prey:[51]

> Rav Kahana said in the name of Rav Shimi bar Ashi: There is no "clawing" with a fox. [The Talmud asks:] Is this so? Surely when Rav Dimi came [from the Land of Israel to Babylonia], he said that there was an incident in which a fox clawed a ewe in the baths at Beit Hini, and the matter came before the Sages, and they said that it *is* a case of clawing? Rav Safra said: In that case, it was a cat.
>
> Some relate this differently: Rav Kahana said in the name of Rav Shimi bar Ashi: There is "clawing" with a fox. [The Talmud asks:] Is this so? Surely when Rav Dimi came [from the Land of Israel to Babylonia], he said that there was an incident in which a fox clawed a ewe in the baths at Beit Hini, and the matter came before the Sages, and they said that it is *not* a case of clawing? Rav Safra said: In that case, it was a dog. (Chullin 53a)

Contemporary observations show that both foxes and jackals, when attacking large mammals and birds, do so with their jaws rather than their claws. Elsewhere, the Talmud discusses the bite of a fox as being particularly severe:

> Warm yourself before the fire of the Sages. But be wary with their coals that you not get burnt, for their bite is the bite of a fox, their sting is the sting of a scorpion, their venom is the venom of a serpent, and all their words are like fiery coals. (Mishna Avot 2:10)

Why is a fox's (or jackal's) bite described as being so terrible? These canids do not possess the teeth of a lion or leopard, nor do their jaws possess the crushing power of a hyena's jaws. However, if we compare it to the Mishna's mention of the sting of a scorpion and the bite of a viper, we see that it is referring to chemical rather than physical damage. It therefore seems to be referring to the terrible scourge of rabies. Foxes and jackals are the main vector of rabies in Israel.[52] This may also contribute to their negative image in traditional thought.

Crafty as a Fox

SYMBOLISM

Across countless cultures, for thousands of years, the fox has been renowned for its cunning, its slyness, its craftiness.[53]

TOBIE OOSTHUIZEN / SHUTTERSTOCK

Unlike lions or leopards, a jackal seizes its prey – in this case, a sand grouse – with its teeth

Foxes are agile predators and are capable climbers

The reasons for this are not entirely clear, but it may relate to the fact that small canids such as foxes and jackals are highly opportunistic and adaptable. They are also smaller than other predators, and thus a little quicker and more agile, which probably enhances their reputation.[54]

In Judaism, too, we find the fox playing such a role. As we saw earlier, Scripture compares fraudulent prophets to foxes:

> Your prophets, O Israel, have been like the foxes in the ruins.... They prophesied falsehood and lying divination; they said, "Declares the Lord," when the Lord did not send them, and then they waited for their word to be fulfilled. (Ezek. 13:4–6)

Along these lines, the Talmud states that one of the curses that Isaiah pronounced upon Israel was that they would have poor rulers, expounding a verse to refer to foxes via wordplay:

> "And babes (*taalulim*) shall govern them" (Is. 3:4) – Rav Acha bar Yaakov said: Foxes (*taali*) who are the sons of foxes.[55] (Chagiga 14a)

Earlier, we saw that the fox symbolized Egypt due to its being the least of predators, just as Egypt was least of the kingdoms that oppressed the Jewish people. The Talmud presents the craftiness of the fox as another way in which it symbolizes the Egyptians:

"And God said to Moses: Stretch out your hand over the sea, and the waters shall return..." (Ex. 14:26) – This is what is referred to by "Seize for us the foxes, the little foxes" (Song. 2:15).... R. Eleazar b. R. Shimon said: The Egyptians were sly, and therefore they are symbolized by foxes. Just as the fox goes along and looks behind it, so too the Egyptians looked behind them as they went along, and what did they say? "Come, let us deal slyly with them" (Ex. 1:10). They said, "Let us come and approach them with slyness, and we will see how to subjugate Israel with something that their God cannot use against us in retribution. If we execute them with the sword, He can bring the sword upon us; if we use fire, He can bring fire upon us. We know that He has sworn never to bring another deluge upon the world, so let us execute them with water, which He cannot bring upon us." The Holy One said, "Wicked ones! I have already vowed not to bring another deluge upon the world, but what shall I do instead – I shall bring you to the deluge! And I shall drag each and every one of you into his own deluge, and he shall be destroyed." This is as David says, "They shall be given over to the power of the sword; they shall be a portion for foxes (Ps. 63:11)" – this refers to the wicked Egyptians, who were dragged by the Holy One to the sword of the sea. What does it mean by, "they shall be a portion for foxes"? The Holy One said: "This smiting is arranged for these foxes" [who thought to outwit Him], whom the Holy One preserved and did not bring the ten plagues upon them, and there [in the sea] they died. R. Berechiah said: The first mention of *shualim* (foxes, in Song. 2:15) is written in full (שועלים), and the second is written deficiently – it is written שעלים (without a *vav*, and it can be read as *shaal-yam*) – referring to the path (*shaal*) of the sea (*yam*).[56] R. Yochanan of Tzippori said: What did the pure and modest daughters of Israel do? They would take their children and hide them in cavities. The wicked Egyptians would bring children [of their own] into the houses of the Israelites, and would pinch them to make them cry, and the [Israelite] babies would hear the sound of the other baby crying and would cry with him. Then the Egyptians would take them and throw them into the river. Therefore it says, "Seize for us the foxes, the little foxes..." [who are acting] while "our vineyards are bearing new grapes" (Song. ibid.). Therefore it says that "the waters returned upon the Egyptians" – that their plans rebounded upon them. (*Shemot Rabba* 22:1)

Precisely because the fox is known for being a crafty creature, it also appears as a character that is outwitted by others:

The Rabbis taught: Once, the wicked government decreed that the Jews may not busy themselves with Torah. Pappus b. Yehuda came and found R. Akiva who was assembling groups in public and busying himself with Torah. He said, Akiva, are you not afraid of the government? R. Akiva replied: I shall illustrate this with a parable. To what can this be compared? To a fox that was walking by a river and saw fish swarming from place to place. He said to them, From what are you fleeing? They replied, From the nets that people are bringing to us. He replied, Would you like to come up to dry land, and you and I can live together, just as my ancestors lived together with your ancestors? They replied, Are you really the one who is known as the craftiest of beasts? You are not crafty, but rather you are a fool! If we are afraid in a place where we live, how much more should we fear a place where we cannot live! So, too, with us – if now, when we are sitting and busying ourselves with Torah, about which it is written, "For it is your life, and your length of days," it is so [that we are threatened], all the more so if we avoid it! (Berakhot 61b)

The following parable likewise shows the sneaky fox having his plan foiled:

"As he came out of his mother's womb, so must he depart at last, naked as he came" (Eccl. 5:14). Geniva said: This is analogous to a fox that found a vineyard which was fenced in on all sides. There was one hole, through which he sought to enter, but he could not fit. What did he do? He fasted for three days until he became weak and thin, and entered through the hole. He ate and became fat, but then when he tried to get out, he could not fit through the hole. So he fasted for another three days, until he became weak and thin, just as he was before, and he went out. As he exited the vineyard, he turned his face to look at it, and said, "Vineyard, vineyard, how good are you, and how good are the fruits in you! Everything in you is beautiful and praiseworthy; but what benefit can be derived from you? In the same way that one enters you, one must leave you." And so too is the situation with this world. (*Kohelet Rabba* 5:20)

All such accounts are equally applicable to fox and jackal. In fact, we find that folktales and parables involving these animals are widespread throughout the world, but whereas Greek and Roman versions of these stories speak of the fox, the Arab and Oriental versions speak of the jackal. There is dispute amongst historians as to whether these stories originated with foxes or jackals.[57]

Fox Fables

Stories about the fox (or jackal), in terms of its crafty nature, abound in Jewish tradition.[58] They are so numerous that the fox became the namesake of this genre of literature, which, while known in English as Aesop's fables, is known in Jewish tradition as *mishlei shualim*, fox fables. These were considered to be a valuable part of the repertoire of a Torah scholar. R. Yochanan b. Zakai is praised for the extent of his wisdom, which includes fox fables.[59] Bar Kappara is said to have known three hundred fox fables.[60] The same is reported about R. Meir:

> R. Yochanan said: R. Meir had three hundred fox fables, but we only have three: "The fathers have eaten sour grapes and the children's teeth are set on edge" (Jer. 31:28 and Ezek. 18:2); "An honest balance, honest weights" (Lev. 19:36); "The righteous man is rescued from trouble, and the wicked man takes his place" (Prov. 11:8). (Sanhedrin 38b–39a)

An illustration of the fox and wolf fable cited by Rashi

FREDERICK COLIN TILNEY

These three verses are explained by Rashi to relate to a fable involving a fox and a wolf:

> A fox once tricked a wolf into joining the Jews on Sabbath eve, to help them with their Sabbath preparations and eat with them on Sabbath. When he arrived, the Jews ganged up on him with sticks. The wolf returned to kill the fox, but the fox told him that they beat him due to his father, who once helped them in preparing their banquet and then consumed all the choice parts. Replied the wolf: "And was I beaten for the wrong done by my father?" "Yes," replied the fox, "'The fathers have eaten sour grapes and the children's teeth are set on edge.' But come with me and I will show a place where you can eat and be satisfied." He led him to a well which had a beam across it, and a rope hanging over it with buckets attached at both ends. The fox entered the upper bucket and his weight caused it to descend into the well whilst the lower one was drawn up. "Why are you going in there?" asked the wolf. "There is meat and cheese to eat here and be satisfied," said the fox, showing him the circular cheese-like reflection of the moon in the water. "How can I get down?" asked the wolf. "Go into the upper bucket," replied the fox. The wolf did so, and as his weight caused the bucket to descend, the fox rose up. "How can I get out?" said the wolf. Replied the fox: "The righteous man is rescued from trouble, and the wicked man takes his place. Is it not written, 'An honest balance, honest weights'?" (Rashi to Sanhedrin 39a, s.v. *Avot Yokhlu Voser*[61])

The Midrash relates another fable that reveals the fox's cunning:

> R. Pinchas explained the events of the Book of Esther as follows: A lion made a feast for all the domestic and wild beasts, and made a canopy out of the skins of lions, wolves, and other predators. After eating and drinking, they said, If only there was someone to recite verse for us, and they looked at the fox. He said to them, Will you say Amen to that which I say? And they said, Yes. He said, "May the fate of those above us also be the fate of those below." So, too, He who has shown us the downfall of Bigthan and Teresh and their hanging, will also show us the downfall of Haman. (*Esther Rabba* 7:3)

Another fable about the fox has the fox itself knowing such fables:

> "And Jacob raised his eyes and saw Esau was coming with three hundred men" (Gen. 33:1). R. Levi said: Once, the lion was angry with all the animals. They said, Who will go and appease him? The fox said, Let us all go, for

I know three hundred fables, and I shall appease him. They all replied, Good. He went a little way, and stopped. They said to him, What is happening? He replied, I forgot a hundred fables. They said to him, Two hundred will suffice. He went a little further and stopped. They said to him, What now? He replied, I forgot another hundred. They said to him, Even a hundred will suffice. When they arrived, he said, I have forgotten all of them; let everyone appease him. So, too, with our forefather Jacob. R. Yehuda bar Shimon said: [Jacob said,] I have the ability to prepare a prayer. R. Levi said: [Jacob said,] I have the ability to prepare for war. But when he reached him, "He divided the children among Leah, Rachel, and the two maids" (Gen. 33:1) – he said, let each and every person stand on his own merit. (*Bereshit Rabba* 78:7)

(This story was cited by Rabbi Yitzchak Ze'ev Soloveitchik, colloquially known as the "Brisker Rav," at the onset of the Holocaust, after a planned official "Day of Prayer" for Vilna did not come to fruition. He urged everyone to pray for mercy on their own instead.[62])

Such fox fables continued as a popular tradition during the medieval period. Rav Hai Gaon, the great leader of the talmudic academy of Pumbedita during the early eleventh century, includes a fox fable in one of his legal responsa.[63] Another fox fable is found in a midrash attributed to Rav Moshe HaDarshan, the eleventh-century dean of the Yeshiva of Narbonne; it concerns a lion who successfully lures animals into its den to be eaten, except for the fox, who notices all the footprints leading in and none leading out.[64] The midrashic anthology *Yalkut Shimoni* relates a fable about a fox simultaneously outwitting a donkey and a lion.[65] Berechiah ben Natronai HaNakdan, who probably lived in the twelfth century, published a collection of over a hundred such fables, appropriately titled *Mishlei Shualim*, "Fox Fables." It was based on the classical fables about foxes and other creatures, both from the Talmud as well as Greek sources, but he added biblical quotations and messages in order to adapt the fables for a Jewish readership. Berechiah's collection of fox fables was extremely popular, being printed in many editions, and eventually in English translation.[66]

Perhaps the fox's reputation and symbolism as a crafty creature sheds light upon its use as a Jewish family name. While *shual* never appears as a personal name, Fuchs ("fox") is a common Jewish family name. This may be based on a house name, or due to a family being red-haired like the European red fox. Alternately, it may be because rabbis in Poland in the eighteenth and nineteenth centuries wore special garb with a fox-lined outer garment.[67] But another possibility is that people with a reputation for craftiness were given this name – either as a compliment, or as an insult.

The title page from the 1661 Prague edition of Berechiah HaNakdan's Mishlei Shualim

Rabbi Akiva and the Fox

——————————————— SYMBOLISM

The fox plays a role in famous story about the great R. Akiva who, together with his friends, visited the ruins of the Second Temple:

> When they reached the Temple Mount, they saw a fox emerging from the Holy of Holies. They began weeping, but R. Akiva was laughing. They said to him, "Why are you laughing?" He replied, "Why are you crying?" They said to him, "A place about which it is written, 'And the common person who draws near shall be put to death,' now has a fox walking through it – should we not cry?!" He replied to them, "That is why I am laughing.... Now that Uriah's prophecy has been fulfilled, it is certain that Zechariah's prophecy shall be fulfilled." They said to him: "Akiva, you have comforted us; Akiva, you have comforted us." (Makkot 24b)

Rabbi Yaakov Ettlinger, a leading German rabbi of the nineteenth century, gives a striking explanation of this story.[68] As discussed in the chapter on lions, when the evil inclination for idolatry was driven out of the Temple, it was manifest in the form of a lion. This was because the

193

גַּם תַּנִּין חָלְצוּ שַׁד הֵינִיקוּ גוּרֵיהֶן בַּת עַמִּי לְאַכְזָר כַּיְעֵנִים בַּמִּדְבָּר:
איכה ד:ג

עַל זֹאת אֶסְפְּדָה וְאֵילִילָה אֵילְכָה שׁוֹלָל וְעָרוֹם אֶעֱשֶׂה מִסְפֵּד
כַּתַּנִּים וְאֵבֶל כִּבְנוֹת יַעֲנָה: מיכה א:ח

lion, as a powerful animal, symbolizes the raw power of the desire for idolatry. It was this sin that brought about the destruction of the First Temple. During the period of the Second Temple, however, the Jewish people were busy with Torah and observing the commandments. Their sin, which brought about the Destruction, was a different one: that of baseless hatred. Rabbi Ettlinger explains that "it is the way of the evil inclination, when it wants to cause the righteous to stumble, to deceive them into thinking that they are doing a mitzva by hating and persecuting others." The evil inclination deviously convinces pious people that their piety requires them to despise others, whom they perceive as insufficiently pious. This deviousness, states Rabbi Ettlinger, is symbolized by the fox, the perennial embodiment of craftiness and cunning.

Rabbi Ettlinger further suggests that this sheds light upon why R. Akiva was happy when he saw the fox emerging from the Temple. Just as, when the evil inclination for idolatry was vanquished, it was manifest as a lion fleeing, so too the fox leaving the Temple grounds symbolized that the evil inclination for baseless hatred had weakened. There was now hope for redemption.

Snakes, Owls, and Jackals

IDENTIFICATION

Although it seems that the jackal sometimes shares the name *shual* with the fox, there may be an additional name for it. There is a creature mentioned on numerous occasions in Scripture whose identity is disputed. It is not even clear whether it is a mammal, bird, or reptile. This creature is referred to by the name *tanim*, but there is even dispute as to whether that is the name of a single individual of this species, or if it is the plural form, with an individual being

A jackal feasting on carrion

194

known as a *tan*. There are three opinions altogether: One, that the creature's name is *tanim*, and it is synonymous with the name *tanin* (with an "n" at the end), which elsewhere refers to a serpentine creature (with the plural form being *taninim*); two, that the creature's name is *tan* (with the plural form being *tanim*), and it is a jackal; and three, that the creature's name is *tan* and it is a type of owl.

One critical verse might provide evidence for one of these three views. It is a verse which, according to tradition, is read differently from how it is written:

> Even the *tanin* have bared their breast, nursing their cubs; yet the daughter of my people has become cruel, like *ya'enim* (a type of bird) in the wilderness. (Lam. 4:3)

In a traditional scroll, the creature's name is written as *tanin*. However, there is an oral tradition that it is to be pronounced as *tanim*. There are differing views as to the significance of such differences between the oral reading and the written text (known as *kri uktiv* disputes). Some rabbinic authorities ascribe dual layers of meaning – in which case both names are accurate for the creature, and would be synonyms.[69] Others ascribe these differences to uncertainty as to which is correct – in which case only one of the word-forms here, either *tanin* or *tanim*, is actually accurate.[70]

Now, the *tanin* elsewhere refers to serpentine creatures such as snakes and crocodiles (which are rated by Torah commentators as aquatic serpents), and is often understood to refer to sea-monsters and dragons. Accordingly, this is how many commentaries explain this verse, too.[71] This has led to this verse being commonly translated as "Even the sea-monsters have drawn out the breast" or "Even the dragons have drawn out the breast."

In addition, some traditional commentators likewise explain every mention of *tanim* (as well as *tanin*) to refer to snakes, sea-monsters, or dragons.[72] This, however, does not fit with certain descriptions of the *tanim* given elsewhere, which indicate that they emit a mournful wailing sound:

> For this I shall lament and wail, I will go around delirious and naked, I shall make a lamentation like *tanim*, and a mourning like *benot yaana*. (Micah. 1:8)

The description of the *tanim* making a lamentation is understood to mean that they howl in a mournful-sounding wail.[73] Yet no reptile emits such a sound. Hence, the *tanim*

"The sound of a report! Behold, it is coming, and a great noise from the northern lands, to place the cities of Judah in desolation, a lair of jackals."

(Jer. 10:22)

mentioned in several places in Scripture cannot be serpentine creatures.

Furthermore, the verse in Lamentations describing the *tanim/tanin* as "baring its breast" and "nursing its cubs" does not fit with a serpentine creature. Neither snakes nor crocodiles possess breasts with which to nurse their young. Thus, they are presumably not the *tanim/tanin* of this verse.[74]

While a powerful argument, this does not conclusively prove that the verse in Lamentations is not referring to serpents or sea-monsters. Some argue that it is describing aquatic serpentine creatures and sea-monsters such as whales, which do indeed nurse their young on milk.[75] Others argue that this verse reflects a belief in antiquity that snakes nurse their young on milk.[76] According to both suggestions, this verse is to be understood, in accordance with the Septuagint, as referring to the *taniN*, being identical to the serpentine/aquatic *tanin* of other verses. (The *tanim* mentioned elsewhere would then be birds,[77] in accordance with the Aramaic traditions.[78])

However, it is impossible to accept that the verse in Lamentations refers to an aquatic mammal. This verse also mentions the "*ya'enim* (a type of bird) in the wilderness";

and *benot yaana*, which are presumably the same bird, are mentioned in the same verse as the *tanim* on four other occasions in Scripture, as together representing the denizens of wilderness areas. This verse must then be referring to the same creature – *tanim* that live with *ya'enim* in the wilderness, and therefore not an aquatic *tanin*.

Another argument against the verse referring to a *tanin*, be it snake or marine mammal, is that the verse speaks of "*them* drawing out the breast," in the plural. Yet the plural of *tanin* is *taninim*, not *tanim*. Since the verse is speaking in the plural, *tanim* must be a plural form. If so, the singular form would be *tan*, which is not the same word as the serpentine *tanin* mentioned elsewhere.[79]

A final argument against this verse referring to a *tanin* rather than *tanim*, and thus to a serpentine creature, is that the young are referred to as *gurim*. This term is used elsewhere for the young of lions, and thus seems to mean "cubs," i.e. the young of mammals rather than any kind of serpentine creature.

Accordingly, this verse should probably be understood as not describing a *tanin*, but rather *tanim* (in accordance with the oral tradition). This verse then sheds crucial light on the other references to *tanim* in Scripture. Those other

A jackal emitting its distinctive mournful-sounding howl

CHRIS FOURIE / SHUTTERSTOCK

וְנָתַתִּי אֶת יְרוּשָׁלַ͏ִם לְגַלִּים מְעוֹן תַּנִּים וְאֶת עָרֵי יְהוּדָה אֶתֵּן שְׁמָמָה מִבְּלִי יוֹשֵׁב:

ירמיה ט:י

קוֹל שְׁמוּעָה הִנֵּה בָאָה וְרַעַשׁ גָּדוֹל מֵאֶרֶץ צָפוֹן לָשׂוּם אֶת עָרֵי יְהוּדָה שְׁמָמָה מְעוֹן תַּנִּים:

ירמיה י:כב

וְהָיְתָה חָצוֹר לִמְעוֹן תַּנִּים שְׁמָמָה עַד עוֹלָם לֹא יֵשֵׁב שָׁם אִישׁ וְלֹא יָגוּר בָּהּ בֶּן אָדָם:

ירמיה מט:לג

וְעָנָה אִיִּים בְּאַלְמְנוֹתָיו וְתַנִּים בְּהֵיכְלֵי עֹנֶג וְקָרוֹב לָבוֹא עִתָּהּ וְיָמֶיהָ לֹא יִמָּשֵׁכוּ:

ישעיה יג:כב

וְעָלְתָה אַרְמְנֹתֶיהָ סִירִים קִמּוֹשׂ וָחוֹחַ בְּמִבְצָרֶיהָ וְהָיְתָה נְוֵה תַנִּים חָצִיר לִבְנוֹת יַעֲנָה:

ישעיה לד:יג

וְהָיְתָה בָבֶל לְגַלִּים מְעוֹן תַּנִּים שַׁמָּה וּשְׁרֵקָה מֵאֵין יוֹשֵׁב:

ירמיה נא:לז

וְאֶת עֵשָׂו שָׂנֵאתִי וָאָשִׂים אֶת הָרָיו שְׁמָמָה וְאֶת נַחֲלָתוֹ לְתַנּוֹת מִדְבָּר:

מלאכי א:ג

וְהָיָה הַשָּׁרָב לַאֲגַם וְצִמָּאוֹן לְמַבּוּעֵי מָיִם בִּנְוֵה תַנִּים רִבְצָהּ חָצִיר לְקָנֶה וָגֹמֶא:

ישעיה לה:ז

references describe *tanim* as creatures of desolate areas that emit mournful sounds, and, without taking into account the verse in Lamentations, could refer to either owls or jackals. However, since the verse in Lamentations is also best understood as referring to the same *tanim*, and it describes them as nursing their young, as well as describing the young as *gurim*, then many prefer to identify the *tanim* as mammals,[80] which would be jackals. The identification of *tan* with the jackal was apparently first given in the tenth century by David ben Avraham Alfasi,[81] and again by Rabbi Tanchum Yerushalmi in the thirteenth century,[82] and it has been carried forward into Modern Hebrew.

It might appear strange that the jackal would have two names in Scripture – *tan* and *shual*.[83] However, as discussed, the lion has even more names. In English, animals can likewise have multiple names; cougar, puma, and mountain lion are all the same animal.

The Jackal of Desolation

— SYMBOLISM

The majority of references to the *tanim* – over a dozen – refer to them in exactly the same way: as creatures that symbolize desolation and ruin. The prophet Jeremiah, in his predictions of the destruction of Jerusalem, frequently makes reference to the jackal, by virtue of the terrain that it inhabits:

I shall make Jerusalem heaps of rubble, a lair of jackals, and I shall make the cities of Judah desolate, without inhabitants. (Jer. 9:10)

The sound of a report! Behold, it is coming, and a great noise from the northern lands, to place the cities of Judah in desolation, a lair of jackals. (Jer. 10:22)

Hazor will become a lair of jackals, forever desolate; no man shall ever dwell there, and no person shall ever sojourn there. (Jer. 49:33)

This might provide further indication that *tanim* are jackals, since the *shual* is similarly described as living in areas of desolation:

Because of this our hearts are sick, because of these our eyes are dimmed; for Mount Zion which is desolate, *shualim* walk in it. (Lam. 5:17–18)

It is not only the inhabitants of the Land of Israel that are punished by their land becoming a jackal's lair. This is also the description of the punishments inflicted upon other nations. Isaiah declares such a prophecy regarding the downfall of Babylon, describing how the homes of the nobility are destroyed and become lairs for wild animals:

Wild cats[84] will respond in the mansions, and jackals in the palaces of delight. Her time is soon to come, and her days will not last long. (Is. 13:22)

Its palaces will sprout weeds, thorns and thistles in its fortresses; it will be an abode of jackals, a court of owls. (Is. 34:13)

The same description is given by Jeremiah in describing the destruction of Babylon:

Babylon shall become rubble, a lair of jackals, desolate and whistling, without inhabitant. (Jer. 51:37)

And such a punishment is also foretold for the kingdom of Esau:

But Esau I hated, and I made his hills desolate, and his heritage for the desert jackals.[85] (Mal. 1:3)

Isaiah further speaks of how, after the downfall of Edom, the Land of Israel will be rejuvenated, such that it will no longer be the desolate wilderness inhabited by jackals:

The scorched place will become a pond, and the parched place will become springs of water; in the place where jackals crouched, there will be grassland with reeds and bulrushes. (Is. 35:7)

197

תְּכַבְּדֵנִי חַיַּת הַשָּׂדֶה תַּנִּים וּבְנוֹת יַעֲנָה כִּי נָתַתִּי בַמִּדְבָּר מַיִם נְהָרוֹת בִּישִׁימֹן לְהַשְׁקוֹת עַמִּי בְחִירִי:

ישעיה מג:כ

וּפְרָאִים עָמְדוּ עַל שְׁפָיִם שָׁאֲפוּ רוּחַ כַּתַּנִּים כָּלוּ עֵינֵיהֶם כִּי אֵין עֵשֶׂב:

ירמיה יד:ו

אָח הָיִיתִי לְתַנִּים וְרֵעַ לִבְנוֹת יַעֲנָה:

איוב ל:כט

כִּי דִכִּיתָנוּ בִּמְקוֹם תַּנִּים וַתְּכַס עָלֵינוּ בְצַלְמָוֶת:

תהלים מד:כ

עַל זֹאת אֶסְפְּדָה וְאֵילִילָה אֵילְכָה שׁוֹלָל וְעָרוֹם אֶעֱשֶׂה מִסְפֵּד כַּתַּנִּים וְאֵבֶל כִּבְנוֹת יַעֲנָה:

מיכה א:ח

The beasts of the field shall honor Me, the jackals and the owls, for I will have placed water in the desert, rivers in the wilderness, to provide water for My chosen people. (Is. 43:20)

Returning to Jeremiah's tragic predictions, he also foretells how droughts in the Land of Israel will transform it to arid wilderness:

And the wild asses stand in the high hills, they suck in (*shaafu*) the wind like jackals; their eyes fail, because there is no grass. (Jer. 14:6)

As we shall discuss in the chapter on wild asses, this verse is a reference to the asses exhibiting a behavior known as "flehmen," in which they curl up their upper lip and inhale such that the air passes over the Jacobson's organ (a highly sensitive olfactory receptor) in the roof of their mouth. Although it is sometimes claimed that canids do not exhibit this behavior, there are reports of jackals doing so.[86] But why compare the wild asses to jackals, seeing as the wild asses are better known for this behavior than

jackals are? Perhaps because jackals also innately symbolize drought, due to their being animals that inhabit ruined areas.

As a result of the jackal being a symbol of the physical destruction of places, it also came to represent any state of suffering. Thus, Job, recounting his situation of suffering and despair, describes himself as having been like a jackal:

I was a brother to jackals, and a companion of owls. (Job 30:29)

And a psalm mentions jackals as a symbol for generic suffering:

(Our heart has not turned back, nor have our footsteps strayed from Your path,) Even when You crushed us in the place of jackals, and covered us in the shadow of death. (Ps. 44:20)

However, it is not only due to its environment that the jackal is the symbol of destruction. As noted earlier, it has a distinctive mournful cry:

For this I shall lament and wail, I will go about delirious and naked, I shall make a lamentation like *tanim*, and a mourning like *benot yaana*. (Micah. 1:8)

The unearthly howls of the jackal sound like the bitter cries of a person. Indeed, Holocaust survivors who came to Israel are said to have found the jackals' howling to be deeply disturbing: "It was very hot in the banana groves of the Jordan Valley kibbutz, and life was hard.... At night the wails of the jackals brought back memories of Bergen-Belsen."[87] Thus, due to both the types of environment in which it lives and the unusual sounds that it makes, the jackal is the symbol of destruction. ∎

Notes

1 "The sons of Zophah: Suah, Harnepher, Shual, Beri, Imrah" (1 Chr. 7:36).

2 "One column headed for the Ophrah road that leads to the district of Shual" (1 Sam. 13:17). See too Joshua 19:3.

3 In Europe, this was first pointed out in the seventeenth century by Bochart in the *Hierozoicon*

4 Schonhak, *Toledot HaAretz*, p. 55, and *Easton's Bible Dictionary* relate the Hebrew word *shual* to the Persian *schagal*. Schonhak also suggests that this lies behind the Talmud in Rosh HaShana 4a interpreting the word *shegal* as referring to a dog.

5 Schonhak, *Toledot HaAretz*, p. 55.

6 Yoram Yom-Tov, Shoshana Ashkenazi, Omer Viner, "Cattle Predation by the Golden Jackal *Canis Aureus* in the Golan Heights, Israel," *Biological Conservation* 73 (1995), pp. 19–22.

7 The Mishna (Kilayim 1:6) makes mention of a creature called *kelev hakufri*, "village dog," which is similar to the *shual* but prohibited from being bred to it. The identity of this "village dog" is unclear.

8 Rashi ad loc.

9 "For the House of Israel is the vineyard of the God of Hosts" (Is. 5:7).

10 Cf. *Midrash Bemidbar Rabba* 20:14, where it appears with *nimkarim* rather than *nimsarim*. The *Tanchuma*'s version is surely the accurate version.

11 Maharzav (Zev Wolf Einhorn) to *Midrash Bemidbar Rabba* 20:14.

12 Cf. Isaiah 40:12 and Rashi ad loc.

13 Feliks, *The Animal World of the Bible*.

14 Saul Lieberman, "*Lachpor perot velaatalefim*," *Leshonenu* 29 (5725), pp. 132–135.

15 See the notes of D'arcy Wentworth Thompson to Aristotle, *Historia Animalium* (Oxford, 1910), p. 490a note 6.

16 Lieberman, loc. cit.

17 Albayrak I., Asan N., Yorulmaz T., "The Natural History of the Egyptian Fruit Bat, *Rousettus aegyptiacus*, in Turkey," *Turkish Journal of Zoology* 32 (2008), pp. 11–18.

18 Korine, C., Izhaki, I., and Arad, Z., "Is the Egyptian fruit-bat *Rousettus aegyptiacus* a pest in Israel? An analysis of the bat's diet and implications for its conservation," *Biological Conservation* (1999), 88, pp. 301– 306.

19 Radak.

20 Henry Tristram, *The Natural History of the Bible*, p. 85.

21 Constantin-François Volney, *Travels through Syria and Egypt, in the years 1783, 1784, and 1785* (London: G.G.J. and J. Robinson, 1787), vol. 2, pp. 386–387.

22 See Rashi. Malbim has a novel explanation of the entire verse, according to which it is referring to Saul and company using the sword to drive David out from his hiding places in the wilderness, such that they then become a dwelling place for *shualim*.

23 *Metzudat David*.

24 Feliks, *The Animal World of the Bible*, pp. 36–37.

25 Rabbi Yehuda Leib Tsirelson (1859–1941, Chief Rabbi of Bessarabia) cited in Yitzchak Eshkoli, *Sefer Tzaar Baalei Chayim*, p. 328.

26 Rabbi Mordechai Yaakov Briesch (1895–1976), Responsa *Chelkat Yaakov* 1:30:5.

27 Radak to Judges 15:4.

28 Othniel Margalith, *The Sea Peoples in the Bible* (Wiesbaden: Harrassowitz, 1994), pp. 105–106.

29 See, for example, the lengthy discussion in Thaddeus Harris, *The Natural History of the Bible*, 1824 edition, pp. 147–157. For extensive discussion of the consternation surrounding this topic from the seventeenth to twentieth centuries, see David M. Gunn, *Judges Through The Centuries* (Blackwell, 2005), pp. 203–206.

30 Benjamin Kennicott, *Remarks on Select Passages in the Old Testament* (Oxford, 1737), p. 100; Gregory Sharpe, *Introduction to Universal History* (1755).

31 In the Jewish world, this was first noted by Baruch Lindau in *Reishit Limudim* (1789) 6:7:5, which was also cited by Shalom Yaakov Abramowitz in *Toledot HaTeva*, vol. 1, p. 199.

32 David W. MacDonald, "The Flexible Social System of the Golden Jackal, *Canis aureus*," *Behavioral Ecology and Sociobiology* vol. 5, no. 1 (1979), pp. 17–38.

33 Constantin-François Volney, *Travels through Syria and Egypt, in the years 1783, 1784, and 1785*, vol. 1, p. 321.

34 Ibid., vol. 2, pp. 386–387.

35 Cambridge: Deighton, Bell and Co., 1864.

36 *The Natural History of the Bible*, p. 87.

37 Martin Wallen, *Fox* (Reaktion Books, 2006), pp. 58, 82–83, 89.

38 See Othniel Margalith, in "Samson's Foxes," *Vetus Testamentum*, vol. 35, Fasc. 2 (Apr., 1985), pp. 224–229, and in *The Sea Peoples in the Bible*, pp. 105–109, and the criticism by Gregory Mobley, in *Samson and the Liminal Hero in the Ancient Near East* (Bloomsbury, 2006), p. 11.

39 The text in the Jerusalem Talmud (Ketubot 7:3, 31b) is different: שאין עפר פריו מת שועל. Saul Lieberman, in "*Lachpor perot velaatalefim*," *Leshonenu* 29 (5725), pp. 132–135, writes that it should be translated as "the fruit-seeking fox is not dead," and argues that it refers to the flying fox (fruit

40 See Rashi and Ritva.

41 Ketubot 111b.

42 Pesachim 35a; Menachot 70a.

43 Yehuda Feliks, "Regarding the question of the identity of *shibbolet shual*" (Hebrew), *Jubilee Volume in Memory of Rabbi Abraham Isaiah Dolgin* (Jerusalem, 2001), pp. 171–178.

44 For a detailed discussion, see Zohar Amar, *Chameshet Minei Dagan* (Makhon Har Bracha, 2010), pp. 60–67.

45 Frederick Thomas Elworthy, *The Evil Eye: An Account of this Ancient and Widespread Superstition* (London: John Murray, 1895), p. 206.

46 Mishna Shabbat 6:10; see Shabbat 67a and Rashi ad loc.

47 Sanhedrin 65b.

48 Rabbi Yom Tov Lippman Heller, *Tosafot Yom Tov* ad loc.

49 Maimonides, *Mishneh Torah, Hilkhot Talmud Torah* 5:4.

50 Unfortunately, these laws give rise to difficult contradictions with our knowledge of zoology. One difficulty is that the Talmud states that the result of such maulings is that venom is injected into the prey animal (Chullin 53a). Needless to say, this is not consistent with modern zoological knowledge of these predators. One solution presented for such difficulties by Rabbi Aryeh Carmell (in Rabbi Eliyahu Dessler, *Mikhtav MiEliyahu*, vol. IV, p. 355, footnote 4) is that the Talmud is not referring to a chemical venom generated by the animal, but rather to infections caused by bacteria accumulating in the animal. As Gordon Grice notes in *The Red Hourglass: Lives of the Predators* (London: Penguin Books, 1998), "Many people mauled by lions have died from wounds that should have been survivable: the meat caked under the attackers' claws and teeth injected the victims with disease, and they died in a gangrenous fever" (p. 104). This answer is offered with regard to why the cat is listed as a creature whose mauling is considered a fatal defect, whereas a dog is not (see Chullin 53a); cats have long retractable claws, and thus dirt can accumulate beneath them, whereas dogs have short, blunt claws. However, this explanation falls short with our discussion, since the wolf is listed as an animal that can cause such damage, even though it is physiologically essentially the same as a dog rather than a cat. A second difficulty is that the Talmud (Chullin 53a) rules that these maulings which are rated as causing fatal defects refer to maulings inflicted with the claws, not with the teeth. This, too, conflicts with contemporary observations of members of the dog family, which reveal that they never attack prey with their claws, only with their teeth. These contradictions resist simple resolutions that preserve the correctness of both the Talmud and modern zoology.

51 Rabbi Moshe Yona Zweig discusses whether there is *derusa* with a jackal. See *Ohel Moshe, Mahadura Tanyana* (Jerusalem, 1960), responsum #44–45, pp. 90–92.

52 Mendelson and Yom Tov, *Fauna Palaestina: Mammals of Israel*, pp. 182, 193. The "little fox" – the fruit bat, otherwise known as the flying fox – is also a transmitter of rabies, although there are no recorded cases in the Israeli population.

53 Hans-Jörg Uther, "The Fox in World Literature: Reflections on a Fictional Animal," *Asian Folklore Studies*, vol. 65, no. 2 (2006), pp. 133–160.

54 I am indebted to Professor David Macdonald, one of the world's greatest authorities on canid behavior, for these insights.

55 The plural form *taalulim* is expounded as referring to their not just being foxes, but even the sons of foxes.

56 See Isaiah 40:12.

bat). Accordingly, he explains the Jerusalem Talmud to mean that even though the flying fox appears dead by day, it comes alive at night; so, too, even though an unhygienic woman is unappealing by day, her husband will be able to have relations with her at night. Lieberman proposes that the Babylonian version of the parable, which indeed refers to an actual fox, emerged from a corrupted text.

57 Otto Keller, in *Untersuchungen über die Geschichte der griechischen Fabel* (Leipzig, 1862), argued that these stories originated with jackals. His evidence was that some of these fables describe the fox as a follower of the lion, which has no basis in reality regarding the fox, but which is true of the jackal. Others found such arguments inconclusive, and argued that the fox, as the craftier animal, was the origin of these fables; see Albrecht Weber, *The History of Indian Literature* (London, 1882), pp. 211–212.

58 See Dan Ben-Amos, *Folktales of the Jews: Tales from Eastern Europe*, vol. II, pp. 298–300.

59 Bava Batra 134a.

60 *Midrash Vayikra Rabba* 28:2. The Midrash relates that R. Shimon forgot to invite Bar Kappara to the wedding of his son. Upon realizing his error, he made a second banquet and invited Bar Kappara. At this meal, Bar Kappara entertained the guests with three hundred fox parables when each course was served, causing them to leave the food untouched.

61 While this fable is widespread in medieval literature, Rashi is the earliest source known for it. G. H. McKnight, "The Middle English Vox and Wolf," *PMLA*, vol. 23, no. 3 (1908), pp. 497–509.

62 Shimon Yosef Meller, *The Brisker Rav* (Jerusalem: Feldheim, 2007), vol. 1, pp. 452–453.

63 Rav Hai Gaon, Responsa 13.

64 *Midrash Bereshit Rabbati, Parashat Toledot*. The same fable is found in Berechiah HaNakdan's *Mishlei Shualim*, number 23.

65 *Midrash Yalkut Shimoni, Va'era* 182.

66 The first printed edition appeared in Mantua, in 1557. An English translation by Moses Hadas appeared in 1967, entitled *Fables of a Jewish Aesop*; it was republished in 2001 by David R. Godine, New Hampshire.

67 Benzion C. Kaganoff, *A Dictionary of Jewish Names and their History* (New York: Schocken, 1977), p. 153.

68 Rabbi Yaakov Ettlinger, *Arukh LeNer* to Makkot 24b.

69 Malbim, introduction to Jeremiah; Maharal, *Tiferet Yisrael* 66; Radbaz, responsum 1020, vol. 3 no. 594. In *Sefer HaShorashim*, Radak states that the aquatic creature named *tanin* is sometimes called *tanim* due to the letters *mem* and *nun* often being interchanged.

70 Radak, introduction to commentary on Joshua.

71 *Targum Yonatan*, Ibn Yachya, and commentary of Rabbeinu Shmuel Vidash ad loc.; Ibn Janach, *tan*; Bochart, *Hierozoïcon*, vol. II p. 429. Rabbi Yaakov of Lisa, *Palgei Mayim* ad loc., also interprets it as a snake, but sees it as a metaphor for the enemies of the Jewish people. The Septuagint has "*dracon*."

72 *Metzudat Tziyon* and Malbim consistently explain *tanim* to be a type of serpent. One reason why some see the *tanin* and *tanim* as being synonymous is that, aside from the variant versions of the verse in Lamentations, there is a verse in Ezekiel 29:3 undoubtedly referring to a crocodile (i.e. the serpentine *tanin*), in which many texts render the word as *tanim*.

73 Radak, *Metzudat David* ad loc.

74 This point was first made in the thirteenth century by Tanchum HaYerushalmi. See p. 126 in Avi Tal, "Rabbi Tanchum HaYerushalmi's Exegetic Methods in his Commentary on the Books of II Kings, Isaiah, Jeremiah and Ezekiel" (Hebrew), in Ayelet Oettinger and Danny Bar-Maoz (eds.), *Mitov Yosef: Jubilee Volume in Honor of Joseph Tobi*, vol. III (Haifa, 5771), pp. 120–144.

75 Yehuda Feliks, *Nature and Man in the Bible*, pp. 101–102.

76 Othniel Margalith, "Samson's Foxes," *Vetus Testamentum*, vol. 35, Fasc. 2 (Apr., 1985), pp. 224–229. As evidence, he points to clay cobras from Bet Shean which are seemingly formed with breasts. See Arlette David, "Clay Cobras Clay Cobras: Ramesside Household Cult or Apotropaic Device?" in *Excavations at Tel Beth-Shean 1989–1996*, vol. III, eds. N. Panitz-Cohen and A. Mazar (Jerusalem: The Hebrew University and the Israel Exploration Society), pp. 556–60.

77 Yehuda Feliks, in *The Animal World of the Bible*, p. 36, argues that since the *tanim* are usually mentioned as living in areas of desolation along with ostriches, this indicates that they are a type of owl rather than jackals. However, this argument is far from conclusive, since the *shual* is also described as living in areas of desolation. Othniel Margalith, "Samson's Foxes," argues that the *tanim* are always listed amongst birds; however, these identifications are subject to dispute.

78 *Targum Yonatan* always gives the Aramaic translation of *yerudin* (or *yerurin*). The Talmud Yerushalmi (Kilayim 8:4) and Tosefta (Kilayim 5:6) states that *yerudot* are birds.

79 Margalith, loc. cit., argues that these words were indeed emended.

80 This is, however, not absolutely straightforward. In antiquity, it was believed that there was a type of owl of ill-omen which nurses its young on milk, called a *strix*. Such a bird would match all descriptions of the *tanim* and would also be supported by the Aramaic translations of *yerudin/yerurin*, as per the description of these as unusual birds in the Talmud Yerushalmi (Kilayim 8:4). It would also better account for why the verse states that "even" the *tanim* nurses its young. Furthermore, if the teats are normally under the bird's plumage, that is why they would have to be "unsheathed" (*chaltzu*). In addition, the Talmud Bavli, Sanhedrin 59b, mentions a "*yarod nala*," and according to Sokoloff, *A Dictionary Of Jewish Babylonian Aramaic*, s.v. נלא, the term *nala* refers to a demon or vampire; this would be further evidence for the Sages identifying it as the strix, which was believed to be a demonic bird that sucked people's blood.

81 Solomon Skoss, *The Hebrew-Arabic Dictionary of the Bible, Known As, Kitab Jami' Al-Alfaz, of David Ben Abraham Al-Fasi*, vol. II (New Haven: Yale University Press, 1945), p. 741.

82 As cited by Wilhelm Gesenius, *Hebrew and Chaldee Lexicon*, and in turn by Yosef Schonhak, *Toledot HaAretz*, p. 57. See pp. 125–7 in Avi Tal, "Rabbi Tanchum HaYerushalmi's Exegetic Methods in his Commentary on the Books of II Kings, Isaiah, Jeremiah and Ezekiel" pp. 120–144.

83 It should also be noted that according to some, the *iyyim* mentioned in Isaiah 13:22, 34:14 and Jeremiah 50:39 are jackals, whereas others identify them as a type of wild cat, probably the caracal. See the chapter on the caracal for further discussion.

84 The term used is *iyyim*, which also appears in Isaiah 34:14 and Jeremiah 50:39, where they appear alongside creatures called *tziyyim*. Bochart and Feliks (*The Animal World of the Bible*, p. 36) identify these *iyyim* as jackals; this is predicated on the view that *tanim* are *not* jackals. Others identify *iyyim* as wild cats, such as caracals, or hyenas. Tanchum HaYerushalmi suggests that the terms *tziyyim* and *iyyim* are non-specific references to animals that inhabit remote areas.

85 Here the word is *tanot* rather than *tanim*; Ibn Ezra states that this is the feminine construct, but the reason for this difference is unclear.

86 R. F. Ewer, *The Carnivores* (Cornell University Press, 1986), p. 134. Alternately, the verse may be saying that wild asses suck in the air and appear like jackals raising their muzzles in the air – which they do in order to sniff the wind.

87 Tom Segev, *The Seventh Million* (New York: Hill and Wang, 1993), p. 154.

CARACAL

Caracal

Iyyim / Tziyyim

Wild Cats of Israel

———————————————— NATURAL HISTORY

There are four different species of wild cats in the Land of Israel: the jungle cat, the sand cat, the wildcat, and the caracal. The jungle cat (also known as the swamp cat), *Felis chaus*, is a long-legged cat that lives near water and swims well. The sand cat, *Felis margarita*, is a small cat that lives only on the sands in the Arava desert. The wildcat, *Felis silvestris*, is the ancestor of the domestic cat. Wildcats in Israel are much smaller than wildcats in Europe, and interbreed

Largest and most prominent of the wild cats in Israel is the caracal, *Caracal caracal*. It weighs up to thirty pounds, and has long legs and a relatively short tail. The caracal's most distinctive feature are its ears, which bear long tufts of black hair, similar to a lynx, though the function of these tufts is unknown. Caracals are now found throughout Israel, having benefited from a boon in their favored prey (hares) following a poisoning campaign against their competitors, jackals. They are best known for their astonishing ability to suddenly leap up to seven feet into the air and catch birds in flight.

Jungle cat

Sand cat

Wildcat

Caracal

202

A snarling caracal

The Caracals of the Ruins

——— IDENTIFICATION

There are no unequivocal references to wild cats in Scripture. However, there are two terms, *iyyim* and *tziyyim*, each of which has been identified by some as referring to wild cats.

When the prophet Isaiah describes the destruction of Babylon, he presents an image of a ruined city inhabited by wilderness animals. No less than six creatures are described in these verses, but unfortunately many of them are difficult to identify with any degree of certainty:

> And *tziyyim* shall crouch there, and their houses will be filled with *ochim*; *benot yaana* shall dwell there, and *se'irim* shall dance there. And *iyyim* shall answer in their castles, and jackals in the palaces of pleasure; her hour is close to coming, and her days shall not last long. (Is. 13:21–22)

וְרָבְצוּ שָׁם צִיִּים וּמָלְאוּ בָתֵּיהֶם אֹחִים וְשָׁכְנוּ שָׁם בְּנוֹת יַעֲנָה
וּשְׂעִירִים יְרַקְּדוּ שָׁם: וְעָנָה אִיִּים בְּאַלְמְנוֹתָיו וְתַנִּים בְּהֵיכְלֵי עֹנֶג
וְקָרוֹב לָבוֹא עִתָּהּ וְיָמֶיהָ לֹא יִמָּשֵׁכוּ:

ישעיה יג:כא-כב

וּפָגְשׁוּ צִיִּים אֶת אִיִּים וְשָׂעִיר עַל רֵעֵהוּ יִקְרָא אַךְ שָׁם הִרְגִּיעָה
לִילִית וּמָצְאָה לָהּ מָנוֹחַ:

ישעיה לד:יד

Later, describing the destruction of Edom, Isaiah again conjures up the image of wild beasts inhabiting the ruins, and again enumerates the *iyyim* and *tziyyim*:

> It shall be a home of jackals, an abode of *benot yaana*. *Tziyyim* shall meet *iyyim*, the *sa'ir* shall greet his friend . . . (Is. 34: 14)

203

And Jeremiah, prophesying regarding the destruction of Babylon, likewise describes its desolation in terms of the animal life that will take over, and mentions the same animals:

> Therefore, *tziyyim* and *iyyim* shall take residence, and owls shall dwell there; it shall never be settled again, nor inhabited throughout the ages. (Jer. 50:39)

What are the *iyyim* and *tziyyim* of these verses? Several commentaries do not even attempt to identify them.[1] However, the Aramaic translation of *Targum Yonatan* (Yonatan ben Uziel), also cited by Rashi, consistently renders *tziyyim* as martens, and *iyyim* as *chatulin*, which means "cats." This would not refer to the domestic cat,[2] but rather to wild cats. Others identify the *iyyim* as jackals, but the *tziyyim* as cats.[3]

If the *iyyim* or *tziyyim*[4] refer to wild cats of some sort, then to which particular type of cat do they refer? Isaiah states that "the *iyyim* shall answer in their castles," which

seems to describe these creatures as emitting a distinctive calling sound. Caracals emit a range of sounds, including growling, hissing, purring, barking, and a call sometimes known as the "wah-wah call."

The verses also describe these *tziyyim* and *iyyim* as inhabiting desolate, ruined areas. Caracals are superbly adapted for living in arid areas; they can survive without drinking for long periods, as their water requirements are satisfied with the body fluids of prey. But they also prefer areas with good cover from vegetation or rocks. A desolate wasteland, with ruined buildings, would thus provide an ideal habitat.

The features of the cat described in these verses, put together, seem to best describe the caracal. Describing the cries of caracals amidst the ruins would conjure up the image of the retribution planned for Babylon and Edom. ∎

Notes

1 Radak, *Metzudat Tziyon*, and Malbim merely note that they are types of animal; Tanchum Yerushalmi suggests that the terms *tziyyim* and *iyyim* are non-specific references to animals that inhabit remote areas.

2 It is also possible that some of the references to the cat in the Talmud are referring to wild cats, such as the ruling that "There is mauling by a cat and a mongoose with kids and lambs" (Chullin 52b).

3 Bochart, *Hierozoicon*, p. 862; Gesenius, also cited by Schonhak, *Toledot HaAretz*, p. 60; and Feliks, *The Animal World of the Bible*, p. 36. This is predicated on the view that the animals in these verses that we have translated as jackals, *tanim*, are instead something else.

4 It is unclear if the singular forms would be *iy* and *tziy* (as Schonhak proposes), or *iyya* and *tziyya*.

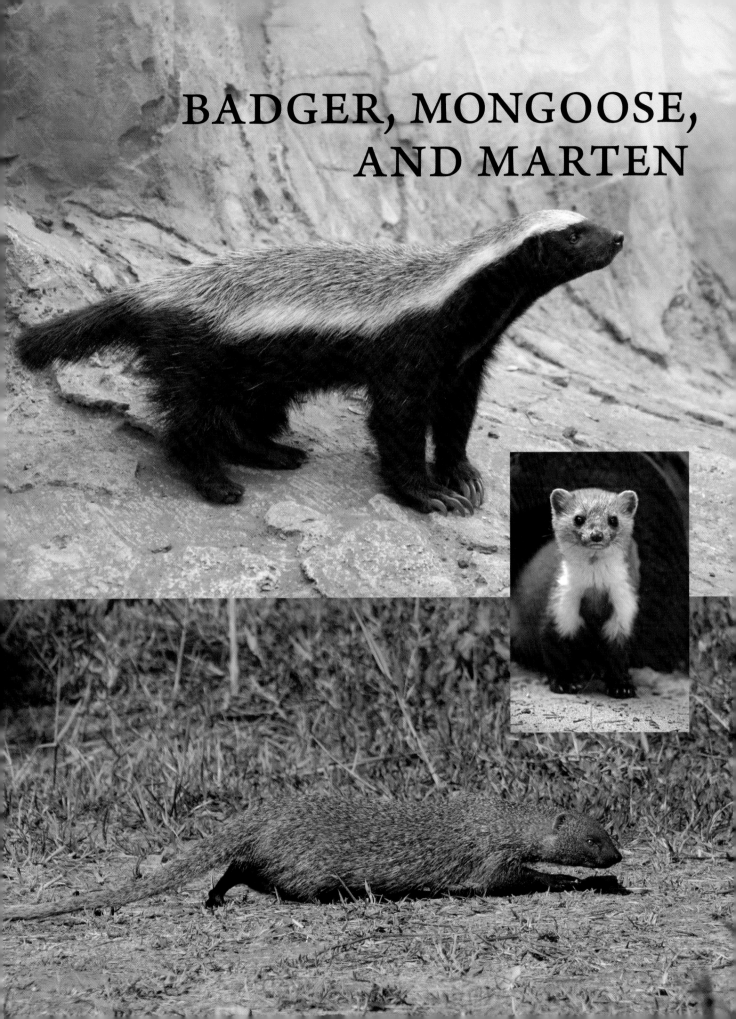

BADGER, MONGOOSE, AND MARTEN

Badger, Mongoose, and Marten

Chuldat Sena'im, Nemiya, Mandaris (Bardelas)

Mongoose, Honey Badger, and Other Small Carnivores

—————————— NATURAL HISTORY

There are several smaller wild animals mentioned in rabbinic literature that are difficult to identify with certainty – the *chuldat sena'im*, the *nemiya*, and the *mandaris*. The potential candidates are the honey badger, the Egyptian mongoose, and the stone marten, but it is difficult to determine which name refers to which creature; it is also possible that the same creature is referred to with more than one of these names. (Another animal sometimes proposed to be mentioned under one of these names is the genet, but it does not seem that genets were ever native to the area.[1]) As such, we shall discuss all these animals together.

There are two species of badger in Israel, which are not particularly closely related. The European badger (*Meles meles*) is grey, with black-and-white stripes on its face. It is a powerfully built animal which digs complex dens in the ground. European badgers are omnivorous and eat a wide range of foods.

The honey badger (*Mellivora capensis*) is also known as the ratel. It is strikingly colored, with the lower half of its body and head dark black, and a broad white mantle extending to the top of its head. Honey badgers are leg-endary for their power, aggression, and near-invincibility. They are mainly carnivorous, but also have a taste for honey, and rip open bee-hives without concern for the stings that they receive. In Israel, it is a rare animal, though it is spread across the country; it is also found in Africa, Arabia, and, significantly, in Iran and Iraq, i.e. the home of the Babylonian Talmud.

The Egyptian mongoose, *Herpestes ichneumon*, is widely distributed in Africa, extending north around the edge of the Mediterranean through to Syria and Turkey. It is a common animal in Israel today; many immigrants from North America, unfamiliar with the mongoose, have been bewildered upon seeing one slinking across the road. (Other, similar species of mongoose live in southern Asia, reaching northwest into Iraq, and thus would have been known to the Sages of the Babylonian Talmud.[2]) The body length is a little less than two feet, with a tail almost as long, and the legs are short. Mongooses are well known for killing snakes, even venomous ones; this makes them valuable creatures and offsets the damage that they cause to poultry farms.

Other small carnivores native to the region are the stone marten (*Martes foina*, also known as the beech marten) and marbled polecat (*Vormela peregusna*), which are both members of the weasel family. The marten is a handsome and very agile animal that somewhat resembles a mink. The

European badger

Honey badger

206

marbled polecat is a colorful and small weasel-like animal. As we shall discuss, it appears that both of these animals may fall into the category of the *chulda* mentioned as being a type of *sheretz* – a small creature that does not fall into the Torah's category of *chayot*, wild animals. As such, the primary discussion regarding these animals will take place in a later volume dealing with *sheratzim*.

The *Chuldat Sena'im* – Between *Chaya* and *Sheretz*

———————————————————— LAW AND RITUAL

The first animal that we shall investigate is variously called the *chuldat hasena'im, chuldat sena'im,* and *chuldat senayim.* The Torah states that *tuma,* ritual impurity, is contracted from the carcasses of dead animals:

> Everything that walks on its hands, among all animals that walk on four legs, are contaminated to you; whoever touches their carcasses shall be contaminated until evening. (Lev. 11:27)

The Midrash derives that the word "everything" serves to include those animals that, for one reason or another, one might have thought do not fall into this category:

> "Everything that walks" – to include the porcupine, the *chuldat hasena'im,* the ape, and the otter. (Sifra, Shemini 6)

Why does the Sifra need to exegetically derive that the *chuldat hasena'im* is included amongst the animals in the verse? The reason is that these laws of ritual impurity are being stated with regard to *chayot,* wild animals, and it is not obvious that the *chuldat hasena'im* falls into this category. Due to its small size, it might be considered to be a *sheretz* – a small, scurrying creature, which is subject to different laws of ritual impurity.

In order to contract *tuma* from a dead *sheretz,* one must touch it. With a dead *chaya,* on the other hand, there is a greater stringency – one becomes ritually impure by carrying it, even if one is not touching it. On the other hand, there is a way in which the situation with a *sheretz* is more stringent. In order to contract *tuma* from a dead *chaya,* one must be carrying a portion of its carcass at least equivalent to an olive in size. But in order to contract *tuma* from a dead *sheretz,* one need only touch a portion of its carcass equivalent to the size of a lentil.

The question regarding the category in which to place the *chuldat hasena'im* is reflected in a discussion in the Mishna regarding which animals are classified as being a *chaya* rather than a *sheretz.* The Mishna notes that two ani-

Egyptian mongoose eating a catfish

mals, despite being on the smaller end of the scale, are still large enough to qualify as being *chayot*:

> The porcupine and the *chuldat senayim* are a type of *chaya.* (Mishna Kilayim 8:5)

This follows the Midrash Sifra cited above. However, the Mishna proceeds to cite a dissenting view. While Beit Shammai were in agreement that the porcupine is large enough to qualify as a *chaya,* they were unsure if the same was true for the *chuldat senayim*; it might be classified as a *sheretz,* like an ordinary *chulda.* They therefore gave it the stringencies of both a *chaya* and a *sheretz*:

> The *chuldat senayim* – R. Yose says that Beit Shammai say: It transmits *tuma* if carried in the quantity equivalent to an olive (like a *chaya*), and if touched in a quantity equivalent to a lentil (like a *sheretz*). (Ibid.)

Thus are the laws of *tuma* as discussed with regard to the *chuldat sena'im.* Let us now turn to investigating its identity.

The *Chuldat Sena'im* – Digging in the Bush

———————————————————— IDENTIFICATION

What is the *chuldat sena'im*? The word *sena'im*[3] is likely to be the plural of *sneh,* which means "bush." It thus appears to refer to a particular variety of *chulda* that lives in the bushes. However, this does not shed much light upon its identity.

(The ordinary variety of *chulda* is described elsewhere in the Talmud as a small predator that lives in areas of human habitation and also eats grain products. This appears to be a member of the weasel family. But it is not the weasel itself, which probably did not live in the area and never eats grain products. Nor could it be the marbled polecat, which likewise never eats grain products. The only small predator that lives in areas of human habitation and also eats grain products is the stone marten, though the term

207

chulda could be a generic term for all similar members of the weasel family.[4])

From the discussion cited above regarding whether the *chuldat senayim* is a *chaya* or a *sheretz*, we have clues regarding its size. We know that it is somewhat bigger than an ordinary *chulda*, which is unequivocally classified as a *sheretz*. We also know that the *chuldat senayim* is somewhat smaller than a porcupine, since Beit Shammai ruled that the porcupine is large enough to qualify as a *chaya*, but were unsure if the same was true for the *chuldat senayim*. Unfortunately, none of this assists in conclusively identifying the *chuldat senayim*.

There are, however, further mentions of the *chuldat senayim* which may shed light on it. One occurs in the context of a discussion in the Talmud about certain animals that may not be raised due to their destructive habits. The Talmud notes that other animals may be raised due to their utility:

> R. Yishmael said: One can raise *kufri* dogs, cats, monkeys, and *chuldat sena'im*, because they are used for cleaning the house (from mice – Rashi). (Bava Kama 80a)

R. Yishmael was a *Tanna* from the Land of Israel. The Sages of the Babylonian Talmud, seeking to identify the *chuldat sena'im* of which he spoke, were not able to agree to its identity:

> What is the *chuldat sena'im*? Rav Yehuda said: The digging animal – and some say, the prickly animal – that has small legs, and forages amongst the bushes. And why is it rated as a *sheretz*? Because of its short legs. (Ibid.)

If the *chuldat sena'im* is a "prickly animal," one might think that it is the hedgehog or the porcupine (and this may also involve the idea that since *sneh* can refer to a thorn bush, the *chuldat sena'im* may an animal that *resembles* a thorn bush). However, nobody would raise porcupines or hedgehogs to clean the house from vermin; the former eats grain, and the latter only eats insects. Furthermore, the *chuldat sena'im* is mentioned above as being a different animal from the porcupine.

If the *chuldat sena'im* is a digging animal, on the other hand, it could perhaps refer to a badger; both the European badger and the honey badger are ardent diggers, and they would eat or scare away vermin. However, it is difficult to

Stone marten

imagine that anyone would raise either type of badger in their home. Badgers are irascible animals that are not easily raised in captivity.

Perhaps a better candidate is the mongoose. It has long claws for digging and often lives in burrows (albeit that these are usually taken over from other animals rather than being excavated by the mongoose itself). As such, it would well match Rav Yehuda's description.

(Rambam states that *chuldat hasena'im* is an animal that is similar to the *chulda* but from the fox family.[5] This is a perplexing definition that may refer to the marten, as some identify the *chuldat sena'im*.[6] However, it could perhaps refer to the mongoose.)

The aforementioned statement from R. Yishmael states that one may raise a *chuldat sena'im*. A dissenting midrash states that the drawbacks outweigh the gains:

> "There are many things that increase futility" (Eccl. 6:11) – for example, those who raise monkeys, cats, *chuldat hasena'im*, apes, and otters. What is the benefit of them? Either a swipe, or a bite. (*Kohelet Rabba* 6:11)

Although the Midrash regards the raising of such animals as a bad idea, the implication is that it nevertheless does take place – and R. Yishmael views the practice as worthwhile. Martens and polecats may well have been raised in homes for such purposes. But the mongoose is perhaps an even better candidate. It is an animal that was commonly raised in homes, and would be a good match for *chuldat sena'im*.

The *Nemiya*

IDENTIFICATION

Another small carnivore mentioned in rabbinic literature is the *nemiya*. The Mishna rules that if one is placing a ladder on one's property, one must ensure that it is not so close to a neighbor's dovecote that an animal could use it to reach the doves and eat them:

> One must distance a ladder at least four cubits from the dovecote [of one's neighbor], such that a *nemiya* cannot leap into it. (Mishna Bava Batra 2:5)

What is the *nemiya*?[7] This mishna indicates that the *nemiya* is an animal that enters human settlement, climbs ladders, eats birds, and can take short jumps, but not to a distance of four cubits (about six feet).[8] The mongoose certainly best matches this description;[9] as a result, the mongoose is commonly identified as the *nemiya*, and it is called *nemiya* in Modern Hebrew. However, the Mishna's description could also match the honey badger, which is often a serious poultry predator. Honey badgers eat birds,

Marbled polecat

and climb trees in order to raid nests.[10] Although honey badgers are apparently unable to jump any distance, it is certainly possible that having witnessed a honey badger climb up to a dovecote, the Sages instructed that ladders must be placed at a safe distance. Nevertheless, the mongoose is still a better fit.

There is also a reference to the *nemiya* in the Jerusalem Talmud, with regard to their excrement:

> [When reciting *Shema,*] one must distance oneself four cubits from the excrement of pigs, *nemiyot,* and chickens. (Y. Berakhot 3:5, 27b)

This could refer to the foul-smelling spray emitted by the honey badger. Alternately, and perhaps slightly more likely, it could refer to the distinctive dung-heaps maintained by mongooses at various sites in their range.[11]

The third and final[12] reference is in the Babylonian Talmud. This occurs in the context of a discussion about the laws of *derusa,* perhaps best translated as "mauling." Certain wild animals are classified as lethal predators of certain domestic animals and birds, such that if they maul them, the domestic animal or bird is considered to be mortally wounded and is no longer kosher for slaughter. After discussing large wild animals, the Talmud describes which small wild animals are classified as lethal predators, capable of inflicting such a mauling, for which domestic animals and birds:

> Rav Amram said in the name of Rav Chisda: There is mauling by a cat and a *nemiya* with kids and lambs; there is mauling by a *chulda* (marten) with birds. (Chullin 52b)[13]

Mongooses are extremely unlikely to kill kids or lambs (and this is certainly an impossibility with martens or polecats).[14] European badgers are known to kill lambs on very rare occasions. Honey badgers, however, are reported to

209

KLAUS RUDLOFF

With their powerful claws and jaws, honey badgers are formidable predators

be responsible for many instances of predation upon small livestock.

Thus, the first two references to the *nemiya* are a *slightly* better fit for the mongoose, while the third reference vastly better fits the honey badger. It may therefore be preferable to identify the *nemiya* as the honey badger. However, this is not conclusive. It is also possible that *nemiya* is a generic term for both animals;[15] alternatively, perhaps the first two references from the Mishna and Jerusalem Talmud, written in the Land of Israel, were referring to the mongoose, while Rav Chisda, living in Babylonia, was referring to the honey badger.[16]

The *Bardelas* and the *Mandaris*
———————————————————————— IDENTIFICATION

There are scattered references throughout the Talmud to a creature by the name of *bardelas*. As discussed in the chapters on the cheetah and hyena, the *bardelas* of the Mishna's list of dangerous wild animals was understood by the Jerusalem Talmud to be the cheetah, while the Sages of Babylonia interpreted it as referring to the hyena. However, there appears to be another reference to the *bardelas* which refers

to a different creature.[17] There is a reference to a *bardelas* in the Tosefta that does not appear to be referring to the large wild animal mentioned in the Mishna:

> R. Yehuda said: There was an incident with a bondmaid of a certain oppressor in Rimon, who threw her miscarried fetus into a pit, and a priest came and looked to see what she had aborted. The case came before the Sages, and they immediately declared him clean, because the *chulda* and *bardelas* drag it away immediately. (Tosefta, Oholot 16:13)

This case is also cited in the Talmud, which notes that in such a case the *chulda* and *bardelas* are certain to take advantage of such an opportunity.[18] Now, a cheetah would certainly not be likely to enter into a pit in an area of human habitation in order to scavenge. And the Tosefta, written in the Land of Israel, would not have used the name *bardelas* for the hyena. But as it turns out, the animal being described here might not be a *bardelas* at all. This story also appears in the Talmud Yerushalmi,[19] where in the Leiden manuscript of the Yerushalmi, the word *bardelas* does not appear; instead, it mentions the *mandaris* (מנדרס). It appears that at some point the similar-sounding term *bardelas* was substituted for the unfamiliar term *mandaris*. But what is a *mandaris*? Interestingly, the mysterious *mandaris* also appears in manuscripts of another rabbinic text:

> There are maulings for which [a guardian] is obligated to pay, and there are mauled animals for which he does not pay. Which is the mauling for which he must pay? For example, mauling by a cat, fox or *nemiya*.... And which is the mauling for which he is exempt from payment? For example, mauling by a wolf, and a lion, and a bear, and a leopard, and a *bardelas* (cheetah), and a snake...for in any case where it is impossible for him to rescue it, he is exempt from paying. (*Mekhilta DeRabbi Yishmael, Mishpatim* 16)

Here, we have the *nemiya* mentioned alongside the cat and fox as being a predator which can easily be fended off by people. Yet in various manuscripts of this midrash, the word *nemiya* does not appear; instead, they mention a *maris* (מריס) or *mindaris* (מינדרס).[20] Thus, we have two contexts

mentioning the *mandaris/mindaris*, together presenting a description of a small, opportunistic predator/scavenger that lives in areas of human habitation.

There are two animals that would best match this description: the mongoose and the marten. The advantage of explaining it to be the mongoose is that the *mindaris* is mentioned alongside the *chulda* as a separate creature, and it seems likely that the *chulda* is the marten, which would mean that the *mindaris* should be a different creature. But on the other hand, there would appear to be a strong etymological link between *mindaris* and marten; in Latin, the marten was also known as the *madrus*.[21] Another Latin name for the marten was *martalus*[22] and perhaps *mardulis*,[23] which might be an indication of how the *mandaris* became the *bardelas* in the discussion regarding scavenging from pits.

In summary, then, it appears that the *bardelas* mentioned alongside the *chulda* as an opportunistic scavenger is in fact a *mandaris*. It further appears that the *mandaris* is either the mongoose or marten. ∎

Mongooses are a familiar sight in Israel today

Notes

1 Heinrich Mendelssohn and Yoram Yom-Tov, *Fauna Palaestina: Mammalia of Israel*, p. 200. The dead type specimen that earned the name *Genetta terrasanctae* was simply a North African genet (*Genetta genetta*) that had been brought to Israel and not been identified properly. There were only ever two reports of genets in Palestine, in the nineteenth and early twentieth century, but these are now suspected to have been mistaken identifications of marbled polecats. The matter is not entirely clear. There certainly were never genets in Babylonia.

2 Omar F. Al-Sheikhly, David Mallon, "The Small Asian Mongoose *Herpestes javanicus* and the Indian Grey Mongoose *Herpestes edwardsii* in Iraq (Mammalia: Carnivora: Herpestidae)," *Zoology in the Middle East* (2013), 59:2 pp. 173–175.

3 Note that sometimes it appears as *sena'im*, and sometimes as *senayim*.

4 See David Talshir, *Shemot Chayim* (Jerusalem: Bialik, 2012), pp. 95–106.

5 Commentary to the Mishna, Kilayim 8:5. See Zohar Amar, "The *Chamos* – The Identity of the *Chulda* in the Mishna by Maimonides" (Hebrew), *Leshonenu* 73 (5771), pp. 327–333.

6 Menachem Dor, *HaChai BiYemei HaMikra, HaMishna VeHaTalmud*, p. 73.

7 Rashi (to Chullin 52b) cites a view that identifies it as a marten. However, as we have argued, the marten is more likely to be the *chulda*. Rashi, living in France, would not have been aware of other candidates, such as the mongoose or honey badger. See too Rashi to Isaiah 13:21 and Isaiah 34:14, who identifies the *tziyyim* of those verses as referring to the *nemiya*, which he identifies as the marten.

8 The Midrash (*Bereshit Rabba* 20:4) states that the gestation period of the *nemiya* is seventy days. However, a number of gestation periods given for different animals in the Midrash stand in conflict with empirical observation.

9 Menachem Dor, *HaChai BiYemei HaMikra, HaMishna VeHaTalmud*, p. 73. Moshe Ra'anan argues that the subsequent discussion in the Talmud shows that it is talking about an *immediate* risk. As such, it must be referring to an animal that frequents human habitation to the extent that it may well be poised and ready to run up the ladder, which would be the mongoose. See http://daf-yomi.com/DYItemDetails.aspx?itemId=2429

10 Keith and Colleen Begg, "Badgers and Birds: Interaction Satisfaction," *Africa – Birds and Birding* (December 2004/January 2005), 9:6 pp. 32–41.

11 Mendelsohn and Yom-Tov, *Fauna Palaestina*, p. 201.

12 Lewysohn, in *Die Zoologie des Talmuds*, p. 90, notes that some editions of the Jerusalem Talmud, Shekalim 12b (which should read 29b), tell of a *nemiya* that seized some meat from a person in the market; however, most editions instead have it as a *dayta*, kite, which makes more sense. There is also a statement in *Yalkut Shimoni*, Genesis 3, that the gestation period of a *nemiya* is 70 days.

13 Note that this passage indicates that a *nemiya* is a larger animal than a *chulda*, and is presumably rated as a *chaya* rather than a *sheretz*. However, Rashi to Shabbat 146b, s.v. *mishum richsha*, states that it is classified as a *sheretz*.

14 There are unconfirmed reports of the small Asian mongoose (*Herpestes javanicus*) killing lambs and newborn calves in the West Indies; see Howard Everest Hinton, A. M. Sarah Dunn, *Mongooses: Their Natural History and Behaviour* (University of California Press, 1967), p. 73. However, these seem unlikely, and there are no such reports concerning the Egyptian mongoose.

15 The *Arukh* says that the *nemiya* is "a small animal such as a cat or similar."

16 Rabbi Moshe Linde, cited by Yosef Schonhak, *Toledot HaAretz*, p. 195, states that that the *kilbit*, a creature described in the Talmud (Shabbat 76b) as terrorizing the leviathan is the mongoose, which terrorizes the crocodile by stealing its eggs. However, it appears unlikely that the leviathan of the Talmud is the crocodile.

17 The ensuing analysis is based upon Zev Ben-Chaim, "Erkhei Milim," in S. Abramsky, ed., *Samuel Yeivin Jubilee Volume* (Jerusalem: Israel Society for Biblical Research, 1970), pp. 432–435. This is also referenced by Avraham Ofir-Shemesh, "The *Bardelas* in Ancient Rabbinic Literature: A Test Case of Geographic Identification" (Hebrew), *Mo'ed* 14 (5764), pp. 70–80.

18 Pesachim 9a–b.

19 Pesachim 1:3.

20 See Zev Ben-Chaim, "Erkhei Milim," pp. 432–435.

21 J. F. Niermeyer, *Mediae Latinitatis Lexicon Minus* (Leiden, The Netherlands: Brill, 1976), p. 658.

22 Ibid.

23 Zev Ben-Chaim, "Erkhei Milim," fn. 16; Yaakov Epstein, *Mevo'ot LeSifrut HaAmora'im*, vol. 1 (Jerusalem: Magnes Press, 1963), p. 150.

PART TWO

———

Kosher Wild Animals

Kosher Wild Animals: Introduction

The Ten Types of Kosher Mammals

For a terrestrial animal to be kosher, it must possess two characteristics: it must have split hooves, and it must bring up its cud:[1]

> These are the creatures that you may eat from among all the land animals: any animal that forms a hoof, which is fully split, and that brings up the cud – such you may eat. (Lev. 11:2-3)

In Deuteronomy, the Torah presents a list of ten kosher mammals that match these requirements. It is not possible to identify all of the last five animals in this list with certainty; in the relevant chapters for each animal, we shall explain the reasoning behind the translations that we have chosen:

> This is the animal that you shall eat; the ox, the sheep, and the goat; the deer, the gazelle, the hartebeest (*yachmur*), the ibex (*akko*), the oryx (*dishon*), the aurochs (*teo*), and the wild sheep (*zamer*). (Deut. 14:4)

The list is divided into two parts. The first three animals – cattle, sheep, and goats – are the domestic kosher animals. The next seven animals, set aside in a second verse, are *chayot* – wild animals.[2]

It can be presumed that the animals are listed in some sort of overall meaningful order. But which order is it? Ralbag (Gersonides) writes that the list is in order of decreasing prestige. First are the domestic animals, which are of greater importance from a human perspective, and after this are the wild animals.

The order of decreasing prestige may also be applied with regard to the individual animals within the list, at least for the most part. If we look at the list of kosher domestic animals – cattle, sheep, and then goats – the order is one of decreasing importance in terms of food value, use as offerings, and market price.

Top: Deer chewing its cud. Bottom: Lower view of the hoof of a deer.

While a similar pattern ought to exist with the list of kosher wild animals, it is a little more difficult to discover. However, there is a clear difference between the first two or three animals, and the rest of the list. We find that the first two wild animals in the list—the deer and gazelle—are mentioned in Scripture far more than the rest, and the hartebeest (which immediately follows them) is grouped with them on one such occasion. Deer and gazelle were apparently the most common of the wild animals, and thus the most significant food source. The rest of the animals were apparently less common, and identifying them is more of a challenge. It is difficult to determine the significance in the order in which these last animals are listed.

A hartebeest

An Exhaustive List?
THEOLOGY, PHILOSOPHY, AND SCIENCE

When discussing the laws of kosher and non-kosher birds, the Torah lists all the non-kosher birds, teaching us that all the rest are kosher. But with the laws of kosher and non-kosher animals, on the other hand, the Torah lists all the kosher animals rather than all the non-kosher animals. The Talmud explains the reason for this:

> It was taught: Rebbi says, it is revealed and known before the One who spoke and the world came into being that the non-kosher animals are more numerous than the kosher ones, therefore Scripture enumerated the kosher ones.... One should always teach his student in a concise manner.[3] (Chullin 63b)

This indicates that the Torah's list of ten kosher animals includes every kosher animal in the world. This is explicitly stated in the Midrash:

> Let our rabbis teach us, how many kosher animals are there in the world? Thus taught our rabbis: There are ten kosher animals – the deer, gazelle, hartebeest, ibex, oryx, aurochs, wild sheep, ox, sheep and goat. There are no others in the world. (*Midrash Tanchuma, Shemini* 7)

The Talmud later also spells this out, although it emerges that not everyone agrees with this:

> This is as per Rav Yitzchak's statement that Scripture enumerated ten animals, and there are no more. (Chullin 80a)

Thus, following Rav Yitzchak's view, the Torah's list of ten kosher animals is exhaustive.[4] But the modern science of zoology counts 172 species that are definitely kosher: thirty-eight species of deer, four species of musk deer, the giraffe and okapi, the pronghorn, twenty-four species of wild cattle, seventeen species of duiker, twenty-three species of grazing antelope, thirty-two species of gazelle and dwarf antelope, four species of chevrotain, and twenty-seven species of goat antelope.[5] Can these all be included in the ten types mentioned in the Torah?[6]

Most of these species, such as the deer, gazelles, antelope, and cattle can certainly be included in the Torah's list without difficulty. But some are very different and are thus more difficult to include in these categories, even if we utilize a system of folk taxonomy in which new animals are grouped with familiar animals of similar appearance. Most problematic is the giraffe, and its smaller relative, the okapi. Some identify the giraffe as one of the ten animals in the Torah's list, which would avoid this difficulty; but others disagree and consider such an identification to be problematic. Furthermore, it would seem difficult to classify the enormous, strange-looking moose, the tiny, tusked musk deer, and the even smaller chevrotain, as varieties of the types in the Torah's list.

All this may lend support to Rav Acha bar Yaakov, who objects to Rav Yitzchak's view that the list is exhaustive:

> Rav Acha bar Yaakov asked: "I would say that 'deer and gazelle etc.' (the list of ten animals) are specifics, 'every animal' (the Torah's ensuing general rule that any animals with two kosher signs may be eaten) is a generality, and in cases of specifics followed by a generality, the generality serves to add to the specifics, in which case there are more!" (Ibid.)

The Talmud proceeds to counter Rav Acha bar Yaakov's view by arguing that if there are more such animals, the Torah would not have given a list. Still, Rav Acha bar Yaakov's view that the Torah's list is *not* exhaustive would certainly seem easier to reconcile with the species that we know, than the view of Rav Yitzchak. Furthermore, it is not too difficult to come up with a reason as to why the Torah specified these ten types. Most simply, they are the ten types of kosher animals that are local to the region. Some suggest that there are other Sages, too, who do not consider the list of ten types of kosher animals to be listing every such animal in the world.[7]

Top: A moose.
Bottom: A chevrotain.

However, even according to the view of Rav Yitzchak that the list indeed includes all kosher animals, it is not entirely clear if this means that it includes all the kosher animals from the *region*, or all those on the *planet*. A number of rabbinic authorities point out that the "world" of the Sages need not refer to the entire universe, or even to the entire planet; rather, there are cases where it refers to the area of human settlement familiar to them.[8] Accordingly, the Torah is only enumerating all the kosher animals in the region, and species such as the moose and musk deer would not present a difficulty.

Practical Differences Between Wild and Domestic Animals

—————————————————————————————— LAW AND RITUAL

Though both the groups of domesticated and wild animals include kosher members, there are several differences in Jewish law between rules governing the slaughtering and eating of domesticated and wild animals.

One difference is that sacrificial offerings may only be brought from domestic animals. The Midrash suggests a reason for this exclusion of wild animals from sacrificial practice:

R. Berechiah bar Shimon said: The Holy One, blessed be He, said: "I have given over ten kosher animals to you. Three are in your possession, and seven are not in your possession. The three that are in your possession are the ox, sheep and goat. The seven that are not in your possession are the deer, gazelle, hartebeest, etc. I have not bothered you for them, and I have not told you to ascend the hills and struggle through the forests in order to bring offerings from the types that are not in your possession; only from that which is in your possession, which has grown at your trough. (*Midrash Yalkut Shimoni, Vayikra* 21:643)

A second difference is that while one may not eat certain fats, called *chelev*, of kosher domestic animals, no such restriction exists with kosher wild animals.[9] A third difference is that after slaughtering a kosher wild animal (or bird), one must cover some its blood with earth:

Any man of the Children of Israel, or of the strangers who sojourn among you, who hunts and traps any beast or bird that may be eaten; he shall pour out its blood, and cover it with earth. For with the soul of all flesh, its blood is with its soul. (Lev. 17:13–14)

The commentaries explain that an animal's blood, flowing around its body, represents its animate spirit. It should therefore receive a burial, just as a dead human being is buried, out of respect.[10] The question is as to why this commandment is only applicable to wild animals and birds but not to domestic animals. One answer given is these animals possess greater vitality; they are more "alive," and we must show respect for this greater degree of life by giving a token burial to the creature's blood. Another answer given is that whereas domestic animals are farmed, wild animals and birds are hunted in a way that is often cruel, and one must compensate for this often-savage method of capturing an animal.[11]

Distinguishing Between Domestic and Wild Animals
IDENTIFICATION

How is a person to determine whether an animal is classified as a domestic or a wild animal? Its behavior alone is not necessarily an indication; an individual domestic animal might act in a wild manner, and a wild animal can be docile, if raised in captivity. The Sages of the Talmud provide characteristics via which wild and domestic animals can be distinguished:

The Rabbis taught: These are the signs of a wild animal...such that its *chelev*-fat is permitted: any creature that has horns and hooves. R. Dosa said: If it has horns, you do not need to ascertain if it has hooves, but if it has hooves, you still need to ascertain if it has horns. (Chullin 59b)

The hooves spoken of here are a particular type of hoof. Not only must they be split (in order for the animal to be kosher), but in order to demonstrate that the animal is a wild animal, the hooves must be pointed.[12] The horns spoken of here are, at this stage of the Talmud's discussion, not specified as being of any particular nature. But the Talmud immediately points out that defining any animal with (pointed) hooves and horns as a wild animal is problematic:

But consider the goat, which has horns and hooves, and yet its *chelev*-fat is forbidden (i.e. it is a domestic animal)! (Chullin 59b)

The Talmud answers this by explaining that in order to be rated as a wild animal with permissible *chelev*-fat, a particular type of horn is required. After engaging in some back-and-forth regarding the precise characteristics required, it reaches the following conclusion:

> Where the horns are branched, there is no need for a ruling or a judge (as it is certainly a wild animal); but where they are not branched, we require that they are layered, circular (in cross-section) and ringed,[13] with rings that are close together.[14] (Ibid.)

It may be asked that following these characteristics would seem to lead to the problematic result that a number of species that are surely wild animals would not be rated as such. The horns of the kudu and eland antelope, for example, are not ringed, and yet these are surely wild animals. But it should be remembered that these characteristics are only being provided for a particular scenario: namely, where a person does not know how to identify an animal, in terms of which it is of the three domestic and seven wild animals in the Torah's list. In such a situation, the Talmud is giving certain necessary conditions for the animal to be certainly classified as a wild animal, such that its *chelev*-fat can be eaten. It is not saying that any animal that does *not* match these criteria is classified as a domestic animal. ▪

A greater kudu. Note that is horns are not ringed.

ECOPRINT / SHUTTERSTOCK

Notes

1 The precise definition of these characteristics is discussed in *The Camel, The Hare And The Hyrax*, by this author.

2 As we shall see in the chapter on the aurochs, however, there is a view in the Talmud that the aurochs is a domestic animal.

3 One can ask that if the goal is to be concise, why list all the kosher animals at all; surely it is adequate merely to list the two signs via which animals are kosher? Maharam Shif suggests that the purpose is not be concise but rather to *teach* the notion of being concise, and this is accomplished via the contrast between birds, where the non-kosher varieties are listed, and animals, where the kosher varieties are listed.

4 This view is also adopted by Rambam, in *Mishneh Torah, Hilkhot Maakhalot Assurot* 1:8.

5 D. MacDonald, ed., *The Encyclopedia of Mammals* (Oxfordshire: Andromeda Oxford, 2001).

6 An effort to do so was made by Mordechai Kislev, "Establishing the Identities of the Ten Kosher Ruminants Via Taxonomy" (Hebrew), *Sinai* 125 (5760), pp. 216–225. Rabbi Yosef Schwartz, in *Divrei Yosef* (Jerusalem: Israel Bek, 5622), p. 64, likewise sought to place newly discovered kosher animals within the ten types mentioned in the Torah.

7 *Arukh HaShulchan* (*Yoreh De'ah* 79:4) suggests that this could be the position maintained by those who view the *koy*, an unusual animal discussed in the Talmud, as a distinct species.

8 Rabbi David Gans, a student of the Maharal of Prague, notes that the word *olam* sometimes refers to the entire universe; sometimes to planet Earth; and sometimes to a limited region, such as in the Talmud's references to warfare coming to the *olam*. Rabbi Gans uses this to explain the statement that "Jerusalem is in the center of the world" – he explains that it refers to the areas inhabited in biblical and talmudic times (*Nechmad VeNa'im* 89). Rabbi Gedalyah Nadel, one of the foremost disciples of the Chazon Ish, in *BeTorato Shel Rabbi Gedalyah* (Maale Adumim: Shilat, 2004), p. 118, brings further evidence for the "world" of the Torah being of limited scope, in the context of explaining that the Deluge was limited to biblical lands. The Talmud rules that someone who makes an oath to abstain from drinking the waters of the Euphrates is "prohibited from all the waters in the world." Now, while there are many tributaries of the Euphrates, there is certainly no chance that, say, a stream in America is connected to the Euphrates! Hence, concludes Rabbi Nadel, when the Talmud speaks about the "world," it refers to the world of the Sages.

9 Leviticus 7:23.

10 Rabbi Chayim ben Attar, *Or HaChayim* ad loc.

11 Rabbi Shaul HaLevi Mortera, *Givat Shaul* (Warsaw, 1901), *Parashat Vayeshev*, p. 87.

12 Rashi, according to the explanation of Maharam Shif; Rosh; Rabbeinu Yerucham, cited by *Beit Yosef, Yoreh De'ah* 80; see also *Tosafot* to Chullin 59a, s.v. *Eilu*.

13 The more precise, but less familiar, translation is "annulated." This is used to refer to horns which consist of ring-like segments.

14 It is difficult to implement this today, due to the lack of clarity regarding the precise meaning of the Talmud's terms.

DEER

Deer

אַיָל

Ayal

The Deer of Israel

NATURAL HISTORY

Deer used to be common in Israel, and they are mentioned in Scripture on twenty-one occasions. But their popularity as targets for hunting, and the deforestation of the land, did not bode well for them. In 1868, the German Templars, a Protestant sect, established a settlement in Haifa, and hunted the local deer nearly to extinction.[1] In addition, the rich forests that used to cover Israel were gradually destroyed. Eventually, deer disappeared from the wild completely.

Several species of deer were found in the Land of Israel in biblical times. The largest and most spectacular was the red deer (*Cervus elaphus*), which is very similar to the elk of North America, and weighs up to five hundred pounds. Skeletal remains show that the red deer used to live in the Land of Israel; it is not known when it disappeared from the region.[2]

Roe deer, also known as roebuck (*Capreolus capreolus*) are distinguished by their small size and very small antlers. They were found in the region of Mount Carmel and the Upper Galilee until the early twentieth century, with the last individual being shot in 1912.[3]

The most common type of deer in the area appears to have been the fallow deer. These are easily distinguished by their beautiful coloration: white spots and stripes against a brown background. The local variety is known as the Persian (or Mesopotamian) fallow deer, which is larger than European fallow deer and has very different antlers. European fallow deer have a broad and flat "palm" at the top of their antlers (technically known as "palmated"), while the antlers of Persian fallow deer are barely palmated. Some zoologists regard the Persian fallow deer as a subspecies of the European fallow deer (*Dama dama*), hence classifying it as *Dama dama mesopotamica*. Others classify it as an entirely separate species, *Dama mesopotamica*; this is in part based on the fact that remains of both types of fallow deer have been found in Israel, indicating that they formed distinct reproductive populations.[4] Fallow deer disappeared from the Land of Israel sometime in the last century.

In recent years, there have been some spectacular efforts to return deer to the wild in Israel; we shall discuss these at the end of the chapter.

The red deer (left) is much larger than the roe deer (right) and has much larger antlers with many more branches

KEV CHAPMAN / FLICKR

222

TINA WHITE

EYAL BARTOV

The European fallow deer (left) is distinguishable from the Persian fallow deer (right) by its broader antlers, though it is overall a smaller animal

Deer, Harts, Hinds, and Rams

———————————————————— IDENTIFICATION

The identity of the *ayal* as the deer is certain and unequivocal. It has the same name in numerous regional languages; there is a universal tradition regarding its identification; and it perfectly and uniquely matches the descriptions given in Scripture and Talmud (notably, of possessing branching horns).

There is a widespread misconception that the name *tzvi* also refers to the deer, whereas in fact *tzvi* is the gazelle, as we shall discuss in the chapter on the gazelle. This confusion appears amongst people from Europe and North America. The reason for the misidentification is that gazelles do not live in those parts of the world, and thus people were not familiar with them. As a result, the name *tzvi* was mistakenly transposed to the most similar local animal, which is the deer. Since it appeared strange to have two animals, the *tzvi* and *ayal*, translated as "deer," this led some to translate *ayal* as "hart" instead.[5] However, "hart" is merely the term for a male deer (with "hind" referring to the female). Thus, to translate *ayal* and *tzvi* as "hart and deer" is to identify them as "male deer and deer," which clearly does not make sense.

Another cause of popular confusion is that there is another animal with a very similar name, the *ayil*. The word *ayil* is comprised of the same letters as *ayal*, but vocalized differently. Whereas an *ayal* is a deer, an *ayil* is a ram (adult male sheep).[6]

Some distinguish between roe deer and fallow deer, identifying only the roe deer as the *ayal*, with the fallow deer being another animal in the Torah's list of kosher animals: the *yachmur* (which became the name of the fallow deer in Modern Hebrew).[7] There are, however, difficulties with identifying the *yachmur* as the fallow deer. The system of classification used in the Torah is generally much less

מְשַׁוֶּה רַגְלַי כָּאַיָּלוֹת וְעַל בָּמוֹתַי יַעֲמִדֵנִי:

שמואל ב כב:לד, תהלים יח:לד

יְהוִה אֲדֹנָי חֵילִי וַיָּשֶׂם רַגְלַי כָּאַיָּלוֹת וְעַל בָּמוֹתַי יַדְרִכֵנִי לַמְנַצֵּחַ בִּנְגִינוֹתָי:

חבקוק ג:יט

specific than that used in modern zoology; it seems unlikely that the Torah would list two species of deer under separate names.[8] Even more problematic is that the gazelle is listed in the Torah in between the *ayal* and the *yachmur*; it seems incongruous to have two species of deer separated by the gazelle. Finally, in light of the fact that fallow deer were very common (much more so than roe deer), it would be strange for the fallow deer to be the *yachmur*, which is barely mentioned in Scripture.[9]

It thus appears preferable to identify the *yachmur* as the hartebeest, which is discussed in its own chapter. *Ayal* would be a generic category for all species of deer. Aside from their all being similar in general body shape, deer all share the feature, unique to their family, of branched horns, properly known as antlers, which fall off and grow anew each year.

Fleet of Foot

———————————————————— SYMBOLISM

The deer often appears in Scripture as a symbol of speed, such as in a verse uttered by King David that appears twice:

> He sets my feet like those of deer, and stands me upon my high places. (II Sam. 22:34; Ps. 18:34)

A very similar description is given by Habakkuk:

> My Lord God is my strength; He places my feet like those of deer, and enables me to walk upon the heights. (Hab. 3:19)

223

When God sets someone's feet like those of deer, it means that He enables them to move swiftly, either in pursuit of their goals or (as better suits the case of David) in escape from their enemies. With a need to be able to flee from danger, fallow deer can reach a maximum speed of 30 mph over short distances. Roe deer are even faster, reaching up to 48 mph. The swiftness of deer is referred to in the *Nishmat* prayer that is recited on Shabbat morning:

> Even if our mouths were as full of song as is the sea, and our tongues as full of rejoicing as the multitude of waves, and our lips as full of praise as the expanse of the sky, and our hands spread like the vultures of the heavens, and our feet as light as those of deer – we could not adequately thank you, God our Lord. (*Nishmat Kol Chai*[10])

The swiftness and agility of deer here represents an exuberance that could be employed as praise of the Creator – and yet is still insufficient.

The deer's great speed may also shed light on a possible reference to a deer in the Talmud:

> R. Akiva became wealthy from the deer of a ship. (Nedarim 50a)

The animal being described here is not a real creature, but rather a component of a ship that R. Akiva found abandoned on a beach. However, there is disagreement as to whether the animal mentioned here is a ram (*ayil*)[11] or a deer (*ayal*).[12] If the latter, then the reference would be to a figurehead that was modeled after a deer due to its speed. (One famous such ship, in which Sir Francis Drake circumnavigated the globe, not only had a deer as its figurehead, but was even named the Golden Hind.[13]) The swiftly running deer is a symbol adopted by those who wish to portray themselves as achieving great speed – which is why it was also adopted as the emblem of the Israel Postal Authority.[14]

VOLODYMYR BURDIAK

Naphtali Is a Hind

SYMBOLISM

The deer first appears in the Torah in Jacob's blessing for his son Naphtali:

> Naphtali is a deer set loose, bearing pleasant speech. (Gen. 49:21)

Simply speaking, this verse is describing Naphtali as possessing the speed, and perhaps the grace and beauty, of a deer. He sets about his tasks with swiftness, and presents his messages with pleasantness. (Some translate the last phrase, *hanoten imrei shafer*, not as "bearing pleasant speech," but as "giving forth beautiful branches," referring to its branched antlers.[15])

Ramban (Nahmanides) sees this blessing as a reference to an ancient custom in which kings would send messages of goodwill to other kings by tying the message to the horns of a deer, which would, upon being released, automatically run to the place where it was born. By raising deer that had been born in different kingdoms, it was possible to send messages to wherever one wanted. The deer is thus the bearer of good news; likewise, Naphtali, whose land provided rich produce, was a source of good tidings for the nation.[16]

Of interest in this blessing is that Naphtali is compared to an *ayala*, which is a hind – a female deer (doe). One would have expected him to be compared to an *ayal* – a male deer (hart or stag). One possibility is that the female deer is mentioned because she is swifter:

> "For the Conductor, on the morning hind" (Ps. 22:1) – This is as Scripture states, "My Lord God is my strength, and He sets my feet like those of hinds" (Hab. 3). R. Pinchas said: It does not say "like those of harts," but rather, "like those of hinds" – for the feet of hinds are swifter than those of harts. (*Midrash Tehillim* 22)

There is also a statement in the Midrash that this alludes to an important female descendant of Naphtali:

> "Naphtali is a deer set loose" – All the other tribes were compared to male [animals], but Naphtali was compared to females, because Devorah the Prophetess descended from him. (*Yalkut Midrashei Teiman, Vaychi*)

Another Midrash elaborates upon this, and notes that there is another woman who is symbolized by the deer:

> "And they hung Haman" (Est. 7:10) – This is what is meant when it is written, "My Lord God is my strength, and He places my feet like those of hinds" (Hab. 3:19). It does not say "like those of a hart," nor "like those of harts"; what does it teach us with "like those of hinds"?

The tribe of Naphtali, depicted in a stained glass window in a synagogue

> Like two hinds – two righteous women who are symbolized by hinds, and they are Devorah and Esther. Devorah was from the tribe of Naphtali, about whom it is written, "A hind set loose," and regarding Esther it is written, "For the Conductor, on the morning hind" (Ps. 22:1). (*Midrash Aggadat Esther* 7[17])

Later, we shall explore the parallel between the deer and Esther in more detail.

As the motif in Jacob's blessing for his son Naphtali, the deer became the symbol for the tribe of Naphtali, appearing on the tribe's banner in the wilderness:

> Naphtali's [stone on the priestly breastplate] was amethyst and the color of his flag was similar to clear wine, the redness of which is not strong. And there was an illustration of a deer on it, as "Naphtali is a deer set loose." (*Bemidbar Rabba* 2:7)

225

◄ *A deer running swiftly*

Following Jacob's son Naphtali, the name Naphtali is first recorded as having been used in 1308, in Brandenburg, Germany. Just thirty years later, we find the name Naphtali Hirsch, with *hirsch* being German for "deer." This is the earliest known case of a Jew being named after an animal in post-biblical times.[18]

The Swiftness of Naphtali

————————————————————— SYMBOLISM

The blessing of Naphtali being an *ayala shelucha*, a "deer set loose," is interpreted by the Midrash in some interesting ways:

> "Naphtali is a deer set loose (*shelucha*)" – that his emissaries (*sheluchim*) were great in Torah, which is called "a loving deer and a graceful ibex" (Prov. 5:19). Why are the words of Torah compared to a deer? Just as this deer is pious, so too those who fulfill Torah are pious. (*Midrash Bereshit* 49:21)

This relates to a midrash elsewhere, which describes the piety of the deer in terms of its relationship with its young.[19]

Then the lame shall leap like a deer, and the tongue of the dumb shall shout with joy, for waters shall burst forth in the desert, and streams in the wilderness.

(Is. 35:6)

Female deer are excellent mothers, providing a high degree of maternal care. The symbolic relationship of deer to Torah is also reflected in a poem recited by some during the morning prayer of Shavuot, in which the deer appears as a metaphor for Torah itself: *Ayelet ahuvim, matnat Sinai* ("Beloved deer, gift of Sinai").

But most statements in the Midrash about Naphtali's blessing explain it more in line with the straightforward meaning of the verse, in which it is describing the fleetness of a deer set loose. According to one interpretation, the speed of deer parallels the rapidity with which crops developed in Naphtali's portion of land:

> Naphtali is a deer set loose – this refers to the valley of Ginnosar, which ripens its produce swiftly like a deer. (*Midrash Tanchuma, Vaychi* 13[20])

Most interpretations, however, focus on the blessing referring to the speed of Naphtali himself:

> R. Yudan said: The prince of the tribe of Naphtali brought offerings corresponding to the patriarchs and the matriarchs. Why? Because Naphtali greatly honored his father. His father would send him to whichever place he wished, and Naphtali would be swift with his mission. And [his father] received satisfaction from him, and his speech was always pleasant. Therefore his father blessed him with the swift hind, for he sped with his task like a deer; and therefore he blessed him with pleasant sayings, for his speech was pleasant. (*Bemidbar Rabba* 14:11)

According to another midrash, Naphtali did not only employ his speed in honor of his father, but also in the service of God:

> Naphtali is a deer set loose – this teaches that Naphtali was as fast on his feet as a deer to fulfill the will of his father.... Another explanation: That he ran like a deer to fulfill the will of our Father in Heaven. (*Midrash Bereshit* 49:21)

The Talmud gives a specific example of Naphtali's speed. This occurs in the context of the tribes seeking to bury their father Jacob in the Cave of Machpelah:

> When they arrived at the Cave of Machpelah, Esau came and complained.... He said to them, Show me the contract! They said, The contract is in Egypt. Who should go to retrieve it? Naphtali should go swiftly, because he is a deer, as it is written, "Naphtali is a swift deer, giving sayings of pleasantness" – R. Avahu said, Do not read *imrei shafer* ("sayings of pleasantness"), but rather, *imrei sefer* ("the sayings of the document"). (Sota 13a[21])

Beloved Deer

Deer are a central motif in Song of Songs, appearing on seven occasions. In a verse that appears twice, they are mentioned as objects of an oath:

> I adjure you, daughters of Jerusalem, by gazelles or by hinds of the field: Do not arouse or awaken love until it so desires! (Song. 2:7, 3:5)

Here, too, the Midrash sees deer as representing the tribe of Naphtali.[22] But the plain meaning of the verse teaches us of the high regard in which deer were held. The fact that gazelles and deer are used as objects of an oath indicates their value; one only swears upon that which is very precious. The Midrash interprets the deer here as representing some very important concepts:

> "I adjure you, O maidens of Jerusalem... by hinds of the field"... R. Chanina said:... These are the tribes, just as it says, "Naphtali is a swift hind"... R. Yehuda, son of R. Shimon said: He adjured them by the circumcision... that they spill their blood like the blood of the gazelle and deer. And the Rabbis said: He adjured them by the generations of persecution... that their blood is spilled in sanctification of My Name like the blood of the gazelle and deer. (*Shir HaShirim Rabba* 2:18)

Further indication of the preciousness of deer comes from the other mentions of deer in Song of Songs, in which they symbolize (according to rabbinic tradition) extremely important characters. In one verse, which appears twice, they represent Moses and Aaron, the sustainers of the Jewish people:

> Your two breasts are like two fawns, twins of a gazelle. (Song. 4:5, 7:4)

And in other verses, the deer is understood to represent no less than God Himself:

> My beloved is like a gazelle or a deer fawn; behold, he stands behind our wall, looking through the windows, peering through the lattice. (Song. 2:9)

> When the day breaks, and the shadows flee, turn, my beloved, swift as a gazelle or a deer fawn, for the distant hills! (Song. 2:17)

This image is so central to Song of Songs that it appears in the very final verse:

> Hurry, my beloved, like a gazelle or a deer fawn, to the hills of spices! (Song. 8:14)

In the fifteenth-century compilation of Jewish texts from Italy known as the Rothschild Miscellany, deer are illustrated in the opening chapter of Psalms

In all these verses, deer appear together with gazelles. And on each occasion, it is either fawns[23] or female deer (hinds) that are mentioned. Presumably this is because fawns and hinds possess greater grace and beauty, similar to that of the gazelle, than the larger, tougher stags. Hinds are also mentioned as metaphors for objects of love in a different verse:

הִשְׁבַּעְתִּי אֶתְכֶם בְּנוֹת יְרוּשָׁלַם בִּצְבָאוֹת אוֹ בְּאַיְלוֹת הַשָּׂדֶה אִם תָּעִירוּ וְאִם תְּעוֹרְרוּ אֶת הָאַהֲבָה עַד שֶׁתֶּחְפָּץ:

שיר השירים ב:ז, ג:ה

שְׁנֵי שָׁדַיִךְ כִּשְׁנֵי עֳפָרִים תְּאוֹמֵי צְבִיָּה הָרוֹעִים בַּשּׁוֹשַׁנִּים:

שיר השירים ד:ה

שְׁנֵי שָׁדַיִךְ כִּשְׁנֵי עֳפָרִים תָּאֳמֵי צְבִיָּה:

שיר השירים ז:ד

דּוֹמֶה דוֹדִי לִצְבִי אוֹ לְעֹפֶר הָאַיָּלִים הִנֵּה זֶה עוֹמֵד אַחַר כָּתְלֵנוּ מַשְׁגִּיחַ מִן הַחַלֹּנוֹת מֵצִיץ מִן הַחֲרַכִּים:

שיר השירים ב:ט

עַד שֶׁיָּפוּחַ הַיּוֹם וְנָסוּ הַצְּלָלִים סֹב דְּמֵה לְךָ דוֹדִי לִצְבִי אוֹ לְעֹפֶר הָאַיָּלִים עַל הָרֵי בָתֶר:

שיר השירים ב:יז

בְּרַח דּוֹדִי וּדְמֵה לְךָ לִצְבִי אוֹ לְעֹפֶר הָאַיָּלִים עַל הָרֵי בְשָׂמִים:

שיר השירים ח:יד

"Hurry, my beloved, like a gazelle or
a deer fawn, to the hills of spices!"

(Song. 8:14)

אֵילֶת אֲהָבִים וְיַעֲלַת חֵן דַּדֶּיהָ יְרַוֻּךָ בְכָל עֵת בְּאַהֲבָתָהּ תִּשְׁגֶּה
תָמִיד:

משלי ה:יט

וַיֵּצֵא מִבַּת צִיּוֹן כָּל הֲדָרָהּ הָיוּ שָׂרֶיהָ כְּאַיָּלִים לֹא מָצְאוּ מִרְעֶה
וַיֵּלְכוּ בְלֹא כֹחַ לִפְנֵי רוֹדֵף:

איכה א:ו

כִּי גַם אַיֶּלֶת בַּשָּׂדֶה יָלְדָה וְעָזוֹב כִּי לֹא הָיָה דֶּשֶׁא:

ירמיה יד:ה

כְּאַיָּל תַּעֲרֹג עַל אֲפִיקֵי מָיִם כֵּן נַפְשִׁי תַעֲרֹג אֵלֶיךָ אֱלֹהִים:

תהלים מב:ב

גַּם בַּהֲמוֹת שָׂדֶה תַּעֲרוֹג אֵלֶיךָ כִּי יָבְשׁוּ אֲפִיקֵי מָיִם וְאֵשׁ אָכְלָה
נְאוֹת הַמִּדְבָּר:

יואל א:כ

She will be like the loving hind and charming ibex; her breasts shall satisfy you at all times; and you will always be intoxicated with her love. (Prov. 5:19)

According to the pioneering figure in biblical zoology, Professor Yehuda Feliks, the references to deer in Song of Songs are best understood in light of their actual behavior.[24] Upon reaching a year in age, male fawns disperse from the birth area and leave the maternal herd. This separation appears to be a tragic state of affairs, but it is of limited duration; hence, Solomon adjures by the deer that one must bide one's time: "Do not wake or rouse Love until it please!" Once the mating season arrives, the young males come rushing to find the females. In their desire to mate, they lose all fear, even approaching human habitation to find the object of their love: "My beloved is like a gazelle or a deer fawn; behold, he stands behind our wall, looking through the windows, peering through the lattice." This is keenly anticipated by the hinds: "Hurry, my beloved, like a gazelle or a deer fawn, to the hills of spices!"

Deer and Water

SYMBOLISM

A frequent theme in Scripture concerning deer is their tragic desperation when they cannot find food or water:

All the splendor of the daughter of Zion is gone from her; her leaders were like deer that found no pasture, and traveled on from the pursuer without strength. (Lam. 1:6)

When Jeremiah describes the droughts that would befall Jerusalem, he attempts to motivate people by not only describing their own suffering, but also by conjuring the haunting imagery of the deer, a loving mother, forced to abandon her young:

Even the hind in the field has given birth, and deserted [her fawn], because there is no grass. (Jer. 14:5)

But by far the most famous verse about a deer's desperation for water is the metaphor employed by David for his desire to unite with God:

Like a deer crying for streams of water, so does my soul cry for You, O God. My soul thirsts for God, for the living Lord; when shall I come and behold the face of God? (Ps. 42:2–3)

Ke'ayal taarog, "Like a deer crying" – some commentators explains that just as lions roar, bears growl, oxen low, and birds chirp, the vocalization of deer has its own word.[25] There is one other occurrence of this word in Scripture, describing the distress of unnamed animals amidst drought:

Even the beasts of the field cry out (*taarog*) to You, for the streams of water have dried up. (Joel 1:20)

According to the view that *taarog* is a vocalization unique to deer, these would be the animals being described in this verse. Others are of the view that *taarog* refers not to the call of a specific animal, but to a cry emitted under specific circumstances – a desperate thirst.[26] There are reports of stags calling loudly during drought.[27]

The comparison of a person thirsting for God to a deer thirsting for water is significant in rabbinic thought, since the deer's eventual ability to obtain water is presented in terms of its successful relationship with God. One saying has God providentially enabling the deer to access potentially dangerous water sources:

This deer is weak in limb, and it is thirsty and afraid of wild beasts. What does the Holy One do? He causes a spirit of madness to enter it, and it stamps its hooves and clatters its antlers, and the wild beasts hear the sound and flee. (*Midrash Shmuel* 9:2[28])

Another midrash speaks of the deer meriting God's providence due to its compassionate nature:

You find with this deer, that when it is thirsty, it digs a hole, and inserts its antlers, and lows, and water rises up from the deep, as it says, "As a deer yearning for streams of water." And the Rabbis said: This is the most pious of animals, and it has much compassion upon its young; and when the animals are thirsty, they gather to it, because they know that its deeds are pious, so that it should raise its eyes upon high, and the Holy One will have compassion upon them ... when David saw that the Holy One answers it, he began to compose this psalm regarding it: "For the Conductor, on the morning hind" (Ps. 22:1). (*Midrash Tehillim* 22)

229

*"Like a deer crying for streams of water,
so does my soul cry for You, O God!"*

(Ps. 42:2)

NATAN SLIFKIN

Given the close association with deer and drought, it is natural that when Scripture describes the redemption in terms of the desert turning green, it speaks of the "lame" (i.e. Israel, weakened through exile) leaping with joy like deer:

> Then the lame shall leap like a deer, and the tongue of the dumb shall shout with joy, for waters shall burst forth in the desert, and streams in the wilderness. (Is. 35:6)

Fallow deer can leap up to five feet high and sixteen feet in distance. With the desperation that they exude when thirsty, and the exuberance that they are able to demonstrate, they are a superb metaphor for the joy of redemption.

Head to Tail

SYMBOLISM

As we have seen, most references to deer in the Torah, Talmud, and Midrash are extremely positive in nature. But there are also references to negative aspects of its symbolism. Let us return to a verse that we cited earlier:

> Gone from fair Zion are all that were her glory; her leaders were like deer that could not find pasture; they traveled weakly before the pursuer. (Lam. 1:6)

At face value, the verse is simply presenting the tragic imagery of deer that thirst for pasture. This is how one midrash explains it:

"Her leaders were like deer that could not find pasture" (Lam. 1:6) – R. Abahu said: When Israel are soft, they are compared to sheep, as it says, "And I shall give my sheep, the sheep of my pasture" (Ezek. 34). And when they are hard, they are compared to deer, as it says, "Its officers were like deer" – Just as deer are tired during a scorching wind, and cannot bear the heat of the sun, so too Israel could not bear the burden of the nations, as it says "they traveled weakly before the pursuer" (Lam. 1:6). (*Midrash Lekach Tov*, Lam. 1:4; *Midrash Eikha* 1)

Such symbolism is reflected by the illustrations of deer in thirteenth- and fourteenth-century illuminated prayerbooks. These accompany a poem recited by some during the morning prayer of Shavuot: *Ayelet ahuvim, matnat Sinai* ("Beloved deer, gift of Sinai"). The deer is often illustrated as being hunted by hounds and a demonic hunter; it had come to symbolize the Jewish people being persecuted.[29]

However, another midrash, along with the Talmud, interprets the deer to which the leaders are compared as symbolizing the negative behavior that brought on divine wrath in the first place:

> "Her leaders were like deer that could not find pasture" (Lam. 1:6) – ...Just as these deer, during a scorching

Deer running through the snow in single file

EDUARD KYSLYNSKYY / SHUTTERSTOCK

wind, turn their faces beneath each other, so too the great ones of Israel would see an act of sin and would turn their faces from it. The Holy One, blessed is He, said to them: The hour will come when I will treat you in the same way. (*Eikha Rabba* 1:34[30])

The Talmud draws a similar lesson, except that instead of referring to deer turning their heads downwards during a hot wind, it describes the way that deer walk.

Jerusalem was only destroyed because people did not rebuke each other, as it says, "Her leaders were like deer that could not find pasture" (Lam. 1:6) – Just as with this deer, the head of one is at the tail of the next, so too the Jews of that generation turned their faces downwards and did not rebuke each other. (Shabbat 119b; *Midrash Lekach Tov*, Lam.1:21)

Deer are well known for walking in single file. This is especially the case when they feel threatened; the benefit of this behavior is that each deer can be warned of danger by the deer in front of it. But, in this passage in the Talmud, this head-to-tail pattern of movement symbolically represents turning a blind eye to sin, and ingratiating oneself with people committing evil, instead of looking them in the eye and protesting their actions.[31]

The Morning Deer

SYMBOLISM

One of the psalms begins with a well-known but curious phrase mentioning deer:

"For the Conductor, on the morning hind (*ayelet hashachar*); a Psalm of David." (Ps. 22:1)

The meaning of the phrase *ayelet hashachar* is unclear. Many of the commentaries explain it to refer to a musical instrument.[32] Literally, however, the words mean "morning hind." The Midrash gives a seemingly obscure connection between deer and the morning:

"The morning hind" – this is as Scripture states, "Do not rejoice over me, my enemy! Although I have fallen, I rise again; although I dwell in darkness, God is my light"

The branching rays of the morning sun parallel the branching antlers of a deer

(Micah 7:8). David said: For the Conductor, for the One who leaps like a deer and illuminates the world when it is dark. (*Midrash Tehillim* 22)

The description of God "leaping like a deer and illuminating the world" may be a reference to a symbolic connection between the antlers of a deer and the morning sun:

Rebbi said: A shaft of light from the moon is not comparable to a shaft of light from the sun. A shaft of light from the moon extends in a straight line like a stick, whereas a shaft of light from the sun diffuses to here and there.... R. Abahu said: What is Rebbi's reason? For it is written, "For the Conductor, on the morning hind" – Just as the antlers of the deer[33] branch here and there, so too the light of the morning sun spreads here and there. (*Yoma* 28b–29a)

The antlers of a deer have protrusions spreading in all directions. This parallels the rays of the dawning sun, piercing the morning clouds.[34] The Talmud Yerushalmi relates this "morning deer" to the Purim victory:

There was a story with R. Chiyya the Great and R. Shimon b. Chalafta. They were traveling in the Arbel valley at dawn, and saw the rays of the Morning Deer. R. Chiyya the Great said to R. Shimon b. Chalafta: "Eminent one! So is the redemption of Israel; at first it shines softly, but as time elapses, it increases.... Thus, at the beginning, "Mordekhai sat at the gate of the king" (Est. 2:21); then, "Haman took the garments and the horse" (ibid. 6:11); then, "Mordekhai returned to the gate of the king" (ibid. 12); then, "Mordekhai emerged from before the king in the royal robes" (ibid. 8:15); and finally, "For the Jews, there was light and rejoicing" (ibid.). (*Y. Berakhot* 1:1, 4b)

This is in line with how the psalm of the "morning deer" in its entirety is explained by the Midrash and Talmud as prophetically referring to the events of the Book of Esther, with one verse from the psalm being the prayer uttered by Esther herself.[35] As we saw earlier, the Midrash mentions a connection between Esther and deer:

"And they hung Haman" (Es. 7:10) – This is what is meant when it is written, "My Lord God is my strength, and He places my feet like those of hinds" (Hab. 3:19). It does not say "like those of a hart," nor "like those of harts"; what does it teach us with "like those of hinds"? Like two hinds – two righteous women who are symbolized by hinds, and they are Devorah and Esther. Devorah was from the tribe of Naphtali, about whom it is written, "A hind set loose," and regarding Esther it is written, "To the

This red deer has greatly branched antlers, indicating considerable age

Conductor, on the morning hind" (Ps. 22:1). And why are they symbolized by deer? R. Yehuda son of R. Shimon said: If you find a house to have a snake, you smoke it out using [a fire made from] the antlers of deer[36] and the hair of a woman, and immediately the snake flees. So, too, with Devorah and Esther; Devorah did not move until she had destroyed Sisera and all his troops, and Esther did not move until Haman and his ten sons were hung. Therefore it states, "and He steadies my feet like those of hinds" – two hinds. (*Midrash Aggadat Esther* 7[37])

The Talmud, after describing the symbolic relationship between deer and morning, asks about the connection to Esther:

R. Zeira said: Why is Esther compared to a deer? (*Yoma* 29a)

One answer given by the Talmud to R. Zeira's question interprets the "*shachar*/morning" in the sense of *Shacharit*,

233

הֲיָדַעְתָּ עֵת לֶדֶת יַעֲלֵי סָלַע חֹלֵל אַיָּלוֹת תִּשְׁמֹר: תִּסְפֹּר יְרָחִים
תְּמַלֶּאנָה וְיָדַעְתָּ עֵת לִדְתָּנָה: תִּכְרַעְנָה יַלְדֵיהֶן תְּפַלַּחְנָה חֶבְלֵיהֶם
תְּשַׁלַּחְנָה: יַחְלְמוּ בְנֵיהֶם יִרְבּוּ בַבָּר יָצְאוּ וְלֹא שָׁבוּ לָמוֹ:

איוב לט:א–ד

the morning prayers. Accordingly, it relates Esther's prayer to the deer:

> We shall expound it in accordance with R. Binyamin bar Yefet in the name of R. Eleazar, who said: Why are the prayers of the righteous likened to a deer? To tell you that just as when a deer grows older, its antlers increasingly branch, so too when the righteous persist in their prayers, they are listened to. (Yoma 29a)

A deer sheds its antlers and grows new ones each year. They become progressively more branched (although, contrary to popular belief, the number of points on a deer's antlers do not correlate precisely with its age), stretching forth. Likewise, the prayers of the righteous eventually penetrate to God.

R. Zeira himself, however, answered his question differently:

> R. Zeira said: Why is Esther compared to a deer? To teach you that just as the womb of the hind is narrow,

and it is as beloved to its mate each time just as the first time, so too Esther was beloved to Ahasuerus each time just as the first time. (Yoma 29a)

The narrow womb of the hind is a motif that finds expression in several places in rabbinic literature, as we shall now explore.

The Narrow Womb: Conception and Birth
— SYMBOLISM

In the Book of Job, after Job has been inflicted with unimaginable suffering, he bemoans his fate. God's cryptic response includes a mention of the hind:

> Do you know when the ibex of the rocks will give birth? Can you anticipate the labor pangs of the hind? Will you count the months to the fulfillment of her term, and do you know the moment of her giving birth, when they crouch to bring forth their young, ridding themselves of their agony? Their young will grow robustly, fattening in the meadow; they have gone, and return no more. (Job 39:1–4)

At its most basic level, God's response to Job serves to humble him. Job is seeking to understand why such terrible events befell him; God in turn explains to Job that he

A hind taking care of her newborn fawn

should not expect to understand the ways of the Creator of the universe. "Where were you when I founded the world?" God asks. God presents examples from the animal kingdom which demonstrate man's limitations. He will then no longer expect to understand the ways of God.

With the hind, the limitation that it demonstrates is that of human knowledge. The very pattern of birthing in ibex, deer, and other ruminants is still somewhat of a riddle to modern zoology (and this is further discussed in the chapter on the ibex). With many of these species, the females synchronize giving birth such that they all give birth within a span of two to three weeks. This may be of benefit in that predators are swamped by the number of new young, and cannot make a serious impact on the population. Other suggested factors in synchrony include benefits from spring grass, social stimulation from female conspecifics, and even the lunar cycle.[38] But there is also a great degree of variance, for reasons that are unclear. With all the studies of modern science, zoologists are still having a hard time figuring out anticipating the labor pangs of the hind; it was certainly difficult for man in the ancient world to do so!

Anticipating the birth of a roe deer would have been particularly difficult, since they practice delayed implantation. This means that the embryo is not immediately implanted in the uterus, but is instead maintained in a dormant state for several weeks or months. As a result, the roe deer gives birth at a totally different time than would be expected based on similar species.[39]

Above, we saw that the Talmud describes the deer's womb as being narrow. In discussing the parallel to Esther, the Talmud explains the narrow womb as causing the hind to be more beloved to its mate; elsewhere, the Talmud states that it causes mating difficulties.[40] With regard to the description of the "labor pangs of the hind" in the Book of Job, the Talmud again interprets this in light of the deer's womb being narrow. According to the Talmud, God's response to Job here is not merely humbling him with the mysteries of the natural world, but also addressing the issue of providence. The hind is mentioned in response to a specific accusation that Job raised:

> Job said before God, Master of the Universe! Perhaps a whirlwind passed before You, and You confused *Iyov* (Job) with *oyev* ("enemy")? (Bava Batra 16a)

Job's charge was that God is not sufficiently involved in the affairs of this world, leaving its fate to arbitrary forces that do not care for what people actually deserve. The end result is that the righteous Job is treated no differently from an enemy of God. The Talmud elaborates on God's reply, explaining how His mention of the ibex and the deer spe-

cifically addresses this charge, showing that He carefully engineers every aspect of the events of this world:

> [God said:] "Can you anticipate the labor pangs of the hind?" The birth canal of this hind is narrow, so when she crouches to give birth, I prepare a serpent for her that bites her in the birth canal, which becomes loose, and she gives birth. If [the serpent would bite her] a moment too early or a moment too late, she would immediately die. I do not confuse one moment with another – would I confuse *Iyov* with *oyev*?! (Bava Batra 16a–b[41])

Taken at face value, these descriptions do not concur with our knowledge of what actually happens; deer are observed to give birth without any assistance from snakes.[42] Some suggest that the Talmud is recording the zoological beliefs of the era.[43] Others argue that the Talmud is speaking of mystical matters.[44] Another possibility is that the Talmud is using poetic language to describe these animals giving birth. The great medieval commentator Ralbag (Gersonides) writes that "if the matter is true, then the explanation of the verse is so; but if not, then the intent of it, according to what I think, is that this animal gives birth with great difficulty, and accordingly the newborn is in great peril, were it not for God's providence, to cause the young to be produced in such a way that they do not die at birth."[45]

Since the process of deer giving birth is considered to be very difficult, this sheds light on a psalm that is recited during Shabbat morning prayers when the Torah is returned to the Ark:

> The voice of God causes hinds to give birth, and strips forests bare; while in His Temple, all say, Glory! (Ps. 29:9)

The verse is describing God's power as reflected in a thunderstorm – metaphorically referred to as His "voice."[46] Thunderstorms are known to cause pregnant animals to abort their young.[47] This verse is saying that even deer, whose womb is narrow and who normally have difficulty passing out their young, will do so as a result of the power of God's thunder. The Midrash expounds this verse as symbolizing the history and destiny of the Jewish people:

> To what can Israel be compared, in this world vis-à-vis their Father in Heaven? To this deer that carries its young in pain and gives birth in pain. At the beginning, there is difficulty, but there is relief at the conclusion, as it says, "The voice of God causes hinds to give birth" (Ps. 29:9). (*Midrash Tanna DeVei Eliyahu* 2)

235

A mosaic of a fallow deer from the Maon Synagogue in the Negev Desert, from around the fifth century

Eating Deer

———————————————— LAW AND RITUAL

The Torah's list of kosher animals is divided into two parts: domestic and wild animals. The deer is first on the list of kosher wild animals:

> This is the animal which you shall eat: cattle, sheep, and goats; the deer, the gazelle, the hartebeest, the ibex, the oryx, the aurochs, and the wild sheep. (Deut. 14:4–5)

Its position in first place probably reflects its prominence in terms of being one of the more common wild animals, and perhaps also in terms of it being a more popular food item.[48] The deer also receives first billing in a list of three wild animals that were served at King Solomon's table:

> Solomon's daily provisions consisted of thirty *kors* of semolina, and sixty *kors* of flour, ten fattened oxen, twenty pasture-grazed oxen, and one hundred sheep, besides deer and gazelle and hartebeest and fattened geese. (1 Kings 5:2–3)

Deer would have been well suited to the royal table. Venison is highly desirable, even today: it has a richer flavor than beef, a finer texture, and is far healthier.

Deer are also mentioned as food on three other occasions in the Torah, each time as an example of something that can be eaten without restriction.[49] One such mention

occurs in the context of a reference to livestock consecrated as offerings, which were redeemed and may then be eaten as freely as wild animals that are never viable as offerings in the first place:

> However, you may kill and eat flesh within all your gates, after all the desire of your soul, according to the blessing of the Lord your God which He has given you: the unclean and the clean may eat of it, as of the gazelle, and as of the deer. (Deut. 12:15)

A similar reference occurs in a different context. Firstborn animals must usually be brought to the Temple as an offering; but in the case of their possessing a blemish, they can be eaten as freely as a wild animal:

> You shall eat it within your gates: the unclean and the clean shall eat it alike, as the gazelle, and as the deer. (Deut. 15:22)

Another reference occurs in the context of the general dispensation to eat meat. Originally, the Children of Israel could only eat livestock if the animal was brought as a peace-offering to the Tabernacle. Moses instructed them that once they entered the Land of Israel, it would be possible to eat meat freely, just as wild animals that are never viable as offerings:

> Just as the gazelle and as the deer is eaten, so you shall eat of it: the unclean and the clean may eat of it alike. (Deut. 12:22)

However, some rabbinic commentators explained these comparisons to deer and gazelle as actually presenting a *limitation* on the consumption of meat. Deer and gazelle are eaten only infrequently, since they are not farmed and must be captured. By the same token, a person should only eat meat on an occasional basis.[50]

236

אַיָּל וּצְבִי וְיַחְמוּר וְאַקּוֹ וְדִישֹׁן וּתְאוֹ וָזָמֶר:

דברים יד:ה

עֲשָׂרָה בָקָר בְּרִאִים וְעֶשְׂרִים בָּקָר רְעִי וּמֵאָה צֹאן לְבַד מֵאַיָּל וּצְבִי וְיַחְמוּר וּבַרְבֻּרִים אֲבוּסִים:

מלכים א ה:ג

רַק בְּכָל אַוַּת נַפְשְׁךָ תִּזְבַּח וְאָכַלְתָּ בָשָׂר כְּבִרְכַּת יהוה אֱלֹהֶיךָ אֲשֶׁר נָתַן לְךָ בְּכָל שְׁעָרֶיךָ הַטָּמֵא וְהַטָּהוֹר יֹאכְלֶנּוּ כַּצְּבִי וְכָאַיָּל:

דברים יב:טו

בִּשְׁעָרֶיךָ תֹּאכְלֶנּוּ הַטָּמֵא וְהַטָּהוֹר יַחְדָּו כַּצְּבִי וְכָאַיָּל:

דברים טו:כב

אַךְ כַּאֲשֶׁר יֵאָכֵל אֶת הַצְּבִי וְאֶת הָאַיָּל כֵּן תֹּאכְלֶנּוּ הַטָּמֵא וְהַטָּהוֹר יַחְדָּו יֹאכְלֶנּוּ:

דברים יב:כב

Kosher deer meat – venison – has remained a kosher but rare delicacy.[51] In nineteenth-century England, the wife of Sir Moses Montefiore published a cookery book which included recipes for venison.[52] When the first Jewish lord mayor of London, David Salomons, was elected in 1855, and was awarded the traditional royal gift of venison from the queen's herd of deer, he sent a *shochet* (ritual slaughterer) so that he would be able to eat it.[53] Kosher venison was available in England in the late nineteenth and early twentieth century, when a group of *shochtim* were given an annual opportunity to catch and slaughter deer on the estate of the Rothschild family. Today, kosher venison is no longer available in the UK, because of agricultural regulations that deer must be shot in the open field, not brought into an abattoir.[54] But kosher venison can be purchased in Israel and the United States.[55]

A Deer by Another Name

——————————————— LAW AND RITUAL

As noted earlier, and as discussed extensively in the chapter on gazelles, Europeans transposed the name *tzvi* from the gazelle to the deer, due to the absence of gazelles from that region. As a result, some references to the *tzvi* in post-talmudic literature actually refer to the deer rather than the gazelle. As Rashi notes, "it seems that the animal which we call *tzvi* is not the *tzvi* of the Talmud [or of Scripture]."[58]

One example is with the laws of shofar. There are two basic types of animal horn. Those of sheep, antelope, cattle, and suchlike consist of a sheath of keratin (the same substance from which our fingernails are made) covering a

bony core. This core can be removed and discarded, and the keratin sheath is then a naturally hollow structure that, with the tip sawn off, becomes an instrument that can be sounded, i.e. a shofar.

Other animals, such as deer and giraffe, have horns that are made of solid bone, without a keratin sheath. It is theoretically possible to drill a hole through these horns and turn them into musical horns that can be sounded, although it would not be easy. However, these would not be kosher for use as a shofar, since they are not naturally hollow.[59]

Some halakhic works discussing the prohibition of using a solid horn give the example of the horns of the *tzvi*. This does not refer to the *tzvi* of the Torah, the gazelle; it has horns that are hollow and are kosher for usage as a shofar. Instead, these works are referring to the animal called *tzvi* in Europe, which is the deer, the horns of which are not hollow and may not be used for a shofar.

Another example of the European influence can be seen in the laws of *tereifot*, physical defects that render an animal non-kosher. One such defect is the absence of a gall-bladder. The *Shulchan Arukh* rules that a missing gall-bladder is not a defect in a *tzvi*, since this is the norm for the species.[60] Now, gazelles do have gall-bladders; but deer do not. The *Shulchan Arukh* is referring to a deer by the name *tzvi*, due to the transposition of names; whereas several other authorities record the phenomenon instead with the deer's original name of *ayal*.[61]

The Fragrance of the Deer

Venison is not the only consumer item that deer produce. There is another deer product that is discussed in Torah literature:

> On every kind of incense, we pronounce the blessing "Who creates fragrant trees," except for musk, because it is from an animal; its blessing is, "Who creates types of fragrances." (Berakhot 43a[56])

Musk comes from the musk deer – a very small type of deer, lacking antlers but bearing fangs, which lives in southern Asia. Males bear a gland from which musk, an immensely valuable substance used for perfumes and incense, is derived. A number of rabbinic authorities claim that the anointing oil for the Tabernacle in the wilderness was made using musk.[57]

Return of the Deer

The reintroduction of the Persian fallow deer to the Land of Israel is one of the most remarkable stories in the history of conservation.[62] Roe deer have been brought to Israel from Europe (where they are readily found), and have been reintroduced into the wild. However, reintroducing the Persian fallow deer to Israel has not been so simple. For a while, the species was thought to be entirely extinct. In the 1950s, however, it was discovered that a tiny colony of Persian fallow deer remained in Iran. General Avraham Yoffe, a founding member of the Hagana, and commander of the army division that captured Sharm el-Sheikh in 1956, was the head of the newly-created Israeli Nature and Parks Authority, and he was determined to bring the deer back to Israel.

Yoffe managed to strike a deal with Prince Abdul Reza, the brother of the Shah, who was an avid hunter. The ibex with the biggest horns in the world lived in the Negev desert in Israel. Yoffe offered the prince the opportunity to hunt this ibex, in exchange for a pair of fallow deer. Prince Reza came to Israel, shot the ibex, and offered Yoffe not one, but two pairs of deer.

In 1978, General Yoffe flew to Iran to capture the deer, but suffered a mild heart attack upon arrival. As he was carried back to the airplane on a stretcher, he pleaded with Brigadier General Yitzchak Segev, the Israeli military attaché in Tehran, to find a way to get the deer. But shortly afterwards, the Islamic revolution gathered steam, with drastic rioting taking place, and the fall of the Shah was imminent. Israel frantically launched a mission to evacuate the Jews of Iran, and Yoffe frantically launched a mission to evacuate the deer. He sent zoologist Mike Van Grevenbroek to assist Brigadier General Segev in capturing the deer, with a blow-gun (for shooting tranquilizing darts) disguised as a cane. They drove to the nature reserve, captured the deer, and brought them to Tehran, where they planned to house them in the zoo until a flight could be arranged.

However, meanwhile, Prince Reza had fled the country. The person in charge of the royal zoo was Erwin Muller, a former Gestapo agent, and he refused to house the deer, insisting that they would not go to Israel. The deer had to be quickly housed at the Israeli embassy! But an export license was also required for the deer, which only Muller could issue. However, at that point the rioting was increasing, and Muller was terrified that the rioters would kill the Shah's beloved cheetah and leopard. He agreed to let the Israelis take the deer, if they would also find a good home for the cheetah and leopard. The Israelis agreed, but by the time they arrived at the zoo, the angry mob had already killed the big cats. Brigadier General Segev attempted to console the weeping Muller, and managed to put the deer on the last El Al flight out of Tehran.

Arriving at Israel, they were met by a tearful General Yoffe. The precious deer were housed in the Har-Bar nature reserve in the Carmel, and began to breed. But ten years later, a massive fire swept through the Carmel forest, killing all the wildlife. The deer, however, survived, due to huddling in a clearing that had been made around a monument in honor of a soldier who had fallen in the line of duty. The monument had been erected by the soldier's father – none other than Brigadier General Segev. The deer continued to reproduce extremely successfully, and some of their descendants have been returned to the wild in Israel. ∎

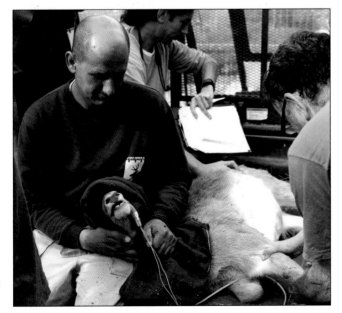

Persian fallow deer from the Tisch Family Zoological Gardens in Jerusalem being released into the Jerusalem Hills

Notes

1 Yisrael Aharoni, *Zikhronot Zoolog Ivri*, vol. II, pp. 92–102. In a twist of poetic justice, the Templars themselves were subsequently deported by the British for being Nazi sympathizers. However, some of them had tried to help the Jews in Germany.

2 Mazin B. Qumsiyeh, *Mammals of the Holy Land*, p. 204, reports that red deer were found in Jordan until the medieval period.

3 Bodenheimer, *Animal Life in Palestine*, p. 114; Mazin B. Qumsiyeh, *Mammals of the Holy Land*, p. 203.

4 W. W. Ferguson, Y. Porath, Samuel Michael Paley, "Late Bronze period yields first osteological evidence of *Dama dama* (Artiodactyla; Cervidae) from Israel and Arabia," *Mammalia* 49 (1985), pp. 209–214.

5 E.g. *The Stone Chumash* (New York: Mesorah Publications, 1993), Deuteronomy 12:15.

6 There is a long history of the two animals being mistakenly transposed. See *Arukh HaShulchan* (*Orach Chayim* 586:3), and the comments of Chakham Tzvi (Responsa #34), Rabbi Akiva Eiger, and Chatam Sofer to *Taz* 586:1.

7 Menachem Dor, *HaChai BiYemei HaMikra HaMishna VeHaTalmud*, p. 31.

8 See Mordechai Kislev, "Methods of Identifying the Ten Types of Kosher Ruminants via Taxonomy" (Hebrew), *Sinai* 125 (Adar 5761/2000), pp. 216–225; Zohar Amar, "Regarding the Identification of the *Ayal*, the *Tzvi*, and the *Yachmur*" (Hebrew), *Al Atar* 15 (5769), pp. 7–20.

9 Ibid.

10 Also *Tanna DeVei Eliyahu Rabba* 31.

11 See the commentary attributed to Rashi printed in Nedarim ad loc., and Daniel Sperber, *Nautica Talmudica* (Brill, 1986), p. 51. The term "ram" may be figurative, just as the English term "naval ram" refers to a battering ram protruding from a ship beneath the water, named after a male sheep's habit of head-butting his enemies.

12 Ran to Nedarim ad loc.

13 However, that ship may have been named and modeled after its patron, who had a deer in his armorial crest.

14 Ironically, the first postal service in Israel was established in the nineteenth century by the German Templars – the very people who hunted the local deer to near-extinction, as noted above.

15 Malbim; Mandelkorn, *Concordance*; see Yisrael Aharoni, "*Ayala VeTachash*," *Tarbiz* 8:3–4 (Tammuz 5697), pp. 319–339.

16 Ramban relates his explanation to a similar account in the Talmud Yerushalmi, Shevi'it 9:2. That account concerns a *tavya*, which, while often translated as deer, actually refers to a gazelle. The gazelle would appear to be a more suitable animal for such a practice, since deer shed their antlers.

17 A briefer version appears in *Midrash Tehillim* 22.

18 Alexander Beider, *A Dictionary of Ashkenazic Given Names*.

19 *Midrash Tehillim* 22, discussed later.

20 Also *Midrash Bereshit Rabba* 99:13. *Midrash HaGadol* adds that the produce of Ginnosar is "full and easy to eat, like venison."

21 A briefer version is in *Midrash Bereshit Rabba* 98:17, with a similar version in *Midrash Pirkei DeRabbi Eliezer* 39.

22 *Midrash Shir HaShirim Rabba* 2:18.

23 The term used for a fawn is *ofer* or *ofer haayalim*, which *Midrash Shir HaShirim Rabba* 2:23 defines as referring to a young deer. The term that it uses, *urzela*, is used elsewhere for the young of another hoofed mammal, the *re'em* (Bava Batra 74b; see Rashbam ad loc.). The word *ofer* may be related to *ofra* which appears in Scripture as the name of a person (1 Chr. 4:14) and of places (Josh. 18:23, 1 Sam. 13:17, and Judges 6:11). Ofer is used in Israel today as a personal name.

24 Yehuda Feliks, *Nature and Man in the Bible*, "The Faunal Motif in the Song of Songs," pp. 270–274.

25 Rashi, citing Dunash ben Labrat; *Metzudot*.

26 Radak and Malbim to Joel 1:20.

27 George Cansdale, *All the Animals of the Bible Lands*, p. 92.

28 In *Midrash Bereshit Rabba* 12:9, this passage appears with regard to the ibex rather than the deer.

29 Marc Michael Epstein, *Dreams of Subversion in Medieval Jewish Art and Literature* (Penn State University Press, 1997), p. 22.

30 In *Yalkut HaMekhiri*, Isaiah 5:7 it reads "turn their faces away from each other."

31 Cf. Chakham Yosef Chayim, *Ben Yehoyada* to Shabbat 119b.

32 Rashi, Radak, Ibn Ezra, *Metzudot*.

33 Rashi and Ritva note that the verse speaks of the female deer, and female deer lack horns; they conclude that the Talmud is taking the verse as speaking of the species of deer in general. Rabbi Yaakov Emden, *Hagahot Yaavetz* ad loc., claims that Rashi mistakenly understood the Talmud to be referring to the female sheep, and that the female deer does in fact have horns. In fact the only female deer with antlers are reindeer (caribou), which only live in the Arctic and sub-Arctic region. On rare occasions, roe deer and red deer females develop antlers, but these are nothing more than small stubs, hardly matching the branching described by the Talmud. Thus, Rashi's explanation remains preferable. See too Rabbi Menachem Manish Halperin, *Menachem Meishiv Nefesh* (Brody, 1906) to Yoma 29a.

34 The Jerusalem Talmud relates it to a seemingly different form of morning illumination, the nature of which is unclear: "R. Yose son of R. Bun said: Regarding the 'morning deer,' those who explain it to be the morning star (Venus) are mistaken, for it (Venus) sometimes rises early and sometimes rises late. Rather, what is it? It is like two horns of light that rise in the east and illuminate the sky" (Y. Berakhot 1:1, 4b).

35 Megilla 15b.

36 The notion that burning antlers drives away snakes is mentioned in numerous works in antiquity, such as Pliny, *Natural History*, Book 8, 35.

37 Briefer version in *Midrash Tehillim* 22.

38 Allen T. Rutberg, "Adaptive Hypotheses of Birth Synchrony in Ruminants: An Interspecific Test," *The American Naturalist*, Vol. 130, No. 5 (Nov., 1987), pp. 692–710.

39 Shaul Efrati, "The Voice of God Causes Hinds to Give Birth – The Gestation of the Hind as a Key to Understanding a Number of Expressions in our Sources" (Hebrew), *Al Atar* 6 (5760), pp. 13–22.

40 This is in a passage regarding the *yachmur* (hartebeest), which is discussed in that chapter: "With regard to the clumps (that are secreted) by a female *yachmur*, the Rabbis proposed that they were eggs and were therefore forbidden (for human consumption, since they are a detached part of a living animal). Rav Safra said: It was really the seed of a stag which sought to mate with a hind, but since the hind's womb is narrow it rejected it, and thus the stag pursued the female *yachmur*, but its seed had already congealed (and is thus excreted as clumps; and since seed is rated as mere waste matter, it is not forbidden for human consumption)" (Bekhorot 7b).

41 A similar account is in *Midrash Shmuel* 9:2: "The deer has compressed organs, and it is difficult for her to bear young. What does the Holy One do? He provides a serpent for her that bites her, which causes her body to loosen. When she gives birth, what does the Holy One do? He provides grasses for her to eat and become healed. That is what is meant by, 'He does great things, unbeknownst to us' (Job 37:5)."

42 Unfortunately I have not been able to find any mention in contemporary zoological literature of deer having a narrow womb. John Fletcher, "Reproduction," in T.L. Alexander, ed., *Management and Diseases of Deer*

(London: Veterinary Deer Society, 1986), pp. 173–177, writes that calving problems are rare in wild deer, and in personal correspondence with this author wrote that all deer species are renowned for ease of parturition.

43 Avraham Korman, *HaAggada UMahuta*, p. 23. Precedent for such an approach is found in many other sources, such as with Rambam and Rabbi Samson Raphael Hirsch.

44 Rabbi Yitzchak Isaac Chaver, *Afikei Yam* ad loc.

45 Ralbag, commentary to Job 39:1.

46 Ibn Ezra, commentary ad loc.

47 "There are singular cases on record of whole herds of cows slinking their calves after being terrified by an unusually violent thunderstorm" – William Youatt, *Cattle: Their Breeds, Management, and Diseases* (London: Baldwin and Cradock, 1834), p. 530.

48 Zohar Amar, Ram Bouchnick, and Guy Bar-Oz, "The Contribution of Archaeozoology to the Identification of the Ritually Clean Ungulates Mentioned in the Hebrew Bible," *Journal of Hebrew Scriptures* (2010), 10:1.

49 These verses are also discussed in the Babylonian Talmud, Bekhorot 15a–b, 33a, and Chullin 28a.

50 *Keli Yakar* to Genesis 27:3; also Abarbanel to Isaiah 11:8.

51 See Zohar Amar and Ari Zivotofsky, "*Kashrut HaAyil VeHaTzvi*," *Tehumin* 29 pp. 162–172.

52 Judith Cohen Montefiore, *The Jewish Manual* (London: T&W Boone, 1846). The book was published anonymously, under the authorship of "A Lady"; the identity of the author was, however, an open secret, and was officially released after her death.

53 Naomi Schaefer Riler, "The Chosen People on the Sceptered Isle," *The Wall Street Journal*, September 22, 2006.

54 London Beth Din, http://www.kosher.org.uk/what.htm.

55 Recently, some have cast aspersions on the kosher status of venison from red deer (elk). The reason is that red deer possess upper canines, and the Talmud states that animals with upper teeth are non-kosher. However, there is no reason to doubt the kosher status of red deer. The principle regarding upper teeth is just an aid to identifying animals that ruminate and have split hooves; when the existence of such features can be clearly established (as is the case with red deer), the presence of upper canines is irrelevant. The principles were not intended to be determinative, merely indicative, based on the majority of cases, as is the nature of many such talmudic principles. Both the Talmud's principle that animals with upper teeth are non-kosher, and its principle that those lacking upper teeth are kosher, have exceptions; yet nobody would propose that the white rhinoceros and anteater, which lack upper teeth, are kosher! For further discussion, see *The Camel, The Hare And The Hyrax*, by this author; and Ari Zivotofsky and Daniel Zivotofsky, "*Kabel Nivi KeMarbit Teshura*," *HaMaayan*, Tevet 5768, 48:2, pp. 15–25.

56 Also Talmud Yerushalmi, Berakhot 6:6.

57 See the commentaries of Rav Saadia Gaon, Abarbanel, and Ibn Ezra to Exodus 30:23, and Rambam, *Mishneh Torah*, *Hilkhot Kelei HaMikdash* 1:3. Raavad (ad loc.) objects that surely blood, and especially that of a non-kosher animal, would not be used for a sacred rite. He was apparently under the impression that the musk of which Rambam spoke was obtained from a civet (a non-kosher animal), which is also sometimes used as a source of musk; however, Rambam speaks of it coming from India, which indicates that he was referring to the musk deer. Furthermore, although Rambam describes the musk as being the "blood" of the animal, it is actually a glandular secretion. See too Ramban, commentary to Exodus 30:23, who relates that the musk is collected via secretions deposited by the deer in the wild; this is also the account given by Oliver Goldsmith, *A History of the Earth and Animated Nature* (London: Blackie and Son, 1857), vol. 1 p. 316. Cf. Chatam Sofer, *Drush LeErev Rosh Chodesh Adar* 5560, who finds a significant connection to Purim in the deer's musk being collected while the animal is alive. However, other studies indicate that musk was always harvested via killing the deer and removing the musk pod from its body. See too *Tur* and *Bach* to *Orach Chayim* 216:2.

58 Rashi to Chullin 59b, s.v. *veharei tzvi*.

59 *Shulchan Arukh, Orach Chayim* 586:1. According to some, the basis for this ruling is that the word *shofar* implies something that is naturally prepared and beautiful (from the word *shafra*, Psalms 16:6), which rules out a horn that has to be drilled in order to be turned into a shofar (Ritva to Rosh HaShana 26a citing Ramban. Others state that the word *shofar* innately refers to a naturally hollow structure, which is reflected in the word *shefoferet*, "tube" or "sheath" (Rashba and Ran to Rosh HaShana 26a; see Mishna Shabbat 2:4, which refers to the shell of an egg as a *shefoferet*, and Baal HaTurim to Exodus 1:15).

60 *Shulchan Arukh, Yoreh De'ah* 42:8.

61 See Zohar Amar, "Regarding the Identification of the *Ayal*, the *Tzvi*, and the *Yachmur*" (Hebrew), *Al Atar* 15 (5769), pp. 18–19; idem; "The Gall-Bladder – A Method of Distinguishing between the Gazelle and the Deer" (Hebrew), *HaMaayan*, Tevet 5769, pp. 14–18.

62 Ronen Bergman, *The Secret War with Iran* (Free Press, 2008), pp. 23–24; Charles Levinson, "How Bambi Met James Bond to Save Israel's 'Extinct' Deer," *The Wall Street Journal*, February 1, 2010.

GAZELLE

Gazelle

Tzvi

Gazelle vs. Deer

——————————— IDENTIFICATION

The *tzvi* is one of the most commonly misidentified creatures in the Torah, at least in certain parts of the world. Europeans, and in turn North Americans, have long identified it as a deer; hence, a common Jewish name is Tzvi Hirsch, since *hirsch* is Yiddish for "deer."

However, nearly a thousand years ago, Rashi pointed out that the deer does not match the Talmud's description of the *tzvi*. This occurs in the context of the Talmud trying to determine physical characteristics by which to differentiate domestic animals from wild animals – with practical ramifications such as that certain fat from wild animals is permitted for consumption. The Talmud suggests that a differentiating characteristic is that only the horns of wild animals are branched. An objection is raised to this from the *tzvi*:

> But surely those of the *tzvi* are not branched, and yet its fat is permitted (i.e. it is certainly a wild animal)! [Rather, where they are not branched,] they must be rounded. (Chullin 59b)

Rashi, in his commentary to the Talmud, plaintively asks, "I do not know what it is saying! The horns of a *tzvi* are certainly branched!" Deer indeed possess branched horns; hence, the deer cannot be the *tzvi* of the Talmud (and Torah). Furthermore, the Talmud elsewhere refers to the branching horns of the deer, which it identifies as the *ayal* rather than the *tzvi*.[1] Rashi continues to observe, "It appears to me that the creature which we call a *tzvi*, they did not call a *tzvi*."

Seeking an animal that matches the Talmud's description of the *tzvi* not having branched horns, Rashi proceeds to suggest that the *tzvi* is the steenbok. This is the ibex, a type of wild goat. However, identifying the *tzvi* as the ibex is

A deer has branched antlers, whereas the gazelle has unbranched horns

The horns of the dorcas gazelle (right) are more curved than those of the mountain gazelle (left)

problematic. The ibex is universally accepted to be identical with the *ya'el* of Scripture, and the *akko* in the Torah's list of kosher animals. The *tzvi* appears in the same list as the *akko*, demonstrating that they are different types of animals. In fact, Rashi himself, in explaining the terms *ya'el* and *akko*, identifies them as the ibex.[2] Hence, the *tzvi* cannot be the ibex.[3]

Rav Saadia Gaon, however, identifies the *tzvi* as the animal with the almost identical name in Arabic, the *tavi*, which is the gazelle. This perfectly matches the Talmud's understanding of it being an animal with horns that are not branched. As we shall see, it also perfectly matches all other scriptural, talmudic, and midrashic descriptions of the *tzvi*. And, due to the gazelle possessing a similar name in other languages, there is no reason not to identify the gazelle as the *tzvi* of the Torah, Talmud, and Midrash.[4]

Why, then, did Rashi and other European scholars not identify the *tzvi* as the gazelle? The answer is extremely straightforward: there are no gazelles in Europe. Consequently, when Jews were originally dispersed to Europe, they transposed the name *tzvi* to the most similar animal, which is the deer.[5] Only Rav Saadia Gaon, and other Jews who lived in Africa and the Middle East and were thus familiar with gazelles, maintained the original and correct identification of the *tzvi*.

One result of the move to Europe is that Naphtali Tzvi became a very common Ashkenazi name. It is popularly thought that Jacob blessed his son Naphtali with the symbolism of the *tzvi*. However, in fact, it is the deer (*ayal*) rather than the *tzvi* that is connected with Naphtali in the Torah, as explained in the chapter on deer. But since, in Europe, there was no differentiation between a *tzvi* and an *ayal* – since they only had one type of animal – the name Naphtali became linked to the *tzvi*. In the same vein, the name Tzvi Hirsch developed due to a belief that the *hirsch* (which is Yiddish for "deer") is the *tzvi*. Similarly, some references to the *tzvi* in post-talmudic literature actually refer to the deer rather than the gazelle, as discussed in the chapter on deer.

Gazelles in the Wild

NATURAL HISTORY

As mentioned, one difference between gazelles and deer is that the horns of deer are branched. But there are also other differences. The horns of deer, properly called antlers, are made of solid bone, whereas the horns of gazelle are made of a keratin sheath surrounding a bony core, and can thus be made into shofars once the core is removed. Gazelles are overall much smaller than deer, with larger eyes, and their coat is sandy in color, with a white belly.

There are two species of gazelles in Israel today. The mountain gazelle, *Gazella gazella*, is known in Modern Hebrew as *tzvi eretz yisraeli* ("Land of Israel gazelle"). It is the most slender of all species of gazelle. There are several thousand mountain gazelles in Israel today, the vast majority of which live in northern and central Israel. Most of these are the subspecies known as the Palestine mountain gazelle (*Gazella gazella gazella*); a tiny population of another subspecies, the Arava or Acacia gazelle (*Gazella gazella acacia*), lives in the southern part of the Negev desert.

The dorcas gazelle, *Gazella dorcas*, is known in Modern Hebrew as *tzvi midbar* ("desert gazelle"). It is smaller than the mountain gazelle, but with longer ears. It has a bushier tail, and its horns are more curved. In Israel today, dorcas gazelles live in the Judaean and Negev deserts, and in the Arava. Although mountain and dorcas gazelles sometimes form mixed herds, hybridization of the mountain gazelle and the dorcas gazelle has not been observed in the wild; it sometimes occurs in captivity, but the offspring seldom reproduce.[6]

A third species of gazelle, the goitered gazelle (*Gazella subguttorosa*) lives in present-day Jordan. It is possible that in the biblical period, it also lived west of the river Jordan. Scripture makes references to the "twins of a gazelle,"[7] and unlike the mountain gazelle and dorcas gazelle, which always bear a single young, the goitered gazelle usually gives birth to twins.

243

Swift as a Gazelle

SYMBOLISM

A primary attribute of the gazelle, expressed in its symbolism, is its speed. A gazelle can run at speeds of up to forty miles an hour; usually, the most one sees of a gazelle is a flash of its white rump as it disappears into the distance. Cheetahs are faster over very short distances, but gazelles can sustain their high speed for longer.

The prophet Isaiah, when foretelling the retribution against Babylon, states that when it happens, any foreigners who happen to be present will flee with the speed of gazelles back to their homelands:

> It will happen that like a pursued gazelle, and like sheep that no one gathers, they will each turn to their own people, and will each flee to their own land. (Is. 13:14)

A person who has been ensnared in financial obligations is urged to salvage his situation with the speed of a gazelle evading hunters:

> Save yourself like a gazelle from the hand (of the hunter), like a bird from the hand of the fowler. (Prov. 6:5)

The Mishna, when speaking of people who have invested their money in situations where it cannot be reclaimed, describes them as having "placed their money on the horn

וְהָיָה כִּצְבִי מֻדָּח וּכְצֹאן וְאֵין מְקַבֵּץ אִישׁ אֶל עַמּוֹ יִפְנוּ וְאִישׁ אֶל אַרְצוֹ יָנוּסוּ:

ישעיה י״ג:י״ד

הִנָּצֵל כִּצְבִי מִיָּד וּכְצִפּוֹר מִיַּד יָקוּשׁ:

משלי ו׳:ה׳

וַיִּהְיוּ שָׁם שְׁלֹשָׁה בְּנֵי צְרוּיָה יוֹאָב וַאֲבִישַׁי וַעֲשָׂהאֵל קַל בְּרַגְלָיו כְּאַחַד הַצְּבָיִם אֲשֶׁר בַּשָּׂדֶה:

שמואל ב ב׳:י״ח

וּמִן הַגָּדִי נִבְדְּלוּ אֶל דָּוִיד לַמְצַד מִדְבָּרָה גִּבֹּרֵי הַחַיִל אַנְשֵׁי צָבָא לַמִּלְחָמָה עֹרְכֵי צִנָּה וָרֹמַח וּפְנֵי אַרְיֵה פְּנֵיהֶם וְכִצְבָאִים עַל הֶהָרִים לְמַהֵר:

דברי הימים א י״ב:ט׳

of a gazelle."[8] A gazelle runs away so swiftly that anything attached to its horns would be irretrievable.

On two occasions, Scripture praises swift runners as being similar to gazelles:

> And there were three sons of Zeruiah there: Joab, and Abishai, and Asahel; Asahel was as swift of foot as one of the gazelles that are in the field. (II Sam. 2:18)

> Some of the Gadites, mighty men of valor, joined David in the stronghold in the wilderness, men fit for the service of war, armed with shield and spear; whose faces were like the faces of lions, and who were swift as the gazelles upon the mountains. (I Chr. 12:9)

This swiftness can also be used for negative ends. The Talmud, homiletically expounding the word *tzvi* as used with a different meaning in Scripture, explains it as alluding to the swiftness of Nebuchadnezzar's conquest:

> What does it mean by, "And I will give glory (*tzvi*) in the land of the living" (Ezek. 26:20)? It is written with regard to Nebuchadnezzar, regarding whom the Merciful One said: I shall bring against them a king who is as swift as a gazelle. (Ketubot 111a)

This appears to be the only place in all rabbinic literature where the gazelle appears in a negative context. However, the most famous reference to the gazelle's speed occurs in a positive context, with the Mishna urging people to emulate this swiftness – for the right goals:

> Yehuda b. Teima said: Be as brazen as a leopard, as light as a vulture, as swift as a gazelle, and as powerful as a lion to fulfill the will of your Father in Heaven. (Mishna Avot 5:20)

When going to perform an act of kindness, or any other fulfillment of God's will, one is urged to waste no time and to act with alacrity. The gazelle presents the perfect metaphor.

DR. JEFFREY M. LEVINE

In the historic Rymanow synagogue, the tzvi *is depicted as a deer, as is typical for Europe*

244

The Beloved Gazelle

הִשְׁבַּעְתִּי אֶתְכֶם בְּנוֹת יְרוּשָׁלַם בִּצְבָאוֹת אוֹ בְּאַיְלוֹת הַשָּׂדֶה אִם תָּעִירוּ וְאִם תְּעוֹרְרוּ אֶת הָאַהֲבָה עַד שֶׁתֶּחְפָּץ:
שיר השירים ב:ז, ג:ה

שְׁנֵי שָׁדַיִךְ כִּשְׁנֵי עֳפָרִים תְּאוֹמֵי צְבִיָּה הָרֹעִים בַּשּׁוֹשַׁנִּים:
שיר השירים ד:ה

שְׁנֵי שָׁדַיִךְ כִּשְׁנֵי עֳפָרִים תָּאֳמֵי צְבִיָּה:
שיר השירים ז:ד

Gazelles are a central motif in Song of Songs, appearing on seven occasions alongside deer. In a verse that appears twice, they are mentioned as objects of an oath:

> I adjure you, daughters of Jerusalem, by gazelles or by hinds of the field: Do not arouse or awaken love until it so desires! (Song. 2:7, 3:5)

The verse teaches us of the high regard in which gazelles were held. The fact that gazelles and deer are used as objects of an oath indicates their value; one only swears upon very precious things. The Midrash, using wordplay with the Hebrew term for gazelles, interprets it as representing some very important concepts:

> "I adjure you, daughters of Jerusalem" – By what did he adjure them? R. Eliezer said: He adjured them by the heavens and the earth; "by gazelles (tzevaot)" – the Host of Above, and the host of Below, with two hosts (tzevaot); hence it says "by tzevaot".... R. Chanina said: He adjured them by the patriarchs and the matriarchs; "by tzevaot" – these are the patriarchs, who fulfilled My desire (tzivyoni), and through whom My desire was carried out.... R. Yehuda son of R. Shimon said: He adjured them by the circumcision; tzevaot meaning the host (tzava) which bears a sign (ot). And the Rabbis said: He adjured them by the generations of persecution; "by tzevaot" – that they fulfilled My desire (tzivyoni), and through them My desire was carried out...and their blood is spilled in sanctification of My Name like the blood of the gazelle and deer. (Shir HaShirim Rabba 2:18[9])

Further indication of the preciousness of gazelles comes from the other mentions of gazelles in Song of Songs, in which, according to rabbinic tradition, they symbolize extremely important characters. Consider the following verse, which appears twice:

> Your two breasts are like two fawns, twins of a gazelle. (Song. 4:5, 7:4)

The commentaries understand this verse as referring to Moses and Aaron. They were the sustainers of the Jewish

Gazelles are most often seen swiftly running away

people, just as breasts sustain a nursing child. And in other verses, the gazelle is understood to represent no less than God Himself:

> My beloved is like a gazelle or a deer fawn; behold, he stands behind our wall, looking through the windows, peering through the lattice. (Song. 2:9)

> When the day breaks, and the shadows flee, turn, my beloved, swift as a gazelle or a deer fawn, for the distant hills! (Song. 2:17)

This image is so central to Song of Songs that it appears in the very final verse:

> Hurry away, my beloved, like a gazelle or a deer fawn, to the hills of spices! (Song. 8:14)

The preciousness of the gazelle is also reflected in rabbinic literature. The Midrash presents a beautiful parable in which a gazelle is beloved and represents the great preciousness to God of a convert:

> The Holy One greatly loves converts. To what is it comparable? To a king who had a flock, which would go out to graze in the fields and be gathered in at dusk, in the same way every day. Once, a single gazelle came in with the flock. It went amongst the goats and grazed together with them. When the flock came in to the pen, it entered

along with them; when they went out to graze, it accompanied them. They told the king that the gazelle was accompanying the flock and grazing with them, every day going out with them and coming in with them. The king loved it. When it went out to the fields, he would appoint a fine shepherd to tend to its needs; he warned that nobody should strike it. When it came in with the flock, he told them to give it to drink. He loved it very much. They said to him, "Our lord! You have so many goats, so many sheep, so many kids, and you do not warn us about them; yet about this gazelle, you instruct us every day!" The king replied: "The sheep, whether they want or not, go out to graze in the fields every day and come back to sleep in the pen every evening. But gazelles sleep in the wilderness; it is not their custom to enter human settlements. Shall we not be grateful to this one, who left the vast expanse of the wilderness, the place of all the wild animals, and came to be in my yard?"

דּוֹמֶה דוֹדִי לִצְבִי אוֹ לְעֹפֶר הָאַיָּלִים הִנֵּה זֶה עוֹמֵד אַחַר כָּתְלֵנוּ מַשְׁגִּיחַ מִן הַחַלֹּנוֹת מֵצִיץ מִן הַחֲרַכִּים:

שיר השירים ב:ט

עַד שֶׁיָּפוּחַ הַיּוֹם וְנָסוּ הַצְּלָלִים סֹב דְּמֵה לְךָ דוֹדִי לִצְבִי אוֹ לְעֹפֶר הָאַיָּלִים עַל הָרֵי בָתֶר:

שיר השירים ב:יז

בְּרַח דּוֹדִי וּדְמֵה לְךָ לִצְבִי אוֹ לְעֹפֶר הָאַיָּלִים עַל הָרֵי בְשָׂמִים:

שיר השירים ח:יד

This springbok – a relative of the gazelle – is "pronking"

So, too, we need to be grateful to the convert who left his family, and his father's home, and his nation, and all the nations of the world, and came to us. (*Bemidbar Rabba* 8:2; *Midrash Tehillim* 146)

Why is the gazelle regarded in such a positive light? Perhaps it is because of its fragile beauty. With its large eyes, delicate build, and graceful movement, the gazelle is much beloved.

Gazelle Analogies

— SYMBOLISM

In the Book of Song of Songs, the subject of the author's love – which, according to rabbinic tradition, is God Himself – is compared to a gazelle. The Midrash expounds upon this analogy, drawing several parallels between God and the characteristics of gazelles. One parallel, which appears in two places, focuses upon the gazelle leaping:

> "My beloved is like a gazelle or a deer fawn" (Song. 2:9) – R. Yitzchak said, Israel said before the Holy One: Master of Worlds! Truly, You approach us first; "my beloved is like a gazelle" – just as the gazelle leaps, so too the Holy One leaped and jumped from Egypt to the Sea (of Reeds), and from the Sea to Sinai. (*Bemidbar Rabba* 11:2)

> "My beloved is like a gazelle or a deer fawn" (Song. 2:9) – Just as the gazelle leaps from place to place and from fence to fence and from tree to tree and from booth to booth, so too the Holy One leaps and jumps from this gathering to that gathering. And why is all this necessary? In order to bless Israel. (*Bemidbar Rabba* 11:2; *Shir HaShirim Rabba* 2:23)

The description of gazelles leaping may refer to the high leaps of nearly eight feet that they sometimes take in the course of fleeing from predators.[10] Alternately, it may be a reference to a particular habit known as "stotting" or "pronking," whereby gazelles bounce high into the air with all four legs simultaneously. (This behavior occurs when sensing a possible threat, though its function is unclear, since it means that the gazelle is not able to put as much distance between it and its pursuer. A number of explanations have been suggested; it may help the gazelle to spot potential threats, to advertise danger to other gazelles, or to show off its fitness to potential predators and discourage them from attempting pursuit.)

Another analogy refers to the gazelle's habit of disappearing, once spotted:

> "My beloved is like a gazelle or a deer fawn" (Song. 2:9) – R. Yitzchak said, Israel said before the Holy One: Master of Worlds! You told us that You would approach us first;

JO CREBBIN / SHUTTERSTOCK

A gazelle is always ready to spring away in the blink of an eye

> "my beloved is like a gazelle" – just as the gazelle appears and then is hidden, so too the first redeemer appeared and then was hidden. (*Bemidbar Rabba* 11:2)

The Midrash proceeds to explain that Moses, after his first meeting with Pharaoh, disappeared for three months, before returning to successfully lead the Children of Israel out of Egypt. This is analogous to the timid gazelle; one catches a glimpse of it, then it runs and hides, and finally one's patience is rewarded by it emerging into view.

The final reference to gazelles in Song of Songs, is where the author urges his beloved to "be like a gazelle," and the Midrash relates this to the gazelle being a kosher animal:

> "Be like a gazelle" – make us pure, like the gazelle. (*Shir HaShirim Rabba* 8:15)

Another exegesis on this final mention makes reference to a gazelle's alertness. A gazelle does not use its senses of smell and hearing to detect predators, but rather its vision. This is its most acute sense, enabling it to spot danger from great distances; gazelles can see a waving arm from a distance of half a mile.[11] For this reason, gazelles cannot afford to close their eyes for long. When they do sleep, it is just a very light sleep of just a few minutes at a time. This has ramifications in Jewish law. Ordinarily, it is prohibited to capture an animal on Shabbat. If the animal is already relatively immobile for some reason, then there is no biblical prohibition, since the animal is rated as effectively already caught. A sleeping gazelle, however, is not considered already caught:

> One who captures (on Shabbat) a gazelle that is lame, blind, sick, or young, is exempt. If it is sleeping, he is liable, for one eye is closed and one eye is open.[12] (Y. Shabbat 14:1, 74b)

247

The Midrash, in expounding the final verse in Song of Songs, likewise makes reference to the gazelle sleeping with one eye open:

> "Be like a gazelle" (Song. 8:14) – Just as the gazelle, when it is sleeping, it keeps one eye open and one eye closed, so too when Israel does the will of the Holy One, He watches over them with two eyes…and when they do not do the will of the Holy One, He watches over them with one eye. (*Shir HaShirim Rabba* 8:16)

The last phrase in this midrash can be interpreted as making a positive or negative statement. It could be the latter, referring to God being less involved with the Jewish people when they sin. But it could be a positive statement, stating that even when the Jewish people sin, God does not completely abandon them; like the gazelle, He is never completely "asleep," and always has one eye open, watching His children.

A Land of Gazelle

— SYMBOLISM

The Hebrew word *tzvi* appears in Scripture with two meanings. Aside from referring to the gazelle, it also has the meaning of beautiful, desirable, and precious. Scholars are in dispute as to whether the etymology is actually one and the same. However, even if they are two different words, the connection is an easy one to make, since the gazelle is indeed a very beautiful animal.

In its other meaning, the word *tzvi* appears on many different occasions in Scripture. However, there is one instance in particular that is interpreted as alluding to the gazelle: a verse that describes the Land of Israel as being *tzvi*.

> Rav Chisda said: What does it mean when it states, "And I shall give you a desirable land, an inheritance of *tzvi*" (Jer. 3:19)? Why is the Land of Israel compared to a gazelle?…. Just as the gazelle is swiftest of all the wild animals, so to the Land of Israel is swiftest of all lands to ripen its produce. (Ketubot 112a[13])

This is but one of several different analogies that are drawn between the positive aspects of the gazelle and the Land of Israel:

> Another explanation: Just as this gazelle is easy to eat, so too the Land of Israel's produce is easy to eat. (*Shemot Rabba* 32:2)

According to some, this means that gazelles are easy to eat in that they can be freely caught rather than having to be purchased.[14] According to others, it means that their

A female springbok tending to her newborn fawn

meat is tender and easily consumed.[15] The analogy would accordingly refer to the produce of Israel being freely found, or easily digested.

Another application of this analogy refers to the fact that when the hide of a dead gazelle is flayed from its body, it appears too small to have ever been able to cover the gazelle's body:

> Why is the Land of Israel compared to a gazelle? Another explanation: To tell you that just as with the gazelle, its skin cannot encompass its flesh, so too the Land of Israel cannot contain its produce. (Ketubot 112a[16])

This aspect of the analogy is also used to describe the way in which the Land of Israel expands to contain its human inhabitants:

> R. Yochanan said that the "Village of Males" was so called because women used to bear males first and finally a girl and then no more. Ulla said: I have seen that place, and it would not hold even sixty myriads of reeds. A certain Sadducee said to R. Chanina: You tell a lot of lies. He replied: It is written, "a land of *tzvi*"; just as the skin of the gazelle cannot hold its flesh, so too with the Land of Israel, when it is inhabited there is plenty of space, but when it is not inhabited it contracts. (Gittin 57a)

Rabbi Yehuda Aryeh Leib Alter, better known by the name of his works, *Sefat Emet*, explains this concept in a deeper way. The Land of Israel is compared to the gazelle, whose skin cannot encompass its body; its outer form is less than its inner being. So too, the Land of Israel is small in physical dimensions, but its inner form – its spiritual size – is great.[17]

The Gazelle in the Mishna and Talmud
——————————— LAW AND RITUAL

The gazelle is mentioned on several occasions in the Mishna. As we have seen, two of these instances relate to its swiftness.[18] Another reference to the gazelle occurs in the laws of *kilayim*, animals that are forbidden to be crossbred or harnessed to the same plough:

> Goats and gazelles…even though they are similar to each other, are prohibited mixtures with each other. (Mishna Kilayim 1:6)

Goats and gazelles are somewhat similar, in terms of both being split-hooved ruminants of a similar size and with roughly similar horns. One view in the Talmud even suggests that it is possible for a union between them to result in offspring.[19] The Mishna here stresses that notwithstanding their similarities, it is forbidden to crossbreed them or work them together.

Other references to the gazelle in the Mishna do not relate to the specific nature of the gazelle, but rather mention it simply as an example of a wild animal. For example, when the Mishna enumerates the thirty-nine types of actions that are prohibited on Shabbat, one of which is trapping, it speaks of one who traps a gazelle.[20] Subsequently, the Mishna elaborates upon the laws of trapping gazelles, recording a dispute as to the size of the area within which a gazelle is considered to be confined:

> R. Yehuda says: One who traps a bird into a cabinet, or a gazelle into a house, is liable (for having transgressed the prohibition of trapping). But the Sages say: He is indeed liable for trapping a bird into a cabinet, but for a gazelle he is liable even for trapping it into a garden, yard or enclosure. (Mishna Shabbat 13:5)

The Mishna then proceeds to discuss various scenarios relating to the capture of gazelles on Shabbat, such as the division of liability if two people jointly captured it.[21] In all these references to the gazelle, there is no particular significance to the gazelle per se, other than that it is presumably mentioned due it being the most common wild animal (or the most commonly trapped wild animal).[22]

In the Talmud, the gazelle is mentioned on numerous occasions, often by its Aramaic name of *tavya*. However, in the vast majority of these cases, the gazelle is likewise simply mentioned as an example of a wild animal. For example, in presenting an example of a wild animal that does not normally eat meat, the Talmud mentions the gazelle.[23] Elsewhere, the gazelle is presented, along with a few other animals, as an example of something that does not have to work at a trade for a living, in contrast to man.[24] And in discussing foodstuffs than can be moved on Shabbat due to their utility as animal fodder, the Talmud mentions that squall plants are food for gazelles.[25]

These male springbok are using their horns to duel with each other

אַיָּל וּצְבִי וְיַחְמוּר וְאַקּוֹ וְדִישֹׁן וּתְאוֹ וָזָמֶר:

דברים יד:ה

עֲשָׂרָה בָקָר בְּרִאִים וְעֶשְׂרִים בָּקָר רְעִי וּמֵאָה צֹאן לְבַד מֵאַיָּל וּצְבִי וְיַחְמוּר וּבַרְבֻּרִים אֲבוּסִים:

מלכים א ה:ג

רַק בְּכָל אַוַּת נַפְשְׁךָ תִּזְבַּח וְאָכַלְתָּ בָשָׂר כְּבִרְכַּת יְהוָֹה אֱלֹהֶיךָ אֲשֶׁר נָתַן לְךָ בְּכָל שְׁעָרֶיךָ הַטָּמֵא וְהַטָּהוֹר יֹאכְלֶנּוּ כַּצְּבִי וְכָאַיָּל:

דברים יב:טו

בִּשְׁעָרֶיךָ תֹּאכְלֶנּוּ הַטָּמֵא וְהַטָּהוֹר יַחְדָּו כַּצְּבִי וְכָאַיָּל:

דברים טו:כב

אַךְ כַּאֲשֶׁר יֵאָכֵל אֶת הַצְּבִי וְאֶת הָאַיָּל כֵּן תֹּאכְלֶנּוּ הַטָּמֵא וְהַטָּהוֹר יַחְדָּו יֹאכְלֶנּוּ:

דברים יב:כב

Eating Gazelles

LAW AND RITUAL

Many of the references to the gazelle in the Talmud relate to it as an animal that is being utilized for food. The gazelle appears in the Torah as second in the list of kosher wild animals:

This is the animal which you shall eat: cattle, sheep, and goats; the deer, the gazelle, the hartebeest, the ibex, the oryx, the aurochs, and the wild sheep. (Deut. 14:4–5)

We are also told that it was one of three wild animals served at King Solomon's table:

Solomon's daily provisions consisted of thirty *kors* of semolina, and sixty *kors* of flour, ten fattened oxen, twenty pasture-grazed oxen, and one hundred sheep, besides deer and gazelle and hartebeest and fattened geese. (1 Kings 5:2–3)

The Talmud also reports of a gazelle that was slaughtered and presented at the table of the Exilarch (*resh galuta*); it was an apparently ordinary event, at least for the Exilarch, of interest only because it was slaughtered on the second day of a Diaspora festival.[26]

Gazelles are also mentioned as food on three other occasions in the Torah, each time as an example of something that can be eaten without restriction.[27] One such mention occurs in the context of a reference to livestock consecrated as offerings, which were redeemed and may then be eaten as freely as wild animals that are never viable as offerings in the first place:

However, you may kill and eat flesh within all your gates, after all the desire of your soul, according to the blessing of the Lord your God which He has given you: the unclean and the clean may eat of it, as of the gazelle, and as of the deer. (Deut. 12:15)

A similar reference occurs in a different context. First-born animals must usually be brought to the Temple as an offering; but in the case of their possessing a blemish, they can be eaten as freely as a wild animal:

You shall eat it within your gates: the unclean and the clean shall eat it alike, as the gazelle, and as the deer. (Deut. 15:22)

Another reference occurs in the context of the general dispensation to eat meat. Originally, the Children of Israel could only eat livestock if the animal was brought as a peace-offering to the Tabernacle. Moses instructed them that once they entered the Land of Israel, it would be possible to eat meat freely, just as wild animals that are never viable as offerings:

Just as the gazelle and as the deer is eaten, so you shall eat of it: the unclean and the clean may eat of it alike. (Deut. 12:22)

However, some rabbinic commentators explained these comparisons to deer and gazelle as actually presenting a *limitation* on the consumption of meat. Deer and gazelle are eaten only infrequently, since they are usually not farmed and must be captured. By the same token, a person should only eat meat on an occasional basis.[28]

The Talmud indicates that while gazelle meat is not equally available to everyone, it is equally valued by everyone. This results from a discussion regarding which categories of work are permitted on festivals:

Rav Papa said: Scripture states, "[No work at all may be done on them;] only that which is eaten by everyone, [that alone may be prepared for you]" (Ex. 12:16) – This refers to something that is equally [consumed] by everyone. Rav Acha son of Rava asked Rav Ashi: If so, then if he came across a gazelle on the festival, it should be forbidden to slaughter it, since it is not equally [consumed] by everyone! Rav Ashi replied: I say, something that is needed by (i.e. useful for) everyone, and gazelle is needed by everyone. (Ketubot 7a)

However, it appears that in some parts of the world, and during certain eras, gazelles were commonly raised by Jews for food.[29] An early indication of this is seen in the Talmud's discussion regarding which items are considered commonly used for animal food and thus may be moved on Shabbat. It rules out items can that be used for elephant food, since it is uncommon to have an elephant, but it permits squall plants, due to their being food for gazelles; apparently, gazelles were frequently kept in captivity.[30] One nineteenth-century rabbinic authority from

250

"Hurry away, my beloved, like a gazelle or a deer fawn, to the hills of spices!"

(Song. 8:14)

The hide of a gazelle

Iraq mentions that they possess a tradition regarding the status of gazelles as a kosher wild animal, indicating that gazelle meat was available.[31] Another authority from the same period refers to a common custom in Baghdad of raising gazelles at home for food.[32] Rabbi Yosef Schwartz, who reported on the natural history of the Holy Land in the nineteenth century, attests that gazelles were eaten by the Jewish community.[33]

Writing Torah Scrolls on Gazelle Hide
———————————————— LAW AND RITUAL

The Talmud describes how R. Chiyya not only taught Torah, but prepared the materials for it with utmost dedication:

> R. Chiyya said: I endeavor such that Torah should not be forgotten from Israel. For I bring flax, and plant it, and make nets and catch gazelles. I feed their meat to orphans, and I make parchment from the hides of the gazelles, and I go to a town which does not have teachers of children, and write out the Five Books of the Torah for five children. (Ketubot 103b[34])

Why did he make parchment from gazelle hides? Elsewhere, we see that gazelle hides are particularly treasured:

> If one sells...a scroll [allegedly] of gazelle hide, and it turns out to be ordinary parchment...the sale is not valid. (Tosefta, Bava Batra 4:7, Zuckermandel ed., p. 403)

Gazelles are harder to come by than cows, and a gazelle's hide is much smaller than that of a cow (it takes about sixty gazelle hides to make a Torah scroll). Thus, making a scroll out of gazelle hides would be vastly more difficult and expensive than making a scroll out of cow hide. Yet people were willing to invest in such items.[35] The Sages elsewhere describe a Torah scroll made from gazelle hide as being the most beautiful kind, which one should strive to obtain:

> A person is obligated to make beautiful *tzitzit*, and beautiful *mezuzot*, and to write a beautiful Torah scroll, with beautiful ink, a beautiful quill, an excellent scribe, beautiful parchment, on the hides of gazelles[36]...as it says, "This is my God, and I shall glorify Him" (Ex. 15:2) – perform the commandments with splendor. (Talmud, Soferim 3:13)

There is also testimony from the period of the Geonim that gazelle parchment was the preferred choice for *tefillin*,[37] and evidence that it was used for *mezuzot*.[38] Later, there is evidence that the most prized Torah scrolls were written in Iraq on parchment made from gazelle hides. Over fifty Torah scrolls, each over one hundred years old, were evacuated from Iraq at the end of the twentieth century, and many of them were written on gazelle parchment. (Calculations indicate that many thousands of gazelles must have been used annually for producing these scrolls, which indicates that they were actually raised on farms for this purpose.[39])

We see that gazelle hide is rated as a highly desirable raw material to use for parchment. This may not only be due to its physical characteristics; it may also be due to the positive symbolism of the gazelle in Jewish thought. (Note that this is despite the fact that Temple offerings are brought from domestic animals and may not be brought from gazelles.)

The Homing Instinct
———————————————— SYMBOLISM

As noted earlier, the gazelle is mentioned in the very final verse of Song of Songs:

> Hurry away, my beloved, like a gazelle or a deer fawn, to the hills of spices! (Song. 8:14)

The Midrash homiletically reads this verse as alluding to the fate of the Jewish people as a whole:

> "Hurry away, my beloved" – When? On the day that the Holy Temple was destroyed. "Like a gazelle" – Just as the gazelle journeys to the end of the world but returns to its place, so, too, the nation of Israel – even though they are scattered throughout the world, they are destined to return, as it is written, "I shall go, I shall return to my place" (Hos. 5:15). (*Midrash Yalkut Shimoni*, Song. 8:994)

In order to buttress this explanation regarding the nature of gazelles, the Midrash proceeds to refer to a story from the Talmud regarding the Roman Emperor Diocletian, who ruled over the Land of Israel at the end of the third century of the Common Era:

Diocletian oppressed the inhabitants of Paneas. They said to him, "We are leaving." A wise counselor said to him, They will not leave, and if they do, they will return. Should you wish to test this, take some gazelles, send them to a faraway land, and in the end they will return to their place. He did this; he brought gazelles, and coated their horns with silver, and sent them off to Africa; at the end of three years they returned to their place. (Y. Shevi'it 9:2, 25b[40])

Many animals are known to possess extraordinary homing instincts. No scientific research has been performed on homing instincts in gazelles, and very little is known about homing instincts in other large animals. However, there is a record of transplanted white-tailed deer making a three hundred mile return journey.[41]

In the aforementioned midrash, the fleeing gazelle symbolizes the nation of Israel, dispersed from its land. In the Zohar, the analogy is reversed, with the fleeing gazelle representing God:

There is no animal in the world like the gazelle or young deer, which, when it is fleeing, it travels a little and turns its head to look back at the place from which it is fleeing, and is constantly looking behind it. So, too, Israel said: Master of the Universe! If we have caused You to depart from us, may it be Your will that You depart like the gazelle or young deer, which flees and turns its head back toward the place where it left. This is as it states, "But despite all this, when they are in the land of their enemies, I will not be disgusted by them, and nor will I reject them, to obliterate them" (Lev. 26:44). (Zohar, II, Ex. 236)

The gazelle, always a symbol of love, represents the hope of an exiled people that they will reunite once again with their beloved Creator.   ∎

The rare Acacia gazelle from the Negev desert

Notes

1 "Just as the antlers of the deer (*ayal*) branch here and there, so too the light of the morning sun spreads here and there" (Yoma 28b–29a).

2 Rashi, commentary to Talmud, Rosh HaShana 26b and to Deuteronomy 14:5.

3 Rashi's grandson, the Tosafist Rabbeinu Tam, seeks to maintain the identification of the *tzvi* as the deer, in light of the deer matching midrashic descriptions of the *tzvi* having tight skin and being extremely alert. This forces him to emend the talmudic text to read that the horns of a wild animal must be *mevutzalot*, curved at the tip (instead of reading that they must be *mefutzalot*, branched), thus leading the Talmud to object that the deer's horns are not curved at the tip and yet it is a wild animal. This emendation is difficult and, as we shall see, unnecessary in light of our knowledge of gazelles.

4 See Zohar Amar, "Regarding the Identification of the *Ayal*, the *Tzvi*, and the *Yachmur*" (Hebrew), *Al Atar* 15 (5769), pp. 7–20; Zohar Amar and Ari Zivotofsky, "*Kashrut HaAyil VeHaTzvi*," *Tehumin* 29, pp. 162–172.

5 Some people are understandably reluctant to ascribe any lack of knowledge to a figure as revered as Rashi, and to negate a long-standing tradition of identifying the *tzvi* as the deer. However, it should be noted that no less an authority than Chatam Sofer (commentary to Nidda 18a) negates statements about anatomy given by Rashi and *Tosafot*, observing that they were not physicians; all the more so, they did not possess knowledge of the wildlife of distant countries. Rabbi Yosef Karo, in his *Kesef Mishneh* comments on the *Tur* by Rabbi Yaakov, son of Rosh, discounts a ruling of his regarding sugarcane on the grounds that sugarcane did not grow in his region and he was unfamiliar with how it is eaten (*Hilkhot Berakhot* 8:5). Radvaz (Responsa Radvaz 6:2:2206) negates the view of Rabbi Eliyahu Mizrachi (and effectively many others) who identified the "River of Egypt," stated to be the border of the Land of Israel, as the river Nile, pointing out that they were unfamiliar with the geographical reality due to their living in Europe. Rabbi Akiva Yosef Schlesinger (1835–1922) writes that European medieval authorities who rated the halakhic quantity of an olive in terms of a large fraction of an egg did so only because they did not have access to actual olives (*Tel Talpiot*, Shevat 5661, p. 103).

6 Mendelssohn and Yom-Tov, *Fauna Palaestina: Mammalia of Israel*, p. 249.

7 Song of Songs 4:5, 7:4.

8 Mishna Ketubot 13:2.

9 Similar such wordplay appears in *Midrash Shir HaShirim Rabba* 8:15: "When Israel recites the *Shema* prayer distractedly, one starting earlier and one later, and they do not focus their minds in reciting *Shema*, a divine spirit cries out and says, 'Flee, my beloved, and be like a gazelle' – like the Host (*tzava*) of Above, who praise Your Glory with a single voice and a single expression."

10 Mendelssohn and Yom Tov, *Fauna Palaestina: Mammalia of Israel*, p. 256.

11 Ibid., pp. 266–7.

12 This should not be understood in a literal sense. There are some birds and aquatic mammals that literally sleep with one eye open, in a form of sleep known as unihemispheric slow-wave sleep. However, this has not been observed with gazelles, which only metaphorically sleep with one eye open, i.e. they sleep very lightly and easily regain full alertness.

13 Also *Midrash Shemot Rabba* 32:2; *Midrash Tanchuma, Re'eh* 8.

14 Commentary of *Etz Yosef* ad loc.

15 Radal and *Eshed HaNechalim* ad loc.

16 Also *Midrash Shemot Rabba* 32:2; similarly in *Midrash Tanchuma, Mishpatim* 17.

17 *Sefat Emet*, Numbers, end of *Parashat Masei*.

18 Ketubot 13:2 and Avot 5:20.

19 "Rav Chisda said: Which is the *koy* that R. Eliezer and the Sages argued about? It is the offspring of a goat and a gazelle" (Chullin 79b). Others dispute Rav Chisda, and modern biology considers it to be impossible for there to be such offspring, due to the great genetic dissimilarity between goats and gazelles. For further discussion, see section on the *koy* in the chapter on the wild sheep.

20 Mishna Shabbat 7:2.

21 Mishna Shabbat 13:6–7.

22 The remaining references to gazelles in the Mishna, Maaser Sheni 3:11 and Bava Metzia 1:4, fall into the same category.

23 Bava Kama 19b.

24 Kiddushin 82b.

25 Shabbat 128a. The Midrash (*Bereshit Rabba* 65:17) also refers to gazelles reaching up to eat from the *kinamon* tree. However, the identity of this tree is unclear; while there is a linguistic resemblance to cinnamon, it does not appear that cinnamon trees were present in the area. See Zohar Amar, *Tzimchei HaMikra* (Jerusalem: Reuven Mas, 2012), p. 183.

26 Eiruvin 39b.

27 These verses are also discussed in the Babylonian Talmud, Bekhorot 15a–b, 33a, and Chullin 28a. Note that whereas the gazelle is listed after the deer in the list of ten kosher animals, these other verses mention the gazelle before the deer. The reason for this is unclear.

28 *Keli Yakar* to Genesis 27:3; also Abarbanel to Isaiah 11:8.

29 Zohar Amar and Ephraim Nissan, "Captive Gazelles in Iraqi Jewry in Modern Times in Relation to Cultural Practices and Vernacular Housing," *Journal of Modern Jewish Studies* 8:1 (2009), pp. 23–39; Zohar Amar and Ari Zivotofsky, "*Kashrut HaAyil VeHaTzvi*," *Tehumin* 29, pp. 162–172.

30 Shabbat 128a. See too Rambam, *Mishneh Torah, Hilkhot Shabbat* 26:16–17, and Rabbi Yosef Karo, *Beit Yosef, Orach Chayim* 308:29.

31 As opposed to it being rated as a domestic animal. Rabbi Abdallah Avraham Yosef Somech, *Zivchei Tzedek* (Baghdad, 1899), vol. 1, *Yoreh De'ah* 80:2.

32 Rabbi Yosef Chayim, *Ben Ish Chai*, Second Year, *Parashat Va'era*.

33 Rabbi Yosef Schwartz, *Tevuot HaAretz* (Third edition, Jerusalem, 1900), p. 364.

34 Similarly in Bava Metzia 85b, and Y. Megilla 4:1.

35 For a full discussion, see Meir Bar-Ilan, "Writing *Sifrei Torah, Tefillin, Mezuzot* and Amulets on the Hides of Gazelles" (Hebrew), *Beit Mikra* 30 (5745), pp. 375–381. Available online at http://faculty.biu.ac.il/~barilm/sifmezma.html.

36 The text reads צבועין, but this is clearly a scribal error, and the correct word should be צבאין, as per the emendation of the Vilna Gaon. See the text attributed to Rabbi Yehuda of Barcelona reproduced in Elkan Adler, *Ginzei Mitzrayim*, Oxford, 1897, and Saul Lieberman, *Tosafot Rishonim*, vol. II, p. 139.

37 *Halakhot Ketzuvot*, Margoliyos ed. (Jerusalem, 5702), p. 148.

38 Yehuda HaDasi, *Eshkol HaKofer*, cited by Bar-Ilan, "Writing Sifrei Torah.".

39 Zohar Amar and Ephraim Nissan, "Captive Gazelles in Iraqi Jewry in Modern Times in Relation to Cultural Practices and Vernacular Housing," *Journal of Modern Jewish Studies* 8:1 (2009), pp. 23–39.

40 Cf. Ramban, commentary to Genesis 49:21, who cites this story and transposes it with the deer with which Naphtali is blessed.

41 Lynn Rogers, "Homing Tendencies of Large Mammals: A Review," in L. Nielsen and R.D. Brown, eds., *Translocation of Wild Animals* (Wisconsin: Wisconsin Humane Society, 1988), pp. 76–92.

HARTEBEEST

Hartebeest

יחמור (?)

Yachmur

The Riddle of the *Yachmur*

———————————————— IDENTIFICATION

For a land animal to be kosher, it must have split hooves and chew the cud. The Torah lists ten animals that match these requirements:

> This is the animal which you shall eat: cattle, sheep, and goats; the deer, the gazelle, the *yachmur*, the ibex, the oryx, the aurochs, and the wild sheep. (Deut. 14:4–5)

It is difficult to identify the *yachmur* with any certainty, and it seems that even in antiquity the meaning of the term was unclear.[1] The only other occurrence of the word in Scripture sheds little light: a reference to the *yachmur* being served at King Solomon's table, along with deer and gazelle:

> Solomon's daily provisions consisted of thirty *kors* of semolina, and sixty *kors* of flour, ten fattened oxen, twenty pasture-grazed oxen, and one hundred sheep, besides deer and gazelle and *yachmur* and fattened geese. (I Kings 5:2–3)

The *yachmur* is also grouped together with the deer and gazelle in a midrash:

> When the sun shone upon the manna, it melted away, and ran in streams to the great sea. Deer, gazelles, and

אַיָּל וּצְבִי וְיַחְמוּר וְאַקּוֹ וְדִישֹׁן וּתְאוֹ וָזָמֶר:

דברים יד:ה

עֲשָׂרָה בָקָר בְּרִאִים וְעֶשְׂרִים בָּקָר רְעִי וּמֵאָה צֹאן לְבַד מֵאַיָּל וּצְבִי וְיַחְמוּר וּבַרְבֻּרִים אֲבוּסִים:

מלכים א ה:ג

yachmurim, and all the animals, came to drink from it; afterwards, the nations would hunt them and eat them, and would taste in them the taste of that manna that descended for Israel. (*Midrash Mekhilta, Beshallach-Vayisa 4, s.v. Vayelaktu*)

There have been a variety of suggestions regarding the identity of the *yachmur*. Some suggestions are extremely far-fetched;[2] in the mainstream are two basic approaches regarding the identity of the *yachmur*.

One approach is that the *yachmur* is a deer. It would have to be a particular single species of deer, since the *ayal*, two places earlier in the Torah's list, is certainly a deer. Several scholars suggest that the *yachmur* would specifically be the fallow deer, and the *ayal* would be the roe deer.[3]

The basis for identifying the *yachmur* as the fallow deer is that the Aramaic translations of the Torah, as well as Rav

Fallow deer and roe deer, identified by some as the yachmur

Saadia Gaon, render the *yachmur* simply as *yachmur*. This indicates that they believed it to be the animal with the same name in other languages. The fallow deer is indeed called by the name *yachmur* in certain Arabic dialects in region of Iraq and Iran. Identifying the *yachmur* of the Torah as the fallow deer is very widely accepted, and based on this, the fallow deer is called *yachmur* in Modern Hebrew. (Some buttress this identification by basing the word *yachmur* on a root referring to a reddish or clay-coloration; however, this would be equally applicable to many different animals.)

There are, however, substantial difficulties with identifying the *yachmur* as the fallow deer, and consequently interpreting the *ayal* as referring to the roe deer. The system of classification used in the Torah is generally much less specific than that used in modern zoology; it seems unlikely that the Torah would list two species of deer under separate names.[4] Even more problematic is that the gazelle appears in between the *ayal* and the *yachmur*; it seems incongruous to have two species of deer separated by the gazelle. Finally, in light of the fact that fallow deer were very common and roe deer were rare, it would be strange for the roe deer to be an animal that is mentioned on many occasions in Scripture and for the fallow deer to be an animal that is barely mentioned at all.[5]

Some of these problems would, however, be solved by positing that the *ayal* is the fallow deer and the *yachmur* is the roe deer. One could suggest that size is a factor in the Torah's order of animals, with the diminutive and rare roe deer therefore being listed after the gazelle.[6]

However, it may be preferable to adopt a different approach, which is to identify the *yachmur* as the hartebeest.[7] This is an odd-looking type of antelope, with a long, thin head and distinctive lyre-shaped horns. The hartebeest is so unusual in appearance that Arabs long believed it to be a type of bovine rather than an antelope, and called it *bekk'r-el-wash*, "wild cattle."[8] The Dutch settlers in Africa considered it most similar to a deer, and named it *hertebeest*, which means "deer-beast," and this eventually became the animal's English name of hartebeest. It appears that the hartebeest was a prominent animal in biblical Israel, and thus it would deservedly take third place in the Torah's list after deer and gazelle.[9]

The Septuagint (the ancient Greek translation of Scripture, adapted from a translation originally made by the Jewish Sages), and the Vulgate (the Latin translation of Scripture produced by Jerome in consultation with Jewish scholars), both translate the *yachmur* as the *bubalus*. This may refer to the now extinct subspecies of the hartebeest known as the bubal hartebeest, which lived in northern Africa. However, it may instead refer to the water buffalo

(not to be confused with the African buffalo or bison), which was sometimes also known by that name (its scientific name is *Bubalus bubalis*); and indeed, there are those who identify the *yachmur* as the buffalo.[10] It is, however, difficult to accept the water buffalo as a candidate for the *yachmur*; first, it would probably be considered a domestic animal, whereas the *yachmur* is listed amongst wild animals, and second, the water buffalo was probably not found in biblical lands during the biblical period.

For those who do not identify the *yachmur* as the hartebeest, the hartebeest must be one of the other animals in the Torah's list of kosher animals, since it is a kosher animal that was common in the region. One suggestion is that it is the *teo*;[11] however, it is preferable to translate the *teo* as referring to the aurochs. Another suggestion is that the hartebeest is the last animal in the list, the *zamer* (which others identify as the wild sheep or giraffe).[12] The Aramaic translation by *Targum Onkelos* of this animal is *ditza*, a word that elsewhere refers to rejoicing or dancing. This may refer to the hartebeest "pronking," a distinct form of motion in which the hartebeest leaps up high into the air with all four legs.

This Coke's hartebeest (Alcelaphus buselaphus cokii) *is engaged in the act of pronking*

257

This is the last ever photograph of a bubal hartebeest, taken at London Zoo in 1895.

The Hartebeest of Israel

NATURAL HISTORY

The hartebeest of the Torah would specifically be the sub-species known as the bubal hartebeest (*Alcelaphus busela-phus buselaphus*), also known as the bubal antelope or just the bubal. It stood about 43 inches high at the shoulder, and was sandy in coloration. The bubal hartebeest is recorded as having grazed in herds of a hundred to two hundred animals, and must have made a spectacular sight.

The bubal hartebeest lived in Israel until at least two thousand years ago,[13] and there are reports that it was still found on the east bank of the Dead Sea in the nineteenth century.[14] It was formerly widespread in north Africa, but subsequently it was driven to extinction altogether, with the last individuals recorded in Morocco in 1925. However, five other subspecies of hartebeest survive, as well as two similar species, the red hartebeest and Lichtenstein's hartebeest.

The primary difference between the different species and subspecies of hartebeest is in the shape of their horns. With some of these, it would be near-impossible to make a shofar from the horn, for practical rather than halakhic reasons; the horn is so sharply bent that the bony core cannot be pulled out from the keratin sheath.

◀ *A red hartebeest* (Alcelaphus buselaphus caama) *in the Kalahari desert*

The *Yachmur* in the Talmud

IDENTIFICATION

There is a single mention of the *yachmur* in the Talmud. It is described as producing unusual secretions, the nature of which was disputed by the Sages. This takes place amidst an extensive discussion regarding whether various animal products are permitted for consumption. Certain animal products are considered to be waste matter rather than food; accordingly, if for some reason a person wanted to eat them, he may do so even they do not come from a kosher animal. Conversely, some products of kosher animals are not permissible for food, if the animal from which they are derived is still alive, due to the prohibition of eating any part of a kosher animal that has not been slaughtered. With these principles in mind, the Talmud discuss the status of certain mysterious secretions produced by the *yachmur*:

> With regard to the clumps (that are secreted) by a female *yachmur*, the Rabbis proposed that they were eggs[15] and were therefore forbidden (for human consumption, since they are a detached part of a living animal). Rav Safra said: It was really the seed of a stag which sought to mate with a hind, but since the hind's womb is narrow it rejected it, and thus the stag pursued the female *yachmur*, but its seed had already congealed (and is thus excreted as clumps; and since seed is classified as mere waste matter, it is not forbidden for human consumption). (Bekhorot 7b[16])

259

The phenomenon described by the Talmud is not recorded in contemporary zoological studies, and it is difficult to correlate it with any known phenomena;[17] it therefore does not assist in the identification of the *yachmur*.[18] But in any case, the hartebeest never lived in the region of Babylon, and thus the Babylonian Sages would not have been discussing it. One might argue that this shows that the *yachmur* is not the hartebeest. However, this is not necessarily the correct inference. It could well be that the *yachmur* of the Torah is the hartebeest, but that in the absence of the hartebeest from Babylonia, the Babylonian sages transposed the name to a local animal. As such, the meaning of the term in the Talmud does not shed light on the meaning of the term in the Torah.   ∎

Notes

1   Leo Wiener, *Contribution Towards a History of Arabico-Gothic Culture, Volume IV: Physiologus Studies* (Philadelphia: Innes & Sons, 1921), Chapter One: The Bubalus in the Bible, pp. 1–10.

2   Abarbanel, commentary to 1 Kings 5:3, identifies it as a buffalo – a view that we shall later discuss. Chizkuni identifies it as the *bivra*, which appears to refer to the beaver. He refers to the Talmud's account of the *yachmur*'s secretions (discussed later), which he apparently takes to refer to the beaver's secretion of castoreum. However, Rabbi Yosef Schwartz, in *Divrei Yosef* (Jerusalem: Israel Bek, 5622), p. 159 and *Tevuot HaAretz*, p. 365, points out that the beaver is a non-kosher animal. Rabbi Schwartz in turn identifies the *yachmur* as the gnu/wildebeest (*Tevuot HaAretz* p. 364 and *Divrei Yosef* pp. 64–65), but this is unlikely, since the gnu only lives in the southern part of Africa. Shalom Yaakov Abramowitz, in *Toledot HaTeva* vol. 1 p. 400, suggests that it is the moose; but this, too, does not live anywhere near biblical lands.

3   Yisrael Aharoni, *Zikhronot Zoolog Ivri*, vol. 1, p. 224; Yehuda Feliks, *The Animal World of the Bible*, p. 12; Elkanah Bialik, "HaYachmur," *Bet Mikra* 3 (5718), pp. 20–25; Yisrael Meir Levinger and Menachem Dor, "The Seven Kosher Mammals" (Hebrew), *Torah UMadda* vol. 5 (5735–1975), pp. 37–50; Yisrael Meir Levinger, *Meor LeMasekhet Chullin* p. 46; Menachem Dor, *HaChai BiYemei HaMikra, HaMishna VeHaTalmud* p. 35; Moshe Ra'anan, "Yachmur" (Hebrew), Daf Yomi Portal, at http://daf-yomi.com/DYItemDetails.aspx?itemId=13884. Others reverse it, identifying the *ayal* as the fallow deer, and the *yachmur* as the roe deer; this is based on the fallow deer being a much more common animal, and the *ayal* being mentioned in Scripture on many more occasions than the *yachmur*. See Bialik, "HaYachmur."

4   See Mordechai Kislev, "Methods of Identifying the Ten Types of Kosher Ruminants via Taxonomy" (Hebrew), *Sinai* 125 (Adar 5761/2000), pp. 216–225; Zohar Amar, "Regarding the Identification of the *Ayal*, the *Tzvi*, and the *Yachmur*" (Hebrew), *Al Atar* 15 (5769), pp. 7–20.

5   Ibid

6   See Bialik, "HaYachmur," and Zohar Amar, Ram Bouchnick, and Guy Bar-Oz, "The Contribution of Archaeozoology to the Identification of the Ritually Clean Ungulates Mentioned in the Hebrew Bible," *Journal of Hebrew Scriptures* (2010), 10:1.

7   Thomas Shaw, *Travels or Observations Relating to Several Parts of Barbary and the Levant* (1738), Section VI, p. 415; Henry B. Tristram, *The Natural History of the Bible*, p. 84; Amar, Bouchnick, and Bar-Oz, "The Contribution of Archaeozoology.".

8   Thomas Shaw, *Travels or Observations Relating to Several Parts of Barbary and the Levant*, p. 415. This Arabic name for the hartebeest is also recorded by Ishtori HaParchi, *Kaftor VaFerach,* ch. 48.

9   Amar, Bouchnick, and Bar-Oz, "The Contribution of Archaeozoology."

10 Abarbanel, commentary to 1 Kings 5:3.

11 Ishtori HaParchi, *Kaftor VaFerach* ch. 48.

12 Menachem Dor, *HaChai BiYemei HaMikra, HaMishna VeHaTalmud*, p. 40.

13 Ella Tsahar, Ido Izhaki, Simcha Lev-Yadun, Guy Bar-Oz, "Distribution and Extinction of Ungulates during the Holocene of the Southern Levant" *PLoS One* 2009; 4(4):e5316.

14 Henry B. Tristram, *The Natural History of the Bible*, p. 84.

15 The meaning of this term is disputed. Rashi explains it to refer to objects with the appearance of testicles, that were presumed to have become detached from the male *yachmur* during mating. Rabbeinu Gershom, on the other hand, appears to explain the Rabbis to be referring to eggs.

16 Codified in *Shulchan Arukh, Yoreh De'ah* 81:3; see too *Turei Zahav* ad loc.

17 Animals such as deer, antelope, and hartebeest have various scent glands that can produce waxy secretions, but these would not appear to be the egg-like "clumps" discussed in the Talmud. The only clumped products from kosher animals that might be used for food are bezoar stones. These are masses found in the stomach or intestines of animals, especially ruminants, and in particular the bezoar ibex. Bezoar stones were used to make antidotes for poisons. However, it is difficult to claim that these are the subject of the Talmud's discussion, since the Talmud indicates that these objects are secreted by the animal, whereas bezoar stones are extracted from the animal after its death.

18 As noted above in endnote 2, Chizkuni identifies the *yachmur* as the *bivra*, which appears to refer to the beaver, due to his interpreting the account of the *yachmur*'s secretions as referring to the beaver's secretion of castoreum. Castoreum is a clumpish secretion that is used as flavoring in certain foods. However, the *yachmur* could not be the beaver, which is not a kosher animal. Even arguing that castoreum is the substance described in the Talmud, and was mistakenly believed to be secreted by a kosher animal, is problematic, since beavers did not live anywhere near biblical or talmudic lands.

IBEX

יעל, אקו

Ibex

Ya'el, Akko

The *Akko*, the *Ya'el*, and the Ibex
— IDENTIFICATION

Amongst the animals listed in the Torah as being kosher is one called the *akko*:

> These are the animals that you may eat: the ox, sheep, and goat; the deer, gazelle, hartebeest, *akko*, oryx, aurochs, and wild sheep. (Deut. 14:4–5)

While there is some dispute and uncertainty regarding some of the animals in the list, there is a universal tradition that the *akko* refers to a wild goat. The primary type of wild goat to which it refers is the ibex, a goat with distinctive sweeping ridged horns that lives on rocky mountains and is renowned for its agility.[1] The ibex is better known in Hebrew by another name, *ya'el*, under which it appears in several instances in Scripture. The first mention of it provides clear evidence for its identity:

> It came to pass, when Saul returned from following the Philistines, that it was told to him, saying, Behold, David is in the wilderness of Ein Gedi. Then Saul took three thousand select men from all Israel, and went to seek David and his men upon the rocks of the *ya'elim*. (1 Sam. 24:1–2)

An ibex at Ein Gedi, near the shore of the Dead Sea

> אַיָּל וּצְבִי וְיַחְמוּר וְאַקּוֹ וְדִישֹׁן וּתְאוֹ וָזָמֶר:
> דברים יד:ה
>
> וַיִּקַּח שָׁאוּל שְׁלֹשֶׁת אֲלָפִים אִישׁ בָּחוּר מִכָּל יִשְׂרָאֵל וַיֵּלֶךְ לְבַקֵּשׁ אֶת דָּוִד וַאֲנָשָׁיו עַל פְּנֵי צוּרֵי הַיְּעֵלִים:
> שמואל א כד:ב
>
> הָרִים הַגְּבֹהִים לַיְּעֵלִים סְלָעִים מַחְסֶה לַשְׁפַנִּים:
> תהלים קד:יח

From biblical times through today, one can go to the wilderness of Ein Gedi – which literally means "the wellspring of the goat" – and see the *ya'elim*, ibex, climbing upon the rocks. The name *ya'el* is explained to be based on the verb *yaal*, which means "he shall ascend," and would be an appropriate description of these superb climbers.

Ibex in Israel today are mainly found in the Judaean and Negev deserts. Although the total population in Israel is only around 1,500, they can be easily seen in Ein Gedi and the Ramon Crater, where they are not at all shy and allow people to approach quite close. Ibex have also been introduced to the Golan Heights.

High Hills and Their Purpose
— THEOLOGY, PHILOSOPHY, AND SCIENCE

Psalm 104 is popularly known by its first two words, *Barkhi Nafshi*. It is recited on Rosh Chodesh, the first day of each new month, and it speaks of the beauty of the natural world. One verse mentions the ibex:

> The high hills are for the ibex, the rocks are a refuge for the hyraxes. (Ps. 104:18)

This verse is a description of the survival strategies of animals in the Judaean desert. Ibex, powerfully built but with short legs, excel at negotiating steep hillsides, an ideal way of escaping predators. Hyraxes live in the same area, but due to their small size, they have a different escape strategy – when enemies approach, they quickly dart down to hide amongst the rocks.

However, the Midrash reads the verse carefully to deduce an important religious perspective:

"The high hills are for the ibex…"

(Ps. 104:18)

R. Yuden said: It does not state, "In the high hills *are* the ibex," but rather, "The high hills are *for* the ibex." Why were the high hills created? *For* the ibex....[2] "The rocks are a refuge for hyraxes" – These hyraxes hide under rocky outcrops from birds flying overhead, that they should not eat them. And if the Holy One created His world in such a way on behalf of a non-kosher animal, how much more so did He create it for the merit of Abraham! (*Bereshit Rabba* 12:9)

The high hills existed before the ibex. But the Midrash states that this does not mean that ibex suit their habitat simply as a happy coincidence, or as a consequence of having been formed or developed to suit the hills. Although the terrain appeared first, it was created with the ultimate end goal of providing an appropriate environment in which these animals can thrive. God created the world and there is a hierarchy in creation. Man, as the goal of creation, is the most important creature. Following man are animals, and then come plants and inanimate matter. Ibex are therefore more important than terrain. God created the terrain to suit the ibex. The high hills are *for* the ibex, created specifically to suit their needs and to give them a way to evade predators. And the rocks are likewise *for* the hyrax, even though the hyrax is a non-kosher animal. The Midrash concludes that on a larger scale, the creation of the entire world was for the sake of (or justified by) the merit of Abraham.

Birth of the Ibex

SYMBOLISM

In the Book of Job, after Job has been inflicted with unimaginable suffering, he bemoans his fate. God's cryptic response includes a mention of the ibex:

> Do you know when the ibex of the rocks will give birth? Can you anticipate the labor pangs of the hind? Will you count the months to the fulfillment of her term, and do you know the moment of her giving birth, when they crouch to squeeze out their young, ridding themselves of their agony? Their young will grow robustly, fattening in the meadow; they have gone, never to return to them. (Job 39:1–4)

At its most basic level, God's response to Job serves to humble him. Job is seeking to understand why such terrible events befell him; God in turn explains to Job that he should not expect to understand the ways of the Creator of the universe. "Where were you when I founded the world?" God asks. God presents examples from the animal kingdom which demonstrate man's limitations. He will then no longer expect to understand the ways of God.

With the ibex, the limitation that it demonstrates is that of human knowledge. "Do you know when the ibex of the

264

rocks will give birth?" As intimately familiar as man was with the animals that shared his environment, the birthing process of the ibex was always a mystery. Copulation with ibex lasts only a few seconds and is almost never observed; thus, one could not anticipate when birth would take place. The birth itself is hidden from view. Ibex select birth sites that are especially difficult to reach – high up, and on steep terrain. This fulfills the double function of protecting the vulnerable birthing mother and young from predators, and of forcing the young to quickly learn how to navigate difficult topography.[3] Delivering the young takes about an hour, and the newborn kid is standing within fifteen minutes. In the first thirty years of the State of Israel, despite intensive studies by naturalists, the ibex was observed giving birth in its natural habitat on only four occasions.[4]

According to the Talmud, God's response to Job here is not merely humbling him with the mysteries of the natural world, but also addressing the issue of providence. The ibex is mentioned in response to a specific accusation that Job raised:

> Job said before God, Master of the Universe! Perhaps a whirlwind passed before You, and You confused *Iyov* (Job) with *oyev* ("enemy")? (Bava Batra 16a)

Job's charge was that God is not sufficiently involved in the affairs of this world, leaving its fate to arbitrary forces that do not care for what people actually deserve. The end result is that the righteous Job is treated no differently from an enemy of God. The Talmud elaborates on God's reply, explaining how His mention of the ibex and the deer specifically addresses this charge, showing that He carefully engineers every aspect of the events of this world:

> "Do you know when the ibex of the rocks will give birth? Can you anticipate the labor pangs of the hind?" [God said:] This ibex is cruel to its offspring; when she crouches to give birth, she goes up to the top of a mountain, so that [her offspring] will fall from her and die. But I prepare a vulture for it, which takes it on its wings and sets it before her. And if it were to be a moment too early or a moment too late, [the newborn] would die immediately. I do not confuse one moment with another – would I confuse *Iyov* with *oyev*?! (Bava Batra 16a–b)

Taken at face value, these descriptions do not concur with our knowledge of what actually happens; ibex are observed to give birth without any assistance from vultures.

Some suggest that the Talmud is recording the zoological beliefs of the era.[5] Others argue that the Talmud is speaking of mystical matters.[6] Another possibility is that the Talmud is using poetic language to describe these animals giving birth. Ralbag writes that "if the matter is true, then the explanation of the verse is so; but if not, then the intent of it, according to what I think, is that this animal gives birth with great difficulty, and accordingly the newborn is in great peril, were it not for God's providence, to cause the young to be produced in such a way that they do not die at birth."[7] It is indeed the case that ibex births are perilous procedures, in that they take place on steep sides of mountains.

The Charm of the Ibex

— SYMBOLISM

In Scripture, there is a heroic character named after the ibex.[8] Yael was the brave woman who killed Sisera, captain of the enemy forces of King Yabin, by luring him into her tent, and driving a tent peg into his skull while he slept.[9] In recent times, the name Yael has been resurrected and is now very popular. Its appeal may be due to the biblical character, but it may also be based on the animal itself (after whom Yael of Scripture was presumably named). Scripture describes the ibex in extremely positive terms:

> She will be like the loving hind and charming ibex (*ya'elet chen*); her breasts shall satisfy you at all times; and you will always be intoxicated with her love. (Prov. 5:19)

The plain meaning of the word is that it refers to a female ibex.[10] Some commentaries interpret the word *ya'elet* as a

A mother ibex with two kids, entirely unfazed by standing on the edge of a cliff

"A charming ibex" – with golden eyes and a natural smile

verb meaning "raising up," such that the verse is saying that "she raises charm,"[11] but this would appear to be a reference to a homiletic exegesis presented in the Talmud. This occurs in the context of a discussion about a leper colony, from whom most of the Sages kept a safe distance; R. Yehoshua, however, conducted himself differently:

> R. Yehoshua would mingle with them and engage in Torah. He said, "'A beloved hind and a *ya'elet chen*' – if the Torah raises (*maala*) charm upon those who learn it, shall it not protect them?" (Ketubot 77b)

In the talmudic period, the phrase *ya'elet chen* was used to describe how a bride, even without make-up, possessed natural beauty:

> Rav Dimi said: This is how they sing for a bride in the West (in the Land of Israel): "Without eye-color, mascara or braiding, and yet a charming ibex!" (Ketubot 17a[12])

The phrase *ya'elet chen* was also used by Rabbi Yehuda HaLevi, author of the *Kuzari*, to begin several of his poems.

The Horn of the Ibex

———————————————————————— LAW AND RITUAL

The ibex's most distinctive feature are its horns. While the horns of females are relatively small, measuring around eight inches, those of the males are enormous, reaching as much as three to four feet in length. They form a sweeping curve up and behind the ibex's head. The horns of the male ibex have two to three dozen large ridges on the top

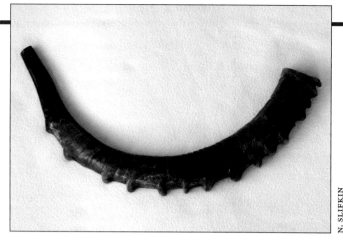

A shofar made from an ibex horn

N. SLIFKIN

(the number is not related to their age). Some suggest that these serve to enable males to lock their horns together when competing with each other, without them slipping.[13] Others propose that these serve a structural function in strengthening the horn.[14]

The Mishna notes that the horn of the ibex was used to make a shofar. According to one opinion, this ibex shofar was used for both Rosh HaShana and to announce the Jubilee year, while according to another view, it was only used to announce the Jubilee year:

> The shofar of Rosh HaShana is of an ibex, straight, and with its mouthpiece coated with gold ... and that of fast days is of rams (lit. "males"), bent.... The Jubilee is equal to Rosh HaShana with regard to the blowing and the blessings. R. Yehuda says: On Rosh HaShana we blow with that of rams, and on the Jubilee with that of ibex. (Mishna Rosh HaShana 3:3–5)

> In what do they argue? R. Yehuda maintains that on Rosh HaShana, the more one bends oneself (in contrition), the better (and thus one should use the bent horn of a ram) ... while the first *Tanna* maintains that on Rosh HaShana, the more one is outstretched (in supplication), the better (and thus one should use an ibex horn). (Rosh HaShana 26b)

The difficulty with this mishna is that the horn of an ibex is *not* straight. All ibex horns are curved. How, then, can the Mishna describe the shofar as being made from the straight horn of an ibex?

One suggestion is that the Mishna is talking about an oryx rather than an ibex, which does indeed possess straight horns.[15] Since the *ya'el* of Scripture is clearly the ibex, we would have to posit that either the Sages of the Mishna used the term in reference to a different animal, or that they saw it as a generic category that includes both oryx and ibex. The former is difficult, since the Sages of the

The sweeping curved horns of an adult male ibex

ALEX KANTOROVICH

An ibex rearing up, in order to crash its horns down with maximum force ▶

Mishna lived in the Land of Israel and would have been very familiar with both ibex and oryx. The latter view is somewhat plausible; there are certain similarities between the oryx and ibex in that both live in desert surroundings, and have ridged horns. However, it is nevertheless a difficult proposal; the oryx is very dissimilar to the ibex in habits, physiology, and coloration, and is far more distantly related to it than is a sheep.

If the Mishna is indeed referring to the ibex, as appears to be the case, is there a way of understanding how it describes the horn as being straight? Perhaps the answer lies in the juxtaposition of the Mishna's description of the ibex horn with its description of a ram's horn. In comparison to the twisted, tight coils of a ram's horn, the horn of the ibex is *relatively* straight.[16]

The Talmud rules in accordance with R. Yehuda's opinion, that a ram's horn should be used for the shofar of Rosh HaShana and an ibex horn only for the Jubilee year. However, although it is preferable to use a ram's horn for Rosh HaShana, if a person did use an ibex horn he has fulfilled his obligation. Due to the unique nature of the ibex horn, there is some interest in obtaining them, and they can occasionally be acquired – albeit at a very steep price.

Ibex and Other Wild Goats

LAW AND RITUAL

There is considerable dispute amongst zoologists as to how to classify the various types of wild goats and ibex. The ibex of Israel, more precisely called the Nubian ibex, is sometimes categorized as a local variety of the Alpine ibex, *Capra ibex*, which is best known from the European Alps. Others consider it to be sufficiently different from this European variety to be defined as a distinct subspecies, *Capra ibex nubiana*, while still others rate it as an entirely separate species, *Capra nubiana*. (Other ibex species include the Spanish ibex, the Siberian ibex, and the Walia ibex.)

The biblical term *akko* would probably also refer to the bezoar goat, also known as the bezoar ibex or wild goat, *Capra aegagrus*. This is the ancestor of the domestic goat, and it was found in the mountains of Syria and Lebanon until the beginning of the twentieth century. The bezoar goat can most easily be distinguished from the Nubian ibex by its horns, which bear only a few small ridges, or none at all. Its coloration is also different; whereas the Nubian ibex is an even sandy color, the bezoar goat is a striking mix of light gray with dark brown and black stripes.

The uncertainty surrounding the classification of goats of various types is also found in the Talmud. An extended discussion involves the question of whether a certain type

A bezoar goat. Note the smoothness of the horns, relative to the ridged horns of the Nubian ibex

of goat is to be defined as a domestic animal (in which case they may be brought as offerings) or a wild animal:

> Rav Hamnuna said: Forest goats[17] are fit for the altar. He was following that which R. Yitzchak said: Scripture enumerated ten (kosher) animals, and there are no others; and since these forest goats are not rated amongst the wild animals, this shows that they are a variety of (domestic) goat…. Rav Acha son of Rav Ikka asked: But perhaps they are a variety of *akko* (and are thus wild animals)?…. Rav Chanan said to Rav Ashi: Ameimar permitted their fat for consumption (which means that he rated them as wild animals). (Chullin 80a)

It is unclear which species of animals the Talmud is describing here. As reflected in the translation above, Rashi understands the term the Talmud uses to describe these goats, *debala,* as meaning "forest," and identifies the species in question as living in Lebanon. According to this interpretation the reference may well be to the bezoar goat, which, as mentioned above, lives in Lebanon and Syria."[18] However, more recent scholars translate this term as referring to a rural area and not to a forest. According to this view, the Talmud may be referring here to the wild goats of the Caucasus mountains, which are known as the East Caucasian tur (*Capra cylindricornis*).[19]

An East Caucasian tur ▶

The Mishna also discusses the classification of ibexes when describing which animals are considered to be forbidden mixtures:

> The wolf and the dog, the *kufri* dog and the fox, the goats and the gazelles, the ibex and the ewes, the horse and the mule, the mule and the donkey, the donkey and the onager – even though they are similar to each other, they are forbidden mixtures with each other. (Mishna Kilayim 1:6)

While the Mishna here states that ibex are forbidden to be crossbred with sheep, it states nothing about whether they are forbidden mixtures with goats. Ibex are far more similar to goats than they are to sheep, and they can breed with them to produce fertile offspring. One might infer from the Mishna's mention of sheep that ibex may be crossbred with goats, but this seems unlikely, given that they are listed as separate types in the Torah's list of kosher animals.

At one point, resolving the permissibility of ibex-goat hybrids would have been a very practical halakhic question. In the 1980s, a herd of hybrid ibex-goats, which is called *ya'ez* in modern Hebrew (a combination of *ya'el* and *ez*), was developed for experimental purposes at Kibbutz Lahav in the Negev desert. This was done as an attempt to provide meat with the taste of ibex, but with an animal that was as easy as a goat to manage. The superiority of the taste of wild goats such as ibex is perhaps alluded to in the Talmud, which notes that the wild goat sells for a higher price than the domestic goat.[20]

The question of whether it is permissible to hybridize wild goats with domestic goats is now largely academic, since the practice turned out to be problematic from an agricultural standpoint. The entire herd of ibex-goats at Kibbutz Lahav was destroyed due to a Brucellosis infection. At the moment, the only mixing of ibex with goats occurs with the Bedouin, who sometimes raise ibex kids amongst their goat herds. ∎

Notes

1 Rav Saadia Gaon translates the *akko* with the Arabic name *wa'al*. *Targum Onkelos* and *Targum Yonatan* translate *akko* as *ya'ela*. Rashi and Chizkuni note that this is an animal called *steinbok*, which refers to the ibex (and is not to be confused with the animal called steenbok or steinbok in English today, which is an antelope from South Africa); *steinbok* literally means "rock goat" in German. Me'iri, in his commentary to Rosh HaShana 26a, states that the *akko* is identical with the *ya'el*, and explains it to be the *steinbok*. Radak in *Sefer HaShorashim* states that the *akko* is the wild goat. Rabbi Yosef Schwartz, in *Tevuot HaAretz* p. 365, describes it as similar to a goat but exceedingly agile, and identifies it as the *steinbok*, which is known as *al-beden* in Arabic. Tristram, in *The Natural History of the Bible*, p. 95, notes that *beden* is the Arabic term for the ibex.

2 The Midrash interjects at this point to relate another aspect of providence regarding the ibex: "The ibex is weak, and is afraid of wild beasts. When she wishes to drink, the Holy One causes a spirit of madness to enter her, and she clatters her horns, and the beasts hear the sound and flee." In *Midrash Aggadat Shmuel* 9, this passage appears with regard to the deer rather than the ibex.

3 A. Dematteis, L. Martino, et al., "Characterization of Ibex Birth Sites in Southern Italian Cotian Alps," paper delivered at 2nd Meeting of the Alpine Ibex European Specialist Group, 2–3 December 2004.

4 Avinoam Danin, "Do You Know When the Ibexes Give Birth?" *Biblical Archeology Review* 5:6 (Nov/Dec 1979), pp. 50–51.

5 Avraham Korman, *HaAggada UMahuta*, p. 23.

6 Rabbi Yitzchak Isaac Chaver, *Afikei Yam* ad loc.

7 Malbim likewise states simply that God enables the mother ibex to overcome difficulties of birth. Maharal (*Chiddushei Aggadot* ad loc.), consistent with his novel approach to such statements, explains the Talmud to be describing metaphysical aspects of the process of childbirth that are symbolized by vultures and snakes.

8 There is also a person by the name of Yaalah, mentioned in Ezra 2:56 and Nehemiah 7:58.

9 Judges 4:17–21.

10 *Targum Yonatan*, Gra, Malbim.

11 *Metzudat David* ad loc.

12 The Talmud also states (ibid. and Sanhedrin 14a) that this praise was given upon the ordination of R. Zeira, which, in light of his appearance being recorded as short and unbecoming, was apparently a jest.

13 Mendelssohn and Yom Tov, *Fauna Palaestina*, p. 271.

14 F. Alvarez, "Horns and fighting in male Spanish ibex, *Capra pyrenaica*," *Journal of Mammalogy* (1990) 71:4, pp. 608–616.

15 Ari Zivotofsky, "*Shofar MiKarnei Re'em, Ya'el VeAyil*," *Tehumin* 27 (5767), p. 116.

16 Me'iri to Rosh HaShana 26a. See Moshe Ra'anan, "The Status of an Ibex Horn regarding the Blowing of the Shofar" (Hebrew), *Tehumin* 28 (5768), pp. 425–437. See too Rabbi Yosef Kapach, "*Shofar Shel Rosh HaShana*," *Sinai* 69 (1970), pp. 209–212.

17 The Aramaic term is עזי דבאלא. Rashi renders this as "goats of Lebanon" and explains *bala* to mean "forest." Sokoloff, in *A Dictionary of Jewish Babylonian Aramaic* p. 220, renders *bala* as a rural area. See too Lewysohn, *Die Zoologie des Talmuds*, p. 126.

18 Rabbi Yosef Schwartz, in *Tevuot HaAretz* p. 365, notes that ibex are abundant in Lebanon, and judges that they are the "wild goats" of the Talmud; he professes surprise that it could at all be considered a domestic animal, since it is clearly the *akko* of the Torah.

19 Lewysohn, *Die Zoologie des Talmuds*, p. 126.

20 This is stated during a battle of wits between a Sadducee eunuch and the bald R. Yehoshua: "A eunuch said to R. Yehoshua the Bald:.... Goats are bald (they have no wool), they sell for four (coins). R. Yehoshua replied: People pay eight for a castrated wild goat!" (Shabbat 152b). The word that appears in the printed Talmud is עיקרא. However, Rabbeinu Chananel and *Arukh* have the variant איקא, which is close to the *akko* of the Torah.

ORYX

Oryx

דישון

Dishon

Rim, Addax, and Oryx

————————————————— IDENTIFICATION

אַיָּל וּצְבִי וְיַחְמוּר וְאַקּוֹ וְדִישֹׁן וּתְאוֹ וָזָמֶר:

דברים יד:ה

Among the ten animals listed as kosher in the Torah is the *dishon*:[1]

> These are the animals that you may eat: the ox, sheep, and goat; the deer, gazelle, hartebeest, ibex, *dishon*, aurochs (*teo*), and wild sheep. (Deut. 14:4–5)

The identity of the *dishon* is not entirely clear, and diverse possibilities have been suggested.[2] The Aramaic translations all render the *dishon* with the name *rim* or *rimu*.[3] But the identity of the *rim* is itself not entirely clear.

One possibility that the *rim* is identical with the biblical *re'em*, an animal described on several occasions in Scripture (and sometimes referred to in Scripture as the *rim*).[4] However, it seems that the *re'em* of Scripture is the aurochs, huge wild ancestor of domestic cattle, as discussed in the next chapter. It further seems likely that the aurochs appears under the name *teo* in Deuteronomy's list of kosher animals quoted above, as an alternative name for the *re'em*. Accordingly, if the *teo* in this list is the aurochs, then the *dishon* in this list cannot also be the aurochs. Thus, the Aramaic translation of *dishon* as *rim* cannot refer to the biblical *re'em*.

But there is another possible meaning of the word *rim*. In Arabic, *rim* refers not to the aurochs, but to the Arabian oryx, *Oryx leucoryx*, a graceful white antelope with magnificent straight black horns. (The name *rim* may be related to the word *ram*, "high," referring to the upwards-pointing horns of the oryx.) This appears to be the creature to which the Aramaic translators were referring when they rendered *dishon* as being the *rim/rimu*. Indeed, the Aramaic translators would not have been familiar with the aurochs, which had disappeared from the area by then.[5]

Similarly, in later rabbinic Hebrew the name *re'em* appears to sometimes refer to the oryx and not the aurochs. Thus, at one point the Midrash describes the *re'em* as follows:

> "His firstborn ox, grandeur is his, and his horns are like the horns of a *re'em*" – The ox is of great strength, but its horns are not beautiful; the horns of a *re'em* are beautiful,

272

The Arabian Oryx

The addax is easily distinguished from the oryx by its spiral horns

but it is not strong; he thus gave to Joshua the strength of an ox and the horns of a *re'em*. (*Sifrei, Vezot HaBerakha* 12)

This description of the *re'em* as possessing beautiful horns but lacking strength cannot possibly refer to the mighty aurochs, but matches the oryx perfectly. [6] (In Modern Hebrew the word *re'em* likewise refers to the oryx.)

Based on this understanding of the Aramaic translators' rendering of *dishon* as *rim*, many contemporary scholars of biblical zoology identify the *dishon* as the oryx.[7] The Hebrew name *dishon* may relate to the root *dash*, meaning "tread" or "trample." This could relate to the extremely broad hooves of the oryx, which aid it both for walking on loose sand and for digging in dirt.[8]

Other scholars suggest identifying the *dishon* as a type of spiral-horned antelope known as the addax, *Addax nasomaculatus*. This opinion is based on the Septuagint (the ancient Greek translation of Scripture, adapted from a translation originally made by the Jewish Sages) and the Vulgate (the Latin translation of Scripture produced by Jerome in consultation with Jewish scholars). Both of these translate the *dishon* as *pygargus*, which is Anglicized as "pygarg" in many English Bible translations. The word *pygargus* literally means "white-rumped," and would suit the addax, a kosher animal that is not mentioned elsewhere in the list. While in the summer, the addax is uniformly white over its entire body, in the winter it turns grayish-brown, with only its hindquarters and legs remaining white. On the basis of this understanding of the ancient Greek and Latin translations, many scholars identify the *dishon* as the addax.[9]

One objection raised to this translation of *dishon* is that the addax was never native to the Land of Israel.[10] However, the addax did live in surrounding regions. It was found in Jordan until the end of the nineteenth century and in Egypt until the mid-twentieth century. As such, it would have been known to the Children of Israel in biblical times.

But there is another point to consider. The oryx was an even more familiar animal than the addax, and must also be in the Torah's list of ten kosher animals. The most likely candidate is the *dishon*.

It would therefore seem best to explain *dishon* as a general category including both oryx and addax. They are similar; both are antelope, white in coloration, with long horns that point upwards. But perhaps the primary reference – to borrow a phrase from zoology, the "type specimen" – should be taken as the oryx, since that is the animal native to the Land of Israel.

The scimitar-horned oryx was once widespread in northern Africa but is now extinct in the wild

The Oryx of Israel

The Arabian oryx is the smallest member of the oryx family. It stands a little over three feet tall at the shoulder, and weighs around 150 pounds, with horns measuring around two feet in length. Its horns are so symmetrical that, from the side, it appears to only have one horn; indeed, in the past, it was claimed that the oryx only has one horn, and it seems to have contributed to the legend of the unicorn.[11]

Oryx possess extraordinary adaptations which enable them to survive in the desert. They keep themselves hydrated in the desert heat by feeding at night, when the vegetation absorbs more moisture from the air. They also breathe very deeply at night, in order to absorb moisture from the air.[12] Their white coat, which reflects the sun, is made up of hollow hairs which act as insulation against heat.[13]

Nevertheless, in the brutal desert conditions, an oryx will still become very hot, with its body temperature rising as high as 113 degrees Fahrenheit. The oryx's ability to withstand temperatures that would kill other animals is still not fully understood by biologists. However, in part the oryx survives the extreme heat by ensuring that its brain does not get as hot as the rest of its body. It accomplishes this through an amazing cranial cooling system. As the blood enters the oryx's head, it enters a special network of arteries. These transmit its heat to an adjacent network of veins carrying blood that has been cooled via the flow of air in the oryx's nasal passages.

The Arabian oryx used to be common across the Middle East. Rock carvings depicting the hunting of oryx, which date back over three thousand years, can be seen in Timna Valley near Eilat. But the oryx became a favored target for Arab hunters, and it disappeared from the Land of Israel before the First World War. With the invention of the rifle and the jeep from which to shoot it, the oryx became entirely extinct in the wild by the mid-twentieth century. However, a handful of captive Arabian oryx remained in private game collections of Arab royalty. A British conservation group tried to bring them to Israel, but political pressures prevented it, and in 1963 the nine oryx were instead brought to the Phoenix zoo, where they bred readily and began to be distributed amongst various zoos.

General Avraham Yoffe, the legendary first head of the Israel Nature and Parks Authority, was determined to return the oryx to the Land of Israel.[14] He detested the name "Arabian oryx," insisting that "we shall not call them by the name of the people who have presided over their near extinction!" Yoffe preferred to instead call them "biblical oryx," arguing

Two gemsbok oryx jousting

that they were first mentioned in the Bible, and tried desperately to obtain some. However, due to the Arab source of the oryx at the Phoenix zoo, Israel was not permitted to receive any. But in 1967 the Los Angeles Zoo obtained a pair of Arabian oryx from Saudi Arabia, and managed to breed them. In 1978, as a result of the personal friendship between the president of the zoo's society and General Yoffe, four pairs of oryx were sent to the Hai-Bar nature reserve in the Arava desert. Today, there are Arabian oryx in several zoos in Israel, and dozens have been released into the wild. Many biblical animals have disappeared from the Land of Israel; the oryx was the first to re-appear.

The Shofar of the Oryx

———————————————— LAW AND RITUAL

The horns of the southern African oryx (*Oryx gazella*), also known as the gemsbok, are sometimes made into shofars. They make striking instruments; long, straight, and deep brown or black in color. Such shofars have recently become widely available, and are sometimes sold with a sticker attesting to rabbinic certification.

But are they kosher for such usage? In Jewish law, the ideal horn to use for a shofar for Rosh HaShana is that of a ram.[15] The ram is reminiscent of Abraham's binding of Isaac, which is an important aspect on the Day of Judgment. Some authorities maintain that one is obligated to use a ram's horn, if it is available.[16] Others are of the view that while the ram's horn is the preferred way to fulfill the mitzva, one can still choose to fulfill one's obligation with a shofar made from the horns of other animals.[17]

Yet there is another serious drawback. The Talmud rules that the shofar for Rosh HaShana should be made from a bent horn (such as that of a ram), since "on Rosh HaShana, the more one bends oneself (in contrition), the better."[18] It should be noted that while this is ruled to be the way in which one should perform the mitzva, if one blows shofar with a straight shofar, one has fulfilled the obligation.[19] Nevertheless, from the outset, if one has a choice between a straight and curved shofar, one is obligated to use the shofar that is curved. As such, if one has a choice (which, with the abundance of ram's horn shofars available, is always the case today), one may not use an oryx shofar. ∎

◀ *Arabian oryx at the Hai-Bar nature reserve*

Notes

1 Dishon also appears in the Torah as an Edomite name (Gen. 36:21, 25 and 1 Chr. 1:41).

2 Rav Saadia Gaon translates *dishon* with the Arabic name *aruy*, which means "ram," and is presumed to refer to the Barbary sheep, *Ammotragus lervia*, also known as the aoudad.

3 *Onkelos, Targum Yerushalmi, Peshita.*

4 In several instances, Rav Saadia Gaon identifies the *re'em* with the Arabic *rim*. See too *Tosafot* to Zevachim 113b s.v. *Urzila d'rima.*

5 Yehuda Feliks, "*Re'em, Teo, VeShor HaBar,*" *Leshonenu* (5740) 44:2, pp. 124–137; ibid., *Nature and Man in the Bible*, p. 263; Menachem Dor, *HaChai BiYemei HaMikra, HaMishna VeHaTalmud*, p. 37.

6 It seems that by the time the Midrash was written, the aurochs had largely or entirely become extinct in that area. Accordingly, the name *re'em* (and its local variants of *rim* and *rimu*) was transferred to another animal with impressive horns: the oryx. See Elkanah Bialik, "*Re'em,*" *Bet Mikra* 54 (1972/3), pp. 382–386; Yehuda Feliks, "*Re'em, Teo, VeShor HaBar,*" pp. 124–137.

7 Menachem Dor, *HaChai BiYemei HaMikra, HaMishna VeHaTalmud*, p. 37; Zohar Amar, Ram Bouchnick, and Guy Bar-Oz, "The Contribution of Archaeozoology to the Identification of the Ritually Clean Ungulates Mentioned in the Hebrew Bible," *Journal of Hebrew Scriptures* (2010), 10:1.

8 Menachem Dor, *HaChai BiYemei HaMikra, HaMishna VeHaTalmud*, p. 37.

9 Bochart bases the identification on it being white-rumped. Tristram, *The Natural History of the Bible* (Pygarg, pp. 126–7), who was unaware of its winter coloration, still identified the *dishon* as the addax via a process of elimination. The Israeli zoologists Aharoni, Bodenheimer, and Feliks all identify the *dishon* as the addax.

10 Menachem Dor, *HaChai BiYemei HaMikra, HaMishna VeHaTalmud*, p. 37, and Amar, Bouchnick, and Bar-Oz, "The Contribution of Archaeozoology to the Identification of the Ritually Clean Ungulates Mentioned in the Hebrew Bible," 10:1.

11 For further discussion, see *Sacred Monsters* by this author.

12 Chris Lavers, *Why Elephants Have Big Ears: Understanding Patterns of Life on Earth*, pp. 117–119.

13 Bill Clark, "The White Oryx Antelope," *Israel – Land and Nature* (1987), pp. 60–64.

14 A lengthy and amusing account can be found in Bill Clark, *High Hills and Wild Goats: Life Among the Animals of the Hai-Bar Wildlife Refuge*, pp. 180–200. See too Bill Clark, "The Biblical Oryx – A New Name for an Ancient Animal," *Biblical Archaeology Review* 10:05, Sep/Oct 1984.

15 Rosh HaShana 16a.

16 *Mishneh Torah, Hilkhot Shofar* 1:1; *Shulchan Aruch, Orach Chayim* 586:1.

17 *Tur, Orach Chayim* 586:1.

18 Rosh HaShana 26b.

19 *Shulchan Arukh, Orach Chayim* 586:1.

NATAN SLIFKIN

A shofar made from an oryx

AUROCHS

Aurochs

Re'em, Teo, Shor HaBar

ראם, תאו, שור הבר

The Legend of the Unicorn

— IDENTIFICATION

The *re'em* is an animal that appears on numerous occasions throughout Scripture. There is much popular confusion about its identity, with some English translations rendering it as "unicorn," and others simply leaving it untranslated. But in fact, the *re'em* can be identified with a great degree of certainty.

Our investigation begins with Balaam's blessing to the Jewish people:

> God brought them out of Egypt, He has as it were the *to'afot* of a *re'em*. (Num. 23:22, 24:8)

The phrase "He has as though the *to'afot* of a *re'em*" has been translated in several different ways, such as "He has as His highest expression of strength"[1] or "He is like the mighty mountains."[2] But many explain that the *re'em* here refers to an animal.[3]

The Septuagint translates *re'em* as "*monokeros*." The Greek *keros* means "horn," and *mono* means "one"; thus, a *monokeros* is an animal with a single horn. Several rabbinic authorities adopted the Septuagint's translation and explained the *re'em* to be a single-horned animal.[4] The phrase "*to'afot* of a *re'em*" is thus sometimes translated as "the glory of a unicorn" or "the strength of a unicorn."[5]

However, the one-horned animal being described by the Septuagint need not be the mythical unicorn;[6] instead, it could be the Indian rhinoceros.[7] If the writers of the Septuagint were referring to the rhinoceros, then it was probably because the *re'em* is described as a horned animal of renown with legendary power. At the time that the Septuagint was written, this was a description that might have seemed to be best matched by the rhinoceros.

But postulating that the rhinoceros is the *re'em* of Scripture involves severe difficulties. The *re'em* is used extensively in Scripture to convey metaphoric imagery and must therefore have been a familiar creature, while the rhinoceros is not found anywhere in biblical lands. Second, the rhinoceros is not a kosher animal; it neither possesses split hooves nor chews the cud. The *re'em*, on the other hand, is generally considered to be one of the kosher animals listed

אֵל מוֹצִיאָם מִמִּצְרַיִם כְּתוֹעֲפֹת רְאֵם לוֹ:

במדבר כג:כב

אֵל מוֹצִיאוֹ מִמִּצְרַיִם כְּתוֹעֲפֹת רְאֵם לוֹ יֹאכַל גּוֹיִם צָרָיו וְעַצְמֹתֵיהֶם

יְגָרֵם וְחִצָּיו יִמְחָץ:

במדבר כד:ח

בְּכוֹר שׁוֹרוֹ הָדָר לוֹ וְקַרְנֵי רְאֵם קַרְנָיו בָּהֶם עַמִּים יְנַגַּח יַחְדָּו אַפְסֵי

אָרֶץ וְהֵם רִבְבוֹת אֶפְרַיִם וְהֵם אַלְפֵי מְנַשֶּׁה:

דברים לג:יז

in Deuteronomy (albeit under a different name), as we shall see later.[8] Furthermore, the reason why the rhinoceros was suggested in the first place to be the *re'em* is that it possesses a single horn, and thus matches the Septuagint's translation of *monokeros*. However, Scripture itself indicates that the *re'em* possesses more than one horn:

> His firstborn ox, grandeur is his, and his horns are like the horns of a *re'em*; with them he shall push the people together to the ends of the earth; and they are the myriads of Ephraim, and they are the thousands of Menasheh. (Deut. 33:17)

The verse speaks of the *horns* of the *re'em*, in the plural; and it also speaks of the horns correlating with the two tribes of Ephraim and Menasheh.[9] Accordingly, the *re'em*

While the rhinoceros may well be the monokeros *of the Septuagint, it is surely not the* re'em *of Scripture.*

278

NEELSKY / SHUTTERSTOCK

must be a two-horned animal rather than a unicorn. A further clue as to its identity can be found in other places where Scripture mentions the *re'em*:

> You raised my *keren* (literally, "horn"; metaphorically, "pride") like that of the *re'em*. (Ps. 92:11)

The description of pride being raised up like the horns of the *re'em* indicates that the horns of the *re'em* were not just magnificent, but also upwards-pointing. But which animal could it be?

In several instances, Rav Saadia Gaon identifies the *re'em* with the Arabic *rim*, which is the oryx.[10] The oryx would also match the Midrash's description of the *re'em* not being strong like an ox:

> "His firstborn ox, grandeur is his, and his horns are like the horns of a *re'em*" – The ox is of great strength, but its horns are not beautiful; the horns of a *re'em* are beautiful, but it is not strong; he thus gave to Joshua the strength of an ox and the horns of a *re'em*. (Sifrei, *Vezot HaBerakha* 12)

Accordingly, some posit that the *re'em* is the oryx, and it is thus named in Modern Hebrew. However, other descriptions of the *re'em* do not match the oryx. In one instance, we see that the *re'em* (here called *reimim* in the plural) is regarded as a dangerous animal, which does not comport with the shy and elusive oryx:

> You saved me from the mouth of the lion, and You answered me from the horns of the *reimim*. (Ps. 22:22)

Furthermore, other verses indicate that the *re'em* is an animal with similarities to domestic cattle. There is a constant juxtaposition or thematic comparison between the *re'em* and domestic cattle. Earlier, we saw the verse which states that "His firstborn ox, grandeur is his, and his horns

PROTASOV / SHUTTERSTOCK

An Arabian oryx, identified by some as the re'em

וַתָּרֶם כִּרְאֵים קַרְנִי בַּלֹּתִי בְּשֶׁמֶן רַעֲנָן:

תהלים צב:יא

הוֹשִׁיעֵנִי מִפִּי אַרְיֵה וּמִקַּרְנֵי רֵמִים עֲנִיתָנִי:

תהלים כב:כב

וְיָרְדוּ רְאֵמִים עִמָּם וּפָרִים עִם אַבִּירִים וְרִוְּתָה אַרְצָם מִדָּם וַעֲפָרָם מֵחֵלֶב יְדֻשָּׁן:

ישעיה לד:ז

וַיַּרְקִידֵם כְּמוֹ עֵגֶל לְבָנוֹן וְשִׂרְיֹן כְּמוֹ בֶן רְאֵמִים:

תהלים כט:ו

הֲיֹאבֶה רֵּים עָבְדֶךָ אִם יָלִין עַל אֲבוּסֶךָ: הֲתִקְשָׁר רֵים בְּתֶלֶם עֲבֹתוֹ אִם יְשַׂדֵּד עֲמָקִים אַחֲרֶיךָ: הֲתִבְטַח בּוֹ כִּי רַב כֹּחוֹ וְתַעֲזֹב אֵלָיו יְגִיעֶךָ: הֲתַאֲמִין בּוֹ כִּי יָשִׁיב זַרְעֶךָ וְגָרְנְךָ יֶאֱסֹף:

איוב לט:ט-יב

are like the horns of a *re'em*" (Deut. 33:17). Other verses echo this theme:

> And *re'emim* shall come down with them, and the steers with the bulls. (Is. 34:7)

> And He caused them to dance like calves; Levanon and Siryon like the young of the *re'em*. (Ps. 29:6)

In the story of Job, the protagonist seeks to understand why terrible suffering has befallen him. God's response is to convey to Job the limitations of man, such that he should not expect to understand the divine plan. As part of this lesson, God contrasts the impossibility of domesticating the *re'em* (here called *reim*) with the work that can be obtained with an ox, thereby illustrating another aspect of the limits of man:

> Would the *reim* be willing to serve you? Would he stay at your feeding-trough? Can you bind the *reim* with ropes to the furrow? Will he level the valleys after you? Would you trust him, because his strength is great, and would you leave your labor to him? Would you believe in him to bring home your seed, and gather it into your barn? (Job 39:9–12)

This contrast actually indicates a similarity with the domestic ox; one only contrasts things which share some sort of fundamental similarity. We further see that the *re'em* is described as an animal possessing great strength (which does not match the oryx).

Some translate the *re'em* as buffalo. This could refer to any one of several entirely different species, but none are viable candidates for the *re'em*. The very impressive African buffalo (*Syncerus caffer*) is native only to sub-Saharan Africa and is therefore presumably not a candidate. The American "buffalo" (*Bison bison*) and the very similar European bison (*Bison bonasus*) did not live in biblical lands during the biblical period; the closest population of bison was

The European bison (at left) and the Asian water buffalo (at right) were not native to biblical lands

in the Caucasus. The Asian water buffalo (*Bubalus arnee*) apparently first appeared in biblical lands only in the eighth century of the Common Era.[11] Thus, the *re'em* is not any kind of buffalo.

From all the references in Scripture, we know the following about the *re'em*: It is similar to domestic cattle, but it is a powerful, dangerous animal, and it possesses two magnificent, upwards-pointing horns. There is an animal that perfectly matches this description, and is even called *rimu* in Akkadian: the aurochs, *Bos primigenius*.

The Mighty Aurochs

——————————— NATURAL HISTORY

The aurochs (pronounced "oar-ox," plural aurochses or aurochsen, and also known as the urus) was a huge wild ox that is familiar to few people today, because it became extinct in 1627. However, due to the recent date of their extinction, we know a lot about them – from descriptions, drawings, and skeletal remains.

Aurochsen are the ancestors of modern cattle, and thus are basically similar to them, which is why Scripture frequently juxtaposes the two. But they were much bigger than domestic cattle; fossil remains indicate that bulls stood six feet at the shoulder and weighed over three thousand pounds. The Roman general Julius Caesar noted that while the aurochs was of "the appearance, color, and shape of a bull," it is "a little below the elephant in size."[12] As we shall see later, there are rabbinic accounts of the *re'em* being gigantic in size; it was certainly the largest land animal throughout much of its range.

Their horns were massive; up to eight inches in diameter and thirty inches in length, and thus suitable for the blessings that "they are the glory (or strength) of the aurochs to Him" (Num. 23:22) and "his horns are like the horns of an aurochs" (Deut. 33:17). The horns pointed forwards and

upwards, as per King David's description of his pride being "raised like the horns of the aurochs" (Ps. 92:11). These horns could be lethal weapons; hence David's expression of gratitude that he was saved "from the horns of the aurochs" (Ps. 22:21).

Aurochsen differed from domestic cattle not only in their form, but also in their behavior. They possessed aggressive dispositions, which, coupled with their great power and horns, made them formidable opponents. Caesar wrote that "their strength and speed are extraordinary; they spare neither man nor wild beast which they have espied.... They cannot be rendered familiar to men and tamed even when taken very young." This perfectly matches the description in God's speech to Job, where He describes an animal that would be superb for agriculture, were it not for the fact that it is untamable.

In biblical times, aurochsen lived in Europe, central Asia, and North Africa. However, they were hunted extensively. By the time of the Mishna and Talmud, they had largely or entirely become extinct in the southern part of their range. It seems that at this time, the name *re'em* (and its local variants of *rim* and *rimu*) was transferred to another animal with impressive horns: the oryx.[13] Thus, the midrash which describes the horns of the *re'em* as being beautiful, but not strong, was indeed referring to the oryx rather than aurochs. But traditions regarding the original *re'em* persisted, resulting in other accounts in the Midrash portraying the *re'em* as being a creature of monstrous size:

> "Save me from the mouth of the lion as you have answered me from the horns of *reimim*" (Ps. 22:22). When David was grazing the sheep, he came across a *re'em* sleeping in the wilderness. Thinking it was a mountain, he climbed upon it to watch the sheep. The *re'em* shook itself and awoke, and David was riding upon it, and reached the heavens. At that moment David prayed, "If You take

me down from this *re'em*, I will build You a temple one hundred cubits in height, like the horn of this *re'em*." Some say he measured it by its length, others say that he measured it by its width. What did the Holy One do? He summoned a lion; when the *re'em* saw the lion, it was afraid, and crouched down before it, because it is the king; and David descended to the ground. (*Midrash Tehillim* 102)

By the early medieval period, the aurochs only remained in small numbers in Eastern Europe, and the transfer of the name *re'em* to more familiar animals continued. The rabbinic scholars of that period noted that animals which were commonly referred to as *re'em* (probably water buffalo) could not be the biblical *re'em*, since they did not match the biblical descriptions.[14] But it was not until the nineteenth century that the aurochs, rediscovered through ancient accounts, drawings, and fossil remains, was realized to be the *re'em*.

Lofty Power and Grandeur

SYMBOLISM

As noted earlier, the aurochs appears in Moses' blessing to the tribes of Ephraim and Menasheh:

His firstborn ox, grandeur is his, and his horns are like the horns of an aurochs; with them he shall push the people together to the ends of the earth; and they are the myriads of Ephraim, and they are the thousands of Menasheh. (Deut. 33:17)

The ox and the aurochs in this verse are correlated with the tribes of Ephraim and Menasheh respectively, with each appearing on the banner of the corresponding tribe:

On the banner of the tribe of Menasheh, there was an illustration of an aurochs, due to "his horns are like the horns of an aurochs"; and due to Gideon son of Yoash, who was from the tribe of Menasheh. (*Bemidbar Rabba* 2:7)

The Midrash here also connects the aurochs to Gideon, who was a powerful hero. This is consistent with the imagery of the aurochs as a symbol of power, with horns representing lofty grandeur.

You raised my *keren* (literally, "horn"; metaphorically, "pride") like that of the aurochs. (Ps. 92:11)

When King David sings that God raised his pride like that of the aurochs, he is not just seeking a symbol of something that points upwards. Horns are always the "pride" of an animal, which is why the Hebrew word *keren* has both meanings, but David is not merely referring to the horns of the aurochs for their shape. Rather, the bearer of these horns, the aurochs itself, also symbolizes the grandeur that God bestowed upon David. The powerful animal and its majestic horns are inseparable in such a motif.

A painting of an aurochs at the Lascaux cave in France

The domestic ox possesses a great degree of strength, and is rated as the "king" of domestic animals – it appears on the Divine Chariot, along with the lion, king of beasts, and the vulture, king of birds. The aurochs, as a wild animal, cannot be the king of its class, since that position is taken by the lion. But it still occupies an important position, which may explain why it is sometimes juxtaposed with the lion: "You saved me from the mouth of the lion, and You answered me from the horns of the aurochs" (Ps. 22:21). In fact, some relate the name *re'em* to the word *ram*, meaning "high."[15] This could refer either to its upwards-pointing horns, or to its lofty status. Recall that the verse "God brought them out of Egypt, He has as though the *to'afot* of a *re'em*" (Num. 23:2) is translated by some not to be referring to an animal, but instead to mean that "He has as His highest expression of strength"[16] or "He is like the mighty mountains." The *re'em* is symbolically and etymologically related to loftiness, power, and mighty mountains.

The Mega-Aurochs of Legend

As we saw earlier, the Midrash presents David as having mistaken an aurochs for a mountain. The Talmud likewise presents an account of an aurochs – just a newborn calf – being the size of a mountain:

> Rabba bar bar Chana said, "I myself saw a young aurochs one day old, and it was the size of Mount Tabor. And how big is Mount Tabor? Forty parasangs. The length of its neck was three parasangs; the resting place for its head was a parasang and a half. It excreted dung and dammed the Jordan River." (Bava Batra 73b)

There were some commentators who interpreted such accounts as referring to a factual reality; some accepted that they were deliberately exaggerated.[17] But many others concluded that these accounts are to be understood allegorically and not literally.

The Gaon of Vilna explained that Rabba bar bar Chana's story is a parable for an overly conceited young Torah scholar, metaphorically described as possessing the horns of an aurochs for fighting the intellectual battles of Torah study. He is compared to Mount Tabor, which the Midrash elsewhere describes as arrogantly wanting to be the place on which the Torah would be given. Forty parasangs, given as the size of Mount Tabor, corresponds to the last forty years of a person's life, following his attaining "thirty years for strength,"[18] and alludes to this student's imagining that he has traveled the full route through maturity. His

An image of an aurochs from the Ishtar Gate of Babylon

The skeleton of an aurochs at the Danish National Museum

head is in the clouds, which are three parasangs above the ground; this is alluded to with the statement that the young auroch's neck was three parasangs long. The description of the resting place of his head being one and a half parasangs alludes to the distance from the edge of the wilderness encampment to Moses' tent at the center, where this person imagines that his status lies. But he never receives the honor that he imagines himself to deserve, and so he responds by trying to destroy the reputation of others. This is represented by his obstructing the flow of the Jordan with his excrement.[19]

But did the Talmud itself understand this account to be allegorical? This passage is cited in a different tractate where it is used in a technical context that is seemingly very literal. The Talmud, in discussing whether the Deluge extended to Israel, raises the question of how the aurochs survived the Deluge if it was not able to take refuge there:

> It is well according to the one that says that the Deluge did not descend to the Land of Israel, and thus the aurochs survived there. But according to the one who says that the Deluge did descend there, where did the aurochs survive? R. Yannai said: They brought calves into the Ark. But surely Rabba bar bar Chana said, "I myself saw a young aurochs one day old, and it was the size of Mount Tabor. And how big is Mount Tabor? Forty parasangs. The length of its neck was three parasangs; the resting place for its head was a parasang and a half. It excreted dung and clogged the Jordan." R. Yochanan said: They inserted its head into the Ark. But the master has said that the resting place for its head was a parasang and a half! Rather, they inserted the tip of its nose into the Ark.... But the Ark was moving! Resh Lakish said: They tied its horns to the Ark. (Zevachim 113b)

This sounds as though the Talmud understood Rabba bar bar Chana's story to be a literal account. However, even here, Rabbi Yosef Chayim (better known as the Ben Ish

Chai) argues that it is not intended to be a literal description of factual reality. Rather, the Sages of the Talmud took the allegory and played it out at face value, to sharpen the minds of their students.[20]

Whether in legend or reality, the aurochs was the largest animal in the region. As such, it also appeared in an aphorism describing the extent of God's providence for the world.

> He sits and sustains everything, from the horns of aurochsen to the eggs of lice. (Shabbat 107b and Avoda Zara 3b)

The phrase describes how God sustains all creatures, from the largest to the smallest, and thus mentions the aurochs. One may wonder why it does not simply state "from aurochsen to lice" – why does it speak of aurochsen horns and lice eggs? One suggestion is that this is because there is a connection between aurochsen horns and lice eggs – the former were used as a raw material from which to make combs to remove the latter![21] Alternately, and perhaps more straightforwardly, the horns of the aurochsen are its most majestic aspect, and the eggs of lice are their smallest aspect, thus enhancing the contrast.

The *Teo*: Wild Ox Confusion

IDENTIFICATION

The aurochs also appears in the Torah under another name. Amongst the ten types of kosher mammals listed in the Torah, one is named the *teo*:

> This is the animal which you shall eat: cattle, young sheep, and young goats; the deer, the gazelle, the hartebeest, the ibex, the oryx, the *teo* (תאו), and the wild sheep. (Deut. 14:4–5)

This *teo* is also mentioned elsewhere in Scripture, with the variant spelling of *t'o*:[22]

> Awake, awake, stand up, O Jerusalem, who has drunk at the hand of the Lord the cup of his fury; you have drunk to the dregs the bowl of staggering.... Your sons have fainted, they lie at the head of all the streets, as a *t'o* (תוא) in a net; they are full of the fury of the Lord, the rebuke of your God. (Is. 51:17, 20)

אַיָּל וּצְבִי וְיַחְמוּר וְאַקּוֹ וְדִישֹׁן וּתְאוֹ וָזָמֶר:

דברים יד:ה

בָּנַיִךְ עֻלְּפוּ שָׁכְבוּ בְּרֹאשׁ כָּל חוּצוֹת כְּתוֹא מִכְמָר הַמְלֵאִים חֲמַת יְהֹוָה גַּעֲרַת אֱלֹהָיִךְ:

ישעיה נא:כ

A recreation of an aurochs battling wolves

The Septuagint and Vulgate render the *teo* of Deuteronomy's kosher list as the oryx. However, as noted in the previous chapter, it seems that the oryx was already mentioned previously in the Torah's list. Likewise, while some suggest that the *teo* is the hartebeest,[23] it appears that the hartebeest was already mentioned in the Torah's list, under the name *yachmur*. The *teo* is often interpreted as referring to a type of buffalo, but as we noted earlier, there was no type of buffalo living in biblical lands during the biblical period.

The notion that the *teo* is a buffalo appears to stem from the Aramaic translations of the Torah. These render *teo* as *torbala* or *torbara*, which literally means "ox of the wild."[24] Since buffalo are bovines, it was assumed that they are the "wild ox" of Scripture. However, the aurochs is a far superior candidate for the name "wild ox." With the extinction of the aurochs in the seventeenth century, and the subsequent confusion regarding various animal names, it is entirely understandable that this identification is largely unknown. (Indeed, some early scholars of biblical zoology, even while identifying the *teo* as the aurochs, conflated the aurochs with the European bison, which probably also contributed to the idea that the *teo* is a "buffalo."[25]) With the knowledge available today, it appears correct to identify the *teo* as the aurochs.[26] This is also the view of R. Yose in the Talmud, as we shall later discuss.

Some biblical scholars (generally Christian or secular scholars) are of the view that the *teo* cannot be the aurochs, since the aurochs has a different name, i.e. *re'em*. But according to the dominant view in the Talmud, the list of kosher animals in Deuteronomy is exhaustive. Even if it does not encompass every species of kosher animal in the planet, it is surely presenting a comprehensive list of kosher animals that were available for the Jewish people. The aurochs, which is a kosher animal, must be in the list somewhere; hence, it must be that it is listed under a different name. In English, an animal can have different names in different contexts; dog/hound, cougar/panther, donkey/ass. Perhaps *teo*

is the technical Hebrew name for the aurochs, while *re'em* is used in poetic contexts.

The "Wild Ox" of the Talmud

IDENTIFICATION

An intricate problem in Jewish law reveals the difficulty of drawing the line between domestic and wild animals. The Sages of the Talmud discuss the status of an animal called *shor habar*, literally "ox of the wild" or "wild ox." There is a dispute as to whether this wild ox is to be defined as a domestic or wild animal in Jewish law:

> The wild ox is a domestic animal. But R. Yose[27] says, it is a wild animal. (Mishna Kilayim 8:6)

According to the Tosefta (a supplementary text to the Mishna), this correlates with a dispute as to whether this wild ox is to be identified as the *teo* of the Torah.

> Five things were stated with regard to the wild ox: It can fall under the prohibition of slaughtering mother and young on the same day; its fat is prohibited; it can be sacrificed on the altar; it is obligated in [its parts being given as] gifts [to the priest]; and it can be purchased with tithed moneys for peace-offerings, but not as meat for satiation; and it is rated as a domestic animal in every way. R. Yose said: It is the *teo* mentioned in the Torah, and it does not fall under the prohibition of slaughtering mother and young on the same day; its fat is permitted; it cannot be sacrificed on the altar; it is exempt from [its parts being given as] gifts [to the priest]; and it can be purchased with tithed moneys for satiation, but not as peace-offerings; ... and it is rated as a wild animal in every way. And the Sages said: The *teo* and the wild ox are distinct animals. (Tosefta, Kilayim 1:6)

A model of an aurochs at Paleosite in Saint-Cesaire

The Jerusalem Talmud likewise correlates the dispute between the Rabbis and R. Yose with the issue of whether the wild ox is the *teo*. According to the Rabbis, the wild ox is simply a domestic ox that has become feral, whereas according to R. Yose, it is a different type of animal, being the *teo* of the Torah:

> "The wild ox is a domestic animal" (– Mishna). The Rabbis say: It was from here (human settlement), and it fled to the wild.[28] R. Yose says: It was always from the wild. Thus, [according to the Rabbis,] an ox with a wild ox is not a forbidden mixture. And this is not in accordance with R. Yose; for R. Yose says that it is a forbidden mixture. And they who translate [the *teo* of Deuteronomy] as "the *turi-bar* (wild ox)" are of the same view as R. Yose. (Y. Kilayim 8:6)

According to the Babylonian Talmud, on the other hand, although the Rabbis who oppose R. Yose maintain that the "wild ox" is a domestic animal, they still identify it as the *teo* of Scripture. According to the Rabbis, the *teo* is a domestic animal that is placed among wild animals in the Torah's list of kosher creatures:

> These wild goats – what is their ruling regarding the altar (i.e. are they rated as domestic or wild animals)? ... The Rabbis and R. Yose only disagree regarding the wild ox, as we have learned in a mishna: (The Rabbis say:) The wild ox is a domestic animal. R. Yose says: It is a wild animal. The Rabbis reason that since it is translated as *tor-bala* ("wild ox"), it is a type of domestic animal, and R. Yose reasons that since it is listed among the wild animals, it is a wild animal. But with these wild goats, everyone says that they are a type of (domestic) goat. (Chullin 80a)

The identity of this "wild ox" is not clear; it is most likely to be the aurochs, but it may refer to some sort of feral cattle (or possibly the Asian water buffalo, which was a familiar animal in the talmudic era). With all three of these, there are reasonable grounds for the Sages to classify them either as domestic species (that have since become feral), or wild species. This is even true of the aurochs; if, according to modern zoologists, it is the *ancestor* of domestic cattle, then it is not unreasonable for the Rabbis to posit that it is the *descendant* of domestic cattle and rated in the same category.

The Return of the *Re'em*

NATURAL HISTORY

In the previous section, we saw that the Sages could not reach a consensus regarding whether the wild ox – which may be the aurochs or feral cattle – is classified as a domestic or wild animal. The line between aurochs and domestic cattle is difficult to draw, from any perspective. Contemporary biologists, tracing the ancestry of domestic cattle to the aurochs, differ as to whether domestic cattle should be rated as a subspecies of the aurochs, or as an entirely different species.

The lack of a clear dividing line between domestic cattle and the wild aurochs does, however, present an interesting opportunity. It means that it may be possible to reconstitute the extinct aurochs. This could be done via selective back-breeding of domestic cattle.

Such a project was started in the 1920s by the German brothers Heinz and Lutz Heck.[29] Unfortunately, their motives were related to Nazi ideology, in trying to recover the "racial purity" of Aryan wildlife and demonstrate its strength. Furthermore, their methods involved looting animals from zoos in countries that Germany conquered. Their efforts were in any case unsuccessful; the resultant animals, known as Heck cattle, are smaller than aurochsen and possess a less athletic build, amongst other differences.

More promising projects are the Polish Foundation for Recreating the Aurochs and the Tauros Programme.[30] These are looking for gene sequences in breeds of primitive cattle that match those found in DNA from the remains of aurochs, and then to selectively breed those cattle in order to combine and reinforce those characteristics that are shared with aurochsen. This should result in an animal that in both appearance and behavior very closely resembles the original aurochs. The resulting cattle will be placed in the wild, to fill the ecological niche of the aurochs. The results are already promising; one young animal already has the coloration of aurochs, with a black coat and a lighter dorsal stripe. One day, the biblical *re'em* may raise its horns again. ∎

A Heck bull – a failed attempt to recreate the aurochs

Notes

1 Rashi, *Targum*.

2 *Lekach Tov*.

3 Rav Saadia Gaon, Ibn Ezra, Radak, Rabbeinu Bechaya, *Daat Zekeinim*, Seforno, Ibn Janach, *HaKetav VeHaKabbala*, *Haamek Davar*.

4 See e.g. Radak, *Sefer HaShorashim*, *Re'em*; Rabbi Hezkiah ben David DeSilva, *Peri Chadash*, *Orach Chayim* 80:1:2. Rav Saadia Gaon also seems to follow this view, translating the *re'em* in this verse as the *karkadan*, which is the name of the unicorn in Arabian legend.

5 For example, in the King James Bible.

6 For extensive discussions of the unicorn in Jewish sources, see *Sacred Monsters* (Jerusalem: Zoo Torah/ Gefen Books, 2011) by this author.

7 Avraham ben Hananiah Yagel (1553–1623), an Italian kabbalist and philosopher who wrote a treatise on natural history which included a lengthy discussion of unicorns, likewise described a rhinoceros with the name *re'em* (*Beit Yaar HaLevanon*, Book IV, chapters 45 and 46, pp. 106b–112a).

8 See *Tosafot* to Zevachim 113b s.v. *Urzila d'rima*. There were, however, some who argued that the *re'em* is a non-kosher animal. See *Peri Chadash* (*Orach Chayim* 80:1:2).

9 Radak nevertheless maintains that the *re'em* possesses only one horn, and asserts that this verse is to be read loosely, as though it states *re'emim* in the plural. But this is not a straightforward explanation; and Rabbi Eliyahu Ashkenazi, in his response to Radak, instead concludes from this verse that the *re'em* does indeed possess more than one horn.

10 This identification is also followed by Bochart in the *Hierozoïcon*. Curiously, though, in Deuteronomy 33:17 Rav Saadia Gaon explains it to refer to the *karkadan*, which refers to either the unicorn or rhinoceros.

11 Zohar Amar and Yaron Seri, "When Did the Water Buffalo Make Its Appearance in Israel?" (Hebrew), *Cathedra* 117 (2005), pp. 63–70.

12 Caesar, *Gallic War*, 6:28.

13 Elkanah Bialik, "Re'em," *Bet Mikra* 54 (1972/3), pp. 382–386; Yehuda Feliks, "Re'em, Teo, VeShor HaBar," *Leshonenu* (5740) 44:2, pp. 124–137.

14 *Tosafot* to Zevachim 113b s.v. *Urzila d'Rima*.

15 Rashi to Numbers 23:22.

16 Rashi, *Targum*.

17 Ramban, *drasha* for Rosh HaShana; Rashbam; Maharsha.

18 Mishna Avot 5:21.

19 Vilna Gaon, commentary on the Aggadot; see too Rashbam. For an English exposition of this approach, see Rabbi Aharon Feldman, *The Juggler and the King*, pp. 46–55.

20 Rabbi Yosef Chayim, *Ben Yehoyada*, Zevachim 113b.

21 Rabbi Yaakov Yisrael Stahl, "A Comb From the Horns of Aurochs to Remove the Eggs of Lice" (Hebrew), *HaMaayan* 51:1 (5771), pp. 69–79.

22 Although the Hebrew word here is *t'o* rather than *teo*, it is generally rated as identical to the *teo* of Deuteronomy, with two of the letters transposed (as sometimes occurs in Hebrew). See Rashi, Ibn Janach, and Radak. The Septuagint, on the other hand, renders the word *t'o* as a vegetable.

23 Suggested to be the view of the Sages by Ishtori HaParchi, *Kaftor VaFerach* ch. 48 (p. 768 in 1899 ed.).

24 *Targum Yerushalmi* has *tori-bar* (תורי־בר) while *Targum Onkelos* has *torbala* (תור־בלא); cf. the *torbala* (תורבלא) of the Talmud. Some understand *bala* to mean "forest"; others understand it to be transposed from the word *bara*, and to mean "the wild."

25 Baruch Linde, *Reishit Limudim*, *shaar* 6; Shalom Yaakov Abramowitz, *Toledot HaTeva*, p. 489. In the eighteenth century, there was one school of thought that there had only ever been one wild bovine in Europe, the European bison. See Ronald Goderie, *The Aurochs: Born To Be Wild* (The Netherlands: Roodbont Publishers, 2013), p. 77.

26 Yosef Schonhak, *Toledot HaAretz*, p. 82; Ludwig Lewysohn, *Die Zoologie des Talmuds*, p. 127 (though he mistakenly believes that the aurochs had fourteen pairs of ribs, like bison, and was not the ancestor of domestic cattle); Zohar Amar, Ram Bouchnick, and Guy Bar-Oz, "The Contribution of Archaeozoology to the Identification of the Ritually Clean Ungulates Mentioned in the Hebrew Bible," *Journal of Hebrew Scriptures* (2010), 10:1. For a survey of different opinions, see Elkanah Bialik, "HaTeo VeHaT'o," *Bet Mikra* 20 (Jerusalem: Tammuz 5716); Yehuda Feliks, "Re'em, Teo, VeShor HaBar," *Leshonenu* (5740) 44:2, pp. 124–137. Feliks prefers not to identify the *teo* as the aurochs, as he considers that it must be different from the *re'em*, and identifies it instead as the European bison. However, as noted, it does not appear that the bison lived anywhere near biblical lands. Furthermore, as we shall discuss, the *teo* could well be identical with the *re'em*.

27 R. Yose appears to have had a particular sensitivity to zoological matters. He differentiates apes from other animals (Mishna Kilayim 8:5) and observes that the *koy* (probably the water buffalo) is an independent species (Chullin 80a).

28 Contrast Malbim to Genesis 1:28, 2:20, 7:3, and Leviticus 11:2, who states that domestic animals are all descended from wild animals.

29 See Diane Ackerman, *The Zookeeper's Wife* (London: W.W. Norton, 2007), pp. 80–86, 91–93, 317–321.

30 See Ronald Goderie, *The Aurochs: Born To Be Wild* pp. 118–140.

WILD SHEEP

Wild Sheep

The Riddle of the *Zamer*

━━━━━━━━━━━━━━━ IDENTIFICATION

For a land animal to be kosher, it must have split hooves and chew its cud. The Torah lists ten animals that match these requirements:

> This is the animal which you shall eat: cattle, sheep, and goats; the deer, the gazelle, the hartebeest, the ibex, the oryx, the aurochs, and the *zamer*. (Deut. 14:4–5)

Identifying the last animal in this list, the *zamer*, is exceedingly difficult. The word appears nowhere else in Scripture, and there is no such name of an animal in other languages from the region.[1] Contemporary scholars sometimes identify it via process of elimination, ruling out animals that are already mentioned earlier in the list, and selecting whichever animal is left. However, this produces differing results depending upon how the earlier animals in the list are identified, and depending upon how one subsumes animals into existing categories (e.g. whether the roe deer and fallow deer are to be considered as two different types of animal, or the same type).

A further consideration is the degree to which the list is presumed to be exhaustive – whether it includes all kosher animals from the region, or all kosher animals in the world – and thus which animals are required to be mentioned. (Again, this will have differing results depending upon how one subsumes animals into existing categories.)

אַיָּל וּצְבִי וְיַחְמוּר וְאַקּוֹ וְדִישֹׁן וּתְאוֹ וָזָמֶר:
דברים יד:ה

The *zamer* is an opportunity to include an animal that cannot be easily subsumed under the previous animals in the list.

One suggestion is that the *zamer* refers to the wild goat, *Capra aegagrus*. It does not seem to have been found in the Land of Israel, but it did live in nearby areas. However, it seems overwhelmingly probable that the wild goat would be subsumed under the category of the *akko* with the very similar ibex, rather than being listed separately from the ibex and not even adjacent to it.

Still others identify the *zamer* as the hartebeest. This is the result of those who do not identify the *yachmur* as the hartebeest, and who still need to fit the hartebeest somewhere into the list of kosher animals; the *zamer* is selected as the only available option.[2] The Aramaic translation by Onkelos of this animal is *ditza*, a word that elsewhere refers to rejoicing or dancing.[3] Advocates of the hartebeest argue that it refers to the hartebeest "pronking" – a form of movement involving high leaps into the air.

More unlikely suggestions include the moose[4] and chamois,[5] neither of which live anywhere near the Land of Israel. There is also an ancient tradition that the *zamer* is the giraffe. This is not as far-fetched as some would suppose,

The wild goat (left) and the hartebeest (right), identified by some as the zamer

and we shall explore this in the following chapter. However, the most widely accepted view in contemporary academic scholarship is to identify the *zamer* as a type of wild sheep.[6] Identifying the *zamer* as a sheep rather than a giraffe is perhaps also supported by the Talmud, which suggests that a certain "forest goat" may be a variety of *zamer*.[7]

The Leap of the Sheep

Of the various species of wild sheep, the most likely candidate for the *zamer* is the mouflon, *Ovis orientalis*, also known as the urial. It is mostly brown in color, with white lower legs and belly, and a black stripe running down its back. The horns of mature rams are large and tightly curled in almost a full circle. Mouflon are thought to have lived in the Land of Israel during antiquity, based on bones found at two archeological sites. These findings are not conclusive, due to the difficulty of distinguishing mouflon bones from those of domestic sheep. However, mouflon did live in

Jordan, and thus certainly qualify as animals that are part of the biblical landscape. Today, wild mouflon are restricted to a few areas in central Asia. The mouflon is thought to be one of two ancestors of domestic sheep, and in 2001 a mouflon was successfully cloned using a domestic sheep as the surrogate mother.

Another possible contender is the much larger Barbary sheep (also known as the aoudad), *Ammotragus lervia*.[8] The Barbary sheep is distinguished by its sandy-brown coat, shaggy hair extending downwards from the throat, and outwards-curving horns that are triangular in cross-section. However, it is not clear if the Barbary sheep ever lived in the region; it is native to North Africa.

Support for identifying the *zamer* as the wild sheep is based upon the assumption that the Torah's list contains all kosher animals from the region, and thus the wild sheep should appear in the list.[9] Furthermore, it is presumably the case that the animals are listed in order of their prominence, and this is in turn suggested to be based upon their abun-

289

A male (ram) and female (ewe) mouflon

dance. The mouflon was found in the region of the Land of Israel, but apparently only rarely, and thus appears at the end of the list. Placing it after the aurochs might also make thematic sense, in that the domestic sheep is mentioned immediately after the domestic cattle, and the wild sheep (mouflon) would be mentioned immediately after the wild cattle (aurochs). The name *zamer* is suggested by some to mean "cut off" and to relate to the short fur of the mouflon, which appears as though it has been shorn.[10] Alternately, it may be based on the word "song," and relate to the Aramaic translation of *ditza*, meaning "dancing." This would match the wild sheep, which is very agile; the Barbary sheep leaps from rock to rock, and can achieve a standing jump of over seven feet. In this vein, one is reminded of the verse from Psalms describing the leaping of sheep:

> The mountains danced like rams, the hills like young sheep. (Ps. 114:6)

The Wild Sheep in the Talmud
—————————————————— IDENTIFICATION

In a number of places, the Talmud discusses a creature known as the *koy*, the identity of which is unclear. The Talmud presents four different opinions regarding its nature:

> The *koy* is the wild ram; but some say that it is the product of a goat and a gazelle. R. Yose says: The *koy* is a distinct type of creature, and the Sages could not determine if it was a wild or a domestic type of animal. Rabban Shimon b. Gamliel says: It is a type of domestic animal, and the House of Dushai used to raise many herds of them. (Chullin 80a)

These four opinions place the *koy* in four different categories: As a wild animal (if it is a wild ram), as a hybrid of a domestic animal with a wild animal, as a creature that is of indeterminate status, and as a domestic animal. The various possibilities about the *koy* present a number of questions regarding its status in Jewish law.[11] As a result, the *koy* has been a favorite topic of rabbinic discussion for many centuries.

But what actually is the animal under discussion? Adding further complexity to the topic is that it is not clear how to understand the talmudic dispute. Simply speaking, the Sages all had the same particular animal in mind, and were arguing as to its ancestry and status. Yet it has also been proposed that the Sages were not in fact talking about a particular animal, but rather about a conceptual category into which several animals could be fitted.[12] Another suggestion is that the animal being discussed is the domesticated form of the Asian water buffalo, *Bubalus bubalis*, with the Sages arguing about whether it is legally equivalent to a wild ram, to a hybrid of a domestic animal with a wild animal, of indeterminate status, or a domestic animal.[13]

In any case, the first opinion mentioned in the Talmud is that the *koy* is the "wild ram" (or is in the same category as the wild ram, depending on one's understanding of the discussion). Some understand this as referring to the mouflon, which would have been familiar to the Sages of the Babylonian Talmud.[14] Yet it is also possible that it refers to the Barbary sheep, which perhaps looks a little more like a hybrid between a goat and a gazelle. It is not only the status of the *koy* but even its identity that remains unclear. ∎

The Asian water buffalo, identified by some as the koy of the Talmud

◀ *The Barbary sheep, also known as the aoudad*

Notes

1 It seems that even the Sages of the Talmud were uncertain regarding its identity. The sole mention of the *zamer* is in Chullin 80a, where Rav Acha is unclear as to whether the "forest goat" is a type of *zamer*, a type of *teo*, or something else. See Rashi ad loc., who explains that there is uncertainty regarding the identities of these animals.

2 Menachem Dor, *HaChai BiYemei HaMikra, HaMishna VeHaTalmud*, p. 40.

3 Cf. the Aramaic translations to Isaiah 32:13 and Job 3:22.

4 Yosef Schonhak, *Toledot HaAretz*, p. 88. Moose (known as elk in Europe) only live in the extreme northern parts of America and Europe.

5 This is found in many English Bible translations; however, the chamois (a type of goat-antelope) does not live anywhere near the Land of Israel.

6 Yehuda Feliks, *The Animal World of the Bible*, p. 18; Yisrael Meir Levinger and Menachem Dor, "The Seven Kosher Mammals" (Hebrew), *Torah UMadda* vol. 5 (5735–1975), pp. 37–50; Yisrael Meir Levinger, *Meor LeMasekhet Chullin* p. 47; Zohar Amar, Ram Bouchnick, and Guy Bar-Oz, "The Contribution of Archaeozoology to the Identification of the Ritu-ally Clean Ungulates Mentioned in the Hebrew Bible," *Journal of Hebrew Scriptures* (2010), 10:1.

7 Chullin 80a.

8 Yisrael Aharoni, *Zikhronot Zoolog Ivri* (Jerusalem: Ariel Publishers, 1943–1946), pp. 22–23; Ephraim Bilik, "Kosher Ungulates in the Bible" (Hebrew), *Bet Mikra* 6 (1961), pp. 28–31.

9 Rav Saadia Gaon places the wild sheep elsewhere in the list: he translates *dishon* with the Arabic name *aruy*, which means ram, and is presumed to refer to the wild sheep.

10 Feliks, *The Animal World of the Bible*, p. 18.

11 See Mishna Bikkurim 2:8–11; Beitza 8a–b, Yoma 74b, Nedarim 18b, Keritot 17b–18a, 21a, Chullin 79b–80a.

12 Moshe Ra'anan, "*Koy Briya Bifnei Atzma Hi – Teo (Jamus)*" at http://www.daf-yomi.com/DYItemDetails.aspx?itemId=13936.

13 Mordechai Kislev, "*Koy – Kashruto Shel Baal Chayim Meyuba*," *Techumin* 17 (5757), pp. 415–432. We shall explore this possibility further in the volume on domestic animals.

14 Feliks, *Animals and Plants of the Mishna*, p 240.

GIRAFFE

Giraffe

זמר(?)
Zamer

An Alternative Candidate for the *Zamer*
IDENTIFICATION

אַיָּל וּצְבִי וְיַחְמוּר וְאַקּוֹ וְדִישֹׁן וּתְאוֹ וָזָמֶר:
דברים יד:ה

For a land animal to be kosher, it must have split hooves and chew the cud. The Torah lists ten animals that match these requirements:

> This is the animal which you shall eat: cattle, sheep, and goats; the deer, the gazelle, the hartebeest, the ibex, the oryx, the aurochs, and the *zamer*. (Deut. 14:4–5)

As noted in the previous entry, on the wild sheep, it is exceedingly difficult to identify the last animal in this list, the *zamer*. The word appears nowhere else in Scripture, and there is no such name of an animal in other languages from the region.[1] As discussed, one widely accepted view in contemporary academic scholarship is to identify the *zamer* as a type of wild sheep. However, the Septuagint – the ancient Greek translation of Scripture by the Jewish Sages in Egypt during the Second Temple period – translates the *zamer* as the *camelopardalis*, or "camel-leopard." This is an ancient term for the giraffe, which looks like a cross between a camel and a leopard, and was believed by many to actually be such a hybrid. The Vulgate – the Latin translation of

Scripture produced by Jerome in consultation with Jewish scholars – likewise translates *zamer* as *camelopardalis*.

Rav Saadia Gaon translates *zamer* with the Arabic word *al-zarafa*, which refers to the giraffe. This was followed by other Spanish and North African rabbinic scholars of the medieval period, such as Rabbi Yona ibn Janach,[2] Rabbi Shlomo ben Natan of Sijilmasa,[3] and Rabbi Shimon ben Tzemach Duran.[4] The latter notes that it "has a long neck and a very large body, to the extent that when it is inside a wall, it stretches its neck outside of the wall, and they have testified to me that they saw it in Fez (Morocco)."

The giraffe is therefore also a possible contender for the *zamer* of the Torah, and one that is supported by strong tradition. It would also match the Aramaic name *zamer*, meaning "rejoicing" or "dancing," which could relate to the graceful and extraordinary appearance of the giraffe when galloping; its long neck swings back and forth like a pendulum. Furthermore, following the view that the Torah's list of ten kosher animals includes all kosher species in the world,

PICHUGIN DMITRY / SHUTTERSTOCK

the giraffe must be included in one of these categories, and the *zamer* provides such an opportunity.[5]

Some also claim that the giraffe is the *tachash* whose skins were used to cover the Tabernacle, and that it is identical with a creature called the *keres* in the Talmud.[6] However, these theories are somewhat fanciful,[7] and there are more reasonable alternative suggestions for the identities of these creatures.[8]

Giraffes in the Ancient Near East
NATURAL HISTORY

Many contemporary scholars in the field of biblical zoology have specifically rejected identifying the *zamer* as the giraffe. The reason for this is that the Torah is presumed to only mention animals that were familiar to the Jewish people, whereas giraffes were not indigenous to the Land of Israel or surrounding regions and are not part of the "world" of the Torah.[9]

However, this is not necessarily correct. It is true that today, giraffes only live in sub-Saharan Africa. But in ancient times their range was more extensive. Wild giraffes once lived in Egypt; archeologists have found over three hundred images of giraffes in the Nile valley and the eastern desert of Egypt, many of which depict giraffes grazing in their natural habitat.[10]

Giraffes disappeared from Egypt around four or five thousand years ago, when the climate became more arid and there was more competition for food from cattle. But even after they disappeared from the wild, they were frequently brought to the region. Giraffes were presented to Egyptian rulers by African peoples; Rameses II appears to have had several specimens.[11] The Egyptians' ability to

A mosaic of a giraffe from a sixth-century synagogue in Gaza

ZEV RADOVAN

transport giraffes from East Africa via the Red Sea meant that they were able to export them from Alexandria to ports around the Mediterranean. The remarkable size, strange form, and great beauty of the giraffe meant that they were prized as tributes and as royal possessions. Giraffes, then, would not have been unknown during the biblical period.

There is evidence that subsequently, giraffes were also brought to the Land of Israel. A drawing of a giraffe from the second century BCE appears in the Sidonian burial caves in Maresha (today part of the Beit Guvrin national park). A beautiful illustration of a giraffe appears in a mosaic in Lod, dated to the third century. There is a record from the fifth century of a giraffe that was transported from the port in Eilat to Gaza, en route to Caesar Anastasias.[12] Further drawings of giraffes, from the sixth century, appear in the ruins of Be'er Shema in the western Negev, on a mosaic floor in Beit She'an (Tel Itztaba), and on the mosaic floor of a synagogue in Gaza.[13]

Galloping giraffes present a spectacular sight

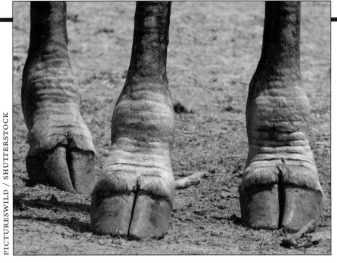

The cloven hooves of a giraffe

A giraffe chewing its cud

Is the Giraffe Kosher?

LAW AND RITUAL

The Torah states that an animal need possess split hooves and chew its cud in order to be kosher. Giraffes clearly possess both of these characteristics.[14] They have fully split hooves that are physiologically identical to those of all kosher animals (albeit much larger!). They are ruminants with a four-chambered stomach, and they regurgitate their food and chew it again. In fact, due to the length of the giraffe's neck, it is possible to observe the bolus of food, bulging under the skin, traveling up and down the neck as it is regurgitated for further chewing. Thus, the giraffe matches the Torah's requirements for an animal to be kosher. The normative position in Jewish law is that this suffices to permit an animal's consumption.

We further have the statements of several authorities that the giraffe is the *zamer* of the Torah, which is listed as a kosher animal. Rabbi Yosef Schwartz, a nineteenth-century scholar who studied the geography, flora, and fauna of the Land of Israel, writes that he examined giraffes in Egypt, found them to possess both kosher signs, and therefore concludes that the giraffe is indeed the *zamer* of the Torah.[15]

In addition, there is another source indicating that a giraffe was historically classified as a kosher animal. There is a view that the parchment of a Torah scroll should measure the same in height as it does in circumference when rolled up on one pole. Whether this actually occurs depends upon several factors, including the overall size of the Torah scroll, the height of the writing, and the thickness of the parchment. In this context, reference is made to the giraffe:

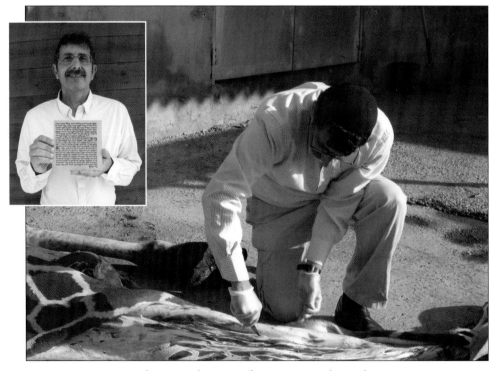

Dr. Zohar Amar skins a giraffe to prepare parchment for mezuzot

Rabbeinu Chananel, may his memory be for a blessing, said that the work of a Torah scroll with parchment requires extra skill to estimate that the circumference of the scroll be equal to the height of it; and some of the early ones wrote in Arabic thus: The skin of the *al-ayl* and the skin of the *al-zarafa* fulfills this requirement. (Rabbi Y. Barzeloni, *Hilkhot Sefer Torah*, p. 20[16])

The giraffe is mentioned as having skin of suitable thickness that will enable a Torah scroll to have the proper dimensions. Since Torah scrolls may only be made from the skin of kosher animals, this shows that the giraffe is a kosher animal.[17]

Thus, giraffes ought to be considered kosher animals that could be eaten today. But while many would indeed rule this way, it is not unequivocal. A number of complexities arise as a result of various statements in halakhic codes.

Like other kosher animals, a giraffe lacks upper incisors

The Talmudic Guide to Identifying Kosher Animals

LAW AND RITUAL

One potential complexity regarding the kosher status of the giraffe relates to its horns. As noted in the introduction to the section on kosher wild animals, the Talmud gives characteristics by which to distinguish between domestic and wild kosher animals. These relate the horns of the animals; the Talmud states that for an animal to be classified as a wild animal, its horns must either be branched, or be layered, circular in cross-section, and tightly ringed.[18] One opinion[19] states that in order for a wild animal to be considered kosher in the first place, it must possess the horn characteristics of kosher species, in addition to split hooves and chewing the cud; otherwise, it is classified as non-kosher. According to this, the giraffe might not be kosher, as its horns are solid, smooth bone and would not appear to match the criteria described in the Talmud.[20]

Most, however, disagree with this lone view.[21] It is pointed out that this argument is only based upon a weak inference from earlier codes, and is contradicted by other inferences from those very same codes. In any case, the Torah only requires that animals possess split hooves and chew the cud, making no mention of horn characteristics. Furthermore, if we are following the Talmud's additional ways of identifying kosher and non-kosher animals, then we should also take into consideration that the giraffe matches other supplementary methods given by the Talmud of identifying kosher animals. One of these is that all animals lacking upper incisors (with the exception of juvenile camels) are kosher, whereas animals with upper teeth are not kosher.[22] Giraffes, like cows, lack upper incisors.

Another method that the Talmud gives for distinguishing between kosher and non-kosher animals is that only kosher animals produce milk that curdles.[23] This test was recently performed on giraffe milk, and it was found to curdle.[24]

But in any case, the additional characteristics of kosher and non-kosher animals given in the Talmud were apparently indicators that were extrapolated from animals local to the area, rather than being determinative for all species in the world.[25] This is further evident from the fact that there are a variety of exceptions to the principle regarding upper incisors.[26] As long as an animal can be clearly determined to possess split hooves and bring up its cud, there is no need to comply with other characteristics.

Is There a Tradition for Eating Giraffe?

LAW AND RITUAL

Another complexity relating to the kosher status of the giraffe is the issue of tradition. The great seventeenth-century halakhist, Rabbi Shabtai HaKohen, in his commentary on *Shulchan Arukh*, *Siftei Kohen* (commonly known by its acronym as "the *Shakh*"), writes the following with regard to the characteristics of horns of kosher animals:

> But since we now have nothing other than which we received by tradition (*mesora*), I have been brief. (*Siftei Kohen* to *Yoreh De'ah* 80:2)

There is debate as to the meaning of the statement that "we only have that which we received by tradition." Simply speaking, he means that a tradition is required in order to definitively distinguish between a domesticated and wild animal. Without such a tradition, one must proceed strin-

*A halakhically-oriented dissection of an aborted
giraffe fetus at the Ramat Gan Zoo*

gently, and the animal's fat would be forbidden like that of a domesticated animal. This is how the view of the *Shakh* is understood by several leading authorities.[27]

However, other authorities understand the *Shakh* to be saying that a tradition is required for animals to be considered at all permissible to eat at all, not just to determine whether they are considered wild or domestic.[28] According to this view, merely possessing the signs of split hooves and chewing the cud does not suffice to permit the consumption of an animal. Thus, these authorities rule that since there is no tradition that the giraffe is kosher, we may not eat it.

One may ask why we would need a tradition for animals. With regard to birds, the Torah permits all except the twenty-four general types mentioned, and so there is good reason to require a tradition, for there is much confusion as to how to identify these twenty-four types. But regarding animals, the Torah clearly states that split hooves and chewing the cud are all that is required. Why would a tradition be necessary?

Chazon Ish suggests that such a tradition might be necessary not to determine whether or not an animal is kosher per se, but rather to establish which types of physical defects render it forbidden from consumption. However, he ultimately insists that there is no need to seek a reason, and that halakhic conservatism alone suffices to justify it. He further claims that this interpretation of the *Shakh* has become communally accepted.

Others, however, challenge all these claims.[29] The normative practice in Jewish law remains that an animal is permissible for consumption if it meets the Torah's requirements of possessing split hooves and chewing the cud, even in the absence of a tradition regarding that type of animal. This is why kosher certification is given to bison meat, even though there is no tradition for eating bison. Accordingly,

a giraffe is also kosher. (The same would be true for the okapi, a strange-looking relative of the giraffe from the dense jungles of central Africa.) There are, however, some sectors of the Orthodox community in Israel which follow the stringency of the Chazon Ish.

In summary, although a giraffe clearly possesses the signs of a kosher animal, the permissibility of eating it depends upon the dispute as to whether a tradition is required.[30] Some further suggest that even if one does take the approach that a tradition is required, a *mesora* does indeed exist, since Rav Saadia Gaon identified the *zamer* as a giraffe, and Rabbeinu Chananel permitted writing a Torah scroll on giraffe skin.[31]

Slaughtering a Giraffe

LAW AND RITUAL

Aside from the question of whether the giraffe is a kosher animal, there is also the matter of *shechita*, ritual slaughter, to be addressed. There is a widespread myth that giraffes cannot be eaten because we do not know where on the neck to slaughter them. This is simply false. The halakha clearly states which part of an animal's neck is suitable for slaughter;[32] it is almost the entire length of the trachea[33] and esophagus.[34] In a cow, this is just over a foot long; in a giraffe, it is almost six feet. Finding the right place for slaughter is easier with a giraffe than with any other animal!

How did such a myth occur? It may well be that it simply began as a joke. Still, some explanations for the myth's origin have been suggested.[35]

The *Shulchan Arukh* states that the animal must be slaughtered in the middle of the neck.[36] This means that it should be slaughtered in the center of the *width* of the neck, as opposed to cutting it from the side. But it may have been misinterpreted to mean that it should be slaughtered in the middle of the *length* of its neck, and that we do not know how to define this place for a giraffe.

The myth that we do not know *where* to slaughter a giraffe might have developed from the more reasonable claim that we do not know *how* to slaughter a giraffe. When an animal is slaughtered, either its head must be supported, or the animal must be hanging upside down, for two reasons. First of all, if the head falls down forcefully onto the knife at the time of the slaughter, this invalidates the slaughter (a problem known as *derusa*). Second, if the precise spot where it is being slaughtered is not clearly visible at the time of the slaughter, some opinions state that this invalidates the slaughter (a problem known as *chalada*). Both of these hazards can be avoided in one of several ways. One can, for example, support the head via a special chin lift, or one can lie the animal down on the ground, or one can hoist the

298

animal by the leg such that the force of gravity will pull the head back (though this last method is considered highly cruel). But all these options are very difficult to implement with a giraffe.

Supporting the giraffe's head is complicated by the fact that giraffes, the tallest of all animals, can reach nineteen feet in height. It would require the construction of a special pen, and the *shochet* (slaughterer) would have to stand on a platform or ladder. Restraining the giraffe, however, would not be easy. Giraffes can weigh four thousand pounds and are immensely strong. A giraffe can kick out with its huge hooves in any direction, with enough force to kill a person.[37]

Forcing a giraffe to lie down on the ground for slaughter, or hoisting it upside down, would be even more problematic. Because the giraffe is so tall, it has special modifications for blood circulation. Its heart measures an enormous two feet in length and weighs twenty-five pounds. This drives the highest known blood pressure in any mammal, more than twice that of a human. The heart beats up to 170 times a minute, also double our own, and pumps approximately sixteen gallons per minute. But with such a powerful heart required to pump blood all the way up to its head, new problems are created when it lowers its head, such as when it drinks. The

rush of blood to the brain would kill the giraffe, were it not to have further special modifications. The elastic walls of the lengthy carotid artery swell to absorb excess blood, and there is also a network of tiny veins that act as temporary collecting vessels. In addition, each jugular vein contains a series of one-way valves that prevent the blood exiting the brain from falling back into it. Yet, as remarkable as this system is, the giraffe is still a very delicate animal. When catching a giraffe, care has to be taken to not chase it for too long, as it can suffer a heart attack due to its high blood pressure. Manually forcing a giraffe down to the ground, or hoisting it up by its leg, would likely have the same result.

Nevertheless, methods of restraining giraffes have been developed.[38] Why, then, has kosher giraffe meat has not yet been made available? The answer appears to be two-fold. First, there is little demand, perhaps related to the giraffe's status as an exotic and endearing animal; even non-Jews do not eat much giraffe meat.[39] Second, there is little supply, due to the practical difficulty of acquiring a giraffe for the purpose. While there are ongoing individual efforts to obtain a giraffe for a halakhically unique exercise, kosher giraffe meat is unlikely to ever be available in supermarkets. ∎

Giraffes kick with tremendous power

Notes

1 It seems that even the Sages of the Talmud were uncertain regarding its identity. The sole mention of the *zamer* is in Chullin 80a, where Rav Acha is unclear as to whether the "forest goat" is a type of *zamer*, a type of *teo*, or something else. See Rashi ad loc., who explains that there is uncertainty regarding the identities of these animals.

2 Rabbi Yona ibn Janach, *Sefer HaShorashim*, *zamer*, also cited by Radak in his *Sefer HaShorashim*.

3 Rabbi Shlomo ben Natan, *Siddur Rabbeinu Shlomo b. Rabbi Natan* (Jerusalem: S. Hagai, 1995), pp. 163 and 170.

4 Rabbi Shimon ben Tzemach Duran, *Yavin Shemua*, *Hilkhot Tereifot* 5b. There is also reference to Rav Saadia Gaon's view in Rabbi Ishtori HaParchi's *Kaftor VaFerach*, chapter 48, but he seems to be merely noting the view rather than necessarily endorsing it.

5 Mordechai Kislev, "Methods of Identifying the Ten Types of Kosher Ruminants via Taxonomy" (Hebrew), *Sinai* 125 (Adar 5761/2000), pp. 216–225, explicitly invokes this reasoning in order to support identifying the *zamer* as the giraffe. However, he also notes that the notion of subsuming all species of kosher animals under the Torah's ten categories is difficult, considering the existence of animals such as Tragulidae (mouse deer). See the introduction to the section on kosher wild animals for further discussion.

6 The suggestion was first raised in the nineteenth-century journal from Vienna, *Kokhavei Yitzchak*. It received more comprehensive treatment in an article by Yaakov Forman, "Tachash," *Tarbitz* 12:3 (1940/41), pp. 218–29, and was more recently proposed by Rabbi Amitai Ben-David in *Sichat Chullin*.

7 Since the most distinctive feature of a giraffe is its height, it would be strange that in the description of the *tachash* (Shabbat 28b), no mention is made of that aspect. With regard to the *keres*, the Talmud (Chullin 59b) describes it as satisfying the condition that a kosher wild animal possesses horns, "even though it only has one horn." This would appear to rule out the giraffe, which always has a minimum of two horns. Maharam Shif suggests that the Talmud is only referring to there being one horn on its forehead, with further horns on top of its head, which is indeed the case with certain giraffes; but this explanation of the Talmud is far from straightforward.

8 See Natan Slifkin, *Sacred Monsters*, second edition (Jerusalem: Zoo Torah/ Gefen Books, 2011), pp. 45–83.

9 Elchanan Bilik, "Kosher Wild Animals in Scripture" (Hebrew), *Bet Mikra* (1961) 6 pp. 28–31; Menachem Dor, *HaChai BiYemei HaMikra, HaMishna VeHaTalmud*, p. 40.

10 Tony Judd, "Presumed Giraffe Petroglyphs in the Eastern Desert of Egypt: Style, Location and Nubian comparisons," *Rock Art Research* 23:1 (May 2006), pp. 59–70; Edgar Williams, *Giraffe* (London: Reaktion Books, 2010), pp. 45–46.

11 Dirk Huyge, "Giraffes in Ancient Egypt," *Nekhan News* 10 (1998), pp. 9–10.

12 Fritz S. Bodenheimer and Alexander Rabinowitz, *Timotheus of Gaza on Animals: Fragments of a Byzantine Paraphrase of an Animal-Book of the 5th Century A.D.* (Paris: Académie internationale d'histoire des sciences, 1949), p. 31.

13 Rachel Hachlili, *Ancient Mosaic Pavements: Themes, Issues, and Trends* (Leiden: Brill, 2009), pp. 72, 168-9, 265.

14 Doni Zivotofsky, Ari Z. Zivotofsky, and Zohar Amar, "Giraffe: A Halakhically-Oriented Dissection," *The Torah u-Madda Journal* 11 (2002–2003), pp. 203–221.

15 Rabbi Yosef Schwartz, *Divrei Yosef*, p. 159b. This was included in the third (1900) edition of *Tevuot HaAretz*.

16 Cited by Rabbi Yitzchak Ratzabi, *Shulchan Arukh HaMekutzar*, 5760, *Yoreh De'ah*, vol. 1, 134:1, note 6 on page 175–176.

17 Dr. Zohar Amar has been researching the laws and practicalities of writing a *mezuza* on parchment made from giraffe skin, regarding which he will soon publish an article in *Mesorah LeYehosef*.

18 Chullin 59b. These are codified in *Shulchan Arukh, Yoreh De'ah* 80:1.

19 *Teshuvot Beit Yaakov* 41 cited by *Pitchei Teshuva, Yoreh De'ah* 80:1.

20 Chullin 59b. For further discussion of these criteria, see the introduction to the section on kosher wild animals.

21 *Pitchei Teshuva, Yoreh De'ah* 80:1; Rabbi Yitzchak Isaac Herzog, Responsa #20.

22 Chullin 59a.

23 Avoda Zara 35b.

24 Zohar Amar, Uzi Merin, and David Iluz, "Curdling of Milk as a Criterion for Determining Kashrut of Animals in the Bible" (Hebrew), *BDD* 21 (March 2009), pp. 75–94.

25 See Rabbi Avraham Chaim Schorr, *Torat Chayim* (Jerusalem, 1962), commentary to Chullin 59a. Cf. Rambam, commentary to the Mishna, Nidda 6:9 (Kapach edition), where he states that the Sages' principles regarding the fins and scales of kosher fish "were arrived at via looking at different species." See too Rabbi Yaakov Gesundheit (1816–1878), *Tiferet Yaakov* to Chullin 64a, s.v. *simanin lav deoraita*, who states that the signs of kosher eggs provided by the Talmud were based upon the Sages' examination of the eggs of common species.

26 See *The Camel, The Hare And The Hyrax* by this author for numerous examples.

27 *Peri Megadim, Siftei Daat* 80:1; *Kaf HaChayim, Yoreh De'ah* 80:5; *Darkhei Teshuva* 80:3; *Kreiti UPleiti* (2), *Pitchei Teshuva, Yoreh De'ah* 80:1; *Beit Yitzchak, Amudei Zahav* 3.

28 Rabbi Avraham Danzig, *Chokhmat Adam* 36:1; Rabbi Yechiel Michel Epstein, *Arukh HaShulchan, Yoreh De'ah* 80:10; Rabbi Yitzchak Tayib, *Erekh HaShulchan, Yoreh De'ah* 80:10 and 82:29; Chazon Ish, *Yoreh De'ah, Hilkhot Behema VeChaya Tehora* 11, letters 4 and 5 (also printed in *Kovetz Igrot*, vol. 1, letter 99 and vol. 2, letter 83), and *Pe'er HaDor*, vol. 4, pp. 226–230.

29 See Rabbi Yitzchak Isaac Herzog, Responsa #20, and the responsum from Rabbi Yisrael Belsky and Rabbi Herschel Schachter, included in the materials distributed at the Orthodox Union conference on the Mesorah of Kosher Birds and Animals, May 2, 2004. See too Rabbi Shmuel Wosner, Responsa *Shevet HaLevi* 10:114.

30 For further discussion, see J. David Bleich, "Survey of Recent Halakhic Periodical Literature," *Tradition* 35:1 (Spring 2001), pp. 70–75; and especially Ari Zivotofsky, "Buffalo, Giraffe, and the Babirusa ("Kosher Pig"): The Halachik and Scientific Factors in Determining their Kashrut Status," *BDD* 12 (Winter 2001), pp. 5–32.

31 Avraham Hamami, "The Giraffe – Its Kashrut for Eating" (Hebrew), *Techumin*, vol. 20 (5760/2000), pp. 89–93.

32 Chullin 45a; *Shulchan Arukh, Yoreh De'ah* 20:1–2.

33 From just below the cricoid (the first cartilaginous ring at the bottom of the larynx) until the level that would be reached by an inflated lobe of the lung.

34 At the top, from the beginning of the section that will collapse closed upon being cut, until the part at the base where it starts to look like the stomach.

35 I am indebted to my colleague Rabbi Dr. Ari Zivotofsky for his input on this topic.

36 *Shulchan Arukh, Yoreh De'ah* 20:3.

37 Edgar Williams, *Giraffe* (London: Reaktion Books, 2010), p. 36.

38 Paul P. Calle and John C. Bornmann, "Giraffe Restraint, Habituation and Desensitization at the Cheyenne Mountain Zoo," *Zoo Biology* (1988) 7, pp. 243–252; Wendy R. Wienter, "Giraffe Squeeze Cage Procedure," *Zoo Biology* (1986), pp. 371–377.

39 See Adam Martin, "What Does Giraffe Meat Taste Like?" *New York* magazine, 2/10/2014, online at http://nymag.com/daily/intelligencer/2014/02/what-does-giraffe-meat-taste-like.html.

PART THREE

Other Wild Animals

HYRAX

Hyrax

The Enigmatic Hyrax

NATURAL HISTORY

Hyraxes, also called conies,[1] rock badgers, rock rabbits, and klipdas, are unfamiliar animals to most English-speaking people (although South Africans are familiar with them by the name "dassies"). However, they are significant animals in Scripture. They are first mentioned in the Torah in the list of four animals that possess only one of the two characteristics required for an animal to be kosher:

> And God spoke to Moses and to Aaron, saying to them: Speak to the Children of Israel, saying, This is the animal that you may eat from all the animals which are on the earth – every animal that forms a hoof that is fully split, and that brings up the cud, you may eat. However, this you may not eat from those that bring up the cud and from those that form a hoof: the camel, for it brings up the cud, but does not form a hoof – it is unclean for you. And the hyrax, for it brings up the cud, but does not form a hoof, it is unclean for you. And the hare, for it brings up the cud, but does not form a hoof, it is unclean for you. And the pig, for it forms a hoof that is fully split, but it does not bring up its cud, it is unclean for you. You shall not eat of their flesh, and you should not touch their carcasses; they are unclean for you. (Lev. 11:1–8)

This list is repeated, in a more concise form, later in the Torah:

> However, this you shall not eat, from those that bring up the cud and from those that have a completely split hoof: the camel, the hare, and the hyrax; for they bring up the cud, but they do not form a hoof; therefore they are unclean to you. And the pig, because it forms a hoof, yet it does not bring up the cud, it is unclean to you; you shall not eat of their meat, nor touch their carcasses. (Deut. 14:7–8)

Hyraxes (the plural form is sometimes written as "hyrax" or "hyraces") are small furry mammals that somewhat resemble very large guinea pigs or woodchucks. However, anatomically, physiologically, and behaviorally they are

וְאֶת הַשָּׁפָן כִּי מַעֲלֵה גֵרָה הוּא וּפַרְסָה לֹא יַפְרִיס טָמֵא הוּא לָכֶם:
ויקרא יא:ה

אַךְ אֶת זֶה לֹא תֹאכְלוּ מִמַּעֲלֵי הַגֵּרָה וּמִמַּפְרִיסֵי הַפַּרְסָה הַשְּׁסוּעָה אֶת הַגָּמָל וְאֶת הָאַרְנֶבֶת וְאֶת הַשָּׁפָן כִּי מַעֲלֵה גֵרָה הֵמָּה וּפַרְסָה לֹא הִפְרִיסוּ טְמֵאִים הֵם לָכֶם:
דברים יד:ז

שְׁפַנִּים עַם לֹא עָצוּם וַיָּשִׂימוּ בַסֶּלַע בֵּיתָם:
משלי ל:כו

entirely different from rodents. According to zoological taxonomy, hyraxes are classified as being most closely related to elephants (!) and are in the category of "subungulates," meaning that they are almost ungulates (hoofed mammals), but not quite.

The species of hyrax found in Israel is *Procavia capensis* (sometimes called *Procavia syriaca*), known in Modern Hebrew as *shafan sela* and in English as the rock hyrax. They are common in many places throughout the country. One unfortunate problem with rock hyraxes is that, in certain parts of Israel, they have been incriminated as reservoir hosts for a species of sand fly which transmits the disease leishmaniasis. Nevertheless, hyraxes are popular animals. They are especially familiar and beloved in the Ein Gedi nature reserve, where they have become very tame and often approach visitors. Being easy to maintain in captivity, these unusual animals are also often found in zoos.

Evidence for the Hyrax

IDENTIFICATION

Historically, there has been considerable confusion with regard to the identity of the *shafan* of the Torah. As we shall discover, there is a reason why this confusion developed; yet there can be no doubt that the *shafan* is indeed the hyrax.[2] There are several different lines of evidence for this. First, there are some verses in Scripture which match the hyrax perfectly:

> There are four in the land that are small, but are exceedingly wise.... The *shefanim* are not a strong folk, but they place their home in the rock. (Prov. 30:24, 26)

Being relatively small animals, hyraxes are preyed upon by eagles, jackals, hyenas, and snakes. They are indeed "not a strong folk."

The verse further states that they place their homes in the rocks. A similar description is given elsewhere:

> The high hills are for the ibex, the rocks are a refuge for the *shefanim*. (Ps. 104:18)

There are different species of hyrax, but the species found in Israel always lives in rocky areas (and hence is called the "rock hyrax"). They have a multitude of tunnels and hiding places in these rocks, and when danger threatens, they all dart into hiding.[3] Hyraxes are so intimately connected with rocks that they are never found far from them. In fact, the recent increase in piles of rocks in Israel due to construction has led to a population boom of hyraxes.[4]

These refuges serve to protect the hyrax from predators, including leopards and hyenas, but principally eagles.[5] Verreaux's eagle is the major predator of hyraxes, feeding upon them almost exclusively.[6] This predation by birds is highlighted in the Midrash:

> "The rocks are a refuge for hyraxes" – These hyraxes hide under rocky outcrops from birds flying overhead, that they should not eat them. (*Bereshit Rabba* 12:9)

At the Bronx Zoo, ibex and hyrax are kept in the same enclosure, just as they live together in the wild – "The high hills are for the ibex, the rocks are a refuge for the hyrax."

ED GAILLIARD

The aforementioned verse provides further important evidence regarding the identity of the *shafan*. It is described immediately after the ibex (a species of wild goat). This suggests a connection between the two, and indeed both ibexes and hyraxes noticeably live in proximity. Ibex and hyrax can be seen living together in the hills surrounding the Dead Sea, especially in the region of Ein Gedi.

As Ibn Ezra states, Arabic names provide strong evidence for identifying animals in Scripture.[7] In the Ehkili

These juvenile hyraxes are demonstrating how they use rocks as a refuge

CHARLES KINSEY

305

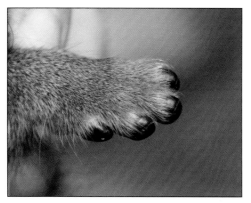  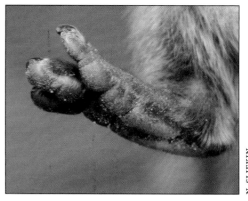

Left: Top view of front foot. Center: Bottom view of front foot. Right: Hind foot.

dialect of Arabic (Sabean) the hyrax is called *thufun*, from the root *thafan*, which is related to the Hebrew word *shafan*.[8] Tristram, the nineteenth-century chronicler of the flora and fauna of the Land of Israel, likewise notes that in Southern Arabia it is known by the similar name *thofun*.[9]

Several rabbinic authorities explain that the Torah specifically wanted to warn against eating those non-kosher animals that were commonly eaten by people in the area.[10] Hyraxes are indeed a popular food item; Tristram notes that hyrax-meat "is much prized by the Arabs."[11]

Various other descriptions of the *shafan* also match the hyrax. According to some commentaries, the Torah is saying that the *shafan* does not possess split feet, while according to others, it is saying that it does not possess hooves at all. Both interpretations match the hyrax. The feet of the hyrax are of a peculiarly solid shape with a rubbery texture. The front foot has four stubby toes, while the hind feet possess three longer toes that are more divided, but there is a solid sole. At the end of the toes are thick nails. Although some zoological texts describe the hyrax's thick nails as hooves, they would not be classified as hoofed animals in the Torah, since these nails do not encase the foot – just as is the case with the nails of the camel.

The Talmud states that, unlike most ruminants, the hare and *shafan* possess upper teeth.[12] This matches the hyrax, which possess large upper incisors. Later, we shall discuss the Torah's description of the hyrax chewing its cud.

The Hyrax in Antiquity

IDENTIFICATION

The Aramaic translation of the Torah, *Targum Onkelos*, renders *shafan* as *tafza*, which means "jumper." This is a vague term that could theoretically describe a variety of animals, but would certainly also well describe the hyrax. Hyraxes are tremendously agile creatures which spectacularly leap from rock to rock in their native habitats.[13]

The Septuagint – the ancient Greek translation of Scripture, made by the Jewish Sages of Alexandria – translates *shafan* as *chyrogrillius*, which is a difficult word to interpret.[14] It has been variously explained to mean "grunting pig"[15] or "bristly animal."[16] Both of these terms could theoretically refer to the hedgehog, which is how many European readers subsequently understood it. However, the hedgehog is not a candidate for the *shafan*; it does not do anything that could be described as bringing up the cud, and nor does it match the scriptural description of the *shafan* being a creature that makes its home inside rocks. Instead, the name *chyrogrillius* presumably refers to the hyrax. If the word means "grunting pig," this would be a fair description, since the hyrax, like a pig, is squat and makes grunting noises. If it means "bristly animal," it would refer to the long, stiff hairs that emerge at intervals all over the hyrax's body, which it uses like whiskers to feel its way in dark tunnels.[17]

In the fifth century, Jerome, who lived in the Land of Israel (and was thus familiar with its wildlife) and consulted with Jewish scholars for his Latin translation of Scripture, also translated *shafan* as *chyrogrillius* in the Vulgate.[18] In correspondence, he explained *chyrogrillius* to refer to a creature that is "no larger than a hedgehog, and resembling both a bear and a mouse"; he notes that it is therefore also called *arktomys*, which literally means "bear mouse."[19] He describes it as being very common in Israel and living in caves in the rocks. Today, *arktomys* is the Latin name for the marmot (known in America as the woodchuck or groundhog), but these are not native to the region of Israel, and they live in tunnels rather than rocks. Jerome was undoubtedly referring to the hyrax, which looks very much like a cross between a bear and a mouse.

In the tenth century, Rav Saadia Gaon translated *shafan* with the Arabic name *wabr*. This is the most common and widespread Arabic name for the hyrax.[20] Rav Saadia would have been familiar with the hyrax from both Egypt and the Land of Israel.

The hyraxes are not a strong folk,
but they place their home in the rock.
(Prov. 30: 26)

307

Europe and the Loss of the Hyrax

In medieval Europe, where the chain of Torah transmission largely occurred, people were entirely unfamiliar with certain animals from the Land of Israel. The name *tzvi* was transposed from the gazelle to the deer, and *nesher* from the vulture to the eagle. Hyraxes likewise live only in Africa and Asia, and were entirely unknown in Europe. As a result, the identity of the *shafan* was lost, and the name *shafan* was usually transposed to the rabbit.[21] (Hence, when Hebrew was revived as a spoken language in modern times, the rabbit was often still referred to with the name *shafan*, and the hyrax was thus given the more specific name of *shafan sela* – "rock *shafan*.")

However, as some European scholars recognized, the *shafan* of Scripture cannot be the rabbit. First of all, there are no rabbits in the Land of Israel. The European rabbit was originally native only to the Iberian Peninsula, subsequently being artificially introduced to northern Africa and other places, but it never lived in the Land of Israel.[22] Furthermore, the scriptural description of the *shafan* as an animal that builds its home and hides among the rocks does not match rabbits, which seek terrain where they can dig tunnels into the earth rather than hiding in rocks.[23] Hyraxes, in contrast, are so closely associated with rocks that they never live anywhere else. There are certain species of rabbits which habitually hide under rocks, of the genus *Pronolagus*, but these are only found in southern Africa.

Some polemicists have attempted to argue that God, and the divinely-inspired authors of Psalms and Proverbs, are not limited to describing animals from the local region.[24] However, even from such a standpoint, it is immensely problematic to claim that the *shafan*, described in Psalms and Proverbs as a familiar animal, is not the hyrax. King David describes the rock-hiding *shafan* in the same verse as the hill-climbing ibex; it is unreasonable in the extreme to propose that instead of referring to a local rock-hiding animal that lives in the exact same vicinity as the ibex in Ein Gedi, he was referring to an animal that does not live in the region. And King Solomon mentions the *shafan* in the context of seeking to relate the ingenuity of an animal that hides under rocks; when there is a local animal that does precisely that, it is extraordinarily unreasonable to propose that he instead is referring to an animal with which his audience would be entirely unfamiliar.

Aware of the problems with identifying the *shafan* as the rabbit, some early European investigators of the wildlife of the Bible sought to learn of a different animal in the Land of Israel that might be a suitable candidate. In the seventeenth century, Samuel Bochart, author of the *Hierozoïcon* – the first comprehensive study of all the animals mentioned in Scripture – argued that the *shafan* is the jerboa.[25] This is a small rodent that has long back legs for jumping and tiny forelimbs. Bochart had never seen a jerboa, but he was under the (mistaken) impression that it lives in rocks, thus matching the scriptural description of the *shafan*. As further evidence, he argued that the Septuagint's term *chyrogrillius* was a word referring to the jerboa, based on the authority of a fourteenth-century Copto-Arabic lexicon.[26] Following Bochart, the identification of the *shafan* as the jerboa was subsequently adopted by several Jewish and non-Jewish scholars;[27] as a jumping animal, it was also understood to be the *tafza* mentioned in the Aramaic *Targum Onkelos*.

Jerboas are rodents, not ruminants, and they are not known to chew the cud. But it is possible that, like rabbits and hares, they engage in the process known as cecotrophy or refection. This refers to their reingesting certain types of fecal pellets that are specifically produced for this purpose; we shall discuss this process in more detail with regard to the hare. Many rodents practice such behavior.[28] Thus, it is possible that the jerboa practices cecotrophy, and that like the hare, the jerboa would be described as "chewing the cud" because of this.

However, the jerboa cannot be the *shafan*. Contrary to the beliefs of Bochart and the other European scholars – who had never seen a jerboa – no species of jerboa makes its home in rocks; all live in tunnels excavated in sand or earth. Furthermore, the Torah is only listing *behemot* and *chayot* – quadrupeds of reasonable size. Jerboas would presumably be classified as *sheratzim*, creeping verminous creatures, which are prohibited from consumption in a different verse.[29] Hence, the jerboa cannot be the *shafan*.

Other writers searched further afield. Some have proposed that the *shafan* is the java mouse deer.[30] This is a tiny deer that occasionally hides under rocks, just as the *shafan*

The lesser jerboa, Jaculus jaculus, *was mistakenly thought by some to be the* shafan

Hyraxes have a range of forms of motion. Often, they leap from rock to rock. At other times, they walk slowly with a stiff gait, as in this picture.

is described, and which chews the cud. It is argued that since the feet of the mouse deer are splayed, with hooves only covering the extremities, they are considered paws with claws rather than cloven hoofs. However, this identification is untenable for the same reasons that the rabbit is untenable. The *shafan* is described as a familiar animal in Scripture and Talmud, whereas the mouse deer is an obscure creature living only in the islands of Indonesia. The description of the *shafan* habitually making its home in the rocks, and mentioned in association with ibexes, clearly matches the hyrax far better than the mouse deer. If the feet of the mouse deer are not going to be considered as "split hooves," then it is more reasonable to propose that we have some additional animals with a single kosher sign than to propose that the mouse deer is the *shafan* of Scripture. But in any case, the feet of mouse deer are not all that different from those of other deer; the part of the foot that touches the ground is entirely split, and the extremities are entirely encased by hoof.

Still others suggested that the *shafan* is a member of the llama family.[31] However, such animals do not hide under rocks.[32] Furthermore, they are only native to South America, whereas the *shafan* is described in the Torah, Psalms, and Proverbs, as well as in the Talmud, as a familiar animal.

The Rediscovery of the Hyrax

IDENTIFICATION

For Europeans, the true identity of the *shafan* was first rediscovered in the eighteenth century by the British travelers Thomas Shaw[33] and James Bruce,[34] who journeyed throughout the Levant and reported on the plants and animals of the Holy Land. They described the hyrax in detail, for the benefit of their European readers who did not know this creature, referring to it by its local names of *daman Israel* and *ashkoko* ("the bristly one"). They noted that it is clearly the *shafan* described in Scripture: a smallish animal that hides in the rocks and is observed to chew its cud. Furthermore, the fact that the hyrax lives together with ibex in the same habitat means that it is clearly being described in the verse, "The high hills are for the ibex, the rocks are a refuge for the *shefanim*." In the nineteenth century, many more first-hand studies were made of the wildlife of the Land of Israel, further spreading the awareness that the hyrax is the *shafan*. Thus, Rabbi Yosef Schwartz, who wrote a book on the geography and natural history of the Land of Israel based on his experiences there, identified the *shafan* as the hyrax, giving it the Arabic name of *wabr* (like Rav Saadia Gaon).[35]

It took a while for knowledge of the hyrax to spread through Europe; in the nineteenth century, while some accepted that it is the *shafan*,[36] others remained unfamiliar with the hyrax and maintained that the *shafan* was either the rabbit or jerboa, working with the mistaken belief that these animals habitually hide in rocks. Eventually, however, as knowledge regarding all these animals increased, it became clear that the rabbit and jerboa could not be the *shafan*, while the hyrax was an excellent match. Thus, in the nineteenth century, Rabbi Meir Leibush (known as Malbim) and Rabbi David Zvi Hoffman both explained that the *shafan* is the hyrax.[37]

By the twentieth century, the hyrax was already becoming well known (and terms for it such as coney and rock-badger became antiquated). All scholars of scriptural zoology accepted it as the *shafan*.[38] The only people to reject identifying the *shafan* as the hyrax are those who are uncomfortable with the scriptural description of it "chewing the cud," due to their particular outlook on biblical interpretation (as we shall explain). However, no other remotely viable candidate for the *shafan* exists.[39]

Does the Hyrax Chew Its Cud?

THEOLOGY, PHILOSOPHY, AND SCIENCE

The Torah describes the *shafan* as *maale gera*, literally "bringing up by way of the throat,"[40] but more simply translated as "chewing its cud." Although hyraxes possess unusual digestive systems, there is no chamber producing "cud" to be chewed.

Yet there have been certain observers who claim to have seen the hyrax chewing its cud. The eighteenth-century traveler Bruce, who rediscovered the hyrax for Europe, kept a captive hyrax specifically in order to examine this, and writes that it does indeed ruminate.[41] In the twentieth century, one zoologist likewise reported having seen hyraxes chewing their cud, albeit for a much shorter period than with regular ruminants.[42]

Nevertheless, the consensus of zoologists is that the hyrax does not ruminate. Animals that ruminate are clearly observed to do so, engaging in this behavior for long periods of time. Studying hyraxes does not reveal such behavior.

But there is another possibility. There is a very limited form of rumination, called "merycism," which is found in some Australian marsupials such as koalas and kangaroos, and in other animals such as proboscis monkeys. With merycism, the animal regurgitates a small amount of food, and it is not chewed as thoroughly as is the case with ruminants, nor does it play as fundamental a role in digestion. Still, this would undoubtedly be sufficient basis for the Torah to describe such a process as "bringing up the cud."

A hyrax demonstrating its ruminant-like method of chewing

Hyraxes frequently make brief chewing movements with their mouths, long after they have eaten. There also appears to be movement in the throat immediately preceding these chewing motions.[43] Perhaps the hyrax engages in merycism, which would account for those who have claimed to observe it ruminating, as well as the Torah's description of it.

However, other zoologists doubt this interpretation of the actions of the hyrax. They argue that hyraxes will work their jaws from side-to-side when confronted with something new and potentially dangerous, as a threatening gesture. It is therefore suggested that all alleged observations of the hyrax chewing its cud may in fact be observations of a form of communication that has nothing to do with food.[44]

Those who are of the view that the hyrax does not regurgitate its food are therefore faced with the question of why the Torah describes it as a ruminant. One approach to this relates to the hyrax's internal physiology. The hyrax possesses a somewhat ruminant-like gut, with three distinct areas for digestion.[45] This in turn means that hyraxes take a long time to digest food, and are able to process fiber efficiently, similar to a ruminant.[46] According to some zoologists and rabbinic authorities, this internal digestive physiology is the basis for the Torah idiomatically describing the hyrax as chewing the cud.[47]

Another approach is based on the fact that the lateral, gyratory chewing movements of the hyrax's jaws resemble those of a cud-chewer.[48] Furthermore, like ruminants, hyraxes engage in chewing actions even when they are not grazing. Superficially, then, a hyrax certainly *looks as though* it is ruminating, and some explain that the Torah therefore describes it as bringing up the cud.[49]

There are several ways of explaining the precise reasoning behind this. One explanation is that these chewing motions cause people to mistakenly think that the hyrax brings up the cud, which is why the Torah had to mention it. Another explanation is that since most animals that chew in this way are cud-chewers, the term "chewing the cud" is

310

WEIXIANG NG

used idiomatically to refer to all animals that chew in such a way.

Alternately, and perhaps preferably, usage can be made of the principle that *dibra Torah kilshon benei adam*, "the Torah speaks like the language of men." This phrase appears in numerous places throughout the Talmud and Midrash, in the rabbinic works of the medieval period, and in the writings of recent scholars, and its meaning varies.[50] But according to several important rabbinic authorities, it means that the Torah packages its messages and laws within the scientific worldview of antiquity.[51] Thus, since the hyrax appears to chew the cud and is commonly thought of as being a cud-chewer, the Torah describes it as such.

The Only Such Animals in the World?
THEOLOGY, PHILOSOPHY, AND SCIENCE

The Talmud states that the four animals listed in the Torah as possessing only one of the two kosher signs are the only such animals in the world:

> The school of R. Yishmael taught: "And the camel, because it (*hu*) brings up the cud etc." – the Ruler of His world knows that there is no creature that brings up the cud and is non-kosher except for the camel (and the other animals listed), therefore Scripture specified it with *hu* ("it," i.e. these animals alone chew the cud but lack split hooves). (Chullin 59a)

Based on the previous discussion, there is a difficulty with this statement. In order to account for why the hyrax is described as bringing up its cud, we noted that the defini-

tion of bringing up the cud has to be expanded to include merycism, a compartmentalized stomach, or ruminant-like chewing. In the section on the hare, we will see that it was also extended by some to include a phenomenon known as cecotrophy. All these features also exist with other animals – kangaroos engage in ruminant-like chewing, koalas and proboscis monkeys engage in merycism, capybaras engage in cecotrophy, and many animals have compartmentalized stomachs. Accordingly, there are more than just four animals with one kosher sign. This would appear to contradict the statement of the school of R. Yishmael that the four animals in the Torah's list are the only such animals in the world.

One approach to this problem is that the word "world" can have different meanings. The word "world" of the Sages presumably does not include other planets. It also need not refer to the entire planet Earth. There are several instances in the Talmud where we see that it refers to a limited region, such as the civilized areas of the world familiar to the Sages.[52] Indeed, in some cases we see that the Sages themselves did not care if their laws regarding animals had exceptions in remote places.[53] Accordingly, since these other animals with one kosher sign live in remote regions such as South America and Australia, they do not conflict with the Talmud's statement. While R. Yishmael presumably did not know of kangaroos, koalas, and proboscis monkeys, he would not have cared to alter his statement even if he would have known of them. In the world of the Torah, the four animals listed as possessing one kosher sign are indeed the only such animals.

A hyrax emerging from the rocks

Elsewhere, the Talmud states that Moses' statements about the laws of kosher animals are evidence for the divine origins of the Torah.[54] The precise reference and meaning of the Talmud's statement is unclear and disputed.[55] But, apparently beginning in the eighteenth century, it was taken as referring to the list of four animals with one kosher sign, and as meaning that these are the only such animals on the planet, in line with the aforementioned exegesis.[56] However, in light of the fact that the list of four animals is best understood as referring to animals from the local region rather than being an exclusive list of all such animals on the planet, this recent interpretation of the argument for the divine origins of the Torah is problematic.

The Median Hyrax

SYMBOLISM

The Sages explained the four kingdoms under which the Jewish people were exiled – Babylon, Persia-Media, Greece, and Rome – as being a motif that is expressed in many different forms in Scripture. They thereby perceived the turbulent events of history as being part of the grand divine plan for creation.[57]

Elsewhere, we have seen that the four wild beasts in Daniel's vision symbolized these four kingdoms. But the same motif was also applied in expounding concepts in the

312

Torah that are not obviously symbolic. Thus, the Torah's list of animals with one kosher sign – the camel, hyrax, hare, and pig – was interpreted by the Sages as referring to the four kingdoms. Unlike the symbolism of the predators in Daniel's dream, which is wholly negative, these animals possess one of the two signs required for an animal to be kosher, and as such they express a certain positive symbolism. The hyrax, second in the list, is understood to allude to the second of the four kingdoms: the joint kingdom of Persia and Media:

> R. Shmuel bar Nachman said: The prophets all saw the kingdoms going about their business. Moses saw the kingdoms going about their business: "The camel" is Babylon... "the hyrax" is Media. The rabbis and R. Yehuda son of R. Shimon [differed regarding this]. The rabbis said: Just as this hyrax has a kosher sign (i.e. bringing up the cud) and a non-kosher sign (i.e. no split hooves), so too the kingdom of Media established both a righteous person (i.e. Darius II) and an evil person (i.e. Ahasuerus).[58] R. Yehuda son of R. Shimon said: Darius II, son of Esther, was pure from his mother's side and impure from his father's side... (i.e. the kosher and non-kosher aspects are expressed in the same person). (*Vayikra Rabba* 13:5)

Perhaps hyraxes were regarded favorably because they are simply adorable, especially babies

The Midrash continues with further parallels, based upon a play on words in the description of the hyrax bringing up its cud:

> Another explanation: … "the hyrax" is Media, "for it raises up the cud" – that it [raised up its voice in] praise of the Holy One, as it says, "So says Cyrus, king of Persia" (Ezra 1:2)…
>
> Another explanation: … "the hyrax" is Media, "for it brings up its cud" – that it 'brought up' Mordekhai, as it says, "And Mordekhai sat at the gate of the king" (Est. 2:21)….
>
> Another explanation: … "the hyrax" is Media, "for it brings up the cud (gera)" – that it dragged (megarer) another kingdom after it (i.e. Greece). (Vayikra Rabba ibid.)

ISRAEL GOVERNMENT PRESS PHOTOGRAPHY OFFICE

Similar such parallels were drawn in other midrashic texts.[59] Later scholars sought to find further grounds for the hyrax to symbolize Persia/Media; one suggestion is that one of the major cities of the Median Empire was Isfahan, which is etymologically similar to *shafan*.[60]

Perhaps most remarkable is how a passage in Proverbs describing four small yet ingenious animals – the ant, hyrax, locust, and spider – was likewise interpreted by the Sages as referring to the four kingdoms. Here, too, the hyrax symbolizes Persia and Media, and a further parallel is added to the metaphor:

> "There are four in the land that are small" (Prov. 30:26) – This alludes to the four kingdoms…. "The hyraxes are not a strong people" – this refers to Media. Just as the hyrax has a kosher sign and a non-kosher sign, so too Media; Ahasuerus the uncircumcised, and Esther the Jew. "And they put their homes amongst the rocks" – that they sought to build the Holy Temple, as it says, "So says Cyrus king of Persia…" (Midrash Mishlei 30:26; Yalkut Shimoni, Mishlei 904)

The hyrax's homebuilding could have been compared to the Persian building of palaces. Instead, it was interpreted as symbolizing the Persian rebuilding of the Temple. This denotes an unusually positive view of both the Persian-Median Empire as well as the non-kosher hyrax.

In a different context, the Midrash notes that the hyrax provides a lesson as to the value of even a non-kosher animal:

> "The rocks are a refuge for hyraxes" – These hyraxes hide under rocky outcrops from birds flying overhead, that they should not eat them. And if the Holy One created His world in such a way on behalf of a non-kosher animal, how much more so did He create it for the merit of Abraham! (Bereshit Rabba 12:9[61])

It seems that, notwithstanding its non-kosher status and subsequent use as a symbol for a foreign empire, the hyrax was always perceived in a positive light. The references to the hyrax in Psalms and Proverbs present it as part of the beauty and wonder of the natural world. We also find that the scribe who served as emissary of the righteous king Josiah (Yoshiyahu) was named Shafan, indicating that the hyrax had positive associations.[62] It seems that there was always a fondness for this familiar, yet somewhat enigmatic, small furry animal.　■

◀ *A hyrax in its rocky habitat*

Notes

1 Note that the term "coney," which is used in some works as a translation of *shafan* (or *arnevet*), usually refers to the rabbit, and was originally used by European and American translators who were unfamiliar with the hyrax. Since then, the word has sometimes also been used to refer to the hyrax.

2 For more extensive discussion, see *The Camel, the Hare and the Hyrax* (Jerusalem: Zoo Torah / Gefen Books, 2011), by this author, as well as various posts at www.rationalistjudaism.com.

3 J.B. Sale, "The habitat of the rock hyrax," *Journal of the East African Natural History Society* (1966) 25, pp. 205–214.

4 Arik Kershenbaum, "Rock hyrax (*Procavia capensis*) den site selection: preference for artificial sites," *Wildlife Research* (2011) 38, pp. 244–248.

5 H. Hoeck, "Hyraxes," in *The Encyclopedia of Mammals* (ed. D. MacDonald, Oxfordshire: Andromeda Oxford, 2001).

6 V. Gargett, *The Black Eagle: A Study* (Randburg, South Africa: Acorn Books, 1990).

7 Ibn Ezra, commentary to Leviticus 11:13.

8 Fulgence Fresnel, *Journal Asiatique*, 3rd series, v. 514, cited in *The Jewish Encyclopedia* (New York and London: Funk & Wagnalls Company, 1901), "Coney."

9 H.B. Tristram, *The Natural History of the Bible* (New Jersey: Gorgias Press, 2002, reprint of 1883 ed.), p. 75.

10 See the commentaries of Chizkuni, *Bekhor Shor,* and Rabbi Chaim Dov Rabinowitz, *Daat Soferim* (Jerusalem, 1986) to Leviticus 11:4.

11 H.B. Tristram, *The Natural History of the Bible*, p. 77.

12 Chullin 59a.

13 K. Rübsamen, I.D. Hume, and W.V. Engelhardt, "Physiology of the Rock Hyrax," *Comparative Biochemistry and Physiology A* (1982) 72:2, pp. 271–277. Rabbi David Zvi Hoffman notes that the word *tafza* could well refer to the hyrax for this reason.

14 See Ilya Dines, "The Textual and Pictorial Metamorphoses of the Animal called *Chyrogrillius*," in *Science Translated: Latin and Vernacular Translations of Scientific Treatises in Medieval* Europe, eds. Michèle Goyens, Pieter De Leemans, and An Smets (Mediaevalia Lovaniensia, Series I, Studia XL), (Leuven: Leuven University Press, 2008), pp. 73–90.

15 This was the etymology given by Heyschius of Alexandria in his fifth-century dictionary; see H.G. Liddell, *A Greek-English Lexicon* (Oxford, 1897), p. 1732.

16 Julius Fuerst, *A Hebrew & Chaldean Lexicon to the Old Testament* (London: Willams & Norgate, 1867, translation by Samuel Davidson), p. 1432.

17 Rosenmüller, *Handbuch der Biblischen Alterthumskunde* (Leipzig: Baumgärtner, 1823–1831) vol 4 part II p. 220, likewise states that the hyrax earns its Amharic name of *aschkoko* due to its possessing hedgehog-like hairs that resemble thorns, called *aschok* in Amharic.

18 Although Jerome used this translation for *shafan* in Leviticus and Deuteronomy, he used *ericii* (hedgehog) for the *shafan* in Psalms, and *lepusculus* (small hare) for the *shafan* in Proverbs; presumably, he decided to use terms that would be more familiar to his readers. See Ilya Dines, "The Textual and Pictorial Metamorphoses of the Animal called *Chyrogrillius*," pp. 73–90.

19 *Letter to Sunnias and Fretela* (403 CE). Cited by Rosenmüller and Rabbi David Zvi Hoffman.

20 H.B. Tristram, *The Natural History of the Bible*, p. 75.

21 An early example of this is with Rabbi Yona ibn Janach of Spain, who identifies Rabbi Saadia Gaon's *wabr* (the Arabic name for hyrax) as the European rabbit.

22 "The cape hare (*Lepus capensis*)...is the only endemic species of lago-
morph known from the Middle East since the Middle Pleistocene" – Eitan Tchernov, Theodora Bar-El, "Lagomorph Remains at Prehistoric Sites in Israel and Southern Sinai," *Paléorient* (2000) 26:1, pp. 93–109. One can find occasional references to rabbits in Israel, but closer investigation inevitably demonstrates these to be mistakes, and to actually be describing hares.

23 Yosef Schonhak, *Toledot HaAretz* (Warsaw: H. Bomberg, 1841) vol. I p. 32, rejects identifying the *shafan* as the rabbit for this reason, as does *Kitvei HaRav Dr. Yosef HaLevi Zeliger* (Jerusalem: Defus Ivri, 1930), p. 236, also cited in *Teshuvot Rabbi Yitzchak HaLevi Herzog, Yoreh De'ah* 23.

24 Yitzchak Betech, *The Enigma of the Biblical Shafan* (Betech, 2013), p. 85.

25 Samuel Bochart, *Hierozoïcon Sive Bipertitum Opus De Animalibus Sacre Scripturae* ("A Natural History of Old: A Two Volume Work on Animals of the Sacred Scriptures") (London, 1663), vol. I, pp. 1001–1017.

26 The Copto-Arabic lexicon by Barakat ibn Kabar was called the *Scala Magna*; in the seventeenth century, Athanasius Kircher made the work available to the West in his trilingual *Lingua Aegyptiaca Restituta*. The *chyrogrillius* is translated into Arabic on p. 165.

27 Rabbi Dr. Ludwig Lewysohn, *Die Zoologie des Talmuds* (Frankfurt am Main, 1858), p. 110 (strangely, although he refers to Rosenmüller in his *Handbuch der Biblischen Alterthumskunde* – who rejected the jerboa in favor of the newly-rediscovered hyrax – Lewysohn makes no mention of the hyrax and misunderstands the term *klipdachs* as referring to the jerboa). Alexander Kohut (1842–1894), in his extended commentary on the *Arukh* entitled *Arukh HaShalem*, identifies the *shafan* as the *Dipus jaculus*, which is a species of jerboa. Yosef Schonhak, *Toledot HaAretz*, vol. I (*Toledot HaChayim*), *maarekhet hayonkim*, p. 32, observes that the jerboa described by these authors lives in tunnels in the sand, and thus cannot be the *shafan*, which is described in Psalms and Proverbs as dwelling in the rocks. Schonhak identifies it instead as the *alkadaga* (which today, in the form of *Allactaga*, refers to a particular genus of jerboas), claiming that this species of jerboa does indeed make its home in the rocks. However, this is not in fact the case.

28 D.M. Stoddart, "Rodents: Equipped for Gnawing," *The Encyclopedia of Mammals* (ed. D. MacDonald, Oxfordshire: Andromeda Oxford, 2001), p. 580

29 Leviticus 11:41. The hyrax is a significantly larger creature than the jerboa and is therefore defined as a *chaya*, albeit barely. Note that in Proverbs, the *shafan* is grouped with the locust, ant, and spider as being one of the small creatures. It is also possible that a creature could be simultaneously a *chaya* and a *sheretz*; see Rambam, *Mishneh Torah, Hilkhot Maakhalot Assurot* 2:23.

30 Rabbi Yaakov Yechezkel HaLevi (1814–1864), *Bikkoret HaTalmud* (Vienna, 1863), pp. 387–9; he also proposes that the *arnevet* is the greater mouse deer. A similar suggestion is proposed by Tzvi Weinberger, "Identifying the Biblical Arneveth with the Musk-Deer and the Shafan with the Mouse-Deer: A Hypothesis" (Hebrew), *BDD* 27 (March 2013).

31 Rabbi Meyer Lubin, "Identification of the *Gamal, Shafan* and *Arnevet*," in *Intercom* magazine, May 1973; Rabbi Dr. Moshe Tendler, "Torah and Science: Constraints and Methodology," in *The Torah u-Madda Journal*, Volume 5, 1994, p. 178.

32 Rabbi Dr. Yosef Zeliger, *Kitvei HaRav Dr. Yosef HaLevi Zeliger* (Jerusalem: Defus Ivri, 1930), pp. 236–237 suggests that the *shafan* and *arnevet* are two undiscovered miniature varieties of camel, one even small enough to hide under rocks, but the conspicuous absence of any fossils or other evidence for such extraordinary creatures renders this highly implausible.

33 Thomas Shaw, *Travels, or Observations Relating to Several Parts of Barbary and the Levant* (1738), p. 376.

34 James Bruce, *Travels to Discover the Source of the Nile, Vol. VI: Select Specimens of Natural History* (1790), pp. 179 ff.

35 Rabbi Yosef Schwartz, *Tevuot HaAretz* (Jerusalem, 1845).

36 See e.g. Ernst Friedrich Rosenmüller, *Handbuch der Biblischen Alterthumskunde* vol 4 part II pp. 213–222; David Scot, "On the *Saphan* of the Hebrew Scriptures," *Memoirs of the Wernian Natural History Society*, vol. 6 (1832), pp. 103–112.

37 Commentaries to Leviticus 11:5.

38 E.g. Shimon Bodenheimer, *HaChai BeEretz Yisrael* (Tel Aviv: Dvir, 1953), p. 245; Menachem Dor, *HaChai BiYemei HaMikra HaMishna VeHaTalmud* (Tel Aviv: Grafor-Daftal books, 1997), p. 56; Yehuda Feliks, *The Animal World of the Bible* (Tel Aviv: Sinai, 1962), p. 45.

39 The notion that the *shafan* is an unknown or extinct animal can be refuted on zoological and zooarcheological grounds. Chapter five of *The Camel, The Hare And The Hyrax* is dedicated to this.

40 Following Ibn Ezra, Chizkuni, Radak, Rashbam, and contemporary linguistic scholarship.

41 James Bruce, *Travels to Discover the Source of the Nile, Vol. VI: Select Specimens of Natural History* (1790), pp. 179ff.

42 Hubert Hendrichs, "*Vergleichende Untersuchung des wiederkau-verhaltens*" [Comparative investigation of cud-chewers], *Biologisches Zentralblatt* (1965) 84:6, pp. 736–739 (German).

43 This author has filmed such behavior in his own captive hyrax, which can be viewed online at www.zootorah.com.

44 J.B. Sale, "Daily food consumption and mode of ingestion in the hyrax," *Journal of the East African Natural History Society* (1966) 25, pp. 215–224; Mendelssohn and Yom Tov, *Fauna Palaestina: Mammalia of Israel*, p. 236.

45 E.T. Clemens, "Sites of organic acid production and patterns of digesta movement in the gastrointestinal tract of the rock hyrax," *Journal of Nutrition* (1977) 107:11, pp. 1954–61.

46 J.R. Paul-Murphy, C. J. Murphy et al., "Comparison of transit time of digesta and digestive efficiency of the rock hyrax, the Barbados sheep and the domestic rabbit," *Comparative Biochemistry and Physiology A* (1982) 72:3, pp. 611–613.

47 Yehuda Feliks, *The Animal World of the Bible*, p. 45, cited approvingly by Rabbi Menachem Kasher, *Torah Sheleima, Vayikra* 11:31.

48 The skull of a hyrax and its musculature is actually very similar to that of ruminants, due to the shared need to extensively masticate the food. See C.M. Janis, "Muscles of the masticatory apparatus in two genera of hyraces (Procavia and Heterohyrax)," *Journal of Morphology* (1983) 176, pp. 61–87.

49 Rabbi David Zvi Hoffman, commentary to Leviticus 11:5, p. 228, in reference to the hare/*arnevet* but also applicable to the hyrax; also cited by Rabbi Yechiel Yaakov Weinberg, *Seridei Esh* (vol. II, 17); Rabbi Menachem Kasher, *Torah Sheleima* to Leviticus 11:32; and Rabbi Amitai Ben-David, *Sichat Chullin* to Chullin 59a. An early reference to this is in H.B. Tristram, *The Natural History of the Bible*, p. 76.

50 See Zion Ukshi, "The Torah Speaks Like the Language of Men – The Development of the Expression and its Nature" (Hebrew), *Derekh Efrata* 9–10 (5761), pp. 39–59.

51 See Rambam, *Guide for the Perplexed* 2:8 and 3:3, with the commentaries of Efodi, Shem Tov, Narvoni, and Abarbanel in *Taanot*, 4, and Rabbi Shlomo Fisher, *Derashot Beit Yishai, Maamar HaMo'ach VeHaLev*, fn. 4; Ralbag, commentary to Genesis 15:4, and commentary to Job, end of ch. 39; Rabbi Dr. Isadore Twersky, "Joseph ibn Kaspi: Portrait of a Medieval Jewish Intellectual," *Studies in Medieval Jewish History and Literature*, volume 1 (Harvard University Press, 1979), pp. 239–242; Rabbi Samson Raphael Hirsch, *Collected Writings* vol. 7 p. 57 and commentary to Genesis 1:6; and Rabbi Avraham Yitzchak Kook, *Eder HaYekar*, pp. 37–38.

52 Rabbi David Gans, a disciple of the Maharal of Prague, in *Nechmad VeNa'im* 89, notes that the word *olam* sometimes refers to the entire universe, sometimes to planet Earth, and sometimes to a limited region, such as with the Talmud's references to warfare coming to the *olam* (Sukka 29a). Rabbi Gans uses this to explain the statement that "Jerusalem is in the center of the world" – he explains that it refers to the areas inhabited in biblical and talmudic times. Rabbi Gedalyah Nadel, one of the foremost disciples of the Chazon Ish, in *BeTorato Shel Rabbi Gedalyah* (Maale Adumim: Shilat, 2004), p. 118, brings further evidence for the "world" of the Torah being of limited scope, in the context of explaining that the Deluge was limited to biblical lands. The Talmud rules that someone who makes an oath to abstain from drinking the waters of the Euphrates is "prohibited from all the waters in the world." Now, while there are many tributaries of the Euphrates, there is certainly no chance that, say, a stream in America is connected to the Euphrates! Hence, concludes Rabbi Nadel, when the Talmud speaks about the "world," it refers to the world of the Sages. In personal discussion with the author, Rabbi Nadel suggested applying this approach to the Talmud's statement regarding the four animals.

53 See the view of Ameimar in Chullin 61b–62a, Chatam Sofer to Chullin 59a, and Responsa Rivash 192.

54 "But was Moses a hunter or trapper? From here there is a refutation of one who says that Torah is not from Heaven" – Chullin 60b.

55 *Tosafot* to Chullin 60b explain the argument as referring to the knowledge of the *shesuah*, a mutant animal that the Talmud infers as being mentioned in Deuteronomy. Rashi to Chullin 60b, and Netziv in his commentary to *Sifrei, Re'eh* 49, understand the argument as referring to the detailed information presented about all the different animals in the Torah's laws of *kashrut*.

56 Naftali Hertz Wessely, *Levanon, Gan Na'ul, HaBayit HaRishon, Cheder 7, Chalon* 7; Maharatz Chayes, commentary to Chullin 60b; Malbim to Leviticus 11:6; Rabbi Petachyah Menken in *Kerem Petachyah* (Jerusalem, 1931), p.118, citing Wessely; Rabbi Barukh HaLevi Epstein (1860–1942) in *Torah Temima* (1902) Leviticus 11:4 note 17.

57 Rivka Raviv, "The Talmudic Formulation of the Prophecies of the Four Kingdoms in the Book of Daniel" (Hebrew), *Jewish Studies, an Internet Journal* (2006), pp. 1–20.

58 This follows the interpretations of *Yefeh To'ar*. According to *Matnot Kehuna*, it refers to Mordekhai and Haman.

59 *Midrash Tanchuma, Shemini* 8, presents further parallels between the four animals with one kosher sign and the four kingdoms. In the version that we have, it has the hyrax representing Greece rather than Media: את השפן זו יון שהשפילה את התורה מפי הנביאים שנאמר (יחזקאל יד) הנה ימים באים נאם ה' והשלחתי רעב וגו' וכתיב ונעו מים עד ים וגו'. Rabbi Shmuel Waldberg, *Darkhei HaShinuyim* (Lemberg, 1870) 10:3, p. 66b says that this is based on an acronym of *shafan* which appears in the phrase שהשפילה את התורה מפי הנביאים. However, Rabbi Meir ben Samuel Benveniste, in *Ot Emet* (Salonica, 1565) (p. 48a in Prague 1624 edition), emends the text in order to make the hyrax represent Media, thus bringing it into line with the other Midrashim: את השפן זו מדי שעשתה את ישראל פאה והפקר להשמיד להרוג ולאבד את כל וגו'. This would appear to be correct, since the other verse is followed by a statement that the mother of Ptolemy was named after a hare, indicating that that section is speaking about Greece rather than Media.

60 Avraham Epstein, *MiKadmoniyut HaYehudim* (Vienna, 1887), vol. 1, pp. 31–35.

61 For a discussion regarding the theological lesson being taught by this midrash, see the chapter on ibex.

62 II Kings chapter 22.

HARE

Hare

Arnevet

Hares and Rabbits

NATURAL HISTORY

The hare is mentioned in the Torah in the list of four animals that possess only one of the two characteristics required for an animal to be kosher:

> And God spoke to Moses and to Aaron, saying to them: Speak to the Children of Israel, saying, This is the animal that you may eat from all the animals which are on the earth – every animal that has a cloven hoof that is fully split, and that brings up the cud, you may eat. However, this you may not eat from those that bring up the cud and from those that have cloven hooves: the camel, for it brings up the cud, but does not have cloven hooves – it is unclean for you. And the hyrax, for it brings up the cud, but does not have cloven hooves, it is unclean for you. And the hare, for it brings up the cud, but does not have cloven hooves, it is unclean for you. And the pig, for it has cloven hooves that are fully split, but it does not bring up its cud, it is unclean for you. You shall not eat of their flesh, and you should not touch their carcasses; they are unclean for you. (Lev. 11:1–8)

> וְאֶת הָאַרְנֶבֶת כִּי מַעֲלַת גֵּרָה הִוא וּפַרְסָה לֹא הִפְרִיסָה טְמֵאָה הִוא לָכֶם:
>
> ויקרא יא:ו
>
> אַךְ אֶת זֶה לֹא תֹאכְלוּ מִמַּעֲלֵי הַגֵּרָה וּמִמַּפְרִיסֵי הַפַּרְסָה הַשְּׁסוּעָה אֶת הַגָּמָל וְאֶת הָאַרְנֶבֶת וְאֶת הַשָּׁפָן כִּי מַעֲלֵה גֵרָה הֵמָּה וּפַרְסָה לֹא הִפְרִיסוּ טְמֵאִים הֵם לָכֶם:
>
> דברים יד:ז

This list is repeated, in a more concise form, later in the Torah:

> However, this you shall not eat, from those that bring up the cud and from those that have a completely split hoof: the camel, the hare, and the hyrax; for they bring up the cud, but they do not have split hooves; therefore they are unclean to you. (Deut. 14:7)

Although the word *arnevet* in Modern Hebrew is often used in reference to the rabbit, the *arnevet* of the Torah is actually the hare rather than the rabbit. Rabbits are by far the more familiar animals to most people today, due to

The European rabbit

The common hare

Unlike rabbits, hares escape predators by running rather than hiding in burrows

their popularity as pets, but they are not the *arnevet* of the Torah. There are no rabbits in the region of Israel, and nor were there any in biblical times; rabbits lived only in the Iberian Peninsula and adjacent France at the time that the Torah was given. The more accurate term for the rabbit in Modern Hebrew is *arnavon*.

The hare of the Torah is the hare known as the common, brown, or cape hare, *Lepus capensis*. It is a larger animal than the familiar rabbit, with proportionally much longer ears and limbs. It is also much more solitary than the gregarious rabbit. The common hare is found throughout many parts of Africa, Asia, and Europe. There are many different subspecies of this hare, which vary in size, color, and relative size of the extremities. Those found in Israel are the Syrian hare (*Lepus capensis syriacus*), the Philistine hare (*L. c. philistinus*), the Sinai hare (*L. c. sinaiticus*), and the Arabian hare (*L. c. arabicus*).

Zoologically, rabbits and hares are in the same family of *Leporidae* within the order of lagomorphs (literally, "hare-shaped"). This family also includes the pikas, which resemble large hamsters. Leporids can be broadly divided into two groups: the hares, which are specialized runners, and the rabbits, which are specialized for burrowing. Due to the great similarity of rabbits and hares, rabbits would presumably be grouped together with hares under the category of *arnevet* for halakhic classification purposes, even

though they are not the primary reference in the Torah; we shall therefore use the terms interchangeably.

Evidence for the Hare

IDENTIFICATION

The identification of the *arnevet* as the hare is based on a long and universal tradition, as well as numerous lines of evidence.

The hare has long been called *arnab* in Arabic. As noted by Ibn Ezra, Arabic names for animals provide evidence for their correct identification in the Torah.[1] Rabbi Yosef Schwartz, a nineteenth-century immigrant to the Land of Israel who wrote about the geography and natural history of the Torah, identified the *arnevet* with the Arabic *arnab*.[2]

The very warning in the Torah against eating the *arnevet* further supports its identification as the hare. As we saw in the case of the hyrax, several rabbinic authorities explain that the Torah specifically warned against eating those animals that had one kosher sign and which were commonly eaten by people in the area.[3] This is true of the hare even in more recent times. Tristram, the nineteenth-century chronicler of the flora and fauna of the Land of Israel, notes that "the flesh of the hare is highly esteemed by the Arabs, who assert that it is clean because it chews the cud, their limitation not extending to the other requisite of dividing the hoof."[4]

The Sages of the Talmud clearly identified the *arnevet* of the Torah as the hare. One of the strongest lines of evidence for this emerges from the account of Ptolemy II Philadelphus (285–247 B.C.E.) forcing the Sages to translate the Torah into Greek:

> There was an incident with King Ptolemy that he placed seventy-two elders into seventy-two rooms without telling them the reason. Then he entered to each one and said to them, "Write the Torah of your teacher Moses for me!" The Holy One placed counsel in the heart of each of them, and they all wrote the same version . . . and they wrote for him "and the *tze'irat haraglayim* (short legs)" instead of writing "and the hare," because King Ptolemy's wife was called "hare" (in its Greek equivalent), that he ought not to say, "The Jews are making fun of me, and they put my wife's name in the Torah."[5] (Megilla 9a–9b[6])

Although here it states that it was Ptolemy's wife's name about which they were concerned, this may be a textual inaccuracy; Ptolemy's wife was called Arsinoe, which is not known to be the name of an animal.[7] Some texts state instead that it was Ptolemy's mother;[8] yet she was called Berenice, which is likewise not known to be the name of an animal. It seems that it actually refers to the father of Ptolemy I Soter, who was called Lagos, which is identical to the Greek word for "hare."[9] The general consensus is that this is the correct understanding of the Talmud.[10] Accordingly, we see that the Sages understood the *arnevet* to be the hare.[11]

There are further lines of evidence from this story that the *arnevet* is the hare. The Talmud states that the Sages translated *arnevet* with the description *tze'irat haraglayim*, "short-legs." Although this description could match many animals, Rashi explains that this refers to its front legs, which are much smaller than its back legs. This description noticeably matches the hare.[12]

The Septuagint translates *arnevet* as *dasypous*, which literally means, "hairy foot." Likewise, there is a version of the text of the Talmud which reads that the *arnevet* was translated as *se'irat haraglayim*, "hairy feet," rather than *tze'irat haraglayim*.[13] Unlike with most other animals, which have

Rabbits and hares are unusual in possessing thick hair on the soles of their feets, rather than pads

pads on the soles of their feet, the feet of rabbits and hares are covered with long, thick brush-like hairs, which provide a better grip and cushion when moving on hard ground.[14]

There are a number of references to the *arnevet* in Torah literature that also support its identification as the hare and rabbit family. Rabbits and hares have been commonly used as food by the nations of the world, and we see that the Talmud mentions this use of the *arnevet*:

> Tzidkiyah found Nebuchadnezzar eating a live[15] hare. He said, Swear to me that you will not reveal this about me and word will not go out. (Nedarim 65a; cf. *Eikha Rabba* 2:18[16])

Rabbits have also long been killed for their soft hair:

> The school of R. Yishmael taught: the word "garment" only includes a garment of wool or flax; how do we know to include camel fur and rabbit fur … ? Therefore it states, "Or a garment …" (Shabbat 27a)

The Midrash describes an interesting use of the rabbit for its fur:

> "And God, the Lord, made garments of skin for Adam and his wife, and He clothed them" (Gen. 3:21) … R. Shmuel bar Nachman said: They were camel fur and rabbit fur; "garments of skin" meaning, garments that are derived from skin. (*Bereshit Rabba* 20:12)[17]

There has been continuous discussion throughout the ages in Jewish law as to whether it is permitted to raise and trade in rabbits and hares for various different purposes. It is forbidden to raise and trade with non-Jews in non-kosher animals that are used for food.[18] On the other hand, one may raise and trade in non-kosher creatures that are kept for purposes other than food, such as ornamental birds that are raised for pleasure, camels that are raised for work, and horses.[19] If one lives in a time and place where rabbits are commonly eaten, but wants to raise rabbits for their fur, or keep a rabbit as a pet, some rabbinic authorities are still stringent and prohibit this,[20] whereas others permit it in these circumstances.[21] It is clear from these sources that there is a long-standing tradition of the rabbit and hare being called *arnevet*.

All other statements concerning the *arnevet* also match the hare. The Talmud states that the *arnevet* possesses upper teeth, which is true of rabbits and hares (unlike the true ruminants).[22] As for the etymology of the name *arnevet*, it is suggested that it relates to the word *ar*, which means "split,"[23] and *niv*, which means "upper lip."[24] The upper lip of a hare is split in two, which is why the hare is called *ar-nevet*.[25] (Humans born with such a feature are termed "hare-lipped.")

The American jackrabbits are actually a kind of hare

Due to long-standing tradition, and its name in other languages, all scholars of scriptural zoology accept that the *arnevet* is the hare. The only people to reject identifying the *arnevet* as the hare are those who are uncomfortable with the scriptural description of it "chewing the cud," due to their particular religious outlook (as we shall explain). However, no other remotely viable candidate for the *arnevet* exists.[26]

Does the Hare Chew Its Cud?

THEOLOGY, PHILOSOPHY, AND SCIENCE

The Torah describes the hare as bringing up its cud, i.e. that it is a ruminant. Zoologists state that, in contrast to the biblical description, rabbits and hares are not ruminants. This was first raised as a difficulty by Bible critics in the eighteenth century.[27]

In response to this problem, some argued that the zoological literature cannot be relied upon, because zoology bases rumination solely on the existence of multiple stomachs, whereas rabbits and hares could regurgitate their food even in the absence of multiple stomachs.[28] Yet the anatomy

321

of rabbits and hares renders them incapable of vomiting.[29] Furthermore, the rabbit has been studied so extensively in the laboratory that it is inconceivable that a phenomenon such as rumination could have gone undetected. Finally, as we shall soon see, rabbits and hares have their own unique method for extracting the maximum nutrition from their food. Regurgitating it for remastication is therefore entirely unnecessary.

If the hare does not ruminate, how can the Torah describe it in such a way? There are two aspects of a hare's digestive processes that are suggested to earn it this description.

Although rabbits and hares do not produce cud for rechewing, they do have digestive systems that are greatly modified for digesting large amounts of cellulose in vegetation. In order to digest their food properly, much of it has to be passed through the gut twice. Special pellets called cecotrophs, entirely different in both appearance and composition to ordinary fecal pellets, are produced from the cecum and reingested for a second round of digestion. This is sometimes referred to as "coprophagy," but more precisely referred to as "refection" or "cecotrophy."[30] Cecotrophy is fundamentally similar to rumination; indeed, some

works refer to it as "pseudo-rumination." Some argue that it qualifies for the term *maale gera*, "bringing up the cud," in the Torah.[31]

A problem with the cecotrophy explanation is that it is difficult to read this into the words *maale gera*, which literally mean "bringing up that which travels by way of the throat."[32] It might be suggested that the phrase is an idiom for any type of ruminant-like behavior, even if the words themselves do not literally refer to such phenomena; but aside from the lack of traditional support for such an approach, it is far from straightforward on a textual level.[33]

Another approach is based on the fact that the lateral, gyratory chewing movements of the hare's jaws resemble those of a cud-chewer.[34] Furthermore, like ruminants, hares engage in chewing actions even when they are not grazing.[35] Superficially, then, a hare certainly looks as though it is ruminating, and some explain that the Torah therefore describes it as bringing up the cud.[36] There are several ways of explaining the precise reasoning behind this. One explanation is that these chewing motions cause people to mistakenly think that the hare brings up the cud, which is why the Torah had to mention it. Another

Rabbits and hares chew with ruminant-like lateral motions of the jaw

Hares standing to fight during courtship

explanation is that since most animals that chew in this way are cud-chewers, the term "chewing the cud" is used idiomatically to refer to all animals that chew in such a way. Alternately, and perhaps preferably, usage can be made of the principle that *dibra Torah kilshon benei adam*, "the Torah speaks like the language of men." This phrase appears in numerous places throughout the Talmud and Midrash, in the rabbinic works of the medieval period, and in the writings of recent scholars, and its meaning varies.[37] But according to several important rabbinic authorities, it means that the Torah packages its messages and laws within the scientific worldview of antiquity.[38] Thus, since the hare appears to chew the cud and is commonly thought of as being a cud-chewer, the Torah describes it as such.

Female Hares

THEOLOGY, PHILOSOPHY, AND SCIENCE

The hare is mentioned in the Torah under the Hebrew name *arnevet*, with the feminine suffix of "*et*," rather than the masculine form of "*arnav*."[39] This is in contrast to most other animals in the Torah, whose names are in the masculine form. Some explain that the Torah is specifically highlighting female hares as representative of the species,[40] while others are of the view that male hares also have this name.[41] But either way, it is incongruous, and several explanations have been proposed for it.

One answer is that in contrast to most mammals, female hares and rabbits are usually larger than males and dominate the society. There is a curious inversion of roles, with males sometimes protecting the young from being attacked by females – the opposite of what takes place with most mammals.[42] It may be due to this that female hares are used in representation of hares in general.

In a slight twist on this explanation, some note that female hares dominate the breeding process. The phrases, "mad as a March hare" and "hare-brained" come from the springtime mating antics of female hares assessing the courting males. The females stand up on their hind legs and cuff the males in the face and ears, sometimes even mounting them. Due to the females taking a leading role in procreation, they are mentioned in the Torah as representative of the species.[43] Another explanation is that, in contrast to most animals, male hares have no easily distinguishable male sexual characteristics and may appear to be females.[44]

In the medieval period, there were suggestions that the feminine version of the name is used because the hare is androgynous,[45] constantly changes its gender,[46] or because there are simply no males to be found.[47] While these characteristics are not true of the hare (and nor of any other mammal), they were widespread beliefs about the hare for centuries, attested to by the Roman naturalist Pliny[48] and many others,[49] stemming from the unusual anatomy and behavior of hares referred to above.

323

The Greek Hare

The Sages explained the four kingdoms under which the Jewish people were exiled – Babylon, Persia-Media, Greece, and Rome – as being a motif that is expressed in many different forms in Scripture. They thereby perceived the turbulent events of history as being part of the grand divine plan for creation.[50]

Elsewhere, we have seen that the four wild beasts in Daniel's vision symbolized these four kingdoms. But even concepts in the Torah that are not obviously symbolic were also interpreted as referring to the same motif. Thus, the Torah's list of animals with one kosher sign – the camel, hyrax, hare, and pig – was interpreted by the Sages as referring to the four kingdoms. Unlike the symbolism of the predators in Daniel's dream, which is wholly negative, these animals possess one of the two signs required for an animal to be kosher, and as such they express a certain positive symbolism. The hare, third in the list, is understood to allude to the third of the four kingdoms – that of Greece:

> R. Shmuel bar Nachman said: The prophets all saw the kingdoms going about their business. Moses saw the kingdoms going about their business: "The camel" is Babylon…"the hyrax" is Media…"the hare" is Greece. "Because it raises up its cud" – that it [raised up its voice in] praise to the Holy One. When Alexander of Macedon saw Shimon HaTzaddik, he proclaimed, "Blessed is the Lord, the God of Shimon HaTzaddik!"

> Another explanation…"And the hare" – This is Greece. "Because it raises up its cud" – that it raises up the righteous (with respect). When Alexander would see Shimon HaTzaddik, he would stand on his feet. They said to him, "Why do you stand up before a Jew?" He replied, "When I go out to battle, I see his visage and I triumph."

> Another explanation…"And the hare" – This is Greece. "Because it raises up its cud (*gera*)" – that it dragged along (*megarer*, based on the word *gera*) another kingdom after it – Edom. (*Vayikra Rabba* 13:5)

Similar such parallels were drawn in other midrashic texts, which also referred to the fact that the Greek ruler Ptolemy bore Lagos, Greek for "hare," as a family name.[51] Later scholars pointed out further grounds for the hare to symbolize Greece.[52] The hare was an important totem in ancient Greece, symbolizing love and fecundity – hares are unique in often conceiving new offspring while still pregnant with offspring from beforehand.[53] Contemporary works on the cultural history of animals point out that the Greeks were "the originators in Europe of a complex symbolic and mythic role for the hare."[54] Images of hares are found on a wide range of Greek coins, vessels, and jewelry.[55]

It is interesting that despite the hare symbolizing a foreign enemy, its symbolism for Greece in the Midrash was largely depicted in positive terms. Perhaps this reflects the fact that the hare in general is an entirely inoffensive creature. As we shall see, the hare was often used in Jewish symbolism.

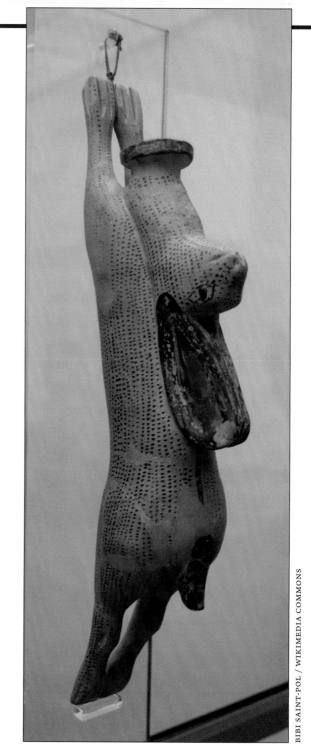

A ancient Greek flask in the shape of a hare

BIBI SAINT-POL / WIKIMEDIA COMMONS

Hares, Hounds, and the Haggada
———————————————— SYMBOLISM

Images of hares appear in all kinds of Jewish contexts. A design of three hares arranged in a circle, such that each ear is used for two hares, originated in China, but eventually made its way to synagogues, where it was common in Germany during the seventeenth and eighteenth centuries. It also often appeared on Jewish tombstones, apparently symbolizing the patriarchs' chain of eternal life.[56]

Beginning in the fifteenth century, many Passover Haggadot featured illustrations of hounds, accompanied by a huntsman, pursuing hares.[57] While this was a common image in medieval illuminated manuscripts, it held particu-lar significance when appearing in a Haggada. There is a mnemonic to help remember the sequence of events when the Passover Seder is held on Saturday night: *YaKNeHaZ*. This acronym stands for *Yayin* (wine), *Kiddush* (sanctification), *Ner* (lighting the candles for Passover), *Havdala* (the blessing for the departure of the Sabbath), and *Zeman* (the *Shehecheyanu* blessing for special occasions). The word *YaKNeHaZ* sounds similar to the German phrase *jag den Has*, meaning "hunt the hare," hence the illustration of such a hunt.

However, there may be more to it than that. In the Augsburg Haggada of 1534, the illustration is of an unsuccessful hunt: the hares are depicted as slipping through the net

325

An illustration of a hare hunt from the fifteenth-century First Cincinnati Haggada

to their freedom, looking over their shoulders at the frustrated hounds. There is more than merely wordplay on *YaKNeHaZ* here. The hares symbolize the Jewish people, persecuted and hunted, escaping to their salvation. Rabbi Yehuda HaLevi presented the concept of the hunted hare as a way for Jews to come to terms with the tribulations of exile; just as the natural world, with its circle of life, reflects divine wisdom, so too all our suffering is clearly part of a larger plan.[58]

This may also shed light on another common illustration in Jewish manuscripts featuring the hare. Beginning in a fourteenth-century Haggada[59] (i.e. predating the *YaKNeHaZ* theme), Esau is depicted as returning to his father Isaac with a hare as the fruit of his hunt. He is also depicted in this manner on the frontispiece of the fourteenth-century Schocken Bible, as well as in other editions of the Haggada. This is especially peculiar in light of the fact that, according to rabbinic tradition, he would only have brought Isaac kosher food!

But perhaps the hare symbolizes Esau's brother Jacob, and by extension, his descendants.[60] The hare has long been known as the animal that survives via its wits. Hares utilize elaborate means to confuse those pursuing their scent trails, such as doubling back on their tracks and leaping sideways to break the trail; they also set up escape routes through gaps in hedges. It thereby symbolizes Jacob, who was pursued by Esau and Laban and had to employ various devious strategies in order to outwit them. The hare's uniquely hairy paws – referred to in the Septuagint's translation of the Torah – may symbolize Jacob's wearing hairy goat hides on his hands when he disguised himself as Esau. Furthermore, inasmuch that the hare bears the internal kosher sign of bringing up the cud, but externally displays the non-kosher feature of lacking split hooves, it symbolizes Isaac's description of Jacob during this episode: "The voice is the voice of Jacob, but the hands are the hands of Esau."[61]

At a larger level, the illustrations also symbolized the Jewish people and their fate during exile. Esau is acting wickedly in bringing non-kosher food to his father, just as his descendants are acting wickedly in their persecution of the Jewish people. Like the hare, the Jewish people lacked strength, and had to survive via their wits and divine compassion. And just as the hare has an external non-kosher sign but an internal kosher sign, the Jewish people might act in a sinful manner, but are pure of heart.[62] ∎

Notes

1 Ibn Ezra, commentary to Leviticus 11:13.

2 Rabbi Yosef Schwartz, *Tevuot HaAretz* (Jerusalem, 1845), p. 367.

3 See the commentaries of Chizkuni, *Bekhor Shor,* and Rabbi Chaim Dov Rabinowitz, *Daat Soferim* (Jerusalem, 1986) to Leviticus 11:4.

4 H.B. Tristram, *The Natural History of the Bible* (New Jersey: Gorgias Press, 2002, reprint of 1883 ed.), p. 99.

5 Maharsha explains that the affront is due to the hare being a non-kosher animal; *Porat Yosef* explains that unlike with other animals, the name for hare is given in the Torah in the feminine gender, and this aberration would give Ptolemy reason to suspect mockery.

6 Also *Midrash Tanchuma, Shemot* 22.

7 Azariah de Rossi, *Meor Einayim, Imrei Bina* 1:7, also cited in *Torah Sheleima,* Leviticus 11 *ot* 33.

8 Y. Megilla 12b; *Midrash Vayikra Rabba* 13:5.

9 Such a transposition can be better understood in light of the fact that *arnevet* is a word in the feminine gender (as discussed later), which may have led people to assume that it must be a female relative. Perhaps the etymological similarity of Ptolemy's mother's name Berenice to *arnevet* also led to this confusion; *Etz Yosef* (loc. cit.) appears to state that confusion occurred for this reason.

10 Ludwig Lewysohn, *Die Zoologie des Talmuds* (Frankfurt am Main, 1858), p. 62; Rabbi David Zvi Hoffman, commentary to Leviticus 11:5, p. 228; *Teshuvot Rabbi Yitzchak HaLevi Herzog, Yoreh De'ah* 23. *Etz Yosef* to *Midrash Vayikra Rabba* 13:5 states that the father and brothers as well as the mother of Ptolemy were known as Lagos. For academic studies of this topic, which conclude that the reference was to Lagos, see Abraham Wasserstein, "On Donkeys, Wine and the Uses of Textual Criticism: Septuagintal Variants in Jewish Palestine," in Lee I. Levine and Daniel R. Schwartz, eds., *Jewish Identities in Antiquity: Studies in Memory of Menahem Stern* (Mohr Siebeck Verlag, Tübingen, 2009), pp. 119–142; David J. Wasserstein, "The Ptolemy and the Hare: Dating an Old Story About the Translation of the Septuagint," *Scripta Classica Israelica* 17 (1998), pp. 77–86; and Nina L. Collins, *The Library in Alexandria and the Bible in Greek* (Leiden: Brill, 2000), pp. 11–13.

11 Rabbi Herzog suggests that even though we see from the story with Ptolemy that the Sages understood the *arnevet* to be the hare, they may have been mistaken; but this is a very difficult approach, and motivated only by discomfort with the description of the *arnevet* chewing its cud. Rabbi Dr. Zev Mishael, *Daat Divrei Chakhamim* (2nd. ed. – Jerusalem, 1929), p. 35, suggests that the Talmud knew it to be a popular misunderstanding that the hare was the *arnevet* and therefore deliberately translated it as *tze'irat haraglayim* to obfuscate its explanation, but this is highly unreasonable.

12 See *Benayahu* for two other explanations as to why it says "little legs" rather than "little arms" (i.e. front legs).

13 Cited by *Torah Temima* and *Pardes Yosef. Torah Sheleima* cites *Dikdukei Soferim* that there is a text reading *tzefirat haraglayim,* which means "shaggy feet."

14 Certain jerboas (a type of rodent) that live in sandy areas have tufts of

bristly hairs on the undersides of their feet, which serve as snowshoes in soft sand, and also help them maintain traction and kick sand back when burrowing. However, the jerboa is not a candidate for the *arnevet*, since it would be defined as as a *sheretz* (vermin) rather than a *chaya* (animal).

15 See Maharsha and *Etz Yosef*. The word used is *chaya*, which Ran states can mean either "raw" or "live."

16 Shlah, *Masekhet Taanit, Matot* 26, has a mystical explanation of this.

17 The Midrash also cites the opinion of R. Yehoshua b. Levi that the garments were *laga'i*. The commentaries *Etz Yosef* and Maharzu, citing Binyamin Mussafia's *Mussaf HaArukh*, explain that *laga'i* is the Greek word for the wool of the *arnevet*.

18 *Shulchan Arukh, Yoreh De'ah* 117.

19 Y. Bava Kama 7:7; *Tosafot*, Bava Kama 82b, s.v. *Lo yigdal*; *She'elot UTeshuvot HaRashba*, 1:489 and 3:223; *Maggid Mishneh, Maakhalot Assurot* 8:16; *Kol Bo*; *Beit Yosef, Yoreh De'ah* 117; *Kaf HaChayim, Yoreh De'ah* II 117:5; *Shakh* to *Yoreh De'ah* 117:1.

20 *Beit Yosef*, citing *ShuT HaRashba* and others that it is forbidden even if one is trading in their skins. *Peri Chadash* states that it is essentially permitted, but nevertheless one should be stringent in accordance with *Beit Yosef* and *Rashba*.

21 See *Kaf HaChayim Yoreh De'ah* II 117:8; *ShuT Chesed LeAvraham, Yoreh De'ah* 9:88b; *Zivchei Tzedek* 43; *ShuT Levushei Mordekhai Tanyana Yoreh De'ah* 50; *Binat Adam, Hilkhot Shechita* 65; *Noda BiYehuda Tinyana* 2:42; *Yad Efraim, Yoreh De'ah* 117:1; *Pitchei Teshuvot* 117:6.

22 Chullin 59a.

23 Cf. *meorat tzifoni*, "the crevice of the asp" (Isaiah 11:8).

24 See Gittin 56a, and Rashi ad loc.

25 Rabbi Yosef Schonhak, *Toledot HaAretz*; *HaKetav VeHaKabbala, Parashat Shemini*.

26 The notion that the *arnevet* is an unknown or extinct animal, suggested by Rabbi Samson Raphael Hirsch, can be refuted on zoological and zooarcheological grounds. Chapter five of *The Camel, The Hare And The Hyrax* is dedicated to this.

27 Voltaire, "The Questions of Zapata" (translated by Dr. Tamponet, of the Sorbonne) in *Toleration and Other Essays* (1755). Translated, with an Introduction, by Joseph McCabe (New York: G.P. Putnam's Sons, 1912).

28 Ludwig Lewysohn, *Die Zoologie des Talmuds*, p. 109, citing Ernst Friedrich Rosenmüller, *Handbuch der Biblischen Alterthumskunde* (Leipzig: Baumgärtner, 1823–1831) vol 4 part II, p. 212, also cited by Rabbi David Zvi Hoffman, commentary to the Torah; Rabbi Natan Adler, *Netina LaGer* to Leviticus 11:6; Rabbi Avraham Korman, "*Devarim Al Amitutam Ve'al Diyukam*," *HaTzofeh* (April 9, 1999), p. 12. Some claim that the source for this is in Aristotle; however, in fact Aristotle makes mention only of hares sharing with ruminants the feature of producing rennet (*Historia Animalium*, III:21). Rabbi Yitzchak HaLevi Herzog, *Teshuvot Rabbi Yitzchak HaLevi Herzog, Yoreh De'ah* 23, cites a Christian theologian who asserts that there is a type of hare in Syria that does indeed bring up the cud, but with which this is difficult to notice.

29 This has many ramifications; for example, like many animals, rabbits groom themselves and ingest their loose hairs. Unlike cats, however, which vomit up the indigestible hair in the form of hairballs, rabbits are unable to do so. It is therefore necessary to prevent the buildup of hairballs in the rabbit's stomach by feeding it high-fiber diets, minimizing stress and boredom, and frequently brushing out loose hairs. Another ramification is with veterinary surgery; it is common to force small animals to fast before undergoing veterinary surgery because they often vomit after coming out of the anesthetic. With rabbits, however, there is no policy to do so, because they cannot vomit. Furthermore, because rabbits cannot vomit, they are used for testing the toxicity of products such as shampoo, bleach, or window cleaner, which are administered orally to them. On rare occasions, rabbits have been known to vomit, but this is very much the exception and it does not seem that it is possible for them to do so in the ordinary course of eating.

30 There are fundamental differences between the coprophagy practiced by animals such as horses, pigs, and gorillas, and the specialized coprophagy practiced by hares and rabbits, and also capybaras. A comprehensive review of this topic is H. Hirakawa, "Coprophagy in leporids and other small mammalian herbivores," *Mammal Review* (2001) 31:1, pp. 61–80, with an important supplement published later in 32:2, pp. 150–152.

31 Rabbi Menachem Kasher, *Torah Sheleima* in *miluim* to 11:32; Rabbi Amitai Ben-David, *Sichat Chullin* to Chullin 59a; Rabbi Dr. Moshe Tendler, "Torah and Science: Constraints and Methodology," *The Torah u-Madda Journal* (1994) vol. 5, p. 178; Rabbi Aryeh Carmell, *Bekhol Derakhekha Daehu* (Ramat Gan: Bar Ilan University Press, 1998) vol. 6, pp. 65–66; and Rabbi Aharon Feldman, personal communication 2000.

32 See the commentaries of Ibn Ezra, Chizkuni, Radak, and Rashbam.

33 For extensive discussion, see *The Camel, The Hare And The Hyrax*, by this author.

34 E. Schneider, in *Grzimek's Encyclopedia of Mammals* (New York: McGraw-Hill Publishing Company, 1990), vol. 4, p. 249; C.M. Janis, "Muscles of the masticatory apparatus in two genera of hyraces (Procavia and Heterohyrax)," *Journal of Morphology* (1983) 176, pp. 61–87.

35 R. M. Lockley, *The Private Life of the Rabbit* (NY: Macmillan, 1964), p. 104; K.Y. Ebino, Y. Shutoh, and W. Takahashi, "Coprophagy in rabbits: autoingestion of hard feces," *Experimental Animals* (1993) 42, pp. 611–613; H. Hirakawa, "Coprophagy in leporids and other small mammalian herbivores," *Mammal Review* (2001) 31:1, pp. 61–80.

36 Rabbi David Zvi Hoffman, commentary to Leviticus 11:5, p. 228; also cited by Rabbi Yechiel Yaakov Weinberg, *Seridei Eish* (vol. II, 17), Rabbi Menachem Kasher, *Torah Sheleima* to Leviticus 11:32; and Rabbi Amitai Ben-David, *Sichat Chullin* to Chullin 59a.

37 See Zion Ukshi, "The Torah Speaks Like the Language of Men – The Development of the Expression and its Nature" (Hebrew), *Derekh Efrata* 9–10 (5761), pp. 39–59.

38 See Rambam, *Guide for the Perplexed* 2:8 and 3:3, with the commentaries of Efodi, Shem Tov, Narvoni, and Abarbanel in *Taanot*, 4, and Rabbi Shlomo Fisher, *Derashot Beit Yishai, Maamar Hamo'ach VeHaLev*, fn. 4; Ralbag, commentary to Genesis 15:4, and commentary to Job, end of ch. 39; Rabbi Dr. Isadore Twersky, "Joseph ibn Kaspi: Portrait of a Medieval Jewish Intellectual," *Studies in Medieval Jewish History and Literature*, volume 1 (Harvard University Press, 1979), pp. 239–242; Rabbi Samson Raphael Hirsch, *Collected Writings* vol. 7 p. 57 and commentary to Genesis 1:6; and Rabbi Avraham Yitzchak Kook, *Adar HaYekar*, pp. 37–38.

39 Radak in *Sefer HaShorashim, shoresh arnav*, cites a view that the name is actually of the masculine gender, but rejects it because the Torah describes it with the feminine words "*maalat gera hi*" as opposed to "*maale gera hu*" in the masculine gender. Compare, however, Deuteronomy 14:7. Interestingly, *Targum Onkelos* and Yonatan ben Uziel translate it with the masculine Aramaic term *arnava*.

40 *Moshav Zekeinim* to Leviticus 11:6.

41 As Ramban to Leviticus 11:6 explains.

42 A.T. Smith, "Rabbits and Hares," in *The Encyclopedia of Mammals* (ed. D. MacDonald, Oxfordshire: Andromeda Oxford, 2001), p. 698.

43 *HaKetav VeHaKabbala; Toledot HaAretz*; cf. *Or HaChayim*.

44 *Midrash Lekach Tov*; Radak, *Sefer HaShorashim, shoresh arnav* (also cited in *Moshav Zekeinim*); Ibn Ezra to Leviticus 11:3, first explanation. Cf. *Sefer Charedim*.

45 I.e. both male and female. See Rabbeinu Bechaya to Leviticus 11:4; *Midrash Lekach Tov*.

46 Ibn Ezra to Leviticus 11:3, second explanation; *Roke'ach*; *Midrash Talpiyot, anaf arnevet*.

47 Ibn Ezra to Leviticus 11:3, first (and preferred) explanation.

48 *Historia Naturalis* VIII:lv.

49 See Sir Thomas Browne, *Pseudodoxia Epidemica* (1646; 6th ed., 1672) III:xvii (pp. 162–166), and Alexander Ross, *Arcana Microcosmi* (1652), Book II, Chapter 10, pp. 151–156.

50 Rivka Raviv, "The Talmudic Formulation of the Prophecies of the Four Kingdoms in the Book of Daniel" (Hebrew), *Jewish Studies, an Internet Journal* (2006), pp. 1–20.

51 *Midrash Tanchuma, Shemini* 8, presents further parallels between the four animals with one kosher sign and the four kingdoms. The printed version has the hare representing Persia/Media: את הארנבת זו מדי שעשתה את ישראל פאה והפקר להשמיד להרוג ולאבד את כל וגו'. However, Rabbi Meir ben Shmuel Benveniste, in *Ot Emet* (Salonica 1565) (p. 48a in Prague 1624 edition) emends the text in order to make the hare represent Greece, thus bringing it into line with the other Midrashim: את הארנבת זו יון שהשפילה את התורה מפי הנביאים שנאמר (יחזקאל יד) הנה ימים באים נאם ה' והשלחתי רעב וגו' וכתיב ונעו מים עד ים וגו'. This would appear to be correct, since this verse is followed by a statement that the mother of Ptolemy was named after a hare, indicating that this section is speaking about Greece rather than Persia/Media.

52 Avraham Epstein, *MiKadmoniyut HaYehudim* (Vienna, 1887), vol. 1, pp. 31–35.

53 This may relate to the belief that it is beneficial for a pregnant woman to eat the ashes of a hare's stomach, recorded in *Moshav Zekeinim*, Leviticus 12:2, citing *Midrash Pirkei DeRabbi Eliezer* (but not found in our versions).

54 Simon Carnell, *Hare* (London: Reaktion Books, 2010), p. 54.

55 Ibid., p. 59.

56 Boris Khaimovich, "On the Semantics of the Motif 'Three Hares Chasing Each Other in a Circle' on Jewish Monuments in Eastern Europe," *East European Jewish Affairs* (2011) 41:3, pp. 157–180.

57 Several of these have been digitized and appear online at http://aleph. nli.org.il/nnl/dig/books_hag.html.

58 Rabbi Yehuda HaLevi, *The Kuzari*, 3:11.

59 Golden Haggadah, Castile 1320, MS Add. 27210 in the British Library, folio 4.

60 Marc Michael Epstein, *Dreams of Subversion in Medieval Jewish Art and Literature* (Penn State University Press, 1997), Chapter Two – The Elusive Hare, pp. 16–38.

61 Genesis 27:22.

62 For further discussion of this imagery, see Marc Michael Epstein, *Dreams of Subversion in Medieval Jewish Art and Literature,* Chapter Two – The Elusive Hare, pp. 16–38; Elliott Horowitz, "Odd Couples: The Eagle and the Hare, the Lion and the Unicorn," Jewish Studies Quarterly 11:3 (August 2004), pp. 243–258.

WILD BOAR

Wild Boar

Chazir Miyaar, Chazir Habar

Pigs of Israel

The wild boar, *Sus scrofa*, is a large, hairy, and potentially dangerous type of pig. Modern zoology classifies it as the ancestor to the domestic pig, with which it can interbreed freely. (Adult male domestic pigs are also called boars. However, in the case of wild boars, even females and piglets are called boars.) They are native to many parts of Europe and Asia, and have been introduced to the Americas and Australasia. Wild boars prefer forest and riverine habitats. In Israel today, they are found throughout the central and northern parts of the country.

Wild boars are rated as major agricultural pests for crops, by eating them, trampling them, and digging for rodents and insects. They also break branches of fruit trees, and cause soil erosion at the edges of ponds and rivers by wallowing and tearing up plants. They are the only wild animals in Israel for which the Nature Reserves Authority issues hunting permits.

The size of wild boars varies with their geographical distribution. Those in Israel weigh up to two or three hundred pounds. Wild boars in northern Europe weigh even more, up to four or five hundred pounds. Exceptional specimens have been recorded weighing as much as six hundred pounds.

Adult male wild boars have tusks that protrude upwards out of the mouth. These are two to four inches in length and serve as weapons as well as tools to aid in foraging. Wild

CZESZNAK ZSOLT / SHUTTERSTOCK

A large male wild boar in Hungary

330

boars usually avoid humans, but if they feel threatened, and especially if there are piglets around, they sometimes attack. They charge with violent power; several hundred pounds of boar slamming its massive skull into a person can cause great injury merely by force of impact. Even more damaging is that upon impact, they slash upwards with their tusks, causing deep lacerations. Such attacks are sometimes fatal.

Boars vs. Pigs

—————— LAW AND RITUAL

In Scripture, the wild boar is referred to as *chazir miyaar*, the "pig of the forest"; the Sages refer to it as *chazir habar*, literally "wild pig." This is in contrast to the domestic pig, which is simply referred to as *chazir*.

In modern zoological science, the domestic pig, which is accepted to be the descendant of the wild boar, is generally rated as a subspecies of the wild boar, and therefore named *Sus scrofa domesticus*. Jewish law, however, has a different system of classifying animals.[1] The Sages rated the domestic pig and wild boar as different types of animals for halakhic purposes, such that it is prohibited to crossbreed them (or to harness them together for agricultural work):

> The pig and the wild boar, even though they are similar to each other, are forbidden mixtures with each other. (Tosefta, Kilayim 1:5)

The extent of the similarities between domestic pig and wild boar are debated in the Mishna:

> These are the creatures whose skin is treated like their flesh (for transmitting ritual impurity): The skin of a human, and the skin of a domestic pig. R. Yose[2] says: Also the skin of a wild boar. (Mishna Chullin 9:2)

The Talmud explains that this dispute relates to the degree of similarity between the skin of wild boar and that of domestic pigs:

> In what do they disagree? One maintains that one (the skin of a wild boar) is hard and the other (the skin of a pig) is soft; the other maintains that it (the skin of a wild boar) is also soft. (Chullin 122a)

Notwithstanding this dispute, all the Sages acknowledged the similarities between the domestic pig and the wild boar, and when discussing the symbolism of these animals, they sometimes grouped them together, as we shall soon see.

The Destructive Beast

—————— SYMBOLISM

In Psalms, a parable is given whereby the Jewish people are compared to a vineyard, and their persecutors are compared to a wild boar that enters the vineyard and destroys the vines:

> A psalm of Assaf: … You plucked up a vine from Egypt; You expelled nations and planted it…. Why did You breach its wall so that every passerby plucks its fruit? The boar of the forest ravages at it, and the animals of the wild graze upon it. (Ps. 80:1, 9, 13–14)

From Mouse to Boar

There is an extremely curious statement in the Jerusalem Talmud about the wild boar:

> The "mouse of the hills" becomes a wild boar. (Y. Shabbat 1:3)[3]

While this statement may have reached us in corrupted form,[4] what could lie behind it? Perhaps it stems from the disparity between adults and young. The piglets of wild boars look strikingly different from the adults. Whereas adults are uniformly very dark brown and rather unprepossessing in appearance, the piglets are light brown

with cream-colored stripes and look quite adorable. They appear to be an entirely different species from the adult

In the Talmud and Midrash, the wild boar symbolizes a particular nation: the Roman Empire and its evolution into Christianity.[5] This linkage is arrived at from several directions.

From a historical standpoint, there were several legions in the Roman Empire which had a wild boar as their emblem. Most notable was the tenth legion, led by Vespasian and Titus, which was involved in the conquest of Jerusalem. Military coins from the period depict wild boar.

From a zoological standpoint, the boar is a highly destructive creature, and also dangerous, as discussed above. The Midrash sees this as symbolizing the destructive and dangerous enemy of Rome:

> "The boar of the forest ravages it" – This is the [Roman] emperor.[6] "And the creatures of the field graze upon it" – these are the officers. (*Midrash Tehillim* 80)

There are other animals that are damaging to agriculture, and other beasts that are dangerous to man, but only the wild boar is harmful to both. The scriptural description of the destruction caused by the wild boar was taken as symbolizing the destruction wreaked by the Roman Empire:

> "The boar of the forest ravages it" – This refers to the Roman Empire....[7] When Israel does not fulfill the will of the Omnipresent, the nations of the world are com-

A Roman antefix roof tile depicting the boar emblem of the Twentieth Legion

pared to the boar of the forest. Just as the boar of the forest is lethal, and damages animals, and injures people, so too whenever Israel does not fulfill the will of the Omnipresent, the nations of the world kill and injure and cause damage. (*Avot DeRabbi Natan* 34:4[8])

Another linkage between the wild boar and Rome emerges from a different psalm:

Wild boar can grow to be huge, and are extremely dangerous; it is rare to be able to approach one in the wild.

■ Rebuke the beast of the reed … (Ps. 68:31)

The Talmud explains this to be a reference to the Messianic Era, when the kingdom of Rome will try to ingratiate itself with the Messiah, and God will rebuke it. The description of a "beast of the reed" is understood as a reference to the wild boar, which often lives in habitats of dense reeds and vegetation alongside riverbanks:

> The Holy One, blessed is He, will say to Gabriel: "Rebuke the beast of the reed" (Ps. 68:31) – …that dwells amongst the reeds, as it is written, "The boar of the forest ravages it, and the crawler of the field feeds on it" (Ps. 80:14). (Pesachim 118b[9])

Likewise, a prophecy regarding the tranquility and safety of the Messianic Era is interpreted in this vein:

> No lion shall be there, and the deviant beast shall not ascend there – they shall not be found there, and the redeemed shall walk it. (Is. 35:9)

Rashi understands the "deviant beast" as the wild boar, representing Rome.[10] It might be considered deviant in terms of it constantly invading human settlement,[11] its unexpected aggression, or its degenerate habits. Symbolically, it represents the oppression of Rome, which will disappear in the Messianic Era.

Another connection between the wild boar and Rome is that in classical Jewish thought, Rome is the fourth of four kingdoms that subjugate the Jewish people, following Babylon, Persia-Media, and Greece. In Daniel's vision, these four kingdoms are symbolized by four different creatures, with Babylon, Persia-Media, and Greece being represented

גְּעַר חַיַּת קָנֶה עֲדַת אַבִּירִים בְּעֶגְלֵי עַמִּים מִתְרַפֵּס בְּרַצֵּי כָסֶף בִּזַּר עַמִּים קְרָבוֹת יֶחְפָּצוּ:

תהלים סח:לא

לֹא יִהְיֶה שָׁם אַרְיֵה וּפְרִיץ חַיּוֹת בַּל יַעֲלֶנָּה לֹא תִמָּצֵא שָׁם וְהָלְכוּ גְּאוּלִים:

ישעיה לה:ט

בָּאתַר דְּנָה חָזֵה הֲוֵית בְּחֶזְוֵי לֵילְיָא וַאֲרוּ חֵיוָה רְבִיעָאָה דְּחִילָה וְאֵימְתָנִי וְתַקִּיפָא יַתִּירָה וְשִׁנַּיִן דִּי פַרְזֶל לַהּ רַבְרְבָן אָכְלָה וּמַדְּקָה וּשְׁאָרָא בְּרַגְלַהּ רָפְסָה וְהִיא מְשַׁנְּיָה מִן כָּל חֵיוָתָא דִּי קָדָמַהּ וְקַרְנַיִן עֲשַׂר לַהּ:

דניאל ז:ז

by the lion, bear, and leopard. The fourth creature is not named as a type of animal, but it does bear a certain degree of similarity to the wild boar:

> After that, as I looked on in the night vision, there was a fourth beast – dreadful, fearsome, and very powerful, with great iron teeth – that devoured and crushed, and stamped the remains with its feet. It was different from all the other beasts which had gone before it, and it had ten horns. (Dan. 7:7)

This beast is described as wreaking havoc not only by devouring, but also by crushing and stamping. Such behavior corresponds to the wild boar, which is the bane of farmers not only due to it eating their crops, but also due to it trampling them. In addition, while the wild boar does not have iron teeth or ten horns, it does have hard, sharp tusks that protrude upwards from its mouth. Thus, there may be some elements of the wild boar present in the imagery of Daniel's fourth beast.

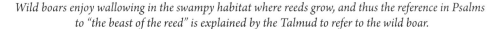

Wild boars enjoy wallowing in the swampy habitat where reeds grow, and thus the reference in Psalms to "the beast of the reed" is explained by the Talmud to refer to the wild boar.

KOO / SHUTTERSTOCK

333

A pig displaying its split hooves

KATOOSHA / SHUTTERSTOCK

Non-Kosher Rome

SYMBOLISM

Another reason for linking the wild boar with Rome is due to the wild boar being essentially a pig. Most references to wild boar in the Midrash relate to its destructive habits and danger, whereas most references to the pig relate to it being a non-kosher animal. As such, the bulk of our discussion regarding the symbolism of the pig as a non-kosher animal will be left for the chapter on the pig in the volume on domestic animals. However, there is a degree of overlap to be discussed here.

The pig appears fourth in the list in Leviticus of four non-kosher animals with one kosher sign. This list of four animals again parallels the four kingdoms that have subjugated the Jewish people, and the pig, as fourth in the list, parallels Rome. But it is not only due to its position in the list that it parallels Rome.

The first three animals in the list, (the camel, the hare, and the hyrax) possess the internal kosher feature of bringing up the cud but do not have split hooves, while the pig has the external kosher feature of split hooves but does not bring up the cud. The pig is the only non-kosher animal whose single kosher sign is external. Furthermore, the pig will often lie down with outstretched hooves, as if to show them off and claim that it is kosher. This is explained by the Midrash to be analogous to Rome, which is considered to be the descendant of Esau. Both Rome and Esau pretended to be upright and just, but in fact committed evil acts:

"And Esau was forty years of age" (Gen. 26:34) – this relates to what is written, "The boar of the forest rav-

ages it." R. Pinchas said in the name of R. Shimon: Of all the prophets, only two, Moses and Assaf, exposed this. Moses said: "And the pig, for it has a split hoof [but does not bring up its cud]" (Lev. 11:7). Assaf said: "The boar of the forest ravages it." Why is it (i.e. Esau/ Edom/ Rome) symbolized by the pig? Just as the pig, when it lies down, stretches its hooves out, as if to say "I am pure," so too this evil kingdom steals and commits violence but justifies itself. And so too Esau; all his forty years, he would ensnare the wives of others and force himself upon them. Yet when he reached forty years of age, he compared himself to his father, and said, "Just as my father married at forty, I shall also marry at forty." (*Bereshit Rabba* 65:1[12])

The wild boar is thus not merely considered to be a harmful menace; it symbolizes the very essence of evil:

"Too long have I dwelled with those who hate peace" (Ps. 120:6). But is there a person that hates peace? Esau hates peace, as it says, "And I shall give peace in the land" (Lev. 26:6); when will it be so? "And I shall banish the dangerous (literally, 'evil') beast from the land" (ibid.); and the "evil beast" is none other than the boar, as it says, "The boar of the forest has ravaged it" – this is the wicked Esau. (*Midrash Tehillim* 120)

No animal is actually evil from a moral standpoint,[13] since animals do not possess free will. But the wild boar, due to its destructive and dangerous nature, as well as its superficially kosher appearance masking a non-kosher status, symbolically represents evil. ∎

◀ *The fearsome tusked visage of an adult male wild boar*

Notes

1 See the section on the classification of animals in the introduction to this work.

2 In the Talmud's version of the Mishna, it is R. Yehuda instead.

3 This is stated immediately following another ancient belief, that the male hyena turns into a female, discussed in the chapter on hyenas.

4 See Rabbi Shmuel Waldberg, *Kitvei Shmuel* (Krakow, 1907), pp. 91–94 (46a–47b).

5 For an academic study of the boar representing Rome in rabbinic thought, see Rivka Raviv, "Shaping the Four Kingdoms in Daniel in the Rabbinical Literature," *Jewish Studies Internet Journal* 5 (2006), pp. 1–20 (Hebrew), and Mireille Hadas-Lebel, *Jerusalem Against Rome* (Peeters Publishing, 2006), pp. 517–521.

6 Literally, "king." In *Midrash Yalkut Shimoni, Tehillim* 80:430, it reads instead Romulus, the legendary founder of Rome.

7 Note that in some versions, the text instead refers to the Cuthim (Samaritans), apparently a result of censorship.

8 The Midrash also notes that in the Hebrew word *miyaar*, "of the forest," the letter *ayin* is traditionally written in superscript. This indicates a variant reading of *miyeor*, which would mean, "of the river." The Midrash explains that, depending upon the behavior of the Jewish people, they are either faced with a dangerous boar of the forest, or a harmless "water pig" (*Avot DeRabbi Natan* 34:4; *Midrash Tehillim* 80; *Midrash Shir HaShirim Rabba* 3:3; *Midrash Vayikra Rabba* 13:5). It is not clear which creature is being described, though it is common for aquatic creatures to be named after terrestrial animals with which they share similarities, such as with sea lions, sea cows, and so on. Possibly the reference is to the *shibbuta*, a large fish which the Talmud (Chullin 109b) describes as tasting like pork.

9 Also *Midrash Shemot Rabba* 35:5.

10 Rashi, commentary ad loc.

11 See Radak, commentary ad loc.

12 Similarly in *Midrash Tehillim* 80.

13 See *Man And Beast* (Jerusalem: Zoo Torah, 2005), by this author.

ONAGER

Onager

עֲרוֹד, פֶּרֶא

Arod, Pere

Wild Ass, Not Feral Donkey

— IDENTIFICATION

Very few people have heard of an onager. Its alternate name of "wild ass" gives away what type of animal it is, but it is a name that is likely to be instantly misleading. There is perhaps a common assumption that the phrase "wild ass" simply refers to a donkey running around without an owner. Yet nothing could be further from the truth. As we shall later discuss, the wild ass is a very different animal from the domestic donkey. Their physical appearance is also quite different from the commonly seen dark grey donkey. Onagers are usually brownish in color with a white belly. They have a black mane and a black stripe stretching from the mane down the center of their back until the tail, which has a tufted tip. Unlike donkeys, they are known for being able to run with great swiftness.

There is no doubt whatsoever that the *arod* of Scripture is the wild ass.[1] Nevertheless, complexities and confusions surround both Hebrew and English names for this animal. The onager is named *arod* in Aramaic texts (the Book of Daniel, the Talmud, and Aramaic translations of the Torah) and once in the Hebrew Book of Job. According to many opinions, the onager is also the *pere* spoken of on numer-

ous occasions in Scripture. It is unclear if the name *arod* is an Aramaic alternative to *pere* that somehow found its way into the Book of Job, or if it is a Hebrew synonym, much like the two names "wild ass" and "onager." The commentaries sometimes give it the descriptive name of *chamor habar*, wild donkey. The English name onager (pronounced "onajer") is from the Greek words *onos*, "donkey," and *agros*, "field." Hence, "onager" is a perfect translation of *chamor habar*. (It should be noted that the *arod* is not to be confused with the reptile of a similar name that is mentioned in the Talmud.[2])

The name of the animal in English is even more complicated. Although the name "wild ass" is commonly used, it is not all that specific. There are actually two species of wild ass, the Asiatic wild ass (which is the onager[3]), *Equus hemionus*, and the African wild ass, *Equus africanus*. The African wild ass is gray in color, with black and white horizontal stripes on the lower parts of its legs. It also has a stockier build and longer ears than the Asiatic wild ass. Some have suggested that both species might be mentioned in Scripture, with the *pere* referring to Asiatic wild ass and the *arod* referring to the African wild ass.[4] Others doubt that the African wild ass was ever found in biblical countries.[5]

An Asiatic wild ass, recognizable by its light brown coloration

An African wild ass, easily distinguished by its gray coloration and striped legs

338

אִיוֹב ו:ה	הֲיִנְהַק פֶּרֶא עֲלֵי דֶשֶׁא אִם יִגְעֶה שּׁוֹר עַל בְּלִילוֹ:
תהלים קד:יא	יַשְׁקוּ כָּל חַיְתוֹ שָׂדָי יִשְׁבְּרוּ פְרָאִים צְמָאָם:
	מִי שִׁלַּח פֶּרֶא חָפְשִׁי וּמֹסְרוֹת עָרוֹד מִי פִתֵּחַ: אֲשֶׁר שַׂמְתִּי עֲרָבָה בֵיתוֹ וּמִשְׁכְּנוֹתָיו מְלֵחָה: יִשְׂחַק לַהֲמוֹן קִרְיָה תְּשֻׁאוֹת נוֹגֵשׂ לֹא יִשְׁמָע: יְתוּר הָרִים מִרְעֵהוּ וְאַחַר כָּל יָרוֹק יִדְרוֹשׁ:
אִיוֹב לט:ה-ח	
	הֵן פְּרָאִים בַּמִּדְבָּר יָצְאוּ בְּפָעֳלָם מְשַׁחֲרֵי לַטָּרֶף עֲרָבָה לוֹ לֶחֶם לַנְּעָרִים:
אִיוֹב כד:ה	

Wild Animals and Wild Asses

───────────────────── IDENTIFICATION

The name *arod*, which all agree refers to the wild ass, only occurs twice in Scripture. There are also numerous verses which speak of the *pere*. In all these verses, some of the commentaries explain *pere* to be a general reference to wild carnivorous animals,[6] but others understand it (in some or all cases) to be another name for the wild ass.[7] Yet there is one verse where it clearly seems to be referring to the wild ass. When Job, immersed in his travails, wishes to tell his friends that he does not complain without justification, he gives the example of the *pere*, which only brays when it lacks food:

> Does the *pere* bray in the grasses? Or the ox low over his fodder? (Job 6:5)

This mention of the *pere* clearly cannot be referring to wild carnivorous beasts, which do not eat grass. One could still perhaps argue that the term generally covers all wild animals, both carnivore and herbivore, and that the verse here is only referring to the herbivores. Still, it seems far more reasonable to explain it as referring specifically to the onager, since the second part of the verse also refers to a specific type of animal. It should also be remembered that the traditional commentators on Scripture all lived in Europe, where there was no knowledge of the onager.

Since it seems that the word *pere* here refers specifically to the onager, we shall interpret its other occurrences in the same way. However, in translating the verses, since Scripture uses two names for this animal, and in order to allude to the other translation of *pere*, we shall translate *pere* as wild ass and *arod* as onager. In discussing the animal, however, we shall use the terms interchangeably.

Donkeys of the Desert

───────────────────── SYMBOLISM

In *Barkhi Nafshi*, the psalm that sings of the harmony of the natural world, King David refers to the springs of water that cascade along the valleys:

> They give drink to every beast of the field; the wild asses quench their thirst. (Ps. 104:11)

The onager is highlighted in this verse as being the quintessential desert creature, which stresses the importance of these oases.[8] Onagers travel over great distances in order to obtain water. The onagers presently in Israel are scattered throughout the hot and dry area of the Ramon Crater, but they all come every several days to a small spring in its eastern corner, Ein Saharonim, in order to drink.[9]

The status of the onager as the archetypical creature of the wilderness may lie behind its lengthy description in God's speech to Job. After Job has complained about the suffering that God inflicted upon him, God responds by describing the onager:

> Who has sent out the wild ass free? Who has loosed the bands of the onager? To him I have given the wilderness for his home, and the barren land for his dwelling. He scoffs at the tumult of the city, and does not listen to the shouts of the driver. The range of the mountains is his pasture, and he searches after every green thing. (Job 39:5–8)

Job is complaining that he doesn't understand why God would inflict such suffering upon him. God's basic reply is that Job should realize his limitations as a human being and should not expect to understand the ways of the Creator. In describing the onager, God is telling Job that he should realize that he is only one very small part of the universe. Onagers are shy animals, generally living far from human habitation. The message here may be that Job is to realize that the world is much larger than just him, or even than mankind. (Later, we shall explore another insight into this passage.)

The supreme suitability of the onager to its desert habitat is also the cause of its mention in another context – as Job's metaphor for the bandits of the wilderness:

> See, they are the wild asses of the desert, going out to do their work, seeking their prey, the plain serves as bread for his accomplices. (Job 24:5)

For those who explain the word *pere* to refer to wild animals in general,[10] this entire verse is comparing the wicked to the wild animals; just as the wild predators seek out their prey, so too do the human bandits seek out their victims. For those who explain the *pere* to be the onager,[11] on the other hand, the phrase "seeking their prey" cannot be a reference to the onager, which is solely herbivorous. Instead, Job is stating that the wicked are as at home in the wilder-

A solitary onager in its desert domain

ness, going about their banditry, as is the onager in its own (quite different) wilderness lifestyle.

It is due to onagers being reclusive in general that when the prophet Hosea speaks of the northern tribes of Israel becoming estranged from God, he speaks in the metaphor of the onager:

> For they have gone up to Assyria, a wild ass alone by himself; Ephraim has hired lovers. (Hos. 8:9)

Onagers are found in small groups of females with their offspring, and there are also bachelor herds, but there are also single males that control large territories.[12] Such a single male would be the reference of this verse; its solitude is enhanced by the innate nature of the onager, which rejects domestication and civilization.

The Wild One

———————————————— SYMBOLISM

The onager is usually depicted in Scripture as the epitome of wildness. The wildness that it represents is not the brutal savagery of a lion or leopard; rather, it is the wildness of being detached from civilization and from following any orders. Daniel refers to onagers in describing to Belshazzar the fate of his father Nebuchadnezzar, who degenerated from man to beast:

340

> And he was driven from the sons of men; and his heart was made like the beasts, and his dwelling was with the onagers; they fed him with grass like an ox, and his body was wet with the dew of heaven; until he learned that the Most High God ruled in the kingdom of men, and that He appoints over it whom He will. (Dan. 5:21)

When Nebuchadnezzar became a beast, his dwelling was with the onagers, representing his great distance from human civilization. The same concept appears in the Book of Job, when Job's friend Tzophar is counseling him for his sufferings. Tzophar's position is that this suffering must be a punishment for some unknown evil that Job has committed. Yet since Job led a tranquil life until now, there must be an explanation for why God did not inflict this suffering previously. Addressing this issue, Tzophar explains:

> That the empty man might attain a heart, the wild ass colt shall become a man. (Job 11:12)

According to one interpretation, Tzophar is telling Job that sometimes God will withhold punishing a person for his sins, granting him time for repentance.[13] If man avails himself of this opportunity, then he can replace his empty life with wisdom and proper ways. Figuratively, this is described as a young onager becoming a man. A young onager represents wildness and irresponsibility.

Others understand the verse in precisely the opposite way – to be describing a person who does not take the opportunity to repent.[14] Accordingly, the verse reads, "The empty man lacks a heart, he is a man born of an onager colt." He recklessly causes damage, without any thought as to his wickedness and the results of his actions.

Whichever the correct understanding, the usage of the metaphor of the onager is the same. The onager represents something wild and reckless. As we shall later see, there are many references in Scripture to the wildness of the onager.

The wildness of the onager is so prominent that the animal's name may even be used synonymously for such wildness. The prophet Hosea speaks of the foolishness of the tribe of Ephraim:

> For he has made wildness (*yafri*) between the brothers. An east wind will come, a wind of God ascending from the wilderness, and his fountainhead will become parched, and his spring will dry up, and it will plunder the treasure of every wondrous article. (Hos. 13:15, following Rashi's translation)

Although most translate the word *yafri* as "flourishes," Rashi cites a view relating it to the *pere*, the onager. Accordingly, it means that Ephraim has caused the wildness of the onager to break out.

כִּי הֵמָּה עָלוּ אַשּׁוּר פֶּרֶא בּוֹדֵד לוֹ אֶפְרַיִם הִתְנוּ אֲהָבִים:

הושע ח:ט

וּמִן בְּנֵי אֲנָשָׁא טְרִיד וְלִבְבֵהּ עִם חֵיוְתָא שַׁוִּיו וְעִם עֲרָדַיָּא מְדֹרֵהּ עִשְׂבָּא כְתוֹרִין יִטְעֲמוּנֵּהּ וּמִטַּל שְׁמַיָּא גִּשְׁמֵהּ יִצְטַבַּע עַד דִּי יְדַע דִּי שַׁלִּיט אֱלָהָא עִלָּאָה בְּמַלְכוּת אֲנָשָׁא וּלְמַן דִּי יִצְבֵּה יְהָקֵים עֲלַהּ:

דניאל ה:כא

וְאִישׁ נָבוּב יִלָּבֵב וְעַיִר פֶּרֶא אָדָם יִוָּלֵד:

איוב יא:יב

The Untamable Onager

—— SYMBOLISM

Returning to God's lengthy description of the onager in His speech to Job, there is another explanation of God's intent that relates to the onager's wildness.

> Who has sent out the wild ass free? Who has loosed the bands of the onager? To him I have given the wilderness for his home, and the barren land for his dwelling. He scoffs at the tumult of the city, and does not listen to the shouts of the driver. The range of the mountains is his pasture, and he searches after every green thing. (Job 39:5–8)

God's message to Job is that he should realize his limitations as a human being and should not expect to understand

An onager colt

the ways of the Creator. Following this idea, God presents examples from the natural world that will humble Job. For example, God described the mighty behemoth, to make Job realize his physical fragility. And God also addresses another aspect of man's arrogance. Man sometimes thinks that he possesses ultimate power over the natural world, able to bend it to his will. God points out to Job that He created the onager as a wild animal, and no man can tame him. Job is thereby humbled, and begins to accept man's limitations. In a deeper parallel, perhaps the idea is that just as man cannot hope to bend the wild ways of the onager to his control, so too he cannot hope to grasp the apparently wild ways of God.

There may be a further depth of insight into God's statement. As noted earlier, there is some dispute amongst zoologists as to whether the wild ass of Scripture is the African or Asiatic wild ass. If it is the latter, then our explanation of God's message becomes far more acute.

For a long period, it was thought that the domestic donkey (*Equus asinus*) was originally domesticated from the Asiatic wild ass (*Equus hemionus*). However, recent studies have concluded that the domestic donkey is in fact a descendant of the African wild ass (*Equus africanus*). The interesting point is that the African wild ass and the Asiatic wild ass are superficially extraordinarily similar. Aside from their close genetic relationship, they look almost identical. And yet, despite their superficial similarities, there is a crucial difference between them. The African wild ass is easily domesticated, resulting in the paradigmatic beast of burden, the donkey. The donkey's name is *chamor*, which some relate to the word *chomer*, raw material, ready to be bent to its master's desire. The Asiatic wild ass, on the other hand – the onager – cannot be domesticated.

It is widely thought that the onager is utterly impossible to tame. This is not quite accurate. The discovery of illustrations from the ancient royal cemetery at Ur, dated to approximately 2500 BCE, show that the Sumerians used onagers for drawing chariots. Furthermore, the Talmud speaks of the onager being used for work:

> What work do large wild animals do? Abaye said: Mar Yehuda of the house of Mar Yochni told me, Onagers pull millstones. (Avoda Zara 16b)

*"Who has sent out the wild ass free? …
To him I have given the wilderness for his home,
and the barren land for his dwelling… The range
of the mountains is his pasture…"*

(Job 39:5–8)

However, neither of these mean that onagers were fully domesticated; it may well mean that they were captured and forced into work, like elephants, but they were not truly docile.[15] In any case, once horses arrived on the scene, which were much more amenable, onagers were abandoned.

It seems that there have been many efforts over history to domesticate the Asiatic wild ass, but all were in vain. Man simply cannot bend it to his will. The explorer Tristram, who chronicled the natural history of the Land of Israel in the nineteenth century, records: "I...saw a wild ass in the oasis of Souf, which had been snared when a colt; but though it had been kept for three years in confinement, it was as untractable as when first caught, biting and kicking furiously at everyone who approached it, and never enduring a saddle on its back. In appearance and colour it could not have been distinguished from one of the finest specimens of the tame ass."[16]

Seen in this light, God's statement to Job takes on new meaning. God describes the Asiatic wild ass – an animal so similar to the African wild ass that is the epitome of servile domestication, and yet so different. Despite the superficial similarities of the Asiatic wild ass to the African wild ass, man cannot tame it. He should therefore be humbled and realize his limitations as a human being – and he will then no longer expect to understand the ways of God.

The Onager and Ishmael

SYMBOLISM

A striking reference to the onager occurs in an unlikely context in the Torah. When God sends an angel to Abraham's wife Hagar to inform her of her future son, the angel states that he will be like an onager:

> The angel of God said to her: Behold, you are pregnant, and you shall give birth to a son; and you shall call him by the name Ishmael, for God has heard your suffering. And he shall be a *pere*-man; his hand shall be against everyone, and everyone's hand shall be against him, and he shall dwell in the face of all his brothers. (Gen. 16:11–12)

What does it mean to be "a *pere*-man"? As in every occurrence of the word *pere*, there is a dispute. Rashi explains it simply to mean that he will enjoy the pursuits of the wilderness, translating *pere* to mean "of the wild" rather than being a reference to the wild ass. Others explain *pere* to mean "wild" as an adjective, describing Ishmael as a wild man,[17] while still others explain *pere* to refer to wild carnivorous beasts.[18] But some explain that the *pere* of this verse is the same as the *pere* that we have been discussing – the onager.[19] Ishmael will be a wild ass of a man, living in the wilderness.[20]

Another verse which mentions the *pere* – again as the symbol of the wilderness – is also taken to allude to Ishmael:

> Because the palaces shall be forsaken; the city with its tumult shall be deserted; the forts and towers shall be for dens forever, a joy of wild asses (*mesos pera'im*), a pasture of flocks. (Is. 32:14)

Rashi interprets the phrase *mesos pera'im* allegorically as "for the lusts of Ishmael." This is clearly based on the words of the angel that Ishmael is represented by the wild ass.

Wild and Domesticated Donkeys
NATURAL HISTORY

The Mishna details several pairs of animals which, even though they are very similar, nevertheless fall under the prohibition of *kilayim*, forbidden mixtures for crossbreeding and for harnessing to the same plough:

> The wolf and the dog, the *kufri* dog and the fox, the goats and the gazelles, the ibex and the sheep, the horse and the mule, the mule and the donkey, the donkey and the onager (*arod*) – even though they are similar to each other, they are *kilayim* with each other. (Mishna Kilayim 1:6)

The donkey and the onager are indeed very similar animals, to the point that telling them apart can only be done in good light:

> [From when is it considered daylight, that one may recite the morning *Shema* prayer?] R. Akiva said: [From when it is light enough to distinguish] between a donkey and an onager.[21] (Berakhot 9b)

But if the domestic donkey and the onager are so similar, why are they considered forbidden mixtures? Is it because they are different species, or is there something more than

that? A later mishna indicates that the differences between them are more significant than their merely being different species:

> The onager is a wild animal. (Mishna Kilayim 8:6)

All animals are divided into two groups: *behemot*, domesticated animals, and *chayot*, wild animals. This mishna rates the onager as a wild animal. As such, it is in a fundamentally different category from the domestic donkey, and they are a forbidden mixture.

In one talmudic discussion, the contrast between the onager and the donkey occurs in a decidedly non-legal context. In seeking to prove a point regarding Sichon, king of the Amorites, the Talmud cites a verse referring to him as "the Canaani, king of Arad." The Talmud explains that the same person was known by three names:

> It was taught: He was Sichon, he was Arad, he was Canaan; Sichon, as he was similar to a foal (*sayach* – a young donkey) in the wilderness; Canaan, after his kingdom; and his name was Arad. Some say: Arad, as he was similar to an onager (*arod*) in the wilderness; Canaan, after his kingdom; and his name was Sichon. (Rosh HaShana 3a)

The name Canaan is related to the symbolism of a donkey.[22] Canaan, son of Ham, was the first person to be cursed with slavery, and thereby became the symbol and archetype of slavery, much like the servile donkey, which is the ultimate beast of burden and the symbol of domestication. The dispute in the Talmud may revolve around the nature of the essence of Sichon, born of a slave nation but fighting against the Jewish people. One view is that he was a Sichon by nature – a *sayach*, a young donkey, servile by nature but happening to run wild in the wilderness. The other opinion is that by nature he was an Arad, an onager, wild to its core.[23]

Of Snuffing and Sucking
SYMBOLISM

Jeremiah uses the parable of an onager to castigate the Jewish people for their sinful ways. Again, the onager appears as the epitome of wildness, reveling in its freedom and utterly untamable:

> [You were like] a wild ass used to the wilderness, sucking in (*shaafa*) the wind in its desire; who can reform its instinct?[24] All those who seek it need not wear themselves out; in its month they shall find it. (Jer. 2:24)

This verse uses an unusual expression in describing the onager's habits: "sucking in the wind." In a later prophecy, describing the droughts that would befall Jerusalem, Jeremiah also makes reference to this behavior:

And the wild asses stand in the high hills, they suck in (*shaafu*) the wind like jackals; their eyes fail, because there is no grass. (Jer. 14:6)

Although many English translations render the word *shaafa* as "sniffing" or "snuffing," it is used elsewhere to refer to inhaling by way of the mouth, e.g. "I opened my mouth and breathed in (*esh'afa*)" (Ps. 119:131), and "I will both lay waste and swallow up (*esh'af*)" (Is. 42:14). This description of inhalation, best translated as "sucking," is exactly what the onager does.

All members of the horse family possess large nostrils and a powerful sense of smell in their nose. But they also possess a second set of highly sensitive olfactory receptors, under the floor of their nasal cavity. These are known as vomeronasal organs or, more commonly, the Jacobson's organ. Although present in all mammals and even in reptiles, they are most highly attuned and used in members of the horse and cat family. The onager uses its Jacobson's organ to detect minute traces of odors in the air; most importantly, pheromone scent signals that are emitted by other onagers. (It seems that with humans, the Jacobson's organ is stimulated in pregnant women, which is the cause of their highly sensitive sense of smell.)

When using its Jacobson's organ, an onager will tilt its head upwards and curl its upper lip back (the behavior mistakenly referred to as laughter when performed by horses). In doing so, air is sucked into the mouth across the Jacobson's organ. This procedure is called flehmen, which means "testing," and it helps the onager trap the scents so that they can be analyzed more carefully. Thus, Jeremiah's description of the onager sucking in the wind seems to be a reference to flehmen behavior. (It would thereby also seem to support the translation of *pere* as wild ass rather than referring to wild beasts in general.)

Since flehmen behavior is primarily used for assessing the sexual receptivity of other onagers, its mention by Jeremiah is even more appropriate: "[You were like] a wild ass used to the wilderness, sucking in (*shaafa*) the wind in its desire; who can reform its instinct?" A reference to the onager seeking to mate all the more illustrates its wild nature and represents the lustful sins of the Jewish people.

Jeremiah concludes his description of the onager by stating that "all those who seek it need not wear themselves out"; it is futile to try to capture it, and there is no

A horse engaging in "flehmen" – arching up its head and curling its upper lip to suck in the air

NICOLE CISCATO / SHUTTERSTOCK

point in wearing oneself out in the attempt. Perhaps this is a reference to his futile efforts in persuading the people to return to the ways of the Torah. The last phrase in Jeremiah's description, "in its month they shall find it," remains difficult to explain. Some explain that there is one month a year when the onager is well fed or sleeping, and it is easily captured, and that this alludes to the month of Av when God exacts retribution from the Jewish people;[25] but this is not in accordance with the known habits of onagers. Others explain it to refer to the first month of an onager's life, when it is too young to flee from capture.[26] Still others explain it to refer to the final month of an onager's pregnancy, when it is heavy with its young and possible to be captured. According to this interpretation, it alludes to the Jewish people eventually growing heavy with sin and then being forcibly straightened out by way of punishment.[27] Another suggestion is that the phrase should be translated differently: "it is [always] found rejuvenated" – the onager is never discovered too weary to run away.[28]

Fascinatingly, the Midrash takes Jeremiah's depiction as portraying a potentially positive picture of the Jewish people. God states that He had hoped that, like the onager, the Jewish people would not take to a human master:

> The Holy One said to Israel: "My child, I thought that you would be free from a king" – how do we know, as it states, "a wild ass, used to the desert" (Jer. 2:24); just as the onager grows up in the desert and does not live in fear of man, so too I thought that you would not have the fear of royalty upon you. But you did not request thus; instead, "in its desire, it sucks in the wind" – and there is no wind other than kingship. How do we know? As it states (regarding Daniel's vision), "And the four winds of heaven stirred up the great sea (from which the four kingships emerged)" (Dan. 7:2). (*Devarim Rabba* 5:8)

It seems that there is indeed a place for independence and the rejection of authority.

An Onager Miscellany

———————————————— LAW AND RITUAL

There are some laws in the Talmud mentioning onagers, which show that despite its symbolism as a wild creature living far from civilization, it was a familiar animal.

The Talmud, in discussing the laws of *chazaka* – acquiring land based on a three-year continuous seizure coupled with a claim to legitimate title – mentions an unusual rule involving onagers. The case involves a farmer who builds a wall on his land to keep the onagers away from grazing on his crops. This wall did not extend to the edge of his property; there was an area of land beyond the wall that was left to the onagers and other animals in order to give them an alternative area to graze. Another person then used this area for three years, without the farmer objecting, and claimed that he had legitimately purchased it. Ordinarily, the farmer's lack of objection would mean that he had indeed sold it to the person. But R. Yehuda rules that the onagers render this case different:

> Rav Yehuda said: A person who seizes land outside an onager-wall, it is not a *chazaka*. Why not? As [the owner] says, the onagers will eat whatever grows there (and he thus did not protest at the time). (Bava Batra 36a)

Another mention of the onager occurs in the context of identifying kosher animals. The Talmud mentions a means of distinguishing kosher from non-kosher animals even in the absence of being able to check their mouth (to determine if the animal brings up its cud) or its feet (to determine if it has split hooves):

> Rav Chisda further said: If a man was walking in the wilderness and found an animal which had a mutilated mouth and its feet were cut off, he should check its flesh. If [the pattern of muscles] runs in a criss-cross direction then it is certainly kosher, if not then it is certainly non-kosher, provided that he can identify an onager. (The Talmud asks:) Did you not say that there is [the exception of] the onager – perhaps there is another type of animal that is similar to an onager [in its possessing criss-crossing flesh, yet not being kosher]! (The Talmud answers:) We have a tradition that there is no other such type of animal. And where should he examine [the flesh]? Abaye, and some say Rav Chisda, stated: Under the rump. (Chullin 59a)

Stating that the onager possesses a different musculature pattern in its rump from that of other animals reflects an extraordinarily thorough familiarity with anatomy.

Return of the Wild Asses

———————————————— JEWISH HISTORY

Onagers were often hunted. This is commonly depicted on ancient illustrations and carvings, and is also mentioned in the Talmud:

> R. Yehoshua b. Beteira said: A case occurred where they were butchering onagers[29] to feed to the lions in the king's court, and the people making pilgrimages for the festival were up to their knees in blood, and nothing was said to them (even though they would enter the Temple and eat consecrated offerings, which proves that the blood does not cause ritual impurity). (Menachot 103b)

Unfortunately, hunting has eventually proven catastrophic for the onager. All the surviving races of wild ass are in a precarious position. Their great running speed, and ability to withstand harsh desert conditions, enabled them to survive despite intensive efforts to hunt them during the last few thousand years. But the invention of firearms, and automobiles from which to shoot them, brought them to the brink of extinction.

The African wild ass, ancestor to the domestic donkey, and thought by some to be the *arod* of Scripture, is highly endangered. Only a few hundred remain in the wild, in the hostile deserts of Ethiopia and Somalia. In 1972, a small number was brought to Israel in a remarkable mission.[30]

It was in June 1972 that General Avraham Yoffe, of Israel's Nature and Parks Authority, heard about a herd of African wild asses in a remote desert village in Ethiopia. The Ethiopian government was willing to sell them for a cash payment of $90,000. Yoffe exerted great efforts to raise the funds in Israel, eventually convincing the Education Ministry of the historical and biblical importance of bringing over the animal, and the Treasury granted him the loan.

But the Israeli Air Force also had to be brought on board. The mission required the use of a gigantic Hercules aircraft, the only military Israeli aircraft capable of taking off and landing on dirt paths. General Motti Hod initially ridiculed the request, saying, "Why African wild ass? Take a regular donkey, paint stripes on his legs, and you have an African wild ass!" Eventually, Yoffe managed to talk him into it.

In September of that year, the huge plane flew to Addis-Ababa, and from there to a makeshift airstrip in Assab. Amidst a cloud of desert dust, the rendezvous was made with a convoy of trucks, carrying a dozen of the precious African wild asses. They were brought safely to the Hai-Bar reserve in Yotvata. The group has successfully bred, and its descendants are now found in zoos around the world.

Such is the situation with the African wild ass. The Asiatic wild ass (onager), which is the *pere* of Scripture as well as probably the *arod*, was also in dire straits. The particular subspecies which lived in the biblical Land of Israel was the Syrian wild ass, *Equus hemionus hemihippus*. Sadly, this became extinct in the last century, with the last sighting occurring in 1927.

However, small numbers of other subspecies of the Asiatic wild ass were still to be found. In 1968–69 Israel managed to obtain some from the Amsterdam Zoo and from a nature reserve in Iran. These were a mixture of Persian onagers (*Equus hemionus onager*) and Mongolian onagers, also known as kulans (*Equus hemionus kulan*).[31] They were brought to Hai-Bar in Yotvata, where they successfully bred.[32] Eventually, it was possible to reintroduce some of their descendants to the wild, and around 250 onagers now roam the Negev.[33] Once again, as God told Job, the wilderness is the home for the onager.   ∎

A group of onagers at Hai-Bar in Israel

Notes

1 The most thorough discussion is that by Zohar Amar, "*Pere VeChamor – Uma Shebenehem*," *Leshonenu* 76:3 (Jerusalem, 5774), pp. 265–284.

2 Berakhot 33a. The word is spelled the same, but vocalized as *arvad*. (*Arwad* is snake in Arabic; see Moshe Piamenta, *A Dictionary of Postclassical Yemeni Arabic*, Volume 1, p. 111).

3 To further complicate the naming issue, while the Asiatic wild ass is commonly called the onager, the name onager is sometimes said to technically apply only to some of the several subspecies of Asiatic wild ass. The race that was formerly prevalent in the region of the Land of Israel was the Syrian wild ass, *Equus hemionus hemihippus*. It is also believed by some that the Persian onager, *Equus hemionus onager*, was also once native to this region.

4 Yehuda Feliks, *Nature and Man in the Bible*, pp. 261–262.

5 Menachem Dor, *HaChai BiYemei HaMikra, HaMishna VeHaTalmud*. p. 51.

6 Me'iri, Malbim, ad loc.

7 *Meztudat Tziyon* in all references to the *pere*; *Targum Yerushalmi* to Genesis 16:12; *Targum Yonatan* to Psalms 104:11; Seforno to Genesis 16:12; and all works of biblical zoology concerning all references.

8 Radak, Me'iri ad loc.

9 Heinrich Mendelssohn and Yoram Yom-Tov, *Fauna Palaestina: Mammalia of Israel*, p. 239.

10 Rashi, Ralbag, Malbim ad loc.

11 *Metzudat Tziyon* ad loc.

12 Heinrich Mendelssohn and Yoram Yom-Tov, *Fauna Palaestina: Mammalia of Israel*, p. 239.

13 Rashi, commentary ad loc.

14 Ramban, commentary ad loc.

15 George Cansdale, *All the Animals of the Bible Lands* (Michigan: Zondervan Publishing House, 1970), p. 95; Menachem Dor, *HaChai BiYemei HaMikra, HaMishna VeHaTalmud*, p. 51; Heinrich Mendelssohn and Yoram Yom-Tov, *Fauna Palaestina: Mammalia of Israel*, p. 240.

16 H.B. Tristram, *The Natural History of the Bible*, p. 43.

17 Rabbi Samson Raphael Hirsch; Netziv, *Haamek Davar*.

18 Ramban, commentary ad loc.

19 *Targum Yonatan* and Seforno ad loc.

20 Seforno explains that Ishmael had an Egyptian mother, and the people of Egypt are likened to donkeys in Ezekiel 23:20.

21 There is another interesting reference by R. Akiva to donkeys; he recounts that when he was an ignoramus, he used to say, "Who will bring me a Torah scholar, that I may bite him like a donkey!" (Pesachim 49b).

22 One of the *piyutim* (liturgical prayers) recited on *Parashat Zakhor*, the remembrance of the evil tribe of Amalek, notes how Amalek pretended to be Sichon: "Remember the one who dwelled in the Negev desert without a yoke, like an onager (*arod*); he changed his clothing and language, emulating the king Arad." The description of him living "without a yoke" is an allusion to Sichon/Arad resembling the *arod*, the onager, a wild ass with no yoke (see *Iyun Tefilla* in *Siddur Otzar HaTefillot*).

23 See Rabbi Tzaddok HaKohen, *Resisei Layla* 52, and *Shem MiShmuel*, *Parashat Vayetze* 5678, for mystical explanations of this passage.

24 Translation based on Malbim ad loc.

25 Rashi and Mahari Kara.

26 Malbim.

27 Radak, *Metzudat David*.

28 Radak.

29 The word is *arudiyot*; an alternate text reads *adiraot*, which means "herds of animals"; see *Shita Mekubetzet* and Rabbeinu Gershom ad loc.

30 Tamara Zieve, "This Week In History: Bringing Biblical Animals Home," *The Jerusalem Post*, September 9, 2012.

31 Heinrich Mendelssohn and Yoram Yom-Tov, *Fauna Palaestina: Mammalia of Israel*, p. 238.

32 See Bill Clark, *High Hills and Wild Goats: Life Among the Animals of the Hai-Bar Wildlife Refuge*, pp. 201–216.

33 Diana Lutz, "The Secret Lives of the Wild Asses of the Negev," Newsroom, Washington University in St. Louis, March 27, 2013.

HIPPOPOTAMUS

Hippopotamus

The River Horse of Israel

NATURAL HISTORY

The hippopotamus, *Hippopotamus amphibius*, is the world's largest land animal after the elephant. Today, the hippopotamus lives only south of the Sahara, in central and southern Africa. Outside of that region, it can only be seen in a zoo, with the world's largest captive population – numbering around forty – living at the Ramat Gan Safari in Israel. (There is also a smaller and less aquatic species, the pygmy hippopotamus *Hexaprotodon liberiensis*, which lives in central Africa.)

But further back in history, the hippopotamus had much broader range. It was plentiful in the Nile river, becoming rare there only in the eighteenth century, with the last known hippopotamus in Egypt being killed around 1816. Earlier in history, during the biblical period, the hippopotamus also lived in the Land of Israel. Bones of hippopotami, dated to the Iron Age, have been found in numerous locations in areas of the coastal region that had freshwater rivers and swamps, reaching north almost as far as Haifa.[1] There is also evidence that they once inhabited Lake Kinneret.[2] Hippopotamus tusks reach twenty inches in length, and are a valued source of ivory; artifacts made from hippopotamus ivory have been found in the Negev and Judaean deserts.[3]

Why did the hippopotamus disappear from the Land of Israel? Many of them were undoubtedly killed, although that is not an easy task. The rest probably died out as a result of interference with their natural habitat. During that period, there was intense growth in human settlement; the fertile coastal region was ideal for agriculture. It was no place for a hippopotamus. With the dense population of Israel today, reintroducing hippopotami to the wild is not a viable option.

A hippopotamus yawns not because it is tired, but as a threat gesture

Behold the Behemoth

IDENTIFICATION

Israelis today usually refer to the hippopotamus as *hippopotam*. But the formal name of the hippopotamus in Modern Hebrew is *sus hayeor*. This means "river horse," which is also the meaning of the term "hippopotamus" in Ancient Greek. However, in Biblical Hebrew, the hippopotamus has a different name.

The Book of Job tells the story of a righteous person, Job, who is tormented by terrible suffering. He cries out to God, protesting his bitter fate, asking how God could act in such a way. God's answer is difficult to understand; at one point, He speaks about a wondrous creature called the behemoth:

> Behold now behemoth, which I made with you; he eats grass like an ox. Behold now, the strength of his loins, and the power in his belly. He stiffens his tail like a cedar; his testicles are bound by twisted cords. His bones are like tubes of bronze; his limbs are like bars of iron. He is the head of the works of God; let Him who made him bring His sword near to him. The mountains bring him forth food, where all the beasts of the field play. He lies under the shady trees, in the cover of the reeds and swamp. The shady trees cover him with their shadow; the willows of the brook surround him. Behold, he plunders a river without hurry; he trusts that he can draw the Jordan into his mouth. He takes in the river with his eyes, his nostrils are as though pierced by hooks. (Job 40:15–25).

◀ *This scene, encountered by the author in Botswana, could have been a familiar sight in the biblical Land of Israel.*

While the word *behemoth* is usually the plural form of *behema* (animal), and merely refers to animals (of unspecified type) in the plural, here the ensuing verses treat it as a singular form. Historically, there was much confusion as to the identity of this creature. Several traditional commentaries explain it to refer to a huge animal, but do not specify which species.[4] For this reason, when Scripture was translated into English, the name of this creature was usually not translated, but instead simply transliterated as *behemoth*. As a result, the word "behemoth" has entered the English language as referring to a massive creature.

But what is the behemoth of the Book of Job? Some have suggested that the behemoth is the elephant.[5] As the largest creature on land, the elephant would certainly qualify for the lavish descriptions that God gives. But while they enjoy occasionally bathing in rivers, the verses seem to indicate that the behemoth is an animal that spends much of its time there. It would also be strange that Scripture would make no mention of its trunk or tusks, which are its most distinctive features. Furthermore, elephants do not eat grass.

הִנֵּה נָא בְהֵמוֹת אֲשֶׁר עָשִׂיתִי עִמָּךְ חָצִיר כַּבָּקָר יֹאכֵל: הִנֵּה נָא
כֹחוֹ בְמָתְנָיו וְאֹנוֹ בִּשְׁרִירֵי בִטְנוֹ: יַחְפֹּץ זְנָבוֹ כְמוֹ אָרֶז גִּידֵי פַחֲדָיו
יְשֹׂרָגוּ: עֲצָמָיו אֲפִיקֵי נְחוּשָׁה גְּרָמָיו כִּמְטִיל בַּרְזֶל: הוּא רֵאשִׁית
דַּרְכֵי אֵל הָעֹשׂוֹ יַגֵּשׁ חַרְבּוֹ: כִּי בוּל הָרִים יִשְׂאוּ לוֹ וְכָל חַיַּת הַשָּׂדֶה
יְשַׂחֲקוּ שָׁם: תַּחַת צֶאֱלִים יִשְׁכָּב בְּסֵתֶר קָנֶה וּבִצָּה: יְסֻכֻּהוּ צֶאֱלִים
צְלָלוֹ יְסֻבּוּהוּ עַרְבֵי נָחַל: הֵן יַעֲשֹׁק נָהָר לֹא יַחְפּוֹז יִבְטַח כִּי יָגִיחַ
יַרְדֵּן אֶל פִּיהוּ: בְּעֵינָיו יִקָּחֶנּוּ בְּמוֹקְשִׁים יִנְקָב אָף:

איוב מ:טו-כד

351

"Behold now behemoth,
which I made with you…"

(Job 40:15)

Others suggest that the behemoth is a water buffalo. But the water buffalo, a very familiar animal in those days, would not seem to qualify for the grand descriptions that the verses give. It would also be strange to speak of the water buffalo "eating grass like cattle" when it essentially *is* cattle. Furthermore, it seems unlikely that the water buffalo was present in the area during biblical times.

It seems overwhelmingly likely that the behemoth is the hippopotamus, an animal largely unfamiliar to the medieval European scholars of Scripture.[6] This would be a striking animal to use in presenting the message to Job of the Creator's power. If we analyze the verses, we can see how the hippopotamus perfectly matches the description of the behemoth.

> Behold now behemoth, which I made with you; he eats grass like an ox.

The hippopotamus indeed "eats grass like an ox," albeit in slightly larger quantities. Hippos consume about ninety pounds of various grasses each night, which is the time when all the feeding takes place. The grass is cropped with a plucking motion of the broad, thick lips.

> Behold now, the strength of his loins...

This refers to the hippos' surprising capacity for speed.[7] Although they may look clumsy, hippos are capable of reaching speeds of eighteen miles per hour in short bursts – faster than a human!

> ...and the power in his belly.

Weighing up to four tons, the hippopotamus is a tremendously powerful animal, as the verses describe. Males can stand five feet high and measure fifteen feet in length. Some point out that whereas the power of predators is in their claws, teeth, and venom, the power of the herbivorous hippopotamus lies in its sheer bulk.[8]

> He stiffens (*yachpotz*) his tail like a cedar; his testicles are bound by twisted cords.

The comparison of the behemoth's tail to a cedar is slightly difficult to understand. Some explain that the word *yachpotz* refers to speed, and the verse is saying that the behemoth whips its tail;[9] others say that it refers to the desire of the behemoth to move its tail.[10] The tail is then compared to the size and shape of a cedar tree.[11] This is certainly not the case with the hippopotamus, which has a very short tail.

According to others, however, the word *yachpotz* does not mean that it whips its tail, but that it *stiffens* its tail,[12] which is thus only likened to a cedar in terms of its stiffness,

The short, bristled tail of a hippopotamus

but not in its overall dimensions. The hippo's tail is less than a foot long, but it is broad and stiff. It uses it to slap the water as a method of social interaction. The verse may be referring to the hippo slapping its short but firm tail, like a wooden paddle. It may also allude to the bristles that protrude from either side of it, like the needles on the branch of the cedar.

Alternatively, the "tail" may be a euphemistic reference to its reproductive organ.[13] This is also how the term is explained by many when it occurs elsewhere in Scripture,[14] and it would make sense to be juxtaposed with the latter part of the verse describing its testicles.[15] According to this translation, the word *yachpotz* refers to a physical desire, and the verse would read that "when it is possessed with desire, its member is like a cedar."

> His bones are like tubes of bronze; his limbs are like bars of iron.

The hippopotamus has been trivialized in cartoons and toys. Yet it is still one of the most powerful and dangerous animals in Africa, killing more people than lions, elephants, and buffaloes combined. Although hippopotami are usually herbivorous, they are fiercely territorial and will stomp or chomp anyone sailing a boat near their territory.

> ...He is the head of the works of God; let Him who made him bring near His sword to him.

In the regions of the Middle East where the hippopotamus was formerly found, it was by far the largest animal. Only God Himself can overpower it.

"Behold now behemoth…" – A pictorial representation

MRSIRAPHOL / SHUTTERSTOCK

*"Behold now behemoth, which I made with you;
he eats grass like an ox"*

DIANE TANNER

"Behold now, the strength of his loins…"

N. SLIFKIN

"…and the power in his belly…"

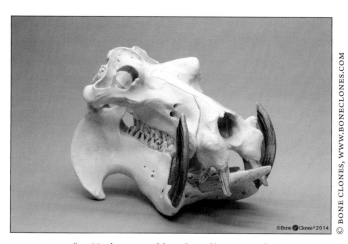

© BONE CLONES, WWW.BONECLONES.COM

"…His bones are like tubes of bronze…."

DONOVAN VAN STADEN / SHUTTERSTOCK

"…He trusts that he can draw the Jordan up into his mouth…."

SHAUN JEFFERS / SHUTTERSTOCK

*"…He takes in the river with his eyes,
his nostrils are as though pierced by hooks."*

354

> The mountains bring him forth food, where all the beasts of the field play.

Despite its size and power, the hippopotamus is a herbivore and does not pose a threat to other animals. When the hippo emerges from the river at night to graze upon grass, other animals can play in its presence.

> He lies under the shady trees, in the cover of the reeds and swamp. The shady trees cover him with their shadow; the willows of the brook surround him.

Hippopotami spend most of their days lying in the river under the shade of reeds.[16] This is because they lose water at very high rate through their skin, about four times as fast as do humans. They also lack sweat glands; instead, they secrete a pink fluid that dries to form a lacquer on their skin and protects them from sunburn.

> Behold, he plunders a river without hurry; he trusts that he can draw the Jordan up into his mouth.

The description of the behemoth being able to drink up a river and draw the Jordan into its mouth is a poetic exaggeration. It is based on the enormous gape of the hippo's mouth, some four feet from jaw to jaw. This is achieved by virtue of the lower jaw being hinged very far back on the skull, enabling it to open to 150°, compared to 45° for a human.

> He takes in the river with his eyes, his nostrils are as though pierced by hooks.

This phrase is exceedingly difficult to translate. The first part is translated by some as that the hippopotamus takes in the river with a glance, looking upon it with the thought of drinking it all.[17] This may well refer to the fact that the hippopotamus usually rests with just its eyes above the surface of the water, on the lookout. Others state that the word *einav* refers not to eyes but to the springs that feed the river, which the behemoth consumes along with the river.[18] The latter part of the phrase is explained by some to mean that the behemoth's nostrils are as if pierced by hooks.[19] This would refer to the enormous nostrils of the hippopotamus.

The Role of the Behemoth

SYMBOLISM

Why does God, in speaking to the tormented Job, speak of the hippopotamus? One answer is that God is telling Job that He is the Creator of the universe and, as such, His ways are beyond the grasp of mortal man. As a way of putting Job in his place, God speaks about the mighty hippopotamus, truly a creature to be in awe of, an animal to remind man how small and fragile he is. Suitably humbled, man will no longer dare to challenge the Creator's ways.[20]

Another explanation of the behemoth's appearance is that God is telling Job how nothing could have prevented Him from rewarding Job, had Job deserved it. If nobody can overcome a hippopotamus, which is merely one of God's creations, then certainly nobody could stand in the way of God rewarding Job. Since God did not reward him, it could not have been for lack of ability, but rather because Job was undeserving.[21]

Yet another explanation builds from the previous few verses:

> Then God answered to Job from the stormy wind, and said, Gird up your loins now like a man; I will put questions to you, and you will enlighten Me. Will you also disavow My judgment? Will you condemn Me, that you may be in the right? Do you have an arm like God? Or can you thunder with a voice like Him? Deck yourself now with majesty and grandeur; and array yourself with glory and beauty. Cast abroad the rage of your wrath; and behold everyone who is arrogant, and abase him. Look on everyone who is arrogant, and bring him low; and tread down the wicked in their place. Hide them in the dust together; and bind their faces in the hiding place. Then will I also confess to you that your own right hand can save you. (Job 40:6–14)

In these verses, God is not addressing Job's question of why bad things happen to good people, but rather his question of why good things happened to bad people. God is telling Job that even if Job were to possess all the power he wanted, he still would not be able to bring himself to destroy the wicked. Job should realize what it would mean to stand from a standpoint of majesty and grandeur, where Job would be able to see world history in all of its intricacy. In such a case, he would realize that the complex interrelationships of this society are worth preserving even if it means leaving the wicked temporarily undisturbed.

As an illustration of this point, God speaks about the behemoth and the leviathan.[22] The behemoth, for all its strength, is a herbivore; the leviathan, a devastating predator. Yet each has its place in the natural world. They both contribute to the harmony of their ecosystem. In the same way, wicked people have their function within broader society. Job must learn to accept that the interdependencies of our world require limitations upon the idea of pure justice.[23]

The Behemoth of Legend

SYMBOLISM

There are other descriptions of the behemoth which certainly do not match the hippopotamus:

> For all the beasts of the forest are Mine, the behemoth among the thousands of the mountains. (Ps. 50:10)

A simple translation of this would be that there are numerous animals (*behemoth* being the plural form of *behema*, "animal"), which live upon the mountains.[24] But the Midrash takes it to refer to the singular creature known as the behemoth:

> "The behemoth upon a thousand mountains" …R. Yochanan said, it is one animal that rests upon a thousand mountains, and a thousand mountains grow all types of grasses for it to eat, as it says, "Surely the mountains bring him forth food" (Job 40:20). And Resh Lakish said, it is one animal that rests upon a thousand mountains, and a thousand mountains grow food that is worthy for the righteous, and it eats it; what is the reason – "And the Sharon shall be a fold of flocks" (Is. 65:10). And the Rabbis say, there is one animal that rests on a thousand

mountains, and a thousand mountains grow different types of animals for it to eat; what is the reason – "where all the beasts of the field play" (Job 40:20)…. And from where does it drink? …R. Yochanan said: Whatever the Jordan brings in over six months it swallows in one draft, as it says, "Behold, he drinks up a river, and hastens not" (Job 40:23). R. Shimon b. Lakish said: Whatever the Jordan brings in over twelve months it swallows in one draft, as it says, "he trusts that he can draw the Jordan up into his mouth" (ibid.)…. And from where does it drink? R. Shimon b. Yochai taught: A river emerges from Eden, and its name is Yuval, and from there it drinks. (*Vayikra Rabba* 22:10)

This behemoth, sometimes referred to as *shor habar*, the "wild ox," is also described in the Talmud:

> Also the "behemoth upon a thousand mountains" (Ps. 50:10), He created male and female; and were they to cohabit with each other, they would destroy the entire world. What did God do? He castrated the male, sterilized the female and preserved her for the righteous in

The huge tusks of a hippopotamus can cause fearsome wounds

the World to Come, as it says, "Behold now, his strength is in his loins" – this refers to the male, "and his force is in the muscles of his belly" – this refers to the female. (Bava Batra 74b)

These descriptions do not match any conceivable creature, let alone the hippopotamus. But some explain that there are two usages of the term behemoth. The physical animal described in the Book of Job is a hippopotamus; but this animal is also used by the Talmud and Midrash as a metaphor for a concept.[25] One of the commentators bases his explanation on the idea that the behemoth represents the physical aspects of the world (whereas its counterpart, the leviathan, is a metaphor for the spiritual aspects).[26]

This may shed light on the scriptural name for the hippopotamus, behemoth. This is a curious word. It is usually a plural form of the word *behema*, animal, and yet here it is the singular form of the name hippopotamus. Some explain that the unusual form of the word indicates that it is referring to a particularly large animal.[27] But there may also be here an indication that the hippopotamus is the ultimate *behema* in another sense. As explained in the introduction to the section on animals, the word *behema* is interpreted by some to relate to the physicality of an animal, the beast that lacks capacity for spiritual development and represents plain materialism. The hippo conveys this concept very powerfully. Its vast, obese, ponderous bulk, together with its enormous mouth, symbolize physicality in its rawest and most extreme form. The hippopotamus is the ultimate *behema*, and it is therefore known as the behemoth.

Why the Hippopotamus Is Not Kosher
———————————————— LAW AND RITUAL

The status of the hippopotamus with regard to kosher signs has historically been the source of considerable confusion. The hippopotamus does not bring up its cud. Although the hippopotamus has multiple stomach chambers, which function in a similar way to those of kosher animals, it does not bring up food from these chambers for re-chewing.[28]

Thus, the hippopotamus is certainly not a kosher animal. But does it lack both signs of kosher animals, or just one? There was a widespread (and mistaken) belief that the hippopotamus possesses cloven hooves. This appears to have originated with the Roman naturalist Pliny, who described the hippopotamus as having "the cloven hoof of an ox."[29] Even today there are those who mistakenly believe this, perhaps due to the hippopotamus being classified in the family of artiodactyls (even-toed ungulates), which includes deer, cows, sheep, and pigs – all animals with split hooves.[30]

N. SLIFKIN

This underwater view of a hippopotamus shows that its feet have soles with toes rather than split hooves

Rabbi Avraham Portaleone (1542–1612) cites Pliny and raises the question of why the hippopotamus is not listed in the Torah as an animal with the kosher sign of split hooves but lacking the kosher sign of chewing the cud, along with the pig.[31] He answers that the Torah does not mention the hippopotamus either because it isn't fit for eating anyway, or because its non-kosher status can be inferred from the pig.[32] Rabbi Portaleone then states that the hippopotamus does not contradict the Talmud's statement that the Torah specified the pig as being the only animal to possess split hooves and not to ruminate,[33] because the Talmud is not making an absolute statement about all creatures; instead, it is only discussing animals that are fit to eat in the first place.[34]

However, in fact the hippopotamus does not raise a difficulty in the first place, because it does not actually have cloven hooves. Although the toes of both the hippopotamus and the pygmy hippopotamus are fully encased by hooves, the animal does not stand on its toes, but rather on the soles of its feet, with the hoofed toes providing only supplementary support. Whether one interprets the Torah's requirement as being that the animal has a full hoof which is split,[35] or one interprets the Torah's requirement as being that the part of the foot that touches the ground is split,[36] the hippopotamus fails on both counts; it does not have a full hoof, and the part of the foot that touches the ground is not split. The hippopotamus lacks both signs of kosher animals.

357

∎

Notes

1 Georg Haas, "On the Occurrence of Hippopotamus in the Iron Age of the Coastal Area of Israel (Tell Qasîleh)," *Bulletin of the American Schools of Oriental Research* 132 (1953), 30–34; Ella Tsahar, Ido Izhaki, Simcha Lev-Yadun, Guy Bar-Oz, "Distribution and Extinction of Ungulates during the Holocene of the Southern Levant" PLoS One 2009; 4(4):e5316; Liora Kolska Horwitz and Eitan Tchernov, "Cultural and Environmental Implications of Hippopotamus Bone Remains in Archaeological Contexts in the Levant," *Bulletin of the American Schools of Oriental Research,* No. 280 (Nov., 1990), pp. 67–76.

2 My colleague Shlomo Horowitz retrieved a tooth from the Kinneret which also appears to be from a hippopotamus.

3 Annie Caubet, "Animals in Syrio-Palestinian Art," in Billie Jean Collins, ed., *A History of the Animal World in the Ancient Near East* (Brill, 2002), p. 233.

4 Ralbag, Ibn Yachya, and Seforno. Ramban suggests that behemoth is a generic term for any large animal; he also notes the tradition that it refers to an animal known in aggadic literature as the *shor habar*, the wild ox.

5 Ibn Ezra records this suggestion but considers its arguments to be inconclusive.

6 Samuel Bochart, *Hierozoïcon*; Yosef Schonhak, *Toledot HaAretz*, p. 98, also citing Gesenius. This identification is accepted by all contemporary scholars in the field of biblical zoology.

7 Seforno.

8 Malbim.

9 Ramban, *Metzudat David,* and *Metzudat Tziyon.*

10 Ramban, Ibn Yachya. Malbim explains it to refer to a sexual desire, in line with his explanation that the "tail" is a reference to its reproductive organ.

11 *Metzudat David* and Ibn Yachya.

12 Rashi ad loc.

13 Malbim, commentary ad loc.

14 Deuteronomy 25:18; see Rashi ad loc. citing *Midrash Tanchuma*; Rabbeinu Bechaya; and *Daat Zekeinim.*

15 Rashi, Ibn Ezra, Ralbag, *Metzudat Tziyon* ad loc.

16 The description of the hippopotamus as an animal that lies in the cover of the reeds led Yehuda Feliks (*The Animal World of the Bible*, p. 24) to suggest that it is the "beast of the reeds" spoken of elsewhere: "Rebuke the beast of the reeds, the herd of bulls, with the calves of the peoples, who seek to ingratiate themselves with pieces of silver; scatter the peoples who delight in war" (Ps. 68:31). However, it is equally possible that the beast of the reeds is the water buffalo.

17 Ibn Ezra, Ramban, Ibn Yachya.

18 *Metzudat David, Metzudat Tziyon,* Malbim.

19 Ibn Ezra, Ramban.

20 Chida, *Chomat Anakh* to Job 40:15.

21 *Metzudat David* to Job 40:15.

22 The account of the leviathan of these verses appears to be a dramatic description of a crocodile.

23 Rabbi Moshe Eisemann, *Iyov* (New York: ArtScroll/Mesorah Publications, 1994).

24 *Metzudat David.*

25 For further discussion, see *Sacred Monsters* (Jerusalem: Zoo Torah/Gefen Books, 2011).

26 Rashba, *Perushei HaHaggadot* to Bava Batra 74a.

27 Ramban.

28 Additionally, hippos possess upper canines and incisors, a feature that the Talmud (Chullin 59a) states is lacking in animals that chew the cud.

29 Pliny, *Natural History* 8:25.

30 See e.g. G.S. Cansdale, *All the Animals of the Bible Lands* (Paternoster Press, 1970), p. 101.

31 Rabbi Avraham Portaleone, *Shiltei HaGiborim* (Mantova, 1612), p. 53b.

32 Note that he does not say that the hippo is the same species as the pig, just that its status can be inferred from the pig.

33 Chullin 59a.

34 He also suggests that the hippopotamus is classified as an aquatic creature, in the same category as fish, and is thus not kosher without fins and scales.

35 Rav Saadia Gaon, Rashbam, Ibn Ezra, Ibn Janach, Ralbag, and Chizkuni to Leviticus 11:26.

36 Rashi to Leviticus 11:26.

ELEPHANT

Elephant

Elephants and the Holy Land

NATURAL HISTORY

There are two types of elephant. The Asian (also called the Indian) elephant, easily trained and used in the logging industry for many generations, is a popular exhibit in zoos. It has a rounded back and distinctive domes on its forehead, a single "finger" at the end of its trunk, and only males possess tusks. The larger African elephant has much bigger ears, two "fingers" at the end of its trunk, and both males and females have tusks.[1] It is the largest land animal in the world.

Although elephants are among the most well-known animals today, and are mentioned on several occasions in the Mishna and Talmud, they are not mentioned in Scripture. This is due to the simple reason that they were not native to the Land of Israel. They did not, however, live as far away as they do today. Asian elephants lived on the banks of the Euphrates until the eighth century BCE.[2] Elephant remains have also been found in Kamid al lawz in Lebanon, just north of the Golan Heights, but it cannot be determined if they are from Asian elephants that were on the Euphrates, or African elephants that were imported.[3]

Although elephants were not found in the Land of Israel,

elephant ivory, on the other hand, was a familiar imported item. The ivory for King Solomon's throne was brought by his fleet from Tarshish, along with other items and creatures of tribute:[4]

> For the king had at sea a fleet of Tarshish with the fleet of Hiram; once every three years the fleet of Tarshish came, bringing gold, and silver, ivory (*shenhabim*), and monkeys, and peacocks. (I Kings 10:22; II Chr. 9:21)

Shenhab is generally understood to refer to ivory.[5] However, some suggest that the term *shenhab* not only refers to ivory, but also to elephants themselves.[6] According to this

כִּי אֲנִי תַרְשִׁישׁ לַמֶּלֶךְ בַּיָּם עִם אֲנִי חִירָם אַחַת לְשָׁלֹשׁ שָׁנִים תָּבוֹא
אֲנִי תַרְשִׁישׁ נֹשְׂאֵת זָהָב וָכֶסֶף שֶׁנְהַבִּים וְקֹפִים וְתֻכִּיִּים:
מלכים א י:כב

כִּי אֳנִיּוֹת לַמֶּלֶךְ הֹלְכוֹת תַּרְשִׁישׁ עִם עַבְדֵי חוּרָם אַחַת לְשָׁלוֹשׁ
שָׁנִים תָּבוֹאנָה אֳנִיּוֹת תַּרְשִׁישׁ נֹשְׂאוֹת זָהָב וָכֶסֶף שֶׁנְהַבִּים וְקוֹפִים
וְתוּכִּיִּים:
דברי הימים ב ט:כא

At left, an Asian elephant; note the domed forehead and rounded back.
At right, an African elephant; note the much larger ears, overall larger size, and different shaped back.

view, perhaps because tusks are one of the most prominent features of the elephant, they became the basis of the animal's name. Similarly, in English, an elephant with large tusks is sometimes called a "tusker."

Ivory Tusks – Fit for a King

Ivory is usually called *shen* in Scripture, which literally means "tooth," but refers here to the type of teeth that are used as a raw material for construction of precious items – the ivory tusks of elephants. There are numerous references to ivory in Scripture, such as in the following verses:

> His hands are rods of gold, studded with topaz; his chest a tablet of ivory, adorned with sapphires. (Song. 5:14)

> Your neck is like an ivory tower, your eyes like pools in Heshbon. (Song. 7:5)

> They lie on beds of ivory, spreading on their couches. (Amos 6:4)

Ivory is identical to dentine, which is the primary substance in all mammal teeth, including those of humans. But whereas human teeth are capped with enamel, some animals have long protruding teeth – called tusks – that are covered with only a thin layer of enamel, which soon wears off. The tusks of hippopotami, walruses, pigs, mammoths, and elephants have all been used as sources of ivory, but elephant ivory is by far the most common type. Elephant tusks, the largest teeth of any creature, have been known to measure over eleven feet in length and to weigh 240 pounds.

Ivory has always been a greatly valued material, used especially to adorn the palaces of kings:

> All your garments have myrrh and aloes and cassia; lutes entertain you from ivory palaces. (Ps. 45:9)

> I will wreck the winter palace together with the summer palace; the ivory palaces shall be demolished, and the great houses shall be destroyed, declares God. (Amos 3:15)

> The other events of Ahab's reign, and all his actions – the ivory palace that he built and all the towns that he fortified – are all recorded in the annals of the kings of Israel. (1 Kings 22:39)

Ivory carvings have been found in archeological excavations of royal palaces throughout Israel, Syria, Cyprus, and the region of Mesopotamia.[7] King Solomon used ivory in the construction of his royal throne:

> Moreover the king made a great throne of ivory (*shen*), and overlaid it with the finest gold. (1 Kings 10:18)

These magnificent tusks were taken from a bull African elephant killed in 1899 in Kenya. One tusk weighed 228 pounds and the other weighed 236 pounds.

Perhaps ivory was not only used for royal furniture due to its aesthetic qualities, but also due to its representing the strength of the world's most powerful animal.

An interesting reference to ivory tusks occurs in the prophecy concerning the downfall of Tyre, which reminisces about the items that it received as tribute during the height of its glory:

> The men of Dedan were your peddlers, many islands traded with you, they brought horns (*karnot*) teeth (*shen*) and peacocks as your tribute. (Ezek. 27:15)

Some of the commentaries state that the horns mentioned in this verse were those of ibex, and the teeth were the tusks of elephants.[8] However, it is difficult to imagine that ibex horns would have been such a valuable item to bring as tribute. Others explain that the phrase *karnot shen* is not to be translated as "horns, tusks" but instead describes a single item, "horns of ivory," i.e. elephant tusks.[9] These are referred to as "horns" because of their being more similar to horns than to teeth.

Since elephant tusks are described here as "horns," one

may wonder if an elephant tusk may be made into a shofar. However, even if this verse is actually classifying tusks as horns, they would nevertheless probably be disqualified as shofars. This is because the Talmud, according to most authorities, disqualifies any horn that is referred to in Scripture as a "*keren*" ("horn") and not as a "*shofar*."[10] Thus, it is precisely this verse which refers to elephant tusks as "horns" which renders them disqualified as a shofar. Furthermore, due to doubt as to whether the horn of a non-kosher animal may be used for the mitzva of shofar, the consensus is that it should not be used if there is a shofar from a kosher animal available.[11]

The Amazing Elephant

SYMBOLISM

In *Perek Shira*, the ancient text that lists the lessons to be learned from the natural world, the elephant's song is one of the easiest to understand:

> The elephant is saying: "How great are Your works, God; Your thoughts are tremendously deep" (Ps. 92:6). (*Midrash Perek Shira*)

This verse is a simple gasp at the wonder of creation. And there is no animal better than the elephant at making one gasp. In nineteenth-century America, the phrase "seeing the elephant" meant having an overwhelming experience. This phrase presumably originated with people who had an overwhelming experience of seeing the greatest animal on land: the elephant. The Talmud prescribes a blessing to be made upon seeing elephants:

> The Rabbis taught: One who sees an elephant, monkey, or *kifof*[12] says, Blessed is He who varies the creations. (Berakhot 58b[13])

Simply speaking, this blessing refers to the elephant's extraordinary size, power, and form (later, we shall explore another possibility). While every animal should be a source of wonder, the elephant's particularly unusual nature is more likely to induce feelings of wonder in a person.[14] Perhaps the reason why many do not pronounce this blessing with God's Name today is that our sensitivity has been blunted even toward elephants. We are so used to seeing them in pictures and natural history documentaries that we have become numb to their wonder. In order to regain the inspiration that the elephant ought to give us, we need to contemplate and meditate upon its wondrousness.

The most obvious remarkable aspect of elephants is their great size. Male Asian elephants are usually nine or ten feet tall at the shoulder. Male African elephants typically stand ten to twelve feet tall at the shoulder and weigh four to seven tons. Exceptional individuals have been measured at fourteen feet in height and weighing over twelve tons.[15]

Elephants enjoy trying their strength by pushing over trees, and they often feast upon the foliage and the bark of the fallen tree. A skillful tree-feller can bring down trees up to five feet in circumference. According to some, the

A herd of elephants being led by a "tusker" bull

elephant's Hebrew name *pil* is related to the word *naphal*, "fall"; the elephant is called the "toppler," after its ability – and its predilection – to knock down trees and buildings.[16]

There are many other remarkable features of elephants. The elephant's trunk, which contains no bone but has tens of thousands of muscles, is an astonishing tool. Strong enough to lift vast weights, it is simultaneously delicate enough to pluck a stalk of grass.

Another extraordinary aspect of elephants is their mode of communication. There have long been stories told of elephant hunters who experienced a quivering sensation of fear as they approached the herd. These accounts have been proven to have a factual basis. Elephants communicate to each other by means of sound waves far below the frequencies that humans can detect without special equipment. However, when standing near a large herd of elephants, the low sound waves can make one feel the air trembling.[17]

In all these ways and more, the elephant is a wondrous animal, which is why it is a fortuitous vision to experience in a dream:

> If a person sees an elephant in a dream, wonders will take place for him. If he sees [several] elephants, a multitude of wonders will take place for him. (Berakhot 56b, 57b)

The Talmud here may also be relating the name of the elephant, *pil*, to the similar word *pele*, wonder. The elephant is wondrous by name, wondrous by nature.

Extreme Elephants

SYMBOLISM

There are a number of references to elephants scattered throughout the Talmud and Midrash which relate to various aspects of the elephant's extreme nature. Earlier, we saw the Talmud's statement that seeing an elephant in a dream portends wondrous events. The Talmud raises a question on this:

> But surely it was taught that all animals are good in a dream except the monkey and the elephant? It is no question; one is where it was saddled, one is where it was not saddled. (Berakhot 57b)

A wild elephant is a truly formidable creature. Even in zoos, elephants have killed more people than any other animal, and the job of elephant keeper ranks as one of the most dangerous jobs in the world. An elephant's great size is a source of wonder, but also a potential source of great danger.

Due to the elephant's great size, it makes a particularly spectacular mount for riding. The Indian elephant trainers, called mahouts, typically straddle the elephant's neck,

363

◂ *A huge African elephant in Botswana*

The Rabbis taught: One who
sees an elephant... says, Blessed
is He who varies the creations.

(Berakhot 58b)

The author, riding an African elephant

but a more dignified method of riding has been by way of the howdah, a sort of carriage that was strapped to the elephant's back. A person sitting upon an elephant is riding higher than anyone else:

> Why was the Torah given in Sivan, and not in other months? It is comparable to the king who was making a wedding for his daughter. One of his important associates said to him, It is befitting for the daughter of a king to ride on an elephant, sitting upon a howdah, raised up above all the nobles of the kingdom. Someone else responded and said, An elephant is too tall, and is not glorious or fine-looking; it is befitting to have her ride upon a horse, and to display her beauty amongst all the nobles of the kingdom. Another man responded, An elephant is tall, and a horse is fine-looking, but they do not have a mouth with which to speak, and hands with which to clap, and feet with which to dance; it is befitting to have her ride upon the shoulders of a person, to display her beauty. Similarly the Holy One; He did not give the Torah in Nissan or Iyyar, because the constellation of Nissan is the lamb and that of Iyyar is the bull, and it is not befitting for them to extol and praise. Therefore, the Holy One gave the Torah in Sivan, because the constellation of Sivan is twins, and twins are human, and a human has a mouth with which to speak, and hands with which to clap, and feet with which to dance. (*Midrash Pesikta Rabbati* 20)

Aside from the brute strength and raw dimensions of the elephant, it is also extreme in terms of its prodigious capacity for food. An elephant drinks up to 25 gallons of water a day and eats up to 350 pounds of vegetation. They are remarkable not only in terms of the overall quantity of food that they consume, but also in the size of the items in their vegetarian diets:

> The Rabbis taught: One may carry squall plants [on the Sabbath], because they are food for gazelles, and mustard, because it is food for doves. R. Shimon b. Gamliel said: One may also carry glass shards, because it is food for ostriches. R. Natan said: This would indicate that one may carry bundles of vines, because they are food for elephants! However, R. Shimon b. Gamliel was of the opinion that ostriches are commonly found, whereas elephants are not. (Shabbat 128a)

The Midrash notes that Noah indeed had to bring such food on the Ark for the elephants:

> He brought vines for the elephants, hay for the gazelles, and glass for the ostriches. (*Bereshit Rabba* 31:14)

About sixty percent of what is excreted from the elephant's intestines, which can measure 116 feet long, is undigested vegetable matter. This provides the grounds for an unusual question in the Talmud:

Rami bar Chama asked: "What is the rule in the case of an elephant that swallowed an Egyptian basket and excreted it?" For what relevance? If you say to annul its ritual impurity, we have already learned this elsewhere…rather, it is necessary for a case where it swallowed palm-leaves, and an Egyptian basket was made [from the excreted vegetation]. (Menachot 69a; Bava Batra 22a)

The elephant is also mentioned in the Talmud as possibly providing a ramification regarding a dispute about using an animal as the wall of a sukka:

If an animal was used as a wall of a sukka, R. Meir disqualifies it, and R. Yehuda permits it…. What is the reason of R. Meir? Abaye said: As the animal might die. R. Zeira said: As the animal might run away. With a tied elephant, according to all reasons it is valid, as even if it dies, its carcass is still ten handsbreadths in height. A difference would arise in the case of an untied elephant; according to the one who says that (in general) we are concerned that the animal might die, there is no concern here (as it would still be ten handsbreadths in height), whereas according to the one who says that we are con-

cerned that it might run away, this concern would apply. (Sukka 23a)

Here, too, the elephant appears as being something extreme – an animal with which even its collapsed body exceeds ten handsbreadths (about three feet), the minimum height for a sukka.[18]

Elephant Limitations

The great size of the elephant makes it the most ridiculous animal to imagine fitting in a small space. It is thus the favored metaphor used by the Sages of the Talmud when they felt that someone's opinion was somewhat of a stretch – or perhaps we should say, a squeeze:

Maybe you are from Pumbedita, where they push an elephant through the eye of a needle! (Bava Metzia 38b)

An elephant fitting through the eye of a needle is the height of absurdity – something quite literally inconceivable:

R. Shmuel bar Nachmani said in the name of R. Yonatan: A person is not shown something [in a dream] unless he thought about it during the day…. Rava said: A proof for this is that people do not dream about a gold palm-tree or an elephant passing through the eye of a needle. (Berakhot 55b)

Yet it is intriguing to think that the largest of animals can be contained in something very small – or be vanquished by something very small. Hence, the widespread notion that elephants are terrified of mice. Unfortunately, however, this is entirely false; confronted by a mouse, an elephant is more likely to step on it than to flee. This myth seems to have stemmed from a defense tactic used by the Romans against Pyrrhus' war elephants in 275 BCE. They coated pigs in pitch and grease and set fire to them; the dying screams of the animals caused the elephants to panic and flee, leading to a saying that "squealing scares elephants."[19]

Nevertheless, elephants are certainly bothered, if not terrified, by an even smaller creature: the mosquito.

The Rabbis taught: There are five fears with which the fear of the weak is upon the mighty: The fear of the gnat upon the lion, the fear of the mosquito upon the elephant, the fear of the gecko upon the scorpion, the fear of the swallow upon the vulture, and the fear of the kilbit-fish upon the whale. R. Yehuda said: What is the scriptural source? "He grants the robbed one power over the mighty" (Amos 5:9). (Shabbat 77b)

ANDAMAN / SHUTTERSTOCK

◀ An elephant eating a palm leaf, just as described in the Talmud

A mother elephant escorting her calf through a pride of lions ▶

The elephant, mightiest of animals, does not fear attacks by lions or hippopotami. The only creature that they have to contend with is one of the smallest of all: the mosquito. There is an expression, being as thick-skinned as an elephant, which is highly misleading. It is true than an elephant's skin is physically thick, up to an inch and a half in some places. Yet elephants are not only emotionally very sensitive – they are physically highly sensitive, too. Mosquitoes and ticks cause elephants to bleed and are an endless source of distress for them.[20] An elephant's tail is too ineffective a whisk, so elephants will sometimes break off branches from trees for this purpose. They enjoy swimming and wallowing in mud for the same reason; it provides them with temporary respite from the insects that plague them.

Of all the other creatures in the world, the only ones that present a constant menace to elephants are parasites. This serves as a reminder never to attribute too much importance to physical size and strength.[21] The mosquito is presented not only as the nemesis of the elephant, but also of the Roman Emperor Titus. The Talmud relates that a mosquito burrowed into his brain and eventually killed him.[22] Just as the tiny mosquito is the foe of the mighty elephant, so too is it the vanquisher of the mighty Roman emperor. Titus himself is linked to elephants; a coin minted on the occasion of his completion of the Colosseum depicts Titus on one

The coin minted on the occasion of Titus completing the Colosseum

side and an elephant on the other. The elephant, a powerful and majestic beast, was the very symbol of his reign.[23]

When a king wishes to put insurgents in their place, he does not send his best troops against them. Rather, he sends his lowest troops, to show the insurgents how small they are in his eyes. By the same token, God causes the mosquito to be the foe of the Roman emperor and the mighty elephant, to show how physical power is nothing next to Him.

Elephants and Monkeys
—————————————— LAW AND RITUAL

The monkey and elephant are a common pair in many places. Not only was the ivory of elephants grouped with

367

monkeys in the tribute sent on the ships of Tarshish to King Solomon, but the Mishna and Talmud list them together in several instances.

The Mishna discusses whether various animals are defined as *behemot*, domestic animals, or *chayot*, wild animals. With kosher animals, this is relevant to determine whether their fat is permitted and whether their blood requires covering. With non-kosher animals, this can be relevant to determine if there is a crossbreeding problem with different varieties, or if a contract to sell all one's *behemot* or *chayot* includes these animals. The Mishna decides the status of the monkey and elephant together:

> The monkey and the elephant are types of *chaya*. (Mishna Kilayim 8:6)

Even though both lend themselves to being trained, they are not considered domestic animals in the legal sense. Thus, if a person were to write that he was selling his domestic animals, this would not include his trained monkey or lumber-lugging elephant.

Another occurrence of elephants in the Talmud is in the context of Shabbat laws. There is a limit of walking beyond two thousand cubits from the edge of town on Shabbat. However, this limit can be extended by placing, before Shabbat, an *eiruv* – a token meal – outside town, thereby symbolically establishing one's location there. The Mishna discusses the legitimacy of using different methods to send the *eiruv* to this location, one of which involves sending it via elephant:

> If he gave it to an elephant, and it transported it to a monkey, it is not a valid *eiruv*. But if he told somebody else to take it from [the monkey], it is valid. (Eiruvin 31b)

Rabbi Shimon ben Zemach Duran (1361–1444), writing a medieval encyclopedia of animals, observes that there is none closer to understanding humans than the elephant.[24] Elephants, which lead highly complex social lives spanning many decades, demonstrate a level of intelligence that is second only to monkeys and dolphins. They even demonstrate unease around dead members of their species, a feature shared only with chimpanzees.

Physiologically speaking, the elephant's intelligence is explained in terms of its huge brain. Its brain weighs up to twelve pounds, the largest brain of any land mammal. In addition, the elephant spends much of its life learning, like man. Most animals are born with their brains weighing about 90 percent of their weight at adulthood. But humans are born with brains weighing only 25 percent of their adult weight. Thus, we spend much of our lifetime learning. Following man in the lifetime growth of the brain is the elephant, whose brain at birth weighs just 35 percent of the adult weight.

Baby elephants spend much time playing as well as learning

STEVE BOWER / SHUTTERSTOCK

*An elephant forms a lifelong bond with its handler and can
be trained to follow dozens of commands*

The common feature of advanced intelligence may also be the reason why the monkey and the elephant are grouped together in a different context:

> Everything that walks on its hands, among all animals that walk on four legs, are contaminated to you; whoever touches their carcasses shall be contaminated until evening (Lev. 11:27). "Everything that walks on its hands" – this is the monkey.... "All animals" – to include the elephant. (*Sifra, Shemini* 6)

The question is raised as to why it is necessary to have a special exegesis to include the elephant more than any other animal. If we look at the preceding section of the Midrash, however, we see that it is necessary to include animals that are somewhat humanlike, in that they have hands rather than feet. Perhaps along the same lines it is necessary to specifically include the elephant, which is also somewhat humanlike in its advanced intelligence. The Midrash is teaching that, notwithstanding the humanlike nature of monkeys and elephants, they are nevertheless included together with animals for the laws of ritual impurity.

The Blessing on Elephants and Monkeys
— SYMBOLISM

The concept of elephants and monkeys sharing similarities with humans is also advanced by some in order to explain the law concerning the blessings that are pronounced upon these animals:

> The Rabbis taught: One who sees an elephant, monkey, or *kifof* says, Blessed is He who varies the creations. (Berakhot 58b[25])

Some explain this blessing to refer to a statement in the Midrash regarding the builders of the Tower of Babel being physically transformed into various animals. While there are those who interpret these statements allegorically,[26] others understand them literally. Accordingly, the blessing is acknowledging God having literally "changed the creations."[27] However, this is a difficult explanation in light of the fact that the blessing is also pronounced upon the elephant. The Talmud only makes reference to people being transformed into monkeys.[28] While there is a midrash that refers to their being transformed into elephants, it appears to be of relatively late authorship.[29]

The most straightforward understanding of this blessing is that it is simply due to these animals being very unusual in comparison to other animals. (By extension, it would therefore also apply to other unusual animals, such as kangaroos or rhinoceroses.) It can be interpreted in a positive or negative manner; either as an expression of joyous wonder at such extreme diversity, or as forcing oneself to acknowledge God's wisdom even in bizarre and aberrant forms of life.

The latter interpretation, while less appealing, is perhaps more likely, for two reasons. One is that the Talmud rules that this blessing is also pronounced upon people with

Elephants can paint pictures; while most are abstract scribbles, some have been trained to paint illustrations

congenital abnormalities.[30] Second is in light of a negative reference to monkeys and elephants; as we saw earlier, there is a statement in the Talmud that "all animals are good in a dream except the monkey and the elephant." In his commentary, Rashi explains that this is due to their being unusual in appearance. Apparently, this is viewed negatively, and thus portends harm in a dream.

Whether viewed positively or negatively, the blessing appears to be contrasting monkeys and elephants with more mundane creatures. However, the thirteenth-century authority Rabbi Menachem Me'iri explains that the Talmud specifies the elephant and monkey due to their both possessing a unique similarity to human beings.[31] This might mean that the blessing is referring to monkeys and elephants being different from other animals ("Who varies the creations") in terms of their unique similarity to human beings. However, it could be that Me'iri is saying something even more remarkable. Perhaps the blessing, with its mention of God "varying the creations," is not commenting on

monkeys and elephants being different from other animals, but instead it is referring to their being different from *people*. The elephant and monkey are both fundamentally similar to man in possessing advanced intelligence and emotions. Intelligence is the defining characteristic of man, and it is also the special characteristic of elephants and monkeys. It is only because they are nevertheless somewhat different from man – with elephants, due to their overall form, and with monkeys, due to the degree of intelligence – that one praises the One who made them different in that way. The blessing is not acknowledging their differing from other animals; it is acknowledging their differing from man.[32]

How to Buy an Elephant

——————— LAW AND RITUAL

In Jewish law, when a person wishes to acquire an item, it is not enough to simply pay for it; he must also perform an act of acquisition. The Mishna discusses various methods of legally acquiring different types of animals. It would always be possible to formally acquire an animal by bringing it into one's property. However, most people wish to complete the acquisition at the market. A physical act of acquisition is necessary in addition to the financial transaction, but the type of act that is required depends on the type of animal concerned. For a large animal, the Mishna says that its reins or mane may be handed over, whereas sheep and goats are acquired by *hagbaha*, lifting them up. The Gemara cites the opinion of R. Shimon that all animals can only be acquired by lifting them up – handing over their reins or mane is never valid. This leads to a question regarding animals that are too heavy to lift up, of which the elephant is the most obvious example:

Rav Yosef asked: "If so, then how, according to R. Shimon, does one acquire an elephant?!"

Abaye responded: "Through *chalifin* (a type of exchange); alternatively, by renting the place on which it is standing (and thereby acquiring it by virtue of the principle that one can acquire what is on one's property)."

R. Zeira said: "He brings four vessels and places them under its feet." (Kiddushin 25b)

R. Zeira explains that according to R. Shimon, an elephant can be acquired by having it step up, one foot at a time, into four pots that one owns. One has thereby acquired the elephant by way of the principle that one acquires whatever is in one's vessels. But the Talmud then proceeds to suggest an entirely different way that an elephant can be acquired:

Alternatively, it is with bundles of vines. (Ibid.)

What does this mean? According to the commentary of Rashi, it means that one stacks up bundles of vines to three handsbreadths in height and makes the elephant stand on them. One has thereby caused the elephant to rise, and has acquired it through *hagbaha*.

In the glosses of *Tosafot*, on the other hand, this explanation is rejected. It is pointed out that if the Talmud were talking about building a platform, it would surely make more sense to speak of using stones or wood. Others raise the objection that a platform of vines would not be of legally different status than the ground itself. *Tosafot* therefore cites Rav Meshullam ben Nathan of Melun, France, as giving a different explanation for this method of acquisition. Noting that bundles of vines are food for elephants (as we cited earlier, from the Talmud and Midrash), Rav Meshullam explains the Talmud's answer to mean that one takes the bundles of vines and hangs them very high up in the air. The elephant will then jump up in the air in order to reach them and eat them. One has therefore caused the elephant to raise itself up and perform *hagbaha* on itself. The authorities Ritva and Ramban concur with this explanation.

(Rav Meshullam is definitely referring to the elephant jumping clear from the ground with all four feet, not rear-

In countries such as India, elephants are often present at the market

371

The elephant, being much larger than the gazelle standing near it, has limbs that are proportionately much thicker

ing up on its back legs. His point is not in innovating a form of movement that is acceptable as *hagbaha*, but rather that one can make the elephant into an emissary to do the *hagbaha* on itself. The *hagbaha* itself must be a regular *hagbaha*, which, as always, requires that the item be entirely raised from the ground.[33])

Do Elephants Jump?

THEOLOGY, PHILOSOPHY, AND SCIENCE

There appears to be a problem with Rav Meshullam's explanation of the Talmud's answer: elephants cannot jump. This is known both empirically and also due to our understanding of animal anatomy. Many people have worked with elephants their whole lives and have observed that they do not jump. And despite intense efforts by circus trainers to make elephants perform an extraordinary range of tricks, and the earth-shattering impact that a jumping elephant act would have, nobody has ever managed to come up with one. It is true that elephants are quite agile in terms of balancing, being able to perform handstands, walk a tightrope, and even ride a tricycle. However, such forced feats, aside from causing distress to the elephant, do not relate to its raw power.

It all boils down to physics. An average cantaloupe melon, at about six inches in diameter, is twice as wide as an average orange. But if you cut the melon in half, the area of the cross-section is four times as great as that of the orange. And the melon weighs not twice, not four times, but eight times as much as the orange. For any given object, if

it increases in length and its proportions remain the same, its cross-sectional area increases at an even greater rate, but its volume at a yet greater rate still. The cross-section is proportional to the length squared, while the volume (mass) is proportional to the length cubed.

Bigger animals are therefore built differently than smaller animals, since the strength of a leg-bone depends primarily upon its cross-sectional area, but the weight increases according to the volume. Imagine a deer that is magically doubled in size to the height of an elephant. The cross-sectional area of its leg bones would quadruple in size, but its weight would increase eightfold. Its legs would therefore not be able to support it. A mouse can support its weight on very slender legs; a deer has thicker legs; and an elephant's legs must be very thick indeed. As a consequence, it has a heavily built skeleton which is necessarily very rigid, and its movements are relatively stiff.

The strength of muscle, like that of bone, also depends on its cross-sectional area. And as an animal increases in size, the cross-sectional area of its muscle does not increase at the same rate as the animal's mass. The bigger an animal, the stronger it is in an absolute sense, but the weaker in a relative sense. Elephants simply lack the muscular strength to propel themselves from the ground.

The posture of an elephant is also necessarily very different from that of smaller animals. A mouse can keep all its legs in a crouching position, ideally suited for moving fast in a dangerous world. A dog or deer stands with its hind legs in a bent position, ready for acceleration. But an elephant does

372

not have enough muscular power to stand in such a way. Elephants therefore stand with their legs positioned like columns beneath them, and run by swinging these pillars back and forth rather than with the flexibility and grace that smaller animals possess. In fact, it is generally considered inappropriate to use the term "running" for elephants, since at no point do all their feet leave the ground.[34]

Elephants are very ponderous beasts and are only too aware of how much support their vast bulk needs. They tread carefully and are reluctant to even take two legs off the ground at the same time. Zoos are able to keep elephants restrained in their enclosures with only a shallow ditch; the elephants usually realize that they are simply incapable of crossing it. The circus acrobatics that elephants are forced to perform (usually by means of prodding them painfully with a spiked stick) cause immense strain. Even something as seemingly simple as going down on its knees puts a tremendous strain on an elephant's joints and intervertebral discs. If an elephant somehow left the ground, coming back down would cause it to suffer severe damage.

Another point to consider is that we are not only discussing any case of an elephant jumping, but rather we are discussing making it jump by hanging food out of its reach. But an elephant has a different strategy in such a situation. First it tries to reach the food with its trunk. If that doesn't work, it tries to increase its reach by standing on its back legs (although only males can do this, and only briefly). If it still couldn't reach, jumping would now require using the force exerted by its hind legs alone – which would be even less conceivable than jumping with all four legs.

Why did Rav Meshullam suggest that one could make the elephant jump? The answer is that he had no reason to believe otherwise. There were no zoos in medieval Europe, and very few elephants. The emperor Charlemagne, king of the Franks, received an elephant as a gift in 797. Frederick II used an elephant in his capture of Cremona in 1214. King Henry III of England received an elephant from Israel in 1254. Alfonso V of Portugal gave an elephant to René d'Anjou in 1477. The Vatican was given an elephant in 1514. But the average person in those times never saw an elephant. Illustrations from that era show that artists, basing themselves on stories, were very unsure about how to depict elephants. They were often portrayed as possessing a body like those of horses or deer, sometimes even with split hooves. Of particular relevance to us is that they are sometimes drawn with the hindlimb structure of lions or dogs, poised with elastic energy. Rav Meshullam ben Nathan, who was born in Provence in 1120 and passed away in Melun in 1180, never saw either a live elephant or an accurate drawing of

one. He thus had every reason to believe that, like other animals, elephants can jump.[35]

It should be noted that our modern knowledge about elephants does not mean that there is any less value in studying this case of the Talmud and *Tosafot*. Consider this: the total number of Jews who ever wanted to purchase an elephant is in any case probably close to zero. Why, then, didn't the Talmud discuss the vastly more likely case of an ox, which is also usually too heavy to pick up? Presumably the Talmud wanted to give an extreme example to illustrate the difficulty of R. Shimon's requirement of *hagbaha*. With this in mind, perhaps it is irrelevant if elephants do or do not jump. The point of the Talmud is just to ask how, according to R. Shimon's view, one would acquire an animal that is too heavy for *hagbaha*. One of the options given is that it could be made to jump. True, the specific example given of an elephant would not work, but Rav Meshullam's explanation of the Talmud's answer is still relevant for other animals. And there can be further ramifications. Some of the later authorities discuss the legal workings of Rav Meshullam's answer; can jumping really suffice as a form of *hagbaha*? This point is of legal interest even if elephants don't jump, as there are many other animals that do. The Talmud uses the example of an elephant because, as the very biggest creature, it is an extreme example that makes the point with greater vividness.

In Synagogues and Scrolls

———————————————— SYMBOLISM

When one thinks of animals that are depicted in synagogues, the lion comes to mind. One also sometimes finds other animals which possess scriptural symbolic significance, such as deer and other animals representing the twelve

The Great Khan Hunting, from the Livre des Merveilles du Monde, *c. 1400. Note the lion-like legs of the elephants, complete with paws, which would indicate an ability to jump.*

When an elephant seeks to reach food that is high up, its first recourse is to stand on its back legs and stretch its trunk. Reaching any higher would require jumping with just two legs – clearly an impossible feat.

374

tribes. But surprisingly, a number of ancient synagogues also contain depictions of elephants.

The synagogue of Maon, which dates back to at least the sixth century CE, has a mosaic floor depicting lions, birds, and two elephants. Much later, in eighteenth-century Poland, one finds several synagogues with paintings of elephants. In the Gwozdiec synagogue, two elephants, bearing howdahs, flank the *Aron HaKodesh* (Ark of the Law). In the Hodorov synagogue, a pair of elephants, bearing castles, appears on the north and south sides of the domed ceiling, forming a triangle with the *Aron HaKodesh*.

Filling the gap between these two periods, we find medieval Jewish manuscripts which also depict elephants. A thirteenth-century illuminated *machzor* (prayerbook for the festivals) from Worms includes a poem entitled *Adon Imnani*, which is written as though composed by the Torah itself, describing her being given to the Jewish people at Sinai; at the bottom of the page is an elephant. And a fourteenth-century illustrated Torah has an elephant, centrally situated and carrying a huge crown, on the title page of the Book of Deuteronomy.

Putting all these together, it appears that the elephant symbolizes Torah. The elephant represents grandeur, power, and majesty, with the added bonus of simultaneously being beneficial to man (unlike the lion). This represents the grandeur, power, and majesty of Torah, the foundation of the world, which likewise serves in benefit of man. This is why the elephant appears in synagogues, surrounding the Ark of the Law where the Torah is kept. This is why the elephant is depicted alongside a poem written about the Torah. And this is why the elephant appears on the title page of the Book of Deuteronomy, which is a review of the Torah.[36]

Title page of the Book of Deuteronomy from a fourteenth-century manuscript. In the center of the Star of David is an elephant.

A mosaic of an elephant from the ancient Maon Synagogue in the Negev, Israel

War Elephants

Today, we think of the elephants as objects of fascination and entertainment in the zoo or circus. Historically, however, the most prominent role of elephants was neither that nor the logging industry, but rather was their use in battle.

> When Antiochus saw that his kingdom was established, he determined to become king of the land of Egypt, in order that he could reign over both kingdoms. And so he invaded Egypt with a strong force, with chariots and elephants and cavalry and a large fleet. (1 Maccabees 1:16–17)

War elephants were the most formidable weaponry that an army could possess. They carried boxes filled with numerous archers, lance-throwers, and men wielding slingshots. The elephants themselves would be protected by a coat of fire-reinforced leather and iron. These animals were trained to dash the enemy soldiers to the ground with their

375

trunks and trample upon them. Their gigantic size, their terrifying trumpeting and, most importantly, the unfamiliarity of many people with them ensured that they struck fear into the hearts of the enemy. Antiochus's army, armed with elephants, was powerful indeed.

His forces numbered one hundred thousand foot soldiers, twenty thousand horsemen, and thirty-two elephants trained for battle.... Early in the morning, the king set out and took his army by a forced march along the road to Beth-Zechariah, and his troops prepared for battle and sounded their trumpets. They offered the elephants the syrup of grapes and mulberries, to arouse them for battle. They distributed the beasts among the phalanxes; with each elephant they stationed a thousand men wearing coats of armor, and with brass helmets on their heads; and five hundred select horsemen were assigned to each beast. They took their position beforehand alongside the elephant; wherever it went, they went with it, never leaving it. On the elephants were covered strong wooden towers; they were fastened on each animal by special harnesses, and on each tower were four armed men who fought from there, as well as its mahout. (1 Maccabees 6:30, 33–37)

The Death of Eleazar – A nineteenth-century illustration by Gustave Dore

As enormous as these elephants are, they are dwarfed by the mountain

The most famous incident involving a war elephant occurred with the tragic death of Eleazar the Maccabee:

> Now Eleazar, called Avaran, saw that one of the beasts was equipped with royal armor, and was taller than all the others, and he presumed that the king was on it. And so he sacrificed his life to save his people, and to win for himself an everlasting name. He courageously ran into the thick of the phalanx to reach it, killing men right and left, and they parted before him on both sides. He ran under the elephant, stabbed it from beneath, and killed it. But it collapsed to the ground on top of him, and he died. (I Maccabees 6:43–46)

It took someone of great faith to remember that God, rather than a huge elephant, determines the outcome of a battle:

> Maccabeus, seeing the hordes that were in front of him, and the assorted of arms, and the ferocity of the elephants, stretched out his hands toward heaven and called upon the Lord who works wonders. For he knew that it is not by arms, but as the Lord decides, that victory is gained for those who deserve it. (II Maccabees 15:21)

For all the great size and power of the elephant, ultimately it is no more than another of God's creations. ∎

Notes

1 Many taxonomists divide the African elephant into two species: the African bush elephant (*Loxodonta africana*) and the smaller African forest elephant (*Loxodonta cyclotis*).

2 Frederick E. Zeuner, *A History of Domesticated Animals* (New York: Harper & Row, 1963), pp. 276–278.

3 Sándor Bökönyi, "Subfossil elephant remains from southwestern Asia," *Paleorient* (1985) 11:2, pp. 161–3.

4 For a discussion regarding the origin and route of the ivory that was brought to King Solomon, see Avinoam Shalem, *The Oliphant: Islamic Objects in Historical Context* (Leiden: Brill, 2004), pp. 19–20.

5 For a discussion of the etymology of this term, see Avinoam Shalem, ibid., p. 14.

6 Rashi, commentary to II Chronicles 9:21. Note that there is a medieval midrash which refers to elephants with the name *shinhab*; see *Sefer HaYashar* to *Parashat Noach* (p. 31 in Berlin 1923 ed.), also cited in *Seder HaDorot* 1973, that we shall discuss later.

7 Oded Borowski, *Every Living Thing: Daily Use of Animals in Ancient Israel* (London: Altamira Press, 1998), p. 194.

8 Rashi, *Targum Yonatan*, and Mahari Kra ad loc.

9 Radak, *Metzudat Tziyon*, and Abarbanel ad loc.

10 Rosh HaShana 26a, according to Ramban s.v. *Veyesh lehakshot* and Ritva s.v. *Od hikshu*. However, cf. Rabbi Yehuda Leib Margoliyos, *Korban Reishit* (Warsaw, 1911); Rabbi Moshe Teitelbaum, *Yismach Moshe, Parashat Ki Tissa*, p. 193a. See Natan Slifkin, *Exotic Shofars: Halachic Considerations*, available at www.zootorah.com.

11 *Mishna Berura* 586:8, citing several authorities. See too *Shaar HaTziyun*, 586:14.

12 The identity of the *kifof* is unclear. Rashi states that the *kifof* is "similar to a monkey but possesses a tail" (apparently contrasting it with the Barbary macaque). See Yisrael Aharoni, "*Kufad, Kipod, Kifof,*" *Tarbitz* 17:2 (Jan. 1946), pp. 1–11.

13 Codified in *Shulchan Arukh, Orach Chayim* 225:8.

14 See Chazon Ish, *Emuna VeBitachon*, ch. 1: "It is too much habituation that blunts the sensitivity of the soul, which should justly feel wonder at every living thing just by virtue of its being alive. In contrast to this, the soul does find wonder from certain species that are not so commonly found, such as is the case with one who sees an elephant or monkey."

15 Mark Carwardine, *Animal Records* (London: Natural History Museum, 2010), p. 72.

16 Gershon ben Shlomo, *Shaar HaShamayim* (thirteenth century).

17 Karl Groning, *Elephants: A Cultural and Natural History* (Cologne, Germany: Konemann, 1999), p. 75.

18 Some claim that there is another reference to the extreme nature of elephants. The Talmud in Shabbat 155b, seeking to explain how a mishna could be describing carcasses that are too tough to be consumed by dogs, suggests that it is referring to "*basar pili.*" Some explain this to mean elephant's flesh, which is very tough. However, the same word appears in Pesachim 76b, where it refers to ordinary meat (from cows) that has cracked due to being so dry and hard.

19 Karl Groning, *Elephants: A Cultural and Natural History,* p. 218.

20 It is unclear if the sound of mosquitos bothers elephants, but they are known to be scared by the buzzing of bees. See L. King, I. Douglas-Hamilton, and F. Vollrath, "African elephants run from the sound of disturbed bees," *Current Biology* 17:19, pp. R832–R833.

21 Cf. Rabbi Bachya ibn Pakuda, who notes that ultimately, the elephant is no more magnificent than a tiny insect: "Wisdom is manifest in the smallest creatures as in the largest. The force of wisdom displayed in the creation of the elephant, in its great body size, is not more marvelous than the force of wisdom displayed in the creation of the ant, in its minuteness" (*Chovot HaLevavot, Shaar HaYichud* 7).

22 Azariah De Rossi, in *Meor Einayim, Imrei Bina* ch. 16, argued that the Sages created this story for didactic purposes. Maharal, *Be'er HaGola* 6, vehemently opposed this approach and argued instead that the account is to be understood as using symbolic language; the "mosquito" is a reference to something small. Rabbi Chaim Eisen notes that Rabbi Samson Raphael Hirsch presented the same general approach as that of De Rossi; see "Maharal's *Be'er ha-Gola* and His Revolution in *Aggadic* Scholarship – in Their Context and on His Terms," *Hakira* vol. 4 (Winter 2007), pp. 137–194.

23 Cf. Janeen Renaghan, *ZooGoer* (The Smithsonian National Zoological Park, 1998) 27:4: "As a majestic foreign beast, the elephant came to symbolize Roman expansion.... In 46 B.C., after the defeat of rival Pompey in Greece and successful campaigns in Asia Minor and Egypt, Caesar held an elaborate triumph in which 40 trained elephants marched alongside him up the steps of the Capitol. Lighted torches burned brightly in the elephants' trunks, illuminating what ultimately would be the legendary dictator's last victory. Not surprisingly, Roman rulers often chose this pachydermal symbol of majestic light and omnipotence to appear on their coins."

24 Rabbi Shimon ben Tzemach Duran, *Magen Avot*, ch. 3 p. 68b. See too Me'iri to Eiruvin 31b.

25 Codified in *Shulchan Arukh, Orach Chayim* 225:8.

26 Maharal, *Chiddushei Aggadot* to Sanhedrin 109a, explains regarding a similar statement about men turning into monkeys during the generation of Enosh that it means that people lost certain human spiritual traits.

27 Rabbi Shlomi Edni, *Melekhet Shlomo*, Kilayim 8:6. See Baruch Placzek, "Anthropoid Mythology," *Popular Science Monthly* (September 1882), p. 656.

28 Sanhedrin 109a.

29 The midrash is *Sefer HaYashar* to *Parashat Noach* (p. 31 in Berlin 1923 ed.), also cited in *Seder HaDorot* 1973.

30 Berakhot 58b.

31 Me'iri, *Beit HaBechira* ad loc.

32 Rabbi Betzalel Stern, in *Ohalekha BeAmitekha* (Jerusalem, 5752) 17:10, interprets the Me'iri as referring to elephants and monkeys being a variation on human beings, but claims that the Me'iri is referring to the aforementioned midrash about people being transformed into elephants and monkeys. However, even if the midrash referring to elephants and monkeys existed in Me'iri's time, it is inconceivable that he would have accepted the midrashic statement as literally true, in light of the fact that Me'iri was a staunch follower of the rationalist school of thought.

33 Ritva likewise notes that the elephant must have all four feet off the ground at the same time. This is also clear from *Ketzot HaChoshen* 273:4.

34 Some claim that there are reports that baby elephants will jump when provoked, and that there is a report of an adult elephant leaping over a ravine. But experts are skeptical of such claims, and in any case they are entirely irrelevant to our discussion. First, baby elephants are not too heavy to be picked up either, which means that the Talmud's question would not apply to them (since it is only discussing how one can acquire an animal that is too heavy to be acquired via the preferred method of picking it up). Second, and more fundamentally, we are not discussing whether it is ever possible for any elephant to jump, but rather whether it is a normal behavior which it would do to obtain food. The Talmud is discussing how, according to R. Shimon's view, it is possible to acquire an elephant, which is too heavy to be picked up. It is not discussing how it is ever possible for an elephant to jump, but rather, generally speaking, how elephants can be acquired. And, generally speaking, making it jump up in the air is not an option.

35 It should be noted, however, that the fact that elephants do not jump does *not* mean that Rav Meshullam was incorrect in his explanation of the Talmud. Rav Meshullam may very well have been correct in explaining that this is what the Talmud was referring to.

36 For extensive discussion, see Marc Michael Epstein, "The Elephant and the Law: The Medieval Jewish Minority Adapts a Christian Motif," *The Art Bulletin*, vol. 76, no. 3 (Sep., 1994), pp. 465–478 and an expanded version in idem, *Dreams of Subversion in Medieval Jewish Art and Literature* (University Park, PA: Pennsylvania State University Press, 1997), pp. 39–69.

MONKEY

Monkey

The Monkeys of Tarshish

— IDENTIFICATION

Monkeys are not found in the Land of Israel, neither today nor in biblical times. Yet they are mentioned in Scripture, in the context of describing the gifts that King Solomon received:

> For the king had at sea a fleet of Tarshish with the fleet of Hiram; once in three years the fleet of Tarshish came, bringing gold, and silver, ivory, and monkeys, and peacocks. (I Kings 10:22; similarly II Chr. 9:21)

There is near-universal consensus that the Hebrew term *kof* refers to a monkey,[1] buttressed by the fact that *kof* refers to the monkey in Arabic, Akkadian, and other regional languages. It should be noted that while many English translations of this verse render it as referring to "apes," this does not refer to the true apes (gorillas, chimpanzees, orangutans, and gibbons); rather, it is an older English usage of the term which refers to monkeys. These verses are the only unequivocal references to monkeys in Scripture; although there are other verses that are taken by some as referring to monkeys.[2]

In order to identify which kinds of monkeys were brought, one would have to know where they were being brought from. But it is difficult to identify the location of Tarshish; it is variously identified as a location in North Africa,[3] Asia, or Europe. Some even understand it to instead refer to a class of ships.[4] It is therefore impossible to state

אֲנִי תַרְשִׁישׁ לַמֶּלֶךְ בַּיָּם עִם אֳנִי חִירָם אַחַת לְשָׁלֹשׁ שָׁנִים תָּבוֹא
אֲנִי תַרְשִׁישׁ נֹשְׂאֵת זָהָב וָכֶסֶף שֶׁנְהַבִּים וְקֹפִים וְתֻכִּיִּים:

מלכים א י:כב

כִּי אֳנִיּוֹת לַמֶּלֶךְ הֹלְכוֹת תַּרְשִׁישׁ עִם עַבְדֵי חוּרָם אַחַת לְשָׁלוֹשׁ
שָׁנִים תָּבוֹאנָה אֳנִיּוֹת תַּרְשִׁישׁ נֹשְׂאוֹת זָהָב וָכֶסֶף שֶׁנְהַבִּים וְקוֹפִים
וְתוּכִּיִּים:

דברי הימים ב ט:כא

with certainty which types of monkeys are being described. However, there are a few species which are the most likely candidates.[5]

If the ships were coming from Africa, then the monkeys may have been Barbary macaques (*Macaca sylvanus*). These are the sole species of monkey to lack a tail, making them somewhat resemble apes (which is perhaps why the famous Barbary macaques of Gibraltar are sometimes referred to as "rock apes"). They were formerly common in North Africa.

Another candidate is the vervet or grivet monkey (similar species from the genus *Chlorocebus*). This is known to have been a popular pet in the ancient world. There is also evidence that it was exported from central Africa to the Aegean region of the Mediterranean via Egypt, as a precious gift.

A third, more remote possibility from Africa is the hamadryas baboon (*Papio hamadryas*) or the olive baboon

Barbary macaque

Vervet monkey

DAN KOSMAYER

NATAN SLIFKIN

Hamadryas baboon

Olive baboon

Gray langur

Rhesus macaque

(*Papio anubis*), which were very popular in Ancient Egypt. It is unclear if they were indigenous to that area in biblical times, but even if not, they were being imported as sacred animals. However, they are aggressive and powerful animals that are particularly unsuitable as pets, and would be unlikely to be presented as gifts.

Finally, if the ships of Tarshish were coming from Asia, then the monkeys they carried would probably have been rhesus macaques (*Macaca mulatta*), but possibly gray langurs (*Semnopithecus entellus*).

Monkeys in Talmudic Law

LAW AND RITUAL

There are numerous references to monkeys in the Talmud.[6] These usually refer to a monkey performing an action that is ordinarily performed by humans, such as a reference to a monkey applying dye to wool.[7] Many of these references occur in legal contexts; there is mention in several areas of

Jewish law as to whether a monkey may be used to fulfill a role that is normally performed by a human. It is not that the Sages of the Talmud were faced with pressing practical situations with monkeys that they needed to resolve. Rather, in order to shed light on the nature of various obligations, the Sages discussed the theoretical case of the obligation being performed by an animal. The example that they chose was a monkey, which is the most viable for such tasks, due to its great intelligence, coupled with its ability to perform tasks that require a high degree of physical dexterity.

For example, in discussing *shechita* – the slaughter of animals for food according to Jewish law – the Sages invoke the example of a monkey in order to illustrate that it can only be performed by a Jew himself:

Shechita performed by a monkey is invalid, as it says, "and *you* shall slaughter and eat" (Deut. 12:21)...not that a monkey slaughtered it. (Tosefta, Chullin 1:1[8])

381

POLISPOLIVIOU / SHUTTERSTOCK

This monkey has been trained to carry a basket of
food, exactly as described in the Talmud

When he returns (the flour to the vessel), he puts it near the side of the vessel, and shakes it such that it falls in on its own; in which case it is as though it was put back by a monkey. (Menachot 7a)

In all the above cases, a monkey is rated as unacceptable. The term *maase kof*, "an act performed by a monkey," entered halakhic discourse to refer to any act that is done without conscious intent. But there are situations where there is a possibility that an action can be performed by a monkey.

There is a limit of walking beyond two thousand cubits from the edge of town on Shabbat. However, this limit can be extended by placing, before Shabbat, an *eiruv* – a token meal – outside town, thereby symbolically establishing one's location there. The Sages discussed the legitimacy of using different methods to send the *eiruv* to this location, and one method involves sending it via monkey:

If he gave it to a monkey, which transported it; or if he placed it on an animal, which transported it – it is a valid *eiruv*. (Tosefta, Eiruvin 2:12; Me'ila 21a)

However, elsewhere the Talmud clarifies that animals are only acceptable for the intermediate stage of transporting the *eiruv*; a human must receive it at the other end:

If he gave his *eiruv* to an elephant, and it transported it to a monkey, it is not a valid *eiruv*. But if he told somebody (at the other end) to take it from [the monkey], it is valid. (Eiruvin 31b)

In other situations, there is a dispute as to whether the conscious intent of a human is required. The Talmud presents such questions in terms of whether a monkey is considered to be equivalent to a human. One such case is with regard to the prohibition of *nolad*, something created on a Festival:

R. Zeira asked: What is the ruling regarding a dish prepared (on a Festival) by a monkey? R. Yose son of R. Bun says: R. Zeira and Rav Hamnuna disagreed regarding this; one said that it is prohibited, and one said that it is permissible. (Y. Beitza 1:3, 5a)

Another disputed case is with regard to the requirement of washing hands for ritual purposes. The law is that a person must have the water poured over his hands, either by himself or by somebody else. The Mishna discusses whether a monkey is acceptable for this task:

A monkey may wash a person's hands; R. Yose disqualifies it. (Mishna Yadayim 1:5)

(Note, however, that this same R. Yose was of the view that apes, as opposed to monkeys, have a legal status similar to humans in some areas, as we shall later see.)

Similarly, the Talmud notes that the scriptural obligation for the priest to take blood from an offering means that he himself must take it, ruling out a monkey:

It is written, "And he shall take [from the blood]" (Lev. 4:25); and thus if a monkey comes and puts it in his hand, he must take it again. (Zevachim 14a)

On other occasions, the Talmud describes an inadequate fulfillment of an obligation as being "as though performed by a monkey," i.e. useless from the perspective of Jewish law, even though a monkey is physically capable of fulfilling the task. One such case is where the showbread in the Temple was arranged prematurely:

Since he did not arrange it according to the requirement, it is as though a monkey arranged it. (Yoma 29b, Menachot 100b)

Another such statement occurs with regard to another aspect of the Temple service. The Talmud discusses a situation where flour must be returned to the place in the container from which it was taken, and it describes a case where the flour is not considered to have been returned correctly:

Medieval Monkey Disputes

Above, we saw that the Mishna records a dispute as to whether a monkey can wash a person's hands. Although the Mishna leaves the question undecided, Rambam rules that it is permissible.[9] But Raavad attacks Rambam's ruling, pointing out that the Talmud[10] requires "human power" for the washing. He further asks how a monkey could possibly be rated as equivalent to a human, and argues that its actions are even less significant than those of a deaf-mute, idiot, or child.

Rabbi Shem Tov ben Avraham ibn Gaon, a fourteenth-century defender of Rambam, counters that a monkey is able to imitate human behavior to a remarkable degree. He further brings several arguments, based upon the Talmud, that a monkey's actions are considered to have a degree of legitimacy.[11] For example, while, as we saw above, show-bread arranged by a monkey is not considered to have fulfilled the biblical requirement, it is nevertheless a deed that has been done. Furthermore, the Talmud derives the legitimacy of transporting an *eiruv* via a deaf-mute, idiot, or child, from the fact that it is permitted to transport it by means of monkey. For these and other reasons, Rabbi Shem Tov argues that Rambam's adoption of the view that a monkey can wash a person's hands is legitimate.

Rabbi Yosef Karo defends Rambam by explaining that, according to Rambam, when the Talmud states a requirement that the washing come from human power, this is not intended to exclude animals. Rather, the Talmud's point is that there must be *someone* pouring, instead of simply dipping one's hands into a water source – and a monkey can be that someone. Rabbi Karo is unsure, however, if only a monkey may pour the water, since it is somewhat intelligent and capable of service, or if a monkey is simply being used as an example and any animal would be kosher for this task.[12]

In Rabbi Yosef Karo's halakhic compendium, the *Shulchan Arukh*, he records both views on the matter.[13] He concludes that although the words of those who permit using a monkey appear correct, one should act stringently and refrain from using a monkey.

In a different context, Rabbi Moshe Sofer notes that there is another case where one may make use of a monkey: to deliver *mishlo'ach manot* (gift baskets) on the holiday of Purim. He explains that it is only where a person bears an obligation to do something himself, and we are reckoning whether an emissary is rated as being equivalent to him, that a monkey is inadequate. However, when the obligation is not for a person to do something himself, but rather to send an emissary – as is the case with the mitzva to send gift baskets on Purim – then a monkey is acceptable.[14]

Monkeys possess such great intelligence and dexterity that they will play with a computer

Monkeys and Elephants

The monkey and elephant are a common pair in many places. Not only was the ivory of elephants grouped with monkeys in the tribute to King Solomon, but the Mishna and Gemara list them together in several instances.

The Mishna discusses whether various animals are rated as domestic animals (*behemot*) or wild animals (*chayot*). With kosher animals, this is relevant to determine whether their fat is permitted and whether their blood requires covering. With non-kosher animals, this can be relevant to determine if there is a crossbreeding problem with different varieties, or if a contract to sell all one's domestic or wild animals includes these animals. The Mishna decides the status of the monkey and elephant together:

> The monkey and the elephant are types of wild animal. (Mishna Kilayim 8:6)

Even though both lend themselves to being trained, they are not considered domestic animals in the technical sense. Thus, if a person were to write that he was selling his domestic animals, this would not include his trained monkey or lumber-lugging elephant.

The Talmud rules that there is a special blessing to be pronounced upon seeing a monkey or an elephant:

> The Rabbis taught: One who sees an elephant, monkey, or *kifof*[15] says, Blessed is He who varies the creations. (Berakhot 58b)

Some explain this blessing to refer to statements in the Midrash (that we shall later explore) regarding certain generations of sinners being physically transformed into monkeys. Accordingly, the blessing is acknowledging God having literally "changed the creations."[16] However, this is a difficult explanation, in light of the fact that the blessing is also pronounced upon the elephant.[17]

The most straightforward understanding of this blessing is that it is simply due to these animals being very unusual in comparison to other animals. (By extension, it would therefore also apply to other unusual animals, such as kangaroos or rhinoceroses.) It can be interpreted in a positive or negative manner; either as an expression of joyous wonder at such extreme diversity, or as forcing oneself to acknowledge God's wisdom even in perverse (in the sense of bizarre and aberrant) forms of life.[18]

The latter interpretation, while less appealing, is perhaps more likely, for two reasons. One is that the Talmud rules that this blessing is also pronounced upon people with congenital abnormalities.[19] Second is in light of a negative reference to monkeys and elephants:

> All animals are good in a dream except the monkey and the elephant. (Berakhot 56b, 57b)

In his commentary, Rashi explains that this is due to their being unusual in appearance. Apparently, this is viewed negatively, and thus portends harm in a dream.

Whether viewed positively or negatively, the blessing appears to be contrasting monkeys and elephants with more mundane creatures. However, the thirteenth-century authority Rabbi Menachem Me'iri explains that the Talmud specifies the elephant and monkey due to their both possessing a unique similarity to human beings.[20] This might mean that the blessing is referring to monkeys and elephants being different from other animals ("Who varies the creations") in terms of their unique similarity to human beings. However, it could be that Me'iri is saying something even more remarkable. Perhaps the blessing, with its mention of God "varying the creations," is not commenting on monkeys and elephants being different from other animals, but instead it is referring to their being different from *people*. The elephant and monkey are both fundamentally similar to man in possessing advanced intelligence and emotions. Intelligence is the defining characteristic of man, and it is also the special characteristic of elephants and monkeys. It is only because they are nevertheless somewhat different from man – with elephants, due to their overall form, and with monkeys, due to the degree of intelligence – that one praises the One who made them different in that way. The blessing is not acknowledging their differing from other animals; it is acknowledging their differing from man.[21]

Monkeys, such as these Barbary macaques, have complex social lives

TRATONG / SHUTTERSTOCK

Of Monkeys and Men

SYMBOLISM

In Jewish thought, the physical universe is divided into four categories: inanimate matter (*domem*), plants (*tzome'ach*), animals (*chai*), and man (*medaber*). Several Jewish philosophers noted that these divisions are not absolute. Instead, there are intermediates between each class:

> Coral is intermediate between inanimate matter and plants. We also find the sea sponge which only has the sense of touch, and is an intermediate between plant and animal stages. We also find the monkey to be intermediate between animals and man. (Rabbi Yosef Albo, *Sefer HaIkkarim* 3:1; see too Malbim, commentary to Genesis 1:20)

Why is the monkey rated as occupying an intermediate position between other animals and man? It may be due to the monkey's humanlike appearance: a somewhat erect posture, grasping hands, and a flat face.[22] Alternately, or in addition, it may be due to the monkey's great intelligence.[23]

Yet despite these attributes of a monkey, which render it a step above other animals, it is nevertheless not rated as equal to a human being. In classical rabbinic thought, the crucial differences between man and monkey are not physical differences, but rather intellectual and spiritual differences.[24] To be sure, monkeys and apes are highly intelligent, and are capable of a wide range of emotions. But they are not made *betzelem Elokim*, in the image of God; and while, like all animals, they possess a spirit (known as *nefesh*), they do not possess a soul (*neshama*). The concepts of the divine image and the soul have been interpreted differently by various rabbinic scholars, but, in general, it means that monkeys possess a lesser spiritual and intellectual stature. Monkeys do not possess true free will to make moral choices between good and evil, and they do not forge a relationship with their Creator. For all their similarities to humans, they are, at the end of the day, much lesser creatures.

It is for this reason that the Talmud, in discussing the relative superiority of different people, uses the metaphor of a monkey vis-à-vis a person:

> Everyone in comparison to Sarah is like a monkey in comparison to a human. Sarah in comparison to Eve is like a monkey in comparison to a human. Eve in comparison to Adam is like a monkey in comparison to a human. Adam in comparison to the Divine Presence is like a monkey in comparison to a human. (Bava Batra 58a)

This passage is explained to refer to the fact that humans are made in the image of God, while monkeys are not. The

© THE ISRAEL MUSEUM, JERUSALEM

In the fifteenth-century century compilation of Jewish texts from Italy known as the Rothschild Miscellany, *the* Nishmat *prayer, in which all the diverse creatures are called upon to praise God, is illustrated with a monkey. Curiously, the monkey is wearing a hooded shawl.*

phrase "like a monkey in comparison to a human being" indicates that the latter has a greater degree of God's image than the former.[25]

The concept of monkeys as inferior versions of humans also finds expression in some statements about the fate of certain people in ancient times:

> Four changes occurred in the days of Enosh, son of Shet: the hills became hard, the dead began to rot, the people's faces came to resemble those of monkeys, and they were easy prey for demons. (*Bereshit Rabba* 23:6)

This is similar to the fate of one of the groups involved in the Tower of Babel, the attempt to rise up against God:

> Those that said, "Let us rise up and make war," became monkeys, spirits, demons, and sprites. (Sanhedrin 109a[26])

Such statements have been interpreted in a variety of different ways. Many interpreted these accounts in their literal sense as referring to a physical transformation.[27] Others state that these people were reincarnated as monkeys.[28] Still others explain that the *tzelem Elokim*, the divine aspect of these people, was removed from them, leaving them not qualitatively different from a monkey.[29]

385

The inferiority of the monkey relative to man is seen in a midrash which observes the progressive states of a person who drinks wine to excess, with the worst stage being compared to the behavior of a monkey:

The Rabbis said: When Noah came to plant a vineyard, Satan came and... brought a lamb and slaughtered it under the vine, and after this he brought a lion and killed it, and then he brought a monkey and killed it under the vine, and dripped their blood into that vineyard, and made him drink from their blood. He alluded to him that before a man drinks wine, he is innocent as a lamb, that knows nothing, and like a ewe that is dumbstruck before being sheared; if he drinks in appropriate quantities, he becomes as powerful as a lion and says there is no one like him in the world. As soon as he drinks too much, he becomes like a pig, dirtying himself with urine and other things. When he becomes drunk, he becomes like a monkey, standing and dancing and fooling around, emitting obscenities from his mouth in front of everyone, and not knowing what he is doing. (*Midrash Tanchuma*, Gen. 13)

Another midrash also compares a person at different stages of life to various animals, again referring to a monkey:

The seven futilities of which Kohelet spoke match the seven forms of existence that a person sees. At a year old he is like a king seated in a canopied litter, and every- one hugs and kisses him. At two and three he is like a pig, sticking his hands in the gutter. At ten years old, he jumps like a young goat. At twenty he is like a neighing horse, adorning himself and seeking a mate. Once he has married a woman, he is [working] like a donkey. When children are born to him, he becomes brazen like a dog to bring them bread and food. When he grows old, he is like a monkey. This is said for a boor; but with Torah students, it is written, "And the king, David, was old" (1 Kings 1:1); even though he was old, he was still king. (*Kohelet Rabba* 1:2)

The comparison between an old man and a monkey is explained in different ways. Some explain it to refer to a decline in a person's mental faculties.[30] Others explain it to mean that he is dirty and bent over like a monkey.[31] Again, we see the monkey being presented as an inferior version of a human being.

In the eighteenth century, Rabbi Eliyahu HaKohen Itamari of Izmir, Turkey, discussed the monkey's similarity to man and its desire to ape his actions.[32] He presents it as an example of the talmudic precept to learn positive attributes from animals. The monkey, perceiving itself to be somewhat similar to humans, attempts to copy their ways and resemble them more fully. So, too, man, who perceives himself to be at least somewhat Godly, should strive to emulate his Creator as much as possible.

Despite their charm, monkeys do not make good pets

Monkeys as Pets

Monkeys tend to be popular due to their antics – we have already seen how they were favored by kings – but they certainly do not make good pets for the average home. This was recognized by the Sages:

> "There are many things that increase futility" (Eccl. 6:11) – for example, those who raise monkeys, cats,[33] mongooses, apes, and otters.[34] What is the benefit of them? Either a swipe, or a bite. (*Kohelet Rabba* 6:12[35])

Monkeys can be highly-strung, mischievous, and downright dangerous. They are powerful animals that can and do bite hard. As the Midrash notes, those who bring home an adorable baby monkey as a cute pet later find themselves regretting it.[36] There is also mention of even more serious harm to humans being caused by monkeys:

> There was a case of a girl who was tidying a house, and a monkey forced itself upon her from behind. The case came before the Sages, and they did not disqualify her from [marrying into] the priesthood. (*Masekhet Derekh Eretz Rabba* 1:7)

It is not unknown for male orangutans to attack the women of local villages in Borneo and Sumatra. Perhaps baboons, which were sometimes imported to other countries, caused similar problems. The Talmud relates that as a consequence of such events, women had to wear protective clothing:

> Ezra decreed that a woman should wear an apron both in front and behind. R. Tanchum bar Chiyya said: This was because of an incident which occurred when a monkey forced itself upon a woman from both in front and behind. (Y. Megilla 4:1)

However, the Talmud does note that in certain circumstances, trained monkeys can be beneficial. In the context of discussing animals that are forbidden to be kept in certain parts of Israel due to their danger to agriculture, some animals are expressly permitted:

> R. Yishmael said: One can raise *kufri* dogs, cats, monkeys, and mongooses, because they are used for cleaning the house (from pests). (Bava Kama 80a[37])

Furthermore, one never knows when a monkey might prove extremely useful, as illustrated by the following story from the Talmud:

> Rav Gamda gave four *zuz* to sailors and asked them to bring back something in exchange. They didn't find anything, so they bought a monkey. The monkey escaped

This lion-tailed macaque is displaying its powerful jaws and large canine teeth

and entered a hole. They dug after it and found it crouching on pearls; the sailors gave them all to Rav Gamda. (Nedarim 50b)

Monkey Hands

The Midrash explains a certain phrase in the Torah to be primarily referring to monkeys:

> Everything that walks on its paws (*holech al kapav*), among all animals that walk on four legs, are contaminated to you; whoever touches their carcasses shall be contaminated until evening (Lev. 11:27). "Everything that walks on its paws" – this is the monkey. (Sifra, *Shemini* 6)

The phrase *holech al kapav* is usually translated as "walks on paws," but the term *kapav* usually refers to the *palms* of the hands (and in conjunction with *regel* means the palm of the foot rather than the sole of the foot). The Midrash takes this to indicate that the verse is referring to animals that possess hands rather than paws. Most mammals walk on their toes, with the digits corresponding to the human palm and sole being well off the ground. But some animals walk on their palms and soles (a stance that is described in zoology by the term "plantigrade"). Such animals are described by the Midrash as "walking on their hands."[38]

387

However, the significance of a monkey's hands is not just that it walks on its palms. As we have seen, the monkey is significant in Jewish law not merely because of its intelligence, but also because of its ability to translate this intelligence into action. The key feature of a monkey that enables it to perform such tasks is its opposable thumb. All mammals have five digits on their front hands, but with most of them, these flex in the same direction (if at all). With monkeys and apes, on the other hand, the first digit is very distinctly a thumb rather than just another finger; that is to say, it bends toward the other fingers. This enables monkeys to grasp objects and manipulate them, a task for which other animals are physically incapable.

For intelligent manipulation, thumbs are required. A thumb is called *bohen* in the Torah; some relate this to the word *bina*, intelligence and understanding.[39] Through the thumb, the fingers enter the service of the intelligent brain. Thus, the monkey's thumbs transform their paws into grasping hands. It is this that enables them to manipulate objects with intelligence; in fact, there is an organization called "Helping Hands" that trains monkeys to work as helpers for quadriplegics.

It is for this reason that some see a reference to monkeys in King Solomon's description of several animals that are small yet remarkable:

> There are four of the land that are small, and yet they are the wisest of the wise.... The *semamit* catches with its hands, and it is in kings' palaces. (Prov. 30:24, 28)

The grasping hand of a monkey

KUNANEK SUPAKOSOL / SHUTTERSTOCK

388

The commentaries differ as to the correct translation of *semamit*, with most understanding it to refer to a spider,[40] and some to a lizard[41] or sparrow.[42] But others interpret it as referring to a monkey, with differing explanations of the verse. Some translate the verse to mean, "The monkey is captured by human hand."[43] The monkey's intelligence, while insufficient to prevent it being captured, is adequate to ensure that it has a place in the palace.[44] Avraham ibn Ezra, however, translates the verse to mean that the monkey grasps with its hands whatever is offered to it. By virtue of its clever antics, it merits being kept by kings in their palaces. Ibn Yachya notes that wisdom is a powerful tool for currying the favor of kings, and is a trait that has served Jews well throughout history.

Apes: The "Wild Men"

IDENTIFICATION

One more possible simian is argued by some to be mentioned in the book of Job, in the context of Eliphaz's description of how God acts benevolently to people:

> For you shall be in league with the *avnei hasadeh*; and the beasts of the field shall be at peace with you. (Job 5:23)

Avnei hasadeh is translated by some as "the stones of the field,"[45] but others[46] understand it to be identical to the *adnei hasadeh* spoken of in the Mishna:

> *Adnei hasadeh* is rated as a *chaya*. R. Yose says: It causes ritual impurity (when dead) in a building like a human being. (Mishna Kilayim 8:5)

The Talmud also discusses this creature:

> *Adnei hasadeh*, says Yaysi Araki, is the man of the field,[47] and it lives via its navel. If its navel is detached, it cannot live. (Y. Kilayim 8:4)

But what does it mean that it "lives via its navel"? Some understood the *adnei hasadeh* to be a humanoid creature that grows from the ground, like a plant, via a cord attached to its navel. But others explained it to refer to more familiar creatures. Rambam explains it to be a creature similar to man, with a relatively advanced form of communication, called *al-nasnas* in Arabic; this apparently refers to a kind of ape.[48] Similarly, Rabbi Yisrael Lipschutz suggests that it refers to the "orangutan."[49] However, he may not have been referring to the ape that is known today by the name "orangutan"; in the eighteenth century, there was much confusion surrounding the great apes (gorillas, chimpanzees, and orangutans) and the names were often interchanged.⁵⁰ The nineteenth-century commentator Rabbi Meir Leibush Wisser (better known as Malbim) states that *adnei hasadeh* refers to chimpanzees as well as orangutans.⁵¹ It seems that the term *adnei hasadeh* was understood by these authorities to refer to all the great apes.⁵² Yet, if we adopt this view, we are still left with a difficulty regarding the statement in the Talmud Yerushalmi about it growing via its navel.

It has been conjectured that the original text of the Talmud may have been altered over time.⁵³ The original statement of Yaysi Araki may have been simply that "*Adnei hasadeh* is the man of the field." The word *tur* (field), written in Hebrew as טור, may have had its middle letter doubled to read טוור, and then subsequently misread and altered to *tabur*, טבור, navel (since ו frequently transposes with ב in the Talmud Yerushalmi). The "field man" thus subsequently became thought of as being explained to be the "navel-man." A medieval explanatory comment, about there being creatures that grow on stalks from the ground, was subsequently incorporated into the talmudic text. Such a misunderstanding would have been especially reasonable in light of the continuation of the Talmud:

> R. Chama bar Ukva said in the name of R. Yose bar Chanina: R. Yose's reason (that the *adnei hasadeh* causes ritual impurity when dead like a human) is that it says, "And whoever in the open field touches [one that is slain by a sword … shall be impure]" (Num. 19:16) – [this phrase serves to include] that which grows on the field. (Y. Kilayim 8:4)

When one is picturing a creature growing from a stalk, the Talmud seems to be strengthening this idea by deducing that the scriptural verse serves to include that which grows on the field, i.e. from the ground. However, those who understand *adnei hasadeh* as referring to an ape would simply interpret this phrase as referring to a creature that *lives* in the field, i.e. in the wild.

Chimpanzees, orangutans, and gorillas are even more intelligent than monkeys – vastly so, in fact. Some individuals have even learned to communicate with humans

Adult male orangutans possess distinctive flanges of skin on their cheeks

in sign language. They are more than just animals, which is why R. Yose is of the opinion that, when dead, they cause ritual impurity like a human being. However, this is the only way in which they are equivalent to humans. They lack a developed *neshama*, and they do not make moral choices between good and evil for which they can be held accountable. They are more than animals, but less than people. ∎

Notes

1 The exception is Abarbanel, who considers that it refers to coral instead.

2 Malbim, in his commentary to Isaiah 13:21, interprets the *ochim* of that verse as referring to monkeys. However, in light of no monkeys existing in the Middle East, this lone view is difficult. Some interpret the *semamit* of Proverbs as referring to a monkey.

3 *Targum Yonatan* (cited by Rashi and Radak), Septuagint, Vulgate.

4 Abarbanel, commentary ad loc.

5 Zoological and archeological/historical information from Marco Masseti and Emiliano Bruner, "The Primates of the Western Palaearctic: a Biogeographical, Historical, and Archaeozoological Review," *Journal of Anthropological Sciences* 87 (2009), pp. 33–91.

6 An early study was published by Baruch Placzek, Chief Rabbi of Brinn

MAZZZUR / SHUTTERSTOCK

(Moravia): "Anthropoid Mythology," *Popular Science Monthly*, September 1882, pp. 655–63.

7 Bava Kama 101a.

8 Codified by Rema, *Shulchan Arukh, Yoreh De'ah* 2:11. *Peri Chadash* (ad loc.) notes that this would be the ruling even if a human supervised the *shechita* and ascertained that it was performed entirely correctly.

9 Rambam, *Mishneh Torah, Hilkhot Berakhot* 6:13.

10 Chullin 107a.

11 *Migdal Oz* ad loc.

12 *Kesef Mishneh* ad loc.

13 *Shulchan Arukh, Orach Chayim*, 159:11–12.

14 Rabbi Moshe Sofer, *Chatam Sofer* to Gittin 22b, s.v. *Veha Lav Benei De'ah Ninhu*; Rabbi Yitzchak Zilberstein, *Chashukei Chemed*, Megilla 7a.

15 The identity of this animal is unclear. Rashi states that the *kifof* is "similar to a monkey but possesses a tail" (apparently contrasting it with the Barbary macaque). See Yisrael Aharoni, "*Kufad, Kipod, Kifof*," *Tarbitz* 17:2 (Jan. 1946), pp. 1–11.

16 *Melekhet Shlomo*, Kilayim 8:6. See Baruch Placzek, "Anthropoid Mythology," in *Popular Science Monthly*, vol. 21 (Sept. 1882), p. 656.

17 There is only one reference to sinners being transformed into elephants, and it is seemingly from a relatively late source: *Sefer HaYashar* to *Parashat Noach* (p. 31 in Berlin 1923 ed.), also cited "in *Seder HaDorot* 1973, in reference to the Tower of Babel.

18 *Tosafot* to Bava Kama 101a, s.v. *d'tzava bahu kufa*, describes monkeys as being ugly.

19 Berakhot 58b.

20 Me'iri, *Beit HaBechira* ad loc.

21 Rabbi Betzalel Stern, in *Ohalekha BeAmitekha* (Jerusalem, 5752) 17:10, interprets the Me'iri as referring to elephants and monkeys being a variation on human beings, but claims that the Me'iri is referring to the aforementioned midrash about people being transformed into elephants and monkeys. However, even if the midrash referring to elephants and monkeys existed in Me'iri's time, it is inconceivable that he would have accepted the midrashic statement as literally true, in light of the fact that Me'iri was a staunch follower of the rationalist school of thought.

22 Cf. Nidda 23a, which compares an owl to a person in that its eyes are situated on the front of its face.

23 Rabbi Pinchas Eliyahu Hurwitz in *Sefer HaBrit* 1:11:5 notes that monkeys menstruate, like humans; Tuvia HaKohen, *Maase Tuvya, Olam Katan* 11, expresses wonder at their being the only animals to do so. The only animals known to modern zoology to menstruate are apes, monkeys, certain other primates, the elephant shrew, and certain bats.

24 For an extensive discussion of the similarities and differences between man and animals in Jewish thought, see Natan Slifkin, *Man and Beast* (Jerusalem: Zoo Torah, 2006).

25 Maharal, *Chiddushei Aggadot* ad loc.

26 A different version is found in *Sefer HaYashar* to *Parashat Noach* (p. 31 in Berlin 1923 ed.), also cited in *Seder HaDorot* 1973.

27 E.g. Rabbi Eliyahu HaKohen Itamari, *Shevet Mussar* 47.

28 *Etz Yosef.*

29 Maharal, *Chiddushei Aggadot* ad loc.

30 Rashash, Radal, and Maharzav.

31 *Matnat Kehuna*. Matityahu Clark, *Etymological Dictionary of Biblical Hebrew* (Jerusalem: Feldheim, 1999), citing *Daat Mikra*, explains the word *kof* to be related to the word *kafaf*, "bent," as is the posture of a monkey.

32 *Shevet Mussar* 47.

33 Sources indicate that the cats of those days were considerably less domesticated than the cats of today. See Rashba (*Torat HaBayit HaKatzar* 2:3), *Chiddushi Maharal, Hilkhot Tereifot*, 57:11, citing Ran and Bava Kama 80b.

34 This is curiously similar to the list of animals mentioned in the Sifrei as walking on their hands.

35 A different version is in *Midrash Yelamdeinu, Parashat Shelach,* cited by *Arukh, Davar*, second entry, in which it makes the milder point that monkeys require feeding, but do not provide food.

36 However, see *Tosafot* to Bava Batra 20a, s.v. *Kivan d'Ika*, who explains a case in the Gemara to be referring to a pet monkey, kept for entertainment purposes.

37 Rabbi Shimon ben Shlomo Duran, *Responsa Yakhin UBoaz* 2:25, permits trade in monkeys.

38 See Malbim, *HaTorah VeHaMitzva* ad loc.

39 Rabbi Hirsch, commentary to Genesis 14:18.

40 Rashi, Radak, *Metzudat David, Metzudat Tziyon*, Ralbag, and Malbim. Accordingly, the verse is either to be understood to mean that she "catches with the work of her hands," i.e. a web, or that it is so tiny that it can be caught in the hand.

41 *Sefer HaArukh* identifies it as the *haltaa* which refers to a type of lizard (perhaps the gecko, which sticks to walls with its hands).

42 Rav Saadia Gaon identifies it as the sparrow, which nests in human habitation and is "caught by hand."

43 Ibn Yachya, Me'iri.

44 According to Me'iri, the sequence of verses is describing the steps that are necessary to succeed in Torah study. The lesson of the monkey that is captured by man teaches us that one should avail oneself of the company of Torah scholars.

45 E.g. by Ibn Ezra, *Metzudat David*, Malbim.

46 Rashi, Rosh in his commentary to Kilayim 8:5, Rabbeinu Bechaya to Deuteronomy 18:10 (who says that the name is *benei hasadeh*, the "sons of the field"), *Sefer HaChinnukh* mitzva 514, Rabbi Ovadiah MiBartenura to Kilayim 8:5. In some versions of the Talmud Yerushalmi, Kilayim 8:4, it states *avnei hasadeh* rather than *adnei hasadeh*.

47 The term used is *bar nash d'tur*. *Tur* has been translated by some as "mountain," but there are convincing arguments that it means "field" – see Saul Lieberman, *Tarbitz* vol. 8 (1937), p. 367, *Tur-Sadeh*. Hence, *bar nash d'tur* means "man of the field" and is a direct translation of *adnei hasadeh*.

48 Rambam, commentary to the Mishna, Kilayim 8:5. However, in *Guide* III, 51, he refers to apes with the Arabic word *kird*. It is possible that the *nasnas* is a mythical creature in Arabic folklore by that name. See too Steven Harvey, "A New Islamic Source of the Guide of the Perplexed," in *Maimonidean Studies*, vol. 2, ed. Isadore Twersky (New York: Yeshiva University, 1991), pp. 31–60.

49 Rabbi Yisrael Lipschutz, *Tiferet Yisrael* commentary to Mishna, Kilayim 8:5.

50 See Frank Spencer, *History of Physical Anthropology*, vol. 1, p. 118.

51 Commentary to Leviticus 11:27.

52 See too Baruch Placzek, "Anthropoid Mythology," pp. 655–663.

53 Daniel Sperber, "Vegetable-Men," *Magic and Folklore in Rabbinic Literature*, pp. 21–25.

PORCUPINE

Porcupine

Kuppod

Hedgehogs and Porcupines of Old World and New

—————————————————— NATURAL HISTORY

Israel is home to both hedgehogs and porcupines. Although commonly confused, hedgehogs and porcupines are very different creatures. Hedgehogs are small, brown, and eat insects. Their quills are short and are firmly attached to their skin. A hedgehog's defense mechanism is to curl up into a ball.

Porcupines, on the other hand, are rodents, and are thus herbivorous, eating roots, fruit, and crops. They are much larger than hedgehogs, and have proportionately much longer quills. There are two families of porcupines: those in the Old World of Asia and Africa, and those in the New World of the Americas. The New World porcupines have scattered quills that are interspersed with bristles, underfur, and hair. Old World porcupines, on the other hand, have clusters of quills.

The species of porcupine found in the Land of Israel is the Indian crested porcupine, *Hystrix indica*. They can measure three feet in length and weigh as much as forty pounds. Their black and white striped quills measure up to twenty inches in length. However, it is the shorter, stiffer quills that do most damage. Unlike hedgehogs, the porcupine does not respond to threats by curling up, but instead stamping its feet, grunting, erecting the quills on its body, and rattling the hollow quills on its tail. If this formidable display does not suffice, they quickly run backwards into their enemy. Contrary to popular myth, they do not shoot their quills. Instead, the quills are so loosely attached to the porcupine that when it backs into its enemy, the quills detach and remain painfully embedded in the flesh. These may cause septic wounds that can be fatal for leopards, their primary natural predators.

A Porcupine in Scripture?

—————————————————— IDENTIFICATION

Determining if there are references to the porcupine in Scripture, Talmud, and Midrash is quite a challenge.[1] On several occasions, Scripture refers to a creature called the *kippod*:

> I will rise up against them, says the Lord of Hosts, and I will wipe out from Babylon name and remnant, kith and kin, says the Lord; and I will make it a home of *kippod*, and pools of water. I will sweep it with a broom of extermination, says the Lord of Hosts. (Is. 14:23)

Pictured on the left is a hedgehog, on the right is a porcupine

MIROSLAV HLAVKO / SHUTTERSTOCK

TRATONG / SHUTTERSTOCK

Likewise in describing the destruction of Edom:

Through the ages it shall lie in ruins; through the eons none shall traverse it. Little owl and *kippod* shall possess it; great owl and raven shall dwell there. He shall measure it with a line of chaos, and with weights of emptiness. (Is. 34:10–11[2])

Several ancient translations and commentaries interpret the *kippod* of Scripture as the hedgehog.[3] The various terms for hedgehog that they use may well refer to the porcupine instead; some languages employ the same word for both animals, and many Europeans, unfamiliar with the porcupine, would refer instead to the hedgehog. Their basis for translating these verses in this way appears to be that in the Mishna and Talmud, as we shall see, the term *kuppod* refers to the hedgehog and/or porcupine.

However, there are also ancient traditions that the *kippod* of Scripture is a type of owl, which fits much better with the context.[4] The *kippod* is grouped together with birds, and is described as inhabiting ruined areas. Such a description matches an owl – which is called *kupda* in various ancient languages of the region – rather than the hedgehog or porcupine. It appears that there is no mention of the porcupine in Scripture[5] – notwithstanding the well-known humorous anecdote about the child who reported that King Solomon had seven hundred wives and three hundred porcupines.

The Porcupine in the Talmud

IDENTIFICATION

In the Mishna and Talmud, we find mention of a creature called *kuppod*. Here it is a term that refers to both hedgehogs and porcupines (as noted earlier, in many languages both creatures share the same name). Note that the hedgehog or porcupine of the Mishna and Talmud is generally referred to as *kuppod* (קופד), in contrast to the *kippod* (קיפוד) bird of Scripture.[6]

Sometimes, the term *kuppod* appears to refer specifically to the hedgehog. For example, the Mishna and Talmud refer to the practice of attaching the skin of the *kuppod* to the udders of a cow, in order to protect it from animals.[7] But it would not be viable to use the skin of the porcupine for such a purpose; its quills are too long and fall out far too easily. The Mishna and Talmud must therefore be referring specifically to the hedgehog.

On other occasions, however, it appears that the term *kuppod* refers specifically to the porcupine. The Mishna specifies that certain animals are rated as being a *chaya* rather than a *sheretz*. A *chaya* is a wild animal of substantive size; a *sheretz* is a small, scurrying creature. There are differ-

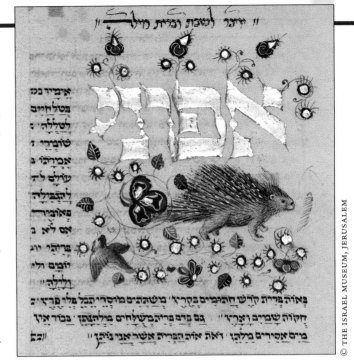

This illustration of a porcupine appears in the Rothschild Miscellany, a fifteenth-century compilation of Jewish texts from Italy. There does not appear to be any connection between the porcupine and the text in which it appears – a hymn recited when there is a brit mila on Shabbat. It seems that the porcupine was merely selected as a decoration, like the leopard and cheetah which also appear in this text.

ences in Jewish law between the two: in order to contract ritual impurity (*tuma*) from a *sheretz*, one must actually touch it when it is dead, in a quantity equivalent to the size of a lentil. With a dead *chaya*, on the other hand, one becomes ritually impure by carrying it, in a quantity equivalent to an olive. The Mishna notes that two animals, despite being on the smaller end of the scale, are still large enough to qualify as being *chayot*:

The *kuppod* and the *chuldat sena'im* are a type of *chaya*. (Mishna Kilayim 8:5)

Similarly, the Midrash expounds a verse regarding the laws of ritual impurity concerning *chayot*:

"Everything that walks on its hands, among all animals that walk on four legs, are contaminated to you…" (Lev. 11:27). "Everything that walks" – to include the *kuppod*, and the *chuldat sena'im*. (Sifra, *Shemini* 6)

A number of European commentaries identify the *kuppod* of this mishna and midrash as the hedgehog.[8] However, the hedgehog is a small, scurrying animal, which is presumably to be classified as a *sheretz* and not a *chaya*. Indeed, according to many views the hedgehog appears in the Torah's list of *sheratzim*, under the name *anaka*.[9] (For this reason, our primary discussion of the hedgehog, including other references in the Talmud to this creature, will

This porcupine feels threatened and has erected its quills

take place in the volume about *sheratzim*.) The Mishna and Midrash are thus presumably referring to the much larger porcupine, which better fits the classification of *chaya* rather than *sheretz*.[10]

The Modern Hebrew name for porcupine, *dorban*, was coined in 1915 by the zoologist Yisrael Aharoni.[11] In part, this choice was related to an Arabic name for the porcupine. It also related to the word *dorban* used in the Talmud to refer to ox-goads,[12] and thus characterizing the pointy-quilled porcupine. ∎

Notes

1 For extensive discussion, see Yisrael Aharoni, "*Kufad, Kipod, Kifof*," *Tarbitz* 17:2 (Jan. 1946), pp. 1–11, and especially David Talshir, *Shemot Chayim* (Jerusalem: Bialik, 2012), pp. 106–124.

2 Similarly Zephaniah 2:14, and Isaiah 34:15, speaking of the *kippoz* but perhaps referring to the *kippod*.

3 Septuagint; Vulgate; Rashi to Isaiah 14:23 (but not to Isaiah 34:11 and 34:15).

4 See e.g. Rashi to Isaiah 34:11 and 34:15; *Metzudot* to Isaiah 14:23; Radak, *Sefer HaShorashim*; Ibn Ezra to Isaiah 34:15.

5 Psalms 68:31 mentions the "beast of the reeds." While the Talmud (Pesachim 118b) explains this to refer to an animal that lives amongst the reeds, and specifies it as the wild boar, Ibn Ezra identifies it as a creature that possesses reeds, i.e. quills; thus, it refers to the hedgehog or porcupine. However, the context of the verse indicates that it is referring to a large beast, such as the hippopotamus, wild boar, or some kind of cattle.

6 See David Talshir, *Shemot Chayim*, p. 113, footnote 37.

7 Mishna Shabbat 5:4, and Shabbat 54b.

8 Rosh, *Pnei Moshe*, Raavad to Sifra, *Shemini* 3:5, and Rabbi Ovadiah Mi-Bartenura.

9 Leviticus 11:29–30.

10 Several of the commentaries support this approach based on the prior reference in the Mishna to the *chuldat sena'im*. Rabbi Shlomo Sirilio and Vilna Gaon (*Shenot Eliyahu* ad loc.) note that there are two types of *chulda*; the *chulda* mentioned in the Torah, which is a *sheretz*, and the *chulda* of the bushes – the *chuldat sena'im* – which is a *chaya*. Likewise, the suffix *sena'im* is *also* referring to the *kuppod*. There is a *kuppod* which is a *sheretz*, and this is the hedgehog. But the similar porcupine, which is a larger and wilder version of the hedgehog, is the *kuppod sen'aim*, the *chaya* variety of *kuppod*.

11 Yisrael Aharoni, *Torat HaChai*, p. 37 in 5675 ed., pp. 65–66 in 5683 ed. For extensive discussion on the adoption of the name *dorban*, and whether it should be vocalized as *dorban* or *darban*, see Talshir, *Shemot Chayim*, pp. 120–124.

12 Chagiga 3b, Mishna Keilim 9:6.

OTTER

Otter

כלב הים

Kelev HaYam

Otter of the River, Seal of the Sea

———————————————— NATURAL HISTORY

There are two semi-aquatic mammals that are native to the Land of Israel. One is the European or common otter (*Lutra lutra*), called *lutra* in Modern Hebrew.[1] The body length is about thirty inches, with a tail about eighteen inches, and they weigh approximately twenty pounds. Otters mainly eat fish, but also other foods; in the water, European otters also eat water snakes, amphibians, crustaceans, and mollusks, while on land, they eat birds, small mammals, and invertebrates. They also occasionally eat fruit.

Formerly common in Israel, the otter population declined drastically in the twentieth century, due to their being hunted for their fur, killed by resentful fish breeders, and habitat loss due to the draining of streams and pollution of rivers. At present there are less than a hundred otters left in Israel, along the Jordan River and in the Golan.

The second semi-aquatic mammal native to the region is the Mediterranean monk seal (*Monachus monachus*). They reach about eight feet in length and weigh six to seven hundred pounds. Males are black, females are dark grey or brown, and both genders have a pale belly.

In the past, monk seals were commonly found throughout the Mediterranean, extending into the Atlantic.[2] But commercial hunting during the era of the Roman Empire and the Middle Ages, followed by killings by fishermen, and the loss of coastal habitat due to urbanization and pollution in the twentieth century, has brought the Mediterranean monk seal to the brink of extinction. With only a few hundred seals left, it is one of the most endangered mammals in the world. The last sighting of a seal in Israel was in 2010.

Terrestrial vs. Aquatic

———————————————— LAW AND RITUAL

There are three references in the Mishna and Midrash to a semi-aquatic creature called *kelev hamayim* or *kelev hayam*, literally "water-dog" or "sea-dog." This is commonly understood to refer to the seal. However, there are those who argue that it is instead the otter that is being discussed.[3] Each view has its strengths and weaknesses. We shall first survey the statements in the Mishna and Midrash, and then return to analyze whether each one better matches the otter or the seal.

The Mishna declares that utensils and items of clothing

The rare Mediterranean monk seal

The European otter

A Hawaiian monk seal (a related species to the Mediterranean monk seal) relaxing in safety on the beach

manufactured from aquatic animals cannot contract *tuma*, ritual impurity. However, it presents one aquatic animal that is an exception:

> Everything in the sea is pure, except for the *kelev hamayim*, since it flees to the land, says R. Akiva. (Mishna Keilim 17:13)

Since the *kelev hamayim*, when faced with danger, seeks refuge on land, it is not defined as an aquatic creature.[4]

The Midrash Sifra also makes mention of the *kelev hayam*, in reference to a different aspect of the laws of ritual impurity: that contracted by touching the carcass of a dead animal:

> Everything that walks on its hands, among all animals that walk on four legs, are contaminated to you; whoever touches their carcasses shall be contaminated until evening. (Lev. 11:27)

> "Everything that walks" – to include the porcupine, the mongoose, the ape, and the *kelev hayam*. (Sifra, *Shemini* 6)

Why do these animals need to specifically be included? In the case of the porcupine and mongoose, it is because one might have thought that they are classified as *sheratzim* (small, vermin-like animals) rather than the wild animals discussed in this verse. In the case of the ape, it is because it

is so humanlike that one might have thought that the laws of animals do not include it. In the case of the *kelev hayam*, it is because of its aquatic nature.[5]

The third and final reference to the *kelev hayam* in rabbinic literature is a perspective on the keeping of various animals as pets:

> "There are many things that increase futility" (Eccl. 6:11) – for example, those who raise monkeys, cats,[6] mongooses, apes, and the *kelev hayam*.[7] What is the benefit of them? Either a swipe, or a bite. (*Kohelet Rabba* 6:12)

Here we are advised that the entertainment value of these animals is offset by the injuries that can be received from them.

Otter or Seal?

IDENTIFICATION

In order to determine whether the *kelev hayam* is the otter or seal, we must explore each of the sources in turn, and analyze whether they better match the otter or seal. First, there is the question of whether the name itself gives an indication as to the animal's identity. Conceptually, both otters and seals could well be referred to as aquatic "dogs." The seal has a very dog-like face. The otter has a somewhat dog-like appearance, and is also similar to dogs in its playful behavior and lending itself to being trained.

397

But in two of the three places where it is mentioned,[8] it is called *kelev hayam*, the "sea-dog," rather than *kelev hamayim*, the "water dog." Certainly, that would fit seals, which exclusively live in the sea. Otters, on the other hand, generally live in rivers rather than the sea (there is a sea-otter, but it only lives in North America). This would seem to conclusively determine that the animal being discussed is the seal. However, the otter does sometimes travel by sea to new habitats; some populations of otters in Israel arrived via sea from Lebanon.[9] Second, it may well be that the original name of the creature was *kelev hamayim*, "water dog," which subsequently was contracted to *kelev hayam*, "sea dog."

If we look at the historical usage of such names, then the otter has a distinct edge in being named as an aquatic dog. Seals were referred to as "sea-dogs" in medieval Europe, but there is less of such a characterization in the Ancient Near East; only in Syriac is the seal called a sea-dog, but the otter is also called a water-dog in Syriac. The otter is also called "water-dog" in Arabic and Akkadian, which is further evidence for understanding the Hebrew term as referring to the otter.[10]

Let us now turn to the three different references to the sea/water-dog, and see whether they indicate that the otter or seal is being discussed.

> Everything in the sea is pure, except for the water-dog, since it flees to the land, says R. Akiva. (Mishna Keilim 17:13)

This description perfectly matches monk seals, which are threatened in the water by sharks, and which seek refuge on open beaches, as the mishna describes.[11] It is a little more difficult to match this mishna to the otter, which usually flees to the water to escape predators on land. However, the otter does make its home (called a "holt") on land, which might be the intent of the mishna. Furthermore, in antiquity, crocodiles were present in the Land of Israel; the otter may well have had to flee the water. Alternately, the mishna may simply be referring to the fact that it is not entirely aquatic and often emerges to the land.

An otter emerging onto dry land

The first reference to the *kelev hayam* is thus inconclusive. Let us turn to the second reference:

"Everything that walks" – to include the porcupine, the mongoose, the ape, and the *kelev hayam*. (Sifra, *Shemini* 6)

This may appear to support the otter rather than the seal; while otters walk on four legs, seals drag themselves on their bellies with their front paws. However, the Sifra could perhaps equally be referring to the seal. The Midrash is not making a scientific statement about the precise nature of animal locomotion; it is noting which creatures are included in the category of terrestrial wild animals. Its point is that notwithstanding the aquatic nature of the *kelev hayam*, it is part of this category.

The second reference is thus likewise inconclusive. We now reach the third and final reference to the *kelev hayam*:

"There are many things that increase futility" (Eccl. 6:11) – for example, those who raise monkeys, cats, mongooses, apes, and the *kelev hayam*. What is the benefit of them? Either a swipe, or a bite. (*Kohelet Rabba* 6:12)

This midrash is presumably not referring to the seal. While seals were occasionally used in the Roman circus, it is extraordinarily unlikely that they could have been raised in homes; they require an aquatic environment. Otters, on the other hand, are often raised as pets, similarly to cats, mongooses, and apes; yet as the midrash says, notwithstanding their endearing and entertaining natures, they can bite viciously.

In defense of identifying the *kelev hayam* as the seal, perhaps one could note that the list of animals in this midrash here is nearly identical to that in the Sifra. Perhaps the *kelev hayam* was somehow transposed to this list, even though it doesn't really belong here. It is also possible that the mishna was referring to the seal, and the midrashim were referring to the otter. Still, overall, this midrash would appear to give the edge to the otter.

In conclusion: While there is certainly no clear conclusion as to whether the *kelev hayam* is the seal or otter, a comparison with other languages, and one of the references, suggests that the otter is the more likely candidate.

Hasidic Insights Regarding Otters

SYMBOLISM

Let us return to the Mishna's ruling regarding the otter (or seal):

Everything in the sea is pure, except for the otter, since it flees to the land, says R. Akiva. (Mishna Keilim 17:13)

Otters are cute and playful and look like fun pets, but they easily amputate fingers

Although, as noted earlier, there is a dispute if R. Akiva's view is followed for legal purposes, it has been popularly utilized for an ideological lesson. The nineteenth-century hasidic thinker Rabbi Tzaddok HaKohen of Lublin is one of several to draw upon R. Akiva's ruling regarding the otter.[12]

Rabbi Tzaddok notes that R. Akiva's ruling tells us how to define one's identity. It means that identity is determined not by where one is born, or where one spends most of one's time. Instead, it is determined by where one flees to in times of fear. There is an aphorism that "there are no atheists in a foxhole." If a person finds refuge in God and Torah, then this says more about who he is than does his upbringing. There are many Jews who are generally lax in their attachment to Judaism, but who attend synagogue during the Days of Awe. The otter teaches us to perceive religious identity in many more people than one would usually assume. ∎

399

Notes

1 Not to be confused with the nutria, a large semi-aquatic rodent from South America that has established itself in the wild in Israel.

2 William M. Johnson and David M. Lavigne, *Monk Seals In Antiquity* (Leiden: Netherlands Commission for International Nature Protection, 1999); William M. Johnson, *Monk Seals in Post-Classical History* (Leiden: Netherlands Commission for International Nature Protection, 2004). See too G.C.L. Bertram, "Notes on the present status of the monk seal in Palestine," *Journal of the Society for the Preservation of the Fauna of the Empire* 47 (1943), pp. 20–21.

3 Yehuda Feliks, *Tzome'ach VeChai BaMishna*; Menachem Dor, *HaChai BiYemei HaMikra, HaMishna VeHaTalmud*, p. 74; David Talshir, *Shemot Chayim* (Jerusalem: Mossad Bialik, 5772/2012), pp. 17–23. For a contrasting view, see Zohar Amar, review of *Shemot Chayim, Leshonenu*.

4 There is a dispute regarding whether R. Akiva's view is adopted. See *Mishneh LeMelekh* to *Mishneh Torah*, Keilim 1:3; *Tosafot Yom Tov* to Keilim 10:1.

5 However, for a different view as to why all these animals are mentioned here, see Malbim, *HaTorah VeHaMitzva* ad loc.

6 The cats mentioned here were probably not the thoroughly domesticated felines of today. See Rashba (*Torat HaBayit HaKatzar* 2:3), *Chiddushi Maharal, Hilkhot Tereifot*, 57:11, citing Ran and Bava Kama 80b.

7 This is curiously similar to the list of animals mentioned in the Sifrei as walking on their hands.

8 And, according to the Kaufman manuscript, even in the Mishna.

9 Amichai Guter, Amit Dolev, et al., "Do Otters Occasionally Visit Israel's Coastal Plain?" IUCN Otter Specialist Group, Bulletin 23:1 (2006), pp. 12–14.

10 For a detailed study, see David Talshir, *Shemot Chayim* pp. 17–23.

11 "Monk Seals In Antiquity."

12 Rabbi Tzaddok HaKohen, *Or Zarua LaTzaddik* (Lublin, 1929), Introduction, p. 1. See too Rabbi Chaim Ephraim Zaitchik, *Torat HaNefesh* (Brooklyn, 1956), *Parashat Shemini*, pp. 425–6.

Bibliography of General Works on Biblical/Talmudic Zoology and the Wildlife of Israel

A more comprehensive bibliography of literature relating to Biblical and Talmudic zoology can be found online at www.BiblicalNaturalHistory.org/resources.

Aharoni, Israel. "On Some Animals Mentioned in the Bible." *Osiris* vol. 5 (1938) pp. 461–478.

Amar, Zohar, Bouchnick, Ram and Bar-Oz, Guy. "The Contribution of Archaeozoology to the Identification of the Ritually Clean Ungulates Mentioned in The Hebrew Bible." *Journal of Hebrew Scriptures* 10:1 (2009). Available online at http://www.arts.ualberta.ca/JHS/Articles/article_129.pdf

Bodenheimer, Friedrich S. *Animal and Man in Bible Lands.* Leiden, Netherlands: E. J. Brill 1960.

———. *HaChai B'Eretz Yisrael.* Tel Aviv: Dvir 1953.

———. *HaChai B'Artzot HaMikra.* Jerusalem: Mossad Bialik 1957.

Cansdale, George. *All the Animals of the Bible Lands.* Michigan: Zondervan Publishing House 1970.

Clark, Bill. *High Hills and Wild Goats: Life Among the Animals of the Hai-Bar Wildlife Refuge.* Boston: Little, Brown and Company, 1990.

Dor, Menachem. *HaChai BiYmei HaMikra, HaMishnah VeHaTalmud.* Tel Aviv: Grafor-Daftal Books, 1997.

Feldman, David. *Yalkut Kol Chai.* Jerusalem: Machon Shaarei Tziyon, 1997.

Feliks, Yehudah. *HaChai b'Mishnah.* Jerusalem: Institute for Mishna Research, 5732/1972.

———. *Nature and Man in the Bible.* Jerusalem: The Soncino Press, 1981.

———. *The Animal World of the Bible.* Tel Aviv: Sinai, 1962.

Lewysohn, Ludwig. *Die Zoologie Des Talmuds.* Frankfurt on Main, 1858.

Qumsiyeh, Mazin B. *Mammals of the Holy Land.* Texas: Texas Tech University Press, 1996.

Schonhak, Yosef. *Toldot HaAretz.* Warsaw: H. Bomberg, 1841.

Schwartz, Yosef. *Tevuot HaAretz.* Jerusalem 1845.

Mendelssohn, Heinrich and Yom-Tov, Yoram. *Fauna Palaestina: Mammalia of Israel.* Jerusalem: The Israel Academy of Sciences and Humanities 1999.

Tristram, Henry B. *The Natural History of the Bible.* London, 1867; New Jersey: Gorgias Press 2002.

Glossary of Rabbinic Sources

Abarbanel, Rabbi Yitzchak
(1437–1508, Spain and Italy)
Author of an extensive commentary on the entire Bible. He was also an important philosopher and statesman.

Aggadat Esther
A midrash on the Book of Esther also referred to as *Midrash HaGadol* on Esther. It is generally attributed to David ben Amram Eladani of Aden, Yemen. He lived sometime between the thirteenth and fifteenth centuries.

Avot DeRabbi Natan
A rabbinic expansion on *Pirkei Avot.* Though it contains material that goes back to the end of the period of the Mishna, the exact date of its final editing is unknown.

Bemidbar Rabba
A late midrash on the fourth book of the Torah, composed in the eleventh or twelfth century. It is made up of two parts. The first is an interpretive midrash covering chapters 1–7 of Numbers. The second part covers the rest of Numbers and is a midrash in the tradition of *Midrash Tanchuma.* The two parts were probably combined into a single work during the thirteenth century.

Bereshit Rabba
The most extensive and earliest midrash on the first book of the Torah. Compiled around the fifth century in the Land of Israel.

Bereshit Rabbati
A medieval midrashic work on the first book of the Torah, based on the work of Rabbi Moshe HaDarshan (eleventh century, Southern France).

Chizkuni
A commentary on the Torah written by Rabbi Chizkiya ben Mano'ach (thirteenth century, Northern France).

Devarim Rabba
A homiletical midrash on the final book of the Torah. It is written in the same style and comes from the same tradition as the *Midrash Tanchuma.* It was edited between the sixth and eighth centuries CE.

Eikha Rabba
An exegetical midrash on the Book of Lamentations, edited in the Land of Israel around the sixth century.

Esther Rabba
A midrash on the Book of Esther. It is made up of two distinct parts. The first part is an exegetical midrash on chapters 1 and 2 of the Book of Esther, written in the Land of Israel around the sixth century CE. The second part is a midrashic retelling of chapters 3–10 of Esther written in Europe around the eleventh century CE. The two works were combined into a single book in the twelfth or thirteenth century.

Etz Yosef
Name of a series of commentaries on various midrashic works, including *Midrash Rabba* and *Midrash Tanchuma,* written by Rabbi Chanoch Zundel ben Yosef (died 1859, Poland).

Hirsch, Rabbi Samson Raphael
(1808–1888, Germany)
Important Orthodox rabbinic leader and thinker. Author of a popular commentary on the Torah.

Ibn Ezra, Rabbi Abraham
(1089–1164, Spain)
Biblical exegete whose commentaries on the Torah focus on the simple meaning of the text. He is also famous as a poet, grammarian, philosopher, astronomer, physician, and mathematician.

Kohelet Rabba
An interpretive midrash on the Book of Ecclesiastes, edited in the period following the completion of the Talmud.

Maharal
Rabbi Judah Loew ben Bezalel of Prague (c. 1520 –1609)
One of the most influential Jewish thinkers of the post-medieval period. In his extensive commentaries to the aggadic (non-legal) sections of the Talmud, he advocated an allegorical approach to this material.

Maharsha
Rabbi Samuel Eliezer ben Judah Edels (1555–1631, Poland)
One of the most influential interpreters of the Talmud. In addition to analysis of halakhic dialectics, his commentary on the Talmud also contains extensive discussion of aggadic (non-legal) passages.

Maharzu
Rabbi Zev Wolf Einhorn (died 1862, Lithuania)
Author of important commentaries on various midrashim. His commentary on *Midrash Rabba* is included in the standard Vilna edition.

Malbim
Rabbi Meir Leibush ben Yechiel Michel Weisser (1809–1879, Poland and Romania)
One of the leading rabbinic figures and most important traditional biblical exegetes of the mid-ninteenth century.

Masekhet Derekh Eretz Rabba
One of the "minor tractates" which are not part of the Talmud but are included in the back of many printings of the Talmud. *Masekhet Derekh Eretz Rabba* deals with, among other things, proper behavior and manners in day-to-day life.

Matnot Kehuna
A commentary on *Midrash Rabba* included in many editions of the work. It was written by Rabbi Yissachar Ber Katz (sixteenth century, Poland and Israel).

Me'iri
Rabbi Menachem HaMe'iri (Southern France, 1259–c.1316)
Rabbi and talmudic scholar.

Mekhilta
An early midrash on the Book of Exodus, edited in the Land of Israel in the third century CE. It focuses on legal sections of the Torah but also contains interpretations of many narrative passages as well.

Metzudot
This term refers to a pair of commentaries on the Prophets and Writings, *Metzudat Tziyon* and *Metzudat David,* written by Rabbi David Altschuler (1687–1769, Poland). *Metzudat Tziyon* explains difficult words while *Metzudat David* provides a verse by verse explanation of the text.

Midrash
Any work of biblical commentary or exposition written by the Sages of the Mishna and the Talmud or developing traditions passed on from them. Some midrashim were edited as late as the end of the Middle Ages.

Midrash Aseret HaDibrot
A collection of inspirational stories whose date and place of composition is uncertain. The stories are organized around the framework of the Ten Commandments.

Midrash Rabba
A collection of originally independent midrashic works written over many centuries in different styles, brought together into a single work in the Middle Ages. *Midrash Rabba* contains ten different midrashim, one for each of the five books of the Torah and the five *Megillot.* Each of the *Rabba* midrashim is discussed in its own entry in this glossary.

Midrash Lekach Tov
A midrashic collection on the Torah and the five *Megillot* composed by Rabbi Tuviah ben Eliezer in Greece during the eleventh century.

Midrash Mishlei
A midrash on the Book of Proverbs, written in the Land of Israel sometime between the seventh and eleventh centuries.

Midrash Shmuel
Also known as *Aggadat Shmuel, Aggadeta DeShmuel,* and *Et Laasot.* A midrash on the Book of Samuel of uncertain date from the Land of Israel.

Midrash Tanchuma
A homiletical midrash on the Torah. Though it contains material from talmudic times, in the form that we have it, it was only edited in the Middle Ages. There are several other midrashim, mostly works included in *Midrash Rabba,* which come from the same tradition as the *Midrash Tanchuma.* They were written in the same style and often contain similar material. *Midrash Tanchuma* and these related works come from the Land of Israel, though some of them may have been edited in Italy or elsewhere in Europe.

Midrash Tanchuma-Buber
An alternate version of the *Midrash Tanchuma* (see above) first published from an ancient manuscript in the nineteenth century by the great scholar of Midrash, Solomon Buber. Buber titled the work *Tanchuma HaYashan,* but there is no reason to believe that it is any older than the standard *Midrash Tanchuma.*

Midrash Tanna'im
This refers to a work by Rabbi David Zvi Hoffman (1843–1921, Austria-Hungry and Germany) in which he sought to reconstruct the lost halakhic midrash on the Book of Deuteronomy, based on later sources.

Midrash Tehillim
A midrash on the Book of Psalms. There is no consensus as to when this work was completed. It is also known as *Midrash Shocher Tov.*

Mishna
Earliest collection of rabbinic law, edited by Rabbi Yehuda HaNasi in the Land of Israel in the early third century CE.

Ovadiah MiBartenura, Rabbi
(1445–1515, Italy and Israel)
Author of one of the most important commentaries on the Mishna.

Perek Shira
First referenced around a thousand years ago, *Perek Shira* lists various elements of the natural world together with verses which represent their "song."

Pesikta DeRav Kahana
A midrashic collection of the talmudic period compiled in the Land of Israel around the fifth century. It contains homilies on the Torah and Haftara readings for the holidays and special Sabbaths.

Pesikta Rabbati
A later midrashic work which draws on and follows the same framework as *Pesikta DeRav Kahana,* presenting homilies on the Torah and Haftara readings for the holidays and special Sabbaths. It contains much post-talmudic material and was not finally edited until the early Middle Ages.

Pirkei DeRabbi Eliezer
A later midrashic text which retells the story of the Torah from Creation though the middle of the Book of Numbers. It was probably edited around the eighth century.

Radak
Rabbi David Kimche (1160–1235, Southern France)
Biblical commentator and grammarian.

Ralbag
Rabbi Levi ben Gershom (Gersonides, 1288–1344, Southern France)
Philosopher, biblical exegete and scientist.

Rambam

Rabbi Moshe ben Maimon, Maimonides (1138–1204, Spain and Egypt)
One of the most important rabbis of the Middle Ages, author of the comprehensive legal code *Mishneh Torah* and the major philosophical work *Moreh Nevukhim*.

Ramban

Rabbi Moshe ben Nachman, Nahmanides (1195–1270, Spain and Israel)
Leading talmudic scholar and kabbalist. His commentary on the Torah remains among the most important ever written.

Rashi

Rabbi Shlomo Yitzchaki (1060–1105, Northern France) One of the most important rabbis of his era, Rashi wrote the standard commentaries on the Talmud and the Bible.

Saadia Gaon

(822–942, Egypt and Babylonia)
The leading rabbinic figure of his day, Rabbi Saadia was among the earliest Jewish philosophers and linguists. He also translated the Torah into Arabic.

Shir HaShirim Rabba

A midrash on the Song of Songs composed in the Land of Israel in the sixth or seventh century.

Shir HaShirim Zuta

Also known as *Aggadat Shir HaShirim,* a brief midrash on the Song of Songs. Its date of composition is debated by scholars.

Shulchan Arukh

The most authoritative code of Jewish law, written by Rabbi Yosef Karo in the Land of Israel and published in 1565.

Sifra

An early legal midrash on the Book of Leviticus, edited in the Land of Israel in the third century CE.

Sifrei

An early midrash on the books of Numbers and Deuteronomy, edited in the Land of Israel in the third century CE. It focuses on legal sections of the Torah but also contains interpretations of many narrative passages as well.

Strashun, Rabbi Samuel

(Lithuania, 1794 –1872)
Talmudic scholar, often referred to by his acronym, Rashash. His commentary on the Talmud is included in most printings of the Talmud. He also wrote a commentary on the *Midrash Rabba*.

Talmud

The central text of rabbinic Judaism. An encyclopedic work of legal commentary and discussion, biblical exegesis, theology, and religious tradition. Compiled around the sixth century in Babylonia.

Tanna DeVei Eliyahu Rabba

A midrashic work organized around themes rather than on a specific biblical text. Its date is debated by scholars.

Targum Onkelos

A translation of the Torah into Aramaic, which was recognized as authoritative by the Talmud. It is commonly attributed to Onkelos, a Roman convert to Judaism who lived in the period following the destruction of the Second Temple in 70 CE.

Targum Yonatan ben Uziel

This term refers to two distinct works. The first is the ancient translations of the Prophets and Writings (*Nakh*) into Aramaic, attributed by the Talmud to the early sage Yonatan ben Uziel. The other is an expansive translation and midrashic exposition on the Torah, written in the post-talmudic period, which was later mistakenly attributed to Yonatan ben Uziel.

Tosafot

This refers to the talmudic commentaries that appear in the margins of all editions of the Talmud. They were written by rabbis who lived in France and Germany in the eleventh and twelfth centuries.

Tosefta

An early halakhic work, edited in the third century in the Land of Israel. It follows the same structure of orders and tractates as the Mishna. It includes many rulings and traditions not included in the Mishna.

Tzaddok HaKohen of Lublin, Rabbi

(1823–1900, Poland)
Leading expositor of hasidic thought.

Vayikra Rabba

An aggadic (non-legal) midrash on the third book of the Torah. Presents homilies and expositions on themes related to the weekly Torah readings. Compiled around the fifth century CE in the Land of Israel.

Yalkut Midrashei Teiman

A midrashic collection on the Torah from Yemen. Its author is unknown.

Yalkut Shimoni

A wide-ranging collection of midrashim arranged in order of the verses on all twenty-four books of the Bible. It preserves many interpretations whose original sources were lost to us. *Yalkut Shimoni* was written in Germany in the thirteenth century by Rabbi Shimon HaDarshan.

Yehuda HaLevi

(c.1075–1141, Spain)
Among the greatest of Jewish poets and philosophers. He was the author of the *Kuzari* and many standard liturgical poems.

Yerushalmi
Also called the Palestinian Talmud, this work records the comments and teachings of the rabbis of the Land of Israel on the Mishna. It was edited in northern Israel around the fifth century.

Yona ibn Janach
(c. 993–c. 1050, Spain)
Leading scholar of Hebrew grammar and linguistics.

Yossipon
A history of the Jews covering the era of the Second Temple and the period following its destruction. Based primarily on the first-century writings of Flavius Josephus, it was composed in Italy in the tenth century.

Zohar
The primary work of the Jewish mystical tradition, known as the Kabbala. The Zohar is traditionally attributed to R. Shimon bar Yochai. The text of the Zohar was first disseminated widely in the thirteenth century in Spain.

Subject Index

Index of Citations from Scripture and Talmud

Torah

Nevi'im

Ketuvim

Talmud Bavli

Talmud Yerushalmi